Learning Web Design

Fourth Edition

A Beginner's Guide to HTML, CSS, JavaScript, and Web Graphics

Jennifer Niederst Robbins

O'REILLY®

Beijing · Cambridge · Farnham · Köln · Sebastopol · Tokyo

Learning Web Design, Fourth Edition

by Jennifer Niederst Robbins

Published by O'Reilly Media, Inc., 1005 Gravenstein Highway North, Sebastopol, CA 95472.

O'Reilly Media books may be purchased for educational, business, or sales promotional use. Online editions are also available for most titles (*safari.oreilly.com*). For more information, contact our corporate/institutional sales department: 800-998-9938 or *corporate@oreilly.com*.

Editor: Simon St. Laurent

Production Editor: Melanie Yarbrough

Copy Editor: Genevieve d'Entremont

Technical Reviewers: Aaron Gustafson, Matt Menzer, Joel Marsh

Interior Designer: Ron Bilodeau

Cover Designer: Mark Paglietti

Indexer: Ellen Troutman Zaig

Print History:

February 2001:	First edition.
March 2004:	Second edition.
June 2007:	Third edition.
August 2012:	Fourth edition.

ISBN: 978-1-449-31927-4
[TI]
[2013-10-04]

CONTENTS

Part II   HTML Markup for Structure

Chapter 4
Creating a Simple Page 49

Chapter 5
Marking Up Text 69

Chapter 6
Adding Links 105

Part III   CSS for Presentation

PREFACE

Hello and welcome to the fourth edition of *Learning Web Design*.

So much has happened since the previous edition! Just when it looked like things were beginning to settle down with the adoption of web standards by the browser creators and the development community, along comes the "Mobile Web" to shake things up again. With the introduction of smartphones and tablets, the Web is finding its way onto small screens and on-the-go contexts where it never appeared before. This has introduced some rigorous challenges for web designers and programmers as we scramble to find ways to make the experience of using our sites pleasing, regardless of how they might be accessed.

As I write, many of these challenges, such as how to deliver the right image to the right device, are still being debated. It's an incredibly lively time for web design, full of experimentation and collaboration. In ways, it reminds me of the Wild West days of the Web back in 1993 when I started my web design career. So much to figure out! So many possibilities! And to be honest, it's also a tricky time to nail these moving-target technologies and techniques down in a book. To that end, I've done my best to point out the topics that are in flux and provide pointers to online resources to bring you up to date.

There are also two new standards—HTML5 (the fifth major revision of Hypertext Markup Language) and CSS3 (Cascading Style Sheets, Level 3)— available to us now that were only rumors the last time I wrote this book. The HTML section of the book now reflects the current HTML5 standard. I cover the parts of the developing CSS3 standard that are ready for prime time, including a new chapter on adding motion and interactivity with Transitions and Transforms. Our tools allow us to do so much more and in a more efficient way than even a few years ago.

Finally, because JavaScript has become such a significant part of web development, this new edition includes two chapters introducing JavaScript syntax and a few of its uses. I'm no JavaScript expert, but I was very lucky to find someone who is. The JavaScript chapters were written by Mat "Wilto"

THE COMPANION WEBSITE

Be sure to visit the companion website for this book at learningwebdesign.com. It features materials for the exercises, downloadable articles, lists of links from the book, book references, and other good stuff.

Marquis, who is a designer and developer at Filament Group, a member of the jQuery Mobile team, and the Technical Editor at *A List Apart*.

As in the first three editions, this book addresses the specific needs and concerns of beginners of all backgrounds, including seasoned graphic designers, programmers looking for a more creative outlet, office assistants, recent college graduates, work-at-home moms, and anyone else wanting to learn how to design websites. I've done my best to put the experience of sitting in my beginner web design class into a book, with exercises and tests along the way, so you get hands-on experience and can check your progress.

Whether you are reading this book on your own or using it as a companion to a web design course, I hope it gives you a good head start and that you have fun in the process.

How This Book Is Organized

Learning Web Design, Fourth Edition, is divided into five parts, each dealing with an important aspect of web development.

Part I: Getting Started

Part I lays a foundation for everything that follows in the book. I start off with some important general information about the web design environment, including the various roles you might play, the technologies you might learn, and tools that are available to you. You'll get your feet wet right away with HTML and CSS and learn how the Web and web pages generally work. I'll also introduce you to some Big Concepts that get you thinking the way modern web designers think about their craft.

Part II: HTML for Structure

The chapters in Part II cover the nitty-gritty of every element and attribute available to give content semantic structure, including the new elements introduced in HTML5. We'll cover the markup for text, links, images, tables, and forms. Part II closes out with an in-depth discussion of HTML5 and how it differs from previous standards.

Part III: CSS for Presentation

In the course of Part III, you'll go from learning the basics of using Cascading Style Sheets for changing the presentation of text to creating multicolumn layouts and even adding time-based animation and interactivity to the page. It also addresses common CSS techniques, including how to create a page using Responsive Web Design.

Part IV: JavaScript for Behaviors

Mat Marquis starts Part IV out with a rundown of JavaScript syntax so you can tell a variable from a function. You'll also get to know some ways that JavaScript is used, including DOM Scripting, and existing

---

Typographical Conventions Used in This Book

The following typographical conventions are used in this book:

Italic

Used to indicate URLs, email addresses, filenames, and directory names, as well as for emphasis.

Colored roman text

Used for special terms that are being defined and for cross-references.

`Constant width`

Used to indicate code examples and keyboard commands.

`Colored constant width`

Used for emphasis in code examples.

`Constant width italic`

Used to indicate placeholders for attribute and style sheet property values.

JavaScript tools, such as polyfills and libraries, that let you put JavaScript to use quickly even if you aren't quite ready to write your own code from scratch.

Part V: Creating Web Graphics

Part V introduces the various file formats that are appropriate for the Web and describes how to optimize them to make their file size as small as possible.

Acknowledgments

I want to thank my editor, Simon St. Laurent, with whom I've had a good run of collaborative projects and I look forward to more. Thanks also go to my contributor, Mat Marquis (*matmarquis.com*), for making JavaScript entertaining and for maintaining good spirits while collaborating with a control freak.

Many smart and lovely people had my back on this edition. I want to thank my primary technical reviewers, Aaron Gustafson (*easy-designs.net*), Joel Marsh (*thehipperelement.com*), and Matt Menzer, for taking so much time out of their schedules to make sure the details in the chapters were spot on. Thanks also go to the following folks for their "surgical strike" reviews: Anthony Calzadilla, Danny Chapman, Matt Haughey, Gerald Lewis, Jason Pamental, and Stephanie Rieger.

I feel fortunate to know so many of the leaders in this field whose books, articles, presentations, slide decks, and personal contact were the fuel that kept me going. I couldn't have done it without the help of these geniuses (in alphabetical order): Dan Cederholm, Josh Clark, Andy Clarke, Chris Coyier, Brad Frost, Lyza Gardner, Jason Grigsby, Stephen Hay, Scott Jehl, Scott Jenson, Tim Kadlec, Jeremy Keith, Sanders Kleinfeld, Peter-Paul Koch, Bruce Lawson, Ethan Marcotte, Eric Meyer, Karen McGrane, Shelley Powers, Bryan Rieger, Stephanie Rieger, Remy Sharp, Luke Wroblewski, and Jeffrey Zeldman.

It takes a village to make a book, and I'd like to extend my appreciation to the contributions of Melanie Yarbrough (production editor and proofreader), Genevieve d'Entremont (copy editor), Rebecca Demarest (figure production), Newgen (page layout), Ellen Troutman Zaig (index), Randy Comer (book cover design), and Ron Bilodeau (book interior design).

Finally, I'd like to thank Edie Freedman (best boss ever) for her patience while this book sucked me into a vortex. And to my dearest darlings, Jeff and Arlo, I'm happy to finally say, "I'm back."

About the Author

Jennifer Robbins began designing for the Web in 1993 as the graphic designer for Global Network Navigator, the first commercial website. In addition to this book, she is the author of *Web Design in a Nutshell* and *HTML5 Pocket Reference* (which is also available as an iOS app), both published by O'Reilly. In the past, Jennifer has spoken at many conferences, including Seybold and South by Southwest, and has taught beginning web design at Johnson and Wales University in Providence, Rhode Island. She is currently a digital product designer for O'Reilly Media, where she is interested in information architecture, interaction design, and making websites, apps, and ebooks pleasant to use. When not on the clock, Jennifer enjoys making things, indie rock, cooking, and being a Mom.

Using Code Examples

This book is here to help you get your job done. In general, you may use the code in this book in your programs and documentation. You do not need to contact us for permission unless you're reproducing a significant portion of the code. For example, writing a program that uses several chunks of code from this book does not require permission. Selling or distributing a CD-ROM of examples from O'Reilly books does require permission. Answering a question by citing this book and quoting example code does not require permission. Incorporating a significant amount of example code from this book into your product's documentation does require permission.

We appreciate, but do not require, attribution. An attribution usually includes the title, author, publisher, and ISBN. For example: *Learning Web Design*, Fourth Edition, by Jennifer Niederst Robbins. Copyright 2012 Littlechair, Inc., 978-1-449-31927-4.

If you feel your use of code examples falls outside fair use or the permission given above, feel free to contact us at *permissions@oreilly.com*.

We'd Like to Hear from You

Please address comments and questions concerning this book to the publisher:

> O'Reilly Media, Inc.
> 1005 Gravenstein Highway North
> Sebastopol, CA 95472
> (800) 998-9938 (in the United States or Canada)
> (707) 829-0515 (international or local)
> (707) 829-0104 (fax)

We have a web page for this book, where we list errata, examples, and any additional information. You can access this page at:

http://oreil.ly/learn_web_design_4e

To comment or ask technical questions about this book, send email to:

bookquestions@oreilly.com

For more information about our books, conferences, Resource Centers, and the O'Reilly Network, see our website at:

http://www.oreilly.com

Colophon

Our look is the result of reader comments, our own experimentation, and feedback from distribution channels. Distinctive covers complement our distinctive approach to technical topics, breathing personality and life into potentially dry subjects. The text font is Linotype Birka; the heading font is Adobe Myriad Pro.

GETTING STARTED

PART I

WHERE DO I START?

The Web has been around for more than 20 years now, experiencing euphoric early expansion, an economic-driven bust, an innovation-driven rebirth, and constant evolution along the way. One thing is certain: the Web as a communication and commercial medium is here to stay. Not only that, it has found its way onto devices such as smartphones, tablets, TVs, and more. There have never been more opportunities to put web design know-how to use.

Through my experience teaching web design courses and workshops, I've had the opportunity to meet people of all backgrounds who are interested in learning how to build web pages. Allow me to introduce you to just a few:

> *"I've been a print designer for 17 years, and now I am feeling pressure to provide web design services."*
>
> *"I work as a secretary in a small office. My boss has asked me to put together a small internal website to share company information among employees."*
>
> *"I've been a programmer for years, but I want to try my hand at design. I feel like the Web is a good opportunity to explore new skills."*
>
> *"I am an artist and I want to know how to get samples of my paintings and sculpture online."*
>
> *"I tinkered with web pages in high school and I think it might be something I'd like to do for a living."*

Whatever the motivation, the first question is always the same: "Where do I start?" It may seem like there is a mountain of stuff to learn, and it's not easy to know where to jump in. But you have to start somewhere.

This chapter attempts to put the learning curve in perspective by answering the most common questions I get asked by people ready to make the leap. It provides an introduction to the disciplines, technologies, and tools associated with web design.

Where Do I Start?

Your particular starting point will no doubt depend on your background and goals. However, a good first step for everyone is to get a basic understanding of how the Web and web pages work. This book will give you that foundation. Once you learn the fundamentals, there are plenty of resources on the Web and in bookstores for you to further your learning in specific areas.

There are many levels of involvement in web design, from building a small site for yourself to making it a full-blown career. You may enjoy being a full-service website developer or just specializing in one skill. There are a lot of ways you can go.

If your involvement in web design is purely at the hobbyist level, or if you have just one or two web projects you'd like to publish, you may find that a combination of personal research (like reading this book), taking advantage of available templates, and perhaps even investing in a visual web design tool such as Adobe Dreamweaver may be all you need to accomplish the task at hand. Many Continuing Education programs offer introductory courses to web design and production.

If you are interested in pursuing web design or production as a career, you'll need to bring your skills up to a professional level. Employers may not require a web design degree, but they will expect to see working sample sites that demonstrate your skills and experience. These sites can be the result of class assignments, personal projects, or a simple site for a small business or organization. What's important is that they look professional and have well-written, clean HTML, style sheets, and possibly scripts behind the scenes. Getting an entry-level job and working as part of a team is a great way to learn how larger sites are constructed and can help you decide which aspects of web design you would like to pursue.

I Just Want a Blog!

You don't necessarily need to become a web designer to start publishing your words and pictures on the Web. You can start your own "blog" or personal journal site using one of the free or inexpensive blog hosting services. These services provide templates that generally spare you the need to learn HTML (although it still doesn't hurt). These are some of the most popular as of this writing:

- WordPress (*www.wordpress.com*)
- Blogger (*www.blogger.com*)
- Tumblr (*www.tumblr.com*)

Another drag-n-drop site design and hosting service that goes beyond the blog is Squarespace (*www. squarespace.com*).

What Does a Web Designer Do?

Over the years, the term "web design" has become a catchall for a process that encompasses a number of different disciplines, from user experience design, to document markup, to serious programming. This section describes some of the most common roles.

If you are designing a small website on your own, you will need to wear many hats. The good news is that you probably won't notice. Consider that the day-to-day upkeep of your household requires you to be part-time chef, housecleaner, accountant, diplomat, gardener, and construction worker—but to you it's just the stuff you do around the house. In the same way, as a solo web designer, you may be a part-time graphic designer, writer, HTML author, and information architect, but to you, it'll just feel like "making web pages." Nothing to worry about.

AT A GLANCE

The term "web design" has come to encompass a number of disciplines, including:

- Visual (graphic) design
- User interface and experience design
- Web document and style sheet production
- Scripting and programming
- Content strategy
- Multimedia

There are also specialists out there whom you can hire to fill in the skills you don't have. For example, I have been creating websites since 1993 and I still hire programmers and multimedia developers when my clients require interactive features. That allows me to focus on the parts I do well (in my case, it's the content organization, interface, and visual design).

Large-scale websites are almost always created by a team of people, numbering from a handful to hundreds. In this scenario, each member of the team focuses on one facet of the site-building process. If that is the case, you may be able to simply adapt your current set of skills (writing, Photoshop, programming, etc.) and interests to the new medium.

I've divided the myriad roles and responsibilities typically covered under the umbrella term "web design" into four very broad categories: design, development, content strategy, and multimedia.

If you are not interested in becoming a jack-of-all-trades solo web designer, you may choose to specialize and work as part of a team or as a freelance contractor.

Design

Ah, design! It sounds fairly straightforward, but even this simple requirement has been divided into a number of specializations when it comes to creating sites. Here are a few of the new job descriptions related to designing a site, but bear in mind that the disciplines often overlap and that the person calling herself the "Designer" often is responsible for more than one (if not all) of these responsibilities.

User Experience, Interaction, and User Interface design

Often, when we think of design, we think about how something looks. On the Web, the first matter of business is designing how the site *works*. Before picking colors and fonts, it is important to identify the site's goals, how it will be used, and how visitors move through it. These tasks fall under the disciplines of Interaction Design (IxD), User Interface (UI) design, and User Experience (UX) design. There is a lot of overlap between these responsibilities, and it is not uncommon for one person or team to handle all three.

The goal of the Interaction Designer is to make the site as easy, efficient, and delightful to use as possible. Closely related to interaction design is User Interface design, which tends to be more narrowly focused on the functional organization of the page as well as the specific tools (buttons, links, menus, and so on) that users use to navigate content or accomplish tasks.

A more recent job title in the web design realm is the User Experience Designer. The UX designer takes a more holistic view—ensuring the entire experience with the site is favorable. UX design is based on a solid understanding of users and their needs based on observations and interviews. According to Donald Norman (who coined the term), user experience design includes "all aspects of the user's interaction with the product: how it is perceived, learned, and used." For a website or application, that includes the visual design, the user interface, the quality and message of the content, and even overall site performance. The experience must be in line with the organization's brand and business goals in order to be successful.

Some of the documents an IxD, UI, or UX designer might produce include:

User research and testing reports

Understanding the needs, desires, and limitations of users is central to the success of the design of the site or web application. This approach of designing around the user's needs is referred to as User-Centered Design (UCD), and it is central to contemporary design. Site designs often start with user research, including interviews and observations, in order to gain a better understanding of how the site can solve problems or how it will be used. It is typical for designers to do a round of user testing at each phase of the design process to ensure the usability of their designs. If users are having a hard time figuring out where to find content or how to move to the next step in a process, then it's back to the drawing board.

Wireframe diagrams

A wireframe diagram shows the structure of a web page using only outlines for each content type and widget (Figure 1-1). The purpose of a wireframe diagram is to indicate how the screen real estate is divided and where functionality and content such as navigation, search boxes, form elements, and so on, are placed, without any decoration or graphic design. These diagrams are usually annotated with instructions for how things should work so the development team knows what to build.

Site diagram

A site diagram indicates the structure of the site as a whole and how individual pages relate to one another. Figure 1-2 shows a very simple site diagram. Some site diagrams fill entire walls!

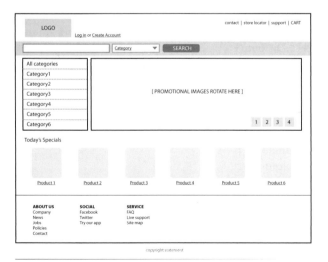

Figure 1-1. Wireframe diagram.

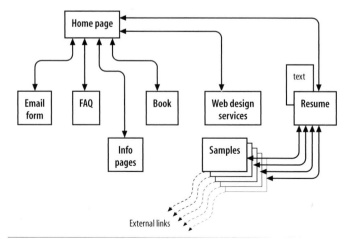

Figure 1-2. A simple site diagram.

Storyboards and user flow charts

A storyboard traces the path through a site or application from the point of view of a typical user (a persona in UX lingo). It usually includes a script and "scenes" consisting of screen views or the user interacting with the screen. The storyboard aims to demonstrate the steps it takes to accomplish tasks, outlines possible options, and also introduces some standard page types. Figure 1-3 shows a simple storyboard. A user flow chart is another method for showing how the parts of a site or application are connected that tends to focus on technical details rather than telling a story. For example, when the user does this, it triggers that function on the server. It is common for designers to create a user flow chart for the steps in a process such as member registration or online payments.

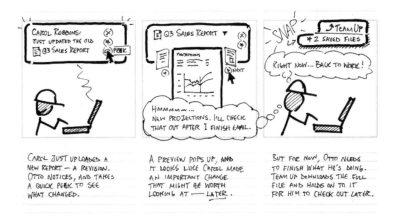

Figure 1-3. A typical storyboard [courtesy of Adaptive Path; drawn by Brandon Schauer].

Visual (graphic) design

Because the Web is a visual medium, web pages require attention to presentation and design. A graphic designer creates the "look and feel" of the site—logos, graphics, type, colors, layout, etc.—to ensure that the site makes a good first impression and is consistent with the brand and message of the organization it represents. Visual designers typically generate sketches of the way the site might look, as shown in Figure 1-4. They may also be responsible for producing the graphic files in a way that is optimized for delivery over the Web (see Chapter 21, Lean and Mean Web Graphics, for image optimization techniques).

If you are interested in doing the visual design of commercial sites professionally, I strongly recommend graphic design training as well as a strong proficiency in Adobe Photoshop (the industry standard) or Adobe Fireworks.

Figure 1-4. Look-and-feel sketches for a simple site.

Style Tiles

Another approach to capturing the look and feel of a site is to create style tiles, which give examples of color schemes, branding elements, content and UI treatments, and mood boards without applying them to a specific page layout. The idea is to agree upon a consistent visual language for the site. For more on this technique, read the article "Style Tiles and How They Work," by Samantha Warren (*www.alistapart.com/articles/style-tiles-and-how-they-work/*), and visit her excellent site where you can download a template at *styletil.es*.

If you are already a graphic designer, you will be able to adapt your skills to the Web easily, although this will not excuse you from acquiring a solid understanding of HTML, CSS, and other web technologies. Because most sites have at least a few images, even hobbyist web designers will need to know how to create and edit images, at minimum.

Again, I want to note that all of these responsibilities may fall into the hands of one designer who creates both the look and the functionality of a site. But for larger sites with bigger budgets, there is an opportunity to find your own special niche in the design process.

Development

A fair amount of the web design process involves the creation and trouble-shooting of the documents, style sheets, scripts, and images that make up a site. At web design firms, the team that handles the creation of the files that make up the website (or templates for pages that get assembled dynamically) is usually called the development or production department.

Web developers may not design the look or structure of the site themselves, but they do need to communicate well with designers and understand the intended site goals so they may suggest solutions that meet those goals.

The broad disciplines that fall under development are authoring, styling, and scripting/programming.

Authoring/markup

Authoring is the term used for the process of preparing content for delivery on the Web, or more specifically, marking up the content with HTML tags that describe its content and function. If you want a job as a web developer, you need to have an *intricate* knowledge of HTML and how it functions on various browsers and devices. The HTML specification is constantly evolving, which means you'll need to keep up with the latest best practices and opportunities as well as bugs and limitations. The good news is, it's not difficult to get started, and from there, you can gradually increase your skills. We'll be dabbling with HTML in Chapter 2, How the Web Works, and then discussing it in great detail in Part II of this book.

NOTE

Many visual designers translate their designs into HTML and CSS documents themselves. In fact, there is a popular argument that in order to call yourself a "web designer," you must be able to build your designs yourself, and nearly everyone agrees that your job prospects will be better if you are able to code as well as design.

Styling

In web design, the appearance of the page in the browser is controlled by style rules written in CSS (Cascading Style Sheets). We'll get deep into CSS in Part III of this book (including what "cascading" means!), but for now just know that in contemporary web design, the appearance of the page is handled separately from the HTML markup of the page. Again, if you are interested in working in web development, knowing your way around CSS and how it is supported (or not supported) by browsers is guaranteed to be part of your job description.

Scripting and programming

As the Web has evolved into a platform of applications for getting stuff done, programming has never been more important. JavaScript is the language that makes elements on web pages do things. It adds behaviors and functionality to elements in the page and even to the browser window itself.

There are other web-related programming languages as well, including PHP, Ruby, Python, and ASP.NET, that run on the server and process data and information before it is sent to the user's browser. See the sidebar "Frontend Versus Backend" for more information on what happens where.

Web scripting and programming definitely requires some traditional computer programming prowess. While many web programmers have degrees in computer science, it is also common for developers to be self-taught. A few developers I know started by copying and adapting existing scripts, then gradually added to their programming skills with each new project. Still, if you have no experience with programming languages, the initial learning curve may be a bit steep.

Teaching web programming is beyond the scope of this book. JavaScript is introduced in Chapter 19, Introduction to JavaScript (teaching JavaScript could fill a whole book itself). It is possible to turn out content-rich, well-designed sites without the need for programming, so hobbyist web designers should not be discouraged. However, once you get into collecting information via forms or serving information on demand, it is usually necessary to have a programmer on the team. You may also ask your hosting company if it offers the functionality you are looking for in an easy-to-use, canned service.

Frontend Versus Backend

You may hear web designers and developers say that they specialize in either the frontend or backend of website creation.

Frontend design

"Frontend" refers to any aspect of the design process that appears in or relates directly to the browser. This book focuses primarily on frontend web design.

The following tasks are commonly considered to be frontend tasks:

- Graphic design and image production
- Interface design
- Information design as it pertains to the user's experience of the site
- HTML document and style sheet development
- JavaScript

Backend development

"Backend" refers to the programs and scripts that work on the server behind the scenes to make web pages dynamic and interactive. In general, backend web development falls in the hands of experienced programmers, but it is good for all web designers to be familiar with backend functionality.

The following tasks take place on the backend:

- Information design as it pertains to how the information is organized on the server
- Forms processing
- Database programming
- Content management systems
- Other server-side web applications using PHP, JSP, Ruby, ASP.NET, Java, and other programming languages

---

Content strategy and creation

Third on our list, though ideally first in the actual website creation process, is the critical matter of the site's content itself. Anyone who uses the title "web designer" needs to be aware that everything we do supports the process of getting the content, message, or functionality to our users. Furthermore, good writing can help the user interfaces we create be more effective.

Of course, someone needs to create the content and maintain it—don't underestimate the resources required to do this successfully. In addition, I want to call your attention to two content-related specialists on the modern web development team: the Content Strategist and Information Architect (IA).

When the content isn't written right, the site can't be fully effective. A Content Strategist makes sure that every bit of text on a site, from long explanatory text down to the labels on buttons, supports the brand identity and marketing goals of the company. Content strategy may also extend to data modeling and content management on a large and ongoing scale, such as planning for content reuse and update schedules.

An Information Architect (also called an Information Designer) organizes the content logically and for ease of findability. She may be responsible for search functionality, site diagrams, and how the content and data is organized on the server. Information architecture is inevitably entwined with UX and UI design, and it is not uncommon for a single person or team to perform all roles.

Multimedia

One of the cool things about the Web is that you can add multimedia elements to a site, including sound, video, animation, and even interactive games. You may decide to add multimedia skills, such as audio and video editing or Flash development (see the "A Little More About Flash" sidebar), to your web design tool belt, or you may decide to go all in and become a multimedia specialist. If you are not interested in becoming a multimedia developer, you can always hire one. Web development companies usually look for people who have mastered the standard multimedia tools, and have a good visual sensibility and an instinct for intuitive and creative multimedia design.

A Little More About Flash

Adobe Flash (previously Macromedia Flash, previously FutureSplash) is a multimedia format created especially for the Web. Flash is used to create full-screen animation, interactive graphics, integrated audio and video clips, and even scriptable games and applications, all at remarkably small file sizes. However, recently Flash use has been on the decline due to a number of developments, including:

- Apple's decision not to support Flash on its iPhones and iPads in favor of non-proprietary HTML5 methods.
- Adobe's decision to stop supporting Flash (its own product) for mobile browsers.
- The new programmable **canvas** element in HTML5 that offers some of the same functionality as Flash.
- Criticism that Flash sometimes gets in the way of user goals. For example, who wants to sit through a movie and soundtrack on a restaurant site when all you really want to know is whether it is open on Sunday?
- The fact that a plug-in is required to play Flash media makes some developers squeamish.

In fact, it is not uncommon to hear web professionals cite that "Flash is dead," but despite suddenly becoming the underdog, Flash still has some advantages if used the right way:

- Because it uses vector graphics, Flash files are small and can be resized without loss of detail.
- It is a streaming format, so movies start playing quickly and continue to play as they download.
- You can use ActionScript to add behaviors and advanced interactivity, allowing Flash to be used as the frontend for dynamically generated content or ecommerce functions.
- The Flash plug-in is well distributed on PCs, so support on desktop browsers is reliable.
- Although HTML5 is promising and rapidly evolving, as of this writing, it cannot match the features and performance of Flash.

Flash is not likely to disappear overnight, but even Adobe is putting its muscle behind HTML5 alternatives.

What Languages Do I Need to Learn?

If you are a visual designer who spends time in Photoshop and Illustrator, you may be put off by needing to learn how to create your designs with text, but I assure you, it's pretty simple to get started. There are also authoring tools that speed up the production process, as we'll discuss later in this chapter.

The following is a list of technologies associated with web development. Which languages and technologies you learn will depend on the role you see yourself in within the web design process. However, I advise *everyone* involved in building websites to know their way around HTML and Cascading Style Sheets, and if you want to do frontend web development for a living, JavaScript know-how is pretty much a job requirement. More technically inclined web professionals may take on server configurations, databases, and site performance, but these are generally not frontend developer tasks (although a basic familiarity with the backend issues never hurts).

AT A GLANCE

Web-related technologies:
- Hypertext Markup Language (HTML)
- Cascading Style Sheets (CSS)
- JavaScript and DOM scripting
- Server-side programming and database management

The World Wide Web Consortium

The World Wide Web Consortium (called the W3C for short) is the organization that oversees the development of web technologies. The group was founded in 1994 by Tim Berners-Lee, the inventor of the Web, at the Massachusetts Institute of Technology (MIT).

In the beginning, the W3C concerned itself mainly with the HTTP protocol and the development of the HTML. Now, the W3C is laying a foundation for the future of the Web by developing dozens of technologies and protocols that must work together in a solid infrastructure.

For the definitive answer on any web technology question, the W3C site is the place to go:

www.w3.org

For more information on the W3C and what it does, see this useful page:

www.w3.org/Consortium/

Hypertext Markup Language (HTML)

You may see HTML and XHTML referred to collectively as (X)HTML.

HTML (HyperText Markup Language) is the language used to create web page documents. There are a few versions of HTML in use today: HTML 4.01 is the most firmly established, and the newer, more robust HTML5 is gaining steam and browser support. Both versions have a stricter implementation called XHTML (eXtensible HTML), which is essentially the same language with much stricter syntax rules. We'll get to the particulars of what makes the various versions different in Chapter 10, What's Up, HTML5?.

HTML is not a programming language; it is a markup language, which means it is a system for identifying and describing the various components of a document such as headings, paragraphs, and lists. The markup indicates the document's underlying structure (you can think of it as a detailed, machine-readable outline). You don't need programming skills—only patience and common sense—to write HTML.

The best way to learn HTML is to write out some pages by hand, as we will be doing in the exercises in this book. If you end up working in web production, you'll live and breathe HTML. But even hobbyists will benefit from knowing what is going on under the hood. The good news is that it's simple to learn the basics.

Cascading Style Sheets (CSS)

While HTML is used to describe the content in a web page, it is Cascading Style Sheets (CSS) that describe how that content should *look*. In the web design biz, the way the page looks is known as its presentation. That means fonts, colors, background images, line spacing, page layout, and so on, are all controlled with CSS. With the newest version (CSS3), you can even add special effects and basic animation to your page.

CSS also provides methods for controlling how documents will be presented in contexts other than the traditional desktop browser, such as in print or on devices with small screen widths. It also has rules for specifying the nonvisual presentation of documents, such as how they will sound when read by a screen reader (although those are not well supported).

NOTE

When this book uses the term "style sheets," it is always referring to Cascading Style Sheets, the standard style sheet language for the World Wide Web.

Style sheets are also a great tool for automating production because you can change the way an element looks across all the pages in your site by editing a single style sheet document. Style sheets are supported to some degree by all modern browsers.

Although it is possible to publish web pages using HTML alone, you'll probably want to take on style sheets so you're not stuck with the browser's default styles. If you're looking into designing websites professionally, proficiency at style sheets is mandatory.

Style sheets are discussed further in Part III.

JavaScript/DOM scripting

JavaScript is a scripting language that is used to add interactivity and behaviors to web pages, including these (just to name a few):

- Checking form entries for valid entries

- Swapping out styles for an element or an entire site

- Making the browser remember information about the user for the next time she visits

- Building interface widgets, such as expanding menus

JavaScript is used to manipulate the elements on the web page, the styles applied to them, or even the browser itself. There are other web scripting languages, but JavaScript (also called ECMAScript) is the standard and most ubiquitous.

You may also hear the term DOM scripting used in relation to JavaScript. DOM stands for Document Object Model, and it refers to the standardized list of web page elements that can be accessed and manipulated using JavaScript (or another scripting language). DOM scripting is an updated term for what used to be referred to as DHTML (Dynamic HTML), now considered an obsolete approach.

Writing JavaScript is a type of programming, so it may be time-consuming to learn if you have no prior programming experience. Many people teach themselves JavaScript by reading books and following and modifying existing examples. Most web-authoring tools come with standard scripts that you can use right out of the box for common functions.

Professional web developers are required to know JavaScript; however, plenty of visual designers rely on developers to add behaviors to their designs. So while JavaScript is useful, learning to write it may not be mandatory for *all* web designers. Teaching JavaScript is outside the scope of this book; I recommend *Learning JavaScript* by Shelley Powers (O'Reilly) as a good starting place if you want to learn more.

Server-side programming

Some simple websites are collections of static HTML documents and image files, but most commercial sites have more advanced functionality such as forms handling, dynamically generated pages, shopping carts, content management systems, databases, and so on. These functions are handled by web applications running on the server. There are a number of programming languages and frameworks (listed in parentheses) that are used to create web applications, including:

- PHP (CakePHP, CodeIngniter, Drupal)

- Python (Django, TurboGears)

The Web Design Layer Cake

Contemporary web design is commonly visualized as being made up of three separate "layers."

The content of the document with its HTML markup makes up the **Structure Layer**. It forms the foundation upon which the other layers may be applied.

Once the structure of the document is in place, you can add style sheets to control how the content should appear. This is called the **Presentation Layer**.

Finally, the **Behavior Layer** includes the scripts that make the page an interactive experience.

- Ruby (Ruby on Rails, Sinatra)

- JavaScript (Node.js, Rhino, SpiderMonkey)

- Java (Grails, Google Web Toolkit, JavaServer Faces)

- ASP.Net (DotNetNuke, ASP.Net MVC)

Developing web applications is programmer territory and is not expected of all web designers. However, that doesn't mean you can't offer such functionality to your clients. It is possible to get shopping carts, content management systems, mailing lists, and blogs as prepackaged solutions, without the need to program them from scratch.

What Do I Need to Buy?

It should come as no surprise that professional web designers require a fair amount of gear, both hardware and software. One of the most common questions I'm asked by my students is, "What should I get?" I can't tell you specifically what to buy, but I will provide an overview of the typical tools of the trade.

Bear in mind that while I've listed the most popular commercial software tools available, many of them have freeware or shareware equivalents that you can download if you're on a budget (try CNET's *Download.com*). With a little extra effort, you can get a full website up and running without big cash.

A Quick Introduction to XML

If you hang around the web design world at all, you're sure to hear the acronym XML (which stands for eXtensible Markup Language). XML is not a specific language in itself, but rather a robust set of rules for creating other markup languages.

To use a simplified example, if you were publishing recipes, you might use XML to create a custom markup language that includes the elements `<ingredient>`, `<instructions>`, and `<servings>` that accurately describe the types of information in your recipe documents. Once labeled correctly, that information can be treated as data. In fact, XML has proven to be a powerful tool for sharing data between applications. Despite the fact that XML was developed with the Web in mind, it has actually had a larger impact outside the web environment because of its data-handling capabilities. There are XML files working behind the scenes in an increasing number of software applications, such as Microsoft Office, Adobe Flash, and Apple iTunes.

Still, there are a number of XML languages that are used on the Web. The most prevalent is XHTML, which is HTML rewritten according to the stricter rules of XML (we'll talk more about XHTML in Chapter 10, What's Up, HTML5?). There is also RSS (Really Simple Syndication or RDF Site Summary), which allows your content to be shared as data and read with RSS feed readers; SVG (Scalable Vector Graphics), which uses tags to describe geometric shapes; and MathML, which is used to describe mathematical notation.

As a web designer, your direct experience with XML is likely to be limited to authoring documents in XHTML or perhaps adding an RSS feed or SVG images to a website. Developing new XML languages would be the responsibility of programmers or XML specialists.

Equipment

For a comfortable web development environment, I recommend the following equipment:

A solid, up-to-date computer. Macintosh, Windows, or Linux is fine. Creative departments in professional web development companies tend to be Mac-based. Although it is nice to have a super-fast machine, the files that make up web pages are very small and tend not to be too taxing on computers. Unless you're getting into sound and video editing, don't worry if your current setup is not the very latest and greatest.

Extra memory. Because you'll tend to bounce between a number of applications, it's a good idea to have enough RAM installed on your computer to allow you to leave several memory-intensive programs running at the same time.

A large monitor. Although not a requirement, a large monitor makes life easier, particularly for a visual designer. (I've seen code-based developers get by just fine on an 11" MacBook Air.) The more monitor real estate you have, the more windows and control panels you can have open at the same time. You can also see more of your page to make design decisions.

If you're using a large monitor, just make sure you design for users with smaller monitors and devices in mind.

A scanner and/or digital camera. If you anticipate making your own images and textures, you'll need some tools for creating them. I know a designer who has two scanners: one is the "good" scanner, and the other he uses to scan things like dead fish and rusty pans.

A second computer. Many web designers find it useful to have a test computer running a different platform than the computer they use for development (i.e., if you design on a Mac, test on a PC). Because browsers work differently on Macs than on Windows machines, it's critical to test your pages in as many environments as possible, and particularly on the current Windows operating system. If you are a hobbyist web designer working at home, check your pages on a friend's machine. Mac users should check out the "Run Windows on Your Mac" sidebar.

Mobile devices. The Web has gone mobile! That means it is absolutely critical that you test the appearance and performance of your site on a mobile browser on a smartphone or tablet device. You may already have a smartphone yourself. If you don't have a budget for devices with multiple platforms, ask your friends if you can spend a few minutes looking at your site on theirs. I have one web developer friend who checks out his designs on the phones at his local mobile carrier store (although you might quickly wear out your welcome).

Run Windows on Your Mac

If you have a Macintosh computer with an Intel chip running OS X (Leopard or later), you don't need a separate computer to test in a Windows environment. It is now possible to run Windows right on your Mac using the free Boot Camp application, which allows you to switch to Windows on reboot.

There are several other VM (Virtual Machine) products for Mac OS that allow you to toggle between Mac and Windows, including:

- VMFusion (*www.vmware.com/fusion*) is a commercial product with a free trial you can download.

- Parallels Desktop for Mac (*www.parallels.com*) is also a commercial product with a free trial.

- Oracle VirtualBox (*virtualbox.org*) is a free program that allows you to run a number of guest operating systems, including Windows and several flavors of Unix.

All VM products require that you purchase a copy of Microsoft Windows, but it sure beats buying a whole machine.

Software

There's no shortage of software available for creating web pages. In the early days, we just made do with tools originally designed for print. Today, there are wonderful tools created specifically with web design in mind that make the process more efficient. Although I can't list every available software release, I'd like to introduce you to the most common and proven web design tools. Note that you can download trial versions of many of these programs from the company websites, as listed in the "Popular Web Design Software Links" sidebar later in this chapter.

Web page authoring

Web-authoring tools are similar to desktop publishing tools, but the end product is a web page (an HTML file and its supporting files). These tools provide a visual "WYSIWYG" (What You See Is What You Get, pronounced "whizzy-wig") interface and shortcuts that save you from typing repetitive HTML and CSS. These tools won't excuse you from learning HTML. Even the most sophisticated tools won't generate HTML as clean or well considered as a professional writing by hand, but they can speed up the process once you know what you're doing.

The following are some popular web-authoring programs:

Adobe Dreamweaver. This is the hands-down industry standard due to its relatively clean code and advanced features.

Microsoft Expression Web (Windows only). Part of Microsoft's suite of professional design tools, MS Expression Web boasts standards-compliant code and CSS-based layouts.

Nvu (Linux, Windows, and Mac OS X). Don't want to pay for a WYSIWYG editor? Nvu (pronounced N-view, for "new view") is an open source tool that matches many of the features in Dreamweaver, and you can download it for free at *nvu.com*.

HTML editors

HTML editors (as opposed to WYSIWYG authoring tools) are designed to speed up the process of writing HTML by hand. They do not allow you to edit the page visually, so you need to check your work in a browser. Many professional web designers actually prefer to author HTML documents by hand, and they tend to recommend the following:

TextPad (Windows only). TextPad is a simple and inexpensive plain-text code editor for Windows.

Sublime Text (Window, Mac, Linux). This inexpensive and up-and-coming text editor looks stripped down but has a lot of functionality (like color coding and full code overviews) that developers love.

NOTE

To do the exercises in this book, all you'll need is the text editor that came with your operating system. No special programs are required.

Coda by Panic (Macintosh only). Coda users like its visual workflow, file management tools, and built-in terminal access.

TextMate by MacroMates (Macintosh only). This advanced text editor features project management tools and an interface that is integrated with the Mac operating system. It is growing in popularity because it is customizable, feature-rich, and inexpensive.

BBEdit by Bare Bones Software (Macintosh only). Lots of great shortcut features have made this the leading editor for Mac-based web developers.

Image-editing and drawing software

You'll probably want to add images to your pages, so you will need an image-editing program. We'll look at some of the more popular programs in greater detail in Part IV. In the meantime, you may want to look into the following popular web-graphics-creation tools:

Adobe Photoshop. Photoshop is undeniably the industry standard for image creation in both the print and web worlds.

Adobe Photoshop Elements. This lighter version of Photoshop is designed for photo editing and management, but some hobbyists may find that it has all the tools necessary for putting images on web pages.

Adobe Illustrator. Because designers need to create logos, icons, and illustrations at a variety of sizes and resolutions, many start with a vector image in Illustrator for maximum flexibility. You can output web graphics directly from Illustrator, or bring them into Photoshop for additional fine-tuning.

Adobe Fireworks. This web graphics program combines an image editor with tools for creating vector-based illustrations. It also features advanced tools for outputting web graphics.

Corel Paint Shop Pro Photo (Windows only). This full-featured image editor is popular with the Windows crowd, primarily due to its low price.

GIMP, "GNU Image Manipulation Program" (Unix, Windows, Mac). This free image-editing program is similar to Photoshop.

Internet tools

Because you will be dealing with the Internet, you need to have some tools specifically for viewing and moving files over the network:

A variety of browsers. Because browsers render pages differently, you'll want to test your pages on as many browsers as possible, both on the desktop and on mobile devices. The following table lists the desktop browsers most commonly used on Windows and Macintosh operating systems:

Windows:	**Macintosh OS X:**
Internet Explorer (the current version and at least two prior versions)	Safari
Chrome	Chrome
Firefox	Firefox
Safari	Opera
Opera	

And don't ignore the mobile browsers! The following list is an overview of the most commonly used mobile web browsers as of this writing (although who knows what mobile browsers will be important by the time you read this?):

- Mobile Safari (iOS)

- Android Browser (Android)

- BlackBerry Browser (RIM)

- Nokia Series 40 and Nokia Browser for Symbian

- Opera Mobile and Mini (installed on any device)

- Internet Explorer Mobile (Windows Phone)

- Silk (Kindle Fire)

A file-transfer protocol (FTP) program. An FTP program enables you to upload and download files between your computer and the computer that will serve your pages to the Web. The web authoring tools listed earlier all have FTP programs built right in. There are also dedicated FTP programs, as listed here:

Windows	**Macintosh OS X:**
WS_FTP	Transmit
CuteFTP	Cyberduck
AceFTP	Fetch
Filezilla	

Terminal application. If you know your way around the Unix operating system, you may find it useful to have a terminal (command-line) application that allows you to type Unix commands on the server. This may be useful for setting file permissions, moving or copying files and directories, or managing the server software.

Windows users can install a Linux emulator called Cygwin for command-line access. There is also PuTTY, a free Telnet/SSH client. Mac OS X includes an application called Terminal that is a full-fledged terminal application, giving you access to the underlying Unix system and the ability to use SSH to access other command-line systems over the Internet.

AT A GLANCE

Popular Web Design Software Links

Web page authoring

Adobe Dreamweaver *www.adobe.com*

Microsoft Expression Web *www.microsoft.com/products/expression*

Nvu (open source web page editor) *www.nvu.com*

HTML editing

TextMate by MacroMates for Mac OS *www.macromates.com*

Sublime Text *www.sublimetext.com*

TextPad for Windows *www.textpad.com*

Coda by Panic Software *www.panic.com/coda/*

BBEdit by Bare Bones Software *www.barebones.com*

Image editing and drawing

Adobe Photoshop *www.adobe.com*

Adobe Photoshop Elements *www.adobe.com*

Adobe Illustrator *www.adobe.com*

Adobe Fireworks *www.adobe.com*

Corel Paint Shop Pro Photo *www.corel.com/paintshoppro*

GIMP *gimp.org*

Browsers

Microsoft Internet Explorer (Windows only) *www.microsoft.com/windows/internet-explorer/*

Firefox *www.firefox.com*

Google Chrome *www.google.com/chrome*

Opera *www.opera.com*

Safari *www.apple.com/safari*

Networking

WS_FTP, CuteFTP, AceFTP, and others for Windows available at: *www.download.com*

Transmit (for Macintosh OSX) *www.panic.com/transmit*

Cyberduck (for Macintosh OSX) *cyberduck.ch*

Fetch (for Macintosh OSX) *fetchsoftworks.com*

Cygwin (Linux emulator for Windows) *www.cygwin.com*

PuTTY (telnet/SSH terminal emulator) *www.chiark.greenend.org.uk/~sgtatham/putty/*

What You've Learned

The lesson to take away from this chapter is: "you don't have to learn everything." And even if you want to learn everything eventually, you don't need to learn it all at once. So relax, and don't worry. The other good news is that, while many professional tools exist, it is possible to create a basic website and get it up and running without spending much money by using freely available or inexpensive tools and your existing computer setup.

As you'll soon see, it's easy to get started making web pages—you will be able to create simple pages by the time you're done reading this book. From there, you can continue adding to your bag of tricks and find your particular niche in web design.

exercise 1-1 |
Taking stock

Now that you're taking that first step in learning web design, it might be a good time to take stock of your assets and goals. Using the lists in this chapter as a general guide, try jotting down answers to the following questions:

- What are your web design goals? To become a professional web designer? To make personal websites only?
- Which aspects of web design interest you the most?
- What current skills do you have that will be useful in creating web pages?
- Which skills will you need to brush up on?
- Which hardware and software tools do you already have for web design?
- Which tools do you need to buy? Which tools would you like to buy eventually?

Test Yourself

Each chapter in this book ends with a few questions that you can answer to see if you picked up the important bits of information. Answers appear in Appendix A.

1. Match these web professionals with the final product they might be responsible for producing.

   A. Graphic designer   _____ HTML and CSS documents

   B. Production department   _____ PHP scripts

   C. User experience designer   _____ Photoshop page sketch

   D. Web programmer   _____ Storyboards

2. What does the W3C do?

3. Match the web technology with its appropriate task:

   A. HTML   _____ Checks a form field for a valid entry

   B. CSS   _____ Creates a custom server-side web application

   C. JavaScript   _____ Identifies text as a second-level heading

   D. PHP   _____ Defines a new markup language for sharing financial information

   E. XML   _____ Makes all second-level headings blue

4. What is the difference between frontend and backend web development?

5. What is the difference between a web-authoring program and an HTML-editing tool?

HOW THE WEB WORKS

I got started in web design in early 1993—pretty close to the start of the Web itself. In web time, that makes me an old-timer, but it's not so long ago that I can't remember the first time I looked at a web page. It was difficult to tell where the information was coming from and how it all worked.

This chapter sorts out the pieces and introduces some basic terminology. We'll start with the big picture and work down to specifics.

The Internet Versus the Web

No, it's not a battle to the death, just an opportunity to point out the distinction between these two words that are increasingly being used interchangeably.

The Internet is a network of connected computers. No company owns the Internet; it is a cooperative effort governed by a system of standards and rules. The purpose of connecting computers together, of course, is to share information. There are many ways information can be passed between computers, including email, file transfer (FTP), and many more specialized modes upon which the Internet is built. These standardized methods for transferring data or documents over a network are known as protocols.

The Web (originally called the World Wide Web, thus the "www" in site addresses) is just one of the ways information can be shared over the Internet. It is unique in that it allows documents to be linked to one another using hypertext links—thus forming a huge "web" of connected information. The Web uses a protocol called HTTP (HyperText Transfer Protocol). That acronym should look familiar because it is the first four letters of nearly all website addresses, as we'll discuss in an upcoming section.

Serving Up Your Information

Let's talk more about the computers that make up the Internet. Because they "serve up" documents upon request, these computers are known as servers. More accurately, the server is the software (not the computer itself) that

IN THIS CHAPTER

An explanation of the Web, as it relates to the Internet

The role of the server

The role of the browser

Introduction to URLs and their components

The anatomy of a web page

The Web is a subset of the Internet. It is just one of many ways information can be transferred over networked computers.

A Brief History of the Web

The Web was born in a particle physics laboratory (CERN) in Geneva, Switzerland, in 1989. There a computer specialist named Tim Berners-Lee first proposed a system of information management that used a "hypertext" process to link related documents over a network. He and his partner, Robert Cailliau, created a prototype and released it for review. For the first several years, web pages were text-only. It's difficult to believe that in 1992, the world had only about 50 web servers, total.

The real boost to the Web's popularity came in 1992 when the first graphical browser (NCSA Mosaic) was introduced, and the Web broke out of the realm of scientific research into mass media. The ongoing development of web technologies is overseen by the World Wide Web Consortium (W3C).

If you want to dig deeper into the Web's history, check out this site:

W3C's History Archives

www.w3.org/History.html

allows the computer to communicate with other computers; however, it is common to use the word "server" to refer to the computer as well. The role of server software is to wait for a request for information, then retrieve and send that information back as quickly as possible.

There's nothing special about the computers themselves…picture anything from a high-powered Unix machine to a humble personal computer. It's the server software that makes it all happen. In order for a computer to be part of the Web, it must be running special web server software that allows it to handle HyperText Transfer Protocol transactions. Web servers are also called "HTTP servers."

There are many server software options out there, but the two most popular are Apache (open source software) and Microsoft Internet Information Services (IIS). Apache is freely available for Unix-based computers and comes installed on Macs running Mac OS X. There is a Windows version as well. Microsoft IIS is part of Microsoft's family of server solutions.

Every computer and device (modem, router, smartphone, cars, etc.) connected to the Internet is assigned a unique numeric IP address (IP stands for Internet Protocol). For example, the computer that hosts *oreilly.com* has the IP address 208.201.239.100. All those numbers can be dizzying, so fortunately, the Domain Name System (DNS) was developed to allow us to refer to that server by its domain name, "oreilly.com", as well. The numeric IP address is useful for computer software, while the domain name is more accessible to humans. Matching the text domain names to their respective numeric IP addresses is the job of a separate DNS server.

It is possible to configure your web server so that more than one domain name is mapped to a single IP address, allowing several sites to share a single server.

Open Source

Open source software is developed as a collaborative effort with the intent to make its source code available to other programmers for use and modification. Open source programs are usually available for free.

No More IP Addresses

The IANA, the organization that assigns IP numbers, handed out its last bundle of IP addresses on February 3, 2011. That's right, no more ###.###.###.###-style IPs. That format of IP address (called IPv4) is able to produce 4.3 billion unique addresses, which seemed like plenty when the Internet "experiment" was first conceived in 1977. There was no way the creators could anticipate that one day every phone, television, and object on store shelves would be clamoring for one.

The solution is a new IP format (IPv6, already in the works) that allows for trillions and trillions of unique IP numbers, with the slight snag that it is incompatible with our current IPv4-based network, so IPv6 will operate as a sort of parallel Internet to the one we have today. Eventually, IPv4 will be phased out, but some say it will take decades.

A Word About Browsers

We now know that the server does the servin', but what about the other half of the equation? The software that does the requesting is called the client. People use desktop browsers, mobile browsers, and other assistive technologies (such as screen readers) as clients to access documents on the Web. The server returns the documents for the browser (also referred to as the user agent in technical circles) to display.

The requests and responses are handled via the HTTP protocol, mentioned earlier. Although we've been talking about "documents," HTTP can be used to transfer images, movies, audio files, data, scripts, and all the other web resources that commonly make up websites and applications.

It is common to think of a browser as a window on a computer monitor with a web page displayed in it. These are known as graphical browsers or desktop browsers and for a long time, they were the only web-viewing game in town. The most popular desktop browsers as of this writing include Internet Explorer for Windows, Chrome, Firefox, and Safari, with Opera bringing up the rear. These days, however, more and more people are accessing the Web on the go using browsing clients built into mobile phones or tablets.

It is also important to keep alternative web experiences in mind. Users with sight disabilities may be listening to a web page read by a screen reader (or simply make their text extremely large). Users with limited mobility may use assistive devices to access links and to type. The sites we build must be accessible and usable for all users, regardless of their browsing experiences.

Even on the desktop browsers that first introduced us to the wide world of the Web, pages may look and perform differently from browser to browser. This is due to varying support for web technologies and the users' ability to set their own browsing preferences.

> **TERMINOLOGY**
>
> ## Server-side and Client-side
>
> Often in web design, you'll hear reference to "client-side" or "server-side" applications. These terms are used to indicate which machine is doing the processing. Client-side applications run on the user's machine, while server-side applications and functions use the processing power of the server computer.

Intranets and Extranets

When you think of a website, you generally assume that it is accessible to anyone surfing the Web. However, many companies take advantage of the awesome information sharing and gathering power of websites to exchange information just within their own business. These special web-based networks are called intranets. They are created and function like ordinary websites, but they use special security devices (called firewalls) that prevent the outside world from seeing them. Intranets have lots of uses, such as sharing human resource information or providing access to inventory databases.

An extranet is like an intranet, only it allows access to select users outside of the company. For instance, a manufacturing company may provide its customers with passwords that allow them to check the status of their orders in the company's orders database. Of course, the passwords determine which slice of the company's information is accessible.

Web Page Addresses (URLs)

Every page and resource on the Web has its own special address called a URL, which stands for Uniform Resource Locator. It's nearly impossible to get through a day without seeing a URL (pronounced "U-R-L," not "erl") plastered on the side of a bus, printed on a business card, or broadcast on a television commercial. Web addresses are fully integrated into modern vernacular.

Some URLs are short and sweet. Others may look like crazy strings of characters separated by dots (periods) and slashes, but each part has a specific purpose. Let's pick one apart.

The parts of a URL

A complete URL is generally made up of three components: the protocol, the site name, and the absolute path to the document or resource, as shown in Figure 2-1.

Figure 2-1. *The parts of a URL.*

❶ `http://`

The first thing the URL does is define the protocol that will be used for that particular transaction. The letters HTTP let the server know to use HyperText Transfer Protocol, or get into "web mode."

❷ `www.example.com`

The next portion of the URL identifies the website by its domain name. In this example, the domain name is *example.com*. The "www." part at the beginning is the particular host name at that domain. The host name "www" has become a convention, but is not a rule. In fact, sometimes the host name may be omitted. There can be more than one website at a domain (sometimes called subdomains). For example, there might also be *development.example.com*, *clients.example.com*, and so on.

❸ `/2012/samples/first.html`

This is the absolute path through directories on the server to the requested HTML document, *first.html*. The words separated by slashes are the directory names, starting with the root directory of the host (as indicated by the initial */*). Because the Internet originally comprised computers running the Unix operating system, our current way of doing things still

NOTE

Sometimes you'll see a URL that begins with https://. *This is an indication that it is a secure server transaction. Secure servers have special encryption devices that hide delicate content, such as credit card numbers, while they are transferred to and from the browser. Look for it the next time you're shopping online.*

follows many Unix rules and conventions, hence the / separating directory names.

To sum it up, the URL in Figure 2-1 says it would like to use the HTTP protocol to connect to a web server on the Internet called *www.example.com* and request the document *first.html* (located in the *samples* directory, which is in the *2012* directory).

Default files

Obviously, not every URL you see is so lengthy. Many addresses do not include a filename, but simply point to a directory, like these:

```
http://www.oreilly.com
http://www.jendesign.com/resume/
```

When a server receives a request for a directory name rather than a specific file, it looks in that directory for a default document, typically named *index.html*. So when someone types the above URLs into his browser, what he'll actually see is this:

```
http://www.oreilly.com/index.html
http://www.jendesign.com/resume/index.html
```

The name of the default file (also referred to as the index file) may vary, and depends on how the server is configured. In these examples, it is named *index.html*, but some servers use the filename *default.htm*. If your site uses server-side programming to generate pages, the index file might be named *index.php* or *index.asp*. Just check with your server administrator or the tech support department at your hosting service to make sure you give your default file the proper name.

Another thing to notice is that in the first example, the original URL did not have a trailing slash to indicate it was a directory. When the slash is omitted, the server simply adds one if it finds a directory with that name.

The index file is also useful for security. Some servers (depending on their configuration) display the contents of the directory if the default file is not found. Figure 2-2 shows how the documents in the *housepics* directory are exposed as the result of a missing default file. One way to prevent people from snooping around in your files is to be sure there is an index file in every directory. Your server administrator may also add other protections to prevent your directories from displaying in the browser.

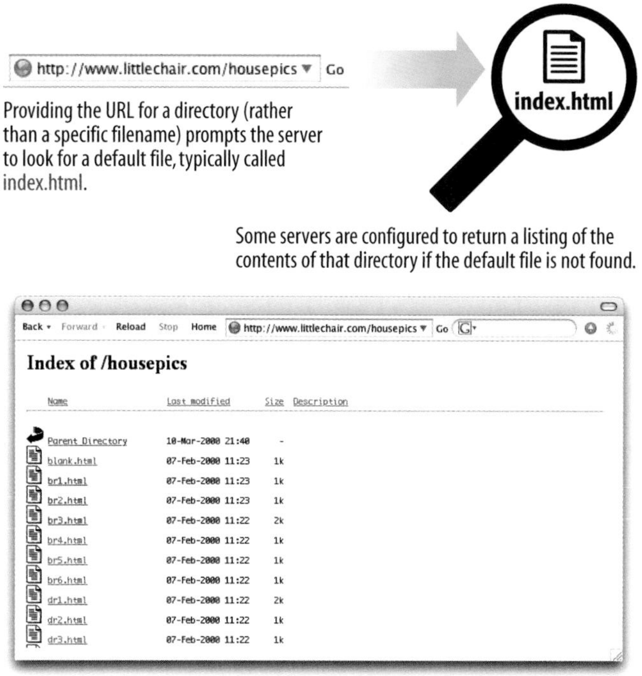

Figure 2-2. Some servers display the contents of the directory if an index file is not found.

Providing the URL for a directory (rather than a specific filename) prompts the server to look for a default file, typically called index.html.

Some servers are configured to return a listing of the contents of that directory if the default file is not found.

The Anatomy of a Web Page

We're all familiar with what web pages look like in the browser window, but what's happening "under the hood"?

At the top of Figure 2-3, you see a minimal web page as it appears in a graphical browser. Although you see it as one coherent page, it is actually assembled from four separate files: an HTML document (*index.html*), a style sheet (*kitchen.css*), and two graphics (*foods.gif* and *spoon.gif*). The HTML document is running the show.

HTML documents

You may be as surprised as I was to learn that the graphically rich and interactive pages we see on the Web are generated by simple, text-only documents. This text file is referred to as the source document.

Take a look at *index.html*, the source document for the Jen's Kitchen web page. You can see it contains the text content of the page plus special tags (indicated with angle brackets, < and >) that describe each element on the page.

Adding descriptive tags to a text document is known as "marking up" the document. Web pages use a markup language called HyperText Markup Language, or HTML for short, which was created especially for documents with hypertext links. HTML defines dozens of text elements that make up documents such as headings, paragraphs, emphasized text, and of course, links. There are also elements that add information about the document (such as its title), media such as images and videos, and widgets for form inputs, just to name a few.

It is worth noting briefly that there are actually several versions of HTML in use today. The most firmly established are HTML version 4.01 and its stricter cousin, XHTML 1.0. And you may have heard how all the Web is a-buzz with the emerging HTML5 specification that is designed to better handle web applications and is gradually gaining browser support. I will give you the lowdown on all the various versions and what makes them unique in Chapter 10, What's Up, HTML5?. In the meantime, we have to cover some basics that apply regardless of the HTML flavor you choose.

A quick introduction to HTML markup

You'll be learning the nitty-gritty of markup in Part II, so I don't want to bog you down with too much detail right now, but there are a few things I'd like to point out about how HTML works and how browsers interpret it.

Read through the HTML document in Figure 2-3 and compare it to the browser results. It's easy to see how the elements marked up with HTML tags in the source document correspond to what displays in the browser window.

---

exercise 2-1 |
View source

You can see the HTML file for any web page by choosing View → Page Source (or View → Source) in your browser's menu. Your browser typically opens the source document in a separate window. Let's take a look under the hood of a web page.

1. Enter this URL into your browser:

   www.learningwebdesign.com/4e/ materials/chapter02/kitchen.html

   You should see the Jen's Kitchen web page from Figure 2-3.

2. Select View → Page Source (or View → Source) from the browser menu. On Chrome and Opera, View Source is located in the Developer menu. A window opens showing the source document shown in the figure.

3. The source for most sites is considerably more complicated. View the source of *oreilly.com* or the site of your choice. Don't worry if you don't understand what's going on. Much of it will look more familiar by the time you are done with this book.

WARNING

Keep in mind that while learning from others' work is fine, the all-out stealing of other people's code is poor form (or even illegal). If you want to use code as you see it, ask for permission and always give credit to those who did the work.

The web page shown in this browser window consists of four separate files: an HTML text document, a style sheet and two images. Tags in the HTML source document give the browser instructions for how the text is structured and where the images should be placed.

index.html

```
<!DOCTYPE html>
<html>
<head>
<title>Jen's Kitchen</title>
<link rel="stylesheet" href="kitchen.css" type="text/css" >
</head>

<body>
<h1><img src="foods.gif" alt="food illustration"> Jen&rsquo;s Kitchen</h1>

<p>If you love to read about <strong>cooking and eating</strong>, would like to find out about
some of the best restaurants in the world, or just want a few choice recipes to add to your
collection, <em>this is the site for you!</em></p>

<p><img src="spoon.gif" alt="spoon illustration"> Your pal, Jen at Jen's Kitchen</p>
<hr>
<p><small>Copyright 2011, Jennifer Robbins</small></p>
</body>
</html>
```

kitchen.css

```
body { font: normal 1em Verdana; margin: 1em 10%;}
h1 { font: italic 3em Georgia; color: rgb(23, 109, 109); margin: 1em 0 1em;}
img { margin: 0 20px 0 0; }
h1 img { margin-bottom: -20px; }
small { color: #666666; }
```

foods.gif *spoon.gif*

Figure 2-3. The source file and images that make up a simple web page.

First, you'll notice that the text within brackets (for example, **<body>**) does not display in the final page. The browser displays only what's between the tags—the content of the element. The markup is hidden. The tag provides the name of the HTML element—usually an abbreviation such as "h1" for "heading level 1," or "em" for "emphasized text."

Second, you'll see that most of the HTML tags appear in pairs surrounding the content of the element. In our HTML document, **<h1>** indicates that the following text should be a level-1 heading; **</h1>** indicates the end of the heading. Some elements, called empty elements, do not have content. In our sample, the **<hr>** tag indicates an empty element that tells the browser to "insert a thematic divider here" (most browsers indicate the thematic divider with a horizontal rule [line], which is how the **hr** element got its initials).

Because I was unfamiliar with computer programming when I first began writing HTML, it helped me to think of the tags and text as "beads on a string" that the browser interprets one by one, in sequence. For example, when the browser encounters an open bracket (**<**), it assumes all of the following characters are part of the markup until it finds the closing bracket (**>**). Similarly, it assumes all of the content following an opening **<h1>** tag is a heading until it encounters the closing **</h1>** tag. This is the manner in which the browser parses the HTML document. Understanding the browser's method can be helpful when troubleshooting a misbehaving HTML document.

But where are the pictures?

Obviously, there are no pictures in the HTML file itself, so how do they get there when you view the final page?

You can see in Figure 2-3 that each image is a separate file. The images are placed in the flow of the text with the HTML image element (**img**), which tells the browser where to find the graphic (its URL). When the browser sees the **img** element, it makes another request to the server for the image file, and then places it in the content flow. The browser software brings the separate pieces together into the final page. Videos and other embedded media files are added in much the same way.

The assembly of the page generally happens in an instant, so it appears as though the whole page loads all at once. Over slow connections or if the page includes huge graphics or media files, the assembly process may be more apparent as images lag behind the text. The page may even need to be redrawn as new images arrive (although you can construct your pages in such a way as to prevent that from happening).

Adding a little style

I want to direct your attention to one last key ingredient of our minimal page. Near the top of the HTML document there is a **link** element that points to the style sheet document *kitchen.css*. That style sheet includes a few lines of instructions for how the page should look in the browser. These are style instructions written according to the rules of Cascading Style Sheets (CSS). CSS allows designers to add visual style instructions (known as the document's presentation) to the marked-up text (the document's structure, in web design terminology). In Part III, you'll really get to know the power of Cascading Style Sheets.

Figure 2-4 shows the Jen's Kitchen page without (left) and with (right) the style instructions. Browsers come equipped with default styles for every HTML element they support, so if an HTML document lacks its own custom style instructions, the browser will use its own (that's what you see in the screenshot on the left). Even just a few style rules can make big improvements to the appearance of a page.

Figure 2-4. The Jen's Kitchen page before (left) and after (right) style rules.

Adding Behaviors with JavaScript

In addition to a document's structure and presentation, there is also a behavior component that defines how things *work*. On the Web, behaviors are defined by a scripting language called JavaScript. We'll touch on it lightly in this book in **Part IV**, but learning JavaScript from scratch is more than we can take on here. Many designers (myself included) rely on people with scripting experience to add functionality to sites. However, knowing how to write JavaScript is becoming more essential to the "web designer" job description.

Putting It All Together

To wrap up our introduction to how the Web works, let's trace a typical stream of events that occurs with every web page that appears on your screen (Figure 2-5).

❶ You request a web page by either typing its URL (for example, *http://jenskitchensite.com*) directly in the browser or by clicking on a link on a page. The URL contains all the information needed to target a specific document on a specific web server on the Internet.

❷ Your browser sends an HTTP request to the server named in the URL and asks for the specific file. If the URL specifies a directory (not a file), it is the same as requesting the default file in that directory.

❸ The server looks for the requested file and issues an HTTP response.

    a. If the page cannot be found, the server returns an error message. The message typically says "404 Not Found," although more hospitable error messages may be provided.

    b. If the document *is* found, the server retrieves the requested file and returns it to the browser.

❹ The browser parses the HTML document. If the page contains images (indicated by the HTML **img** element) or other external resources like scripts, the browser contacts the server again to request each resource specified in the markup.

❺ The browser inserts each image in the document flow where indicated by the **img** element. And *voilà*! The assembled web page is displayed for your viewing pleasure.

Getting Your Pages on the Web

If you would like more information about registering domain names, finding a server to host your site, and transferring files to the server (FTP), download the PDF titled "Getting Your Pages on the Web" at *learningwebdesign.com/pdf/lwd3_getting_on_the_web.pdf*.

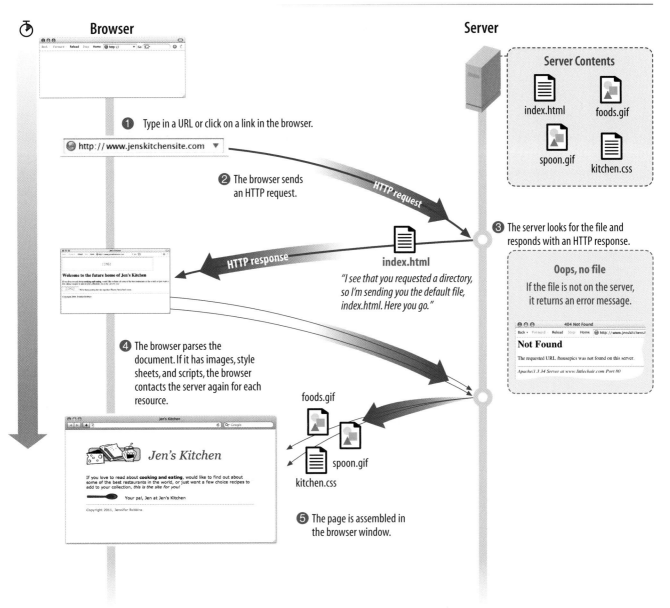

Browser

Server

Server Contents

index.html   foods.gif

spoon.gif   kitchen.css

❶ Type in a URL or click on a link in the browser.

http://www.jenskitchensite.com ▼

❷ The browser sends an HTTP request.

HTTP request

❸ The server looks for the file and responds with an HTTP response.

HTTP response

index.html

"I see that you requested a directory, so I'm sending you the default file, index.html. Here you go."

Oops, no file

If the file is not on the server, it returns an error message.

404 Not Found

Not Found

The requested URL /housepics was not found on this server.

Apache/1.3.34 Server at www.littlechair.com Port 80

❹ The browser parses the document. If it has images, style sheets, and scripts, the browser contacts the server again for each resource.

foods.gif

spoon.gif

kitchen.css

Jen's Kitchen

If you love to read about **cooking and eating**, would like to find out about some of the best restaurants in the world, or just want a few choice recipes to add to your collection, *this is the site for you!*

Your pal, Jen at Jen's Kitchen

Copyright 2011, Jennifer Robbins

❺ The page is assembled in the browser window.

Figure 2-5. How browsers display web pages.

Test Yourself

Let's play a round of "Identify That Acronym!" The following are a few basic web terms mentioned in this chapter. Answers are in Appendix A.

1. HTML	_____	a. Home of Mosaic, the first graphical browser
2. W3C	_____	b. The location of a web document or resource
3. CERN	_____	c. The markup language used to describe web content
4. CSS	_____	d. Matches domain names with numeric IP addresses
5. HTTP	_____	e. A protocol for file transfer
6. IP	_____	f. Protocol for transferring web documents on the Internet
7. URL	_____	g. The language used to instruct how web content looks
8. NCSA	_____	h. Particle physics lab where the Web was born
9. DNS	_____	i. Internet Protocol
10. FTP	_____	j. The organization that monitors web technologies

SOME BIG CONCEPTS YOU NEED TO KNOW

As the Web matures and the number of devices we access it from increases exponentially, our jobs as web designers and developers get significantly more complicated. Frankly, there's a lot more going on out there than I can fit in this book. In the chapters that follow, I will focus on the basic building blocks of web design—HTML elements, CSS styles, a taste of JavaScript, and web graphics production—that will give you a solid foundation for the further development of your skills.

But before we get to the nuts and bolts, I want to introduce some Big Concepts that I think every web designer needs to know. We'll look at ideas and concerns that inform our decisions and contribute to the contemporary web design environment. I'll be referring back to the terminology introduced here frequently.

The heart of the matter is that as web designers, we never know exactly how the pages we create will be viewed. We don't know which of the hundreds of browsers might be used, whether it is on a desktop computer or something more portable, how large the browser window will be, what fonts are installed, whether functionality such as JavaScript is enabled, the speed of the Internet connection, whether the pages are being read by a screen reader, and so on. I think you get the picture. The Big Concepts in this chapter are primarily reactions to and methods for coping with the inescapable element of the Unknown in our medium. They include:

- The multitude of devices

- Web standards

- Progressive enhancement

- Responsive web design

- Accessibility

- Site performance

Because we're just getting started, I will keep the descriptions brief and fairly non-technical. My goal is that you have a basic understanding of what I mean by terms like "progressive enhancement" when you encounter them in a later exercise. Many excellent articles and books have been written on each of these topics and their related production techniques, and I'll provide pointers to resources for further reading.

A Dizzying Multitude of Devices

Until 2007, we could be relatively certain that our users were visiting our sites while sitting at their desks, looking at a large monitor, using a speedy Internet connection. We had all more or less settled on 960 pixels as a good width for a web page. Back then, our biggest concern was dealing with the dozen or so desktop browsers and jumping through a few extra hoops to support quirky old versions of Internet Explorer. And we thought we had it rough!

Although you could access web pages and web content on mobile phones prior to 2007, the introduction of the iPhone and Android smartphones as well as a more widespread 3G network heralded a huge shift in how, when, and where we do our web surfing (particularly in the United States, which lagged behind Asia and the EU in mobile technology). Since then, we've seen the introduction of tablets of all different dimensions, as well as web browsers on TVs and other devices. And the diversity is only going to increase. I think mobile guru Brad Frost sums it up nicely in his illustrations in Figure 3-1.

Figure 3-1. Brad Frost sums up the reality of device diversity nicely (bradfrostweb.com).

The challenge of designing for all of these devices goes beyond addressing differing screen sizes. There is a world of difference between using a site over a broadband connection and over a 3G or EDGE network. There are also varying contexts to consider. Users may be sitting at a desk, enjoying some recreational browsing at home, or getting information quickly on the go. Designers need to resist making assumptions about network speed and context based on the screen size. It's not uncommon to leisurely browse the Web on a smartphone while sitting on the couch at home with a solid WiFi connection. And new iPads with high-resolution displays may be accessing the Internet on a pokey 3G connection. In other words, it's complicated!

Soon, more people will be accessing the Web on their mobile and alternative devices than on a desktop computer. Already a significant portion of Americans use their mobile phones as their *only* access to the Internet. That means it is critical to get it right. But to be honest, as of this writing, we haven't entirely figured out how to make all the content we are accustomed to seeing at our desks fit on our handheld devices with an equally pleasing experience. Great strides are being made, and there is a wonderful spirit of collaboration while we figure it out, but the fact is that our tools and technologies are not quite suited for the task and will take some time to catch up.

What I want you to learn here is that the way you see your design as you're working on it on your nice desktop machine is not how it will be experienced by everyone. This fact should be on the mind of all web design professionals.

Mobile Web?

You may hear designers use the term Mobile Web, but the truth is (as Stephen Hay put it in a tweet in 2011; see Figure 3-2), there is no Mobile Web any more than there is a Desktop Web, or a Tablet Web, or so on. There is just the Web, and it can be accessed from all manner of devices. As of this writing, the term "mobile web" is used as sort of a catchall for describing our efforts to adapt our desktop design skills to accommodate a much wider variety of use cases. And as we are finding out, there is more than one way to crack that nut.

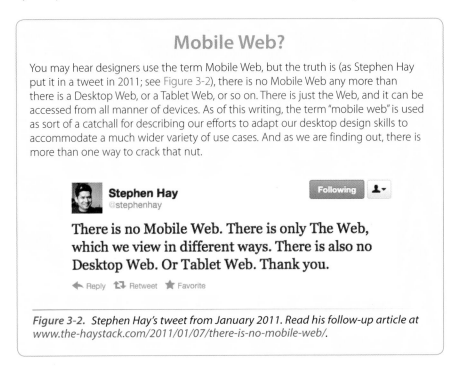

Figure 3-2. Stephen Hay's tweet from January 2011. Read his follow-up article at www.the-haystack.com/2011/01/07/there-is-no-mobile-web/.

For further reading

- In his article "*The Coming Zombie Apocalypse*," Scott Jensen takes a thoughtful look at the onslaught of inexpensive networked devices (*designmind.frogdesign.com/blog/the-coming-zombie-apocalypse-small-cheap-devices-will-disrupt-our-old-school-ux-assumptions.htm*). It is definitely worth a read.

- *Mobile First*, by Luke Wroblewski (A Book Apart). Luke was way ahead of the curve on insisting sites work well on mobile devices, and he shares his perspective in this little book that is jam-packed with ideas.

- The Future Friendly site (*futurefriend.ly*) includes a call to arms composed by many of the brightest mobile designers of the day. They concluded that with the landscape changing so rapidly, we can't make our designs future-proof, but we can make them "future friendly." They assemble a number of tips and resources for doing so.

Sticking with the Standards

Sticking with web standards is your primary tool for ensuring your site is as consistent as possible.

So how do we deal with this diversity? One good start is to follow the HTML, CSS, and JavaScript standards as documented by the World Wide Web Consortium (W3C). Sticking with web standards is your primary tool for ensuring your site is as consistent as possible on all standards-compliant browsers (that's approximately 99% of browsers in current use). It also helps make your content forward-compatible as web technologies and browser capabilities evolve. Another benefit is you can tell your clients that you create "standards-compliant" sites, and they will like you more.

The notion of standards compliance may seem like a no-brainer, but it used to be that everyone, including the browser makers, played fast and loose with HTML and scripting. The price we paid was incompatible browser implementations and the need to create sites twice to make them work for everyone. I talk more about web standards throughout this book, so I won't go into too much detail here. Suffice it to say that the web standards are your friends. Everything you learn in this book will get you headed in the right direction.

For further reading

The bible for standards compliance and how it makes good business sense is *Designing with Web Standards* by Jeffrey Zeldman (New Riders). Go read it (when you're done with this book, of course).

Progressive Enhancement

Progressive enhancement is a strategy for coping with unknown browser capabilities.

With a multitude of browsers comes a multitude of levels of support for the web standards. In fact, no browser has implemented all the standards 100%, and there are always new technologies that are slowly gaining steam. Furthermore, users can set their own browser preferences, so they may have a browser that supports JavaScript but have chosen to turn it off. The point here is that we are faced with a wide range of browser capabilities—from basic HTML support only to all the bells and whistles.

Progressive enhancement is one strategy for dealing with unknown browser capabilities. When designing with progressive enhancement, you start with a baseline experience that makes the content or functionality available to even the most rudimentary browsers or assistive devices. From there, you layer on more advanced features for the browsers that can handle them. You might finish with some "nice to have" effects like animation or rounded corners on boxes that enhance the experience for users with the most advanced browsers, but that aren't really critical to the brand or message.

Progressive enhancement is an approach that informs all aspects of page design and production, including HTML, CSS, and JavaScript.

Authoring strategy

When an HTML document is written in logical order and its elements are marked up in a meaningful way, it will be usable on the widest range of browsing environments, including the oldest browsers, future browsers, and mobile and assistive devices. It may not look exactly the same, but the important thing is that your content is available. It also ensures that search engines like Google will catalog the content correctly. A clean HTML document with its elements accurately and thoroughly described is the foundation for accessibility.

Styling strategy

You can create layers of experience simply by taking advantage of the way browsers parse style sheet rules. Without going into too much technical detail, you can write a style rule that makes an element background red, but also include a style that gives it a cool gradient (a blend from one color to another) for browsers that know how to render gradients. Or you can use a cutting-edge CSS selector to deliver certain styles only to cutting-edge browsers. The knowledge that browsers simply ignore properties and rules they don't understand gives you license to innovate without bringing older browsers to their knees. You just have to be mindful to take care of styling the baseline experience first, then add improvements once the minimum requirements are met.

Scripting strategy

JavaScript is the scripting language that makes web pages interactive and dynamic (updating content on the fly or in response to user input). The Web would be a lot of static brochureware without it. Like other web technologies, there are discrepancies in how browsers handle JavaScript (particularly on non-desktop devices), and some users opt to turn it off entirely. The first rule in progressive enhancement is to make sure basic functionality—such as linking from page to page or accomplishing essential tasks like data submission via forms—is intact even when JavaScript is off. In this way, you ensure the baseline experience, and enhance it when JavaScript is available.

NOTE

Progressive enhancement is the flip side of an older approach to browser diversity called graceful degradation, in which you design the fully enhanced experience first, then create a series of fallbacks for non-supporting browsers.

For further reading

There is no better introduction to the progressive enhancement approach than the book *Adaptive Web Design: Crafting Rich Experiences with Progressive Enhancement*, by Aaron Gustafson (Easy Readers). Aaron is a technical reviewer for this book, but I'd be recommending his excellent primer even if he weren't. See *easy-readers.net/books/adaptive-web-design/* for more information.

Once you have more web development chops, the book *Designing with Progressive Enhancement*, by Todd Parker, Patty Toland, Scott Jehl, and Maggie Costello Wachs (New Riders), is an excellent deep-dive into techniques and best practices. Read more about it at *filamentgroup.com/dwpe/*.

Responsive Web Design

By default, most browsers on small devices such as smartphones and tablets shrink a web page down to fit the screen and provide mechanisms for zooming and moving around the page. Although it technically works, it is not a great experience. The text is too small to read, the links are too small to tap, and all that zooming and panning around is distracting.

Responsive web design is a strategy for dealing with unknown screen size.

Responsive web design is a strategy for providing custom layouts to devices based on the size of the viewport (browser window). The trick to responsive web design is serving a single HTML document to all devices, but applying different style sheets based on the screen size in order to provide the most optimized layout for that device. For example, when the page is viewed on a smartphone, it appears in one column with large links for easy tapping. But when that same page is viewed on a large desktop browser, the content rearranges into multiple columns with traditional navigation elements. It's like *magic*! (Except that it's actually just CSS.)

The web design community has been a-buzz about responsive design since Ethan Marcotte first wrote about it and coined the phrase in his article "Responsive Web Design" on A List Apart in 2010 (*www.alistapart.com/articles/responsive-web-design/*). It's become one of the primary tools we use to cope with unknown viewport size.

Figure 3-3 shows some examples of responsive sites at the typical dimensions for a desktop monitor, tablet, and smartphone. You can see many more inspirational examples at the Media Queries gallery site (*mediaqueri.es*) Try opening a design in your browser and then resizing the window very narrow and very wide, and watch as the layout changes based on the window size. *Très* cool.

Open Medical Device Research Library
www.omdrl.org

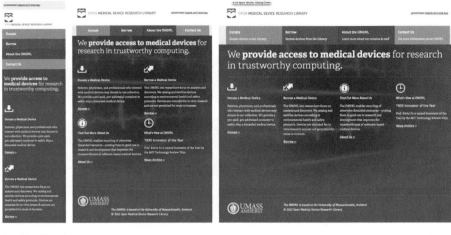

Smashing Magazine
smashingmagazine.org

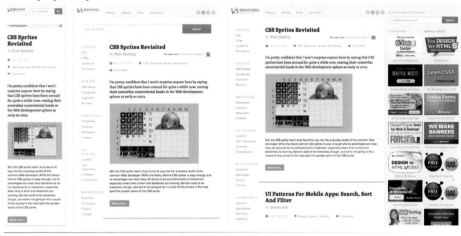

Figure 3-3. Responsive sites' layout changes based on the size of the browser window.

Responsive web design helps with matters of layout, but it is not a solution to all mobile web design challenges. The fact is that providing the best experiences for your users and their chosen device may require optimizations that go beyond adjusting the look and feel. Some problems are better addressed by using the server to detect the device and its capabilities and then making decisions on what to send back. Using progressive enhancement, you can deliver a baseline experience for the most basic browsers and devices, but send enhanced options for devices that can use them.

For some sites and services, it may be preferable to build a separate mobile site (see the "Dedicated Mobile Sites" sidebar) with a customized interface and feature set that takes advantage of phone capabilities like geolocation. That said, although responsive design won't fix everything, it is an important part of the solution for delivering satisfactory experiences on a wide variety of browsers.

Dedicated Mobile Sites

The alternative to a single responsive site is to build an entirely separate site, with a unique URL, that gets served up when requested by a mobile device. Mobile site URLs are commonly prefixed with *m.* or *mobile*. For some types of sites, a dedicated mobile site is the best solution if you know that your mobile users have very different usage patterns than folks seated at a desk. On dedicated mobile sites, the most frequently requested features are highlighted on the first screen, and a lot of the "extra" stuff (like promotions) from the desktop site is simply stripped away. (It makes you wonder what value it adds to the desktop site after all.)

Figure 3-4 compares Walgreens' primary and mobile sites as they appeared mid-2012. You can see that phone users are offered a much more streamlined set of options.

A dedicated mobile site may be the best way to make complex tasks easier for users on smartphones. Luke Wroblewski provides many thoughtful reasons why his service Bagcheck chose a separate site in his article "Why Separate Mobile and Desktop Pages?" (*www.lukew.com/ff/entry.asp?1390*). I recommend you give it a read.

The point here is that responsive web design is not a universal solution. For sites that feature mainly text content, a little layout adjustment may be all that is needed to bring a good reading experience on all devices. For other sites and web applications, a very different experience may be preferred.

The downside of a dedicated mobile site is that it is more than twice the work. It requires additional content planning, design templates, production time, and ongoing maintenance. But if it means giving your visitors the functionality they really need, it is well worth the investment.

Figure 3-4. A comparison of primary and dedicated mobile sites.

NOTE

Even dedicated mobile sites can and should take advantage of responsive techniques to customize their experience from device to device. It isn't necessarily an only one or the other decision. Stephanie Rieger summarizes this point well in her article "Responsiveness is a characteristic," which you can read at stephanierieger.com/responsiveness-is-a-characteristic/.

For further reading

I'll cover responsive web design in more detail in Chapter 18, CSS Techniques, once you have more code experience under your belt. To continue your responsive design education, I recommend the following books.

- Ethan Marcott's book *Responsive Web Design* (A Book Apart) is required reading for budding web designers. It's a short book that is the perfect starting point for learning how responsive web design works and how to try it yourself.

- *Head First Mobile Web*, by Lyza Danger Gardner and Jason Grigsby (O'Reilly). This book includes responsive web design, but expands on it, including techniques that take advantage of scripting and server-side detection. It's also extremely entertaining to read, although you'll need some familiarity with CSS and JavaScript to get the most out of it.

One Web for All (Accessibility)

We've been talking about the daunting number of browsers in use today, but so far, we've only addressed visual browsers controlled with mouse pointers or fingertips. It is critical, however, to keep in mind that people access the Web in many different ways—with screen readers, Braille output, magnifiers, joysticks, foot pedals, and so on. Web designers must build pages in a manner that creates as few barriers as possible to getting to information, regardless of the user's ability and the device used to access the Web. In other words, you must design for accessibility.

Although intended for users with disabilities such as poor vision or limited mobility, the techniques and strategies developed for accessibility also benefit other users with less-than-optimum browsing experiences, such as handheld devices, or traditional browsers over slow modem connections or with the images and JavaScript turned off. Accessible sites are also more effectively indexed by search engines such as Google. The extra effort in making your site accessible is well worth the effort.

There are four broad categories of disabilities that affect how people interact with their computers and the information on them:

Vision impairment. People with low or no vision may use an assistive device such as a screen reader, Braille display, or a screen magnifier to get content from the screen. They may also simply use the browser's text zoom function to make the text large enough to read.

Mobility impairment. Users with limited or no use of their hands may use special devices such as modified mice and keyboards, foot pedals, or joysticks to navigate the Web and enter information.

Auditory impairment. Users with limited or no hearing will miss out on audio aspects of multimedia, so it is necessary to provide alternatives, such as transcripts for audio tracks or captions for video.

Cognitive impairment. Users with memory, reading comprehension, problem solving, and attention limitations benefit when sites are designed simply and clearly. These qualities are helpful to anyone using your site.

The W3C started the Web Accessibility Initiative (WAI) to address the need to make the Web usable for everyone. The WAI site (*www.w3.org/WAI*) is an excellent starting point for learning more about web accessibility. One of the documents produced by the WAI to help developers create accessible sites is the Web Content Accessibility Guidelines (WCAG and WCAG 2.0). You can read them all at *www.w3.org/WAI/intro/wcag.php*. The United States government used the Priority 1 points of the WCAG as the basis for its Section 508 accessibility guidelines (see the sidebar "Government Accessibility Requirements: Section 508"). All sites benefit from these guidelines, but if you are designing a government site, adherence is a requirement.

Government Accessibility Requirements: Section 508

If you create a site receiving federal funding, you are required by law to comply with the Section 508 Guidelines that ensure that electronic information and technology is available to people with disabilities. State and other publicly funded sites may also be required to comply.

The following guidelines, excerpted from the Section 508 Standards at *www.section508.gov*, provide a good checklist for basic accessibility for all websites.

1. A text equivalent for non-text elements shall be provided (e.g., via the "alt" attribute or in element content).

2. Equivalent alternatives for any multimedia presentation shall be synchronized with the presentation.

3. Web pages shall be designed so that all information conveyed with color is also available without color—for example, from context or markup.

4. Documents shall be organized so they are readable without requiring an associated style sheet.

5. Row and column headers shall be identified for data tables.

6. Markup shall be used to associate data cells and header cells for data tables that have two or more logical levels of row or column headers.

7. Pages shall be designed to avoid causing the screen to flicker with a frequency greater than 2 Hz and lower than 55 Hz.

8. When pages utilize scripting languages to display content, or to create interface elements, the information provided by the script shall be identified with functional text that can be read by assistive technology.

9. When a web page requires that an applet, plug-in, or other application be present on the client system to interpret page content, the page must provide a link to a plug-in or applet that complies with §1194.21(a) through (l).

10. When electronic forms are designed to be completed online, the form shall allow people using assistive technology to access the information, field elements, and functionality required for completion and submission of the form, including all directions and cues.

11. A method shall be provided that permits users to skip repetitive navigation links.

12. When a timed response is required, the user shall be alerted and given sufficient time to indicate more time is required.

Another W3C effort is the WAI-ARIA (Accessible Rich Internet Applications) spec, which addresses the accessibility of web applications that include dynamically generated content, scripting, and advanced interface elements that are particularly confounding to assistive devices. The ARIA Recommendation defines a number of roles for content and widgets that authors can explicitly apply using the **role** attribute. Roles include things like **menubar**, **progressbar**, **slider**, **timer**, and **tooltip**, and add an enhanced layer of semantics for those who need it. For the complete list of roles, go to *www.w3.org/TR/wai-aria/roles#role_definitions*.

For further reading

The following resources are good starting points for further exploration on web accessibility:

- The Web Accessibility Initiative (WAI), *www.w3.org/WAI*

- WebAIM: Web Accessibility in Mind, *www.webaim.org*

- *Pro HTML5 Accessibility*, by Joshue O Connor (Professional Apress, 2012)

- *Universal Design for Web Applications: Web Applications That Reach Everyone*, by Wendy Chisholm and Matt May (O'Reilly)

The Need for Speed (Site Performance)

Although the number of users accessing the Internet on slow dial-up connections is shrinking (5–10% in the US as of this writing), the percentage of folks using mobile phones to access the Web is increasing dramatically and is eventually slated to exceed desktop usage. If you have a smartphone, then you know how frustrating it is to wait for a web page to fully display over a cellular data connection.

But site performance is critical regardless of how your users are accessing your site. A study by Google in 2009* showed that the addition of just 100 to 400 milliseconds to their search results page resulted in reduced searches (–0.2 to –0.6%). Amazon.com showed that reducing page load times by just 100ms resulted in a 1% increase in revenue.† Other studies show that users expect a site to load in under two seconds, and nearly a third of your audience will leave your site for another if it doesn't. Furthermore, those people aren't likely to come back. Google has added site speed to its search algorithm, so if your site is a slow poke, it's not likely to show up in that coveted first screen of results. The takeaway here is site performance (down to the millisecond!) matters a lot.

There are many things you can do to improve the performance of your site, and they fall under the two broad categories of limiting file sizes and reducing the number of requests to the server. The following list only scratches the surface for site optimization, but it gives you a general idea of what can be done.

- Optimizing images so they are the smallest file size possible without sacrificing quality. You'll learn image optimization techniques in Chapter 22, Lean and Mean Graphics.

- Minimize HTML and CSS documents by removing extra character spaces and line returns.

- Keep JavaScript to a minimum.

- Add scripts in such a way that they load in parallel with other page assets and don't block rendering.

- Don't load unnecessary assets (such as images, scripts, or JavaScript libraries).

- Reduce the number of times the browser makes requests of the server (known as HTTP requests).

Every trip to the server in the form of an HTTP request takes a few milliseconds, and those milliseconds can really add up. All those little Twitter

NOTE

See the article "Effect of Website Speed on Users, Statistics Reveal Slow Loading Times Cost Sites Serious Money" (munchweb.com/effect-of-website-speed) for more fascinating site performance studies.

---

* "Speed Matters," *googleresearch.blogspot.com/2009/06/speed-matters.html*

† Statistic from "Make Data Matter," PowerPoint presentation by Greg Linden of Stanford University (2006)

widgets, Facebook Like buttons, and advertisements can make dozens of server requests each. You may be surprised to see how many server requests even a simple site makes.

If you'd like to see for yourself, you can use the developer tool in the Chrome browser to see each request to the server and how many milliseconds it takes. Here's how you do it:

1. Launch the Chrome browser and go to any web page.

2. Go to the View menu and select Developer → Developer Tools. A panel will open at the bottom of the browser.

3. Select the Network tab in the tools view and reload the page. The chart (commonly referred to as a waterfall chart) shows you all the requests made and assets downloaded. The columns on the right show the amount of time each request took in milliseconds. At the bottom of the chart, you can see a summary of the number of requests made and the total amount of data transferred.

Figure 3-5 shows a portion of the performance waterfall chart for my site, *Jenville.com*, which is a simple site (but not as simple as I thought!). You can poke around any site on the Web this way. It can be very educational.

Figure 3-5. *Waterfall charts such as this one created by the Chrome Network developer tool show you the individual server requests made by a web page and the amount of time each request takes.*

I won't address site performance much in this book, but I do want you to remember the importance of keeping file sizes as small as possible and eliminating unnecessary server requests in your web design work.

For further reading

There are other techniques that are too technical for this book (and frankly, for me), and I figure if you are reading this book, you are probably not quite ready to become a site performance wizard. But when you are ready to take it on, here are some resources that should help:

- Google's site *Make the Web Faster* (*code.google.com/speed/*) is an excellent first stop for learning about site optimization. It compiles a number of excellent tutorials and articles as well as tools for measuring site speed.

- The books *High Performance Web Sites* and *Even Faster Web Sites* (both by Steve Souders and published by O'Reilly) provide many best practices for speeding up sites. A good understanding of JavaScript and server functionality is required.

Test Yourself

1. The "mobile web" complicates our jobs as web designers. List at least three unknown factors you need to consider when designing and developing a site.

2. Match the technology or practice on the left with the problem it best addresses.

   1. _____ Progressive enhancement   a. Assistive reading and input devices

   2. _____ Server-side detection   b. Slow connection speeds

   3. _____ Responsive design   c. All levels of browser capabilities

   4. _____ WAI-ARIA   d. Determining which device is being used

   5. _____ Site performance optimization   e. A variety of screen sizes

More Site Performance Tools

Try some of these tools for testing site performance:

- WebPagetest (*webpagetest.org*) is a tool that was originally developed for AOL, but is now available for all to use for free under an open source license. Just type in a URL and WebPagetest returns a waterfall diagram, screenshot, and other statistics.

- Yahoo!'s freely available YSlow tool (*yslow.org*) analyzes a site according to 23 rules of web performance, then gives the site a grade and suggestions for improvement.

- For mobile sites, try Mobitest by Blaze (*www.blaze.io/mobile/*), a free tool for testing website performance on various mobile devices.

- There are also a number of slow connection speed simulators so you can get a feel for your users' experiences over less-than-ideal network speeds. Sloppy (*www.dallaway.com/sloppy*) is a web tool where you enter a web address and select a modem speed (and wait and wait). Mac OS users can try Slowy (*slowyapp.com*).

3. Web accessibility strategies take into account four broad categories of disabilities. Name at least three, and provide a measure you might take to ensure content is accessible for each.

4. When would you use a waterfall chart?

5. Responsive web design doesn't solve everything. Describe what it is good for and where it falls short.

HTML MARKUP FOR STRUCTURE

PART **II**

CHAPTER 4

CREATING A SIMPLE PAGE
(HTML Overview)

Part I provided a general overview of the web design environment. Now that we've covered the big concepts, it's time to roll up our sleeves and start creating a real web page. It will be an extremely simple page, but even the most complicated pages are based on the principles described here.

In this chapter, we'll create a web page step by step so you can get a feel for what it's like to mark up a document with HTML tags. The exercises allow you to work along.

This is what I want you to get out of this chapter:

- Get a feel for how markup works, including an understanding of elements and attributes.
- See how browsers interpret HTML documents.
- Learn the basic structure of an HTML document.
- Get a first glimpse of a style sheet in action.

Don't worry about learning the specific text elements or style sheet rules at this point; we'll get to those in the following chapters. For now, just pay attention to the process, the overall structure of the document, and the new terminology.

A Web Page, Step by Step

You got a look at an HTML document in Chapter 2, How the Web Works, but now you'll get to create one yourself and play around with it in the browser. The demonstration in this chapter has five steps that cover the basics of page production.

Step 1: Start with content. As a starting point, we'll write up raw text content and see what browsers do with it.

Step 2: Give the document structure. You'll learn about HTML element syntax and the elements that give a document its structure.

IN THIS CHAPTER

An introduction to elements and attributes

A step-by-step demo of marking up a simple web page

The elements that provide document structure

A simple stylesheet

Troubleshooting broken web pages

HTML the Hard Way

I stand by my method of teaching HTML the old-fashioned way—*by hand*. There's no better way to truly understand how markup works than typing it out, one tag at a time, then opening your page in a browser. It doesn't take long to develop a feel for marking up documents properly.

Although you may choose to use a web-authoring tool down the line, understanding HTML will make using your tools easier and more efficient. In addition, you will be glad that you can look at a source file and understand what you're seeing. It is also crucial for troubleshooting broken pages or fine-tuning the default formatting that web tools produce.

And for what it's worth, professional web developers tend to mark up content manually because it gives them better control over the code and allows them to make deliberate decisions about what elements are used.

Step 3: Identify text elements. You'll describe the content using the appropriate text elements and learn about the proper way to use HTML.

Step 4: Add an image. By adding an image to the page, you'll learn about attributes and empty elements.

Step 5: Change the page appearance with a style sheet. This exercise gives you a taste of formatting content with Cascading Style Sheets.

By the time we're finished, you will have written the source document for the page shown in Figure 4-1. It's not very fancy, but you have to start somewhere.

We'll be checking our work in a browser frequently throughout this demonstration—probably more than you would in real life. But because this is an introduction to HTML, it is helpful to see the cause and effect of each small change to the source file along the way.

Before We Begin, Launch a Text Editor

In this chapter and throughout the book, we'll be writing out HTML documents by hand, so the first thing we need to do is launch a text editor. The text editor that is provided with your operating system, such as Notepad (Windows) or TextEdit (Macintosh), will do for these purposes. Other text editors are fine as long as you can save plain-text files with the *.html* extension. If you have a WYSIWYG web-authoring tool such as Dreamweaver, set it aside for now. I want you to get a feel for marking up a document manually (see the sidebar "HTML the Hard Way").

This section shows how to open new documents in Notepad and TextEdit. Even if you've used these programs before, skim through for some special settings that will make the exercises go more smoothly. We'll start with Notepad; Mac users can jump ahead.

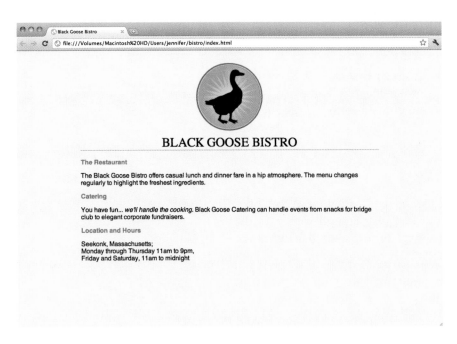

Figure 4-1. In this chapter, we'll write the source document for this page step by step.

Creating a new document in Notepad (Windows)

These are the steps to creating a new document in Notepad on Windows 7 (Figure 4-2):

1. Open the Start menu and navigate to Notepad (in Accessories). ❶

2. Click on Notepad to open a new document window, and you're ready to start typing. ❷

3. Next, we'll make the extensions visible. This step is not required to make HTML documents, but it will help make the file types clearer at a glance. Select "Folder Options…" from the Tools menu ❸ and select the View tab ❹. Find "Hide extensions for known file types" and uncheck that option. ❺ Click OK to save the preference, and the file extensions will now be visible.

NOTE

In Windows 7, hit the ALT key to reveal the menu to access Tools and Folder Options. In Windows Vista, it is labeled "Folder and Search Options."

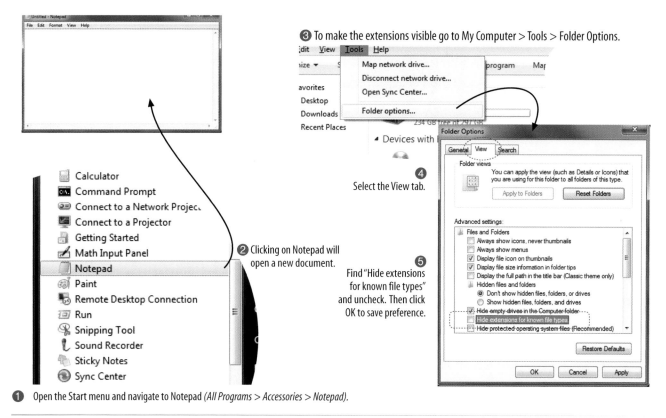

❶ Open the Start menu and navigate to Notepad (*All Programs > Accessories > Notepad*).

Figure 4-2. Creating a new document in Notepad.

Creating a new document in TextEdit (Mac OS X)

By default, TextEdit creates "rich text" documents—that is, documents that have hidden style formatting instructions for making text bold, setting font size, and so on. You can tell that TextEdit is in rich-text mode when it has a formatting toolbar at the top of the window (plain-text mode does not). HTML documents need to be plain-text documents, so we'll need to change the format, as shown in this example (Figure 4-3).

1. Use the Finder to look in the *Applications* folder for TextEdit. When you've found it, double-click the name or icon to launch the application.

2. TextEdit opens a new document. The text-formatting menu at the top shows that you are in Rich Text mode. Here's how you change it.

3. Open the Preferences dialog box from the TextEdit menu.

4. There are three settings you need to adjust:

   On the "New Document" tab, select "Plain text".

   On the "Open and Save" tab, select "Ignore rich text commands in HTML files" and turn off "Append '.txt' extensions to plain text files".

5. When you are done, click the red button in the top-left corner.

6. When you create a new document, the formatting menu will no longer be there and you can save your text as an HTML document. You can always convert a document back to rich text by selecting Format → Make Rich Text when you are not using TextEdit for HTML.

Figure 4-3. Launching TextEdit and choosing Plain Text settings in the Preferences.

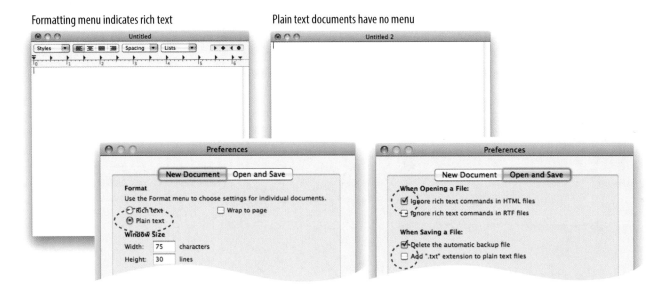

Formatting menu indicates rich text

Plain text documents have no menu

Step 1: Start with Content

Now that we have our new document, it's time to get typing. A web page always starts with content, so that's where we begin our demonstration. Exercise 4-1 walks you through entering the raw text content and saving the document in a new folder.

exercise 4-1 | **Entering content**

1. Type the content below for the home page into the new document in your text editor. Copy it exactly as you see it here, keeping the line breaks the same for the sake of playing along. The raw text for this exercise is available online at *www.learningwebdesign.com/4e/materials/*.

```
Black Goose Bistro

The Restaurant
The Black Goose Bistro offers casual lunch and dinner fare in
a hip atmosphere. The menu changes regularly to highlight the
freshest ingredients.

Catering
You have fun... we'll handle the cooking. Black Goose Catering
can handle events from snacks for bridge club to elegant corporate
fundraisers.

Location and Hours
Seekonk, Massachusetts;
Monday through Thursday 11am to 9pm, Friday and Saturday, 11am to
midnight
```

2. Select "Save" or "Save as" from the File menu to get the Save As dialog box (Figure 4-4). The first thing you need to do is create a new folder that will contain all of the files for the site (in other words, it's the local root folder).

   Windows: Click the folder icon at the top to create the new folder.

   Mac: Click the "New Folder" button.

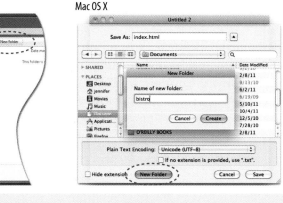

Figure 4-4. Saving index.html in a new folder called "bistro".

Naming Conventions

It is important that you follow these rules and conventions when naming your files:

Use proper suffixes for your files. HTML and XHTML files must end with *.html*. Web graphics must be labeled according to their file format: *.gif*, *.png*, or *.jpg* (*.jpeg* is also acceptable).

Never use character spaces within filenames. It is common to use an underline character or hyphen to visually separate words within filenames, such as *robbins_bio.html* or *robbins-bio .html*.

Avoid special characters such as **?, %, #, /, :, ;, •,** etc. Limit filenames to letters, numbers, underscores, hyphens, and periods.

Filenames may be case-sensitive, depending on your server configuration. Consistently using all lowercase letters in filenames, although not necessary, is one way to make your filenames easier to manage.

Keep filenames short. Short names keep the character count and file size of your HTML file in check. If you really must give the file a long, multiword name, you can separate words with hyphens, such as *a-long-document-title. html*, to improve readability.

Self-imposed conventions. It is helpful to develop a consistent naming scheme for huge sites—for instance, always using lowercase with hyphens between words. This takes some of the guesswork out of remembering what you named a file when you go to link to it later.

What Browsers Ignore

Some information in the source document will be ignored when it is viewed in a browser, including:

Multiple (white) spaces.

When a browser encounters more than one consecutive blank character space, it displays a single space. So if the document contains:

`long,       long       ago`

the browser displays:

long, long ago

Line breaks (carriage returns).

Browsers convert carriage returns to white spaces, so following the earlier "ignore multiple white spaces rule," line breaks have no effect on formatting the page. Text and elements wrap continuously until a new block element, such as a heading (**h1**) or paragraph (**p**), or the line break element (**br**) is encountered in the flow of the document text.

Tabs. Tabs are also converted to character spaces, so guess what? Useless.

Unrecognized markup.

Browsers are instructed to ignore any tag they don't understand or that was specified incorrectly. Depending on the element and the browser, this can have varied results. The browser may display nothing at all, or it may display the contents of the tag as though it were normal text.

Text in comments.

Browsers will not display text between the special **<!--** and **-->** tags used to denote a comment. See the "Adding Hidden Comments" sidebar later in this chapter.

Name the new folder *bistro*, and save the text file as *index.html* in it. Windows users, you will also need to choose "All Files" after "Save as type" to prevent Notepad from adding a ".txt" extension to your filename. The filename needs to end in *.html* to be recognized by the browser as a web document. See the sidebar "Naming Conventions" for more tips on naming files.

3. Just for kicks, let's take a look at *index.html* in a browser. Launch your favorite browser (I'm using Google Chrome) and choose "Open" or "Open File" from the File menu. Navigate to *index.html*, and then select the document to open it in the browser. You should see something like the page shown in Figure 4-5. We'll talk about the results in the following section.

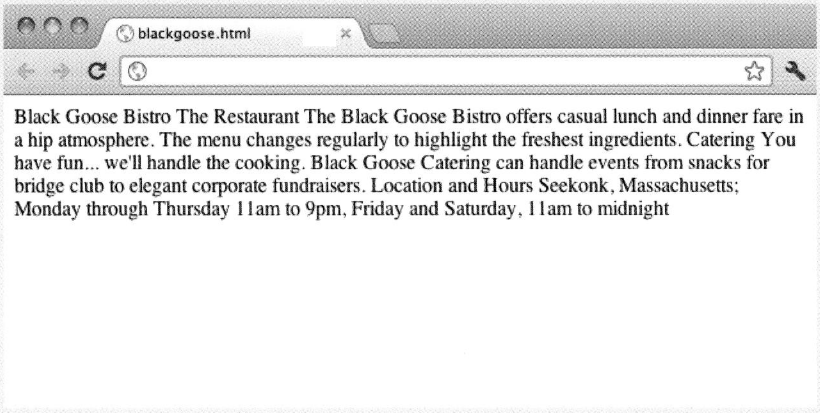

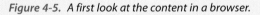

Black Goose Bistro The Restaurant The Black Goose Bistro offers casual lunch and dinner fare in a hip atmosphere. The menu changes regularly to highlight the freshest ingredients. Catering You have fun... we'll handle the cooking. Black Goose Catering can handle events from snacks for bridge club to elegant corporate fundraisers. Location and Hours Seekonk, Massachusetts; Monday through Thursday 11am to 9pm, Friday and Saturday, 11am to midnight

Figure 4-5. A first look at the content in a browser.

Learning from step 1

Our content isn't looking so good (Figure 4-5). The text is all run together—that's not how it looked in the original document. There are a couple of things to be learned here. The first thing that is apparent is that the browser ignores line breaks in the source document. The sidebar "What Browsers Ignore" lists other information in the source that is not displayed in the browser window.

Second, we see that simply typing in some content and naming the document *.html* is not enough. While the browser can display the text from the file, we haven't indicated the *structure* of the content. That's where HTML comes in. We'll use markup to add structure: first to the HTML document itself (coming up in Step 2), then to the page's content (Step 3). Once the browser knows the structure of the content, it can display the page in a more meaningful way.

Step 2: Give the Document Structure

We have our content saved in an *.html* document—now we're ready to start marking it up.

Introducing…HTML elements

Back in Chapter 2, How the Web Works, you saw examples of HTML elements with an opening tag (**<p>** for a paragraph, for example) and closing tag (**</p>**). Before we start adding tags to our document, let's look at the anatomy of an HTML element (its syntax) and firm up some important terminology. A generic container element is labeled in Figure 4-6.

An element consists of both the content and its markup.

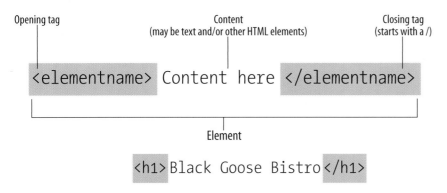

Opening tag   Content (may be text and/or other HTML elements)   Closing tag (starts with a /)

`<elementname>` Content here `</elementname>`

Element

`<h1>`Black Goose Bistro`</h1>`

Figure 4-6. The parts of an HTML container element.

Elements are identified by tags in the text source. A tag consists of the element name (usually an abbreviation of a longer descriptive name) within angle brackets (**< >**). The browser knows that any text within brackets is hidden and not displayed in the browser window.

The element name appears in the opening tag (also called a start tag) and again in the closing (or end) tag preceded by a slash (**/**). The closing tag works something like an "off" switch for the element. Be careful not to use the similar backslash character in end tags (see the tip "Slash vs. Backslash").

The tags added around content are referred to as the markup. It is important to note that an element consists of both the content *and* its markup (the start and end tags). Not all elements have content, however. Some are empty by definition, such as the **img** element used to add an image to the page. We'll talk about empty elements a little later in this chapter.

One last thing…capitalization. In HTML, the capitalization of element names is not important. So **<img>**, **<Img>**, and **<IMG>** are all the same as far as the browser is concerned. However, in XHTML (the stricter version of HTML) all element names must be all lowercase in order to be valid. Many web developers have come to like the orderliness of the stricter XHTML markup rules and stick with all lowercase, as I will do in this book.

TIP

Slash vs. Backslash

HTML tags and URLs use the slash character (/). The slash character is found under the question mark (?) on the standard QWERTY keyboard.

It is easy to confuse the slash with the backslash character (\), which is found under the bar character (|). The backslash key will not work in tags or URLs, so be careful not to use it.

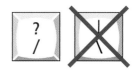

Basic document structure

Figure 4-7 shows the recommended minimal skeleton of an HTML5 document. I say "recommended" because the only element that is *required* in HTML is the **title**. But I feel it is better, particularly for beginners, to explicitly organize documents with the proper structural markup. And if you are writing in the stricter XHTML, all of the following elements except **meta** must be included in order to be valid. Let's take a look at what's going on in Figure 4-7.

Figure 4-7. The minimal structure of an HTML document.

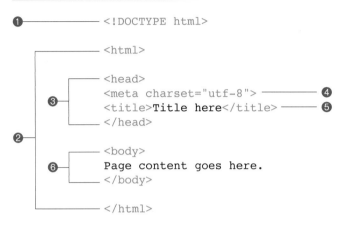

❶ I don't want to confuse things, but the first line in the example isn't an element at all; it is a document type declaration (also called DOCTYPE declaration) that identifies this document as an HTML5 document. I have a lot more to say about DOCTYPE declarations in Chapter 10, What's Up, HTML5?, but for this discussion, suffice it to say that including it lets modern browsers know they should interpret the document as written according to the HTML5 specification.

❷ The entire document is contained within an **html** element. The **html** element is called the root element because it contains all the elements in the document, and it may not be contained within any other element. It is used for both HTML and XHTML documents.

❸ Within the **html** element, the document is divided into a head and a body. The **head** element contains descriptive information about the document itself, such as its title, the style sheet(s) it uses, scripts, and other types of "meta" information.

❹ The **meta** elements within the **head** element provide information *about* the document itself. A **meta** element can be used to provide all sorts of information, but in this case, it specifies the character encoding (the standardized collection of letters, numbers, and symbols) used in the document. I don't want to go into too much detail on this right now, but know that there are many good reasons for specifying the **charset** in every document, so I have included it as part of the minimal document structure.

NOTE

Prior to HTML5, the syntax for specifying the character set with the **meta** *element was a bit more elaborate. If you are writing your documents in HTML 4.01 or XHTML 1.0, your* **meta** *element should look like this:*

```
<meta http-equiv="content-
type" content="text/html;
charset=UTF-8">
```

❺ Also in the **head** is the mandatory **title** element. According to the HTML specification, every document must contain a descriptive title.

❻ Finally, the **body** element contains everything that we want to show up in the browser window.

Are you ready to add some structure to the Black Goose Bistro home page? Open the *index.html* document and move on to Exercise 4-2.

exercise 4-2 | **Adding basic structure**

1. Open the newly created document, *index.html*, if it isn't open already.

2. Start by adding the HTML5 DOCTYPE declaration:

   `<!DOCTYPE html>`

3. Put the entire document in an HTML root element by adding an **<html>** start tag at the very beginning and an **</html>** end tag at the end of the text.

4. Next, create the document head that contains the title for the page. Insert **<head>** and **</head>** tags before the content. Within the **head** element, add information about the character encoding **<meta charset="utf-8">**, and the title, "Black Goose Bistro", surrounded by opening and closing **<title>** tags.

   The correct terminology is to say that the `title` *element is nested within the* **head** *element. We'll talk about nesting more in later chapters.*

5. Finally, define the body of the document by wrapping the content in **<body>** and **</body>** tags. When you are done, the source document should look like this (the markup is shown in color to make it stand out):

```
<!DOCTYPE html>
<html>

<head>
<meta charset="utf-8">
<title>Black Goose Bistro</title>
</head>

<body>
Black Goose Bistro

The Restaurant
The Black Goose Bistro offers casual lunch and dinner fare in
a hip atmosphere. The menu changes regularly to highlight the
freshest ingredients.

Catering Services
You have fun... we'll do the cooking. Black Goose catering can
handle events from snacks for bridge club to elegant corporate
fundraisers.
Location and Hours
Seekonk, Massachusetts;
Monday through Thursday 11am to 9pm, Friday and Saturday, 11am to
midnight
</body>

</html>
```

6. Save the document in the *bistro* directory, so that it overwrites the old version. Open the file in the browser or hit "refresh" or "reload" if it is open already. Figure 4-8 shows how it should look now.

Figure 4-8. The page in a browser after the document structure elements have been defined.

Black Goose Bistro The Restaurant The Black Goose Bistro offers casual lunch and dinner fare in a hip atmosphere. The menu changes regularly to highlight the freshest ingredients. Catering You have fun... we'll handle the cooking. Black Goose Catering can handle events from snacks for bridge club to elegant corporate fundraisers. Location and Hours Seekonk, Massachusetts; Monday through Thursday 11am to 9pm, Friday and Saturday, 11am to midnight

Not much has changed after structuring the document, except that the browser now displays the title of the document in the top bar or tab. If someone were to bookmark this page, that title would be added to his Bookmarks or Favorites list as well (see the sidebar "Don't Forget a Good Title"). But the content still runs together because we haven't given the browser any indication of how it should be structured. We'll take care of that next.

Step 3: Identify Text Elements

With a little markup experience under your belt, it should be a no-brainer to add the markup that identifies headings and subheads (**h1** and **h2**), paragraphs (**p**), and emphasized text (**em**) to our content, as we'll do in Exercise 4-3. However, before we begin, I want to take a moment to talk about what we're doing and not doing when marking up content with HTML.

Introducing…semantic markup

The purpose of HTML is to add meaning and structure to the content. It is *not* intended to provide instructions for how the content should look (its presentation).

Your job when marking up content is to choose the HTML element that provides the most meaningful description of the content at hand. In the biz, we call this semantic markup. For example, the most important heading at the beginning of the document should be marked up as an **h1** because it is the most important heading on the page. Don't worry about what it looks like in the browser…you can easily change that with a style sheet. The important thing is that you choose elements based on what makes the most sense for the content.

In addition to adding meaning to content, the markup gives the document structure. The way elements follow each other or nest within one another creates relationships between the elements. You can think of it as an outline (its technical name is the DOM, for Document Object Model). The underlying document hierarchy is important because it gives browsers cues on how to handle the content. It is also the foundation upon which we add presentation instructions with style sheets and behaviors with JavaScript. We'll talk about document structure more in Part III, when we discuss Cascading Style Sheets, and in Part IV in the JavaScript overview.

Although HTML was intended to be used strictly for meaning and structure since its creation, that mission was somewhat thwarted in the early years of the Web. With no style sheet system in place, HTML was extended to give authors ways to change the appearance of fonts, colors, and alignment using markup alone. Those presentational extras are still out there, so you may run across them if you view the source of older sites or a site made with old tools.

Don't Forget a Good Title

Not only is a **title** element required for every document, it is quite useful as well. The title is what is displayed in a user's Bookmarks or Favorites list and on tabs in desktop browsers. Descriptive titles are also a key tool for improving accessibility, as they are the first thing a person hears when using a screen reader. Search engines rely heavily on document titles as well. For these reasons, it's important to provide thoughtful and descriptive titles for all your documents and avoid vague titles, such as "Welcome" or "My Page." You may also want to keep the length of your titles in check so they are able to display in the browser's title area. Another best practice is to put the part of the title with more specific information first (for example, the page description ahead of the company name) so that the page title is visible when multiple tabs are lined up in the browser window.

In this book, however, we'll focus on using HTML the right way, in keeping with the contemporary standards-based, semantic approach to web design.

OK, enough lecturing. It's time to get to work on that content in Exercise 4-3.

exercise 4-3 | **Defining text elements**

1. Open the document **_index.html_** in your text editor, if it isn't open already.

2. The first line of text, "Black Goose Bistro," is the main heading for the page, so we'll mark it up as a Heading Level 1 (**h1**) element. Put the opening tag, **<h1>**, at the beginning of the line and the closing tag, **</h1>**, after it, like this:

    `<h1>Black Goose Bistro</h1>`

3. Our page also has three subheads. Mark them up as Heading Level 2 (**h2**) elements in a similar manner. I'll do the first one here; you do the same for "Catering" and "Location and Hours".

    `<h2>The Restaurant</h2>`

4. Each **h2** element is followed by a brief paragraph of text, so let's mark those up as paragraph (**p**) elements in a similar manner. Here's the first one; you do the rest.

    ```
    <p>The Black Goose Bistro offers casual lunch and
    dinner fare in a hip atmosphere. The menu changes
    regularly to highlight the freshest ingredients.
    </p>
    ```

5. Finally, in the Catering section, I want to emphasize that visitors should just leave the cooking to us. To make text emphasized, mark it up in an emphasis element (**em**) element, as shown here.

    ```
    <p>You have fun... <em>we'll handle the cooking
    </em>. Black Goose Catering can handle events
    from snacks for bridge club to elegant corporate
    fundraisers.</p>
    ```

6. Now that we've marked up the document, let's save it as we did before, and open (or refresh) the page in the browser. You should see a page that looks much like the one in Figure 4-9. If it doesn't, check your markup to be sure that you aren't missing any angle brackets or a slash in a closing tag.

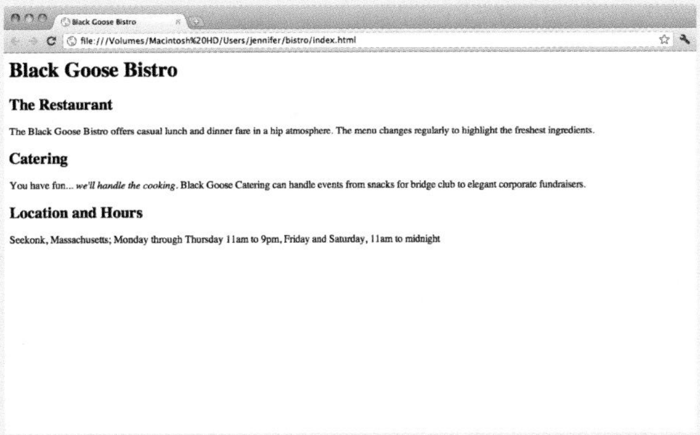

Figure 4-9. _The home page after the content has been marked up with HTML elements._

Now we're getting somewhere. With the elements properly identified, the browser can now display the text in a more meaningful manner. There are a few significant things to note about what's happening in Figure 4-9.

Block and inline elements

Although it may seem like stating the obvious, it is worth pointing out that the heading and paragraph elements start on new lines and do not run together as they did before. That is because by default, headings and paragraphs display as block elements. Browsers treat block elements as though they are in little rectangular boxes, stacked up in the page. Each block element begins on a new line, and some space is also usually added above and below the entire element by default. In Figure 4-10, the edges of the block elements are outlined in red.

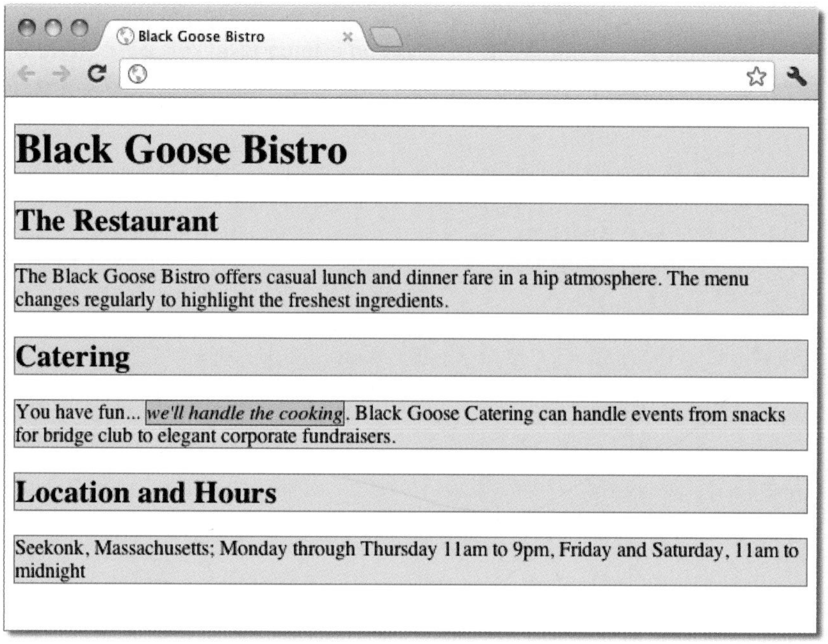

Figure 4-10. The outlines show the structure of the elements in the home page.

Adding Hidden Comments

You can leave notes in the source document for yourself and others by marking them up as comments. Anything you put between comment tags (`<!-- -->`) will not display in the browser and will not have any effect on the rest of the source.

```
<!-- This is a comment -->
<!-- This is a
    multiple-line comment
    that ends here. -->
```

Comments are useful for labeling and organizing long documents, particularly when they are shared by a team of developers. In this example, comments are used to point out the section of the source that contains the navigation.

```
<!-- start global nav -->
<ul>
  ...
</ul>
<!-- end global nav -->
```

Bear in mind that although the browser will not display comments in the web page, readers can see them if they "view source," so be sure that the comments you leave are appropriate for everyone. It's probably a good idea just to strip out notes to your fellow developers before the site is published. It cuts some bytes off the file size as well.

By contrast, look at the text we marked up as emphasized (**em**). It does not start a new line, but rather stays in the flow of the paragraph. That is because the **em** element is an inline element. Inline elements do not start new lines; they just go with the flow. In Figure 4-10, the inline **em** element is outlined in light blue.

Default styles

The other thing that you will notice about the marked-up page in Figures 4-9 and 4-10 is that the browser makes an attempt to give the page some visual hierarchy by making the first-level heading the biggest and boldest thing on the page, with the second-level headings slightly smaller, and so on.

How does the browser determine what an **h1** should look like? It uses a style sheet! All browsers have their own built-in style sheets (called user agent style sheets in the spec) that describe the default rendering of elements. The default rendering is similar from browser to browser (for example, **h1**s are always big and bold), but there are some variations (long quotes may or may not be indented).

If you think the **h1** is too big and clunky as the browser renders it, just change it with a style sheet rule. Resist the urge to mark up the heading with another element just to get it to look better, for example, using an **h3** instead of an **h1** so it isn't as large. In the days before ubiquitous style sheet support, elements were abused in just that way. Now that there are style sheets for controlling the design, you should always choose elements based on how accurately they describe the content, and don't worry about the browser's default rendering.

We'll fix the presentation of the page with style sheets in a moment, but first, let's add an image to the page.

Step 4: Add an Image

What fun is a web page with no image? In Exercise 4-4, we'll add an image to the page using the **img** element. Images will be discussed in more detail in Chapter 7, Adding Images, but for now, it gives us an opportunity to introduce two more basic markup concepts: empty elements and attributes.

Empty elements

So far, nearly all of the elements we've used in the Black Goose Bistro home page have followed the syntax shown in Figure 4-1: a bit of text content surrounded by start and end tags.

A handful of elements, however, do not have text content because they are used to provide a simple directive. These elements are said to be empty. The image element (**img**) is an example of such an element; it tells the browser to get an image file from the server and insert it at that spot in the flow of the text. Other empty elements include the line break (**br**), thematic breaks (**hr**), and elements that provide information about a document but don't affect its displayed content, such as the **meta** element that we used earlier.

Figure 4-11 shows the very simple syntax of an empty element (compare to Figure 4-6). If you are writing an XHTML document, the syntax is slightly different (see the sidebar "Empty Elements in XHTML").

Empty Elements in XHTML

In XHTML, all elements, including empty elements, must be closed (or terminated, to use the proper term). Empty elements are terminated by adding a trailing slash preceded by a space before the closing bracket, like so: **<img />**, **
, **<meta />, and **<hr />**. Here is the line break example using XHTML syntax.

```
<p>1005 Gravenstein Highway
North <br />Sebastopol, CA
95472</p>
```

```
<element-name>
```

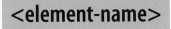

Example: The br element inserts a line break.

```
<p>1005 Gravenstein Highway North<br>Sebastopol, CA 95472</p>
```

Figure 4-11. Empty element structure.

Attributes

Let's get back to adding an image with the empty **img** element. Obviously, an **<img>** tag is not very useful by itself—there's no way to know which image to use. That's where attributes come in. Attributes are instructions that clarify or modify an element. For the **img** element, the **src** (short for "source") attribute is required, and specifies the location (URL) of the image file.

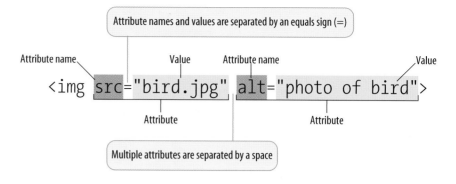

Figure 4-12. An img *element with attributes.*

The syntax for an attribute is as follows:

```
attributename="value"
```

Attributes go after the element name, separated by a space. In non-empty elements, attributes go in the opening tag only:

```
<element attributename="value">
```

```
<element attributename="value">Content</element>
```

You can also put more than one attribute in an element in any order. Just keep them separated with spaces.

```
<element attribute1="value" attribute2="value">
```

For another way to look at it, Figure 4-12 shows an **img** element with its required attributes labeled.

Here's what you need to know about attributes:

- Attributes go after the element name in the opening tag only, never in the end tag.

- There may be several attributes applied to an element, separated by spaces in the opening tag. Their order is not important.

- Most attributes take values, which follow an equals sign (=). In HTML, some attribute values can be reduced to single descriptive words—for example, the **checked** attribute, which makes a checkbox checked when a form loads. In XHTML, however, all attributes must have explicit values (**checked="checked"**). You may hear this type of attribute called a Boolean attribute because it describes a feature that is either on or off.

- A value might be a number, a word, a string of text, a URL, or a measurement, depending on the purpose of the attribute. You'll see examples of all of these throughout this book.

- Some values don't have to be in quotation marks in HTML, but XHTML requires them. Many developers like the consistency and tidiness of quotation marks even when authoring HTML. Either single or double quotation marks are acceptable as long as they are used consistently; however, double quotation marks are the convention. Note that quotation marks in HTML files need to be straight (") not curly (").

- Some attributes are required, such as the `src` and `alt` attributes in the `img` element.

- The attribute names available for each element are defined in the HTML specifications; in other words, you can't make up an attribute for an element.

Now you should be more than ready to try your hand at adding the `img` element with its attributes to the Black Goose Bistro page in the next exercise. We'll throw a few line breaks in there as well.

exercise 4-4 | **Adding an image**

1. If you're working along, the first thing you'll need to do is get a copy of the image file on your hard drive so you can see it in place when you open the file locally. The image file is provided in the materials for this chapter. You can also get the image file by saving it right from the sample web page online at *www.learningwebdesign.com/4e/materials/chapter04/bistro*. Right-click (or Ctrl-click on a Mac) on the goose image and select "Save to disk" (or similar) from the pop-up menu as shown in Figure 4-13. Name the file *blackgoose.png*. Be sure to save it in the *bistro* folder with *index.html*.

2. Once you have the image, insert it at the beginning of the first-level heading by typing in the `img` element and its attributes as shown here:

```
<h1><img src="blackgoose.png" alt="Black Goose logo">Black Goose
Bistro</h1>
```

The `src` attribute provides the name of the image file that should be inserted, and the `alt` attribute provides text that should be displayed if the image is not available. Both of these attributes are required in every `img` element.

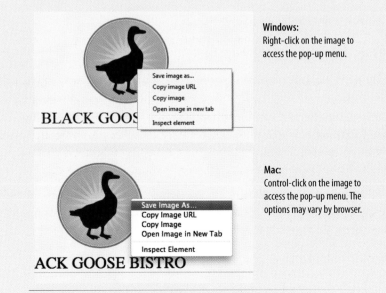

Windows:
Right-click on the image to access the pop-up menu.

Mac:
Control-click on the image to access the pop-up menu. The options may vary by browser.

Figure 4-13. Saving an image file from a page on the Web.

3. I'd like the image to appear above the title, so let's add a line break (**br**) after the **img** element to start the headline text on a new line.

   ```
   <h1><img src="blackgoose.png" alt="Black Goose logo"><br>Black
   Goose Bistro</h1>
   ```

4. Let's break up the last paragraph into three lines for better clarity. Drop a **
** tag at the spots you'd like the line breaks to occur. Try to match the screenshot in Figure 4-14.

5. Now save **index.html** and open or refresh it in the browser window. The page should look like the one shown in Figure 4-14. If it doesn't, check to make sure that the image file, **blackgoose.png**, is in the same directory as **index.html**. If it is, then check to make sure that you aren't missing any characters, such as a closing quote or bracket, in the **img** element markup.

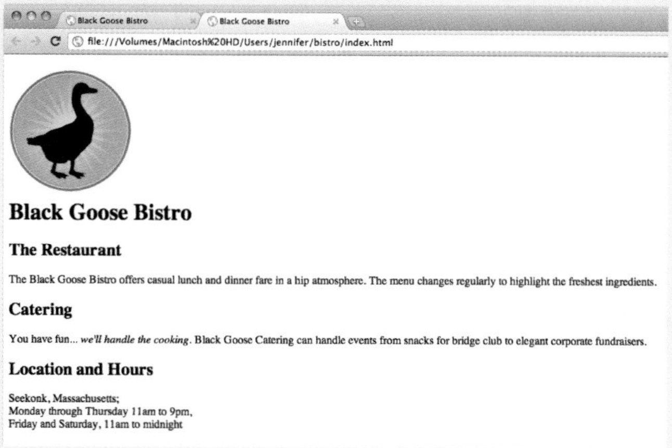

Figure 4-14. The Black Goose Bistro page with the logo image.

YOU TRY IT

Add line breaks (br) to the Location and Hours section so your page matches the example in Figure 4-14.

Step 5: Change the Look with a Style Sheet

Depending on the content and purpose of your website, you may decide that the browser's default rendering of your document is perfectly adequate. However, I think I'd like to pretty up the Black Goose Bistro home page a bit to make a good first impression on potential patrons. "Prettying up" is just my way of saying that I'd like to change its presentation, which is the job of Cascading Style Sheets (CSS).

In Exercise 4-5, we'll change the appearance of the text elements and the page background using some simple style sheet rules. Don't worry about understanding them all right now; we'll get into CSS in more detail in Part III. But I want to at least give you a taste of what it means to add a "layer" of presentation onto the structure we've created with our markup.

exercise 4-5 | **Adding a style sheet**

1. Open *index.html* if it isn't open already.

2. We're going to use the **style** element to apply a very simple embedded style sheet to the page. (This is just one of the ways to add a style sheet; the others are covered in Chapter 11, Style Sheet Orientation.)

   The **style** element is placed inside the **head** of the document. Start by adding the **style** element to the document as shown here:

   ```
   <head>
     <meta charset="utf-8">
     <title>Black Goose Bistro</title>
     <style>

     </style>
   </head>
   ```

3. Now, type the following style rules within the **style** element just as you see them here. Don't worry if you don't know exactly what is going on (although it is fairly intuitive). You'll learn all about style rules in Part III.

   ```
   <style>

   body {
     background-color: #faf2e4;
     margin: 0 15%;
     font-family: sans-serif;
     }

   h1 {
     text-align: center;
     font-family: serif;
     font-weight: normal;
     text-transform: uppercase;
   ```

   ```
     border-bottom: 1px solid #57b1dc;
     margin-top: 30px;
   }

   h2 {
     color: #d1633c;
     font-size: 1em;
   }

   </style>
   ```

4. Now it's time to save the file and take a look at it in the browser. It should look like the page in Figure 4-15. If it doesn't, go over the style sheet code to make sure you didn't miss a semicolon or a curly bracket.

Figure 4-15. The Black Goose Bistro page after CSS style rules have been applied.

We're finished with the Black Goose Bistro page. Not only have you written your first web page, complete with a style sheet, but you've also learned about elements, attributes, empty elements, block and inline elements, the basic structure of an HTML document, and the correct use of markup along the way. Not bad for one chapter!

When Good Pages Go Bad

The previous demonstration went smoothly, but it's easy for small things to go wrong when typing out HTML markup by hand. Unfortunately, one missed character can break a whole page. I'm going to break my page on purpose so we can see what happens.

```
<h2>Catering</h2>
<p>You have fun... <em>we'll handle the cooking.<em> Black Goose
Catering can handle events from snacks for bridge club to elegant
corporate fundraisers.</p>
```

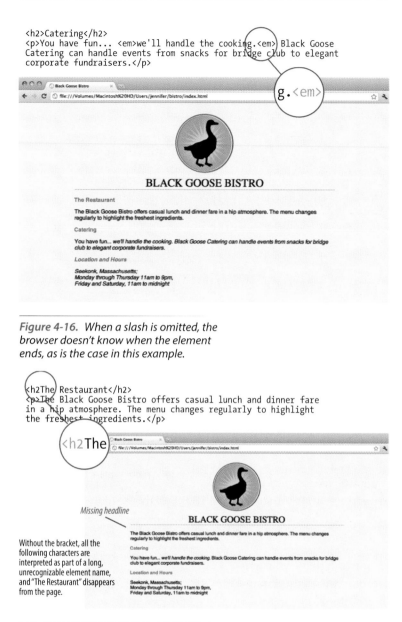

g. `<em>`

Figure 4-16. When a slash is omitted, the browser doesn't know when the element ends, as is the case in this example.

```
<h2The Restaurant</h2>
<p>The Black Goose Bistro offers casual lunch and dinner fare
in a hip atmosphere. The menu changes regularly to highlight
the freshest ingredients.</p>
```

`<h2The`

Missing headline

Without the bracket, all the following characters are interpreted as part of a long, unrecognizable element name, and "The Restaurant" disappears from the page.

Figure 4-17. A missing end bracket makes all the following content part of the tag, and therefore it doesn't display.

What if I had forgotten to type the slash (/) in the closing emphasis tag (`</em>`)? With just one character out of place (Figure 4-16), the remainder of the document displays in emphasized (italic) text. That's because without that slash, there's nothing telling the browser to turn "off" the emphasized formatting, so it just keeps going.

NOTE

Omitting the slash in the closing tag (or even omitting the closing tag itself) for block elements, such as headings or paragraphs, may not be so dramatic. Browsers interpret the start of a new block element to mean that the previous block element is finished.

I've fixed the slash, but this time, let's see what would have happened if I had accidentally omitted a bracket from the end of the first `<h2>` tag (Figure 4-17).

See how the headline is missing? That's because without the closing tag bracket, the browser assumes that all the following text—all the way up to the next closing bracket (>) it finds—is part of the `<h2>` opening tag. Browsers don't display any text within a tag, so my heading disappeared. The browser just ignored the foreign-looking element name and moved on to the next element.

Making mistakes in your first HTML documents and fixing them is a great way to learn. If you write your first pages perfectly, I'd recommend fiddling with the code as I have here to see how the browser reacts to various changes. This can be extremely useful in troubleshooting pages later. I've listed some common problems in the sidebar "Having Problems?" Note that these problems are not specific to beginners. Little stuff like this goes wrong all the time, even for the pros.

Validating Your Documents

One way that professional web developers catch errors in their markup is to validate their documents. What does that mean? To validate a document is to check your markup to make sure that you have abided by all the rules of whatever version of HTML you are using (there are more than one, as we'll discuss in Chapter 10, What's Up, HTML5?). Documents that are error-free are said to be valid. It is strongly recommended that you validate your documents, especially for professional sites. Valid documents are more consistent on a variety of browsers, they display more quickly, and they are more accessible.

Right now, browsers don't require documents to be valid (in other words, they'll do their best to display them, errors and all), but any time you stray from the standard you introduce unpredictability in the way the page is displayed or handled by alternative devices.

So how do you make sure your document is valid? You could check it yourself or ask a friend, but humans make mistakes, and you aren't really expected to memorize every minute rule in the specifications. Instead, you use a validator, software that checks your source against the HTML version you specify. These are some of the things validators check for:

- The inclusion of a DOCTYPE declaration. Without it the validator doesn't know which version of HTML or XHTML to validate against.

- An indication of the character encoding for the document.

- The inclusion of required rules and attributes.

- Non-standard elements.

- Mismatched tags.

- Nesting errors.

- Typos and other minor errors.

Developers use a number of helpful tools for checking and correcting errors in HTML documents. The W3C offers a free online validator at *validator.w3.org*. For HTML5 documents, use the online validator located at *html5.validator.nu*. Browser developer tools like the Firebug plug-in for Firefox or the built-in developer tools in Safari and Chrome also have validators so you can check your work on the fly. If you use Dreamweaver to create your sites, there is a validator built into that as well.

Test Yourself

Now is a good time to make sure you understand the basics of markup. Use what you've learned in this chapter to answer the following questions. Answers are in Appendix A.

1. What is the difference between a tag and an element?

2. Write out the recommended minimal structure of an HTML5 document.

Having Problems?

The following are some typical problems that crop up when you are creating web pages and viewing them in a browser:

I've changed my document, but when I reload the page in my browser, it looks exactly the same.

It could be you didn't save your document before reloading, or you may have saved it in a different directory.

Half my page disappeared.

This could happen if you are missing a closing bracket (**>**) or a quotation mark within a tag. This is a common error when you're writing HTML by hand.

I put in a graphic using the img *element, but all that shows up is a broken image icon.*

The broken graphic could mean a couple of things. First, it might mean that the browser is not finding the graphic. Make sure that the URL to the image file is correct. (We'll discuss URLs further in Chapter 6, Adding Links.) Make sure that the image file is actually in the directory you've specified. If the file is there, make sure it is in one of the formats that web browsers can display (GIF, JPEG, or PNG) and that it is named with the proper suffix (*.gif*, *.jpeg* or *.jpg*, or *.png*, respectively).

---

3. Indicate whether each of these filenames is an acceptable name for a web document by circling "Yes" or "No." If it is not acceptable, provide the reason why.

   a. *Sunflower.html*   Yes   No

   b. *index.doc*   Yes   No

   c. *cooking home page.html* Yes   No

   d. *Song_Lyrics.html*   Yes   No

   e. *games/rubix.html*   Yes   No

   f. *%whatever.html*   Yes   No

4. All of the following markup examples are incorrect. Describe what is wrong with each one, and then write it correctly.

   a. `<img "birthday.jpg">`

   b. `<i>Congratulations!<i>`

   c. `<a href="file.html">linked text</a href="file.html">`

   d. `<p>This is a new paragraph<\p>`

5. How would you mark up this comment in an HTML document so that it doesn't display in the browser window?

   `product list begins here`

Element Review: Document Structure

This chapter introduced the elements that establish the structure of the document. The remaining elements introduced in the exercises will be treated in more depth in the following chapters.

Element	Description
body	Identifies the body of the document that holds the content
head	Identifies the head of the document that contains information about the document
html	The root element that contains all the other elements
meta	Provides information about the document
title	Gives the page a title

CHAPTER 5

MARKING UP TEXT

Once your content is ready to go (you proofread it, right?) and you've added the markup to structure the document (`html`, `head`, `title`, and `body`), you are ready to identify the elements in the content. This chapter introduces the elements you have to choose from for marking up text content. There probably aren't as many of them as you might think, and really just a handful that you'll use with regularity. That said, this chapter is a big one and covers a lot of ground.

As we begin our tour of elements, I want to reiterate how important it is to choose elements semantically—that is, in a way that most accurately describes the content's meaning. If you don't like how it looks, change it with a style sheet. A semantically marked-up document ensures your content is available and accessible in the widest range of browsing environments, from desktop computers and mobile devices to assistive screen readers. It also allows non-human readers, such as search engine indexing programs, to correctly parse your content and make decisions about the relative importance of elements on the page.

With these principles in mind, it is time to meet the HTML text elements, starting with the most basic element of them all, the humble paragraph.

IMPORTANT NOTE

I will be teaching markup according to the HTML5 standard maintained by the W3C (www.w3.org/TR/html5/) as it appeared as of this writing in mid-2012. There is another "living" (therefore unnumbered) version of HTML maintained by the WHATWG (whatwg.org) that is nearly the same, but usually has some differences. I will be sure to point out elements and attributes that belong to only one spec. Both specs are changing frequently, so I urge you to check online to see whether elements have been added or dropped.

You may have heard that not all browsers support HTML5. That is true. But the vast majority of the elements in HTML5 have been around for decades in earlier HTML versions, so they are supported universally. Elements that are new in HTML5 and may not be well supported will be indicated with this marker: NEW IN HTML5 *. So, unless I explicitly point out a support issue, you can assume that the markup descriptions and examples presented here will work in all browsers.*

Paragraphs

`<p>...</p>`

A paragraph element

Paragraphs are the most rudimentary elements of a text document. You indicate a paragraph with the **p** element by inserting an opening `<p>` tag at the beginning of the paragraph and a closing `</p>` tag after it, as shown in this example.

```
<p>Serif typefaces have small slabs at the ends of letter strokes. In
general, serif fonts can make large amounts of text easier to read.</p>

<p>Sans-serif fonts do not have serif slabs; their strokes are square
on the end. Helvetica and Arial are examples of sans-serif fonts.
In general, sans-serif fonts appear sleeker and more modern.</p>
```

Visual browsers nearly always display paragraphs on new lines with a bit of space between them by default (to use a term from CSS, they are displayed as a block). Paragraphs may contain text, images, and other inline elements (called phrasing content in the spec), but they may *not* contain headings, lists, sectioning elements, or any element that typically displays as a block by default.

NOTE

You must assign an element to all the text in a document. In other words, all text must be enclosed in some sort of element. Text that is not contained within tags is called "naked" or "anonymous" text, and it will cause a document to be invalid. For more information about checking documents for validity, see Chapter 4, Creating a Simple Page (HTML Overview).

In HTML, it is OK to omit the closing `</p>` tag. A browser just assumes it is closed when it encounters the next block element. However, in the stricter XHTML syntax, the closing tag is required (no surprise there). Many web developers, including myself, prefer to close paragraphs and all elements, even in HTML, for the sake of consistency and clarity. I recommend folks who are just learning markup, like yourself, do the same.

Headings

`<h1>...</h1>`
`<h2>...</h2>`
`<h3>...</h3>`
`<h4>...</h4>`
`<h5>...</h5>`
`<h6>...</h6>`

Heading elements

In the last chapter, we used the **h1** and **h2** elements to indicate headings for the Black Goose Bistro page. There are actually six levels of headings, from **h1** to **h6**. When you add headings to content, the browser uses them to create a document outline for the page. Assistive reading devices such as screen readers use the document outline to help users quickly scan and navigate through a page. In addition, search engines look at heading levels as part of their algorithms (information in higher heading levels may be given more weight). For these reasons, it is a best practice to start with the Level 1 heading (**h1**) and work down in numerical order (see note), creating a logical document structure and outline.

NOTE

HTML5 has a new outlining system that looks beyond headings to generate the outline. See the sidebar "Sectioning Elements," later in this chapter, for details.

This example shows the markup for four heading levels. Additional heading levels would be marked up in a similar manner.

```
<h1>Type Design</h1>

<h2>Serif Typefaces</h2>
<p>Serif typefaces have small slabs at the ends of letter strokes.
In general, serif fonts can make large amounts of text easier to
read.</p>
```

```
<h3>Baskerville</h3>

<h4>Description</h4>
<p>Description of the Baskerville typeface.</p>

<h4>History</h4>
<p>The history of the Baskerville typeface.</p>

<h3>Georgia</h3>
<p>Description and history of the Georgia typeface.</p>

<h2>Sans-serif Typefaces</h2>
<p>Sans-serif typefaces do not have slabs at the ends of strokes.</p>
```

The markup in this example would create the following document outline:

1. Type Design
    1. Serif Typefaces
       + text paragraph

        1. Baskerville

            1. Description
               + text paragraph

            2. History
               + text paragraph

        2. Georgia
           + text paragraph

    2. Sans-serif Typefaces
       + text paragraph

By default, the headings in our example will be displayed in bold text, starting in very large type for **h1**s, with each consecutive level in smaller text, as shown in Figure 5-1. You can use a style sheet to change their appearance.

NOTE

All screenshots in this book were taken using the Chrome browser on a Mac unless otherwise noted.

Figure 5-1. The default rendering of four heading levels.

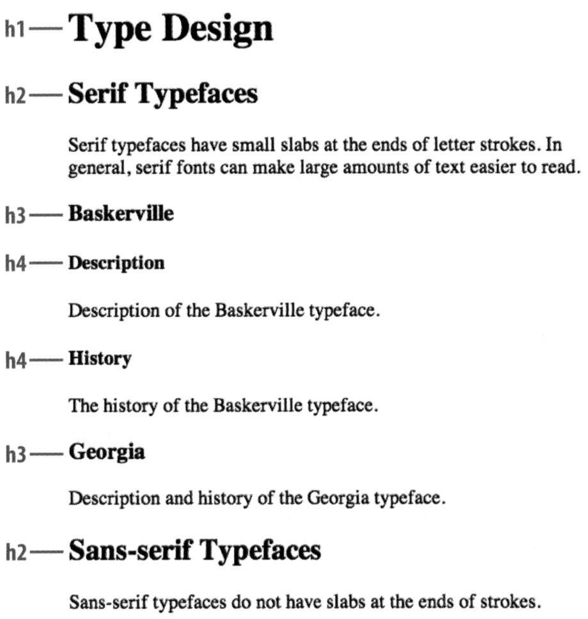

h1 — **Type Design**

h2 — **Serif Typefaces**

Serif typefaces have small slabs at the ends of letter strokes. In general, serif fonts can make large amounts of text easier to read.

h3 — **Baskerville**

h4 — **Description**

Description of the Baskerville typeface.

h4 — **History**

The history of the Baskerville typeface.

h3 — **Georgia**

Description and history of the Georgia typeface.

h2 — **Sans-serif Typefaces**

Sans-serif typefaces do not have slabs at the ends of strokes.

Indicating a Shift in Themes

`<hr>`
A horizontal rule

If you want to indicate that one topic or thought has completed and another one is beginning, you can insert what is called in HTML5 a "paragraph-level thematic break" using the **hr** element. The **hr** element adds a logical divider between sections of a page or paragraphs of text without introducing a new heading level.

In HTML versions prior to HTML5, **hr** was defined as a "horizontal rule" because it inserted a horizontal line on the page. Browsers still render **hr** as a 3D shaded rule and put it on a line by itself with some space above and below by default, but it now has a new semantic purpose. If a decorative line is all you're after, it is better to create a rule by specifying a colored border before or after an element with CSS.

hr is an empty element—you just drop it into place where you want the thematic break to occur, as shown in this example and Figure 5-2. Note that in XHTML, the **hr** element must be closed with a slash: **<hr />**.

```
<h3>Times</h3>
<p>Description and history of the Times typeface.</p>
<hr>
<h3>Georgia</h3>
<p>Description and history of the Georgia typeface.</p>
```

Times

Description and history of the Times typeface.

Georgia

Description and history of the Georgia typeface.

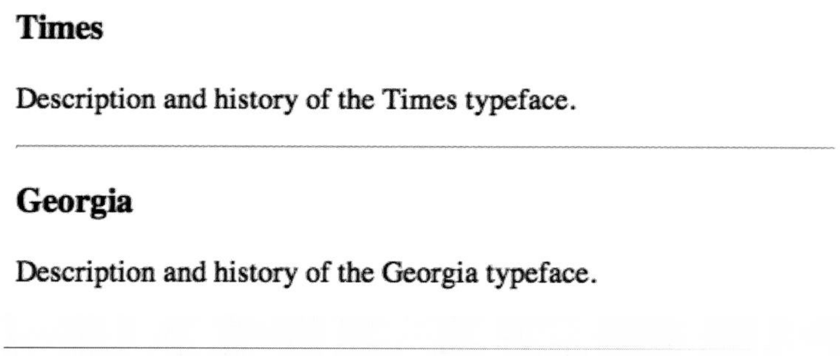

Figure 5-2. The default rendering of a thematic break (horizontal rule).

Heading groups

`<hgroup>...</hgroup>`
A group of stacked headings
NEW IN HTML5

It is common for headlines to have clarifying subheads or taglines. Take, for example, the title of Chapter 4 in this book:

Creating a Simple Page
(HTML Overview)

In the past, marking stacks of headings and subheadings was somewhat problematic. The first line, "Creating a Simple Page," is clearly an **h1**, but if you make the second line an **h2**, you may introduce an unintended new level to the document outline. The best you could do was mark it as a paragraph, but that didn't exactly make semantic sense.

For this reason, HTML5 includes the **hgroup** element for identifying a stack of headings as a group.* Browsers that support **hgroup** know to count only the highest-ranked heading in the outline and ignore the rest. Here is how the **hgroup** element could be used to mark up the title of Chapter 4. With this markup, only the **h1**, "Creating a Simple Page," would be represented in the document outline.

```
<hgroup>
  <h1>Creating a Simple Page</h1>
  <h2>(HTML Overview)</h2>
</hgroup>
```

Lists

Humans are natural list makers, and HTML provides elements for marking up three types of lists:

- **Unordered lists.** Collections of items that appear in no particular order.

- **Ordered lists.** Lists in which the sequence of the items is important.

- **Description lists.** Lists that consist of name and value pairs, including but not limited to terms and definitions.

All list elements—the lists themselves and the items that go in them—are displayed as block elements by default, which means that they start on a new line and have some space above and below, but that may be altered with CSS. In this section, we'll look at each list type in detail.

Unordered lists

Just about any list of examples, names, components, thoughts, or options qualifies as an unordered list. In fact, most lists fall into this category. By default, unordered lists display with a bullet before each list item, but you can change that with a style sheet, as you'll see in a moment.

To identify an unordered list, mark it up as a **ul** element. The opening **<ul>** tag goes before the first list item, and the closing tag **</ul>** goes after the last item. Then, each item in the list gets marked up as a list item (**li**) by enclosing it in opening and closing **li** tags, as shown in this example. Notice that there are no bullets in the source document. They are added automatically by the browser (Figure 5-3).

```
<ul>
  <li><a href="">Serif</a></li>
  <li><a href="">Sans-serif</a></li>
  <li><a href="">Script</a></li>
  <li><a href="">Display</a></li>
  <li><a href="">Dingbats</a></li>
</ul>
```

SUPPORT ALERT

The **hgroup** *element is not supported in Internet Explorer versions 8 and earlier (see the sidebar "HTML5 Support in Internet Explorer," later in this chapter, for a workaround). Older versions of Firefox and Safari (prior to 3.6 and 4, respectively) do not support it according to the spec, but they don't ignore it completely, so you can apply styles to it.*

```
<ul>...</ul>
```
Unordered list

```
<li>...</li>
```
List item within an unordered list

NOTE

The only thing that is permitted within an unordered list (that is, between the start and end **ul** *tags) is one or more list items. You can't put other elements in there, and there may not be any untagged text. However, you can put any type of flow element within a list item (* **li** *).*

---

* Although potentially useful, the future of the **hgroup** element is uncertain. If you are interested in using it for a published site, you should check the HTML5 specification first.

- Serif
- Sans-serif
- Script
- Display
- Dingbats

Figure 5-3. The default rendering of the sample unordered list. The bullets are added automatically by the browser.

Nesting Lists

Any list can be nested within another list; it just has to be placed within a list item. This example shows the structure of an unordered list nested in the second ordered list item.

```
<ol>
  <li></li>
  <li>
    <ul>
      <li></li>
      <li></li>
      <li></li>
    </ul>
  </li>
</ol>
```

When you nest an unordered list within another unordered list, the browser automatically changes the bullet style for the second-level list. Unfortunately, the numbering style is not changed by default when you nest ordered lists. You need to set the numbering styles yourself using style sheets.

But here's the cool part. We can take that same unordered list markup and radically change its appearance by applying different style sheets, as shown in Figure 5-4. In the figure, I've turned off the bullets, added bullets of my own, made the items line up horizontally, and even made them look like graphical buttons. The markup stays exactly the same.

Figure 5-4. With style sheets, you can give the same unordered list many different looks.

Ordered lists

`<ol>...</ol>`
Ordered list

`<li>...</li>`
List item within an ordered list

Ordered lists are for items that occur in a particular order, such as step-by-step instructions or driving directions. They work just like the unordered lists described earlier, except they are defined with the **ol** element (for ordered list, of course). Instead of bullets, the browser automatically inserts numbers before ordered list items, so you don't need to number them in the source document. This makes it easy to rearrange list items without renumbering them.

Ordered list elements must contain one or more list item elements, as shown in this example and in Figure 5-5:

```
<ol>
  <li>Gutenberg develops moveable type (1450s)</li>
  <li>Linotype is introduced (1890s)</li>
  <li>Photocomposition catches on (1950s)</li>
  <li>Type goes digital (1980s)</li>
</ol>
```

1. Gutenberg develops moveable type (1450s)
2. Linotype is introduced (1890s)
3. Photocomposition catches on (1950s)
4. Type goes digital (1980s)

Figure 5-5. The default rendering of an ordered list. The numbers are added automatically by the browser.

If you want a numbered list to start at a number other than "1," you can use the **start** attribute in the **ol** element to specify another starting number, as shown here:

```
<ol start="17">
  <li>Highlight the text with the text tool.</li>
  <li>Select the Character tab.</li>
  <li>Choose a typeface from the pop-up menu.</li>
</ol>
```

The resulting list items would be numbered 17, 18, and 19, consecutively.

Description lists

Description lists are used for any type of name/value pairs, such as terms and their definitions, questions and answers, or other types of terms and their associated information. Their structure is a bit different from the other two lists that we just discussed. The whole description list is marked up as a **dl** element. The content of a **dl** is some number of **dt** elements indicating the names and **dd** elements for their respective values. I find it helpful to think of them as "terms" (to remember the "t" in **dt**) and "definitions" (for the "d" in **dd**), even though that is only one use of description lists in HTML5.

Here is an example of a list that associates forms of typesetting with their descriptions (Figure 5-6).

```
<dl>
  <dt>Linotype</dt>
  <dd>Line-casting allowed type to be selected, used, then recirculated
into the machine automatically. This advance increased the speed of
typesetting and printing dramatically.</dd>

  <dt>Photocomposition</dt>
  <dd>Typefaces are stored on film then projected onto photo-sensitive
paper. Lenses adjust the size of the type.</dd>

  <dt>Digital type</dt>
  <dd><p>Digital typefaces store the outline of the font shape in a
format such as Postscript. The outline may be scaled to any size for
output.</p>
```

Changing Bullets and Numbering

You can use the **list-style-type** style sheet property to change the bullets and numbers for lists. For example, for unordered lists, you can change the shape from the default dot to a square or an open circle, substitute your own image, or remove the bullet altogether. For ordered lists, you can change the numbers to roman numerals (I., II., III. or i., ii., iii.), letters (A., B., C., or a., b., c.), and several other numbering schemes. In fact, as long as the list is marked up semantically, it doesn't need to display with bullets or numbering at all. Changing the style of lists with CSS is covered in Chapter 12, Formatting Text.

`<dl>...</dl>`
A description list

`<dt>...</dt>`
A name, such as a term or label

`<dd>...</dd>`
A value, such as a description or definition

```
            <p>Postscript emerged as a standard due to its support of
graphics and its early support on the Macintosh computer and Apple
laser printer.</p>
      </dd>
</dl>
```

Linotype
   Line-casting allowed type to be selected, used, then
   recirculated into the machine automatically. This advance
   increased the speed of typesetting and printing dramatically.
Photocomposition
   Typefaces are stored on film then projected onto photo-
   sensitive paper. Lenses adjust the size of the type.
Digital type

   Digital typefaces store the outline of the font shape in a
   format such as Postscript. The outline may may be scaled to
   any size for output.

   Postscript emerged as a standard due to its support of
   graphics and its early support on the Macintosh computer and
   Apple laser printer.

Figure 5-6. The default rendering of a definition list. Definitions are set off from the terms by an indent.

> ## Sectioning Roots
>
> The **blockquote** is in a category of elements called sectioning roots. Headings in a sectioning root element will not be included in the main document outline. That means you can have a complex heading hierarchy within a **blockquote** without worrying how it will affect the overall structure of the document. Other sectioning root elements include **figure**, **details**, **fieldset** (for organizing form fields), **td** (a table cell), and **body** (because it has its own outline, which also happens to be the outline of the document).

The **dl** element is only allowed to contain **dt** and **dd** elements. It is OK to have multiple definitions with one term and vice versa. You cannot put headings or content-grouping elements (like paragraphs) in names (**dt**), but the value (**dd**) can contain any type of flow content.

More Content Elements

We've covered paragraphs, headings, and lists, but there are a few more special text elements to add to your HTML toolbox that don't fit into a neat category: long quotations (**blockquote**), preformatted text (**pre**), and figures (**figure** and **figcaption**). One thing these elements do have in common is that they are considered "grouping content" in the HTML5 spec (along with **p**, **hr**, the list elements, and the generic **div**, covered later in this chapter). The other thing they share is that browsers typically display them as block elements by default.

Long quotations

`<blockquote>...</blockquote>`

A lengthy, block-level quotation

If you have a long quotation, a testimonial, or a section of copy from another source, you should mark it up as a **blockquote** element. It is recommended that content within **blockquote** elements be contained in other elements, such as paragraphs, headings, or lists, as shown in this example (see the sidebar "Sectioning Roots").

```
<p>Renowned type designer, Matthew Carter, has this to say about his
profession:</p>

<blockquote>
  <p>Our alphabet hasn't changed in eons; there isn't much latitude in
what a designer can do with the individual letters.</p>

  <p>Much like a piece of classical music, the score is written
down. It's not something that is tampered with, and yet, each
conductor interprets that score differently. There is tension in
the interpretation.</p>
</blockquote>
```

NOTE

There is also the inline element, q, for short quotations in the flow of text. We'll talk about it later in this chapter.

Figure 5-7 shows the default rendering of the **blockquote** example. This can be altered with CSS.

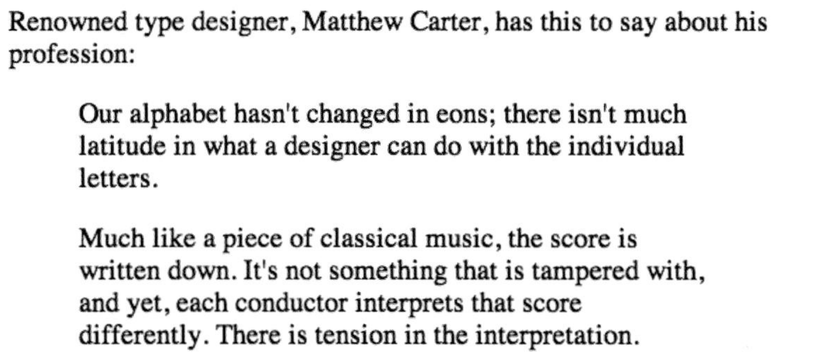

> **Renowned type designer, Matthew Carter, has this to say about his profession:**
>
> > Our alphabet hasn't changed in eons; there isn't much latitude in what a designer can do with the individual letters.
> >
> > Much like a piece of classical music, the score is written down. It's not something that is tampered with, and yet, each conductor interprets that score differently. There is tension in the interpretation.

Figure 5-7. The default rendering of a blockquote *element.*

Preformatted text

In the previous chapter, you learned that browsers ignore whitespace such as line returns and character spaces in the source document. But in some types of information, such as code examples or poetry, the whitespace is important for conveying meaning. For these purposes, there is the preformatted text (**pre**) element. It is a unique element in that it is displayed exactly as it is typed—including all the carriage returns and multiple character spaces. By default, preformatted text is also displayed in a constant-width font (one in which all the characters are the same width, also called monospace), such as Courier.

The **pre** element in this example displays as shown in Figure 5-8. The second part of the figure shows the same content marked up as a paragraph (**p**) element for comparison.

```
<pre>
This is              an            example of
     text with a        lot of
                        curious
                        whitespace.
</pre>
```

`<pre>...</pre>`
Preformatted text

NOTE

The `white-space:pre` *CSS property can also be used to preserve spaces and returns in the source. Unlike the* **pre** *element, text formatted with the* **white-space** *property is not displayed in a constant-width font.*

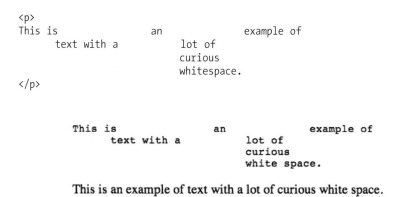

```
<p>
This is              an            example of
     text with a        lot of
                        curious
                        whitespace.
</p>
```

Figure 5-8. Preformatted text is unique in that the browser displays the whitespace exactly as it is typed into the source document. Compare it to the paragraph element, in which line returns and character spaces are reduced to a single space.

Figures

<figure>...</figure>
Related image or resource
NEW IN HTML5

<figcaption>...</figcaption>
Text description of a figure
NEW IN HTML5

The **figure** element is used for content that illustrates or supports some point in the text. A figure may contain an image, a video, a code snippet, text, or even a table—pretty much anything that can go in the flow of web content and should be treated and referenced as a self-contained unit. That means if a figure is removed from its original placement in the main flow (to a sidebar or appendix, for example), both the figure and the main flow should continue to make sense.

Although it is possible to simply drop an image into text, wrapping it in **figure** tags makes its purpose explicitly clear. It also allows you to apply special styles to figures but not to other images on the page.

```
<figure>
    <img src="piechart.png" alt="chart showing fonts on mobile devices">
</figure>
```

A caption can be attached to the figure using the optional **figcaption** element above or below the figure content.

```
<figure>
    <pre><code>
    body {
       background-color: #000;
       color: red;
    }
    </code></pre>
    <figcaption>
        Sample CSS rule.
    </figcaption>
</figure>
```

SUPPORT ALERT

The **figure** and **figcaption** elements are not supported in Internet Explorer versions 8 and earlier (see the sidebar "HTML5 Support in Internet Explorer," later in this chapter, for a workaround). Older versions of Firefox and Safari (prior to 3.6 and 4, respectively) do not support it according to the spec, but allow you to apply styles.

In Exercise 5-1, you'll get a chance to mark up a document yourself and try out the basic text elements we've covered so far.

exercise 5-1 | Marking up a recipe

The owners of the Black Goose Bistro have decided to start a blog to share recipes and announcements. In the exercises in this chapter, we'll assist them with content markup.

Below you will find the raw text of a recipe. It's up to you to decide which element is the best semantic match for each chunk of content. You'll use paragraphs, headings, lists, and at least one special content element.

You can write the tags right on this page. Or, if you want to use a text editor and see the results in a browser, this text file is available online at *www.learningwebdesign.com/4e/materials*. The resulting code appears in Appendix A.

```
Tapenade (Olive Spread)

This is a really simple dish to prepare and it's always a big hit at parties. My father recommends:

"Make this the night before so that the flavors have time to blend. Just bring it up to room temperature
before you serve it. In the winter, try serving it warm."

Ingredients

1 8oz. jar sundried tomatoes
2 large garlic cloves
2/3 c. kalamata olives
1 t. capers

Instructions

Combine tomatoes and garlic in a food processor. Blend until as smooth as possible.

Add capers and olives. Pulse the motor a few times until they are incorporated, but still retain some
texture.

Serve on thin toast rounds with goat cheese and fresh basil garnish (optional).
```

Organizing Page Content

So far, the elements we've covered handle very specific tidbits of content: a paragraph, a heading, a figure, and so on. Prior to HTML5, there was no way to group these bits into larger parts other than wrapping them in a generic division (**div**) element (I'll cover **div** in more detail later). HTML5 introduced new elements that give semantic meaning to sections of a typical web page or application, including sections (**section**), articles (**article**), navigation (**nav**), tangentially related content (**aside**), headers (**header**), and footers (**footer**). The new element names are based on a Google study that looked at the top 20 names given to generic division elements (*code.google. com/webstats/2005-12/classes.html*). Curiously, the spec lists the old **address** element as a section as well, so we'll look at that one here too.

The elements discussed in this section are well supported by current desktop and mobile browsers, but there is a snag with Internet Explorer versions 8 and earlier. See the sidebar "HTML5 Support in Internet Explorer" for details on a workaround.

HTML5 Support in Internet Explorer

Most browsers today support the new HTML5 semantic elements, and for those that don't, creating a style sheet rule that tells browsers to format each one as a block-level element is all that is needed to make them behave correctly.

```
section, article, nav, aside, header, footer,
hgroup { display: block; }
```

Unfortunately, that fix won't work with Internet Explorer versions 8 and earlier (versions 9 and later are fine). Not only do early IE browsers not recognize the elements, but they also ignore any styles applied to them. The solution is to use JavaScript to create each element so IE knows it exists and will allow nesting and styling. Here's what a JavaScript command creating the **section** element looks like:

```
document.createElement("section");
```

Fortunately, Remy Sharp created a script that creates all of the HTML5 elements for IE in one fell swoop. It is called "HTML5

Shiv" (or Shim) and it lives on a Google-run server, so you can just point to it in your documents. To make sure the new HTML5 elements work in IE8 and earlier, copy this code in the **head** of your document and use a style sheet to style the new elements as blocks:

```
<!--[if lt IE 9]>
<script src="http://html5shiv.googlecode.com/svn/
trunk/html5-els.js"></script>
<![endif]-->
```

Find out more about the HTML5 Shiv here: *html5doctor.com/ how-to-get-html5-working-in-ie-and-firefox-2/*.

The HTML5 Shiv is also part of the Modernizr polyfill script that adds HTML5 and CSS3 functionality to older non-supporting browsers. Read more about it online at *modernizr.com*. It is also discussed in Chapter 20, "Using JavaScript."

Sections and articles

<section>...</section>

Thematic group of content

NEW IN HTML5

<article>...</article>

Self-contained, reusable composition

NEW IN HTML5

NOTE

The HTML5 spec recommends that if the purpose for grouping the elements is simply to provide a hook for styling, use the generic div element instead.

Long documents are easier to use when they are divided into smaller parts. For example, books are divided into chapters, and newspapers have sections for local news, sports, comics, and so on. To divide long web documents into thematic sections, use the aptly named **section** element. Sections typically have a heading (inside the **section** element) and any other content that has a meaningful reason to be grouped together.

The **section** element has a broad range of uses, from dividing a whole page into major sections or identifying thematic sections within a single article. In the following example, a document with information about typography resources has been divided into two sections based on resource type.

```
<section>
    <h2>Typography Books</h2>
    <ul>
        <li>...</li>
    </ul>
</section>

<section>
    <h2>Online Tutorials</h2>
    <p>These are the best tutorials on the Web.</p>
    <ul>
        <li>...</li>
    </ul>
</section>
```

Use the **article** element for self-contained works that could stand alone or be reused in a different context (such as syndication). It is useful for magazine or newspaper articles, blog posts, comments, or other items that could be extracted for external use. You can think of it as a specialized **section** element that answers the question "Could this appear on another site and make sense?" with "yes."

To make things interesting, a long **article** could be broken into a number of sections, as shown here:

```
<article>
  <h1>Get to Know Helvetica</h1>
  <section>
    <h2>History of Helvetica</h2>
    <p>…</p>
  </section>

  <section>
    <h2>Helvetica Today</h2>
    <p>…</p>
  </section>
</article>
```

Conversely, a **section** in a web document might be composed of a number of articles.

```
<section id="essays">
  <article>
    <h1>A Fresh Look at Futura</h1>
    <p>…</p>
  </article>

  <article>
    <h1>Getting Personal with Humanist</h1>
    <p>…</p>
  </article>
</section>
```

The **section** and **article** elements are easily confused, particularly because it is possible to nest one in the other and vice versa. Keep in mind that if the content is self-contained and could appear outside the current context, it is best marked up as an **article**.

Sectioning Elements

Another thing that **section** and **article** have in common "under the hood" is that both are what HTML5 calls sectioning elements. When a browser runs across a sectioning element in the document, it creates a new item in the document's outline automatically. In prior HTML versions, only headings (**h1**, **h2**, etc.) triggered new outline items. The new **nav** (primary navigation) and **aside** (for sidebar-like information) are also sectioning elements.

In the new HTML5 outlining system, a sectioning element may have its own internal heading hierarchy, starting with **h1**, regardless of its position in the document that contains it. That makes it possible to take an **article** element with its internal outline, place it in another document flow, and know that it won't break the host document's outline. The goal of the new outlining algorithm is to make the markup meet the needs of content use and reuse on the modern Web.

As of this writing, no browsers support the HTML5 outlining system, so to make your documents accessible and logically structured for all users, it is safest to use headings in descending numerical order, even within sectioning elements.

For more information, I recommend the HTML5 Doctor article "Document Outlines," by Mike Robinson, which tackles HTML5 outlines in more detail than I am able to squeeze in here (*html5doctor.com/outlines/*).

In addition, Roger Johansson's article "HTML5 Sectioning Elements, Headings, and Document Outlines" describes some potential gotchas when working with sectioning elements (*www.456bereastreet.com/archive/201103/html5_sectioning_elements_headings_and_document_outlines/*).

Aside (sidebars)

<aside>...</aside>

Tangentially related material

NEW IN HTML5

The **aside** element identifies content that is related but tangential to the surrounding content. In print, its equivalent is a sidebar, but it couldn't be called **sidebar**, because putting something on the "side" is a presentational description, not semantic. Nonetheless, a sidebar is a good mental model for using the **aside** element. **aside** can be used for pull quotes, background information, lists of links, callouts, or anything else that might be associated with (but not critical to) a document.

In this example, an **aside** element is used for a list of links related to the main article.

```
<h1>Web Typography</h1>
<p>Back in 1997, there were competing font formats and tools for making
them...</p>
<p>We now have a number of methods for using beautiful fonts on web
pages...</p>
<aside>
  <h2>Web Font Resources</h2>
  <ul>
  <li><a href="http://typekit.com/">Typekit</a></li>
  <li><a href="http://www.google.com/webfonts">Google Fonts</a></li>
  </ul>
</aside>
```

The **aside** element has no default rendering, so you will need to make it a block element and adjust its appearance and layout with style sheet rules.

Navigation

<nav>...</nav>

Primary navigation links

NEW IN HTML5

The new **nav** element gives developers a semantic way to identify navigation for a site. Earlier in this chapter, we saw an unordered list that might be used as the top-level navigation for a font catalog site. Wrapping that list in a **nav** element makes its purpose explicitly clear.

```
<nav>
<ul>
  <li><a href="">Serif</a></li>
  <li><a href="">Sans-serif</a></li>
  <li><a href="">Script</a></li>
  <li><a href="">Display</a></li>
  <li><a href="">Dingbats</a></li>
</ul>
</nav>
```

Not all lists of links should be wrapped in **nav** tags, however. The spec makes it clear that it should be used for links that provide primary navigation around a site or a lengthy section or article.

The **nav** element may be especially helpful from an accessibility perspective. Once screen readers and other devices become HTML5-compatible, users can easily get to or skip navigation sections without a lot of hunting around.

Headers and footers

Because web authors have been labeling header and footer sections in their documents for years, it was kind of a no-brainer that full-fledged **header** and **footer** elements would come in handy. Let's start with headers.

Headers

The **header** element is used for introductory material that typically appears at the beginning of a web page or at the top of a section or article. There is no specified list of what a **header** must or should contain; anything that makes sense as the introduction to a page or section is acceptable. In the following example, the document header includes a logo image, the site title, and navigation.

```
<header>
  <img src="/images/logo.png">
  <hgroup>
    <h1>Nuts about Web Fonts</h1>
    <h2>News from the Web Typography Front</h2>
  </hgroup>
  <nav>
    <ul>
      <li><a href="">Home</a></li>
      <li><a href="">Blog</a></li>
      <li><a href="">Shop</a></li>
    </ul>
  </nav>
</header>
```

… page content …

When used in an individual article, the **header** might include the article title, author, and the publication date, as shown here:

```
<article>
  <header>
    <h1>More about WOFF</h1>
    <p>by Jennifer Robbins, <time datetime="11-11-2011"
    pubdate>November 11, 2011</time></p>
  </header>
  <p>...article content starts here...</p>
</article>
```

Footers

The **footer** element is used to indicate the type of information that typically comes at the end of a page or an article, such as its author, copyright information, related documents, or navigation. The **footer** element may apply to the entire document, or it could be associated with a particular section or article. If the footer is contained directly within the **body** element, either before or after all the other **body** content, then it applies to the entire page or application. If it is contained in a sectioning element (**section**, **article**, **nav**, or **aside**), it is parsed as the footer for just that section. Note that although it is called "footer," there is no requirement that

`<header>…</header>`

Introductory material for page, section, or article

NEW IN HTML5

`<footer>…</footer>`

Footer for page, section, or article

NEW IN HTML5

WARNING

Neither **header** *nor* **footer** *elements are permitted to contain nested* **header** *or* **footer** *elements.*

NOTE

You can also add headers and footers to sectioning root elements: body, blockquote, details, figure, td, *and* fieldset.

it come last in the document or sectioning element. It could also appear at or near the beginning if it makes semantic sense.

In this simple example, we see the typical information listed at the bottom of an article or blog post marked up as a **footer**.

```
<article>
  <header>
    <h1>More about WOFF</h1>
    <p>by Jennifer Robbins, <time datetime="11-11-2011"
    pubdate>November 11, 2011</time></p>
  </header>
  <p>...article content starts here…</p>
  <footer>
    <p><small>Copyright &copy;2012 Jennifer Robbins.</small></p>
    <nav>
    <ul>
      <li><a href="">Previous</a></li>
      <li><a href="">Next</a></li>
    </ul>
    </nav>
  </footer>
</article>
```

Addresses

`<address>...</address>`

Contact information

Last, and well, least, is the **address** element that is used to create an area for contact information for the author or maintainer of the document. It is generally placed at the end of the document or in a section or article within a document. An **address** would be right at home in a **footer** element.

It is important to note that the **address** element should *not* be used for any old address on a page, such as mailing addresses. It is intended specifically for author contact information (although that could potentially be a mailing address). Following is an example of its intended use. The "a href" parts are the markup for links…we'll get to those in Chapter 6, Adding Links.

```
<address>
Contributed by <a href="../authors/robbins/">Jennifer Robbins</a>,
<a href="http://www.oreilly.com/">O'Reilly Media</a>
</address>
```

NOTE

You'll get a chance to try out the section elements in Exercise 5-3 at the end of this chapter.

The Inline Element Roundup

Now that we've identified the larger chunks of content, we can provide semantic meaning to phrases within the chunks using what HTML5 calls text-level semantic elements. On the street, you are likely to hear them called inline elements because they display in the flow of text by default and do not cause any line breaks. That's also how they were referred to in HTML versions prior to HTML5.

Text-level (inline) elements

Despite all the types of information you could add to a document, there are only a couple dozen text-level semantic elements in HTML5. Table 5-1 lists all of them.

Table 5-1. Text-level semantic elements

Element	Description
a	An anchor or hypertext link (see Chapter 6 for details)
abbr	Abbreviation
b	Added visual attention, such as keywords (bold)
bdi	**NEW IN HTML5** Indicates text that may have directional requirements
bdo	Bidirectional override; explicitly indicates text direction (left to right, ltr, or right to left, rtl)
br	Line break
cite	Citation; a reference to the title of a work, such as a book title
code	Computer code sample
data	**WHATWG ONLY** Machine-readable equivalent dates, time, weights, and other measurable values
del	Deleted text; indicates an edit made to a document
dfn	The defining instance or first occurrence of a term
em	Emphasized text
i	Alternative voice (italic)
ins	Inserted text; indicates an insertion in a document
kbd	Keyboard; text entered by a user (for technical documents)
mark	**NEW IN HTML5** Contextually relevant text
q	Short, inline quotation
ruby, rt, rp	**NEW IN HTML5** Provides annotations or pronunciation guides under East Asian typography and ideographs
s	Incorrect text (strike-through)
samp	Sample output from programs
small	Small print, such as a copyright or legal notice (displayed in a smaller type size)
span	Generic phrase content
strong	Content of strong importance
sub	Subscript
sup	Superscript
time	**NEW IN HTML5** Machine-readable time data
u	Text that would normally be underlined, such as a formal name or misspelled word
var	A variable or program argument (for technical documents)
wbr	Word break

The Inline Elements Backstory

Many of the inline elements that have been around since the dawn of the Web were introduced to change the visual formatting of text selections due to the lack of a style sheet system. If you wanted bolded text, you marked it as **b**. Italics? Use the **i** element. In fact, there was once a **font** element used solely to change the font, color, and size of text (the horror!). Not surprisingly, HTML5 kicked the purely presentational **font** element to the curb. However, many of the old-school presentational inline elements (for example, **u** for underline and **s** for strike-through) have been kept in HTML5 and given new semantic definitions (**b** is now for "keywords," **s** for "inaccurate text").

Some inline elements are purely semantic (such as **abbr** or **time**) and don't have default renderings. For these, you'll need to use CSS rules if you want to change the way they display.

In the element descriptions in this section, I'll provide both the definition of the inline elements and the expected browser default rendering if there is one.

Obsolete HTML 4.01 Text Elements

HTML5 finally retired many elements that were marked as deprecated (phased out and discouraged from use) in HTML 4.01. For the sake of thoroughness, I include them here in case you run across them in legacy markup or web authoring tool. But there's no reason to use them—most have analogous style sheet properties or are simply poorly supported.

Element	Description
acronym	Indicates an acronym (e.g., NASA); authors should use **abbr** instead
applet	Inserts a Java applet
basefont	Establishes default font settings for a document
big	Makes text slightly larger than default text size
center	Centers content horizontally
dir	Directory list (replaced by unordered lists)
font	Font face, color, and size
isindex	Inserts a search box
menu	Menu list (replaced by unordered lists; however, **menu** is now used to provide contextual menu commands)
strike	Strike-through text
tt	Teletype; displays in constant-width font

Emphasized text

`<em>...</em>`
Stressed emphasis

Use the **em** element to indicate which part of a sentence should be stressed or emphasized. The placement of **em** elements affects how a sentence's meaning is interpreted. Consider the following sentences that are identical, except for which words are stressed.

```
<p><em>Matt</em> is very smart.</p>

<p>Matt is <em>very</em> smart.</p>
```

The first sentence indicates *who* is very smart. The second example is about *how* smart he is.

Emphasized text (**em**) elements nearly always display in italics by default (Figure 5-9), but of course you can make them display any way you like with a style sheet. Screen readers may use a different tone of voice to convey stressed content, which is why you should use an **em** element only when it makes sense semantically, not just to achieve italic text.

Important text

`<strong>...</strong>`
Strong importance

The **strong** element indicates that a word or phrase is important. In the following example, the **strong** element identifies the portion of instructions that requires extra attention.

```
<p>When returning the car, <strong>drop the keys in the red box by the
front desk</strong>.</p>
```

Visual browsers typically display **strong** text elements in bold text by default. Screen readers may use a distinct tone of voice for important content, so mark text as **strong** only when it makes sense semantically, not just to make text bold.

The following is a brief example of our **em** and **strong** text examples. Figure 5-9 should hold no surprises.

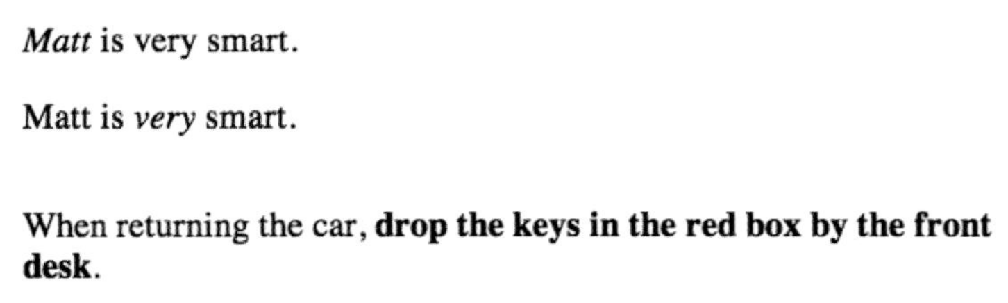

Matt is very smart.

Matt is *very* smart.

When returning the car, **drop the keys in the red box by the front desk**.

Figure 5-9. The default rendering of emphasized and strong text.

The previously presentational elements that are sticking around in HTML5 with fancy new semantic definitions

As long as we're talking about bold and italic text, let's see what the old **b** and **i** elements are up to now. The elements **b**, **i**, **u**, **s**, and **small** were introduced in the old days of the Web as a way to provide typesetting instructions (bold, italic, underline, strike-through, and smaller text, respectively). Despite their original presentational purposes, these elements have been included in HTML5 and given updated, semantic definitions based on patterns of how they've been used. Browsers still render them by default as you'd expect (Figure 5-10). However, if a type style change is all you're after, using a style sheet rule is the appropriate solution. Save these for when they are semantically appropriate.

Let's look at these elements and their correct usage, as well as the style sheet alternatives.

b

HTML 4.01 definition: Bold

HTML5 definition: Keywords, product names, and other phrases that need to stand out from the surrounding text without conveying added importance or emphasis.

CSS alternative: For bold text, use **font-weight**. Example: **font-weight: bold**

Example: `<p>The slabs at the ends of letter strokes are called <b>serifs</b>.</p>`

`<b>...</b>`
Keywords or visually emphasized text (bold)

`<i>...</i>`
Alternative voice (italic)

`<s>...</s>`
Incorrect text (strike-through)

`<u>...</u>`
Annotated text (underline)

`<small>...</small>`
Legal text; small print (smaller type size)

NOTE

It helps me to think about how a screen reader would read the text. If I don't want the word read in a loud, emphatic tone of voice, but it really should be bold, then b *may be more appropriate than* strong.

`i`

HTML 4.01 definition: Italic

HTML5 definition: Indicates text that is in a different voice or mood than the surrounding text, such as a phrase from another language, a technical term, or thought.

CSS alternative: For italic text, use **font-style**. Example: **font-style: italic**

Example: `<p>Simply change the font and <i>Voila!</i>, a new personality!</p>`

`s`

HTML 4.01 definition: Strike-through text

HTML5 definition: Indicates text that is incorrect.

CSS Property: To put a line through a text selection, use **text-decoration**. Example: **text-decoration: line-through**

Example: `<p>Scala Sans was designed by <s>Eric Gill</s> Martin Majoor.</p>`

`u`

HTML 4.01 definition: Underline

HTML5 definition: There are a few instances when underlining has semantic significance, such as underlining a formal name in Chinese or indicating a misspelled word after a spell check. Note that underlined text is easily confused as a link and should generally be avoided except for a few niche cases.

CSS Property: For underlined text, use **text-decoration**. Example: **text-decoration: underline**

Example: `<p>New York subway signage is set in <u>Halvetica</u>.</p>`

`small`

HTML 4.01 definition: Renders in font smaller than the surrounding text

HTML5 definition: Indicates an addendum or side note to the main text, such as the legal "small print" at the bottom of a document.

CSS Property: To make text smaller, use **font-size**. Example: **font-size: 80%**

Example: `<p><small>(This font is free for personal and commercial use.)</small></p>`

The slabs at the ends of letter strokes are called **serifs**.

Simply change the font and *Voila!*, a new personality!

Scala Sans was designed by ~~Eric Gill~~ Martin Majoor.

New York subway signage is set in <u>Halvetica</u>.

(This font is free for personal and commercial use.)

Figure 5-10. The default rendering of b, i, s, u, *and* small *elements.*

Short quotations

Use the quotation (**q**) element to mark up short quotations, such as "To be or not to be," in the flow of text, as shown in this example (Figure 5-11).

```
Matthew Carter says, <q>Our alphabet hasn't changed in eons.</q>
```

According to the HTML spec, browsers should add quotation marks around **q** elements automatically, so you don't need to include them in the source document. And for the most part they do, with the exception of Internet Explorer versions 7 and earlier. Fortunately, as of this writing, those browsers make up only 5–8% of browser usage, and it's sure to be significantly less by the time you read this. If you are concerned about a small percentage of users seeing quotations without their marks, stick with using quotation marks in your source, a fine alternative.

Matthew Carter says, "Our alphabet hasn't changed in eons."

Figure 5-11. Nearly all browsers add quotation marks automatically around **q** *elements.*

`<q>...</q>`
Short inline quotation

REMINDER

Nesting Elements

You can apply two elements to a string of text (for example, a phrase that is both a quote and in another language), but be sure they are nested properly. That means the inner element, including its closing tag, must be completely contained within the outer element, and not overlap.

`<q><i>Je ne sais pas.</i></q>`

Abbreviations and acronyms

Marking up acronyms and abbreviations with the **abbr** element provides useful information for search engines, screen readers, and other devices. Abbreviations are shortened versions of a word ending in a period (Conn. for Connecticut, for example). Acronyms are abbreviations formed by the first letters of the words in a phrase (such as WWW or USA). The **title** attribute provides the long version of the shortened term, as shown in this example:

```
<abbr title="Points">pts.</abbr>
<abbr title="American Type Founders">ATF</abbr>
```

`<abbr>...</abbr>`
Abbreviation or acronym

NOTE

In HTML 4.01, there was an **acronym** *element especially for acronyms, but it has been made obsolete in HTML5 in favor of using the* **abbr** *for both.*

Citations

`<cite>...</cite>`
Citation

The **cite** element is used to identify a reference to another document, such as a book, magazine, article title, and so on. Citations are typically rendered in italic text by default. Here's an example:

```
<p>Passages of this article were inspired by <cite>The Complete Manual
of Typography</cite> by James Felici.</p>
```

Defining terms

`<dfn>...</dfn>`
Defining term

It is common to point out the first and defining instance of a word in a document in some fashion. In this book, defining terms are set in blue text. In HTML, you can identify them with the **dfn** element and format them visually using style sheets.

```
<p><dfn>Script typefaces</dfn> are based on handwriting.</p>
```

Program code elements

`<code>...</code>`
Code

`<var>...</var>`
Variable

`<samp>...</samp>`
Program sample

`<kbd>...</kbd>`
User-entered keyboard strokes

A number of inline elements are used for describing the parts of technical documents, such as code (**code**), variables (**var**), program samples (**samp**), and user-entered keyboard strokes (**kbd**). For me, it's a quaint reminder of HTML's origins in the scientific world (Tim Berners-Lee developed HTML to share documents at the CERN particle physics lab in 1989).

Code, sample, and keyboard elements typically render in a constant-width (also called monospace) font such as Courier by default. Variables usually render in italics.

Subscript and superscript

`<sub>...</sub>`
Subscript

`<sup>...</sup>`
Superscript

The subscript (**sub**) and superscript (**sup**) elements cause the selected text to display in a smaller size, positioned slightly below (**sub**) or above (**sup**) the baseline. These elements may be helpful for indicating chemical formulas or mathematical equations.

Figure 5-12 shows how these examples of subscript and superscript typically render in a browser.

```
<p>H<sub>2</sub>0</p>
```

```
<p>E=MC<sup>2</sup></p>
```

$$H_2 0 \qquad E=MC^2$$

Figure 5-12. Subscript and superscript

Highlighted text

The new **mark** element indicates a word that may be considered especially relevant to the reader. One might use it to call out a search term in a page of results, to manually call attention to a passage of text, or to indicate the current page in a series. Some designers (and browsers) give marked text a light colored background as though it were marked with a highlighter marker, as shown in Figure 5-13.

```
<p> ... PART I. ADMINISTRATION OF THE GOVERNMENT. TITLE IX.
TAXATION. CHAPTER 65C. MASS. <mark>ESTATE TAX</mark>. Chapter 65C:
Sect. 2. Computation of <mark>estate tax</mark>.</p>
```

> ... PART I. ADMINISTRATION OF THE GOVERNMENT. TITLE IX. TAXATION. CHAPTER 65C. MASS. ESTATE TAX. Chapter 65C: Sect. 2. Computation of estate tax.

Figure 5-13. Search terms are marked as mark elements and given a yellow background with a style sheet so they are easier for the reader to find.

`<mark>...</mark>`

Contextually relevant text

`NEW IN HTML5`

SUPPORT ALERT

The **mark** *element is not supported in Internet Explorer versions 8 and earlier (see the sidebar "HTML5 Support in Internet Explorer," earlier in this chapter, for a workaround). Older versions of Firefox and Safari (prior to 3.6 and 4, respectively) do not support it according to the spec, but do allow you to apply styles to it.*

Times and machine-readable information

When we look at the phrase "noon on November 4," we know that it is a date and a time. But the context might not be so obvious to a computer program. The **time** element allows us to mark up dates and times in a way that is comfortable for a human to read, but also encoded in a standardized way that computers can use. The content of the element presents the information to people, and the **datetime** attribute presents the same information in a machine-readable way.

The **time** element indicates dates, times, or date-time combos. It might be used to pass the date and time information to an application, such as saving an event to a personal calendar. It might be used by search engines to find the most recently published articles. Or it could be used to restyle time information into an alternate format (e.g., changing 18:00 to 6 p.m.).

The **datetime** attribute specifies the date and/or time information in a standardized time format illustrated in Figure 5-14. It begins with the date (year, month, day), followed by the letter T to indicate time, listed in hours, minutes, seconds (optional), and milliseconds (also optional). Finally, the time zone is indicated by the number of hours behind (–) or ahead (+) of Greenwich Mean Time (GMT). For example, "–05:00" indicates the Eastern Standard time zone, which is five hours behind GMT.

`<time>...</time>`

Time data

`NEW IN HTML5`

NOTE

The **time** *element is not intended for marking up times for which a precise time or date cannot be established, such as "the end of last year" or "the turn of the century."*

Figure 5-14. Standardized date and time syntax.

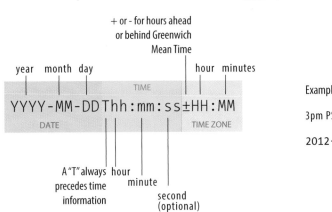

Example:

3pm PST on December 25, 2012

`2012-12-25T15:00-8:00`

The WHATWG HTML specification includes a **pubdate** attribute for indicating that the time is the publication date of a document, as shown in this example. The **pubdate** attribute is not included in the W3C HTML5 spec as of this writing, but it may be included at a later date if it becomes widely used.

```
Written by Jennifer Robbins (<time datetime="2012-09-01T 20:00-05:00"
pubdate>September 1, 2012, 8pm EST</time>)
```

`<data>...</data>`

Machine-readable data

WHATWG ONLY

The WHATWG also includes the **data** element for helping computers make sense of content, which can be used for all sorts of data, including dates, times, measurements, weights, and so on. It uses the **value** attribute for the machine-readable information. Here are a couple of examples:

```
<data value="12">Twelve</data>
<data value="2011-11-12">Last Saturday</data>
```

SUPPORT ALERT

Both time and data are new elements and are not universally supported as of this writing. However, you can apply styles to them and they will be recognized by browsers other than IE8 and earlier.

I'm not going to go into more detail on the **data** element, because as of this writing, the powers that be are still discussing exactly how it should work, and the W3C has not adopted it for the HTML5 spec. Also, as a beginner, you are unlikely to be dealing with machine-readable data yet anyway. But still, it is interesting to see how markup can be used to provide usable information to computer programs and scripts as well as to your fellow humans.

Inserted and deleted text

`<ins>...</ins>`

Inserted text

`<del>...</del>`

Deleted text

The **ins** and **del** elements are used to mark up edits indicating parts of a document that have been inserted or deleted (respectively). These elements rely on style rules for presentation (i.e., there is no dependable browser default). Both the **ins** and **del** elements can contain either inline or block elements, depending on what type of content they contain.

```
Chief Executive Officer: <del title="retired">Peter Pan</del><ins>Pippi
Longstockings</ins>
```

Adding Breaks

Line breaks

`<br>`

Line break

Occasionally, you may need to add a line break within the flow of text. We've seen how browsers ignore line breaks in the source document, so we need a specific directive to tell the browser to "add a line break here."

The inline line break element (**br**) does exactly that. The **br** element could be used to break up lines of addresses or poetry. It is an empty element, which means it does not have content. Just add the **br** element (**
** in XHTML) in the flow of text where you want a break to occur, as shown here and in Figure 5-15.

```
<p>So much depends <br>upon <br><br>a red wheel <br>barrow</p>
```

So much depends
upon

a red wheel
barrow

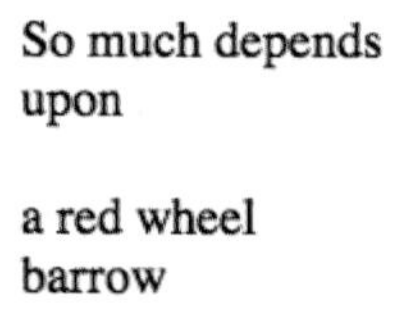

Figure 5-15. Line breaks are inserted at each br element.

Accommodating Non-Western Languages

Because the Web is "world-wide," there are a few elements designed to address the needs of non-Western languages.

Changing direction

The **bdo** (bidirectional override) element allows a phrase in a right-to-left (**rtl**) reading language (such as Hebrew or Arabic) to be included in a left-to-right (**ltr**) reading flow, or vice versa.

> This is how you write Shalom: `<bdo dir="rtl">&#x05E9;&#x05DC;&#x05D5;&#x05DD;</bdo>`

The **bdi** (bidirectional isolation) element is similar, but it is used to isolate a selection that *might* read in a different direction, such as a name or comment added by a user.

Hints for East Asian languages

HTML5 also includes the **ruby**, **rt**, and **rp** elements used to add ruby annotation to East Asian languages. Ruby annotations are little notes that typically appear above ideographs and provide pronunciation clues or translations. Within the **ruby** element, the **rt** element indicates the helpful ruby text. Browsers that support ruby text typically display it in a smaller font above the main text. As a backup for browsers that don't support ruby, you can put the ruby text in parentheses, each marked with the **rp** element. Non-supporting browsers display all the text on the same line, with the ruby in parentheses. Supporting browsers ignore the content of the **rp** elements and display only the **rt** text above the glyphs. The ruby system has spotty browser support as of this writing.

```
<ruby>
字<rp>(</rp><rt>han</rt><rp>)</rp>
汉<rp>(</rp><rt>zi</rt><rp>)</rp>
</ruby>
```

This example was taken from the HTML5 Working Draft at whatwg.com, used with permission under an MIT License.

Unfortunately, the **br** element is easily abused (see the warning). Consider whether using the CSS **white-space** property (introduced in Chapter 12, Formatting Text) might be a better alternative for maintaining line breaks from your source without extra markup.

Word breaks

`<wbr>`

Word break

The word break (**wbr**) element lets you mark the place where a word should break if it needs to (a "line break opportunity" according to the spec). It takes some of the guesswork away from the browser and allows authors to specify the best spot for the word to be split over two lines. Keep in mind that the word breaks at the **wbr** element only if it needs to (Figure 5-16). If there is enough room, the word stays in one piece. Browsers have supported this element for a long time, but it has recently been incorporated into the HTML standard.

```
<p>The biggest word you've ever heard and this is how it goes:
<em>supercali<wbr>fragilistic<wbr>expialidocious</em>!</p>
```

The biggest word you've ever heard and this is how it goes: *supercalifragilistic expialidocious*!

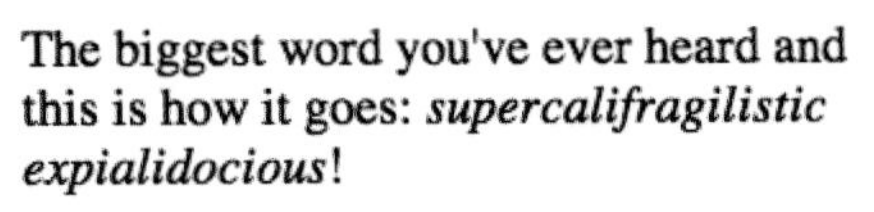

*Figure 5-16. When there is not enough room for a word to fit on a line, it will break at the location of the **wbr** element.*

WARNING

*Be careful that you aren't using **br** elements to force breaks into text that really ought to be a list. For example, don't do this:*

```
<p>Times<br>
Georgia<br>
Garamond
</p>
```

If it's a list, use the semantically correct unordered list element instead, and turn off the bullets with style sheets.

```
<ul>
  <li>Times</li>
  <li>Georgia</li>
  <li>Garamond</li>
</ul>
```

exercise 5-2 | **Identifying inline elements**

This little post for the Black Goose Bistro blog will give you an opportunity to identify and mark up a variety of inline elements. See if you can find phrases to mark up accurately with the following elements:

```
b    br    cite    dfn    em    i    q    small    time
```

Because markup is always somewhat subjective, your resulting markup may not look exactly like the example in Appendix A, but there is an opportunity to use all of the elements listed above in the article. For extra credit, there is a phrase that should have two elements applied to it (remember to nest them properly by closing the inner element before you close the outer one).

You can write the tags right on this page. Or, if you want to use a text editor and see the results in a browser, this text file is available online at *www.learningwebdesign. com/4e/materials*. The resulting code appears in Appendix A.

```
<article>

    <header>

    <p>posted by BGB, November 15, 2012</p>

    </header>

<h1>Low and Slow</h1>

<p>This week I am extremely excited about a new cooking technique

called sous vide. In sous vide cooking, you submerge the food

(usually vacuum-sealed in plastic) into a water bath that is

precisely set to the target temperature you want the food to be

cooked to. In his book, Cooking for Geeks, Jeff Potter describes

it as ultra-low-temperature poaching.</p>

<p>Next month, we will be serving Sous Vide Salmon with Dill

Hollandaise. To reserve a seat at the chef table, contact us

before November 30.</p>


<p>blackgoose@example.com

555-336-1800</p>


<p> Warning: Sous vide cooked salmon is not pasteurized. Avoid it

if you are pregnant or have immunity issues.</p>

</article>
```

Generic Elements (div and span)

What if none of the elements we've talked about so far accurately describes your content? After all, there are endless types of information in the world, but as you've seen, not all that many semantic elements. Fortunately, HTML provides two generic elements that can be customized to describe your content perfectly. The **div** element indicates a division of content, and **span** indicates a word or phrase for which no text-level element currently exists. The generic elements are given meaning and context with the **id** and **class** attributes, which we'll discuss in a moment.

The **div** and **span** elements have no inherent presentation qualities of their own, but you can use style sheets to format them however you like. In fact, generic elements are a primary tool in standards-based web design because they enable authors to accurately describe content and offer plenty of "hooks" for adding style rules. They also allow elements on the page to be accessed and manipulated by JavaScript.

We're going to spend a little time on **div** and **span** (as well as the **id** and **class** attributes) and learn how authors use them to structure content.

`<div>...</div>`
Generic block-level element

`<span>...</span>`
Generic inline element

Divide it up with a div

The **div** element is used to create a logical grouping of content or elements on the page. It indicates that they belong together in some sort of conceptual unit or should be treated as a unit by CSS or JavaScript. By marking related content as a **div** and giving it a unique **id** identifier or indicating that it is part of a **class**, you give context to the elements in the grouping. Let's look at a few examples of **div** elements.

In this example, a **div** element is used as a container to group an image and two paragraphs into a product "listing."

```
<div class="listing">
  <img src="felici-cover.gif" alt="">
  <p><cite>The Complete Manual of Typography</cite>, James Felici</p>
  <p>A combination of type history and examples of good and bad type
design.</p>
</div>
```

By putting those elements in a **div**, I've made it clear that they are conceptually related. It will also allow me to style two **p** elements within listings differently than other paragraphs on the page.

Here is another common use of a **div** used to break a page into sections for layout purposes. In this example, a heading and several paragraphs are enclosed in a **div** and identified as the "news" division.

```
<div id="news">
  <h1>New This Week</h1>
  <p>We've been working on...</p>
  <p>And last but not least,... </p>
</div>
```

> **MARKUP TIP**
>
> It is possible to nest **div** elements within other **div** elements, but don't go overboard. You should always strive to keep your markup as simple as possible, so add a **div** element only if it is necessary for logical structure, styling, or scripting.

Now that I have an element known as "news," I could use a style sheet to position it as a column to the right or left of the page. You might be thinking, "Hey Jen, couldn't you use a **section** element for that?" You could! In fact, authors may turn to generic **div**s less now that we have better semantic grouping elements in HTML5.

Get inline with span

A **span** offers the same benefits as the **div** element, except it is used for phrase elements and does not introduce line breaks. Because spans are inline elements, they can only contain text and other inline elements (in other words, you cannot put headings, lists, content-grouping elements, and so on, in a **span**). Let's get right to some examples.

There is no **telephone** element, but we can use a **span** to give meaning to telephone numbers. In this example, each telephone number is marked up as a **span** and classified as "tel":

```
<ul>
  <li>John: <span class="tel">999.8282</span></li>
  <li>Paul: <span class="tel">888.4889</span></li>
  <li>George: <span class="tel">888.1628</span></li>
  <li>Ringo: <span class="tel">999.3220</span></li>
</ul>
```

You can see how the classified spans add meaning to what otherwise might be a random string of digits. As a bonus, the **span** element enables us to apply the same style to phone numbers throughout the site (for example, ensuring line breaks never happen within them, using a CSS **white-space: nowrap** declaration). It makes the information recognizable not only to humans but also to computer programs that know that "tel" is telephone number information. In fact, some values—including "tel"—have been standardized in a markup system known as Microformats that makes web content more useful to software (see the upcoming "Microformats and Metadata" sidebar).

id and class attributes

In the previous examples, we saw the **id** and **class** attributes used to provide context to generic **div** and **span** elements. **id** and **class** have different purposes, however, and it's important to know the difference.

Identification with id

The **id** attribute is used to assign a *unique* identifier to an element in the document. In other words, the value of **id** must be used only once in the document. This makes it useful for assigning a name to a particular element, as though it were a piece of data. See the sidebar "id and class Values" for information on providing values for the **id** attribute.

This example uses the books' ISBN numbers to uniquely identify each listing. No two book listings may share the same **id**.

---

id and class Values

The values for **id** and **class** attributes should start with a letter (A–Z or a–z) or underscore (although Internet Explorer 6 and earlier have trouble with underscores, so they are generally avoided). They should not contain any character spaces or special characters. Letters, numbers, hyphens, underscores, colons, and periods are OK. Also, the values are case-sensitive, so "sectionB" is not interchangeable with "Sectionb."

```
<div id="ISBN0321127307">
  <img src="felici-cover.gif" alt="">
  <p><cite>The Complete Manual of Typography</cite>, James Felici</p>
  <p>A combination of type history and examples of good and bad type.
  </p>
</div>
```

```
<div id="ISBN0881792063">
  <img src="bringhurst-cover.gif" alt="">
  <p><cite>The Elements of Typographic Style</cite>, Robert Bringhurst
  </p>
  <p>This lovely, well-written book is concerned foremost
   with creating beautiful typography.</p>
</div>
```

Web authors also use **id** when identifying the various sections of a page. In the following example, there may not be more than one element with the **id** of "main," "links," or "news" in the document.

```
<section id="main">
  <!-- main content elements here -->
</section>
```

```
<section id="news">
  <!-- news items here -->
</section>
```

```
<aside id="links">
  <!-- list of links here -->
</aside>
```

Not Just for divs

The **id** and **class** attributes may be used with all elements in HTML5, not just **div** and **span**. For example, you could identify an ordered list as "directions" instead of wrapping it in a **div**.

```
<ol id="directions">
  <li>...</li>
  <li>...</li>
  <li>...</li>
</ol>
```

Note that in HTML 4.01, **id** and **class** may be used with all elements except **base**, **basefont**, **head**, **html**, **meta**, **param**, **script**, **style**, and **title**.

Microformats and Metadata

As you've seen, the elements in HTML fall short in describing every type of information. A group of developers decided that if **class** names could be standardized (for example, always using "tel" for telephone numbers), they could establish systems for describing data to make it more useful. This system is called Microformats. Microformats extend the semantics of HTML markup by establishing standard *values* for **id**, **class**, and **rel** attributes rather than creating whole new elements.

There are several Microformat "vocabularies" used to identify things such as contact information (hCard) or calendar items (hCalendar). The Microformats.org site is a good place to learn about them. To give you the general idea, the following example describes the parts of an event using the hCalendar Microformat vocabulary so the browser can automatically add it to your calendar program.

```
<section class="vevent">
  <span class="summary">O'Reilly Emerging
  Technology Conference</span>,
  <time class="dtstart" datetime="20110306">Mar 6
  </time> -
  <time class="dtend" datetime="20110310">10,
  2011</time>
```

```
  <div class="location">Manchester Grand Hyatt,
  San Diego, CA</div>
  <a class="url" href="http://events.example.com
  pub/e/403">Permalink</a>
</section>
```

The hCard vocabulary identifies components of typical contact information (stored in vCard format), including: address (**adr**), postal code (**postal-code**), states (**region**), and telephone numbers (**tel**), to name a few. The browser can then use a service to grab the information from the web page and automatically add it to an address book.

There is a lot more to say about Microformats than I can fit in this book. And not only that, but there are two additional, more complex systems for adding metadata to web pages in development at the W3C: RDFa and Microdata. It's not clear how they are all going to shake out in the long run, and I'm thinking that this metadata stuff is more than you want to take on right now anyway. But when you are ready to learn more, WebSitesMadeRight.com has assembled a great big list of introductory articles and tutorials on all three options: *websitesmaderight.com/2011/05/html5-microdata-microformats-and-rdfa-tutorials-and-resources/*.

Classification with class

The **class** attribute classifies elements into conceptual groups; therefore, unlike the **id** attribute, multiple elements may share a **class** name. By making elements part of the same class, you can apply styles to all of the labeled elements at once with a single style rule or manipulate them all with a script. Let's start by classifying some elements in the earlier book example. In this first example, I've added **class** attributes to classify each **div** as a "listing" and to classify paragraphs as "descriptions."

```
<div id="ISBN0321127307" class="listing">
  <header>
  <img src="felici-cover.gif" alt="">
  <p><cite>The Complete Manual of Typography</cite>, James Felici</p>
  </header>
  <p class="description">A combination of type history and examples of
good and bad type.</p>
</div>

<div id="ISBN0881792063" class="listing">
  <header>
  <img src="bringhurst-cover.gif" alt="">
  <p><cite>The Elements of Typographic Style</cite>, Robert Bringhurst
</p>
  </header>
  <p class="description">This lovely, well-written book is concerned
foremost with creating beautiful typography.</p>
</div>
```

Notice how the same element may have both a **class** and an **id**. It is also possible for elements to belong to multiple classes. When there is a list of **class** values, simply separate them with character spaces. In this example, I've classified each **div** as a "book" to set them apart from possible "cd" or "dvd" listings elsewhere in the document.

```
<div id="ISBN0321127307" class="listing book">
  <img src="felici-cover.gif" alt="CMT cover">
  <p><cite>The Complete Manual of Typography</cite>, James Felici</p>
  <p class="description">A combination of type history and examples of
good and bad type.</p>
</div>

<div id="ISBN0881792063" class="listing book">
  <img src="bringhurst-cover.gif" alt="ETS cover">
  <p><cite>The Elements of Typographic Style</cite>, Robert Bringhurst
</p>
  <p class="description">This lovely, well-written book is concerned
  foremost with creating beautiful typography.</p>
</div>
```

This should have given you a good introduction to how **div** and **span** elements with **class** and **id** attributes are used to add meaning and organization to documents. We'll work with them even more in the style sheet chapters in Part III.

Some Special Characters

There's just one more text-related topic before we close out this chapter.

Some common characters, such as the copyright symbol ©, are not part of the standard set of ASCII characters, which contains only letters, numbers, and a few basic symbols. Other characters, such as the less-than symbol (<), are available, but if you put one in an HTML document, the browser will interpret it as the beginning of a tag.

Characters such as these must be escaped in the source document. Escaping means that instead of typing in the character itself, you represent it by its numeric or named character reference. When the browser sees the character reference, it substitutes the proper character in that spot when the page is displayed.

There are two ways of referring to a specific character: by an assigned numeric value (numeric entity) or using a predefined abbreviated name for the character (called a named entity). All character references begin with an "&" and end with a ";".

Some examples will make this clear. I'd like to add a copyright symbol to my page. The typical Mac keyboard command, Option-G, which works in my word processing program, may not be understood properly by a browser or other software. Instead, I must use the named entity **©** (or its numeric equivalent, **©**) where I want the symbol to appear (Figure 5-17).

```
<p>All content copyright &copy; 2007, Jennifer Robbins</p>
```

or:

```
<p>All content copyright &#169; 2007, Jennifer Robbins</p>
```

HTML defines hundreds of named entities as part of the markup language, which is to say you can't make up your own entity. Table 5-2 lists some commonly used character references. If you'd like to see them all, the complete list of character references has been assembled online by the nice folks at the Web Standards Project at *www.webstandards.org/learn/reference/charts/entities/*.

All content copyright © 2007, Jennifer Robbins

Figure 5-17. The special character is substituted for the character reference when the document is displayed in the browser.

> **NOTE**
>
> *In XHTML, every instance of an ampersand must be escaped so that it is not interpreted as the beginning of a character entity, even when it appears in the value of an attribute. For example:*
>
> ```
> <img src="sno.jpg" alt="Sifl
> &amp; Olly Show" />
> ```

Table 5-2. Common special characters and their character references

Character	Description	Name	Number
	Non-breaking character space		
&	Ampersand	&amp;	&#038;
'	Apostrophe	&apos;	&#039;
<	Less-than symbol (useful for displaying markup on a web page)	&lt;	&#060;
>	Greater-than symbol (useful for displaying markup on a web page)	&gt;	&#062;
©	Copyright	&copy;	&#169;
®	Registered trademark	&reg;	&#174;
™	Trademark	&trade;	&#8482;
£	Pound	&pound;	&#163;
¥	Yen	&yen;	&#165;
€	Euro	&euro;	&#8364;
–	En-dash	&ndash;	&#8211;
—	Em-dash	&mdash;	&#8212;
'	Left curly single quote	&lsquo;	&#8216;
'	Right curly single quote	&rsquo;	&#8217;
"	Left curly double quote	&ldquo;	&#8220;
"	Right curly double quote	&rdquo;	&#8221;
•	Bullet	&bull;	&#8226;
…	Horizontal ellipsis	&hellip;	&#8230;

Non-breaking Spaces

One interesting character to know about is the non-breaking space (** **). Its purpose is to ensure that a line doesn't break between two words. So, for instance, if I mark up my name like this:

`Jennifer Robbins`

I can be sure that my first and last names will always stay together on a line.

TIP

Remember that indenting each hierarchical level in your HTML source consistently makes the document easier to scan and update later.

Putting It All Together

So far, you've learned how to mark up elements, and you've met all of the HTML elements for adding structure and meaning to text content. Now it's just a matter of practice. Exercise 5-3 gives you an opportunity to try out everything we've covered so far: document structure elements, block elements, inline elements, sectioning elements, and character entities. Have fun!

exercise 5-3 | **The Black Goose Blog page**

Now that you've been introduced to all of the text elements, you can put them to work by marking up the Blog page for the Black Goose Bistro site. The content is shown below (the second post is already marked up with the inline elements from Exercise 5-2). Get the starter text file online at *www.learningwebdesign.com/4e/materials*. The resulting markup is in Appendix A and included in the **materials** folder.

Once you have the text file, follow the instructions listed after the copy. The resulting page is shown in Figure 5-18.

```
The Black Goose Blog

Home
Menu
Blog
Contact

Summer Menu Items
posted by BGB, June 15, 2013
Our chef has been busy putting together the
perfect menu for the summer months. Stop by to
try these appetizers and main courses while the
days are still long.

Appetizers
Black bean purses
Spicy black bean and a blend of mexican cheeses
wrapped in sheets of phyllo and baked until
golden. $3.95

Southwestern napoleons with lump crab -- new
item!
Layers of light lump crab meat, bean and corn
salsa, and our handmade flour tortillas. $7.95

Main courses

Shrimp sate kebabs with peanut sauce
Skewers of shrimp marinated in lemongrass, garlic,
and fish sauce then grilled to perfection. Served
with spicy peanut sauce and jasmine rice. $12.95

Jerk rotisserie chicken with fried plantains --
new item!
Tender chicken slow-roasted on the rotisserie,
flavored with spicy and fragrant jerk sauce and
served with fried plantains and fresh mango.
$12.95

Low and Slow
posted by BGB, November 15, 2012
<p>This week I am <em>extremely</em> excited
```

```
about a new cooking technique called <dfn><i>sous
vide</i></dfn>. In <i>sous vide</i> cooking,
you submerge the food (usually vacuum-sealed in
plastic) into a water bath that is precisely
set to the target temperature of the food. In
his book, <cite>Cooking for Geeks</cite>, Jeff
Potter describes it as <q>ultra-low-temperature
poaching</q>.</p>

<p>Next month, we will be serving <b>Sous Vide
Salmon with Dill Hollandaise</b>. To reserve
a seat at the chef table, contact us before
November 30.</p>


Location: Baker's Corner, Seekonk, MA
Hours: Tuesday to Saturday, 11am to midnight

All content copyright &copy; 2012, Black Goose
Bistro and Jennifer Robbins
```

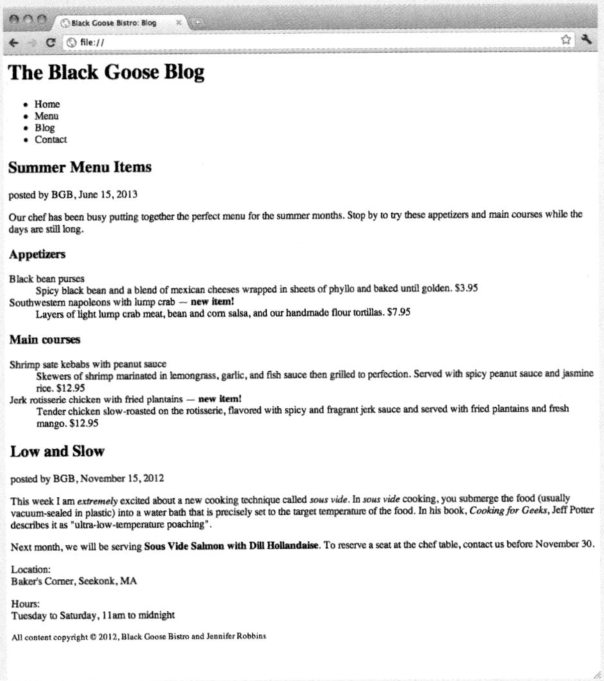

Figure 5-18. The finished menu page.

1. Add all the document structure elements first (**html**, **head**, **meta**, **title**, and **body**). Give the document the title "Black Goose Bistro: Blog."

2. The first thing we'll do is identify the top-level heading and the list of links as the header for the document by wrapping them in a **header** element (don't forget the closing tag). Within the header, the headline should be an **h1** and the list of links should be an unordered list (**ul**). Don't worry about making the list items links; we'll get to linking in the next chapter. Give the list more meaning by identifying it as the primary navigation for the site (**nav**).

3. This blog page has two posts titled "Summer Menu Items" and "Low and Slow." Mark each one up as an **article**.

4. Now we'll get the first article into shape! Let's create a **header** for this article that contains the heading (**h2** this time because we've moved down in the document hierarchy) and the publication information (**p**). Identify the publication date for the article with the **time** element, just as you did in Exercise 5-2.

5. The content after the header is clearly a simple paragraph. However, the menu has some interesting things going on. It is divided into two conceptual sections (Appetizers and Main Courses), so mark those up as **section** elements. Be careful that the closing section tag (**</section>**) appears before the closing article tag (**</article>**) so the elements are nested correctly and don't overlap. Finally, let's identify the sections with **id** attributes. Name the first one "appetizers" and the second "maincourses."

6. With our sections in place, now we can mark up the content. We're down to **h3** for the headings in each section. Choose the most appropriate list elements to describe the menu item names and their descriptions. Mark up the lists and each item within the lists.

7. Now we can add a few fine details. *Classify* each price as "price" using **span** elements.

8. Two of the dishes are new items. Change the double hyphens to an em-dash character and mark up "new items!"

as "strongly important." Classify the title of each new dish as "newitem" (hint: use the existing **dt** element; there is no need to add a **span** this time). This allows us to target menu titles with the "newitem" class and style them differently than other menu items.

9. That takes care of the first article. The second article is already mostly marked up from the previous exercise, but you should mark up the header with the appropriate heading and publication information.

10. So far, so good, right? Now make the remaining content that applies to the whole page a **footer**. Mark each line of content within the footer as a paragraph.

11. Let's give the location and hours information some context by putting them in a **div** named "about." Make the labels "Location" and "Hours" appear on a line by themselves by adding line breaks after them. If you'd like, you could also mark up the hours with the **time** element.

12. Finally, copyright information is typically "small print" on a document, so mark it up accordingly. As the final touch, add a copyright symbol after the word "copyright."

Save the file, name it *bistro_blog.html*, and check your page in a modern browser (remember that IE 8 and earlier won't know what to do with those new HTML5 sectioning elements). How did you do?

Markup tips:

- Choose the element that best fits the meaning of the selected text.
- Don't forget to close elements with closing tags.
- Put all attribute values in quotation marks for clarity.
- "Copy and paste" is your friend when adding the same markup to multiple elements. Just be sure what you copied is correct before you paste it throughout the document.

Test Yourself

Were you paying attention? Here is a rapid-fire set of questions to find out.

1. Add the markup to add a thematic break between these paragraphs.

   ```
   <p>People who know me know that I love to cook.</p>

   <p>I've created this site to share some of my favorite
   recipes.</p>
   ```

2. What's the difference between a **blockquote** and a **q** element?

3. Which element displays whitespace exactly as it is typed into the source document?

4. What is the difference between a **ul** and an **ol**?

5. How do you remove the bullets from an unordered list? (Be general, not specific.)

Want More Practice?

Try marking up your own résumé. Start with the raw text and add document structure elements, content grouping elements, and inline elements as we've done in Exercise 5-3. If you don't see an element that matches your information just right, try creating one using a **div** or a **span**.

6. What element would you use to provide the full name of the W3C (World Wide Web Consortium) in the document? Can you write out the complete markup?

7. What is the difference between a **dl** and a **dt**?

8. What is the difference between **id** and **class**?

9. What is the difference between an **article** and a **section**?

10. Name and write the characters generated by these character entities:

—_____   & _____

   _____   © _____

• _____   ™ _____

Element Review: Text

The following is a summary of the elements we covered in this chapter. New HTML5 elements are indicated by "(5)." The **data** element is included only in the WHATWG HTML version as of this writing.

Page sections

address	author contact information
article (5)	self-contained content
aside (5)	tangential content (sidebar)
footer (5)	related content
header (5)	introductory content
nav (5)	primary navigation
section (5)	conceptually related group of content

Heading content

h1...h6	headings, levels 1 through 6
hgroup	heading group

Grouping content

blockquote	blockquote
div	generic division
figure (5)	related image or resource
figcaption (5)	text description of a figure
hr	paragraph-level thematic break (horizontal rule)
p	paragraph
pre	preformatted text

List elements

dd	definition
dl	definition list
dt	term
li	list item (for **ul** and **ol**)
ol	ordered list
ul	unordered list

Breaks

br	line break
wbr (5)	word break

Phrasing elements

abbr	abbreviation
b	added visual attention (bold)
bdi (5)	possible direction change
bdo	bidirectional override
cite	citation
code	code sample
data (WHATWG)	machine-readable equivalent
del	deleted text
dfn	defining term
em	stress emphasis
i	alternate voice (italic)
ins	inserted text
kbd	keyboard text
mark (5)	highlighted text
q	short inline quotation
ruby (5)	section containing ruby text
rp (5)	parentheses in ruby text
rt (5)	ruby annotations
s	strike-through; incorrect text
samp	sample output
small	annotation; "small print"
span	generic phrase of text
strong	strong importance
sub	subscript
sup	superscript
time (5)	machine-readable time data
u	added attention (underline)
var	variable

ADDING LINKS

If you're creating a page for the Web, chances are you'll want it to point to other web pages and resources, whether on your own site or someone else's. Linking, after all, is what the Web is all about. In this chapter, we'll look at the markup that makes links work—links to other sites, to your own site, and within a page. There is one element that makes linking possible: the anchor (**a**).

```
<a>...</a>
```

Anchor element (hypertext link)

To make a selection of text a link, simply wrap it in opening and closing `<a>...</a>` tags and use the **href** attribute to provide the URL of the target page. The content of the anchor element becomes the hypertext link. Here is an example that creates a link to the O'Reilly Media website:

```
<a href="http://www.oreilly.com">Go to the O'Reilly Media site</a>
```

To make an image a link, simply put the **img** element in the anchor element:

```
<a href="http://www.oreilly.com"><img src="orm.gif" alt="O'Reilly
tarsier logo"></a>
```

Nearly all graphical browsers display linked text as blue and underlined by default. Some older browsers put a blue border around linked images, but most current ones do not. Visited links generally display in purple. Users can change these colors in their browser preferences, and, of course, you can change the appearance of links for your sites using style sheets. I'll show you how in Chapter 13, Colors and Backgrounds.

WARNING

One word of caution: if you choose to change your link colors, keep them consistent throughout your site so as not to confuse your users.

When a user clicks or taps on the linked text or image, the page you specify in the anchor element loads in the browser window. The linked image markup sample shown previously might look like Figure 6-1.

IN THIS CHAPTER

Making links to external pages

Making relative links to documents on your own server

Linking to a specific point in a page

Adding "mailto" and "tel" links

Targeting new windows

AT A GLANCE

Anchor Syntax

The simplified structure of the anchor element is:

```
<a href="url">linked text
or element</a>
```

Figure 6-1. When a user clicks or taps on the linked text or image, the page you specified in the anchor element loads in the browser window.

In HTML5, you can put any element in an a element— even block elements!

Starting in HTML5, you can put any element in an **a** element—even block elements! In the HTML 4.01 spec and earlier, the anchor element could be used for inline content only.

The href Attribute

You'll need to tell the browser which document to link to, right? The `href` (hypertext reference) attribute provides the address of the page or resource (its URL) to the browser. The URL must always appear in quotation marks. Most of the time you'll point to other HTML documents; however, you can also point to other web resources, such as images, audio, and video files.

Because there's not much to slapping anchor tags around some content, the real trick to linking comes in getting the URL correct.

There are two ways to specify the URL:

- **Absolute URLs** provide the full URL for the document, including the protocol (`http://`), the domain name, and the pathname as necessary. You need to use an absolute URL when pointing to a document out on the Web (i.e., not on your own server).

  Example: href="`http://www.oreilly.com/`"

  Sometimes, when the page you're linking to has a long URL pathname, the link can end up looking pretty confusing (Figure 6-2). Just keep in mind that the structure is still a simple container element with one attribute. Don't let the pathname intimidate you.

- **Relative URLs** describe the pathname to a file *relative* to the current document. Relative URLs can be used when you are linking to another document on your own site (i.e., on the same server). It doesn't require the protocol or domain name—just the pathname.

  Example: href="`recipes/index.html`"

In this chapter, we'll add links using absolute and relative URLs to my cooking website, Jen's Kitchen (see Figure 6-3). Absolute URLs are easy, so let's get them out of the way first.

URL Versus URI

The W3C and the development community are moving away from the term URL (Uniform Resource Locator) and toward the more generic and technically accurate URI (Uniform Resource Identifier). On the street and even on the job, however, you're still likely to hear URL.

Here's the skinny on URL versus URI: a URL is one type of a URI that identifies the resource by its location (the L in URL) on the network. The other type of URI is a URN that identifies the resource by name or namespace (the N in URN).

Because it is more familiar, I will be sticking with URL throughout the discussions in this chapter. Just know that URLs are a subset of URIs, and the terms are often used interchangeably.

If you like to geek out on this kind of thing, I refer you to the URI Wikipedia entry: *en.wikipedia.org/wiki/Uniform_ resource_identifier.*

Opening anchor tag

```
<a href="http://www.amazon.com/s/?ie=UTF8&keywords=
bequet+caramel&tag=googhydr20&index=aps&hvadid=79790
39989&ref=pd_sl_1ah68hbamy_b">Bequet Caramels</a>
```

URL   Linked text   Closing anchor tag

Figure 6-2. An example of a long URL. Although it may make the anchor tag look confusing, the structure is the same.

Linking to Pages on the Web

Many times, you'll want to create a link to a page that you've found on the Web. This is known as an "external" link because it is going to a page outside of your own server or site. To make an external link, you need to provide the absolute URL, beginning with `http://` (the protocol). This tells the browser, "Go out on the Web and get the following document."

I want to add some external links to the Jen's Kitchen home page (Figure 6-3). First, I'll link the list item "The Food Network" to the site *www.foodnetwork.com*. I marked up the link text in an anchor element by adding opening and closing anchor tags. Notice that I've added the anchor tags *inside* the list item (`li`) element. That's because only `li` elements are permitted to be children of a `ul` element; placing an `a` element directly inside the `ul` would be invalid HTML.

```
<li><a>The Food Network</a></li>
```

Next, I add the `href` attribute with the complete URL for the site.

```
<li><a href="http://www.foodnetwork.com">The Food Network</a></li>
```

And *voilà*! That's all there is to it. Now "The Food Network" will appear as a link and will take my visitors to that site when they click or tap it.

Figure 6-3. The Jen's Kitchen page

All the files for the Jen's Kitchen website are available online at *www.learningwebdesign.com/4e/materials*. Download the entire directory, making sure not to change the way its contents are organized.

The resulting markup for all of the exercises is provided in Appendix A.

The pages aren't much to look at, but they will give you a chance to develop your linking skills.

---

exercise 6-1 | **Make an external link**

Open the file *index.html* from the *jenskitchen* folder. Make the list item "Epicurious" link to its web page at *www.epicurious.com*, following my example.

```
<ul>
  <li><a href="http://www.foodnetwork.com/">The Food Network</a>
</li>
  <li>Epicurious</li>
</ul>
```

When you are done, you can save *index.html* and open it in a browser. If you have an Internet connection, you can click on your new link and go to the Epicurious site. If the link doesn't take you there, go back and make sure that you didn't miss anything in the markup.

Linking Within Your Own Site

NOTE

On PCs and Macs, files are organized into "folders," but in the web development world, it is more common to refer to the equivalent and more technical term, "directory." A folder is just a directory with a cute icon.

A large portion of the linking you'll do will be between pages of your own site: from the home page to section pages, from section pages to content pages, and so on. In these cases, you can use a relative URL—one that calls for a page on your own server.

Without "http://", the browser looks on the current server for the linked document. A pathname, the notation used to point to a particular file or directory, tells the browser where to find the file. Web pathnames follow the Unix convention of separating directory and filenames with forward slashes (/). A relative pathname describes how to get to the linked document starting from the location of the current document.

Relative pathnames can get a bit tricky. In my teaching experience, nothing stumps beginners like writing relative pathnames, so we'll take it one step at a time. There are exercises along the way that I recommend you do as we go along.

All of the pathname examples in this section are based on the structure of the Jen's Kitchen site shown in Figure 6-4. When you diagram the structure of the directories for a site, it generally ends up looking like an inverted tree with the root directory at the top of the hierarchy. For the Jen's Kitchen site, the root directory is named *jenskitchen*. For another way to look at it, there is also a view of the directory and subdirectories as they appear in the Finder on my Mac (Windows users see one directory at a time).

Important Pathname Don'ts

When you are writing relative pathnames, it is critical that you follow these rules to avoid common errors:

- Don't use backslashes (\\). Web URL pathnames use forward slashes (/) only.

- Don't start with the drive name (D:, C:, etc.). Although your pages will link to each other successfully while they are on your own computer, once they are uploaded to the web server, the drive name is irrelevant and will break your links.

- Don't start with file://. This also indicates that the file is local and causes the link to break when it is on the server.

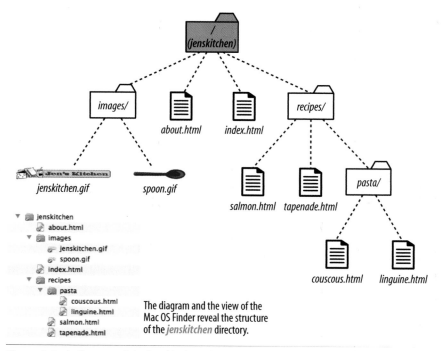

The diagram and the view of the Mac OS Finder reveal the structure of the *jenskitchen* directory.

Figure 6-4. A diagram of the jenskitchen site structure.

Linking within a directory

The most straightforward relative URL points to another file within the same directory. When you link to a file in the same directory, you only need to provide the name of the file (its *filename*). When the URL is a single filename, the server looks in the current directory (that is, the directory that contains the document with the link) for the file.

In this example, I want to make a link from my home page (*index.html*) to a general information page (*about.html*). Both files are in the same directory (*jenskitchen*). So from my home page, I can make a link to the information page by simply providing its filename in the URL (Figure 6-5):

```
<a href="about.html">About the site...</a>
```

A link to just the filename indicates the linked file is in the same directory as the current document.

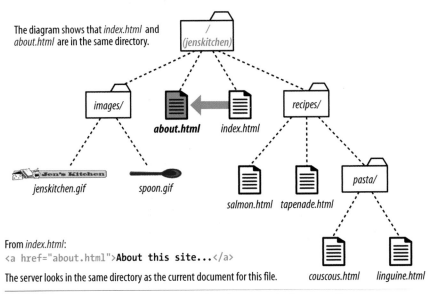

The diagram shows that *index.html* and *about.html* are in the same directory.

From *index.html*:
```
<a href="about.html">About this site...</a>
```
The server looks in the same directory as the current document for this file.

Figure 6-5. Writing a relative URL to another document in the same directory.

---

exercise 6-2 | **Link in the same directory**

Open the file ***about.html*** from the ***jenskitchen*** folder. Make the paragraph "Back to the home page" at the bottom of the page link back to ***index.html***. The anchor element should be contained in the **p** element.

```
<p>Back to the home page</p>
```

When you are done, you can save ***about.html*** and open it in a browser. You don't need an Internet connection to test links locally (that is, on your own computer). Clicking on the link should take you back to the home page.

Linking to a lower directory

But what if the files aren't in the same directory? You have to give the browser directions by including the pathname in the URL. Let's see how this works.

Getting back to our example, my recipe files are stored in a subdirectory called *recipes*. I want to make a link from *index.html* to a file in the *recipes* directory called *salmon.html*. The pathname in the URL tells the browser to look in the current directory for a directory called *recipes*, and then look for the file *salmon.html* (Figure 6-6):

```
<li><a href="recipes/salmon.html">Garlic Salmon</a></li>
```

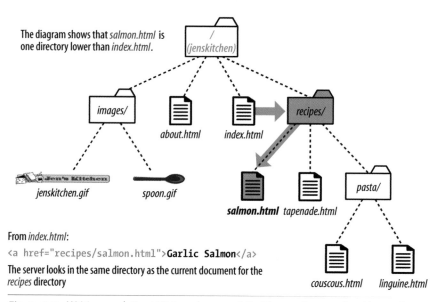

The diagram shows that *salmon.html* is one directory lower than *index.html*.

From *index.html*:

```
<a href="recipes/salmon.html">Garlic Salmon</a>
```

The server looks in the same directory as the current document for the *recipes* directory

Figure 6-6. *Writing a relative URL to a document that is one directory level lower than the current document.*

exercise 6-3 | **Link one directory down**

Open the file ***index.html*** from the ***jenskitchen*** folder. Make the list item "Tapenade (Olive Spread)" link to the file ***tapenade.html*** in the ***recipes*** directory. Remember to nest the elements correctly.

```
<li>Tapenade (Olive Spread)</li>
```

When you are done, you can save ***index.html*** and open it in a browser. You should be able to click your new link and see the recipe page for tapenade. If not, make sure that your markup is correct and that the directory structure for ***jenskitchen*** matches the examples.

Now let's link down to the file called *couscous.html*, which is located in the *pasta* subdirectory. All we need to do is provide the directions through two subdirectories (*recipes*, then *pasta*) to *couscous.html* (Figure 6-7):

```
<li><a href="recipes/pasta/couscous.html">Couscous with Peas and Mint </a></li>
```

Directories are separated by forward slashes. The resulting anchor tag tells the browser, "Look in the current directory for a directory called *recipes*. There you'll find another directory called *pasta*, and in there is the file I'd like to link to, *couscous.html*."

Now that we've done two directory levels, you should get the idea of how pathnames are assembled. This same method applies for relative pathnames that drill down through any number of directories. Just start with the name of the directory that is in the same location as the current file, and follow each directory name with a slash until you get to the linked filename.

When linking to a file in a lower directory, the pathname must contain the names of the subdirectories you go through to get to the file.

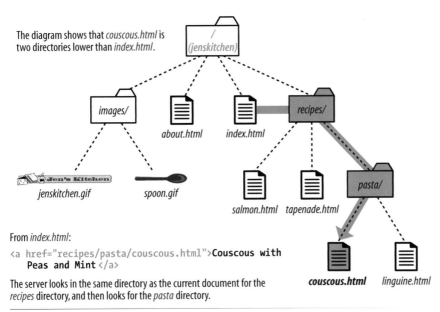

The diagram shows that *couscous.html* is two directories lower than *index.html*.

From *index.html*:

```
<a href="recipes/pasta/couscous.html">Couscous with Peas and Mint </a>
```

The server looks in the same directory as the current document for the *recipes* directory, and then looks for the *pasta* directory.

Figure 6-7. *Writing a relative URL to a document that is two directory levels lower than the current document.*

exercise 6-4 | **Link two directories down**

Open the file ***index.html*** from the ***jenskitchen*** folder. Make the list item "Linguine with Clam Sauce" link to the file ***linguine.html*** in the ***pasta*** directory.

```
<li>Linguine with Clam Sauce</li>
```

When you are done, you can save ***index.html*** and open it in a browser. Click on the new link to get the delicious recipe.

Linking to a higher directory

So far, so good, right? Here comes the tricky part. This time we're going to go in the other direction and make a link from the salmon recipe page back to the home page, which is one directory level up.

In Unix, there is a pathname convention just for this purpose, the "dot-dot-slash" (`../`). When you begin a pathname with `../`, it's the same as telling the browser "back up one directory level" and then follow the path to the specified file. If you are familiar with browsing files on your desktop, it is helpful to know that a "../" has the same effect as clicking the "Up" button in Windows Explorer or the left-arrow button in the Finder on Mac OS X.

Let's start by making a link from *salmon.html* back to the home page (*index.html*). Because *salmon.html* is in the *recipes* subdirectory, we need to back up a level to *jenskitchen* to find *index.html*. This pathname tells the browser to "go up one level," then look in that directory for *index.html* (Figure 6-8):

```
<p><a href="../index.html">[Back to home page]</a></p>
```

Note that we don't need to write out the name of the higher directory (*jenskitchen*) in the pathname. The `../` stands in for it.

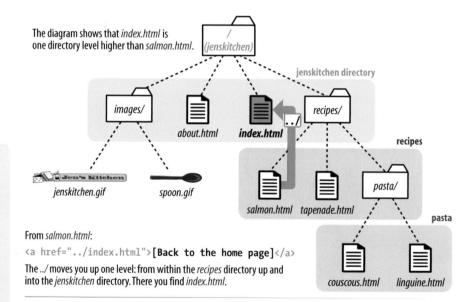

Figure 6-8. *Writing a relative URL to a document that is one directory level higher than the current document.*

But how about linking back to the home page from *couscous.html*? Can you guess how you'd back your way out of two directory levels? Simple: just use the dot-dot-slash twice (Figure 6-9).

A link on the *couscous.html* page back to the home page (*index.html*) would look like this:

```
<p><a href="../../index.html">[Back to home page]</a></p>
```

The first `../` backs up to the *recipes* directory; the second `../` backs up to the top-level directory where *index.html* can be found. Again, there is no need to write out the directory names; the `../` does it all.

NOTE

I confess to still sometimes silently chanting "go-up-a-level, go-up-a-level" for each ../ when trying to decipher a complicated relative URL. It helps me sort things out.

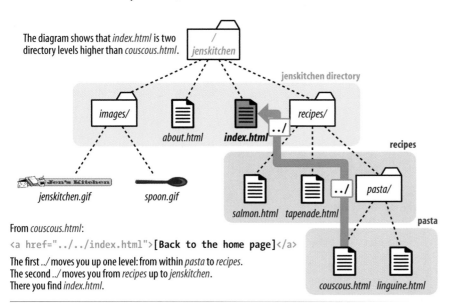

The diagram shows that *index.html* is two directory levels higher than *couscous.html*.

From *couscous.html*:

```
<a href="../../index.html">[Back to the home page]</a>
```

The first ../ moves you up one level: from within *pasta* to *recipes*.
The second ../ moves you from *recipes* up to *jenskitchen*.
There you find *index.html*.

Figure 6-9. Writing a relative URL to a document that is two directory levels higher than the current document.

exercise 6-6 | **Link up two directory levels**

OK, now it's your turn to give it a try. Open the file ***linguine.html*** and make the last paragraph link back to the home page using `../../` as I have done.

```
<p>[Back to the home page]</p>
```

When you are done, save the file and open it in a browser. You should be able to link to the home page.

Site root relative pathnames

All websites have a root directory, which is the directory that contains all the directories and files for the site. So far, all of the pathnames we've looked at are relative to the document with the link. Another way to write a relative pathname is to start at the root directory and list the subdirectory names until you get to the file you want to link to. This kind of pathname is known as site root relative.

In the Unix pathname convention, a forward slash (/) at the start of the pathname indicates the path begins at the root directory. The site root relative pathname in the following link reads, "Go to the very top-level directory for this site, open the *recipes* directory, then find the *salmon.html* file" (Figure 6-10):

```
<a href="/recipes/salmon.html">Garlic Salmon</a>
```

Note that you don't need to (and you shouldn't) write the name of the root directory (*jenskitchen*) in the path—just start it with a forward slash (/), and the browser will look in the top-level directory relative to the current file. From there, just specify the directories the browser should look in.

Site root relative links are generally preferred due to their flexibility.

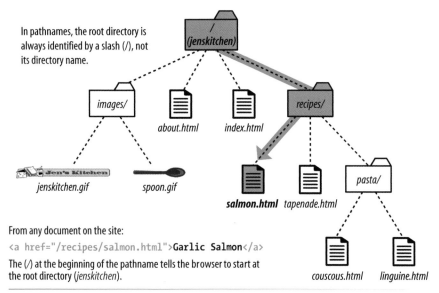

In pathnames, the root directory is always identified by a slash (/), not its directory name.

From any document on the site:

```
<a href="/recipes/salmon.html">Garlic Salmon</a>
```

The (/) at the beginning of the pathname tells the browser to start at the root directory (*jenskitchen*).

Figure 6-10. Writing a relative URL starting at the root directory.

Because this type of link starts at the root to describe the pathname, it will work from any document on the server, regardless of which subdirectory it may be located in. Site root relative links are useful for content that might not always be in the same directory, or for dynamically generated material. They also make it easy to copy and paste links between documents.

On the downside, however, the links won't work on your local machine, because they will be relative to your hard drive. You'll have to wait until the site is on the final server to check that links are working.

It's the same for images

The `src` attribute in the `img` element works the same as the `href` attribute in anchors when it comes to specifying URLs. Since you'll most likely be using images from your own server, the `src` attributes within your image elements will be set to relative URLs.

Let's look at a few examples from the Jen's Kitchen site. First, to add an image to the *index.html* page, the markup would be:

```
<img src="images/jenskitchen.gif" alt="">
```

The URL says, "Look in the current directory (*jenskitchen*) for the *images* directory; in there you will find *jenskitchen.gif*."

Now for the *pièce de résistance*. Let's add an image to the file *couscous.html*:

```
<img src="../../images/spoon.gif" alt="">
```

This is a little more complicated than what we've seen so far. This pathname tells the browser to go up two directory levels to the top-level directory and, once there, look in the *images* directory for an image called *spoon.gif*. Whew!

Of course, you could simplify that path by going the site root relative route, in which case the pathname to *spoon.gif* (and any other file in the *images* directory) could be accessed like this:

```
<img src="/images/spoon.gif" alt="">
```

The trade-off is that you won't see the image in place until the site is uploaded to the server, but it does make maintenance easier once it's there.

> ## A Little Help from Your Tools
>
> If you use a WYSIWYG authoring tool to create your site, the tool generates relative URLs for you. Programs such as Adobe Dreamweaver and Microsoft Expression Web have built-in site management functions that adjust your relative URLs even if you reorganize the directory structure.

exercise 6-7 | Try a few more

Before we move on, you may want to try your hand at writing a few more relative URLs to make sure you've really gotten it. You can just write your answers on the page, or if you want to test your markup to see whether it works, make changes in the actual files. You'll need to add the text to the files to use as the link (for example, "Go to the Tapenade recipe" for the first question). Answers are in Appendix A.

1. Create a link on *salmon.html* to *tapenade.html*.

    Go to the Tapenade recipe

2. Create a link on *couscous.html* to *salmon.html*.

    Try this with Garlic Salmon.

3. Create a link on *tapenade.html* to *linguine.html*.

    Try the Linguine with Clam Sauce

4. Create a link on *linguine.html* to *about.html*.

    About Jen's Kitchen

5. Create a link on *tapenade.html* to *www.allrecipes.com*.

    Go to Allrecipes.com

NOTE

Most of the pathnames in Exercise 6-7 could be site root relative, but write them relative to the listed document for the practice.

Linking to a specific point in a page

Did you know you can link to a specific point in a web page? This is useful for providing shortcuts to information at the bottom of a long, scrolling page or for getting back to the top of a page with just one click or tap. Linking to a specific point in the page is also referred to as linking to a document fragment.

Linking to a particular spot within a page is a two-part process. First, you identify the destination, and then you make a link to it. In the following example, I create an alphabetical index at the top of the page that links down to each alphabetical section of a glossary page (Figure 6-11). When users click on the letter "H," they'll jump down on the page to the "H" heading lower on the page.

Step 1: Identifying the destination

I like to think of this step as planting a flag in the document so I can get back to it easily. To create a destination, use the **id** attribute to give the target element in the document a unique name (that's "unique" as in the name may appear only once in the document, not "unique" as in funky and interesting). In web lingo, this is the fragment identifier.

You may remember the **id** attribute from Chapter 5, Marking Up Text, where we used it to name generic **div** and **span** elements. Here, we're going to use it to name an element so that it can serve as a fragment identifier—that is, the destination of a link.

Here is a sample of the source for the glossary page. Because I want users to be able to link directly to the "H" heading, I'll add the **id** attribute to it and give it the value "startH" (Figure 6-11 ❶).

```
<h1 id="startH">H</h1>
```

Step 2: Linking to the destination

With the identifier in place, now I can make a link to it.

At the top of the page, I'll create a link down to the "startH" fragment ❷. As for any link, I use the **a** element with the **href** attribute to provide the location of the link. To indicate that I'm linking to a fragment, I use the octothorpe symbol (#), also called a hash or number symbol, before the fragment name.

```
<p>... F | G | <a href="#startH">H</a> | I | J ...</p>
```

And that's it. Now when someone clicks on the "H" from the listing at the top of the page, the browser will jump down and display the section starting with the "H" heading ❸.

NOTE

Linking to another spot on the same page works well for long, scrolling pages, but the effect may be lost on a short web page.

NOTE

Remember that **id** *values must start with a letter or an underscore (although underscores may be problematic in some versions of IE).*

Fragment names are preceded by an octothorpe symbol (#).

❶ Identify the destination using the **id** attribute.

```
<h2 id="startH">H</h2>
<dl>
<dt>hexadecimal</dt>
<dd>A base-16 numbering system that uses the characters 0-9 and
A-F. It is used in CSS and HTML for specifying color values</dd>
```

❷ Create a link to the destination. The # before the name is necessary to identify this as a fragment and not a filename.

```
<p>... | F | G | <a href="#startH">H</a> | I | J ...</p>
```

❸

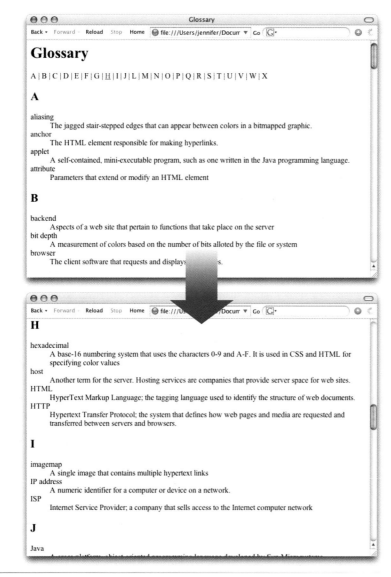

Figure 6-11. Linking to a specific destination within a single web page.

AUTHORING TIP

To the Top!

It is common practice to add a link back up to the top of the page when linking into a long page of text. This alleviates the need to scroll back after every link.

NOTE

Some developers help their brothers and sisters out by proactively adding ids *as anchors at the beginning of any thematic section of content (within a reasonable level, and depending on the site). That way other people can link back to any section in their content.*

exercise 6-8 |
Linking to a fragment

Want some practice linking to specific destinations? Open the file *glossary.html* in the *materials* folder for this chapter. It looks just like the document in Figure 6-11.

1. Identify the **h2** "A" as a destination for a link by naming it "startA" with an **id** attribute.

   ```
   <h2 id="startA">A</h2>
   ```

2. Make the letter "A" at the top of the page a link to the identified fragment. Don't forget the **#**.

   ```
   <a href="#startA">A</a>
   ```

Repeat steps 1 and 2 for every letter across the top of the page until you really know what you are doing (or until you can't stand it anymore). You can help users get back to the top of the page, too.

3. Make the heading "Glossary" a destination named "top."

   ```
   <h1 id="top">Glossary</h1>
   ```

4. Add a paragraph element containing "TOP" at the end of each lettered section. Make "TOP" a link to the identifier that you just made at the top of the page.

   ```
   <p><a href="#top">TOP</a></
       p>
   ```

Copy and paste this code to the end of every letter section. Now your readers can get back to the top of the page easily throughout the document.

Linking to a fragment in another document

You can link to a fragment in another document by adding the fragment name to the end of the URL (absolute or relative). For example, to make a link to the "H" heading of the glossary page from another document in that directory, the URL would look like this:

```
<a href="glossary.html#startH">See the Glossary, letter H</a>
```

You can even link to specific destinations in pages on other sites by putting the fragment identifier at the end of an absolute URL, like so:

```
<a href="http://www.example.com/glossary.html#startH">See the Glossary,
letter H</a>
```

Of course, you don't have any control over the named fragments in other people's web pages (see the note). The destination points must be inserted by the author of those documents in order for them to be available to you. The only way to know whether they are there and where they are is to "View Source" for the page and look for them in the markup. If the fragments in external documents move or go away, the page will still load; the browser will just go to the top of the page as it does for regular links.

Targeting a New Browser Window

One problem with putting links on your page is that when people click on them, they may never come back. The traditional solution to this dilemma has been to make the linked page open in a new browser window. That way, your visitors can check out the link and still have your content available where they left it.

Before I provide the instructions for how to do it, I am going to strongly advise against it. First of all, tabbed browsers make it somewhat less likely that users will never find their way back to the original page. Furthermore, opening new windows is problematic for accessibility. New windows may be confusing to some users, particularly those who are accessing your site via a screen reader or even on a small-screen device. At the very least, new windows may be perceived as an annoyance rather than a convenience. Because it is common to configure your browser to block pop-up windows, you risk having the users miss out on the content in the new window altogether.

So consider carefully whether you need a separate window at all, and I'll tell you how in case you have a very good reason to do it. The method you use to open a link in a new browser window depends on whether you want to control its size. If the size of the window doesn't matter, you can use HTML markup alone. However, if you want to open the new window with particular pixel dimensions, then you need to use JavaScript.

A new window with markup

To open a new window using markup, use the **target** attribute in the anchor (**a**) element to tell the browser the name of the window in which you want the linked document to open. Set the value of target to **_blank** or to any name of your choosing. Remember that with this method, you have no control over the size of the window, but it will generally open as a new tab or in a new window the same size as the most recently opened window in the user's browser.

Setting **target="_blank"** always causes the browser to open a fresh window. For example:

```
<a href="http://www.oreilly.com" target="_blank">O'Reilly</a>
```

If you target "_blank" for every link, every link will launch a new window, potentially leaving your user with a mess of open windows.

A better method is to give the target window a specific name, which can then be used by subsequent links. You can give the window any name you like ("new," "sample," whatever), as long as it doesn't start with an underscore. The following link will open a new window called "display":

```
<a href="http://www.oreilly.com" target="display">O'Reilly</a>
```

If you target the "display" window from every link on the page, each linked document will open in the same second window. Unfortunately, if that second window stays hidden behind the user's current window, it may look as though the link simply didn't work.

Pop-up windows

It is possible to open a window with specific dimensions and various parts of the browser chrome (toolbars, scrollbars, etc.) turned on or off; however, it takes JavaScript to do it. These are known as pop-up windows, and they are commonly used for advertising. In fact, they've become such a nuisance that many browsers have preferences for turning them off completely. Furthermore, in a world where sites are accessed on small, mobile devices, popping up windows at specific pixel dimensions has no place.

That said, if you have a valid reason to open a new browser window at a specific size, I recommend this tutorial article by Peter-Paul Koch at Quirksmode: *www.quirksmode.org/js/popup.html*.

Mail Links

Here's a nifty little linking trick: the **mailto** link. By using the **mailto** protocol in a link, you can link to an email address. When the user clicks on a **mailto** link, the browser opens a new mail message preaddressed to that address in a designated mail program.

A sample **mailto** link is shown here:

```
<a href="mailto:alklecker@example.com">Contact Al Klecker</a>
```

As you can see, it's a standard anchor element with the **href** attribute. But the value is set to **mailto:***name@address.com*.

The browser has to be configured to launch a mail program, so the effect won't work for 100% of your audience. If you use the email address itself as the linked text, nobody will be left out if the **mailto** function does not work (a nice little example of progressive enhancement).

Telephone Links

Keep in mind that the smartphones people are using to access your website can also be used to make phone calls! Why not save your visitors a step by letting them dial a phone number on your site simply by tapping on it on the page? The syntax uses the **tel:** scheme and is very simple.

```
<a href="tel:+18005551212">Call us free at (800) 555-1212</a>
```

When mobile users tap the link, they get an alert box asking them to confirm that they'd like to call the number. This feature is supported on most mobile devices, including iOS, Android, BlackBerry, Symbian, Internet Explorer, and Opera Mini. The iPad and iPod Touch can't make a call, but they will offer to create a new contact from the number. Nothing happens when desktop users click the link. If that bothers you, you could use a CSS rule that hides the link for non-mobile devices (unfortunately, that is beyond the scope of this discussion).

There are a few best practices for using telephone links:

- It is recommended that you include the full international dialing number, including the country code, for the **tel:** value because there is no way of knowing where the user will be accessing your site.

- Also include the telephone number in the content of the link so that if the link doesn't work, the telephone number is still available.

- Android and iPhone have a feature that detects phone numbers and automatically turns them into links. Unfortunately, some 10-digit numbers that are not telephone numbers might get turned into links, too. If your document has strings of numbers that might get confused as phone numbers, you can turn auto-detection off by including the following **meta** element in the **head** of your document.

```
<meta name="format-detection" content="telephone=no">
```

For BlackBerry devices, use the following:

```
<meta http-equiv="x-rim-auto-match" content="none">
```

Test Yourself

The most important lesson in this chapter is how to write URLs for links and images. Here's another chance to brush up on your pathname skills.

Using the directory hierarchy shown in Figure 6-12, write out the markup for the following links and graphics. I filled in the first one for you as an example. The answers are located in Appendix A.

This diagram should provide you with enough information to answer the questions. If you need hands-on work to figure them out, the directory structure is available in the *test* directory in the materials for this chapter. The documents are just dummy files and contain no content.

TIP

The **../** (or multiples of them) always appears at the beginning of the pathname and never in the middle. If the pathnames you write have **../** in the middle, you've done something wrong.

1. In *index.html* (the site's home page), write the markup for a link to *tutorial.html*.

   ```
   <a href="tutorial.html">...</a>
   ```

2. In *index.html*, write the anchor element for a link to *instructions.html*.

3. Create a link to *family.html* from the page *tutorial.html*.

4. Create a link to *numbers.html* from the *family.html* page, but this time, start with the root directory.

Figure 6-12. The directory structure for the Test Yourself questions.

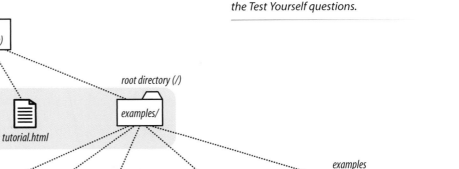

5. Create a link back to the home page (*index.html*) from the page *instructions.html*.

6. In the file *intro.html*, create a link to the website for this book (*www.learningwebdesign.com*).

7. Create a link to *instructions.html* from the page *greetings.html*.

8. Create a link back to the home page (*index.html*) from *money.html*.

We haven't covered the image (**img**) element in detail yet, but you should be able to fill in the relative URLs after the src attribute to specify the location of the image files for these examples.

9. To place the graphic *arrow.gif* on the page *index.html*, use this URL:

   ```
   <img src="                              " alt="">
   ```

10. To place the graphic *arrow.gif* on the page *intro.html*, use this URL:

    ```
    <img src="                              " alt="">
    ```

11. To place the graphic *bullet.gif* on the *friends.html* page, use this URL:

    ```
    <img src="                              " alt="">
    ```

Element Review: Links

There's really only one element relevant to creating hypertext links:

Element and attributes	Description
a	Anchor (hypertext link) element
href="url"	Location of the target file

ADDING IMAGES

A web page with all text and no pictures isn't much fun. The Web's explosion into mass popularity was due in part to the fact that there were images on the page. Before images, the Internet was a text-only tundra.

Images appear on web pages in two ways: embedded in the inline content or as background images. Background images are added using Cascading Style Sheets and are talked about at length in Chapter 13, Colors and Backgrounds. With the emergence of standards-driven design and its mission to keep all matters of presentation out of the document structure, there has been a shift away from using inline images for purely decorative purposes. See the sidebar "Images Move to the Background" on the following page for more information on this trend.

In this chapter, we'll focus on embedding image content into the document using the **img** element. Use the **img** element when the image is the content, such as product shots, gallery images, ads, illustrations, and so on…I think you get the idea.

First, a Word on Image Formats

We'll get to the **img** element and markup examples in a moment, but first it's important to know that you can't put just any image on a web page. In order to be displayed inline, images must be in the GIF, JPEG, or PNG file format. Chapter 21, Web Graphics Basics, explains these formats and the image types they handle best. In addition to being in an appropriate format, image files need to be named with the proper suffixes—*.gif*, *.jpg* (or *.jpeg*), and *.png*, respectively—in order to be recognized by the browser.

If you have a source image that is in another popular format, such as TIFF, BMP, or EPS, you'll need to convert it to a web format before you can add it to the page. If, for some reason, you must keep your graphic file in its original format (for example, a file for a CAD program or an image in a vector format), you can make it available as an external image by making a link directly to the image file, like this:

```
<a href="architecture.eps">Get the drawing</a>
```

IN THIS CHAPTER

Adding images to a web page

Using the src, alt, width, and height attributes

123

Browsers use helper applications to display media they can't handle alone. The browser matches the suffix of the file in the link to the appropriate helper application. The external image may open in a separate application window or within the browser window if the helper application is a plug-in, such as the QuickTime plug-in. The browser may also ask the user to save the file or open an application manually. It is also possible that it won't be able to be opened at all.

Without further ado, let's take a look at the **img** element and its required and recommended attributes.

The img Element

```
<img>
```

Adds an inline image

The **img** element tells the browser, "Place an image here." You've already gotten a glimpse of it used to place banner graphics in the examples in Chapters 4 and 5. You can also place an image element right in the flow of the text at the point where you want the image to appear, as in the following example. Images stay in the flow of text and do not cause any line breaks (HTML5 calls this a phrasing element), as shown in Figure 7-1.

```
<p>I had been wanting to go to Tuscany <img src="tuscany.jpg" alt="">
for a long time, and I was not disappointed.</p>
```

I had been wanting to go to Tuscany for a long time, and I was not disappointed.

Figure 7-1. By default, images are aligned with the baseline of the surrounding text, and they do not cause a line break.

When the browser sees the **img** element, it makes a request to the server and retrieves the image file before displaying it on the page. On a fast network with a fast computer, even though a separate request is made for each image file, the page usually appears to arrive instantaneously. On mobile devices with slow network connections, we may be well aware of the wait for images to be fetched one at a time. The same is true for users still using dial-up Internet connections or other slow networks, like the expensive WiFi at luxury hotels.

When designing mobile web experiences, it is wise to limit the number of server requests in general, which means carefully considering the number of images on the page.

Images Move to the Background

Images that are used purely for decoration have more to do with presentation than document structure and content. For that reason, they should be controlled with a style sheet rather than the markup.

Using CSS, it is possible to place an image in the background of the page or in any text element (a **div**, **h1**, **li**... you name it). These techniques are introduced in Chapter 13, Colors and Backgrounds.

There are several benefits to specifying decorative images only in an external style sheet and keeping them out of the document structure. Not only does it make the document cleaner and more accessible, but it also makes it easier to make changes to the look and feel of a site than when presentational elements are interspersed in the content.

For inspiration on how visually rich a web page can be with no **img** elements at all, look at the examples in the "Select a Design" section of the CSS Zen Garden site at *www .csszengarden.com*.

The **src** and **alt** attributes shown in the sample are required. The **src** attribute tells the browser the location of the image file. The **alt** attribute provides alternative text that displays if the image is not available. We'll talk about **src** and **alt** a little more in upcoming sections.

There are a few other things of note about the **img** element:

- It is an empty element, which means it doesn't have any content. You just place it in the flow of text where the image should go.

- If you choose to write in the stricter XHTML syntax, you need to terminate (close) the empty **img** element with a slash like so: **<img />**.

- It is an inline element, so it behaves like any other inline element in the text flow. Figure 7-2 demonstrates the inline nature of image elements. When the browser window is resized, the line of images reflows to fill the new width.

- The **img** element is what's known as a replaced element because it is replaced by an external file when the page is displayed. This makes it different from text elements that have their content right there in the source (and thus are non-replaced).

- By default, the bottom edge of an image aligns with the baseline of text, as shown in Figures 7-1 and 7-2. Using CSS, you can float the image to the right or left margin and allow text to flow around it, control the space and borders around the image, and change its vertical alignment. We'll talk about those styles in Part III.

> *The* src *and* alt *attributes are required in the* img *element.*

Figure 7-2. Inline images are part of the normal document flow. They reflow when the browser window is resized.

Providing the location with src

src="*URL*"

Source (location) of the image

The value of the **src** attribute is the URL of the image file. In most cases, the images you use on your pages will reside on your server, so you will use relative URLs to point to them. If you just read Chapter 6, Adding Links, you should be pretty handy with writing relative URLs by now. In short, if the image is in the same directory as the HTML document, you can just refer to the image by name in the **src** attribute:

```
<img src="icon.gif" alt="">
```

Developers usually organize the images for a site into a directory called *images*, *assets*, or *graphics*. There may even be separate image directories for each section of the site. If an image is not in the same directory as the document, you need to provide the pathname to the image file.

```
<img src="/images/arrow.gif" alt="">
```

Of course, you can place images from other websites as well (just be sure that you have permission to do so). Just use an absolute URL, like this:

```
<img src="http://www.example.com/images/smile.gif" alt="">
```

Providing alternate text with alt

alt="*text*"

Alternative text

Every **img** element must also contain an **alt** attribute that is used to provide a brief description of the image for those who are not able to see it, such as users with screen readers, Braille, or even small mobile devices. Alternate text (also referred to as alt text) should serve as a substitute for the image content—serving the same purpose and presenting the same information.

```
<p>If you're <img src="happyface.gif" alt="happy"> and you know it clap
    your hands.</p>
```

A screen reader might indicate the image by reading its **alt** value this way:

> *"If you're image happy and you know it clap your hands."*

If an image does not add anything meaningful to the text content of the page, it is recommended that you leave the value of the **alt** attribute empty, as shown in the following example and other examples in this chapter (you may also consider whether it is more appropriately handled as a background image with CSS, but I digress). Note that there is no character space between the quotation marks.

```
<img src="logo.gif" alt="">
```

Do not omit the **alt** attribute altogether, however, because it will cause the document to be invalid (validating documents is covered in Chapter 3, Some Big Concepts You Need to Know). For each inline image on your page, consider what the alternative text would sound like when read aloud and whether that enhances or is just obtrusive to a screen-reader user's experience.

Alternative text may benefit users with graphical browsers as well. If a user has opted to turn images off in the browser preferences or if the image simply fails to load, the browser may display the alternative text to give the user an idea of what is missing. The handling of alternative text is inconsistent among modern browsers, however, as shown in Figure 7-3.

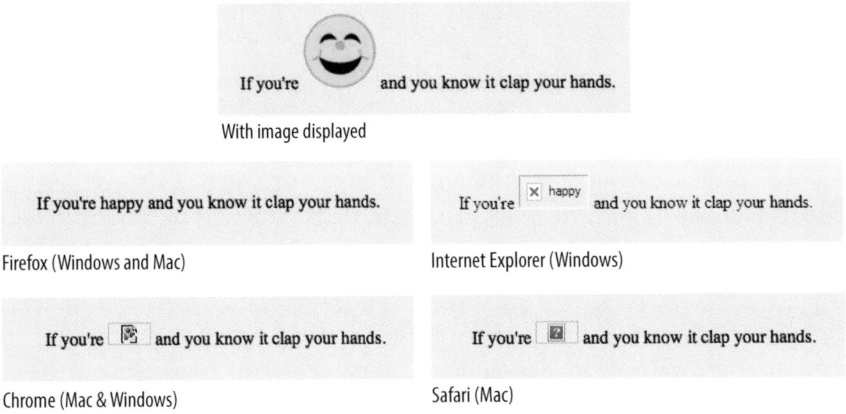

Figure 7-3. *Most browsers display alternative text in place of the image (either with an icon or as inline text) if the image is not available. Safari for Macintosh OS X is a notable exception.*

Image Accessibility

Images and other non-text content are a challenge for users accessing the Web with screen readers. Alternative text allows you to provide a short description of what is in an image for those who can't see it. However, there are some types of images, such as data charts and diagrams, that require longer descriptions than are practical as an **alt** value.

For extremely long descriptions, consider writing the description elsewhere on the page or in a separate document and making a reference or link to it near the image.

HTML 4.01 included the **longdesc** (long description) attribute, but it was dropped in HTML5 due to lack of support. The **longdesc** attribute points to a separate HTML document containing a lengthy description of the image, as in this example:

```
<img src="executivesalaries.png" alt="Executive salaries 1999-2009"
longdesc="salaries-ld.html">
```

In HTML5, the **figcaption** element allows a long description of an image when it is placed in a **figure**.

There is more to say about image accessibility than I can fit in this chapter. I encourage you to start your research with these resources:

* "Creating Accessible Images" at WebAIM (*webaim.org/techniques/images/longdesc*) provides alternatives to the **longdesc** attribute.

* "Chapter 6, The Image Problem" from the book *Building Accessible Websites* by Joe Clark (*joeclark.org/book/sashay/serialization/Chapter06.html*) provides an in-depth look at various levels of image accessibility, but is getting a little dated.

* The Web Content Accessibility Guidelines (WCAG 2.0) at the W3C include techniques for improving accessibility across all web content (*www.w3.org/TR/WCAG20-TECHS/*). Warning: it's pretty dense.

NOTE

Serving different image files for an **img** *element based on device size is handled by JavaScript or a program running on the server. It is beyond the scope of this chapter, but see the "Responsive Images" section in Chapter 18, CSS Techniques.*

Figure 7-4. Browsers resize images to match the provided width and height values. It is strongly recommended not to resize images in this way.

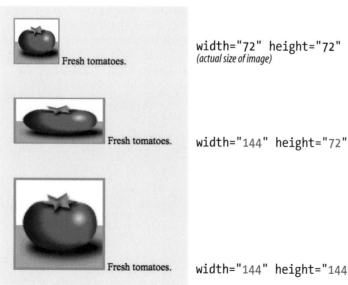

width="72" height="72"
(actual size of image)

width="144" height="72"

width="144" height="144"

Providing width and height dimensions

width="*number*"
Image width in pixels

height="*number*"
Image height in pixels

The **width** and **height** attributes indicate the dimensions of the image in number of pixels. Sounds mundane, but these attributes can speed up the time it takes to display the final page by seconds. Browsers use the specified dimensions to hold the right amount of space in the layout while the images are loading rather than reconstructing the page each time a new image arrives.

And that's great if you are designing one version of your page with one fixed image size. However, in these days of responsive web design, it is common to create several versions of the same image and send a small one to small mobile devices and a larger image for large-screen devices (and rescale the images to fit for sizes in between). If you are scaling images in a responsive design or delivering multiple image sizes, do not use **width** and **height** attributes in the markup.

With this caveat in mind, let's look at how **width** and **height** work for those cases when it is appropriate to use them.

Match values with actual pixel size

Be sure that the pixel dimensions you specify are the actual dimensions of the image. If the pixel values differ from the actual dimensions of your image, the browser resizes the image to match the specified values (Figure 7-4).

Although it may be tempting to resize images in this manner, you should avoid doing so. Even though the image may appear small on the page, the large image with its corresponding large file size still needs to download. It is better to resize the image in an image-editing program and then place it at actual size on the page. Not only that, but resizing with attributes usually results in a blurry and deformed image. In fact, if your images ever look fuzzy when viewed in a browser, the first thing to check is that the **width** and **height** values match the dimensions of the image exactly.

exercise 7-1 | **Adding and linking images**

You're back from Italy and it's time to post about some of your travels. In this exercise, you'll add thumbnail images to a travelog and make them link to pages with full-sized versions.

All the thumbnails and photos you need have been created for you, and I've given you a head start on the HTML files as well. Everything is available at *www.learningwebdesign.com/4e/ materials*. Put a copy of the *tuscany* folder on your hard drive, making sure to keep it organized as you find it. As always, the resulting markup is listed in Appendix A.

This little site is made up of a main page (*index.html*) and three separate HTML documents containing each of the larger image views (Figure 7-5). First, we'll add the thumbnails, and then we'll add the full-size versions to their respective pages. Finally, we'll make the thumbnails link to those pages. Let's get started. Open the file *index.html*, and add the small thumbnail images to this page to accompany the text. I've done the first one for you:

```
<h2>Pozzarello</h2>
```

```
<p><img src="thumbnails/window_thumb.jpg"
alt="view from bedroom window" width="75"
height="100"> The house we stayed in was called
Pozzarello…
```

I've put the image at the beginning of the paragraph, just after the opening **<p>** tag. Because all of the thumbnail images are located in the *thumbnails* directory, I provided the pathname in the URL. I also added a description of the image and the width and height dimensions in pixels (px).

Now it's your turn. Add the image *countryside_thumb .jpg* (100px wide × 75px tall) and *sienna_thumb.jpg* (75 × 100) at the beginning of the paragraphs in their respective sections. Be sure to include the pathname, an alternative text description, and pixel dimensions.

When you are done, save the file and then open it in the browser to be sure that the images are visible and appear at the right size.

Figure 7-5. Travel photo site.

1. Next, add the images to the individual HTML documents. I've done *window.html* for you:

```
<h1>The View Through My Window</h1>
<p><img src="photos/window.jpg" alt="view out the
window of the rolling Tuscan hills" width="375"
height="500"></p>
```

Notice that the full-size images are in a directory called *photos*, so that needs to be reflected in the pathnames.

Add images to *countryside.html* and *sienna.html*, following my example. Hint: all of the images are 500 pixels on their widest side and 375 pixels on their shortest side, although the orientation varies.

Save each file, and check your work by opening them in the browser window.

2. Back in *index.html*, link the thumbnails to their respective files. I've done the first one here.

```
<h2>Pozzarello</h2>
<p><a href="window.html"><img src="thumbnails/
window_thumb.jpg" alt="view from the bedroom
window" width="75" height="100"></a></p>
```

Notice that the URL is relative to the current document (*index.html*), not to the location of the image (the *thumbnails* directory).

Make the remaining thumbnail images links to each of the documents. If all the images are visible and you are able to link to each page and back to the home page again, then congratulations, you're done!

Like a little more practice?

If you'd like more practice, you'll find three additional images (*sweets.jpg*, *cathedral.jpg*, and *lavender.jpg*) with their thumbnail versions (*sweets_thumb.jpg*, *cathedral_thumb.jpg*, and *lavender_thumb.jpg*) in their appropriate directories. This time, you'll need to add your own descriptions to the home page and create the HTML documents for the full-size images from scratch.

For an added challenge, create a new directory called *photopages* in the *tuscany* directory. Move *countryside.html* and *sienna.html* into that directory, and then update the URLs on those pages so that the images are visible again.

Figure 7-6. Inline frames (added with the `iframe` element) are like a browser window within the browser that displays external HTML documents and resources.

A Window in a Window

As long as we're talking about embedding things on a page, I thought I'd tell you about the **iframe** element that lets you embed a separate HTML document or other resource in a document. What you see on the page is a floating or inline "frame" that displays the document with its own set of scrollbars if the embedded document is too long to fit (Figure 7-6).

You place an inline frame on a page similarly to an image, specifying the source (**src**) of its content as well as its width and height. The content in the **iframe** element itself displays on browsers that don't support the element. This example displays a document called *list.html* in an inline frame.

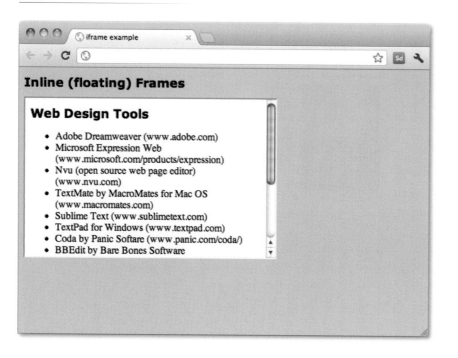

```
<h1>Inline (floating) Frames</h1>

<iframe src="list.html" width="400" height="250">

Your browser does not support inline frames. Read the <a href="list.
    html">list</a>.

</iframe>
```

You don't see inline frames much in the wild, but developers sometimes use them to keep third-party content such as interactive ads or other widgets quarantined so they don't interfere with the scripting and contents of the rest of the page.

Test Yourself

Images are a big part of the web experience. Answer these questions to see how well you've absorbed the key concepts of this chapter. The correct answers can be found in Appendix A.

1. Which attributes must be included in every **img** element?

2. Write the markup for adding an image called *furry.jpg* that is in the same directory as the current document.

3. Why is it necessary to include alternative text? Name two reasons.

4. What is the advantage of including **width** and **height** attributes for every graphic on the page? When should you leave them out?

5. What might be going wrong if your images don't appear when you view the page in a browser? There are three possible explanations.

Element Review: Images

We covered just one element in this chapter:

Element and attributes	Description
`img`	Inserts an inline image.
`src="`*url*`"`	The location of the image file.
`alt="`*text*`"`	Alternative text.
`width="`*number*`"`	Width of the graphic.
`height="`*number*`"`	Height of the graphic.
`usemap="`*usemap*`"`	Indicates a client-side image map.
`title="`*text*`"`	Provides a "tooltip" when the user mouses over the image. Can be used for supplemental information about the image.
`iframe`	Inserts an inline browsing context (window).
`height="`*number*`"`	Height of the frame in pixels.
`src="`*url*`"`	Resource of the display in the frame.
`width="`*number*`"`	Width of the frame in pixels.

TABLE MARKUP

Before we launch into the markup for tables, let's check in with our progress so far. We've covered a lot of territory: how to establish the basic structure of an HTML document, how to mark up text to give it meaning and structure, how to make links, and how to embed images on the page.

This chapter and the next, Chapter 9, Forms, describe the markup for specialized content that you might not have a need for right away. If you're getting antsy to make your pages look good, skip right to Part III and start playing with Cascading Style Sheets. The tables and forms chapters will be here when you're ready for them.

Are you still with me? Great. Let's talk tables. We'll start out by reviewing how tables should be used, then learn the elements used to create them with markup. Remember, this is an HTML chapter, so we're going to focus on the markup that structures the content into tables, and we won't be concerned with how the tables look. Like any web content, the appearance (or presentation, as we say in the web dev biz) of tables should be handled with style sheets, which you'll learn about in Chapter 18, CSS Techniques.

How Tables Are Used

HTML tables were created for instances when you need to add tabular material (data arranged into rows and columns) to a web page. Tables may be used to organize calendars, schedules, statistics, or other types of information, as shown in Figure 8-1. Note that "data" doesn't necessarily mean numbers. A table cell may contain any sort of information, including numbers, text elements, and even images and multimedia objects.

Element	Description	Categories	Parents†	Children	Attributes	Interface
a	Hyperlink	flow; phrasing*; interactive	phrasing	transparent*	globals; href; target; rel; media; hreflang; type	HTMLAnchorElement
abbr	Abbreviation	flow; phrasing	phrasing	phrasing	globals	HTMLElement
address	Contact information for a page or section	flow; formatBlock candidate	flow	flow*	globals	HTMLElement
area	Hyperlink or dead area on an image map	flow; phrasing	phrasing*	empty	globals; alt; coords; shape; href; target; rel; media; hreflang; type	HTMLAreaElement
article	Self-contained syndicatable or reusable composition	flow; sectioning; formatBlock candidate	flow	flow	globals	HTMLElement
aside	Sidebar for tangentially related content	flow; sectioning; formatBlock candidate	flow	flow	globals	HTMLElement
audio	Audio player	flow; phrasing; embedded; interactive	phrasing	source*; transparent*	globals; src; preload; autoplay; mediagroup; loop; controls	HTMLAudioElement
b	Keywords	flow; phrasing	phrasing	phrasing	globals	HTMLElement
base	Base URL and default target browsing context for hyperlinks and forms	metadata	head	empty	globals; href; target	HTMLBaseElement
bdi	Text directionality isolation	flow; phrasing	phrasing	phrasing	globals	HTMLElement
bdo	Text directionality formatting	flow; phrasing	phrasing	phrasing	globals	HTMLElement
blockquote	A section quoted from another source	flow; sectioning root; formatBlock candidate	flow	flow	globals; cite	HTMLQuoteElement

List of elements

w3c.org

PM	7:30	8:00	8:30	9:00	9:30	10:00	10:30
ABC	*The Adventures of Ozzie and Harriet*	The Patty Duke Show	*Gidget*	*The Big Valley*		Amos Burke — Secret Agent*	
CBS	Lost in Space		*The Beverly Hillbillies #8 25.9 rating*	*Green Acres* #11 24.6 rating	The Dick Van Dyke Show #16 23.6 rating	*The Danny Kaye Show*	
NBC	*The Virginian* #25 22.0 rating			*Bob Hope Presents the Chrysler Theatre / Chrysler Presents a Bob Hope Special*		*I Spy*	

wikipedia.org

Providence/Stoughton Line

Print this Schedule
Service Alerts
Holiday Schedule Information
Providence/Stoughton Line Schedule
South Station and Back Bay Schedule

Direction: Inbound Timing: Weekday Redisplay Time

PROVIDENCE/STOUGHTON LINE INBOUND : Weekday Effective 11/14/11

Train Number	800 AM	802 AM	902 AM	804 AM	904 AM	806 AM	832 AM	808 AM	906 AM	810 AM	908 AM	812 AM	834 AM	910 AM	814 AM	912 AM	816 AM	818 PM	914 PM	916 PM
TF Green Airport		05:05				06:13		06:52		07:15					09:23		11:45			
Providence	05:07	05:25		06:07		06:33		07:12		07:35		08:10			09:43		12:05	01:30		
South Attleboro	05:17	05:35		06:16		06:42		07:22		07:45		08:20			09:52		12:15	01:42		
Attleboro	05:27	05:45		06:28		06:52		07:32		07:55		08:30	09:00		10:02		12:25	01:51		
Mansfield	05:36	05:55		06:38		07:04	07:26	07:44		08:05		08:38	09:09		10:10		12:33	01:58		
Sharon	05:44	06:04		06:48		07:13	07:35			08:14		08:47	09:17		10:19		12:42	02:06		
Stoughton			06:28		06:56				07:48		08:28			09:40		10:40			02:20	03:23
Canton Center			06:36		07:04				07:57		08:36			09:49		10:49			02:27	
Canton Junction	05:51	06:11	06:39		07:08		07:41		08:01	08:24	08:40	08:54	09:24	09:52	10:26	10:52	12:50		02:30	03:33
Route 128	05:56	06:16	06:44	06:58	07:14	07:24	07:47		08:07	08:30	08:45	08:59	09:26	09:57	10:31	10:57	12:55	02:16		03:38
Hyde Park	06:01	06:21	06:49		07:19		07:52		08:13	08:36	08:49	09:04		10:02	10:36	11:02	01:00		02:39	03:43
Ruggles	06:11	06:31		07:10					08:23			09:14	09:41		10:46	11:12	01:10	02:29		
Back Bay	06:15	06:35	06:59	07:14	07:28	07:40	08:02	08:11	08:27	08:46	08:58	09:18	09:44	10:12	10:50	11:15	01:15	02:33	02:49	03:53
South Station	06:20	06:40	07:04	07:19	07:33	07:45	08:07	08:16	08:32	08:51	09:03	09:23	09:49	10:17	10:55	11:20	01:20	02:38	02:54	03:58

mbta.org

Figure 8-1. Examples of tables used for tabular information, such as charts, calendars, and schedules.

In visual browsers, the arrangement of data in rows and columns gives readers an instant understanding of the relationships between data cells and their respective header labels. Bear in mind when you are creating tables, however, that some readers will be hearing your data read aloud with a screen reader or reading Braille output. Later in this chapter, we'll discuss measures you can take to make table content accessible to users who don't have the benefit of visual presentation.

In the days before style sheets, tables were the only option for creating multicolumn layouts or controlling alignment and whitespace. Layout tables, particularly the complex nested table arrangements that were once standard web design fare, have gone the way of the dodo. This chapter focuses on HTML tables as they are intended to be used.

The Trouble with Tables

Large tables, such as those shown in Figure 8-1, can be difficult to use on small-screen devices. By default, they are shrunk to fit the screen width, rendering the text in the cells too small to be read. Users can zoom in to read the cells, but then only a few cells may be visible at a time and it is difficult to parse the organization of headings and columns.

To be honest, as of this writing, we are just starting to figure out how best to handle tabular material on small screens. One approach is to replace the table with a graphic representation, such as a pie chart, on mobile devices. Of course, this will work only for certain types of tables. For simple two- or three-column tables, consider using a `dl` list to represent the information instead for more flexibility. Another approach is to put an indication of the table (such as an image of the top of it) that links to a separate screen with the full table for those who are interested. Chris Coyier proposes a clever solution in his article "Responsive Data Tables" (*css-tricks.com/responsive-data-tables/*) that describes how to use CSS to reformat the table as a long, narrow list that fits better in a smartphone screen. See also the clever solution proposed by Filament Group (think of them as the Super Friends of responsive design) at *filamentgroup.com/lab/responsive_design_approach_for_complex_multicolumn_data_tables/*.

There may be new solutions by the time you read this, but it is important to always keep the mobile, small-screen experience in mind as you design any web content.

Minimal Table Structure

Let's take a look at a simple table to see what it's made of. Here is a small table with three rows and three columns that lists nutritional information.

Menu item	Calories	Fat (g)
Chicken noodle soup	120	2
Caesar salad	400	26

Figure 8-2 reveals the structure of this table according to the HTML table model. All of the table's content goes into cells that are arranged into rows. Cells contain either header information (titles for the columns, such as "Calories") or data, which may be any sort of content.

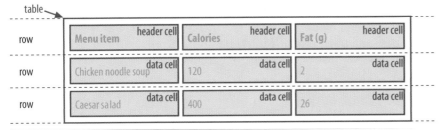

Figure 8-2. *Tables are made up of rows that contain cells. Cells are the containers for content.*

Simple enough, right? Now let's look at how those parts translate into elements (Figure 8-3).

```
<table>
  <tr>
    <th>Menu item</th>  <th>Calories</th>  <th>Fat (g)</th>  </tr>
  <tr>
    <td>Chicken noodle soup</td>  <td>120</td>  <td>2</td>  </tr>
  <tr>
    <td>Caesar salad</td>  <td>400</td>  <td>26</td>  </tr>
</table>
```

Figure 8-3. *The elements that make up the basic structure of a table.*

Figure 8-3 shows the elements that identify the table (**table**), rows (**tr**, for "table row"), and cells (**th**, for "table headers," and **td**, for "table data"). Cells are the heart of the table, because that's where the actual content goes. The other elements just hold things together.

`<table>...</table>`
Tabular content (rows and columns)

`<tr>...</tr>`
Table row

`<th>...</th>`
Table header

`<td>...</td>`
Table cell data

What we don't see are column elements (see note). The number of columns in a table is determined by the number of cells in each row. This is one of the things that make HTML tables potentially tricky. Rows are easy—if you want the table to have three rows, just use three **tr** elements. Columns are different. For a table with four columns, you need to make sure that every row has four **td** or **th** elements; the columns are implied.

Written out in a source document, the markup for the table in Figure 8-3 would look like the following sample. It is common to stack the **th** and **td** elements in order to make them easier to find in the source. This does not affect how they are rendered by the browser.

NOTE

There are two column-related elements in HTML5: col for identifying a column and colgroup for establishing related groups of columns. They were created to add a layer of information about the table that can potentially speed up its display, but they are not part of HTML's row-centric table model. See the sidebar "Advanced Table Elements" for more information.

```
<table>
    <tr>
        <th>Menu item</th>
        <th>Calories</th>
        <th>Fat (g)</th>
    </tr>
    <tr>
        <td>Chicken noodle soup</td>
        <td>120</td>
        <td>2</td>
    </tr>
    <tr>
        <td>Caesar salad</td>
        <td>400</td>
        <td>26</td>
    </tr>
</table>
```

Remember, all the content must go in cells—that is, within **td** or **th** elements. You can put any content in a cell: text, a graphic, or even another table.

Start and end **table** tags are used to identify the beginning and end of the tabular material. The **table** element may directly contain only some number of **tr** (row) elements. The only thing that can go in the **tr** element is some number of **td** or **th** elements. In other words, there may be no text content within the **table** and **tr** elements that isn't contained within a **td** or **th**.

Finally, Figure 8-4 shows how the table would look in a simple web page, as displayed by default in a browser. I know it's not exciting. Excitement happens in the CSS chapters. What is worth noting is that tables always start on new lines by default in browsers.

Advanced Table Elements

The sample table in this section has been stripped down to its bare essentials to make its structure clear while you learn how tables work. It is worth noting, however, that there are other table elements and attributes that offer more complex semantic descriptions and improve the accessibility of tabular content. A thoroughly marked-up version of the sample table might look like this:

```
<table>
<caption>Nutritional Information (Calorie and Fat
    Content)</caption>

<col span="1" class="itemname">
<colgroup id="data">
   <col span="1" class="calories">
   <col span="1" class="fat">
</colgroup>

<thead>
   <tr>
      <th scope="col">Menu item</th>
      <th scope="col">Calories</th>
      <th scope="column">Fat (g)</th>
   </tr>
</thead>

<tbody>
   <tr>
      <td>Chicken noodle soup</td>
      <td>120</td>
      <td>2</td>
   </tr>
   <tr>
      <td>Caesar salad</td>
      <td>400</td>
      <td>26</td>
   </tr>
</tbody>

</table>
```

Row group elements

You can describe rows or groups of rows as belonging to a header, footer, or the body of a table using the **thead**, **tfoot**, and **tbody** elements, respectively. Some user agents (another word for a browsing device) may repeat the header and footer rows on tables that span multiple pages. Authors may also use these elements to apply styles to various regions of a table.

Column group elements

Columns may be identified with the **col** element or put into groups using the **colgroup** element. This is useful for adding semantic context to information in columns and may be used to calculate the width of tables more quickly. Notice that there is no content in the column elements; it just describes the columns before the actual table data begins.

Accessibility features

Accessibility features such as captions for providing descriptions of table content and the **scope** and **headers** attributes for explicitly connecting headers with their respective content are discussed later in this chapter.

An in-depth exploration of the advanced table elements is beyond the scope of this book, but you may want to do more research at the W3C site (*www.w3.org/TR/html5*) if you anticipate working with data-heavy tables.

NOTE

According to the HTML5 spec, a table may contain "in this order: optionally a caption *element, followed by zero or more* colgroup *elements, followed optionally by a* thead *element, followed optionally by a* tfoot *element, followed by either zero or more* tbody *elements or one or more* tr *elements, followed optionally by a* tfoot *element (but there can only be one* tfoot *element child in total)." Got all that?*

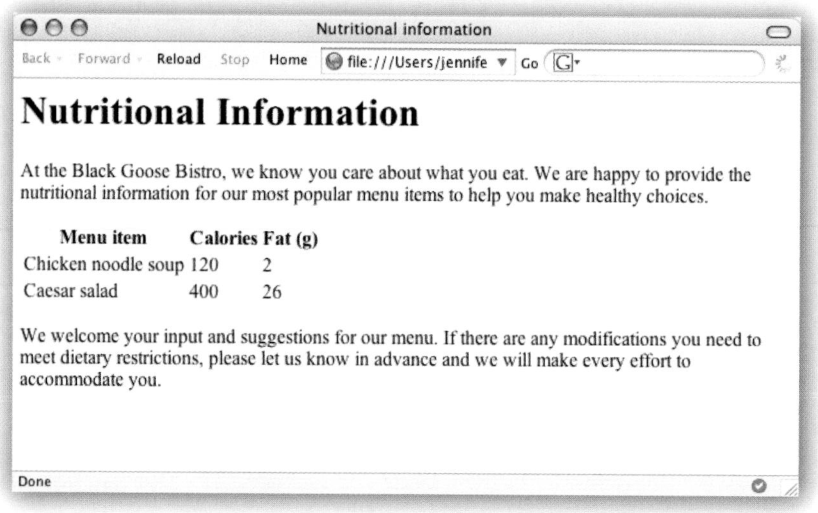

Figure 8-4. The default rendering of our sample table in a browser.

Stylin' Tables

Once you build the structure of the table in the markup, it's no problem adding a layer of style to customize its appearance.

Style sheets can and should be used to control these aspects of a table's visual presentation. We'll get to all the formatting tools you'll need in the following chapters:

In Chapter 12, Formatting Text:

- Font settings for cell contents
- Text color in cells

In Chapter 14, Thinking Inside the Box:

- Table dimensions (width and height)
- Borders
- Cell padding (space around cell contents)
- Margins around the table

In Chapter 13, Colors and Backgrounds:

- Background colors
- Tiling background images

In Chapter 18, CSS Techniques:

- Special properties for controlling borders and spacing between cells

Here is the source for another table. Can you tell how many rows and columns it will have when it is displayed in a browser?

```
<table>
    <tr>
        <td>Sufjan Stevens</td>
        <td>Illinoise</td>
        <td>Asthmatic Kitty Records</td>
    </tr>
    <tr>
        <td>The Shins</td>
        <td>Oh Inverted World</td>
        <td>Sub-pop Records</td>
    </tr>
</table>
```

If you guessed that it's a table with two rows and three columns, you're correct! Two **tr** elements create two rows; three **td** elements in each row create three columns.

Table Headers

As you can see in Figure 8-4, the text marked up as headers (**th** elements) is displayed differently from the other cells in the table (**td** elements). The difference, however, is not purely cosmetic. Table headers are important because they provide information or context about the cells in the row or column they precede. The **th** element may be handled differently than **td**s by alternative browsing devices. For example, screen readers may read the header aloud before each data cell ("Menu item, Caesar salad, Calories, 400, Fat-g, 26").

In this way, they are a key tool for making table content accessible. Don't try to fake headers by formatting a row of **td** elements differently than the rest of the table. Conversely, don't avoid using **th** elements because of their default rendering (bold and centered). Mark up the headers semantically and change the presentation later with a style rule.

That covers the basics. Before we get fancier, try your hand at Exercise 8-1.

exercise 8-1 | Making a simple table

Try writing the markup for the table shown in Figure 8-5. You can open a text editor or just write it down on paper. The finished markup is provided in Appendix A.

(Note that I've added a 1-pixel border around cells with a style rule just to make the structure clear. You won't include this in your version.)

Be sure to close all table elements. Technically, you are not *required* to close **tr**, **th**, and **td** elements, but I want you to get in the habit of writing tidy source code for maximum predictability across all browsing devices. If you choose to write documents using XHTML syntax, closing table elements is required in order for the document to be valid.

Album	Year
Rubber Soul	1968
Revolver	1966
Sgt. Pepper's	1967
The White Album	1968
Abbey Road	1969

Figure 8-5. Write the markup for this table.

Spanning Cells

One fundamental feature of table structure is cell spanning, which is the stretching of a cell to cover several rows or columns. Spanning cells allows you to create complex table structures, but it has the side effect of making the markup a little more difficult to keep track of. You make a header or data cell span by adding the **colspan** or **rowspan** attributes, as we'll discuss next.

Column spans

Column spans, created with the **colspan** attribute in the **td** or **th** element, stretch a cell to the right to span over the subsequent columns (Figure 8-6). Here a column span is used to make a header apply to two columns. (I've added a border around cells to reveal the table structure in the screenshot.)

```
<table>
   <tr>
      <th colspan="2">Fat</th>
   </tr>
   <tr>
      <td>Saturated Fat (g)</td>
      <td>Unsaturated Fat (g)</td>
   </tr>
</table>
```

Fat	
Saturated Fat (g)	Unsaturated Fat (g)

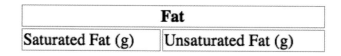

Figure 8-6. The `colspan` *attribute stretches a cell to the right to span the specified number of columns.*

WARNING

Be careful with `colspan` *values. If you specify a number that exceeds the number of columns in the table, most browsers will add columns to the existing table, which typically screws things up.*

Notice in the first row (**tr**) that there is only one **th** element, while the second row has two **td** elements. The **th** for the column that was spanned over is no longer in the source; the cell with the **colspan** stands in for it. Every row should have the same number of cells or equivalent **colspan** values. For example, there are two **td** elements and the **colspan** value is 2, so the implied number of columns in each row is equal.

exercise 8-2 | Column spans

Try writing the markup for the table shown in Figure 8-7. You can open a text editor or just write it down on paper. I added borders to reveal the cell structure in the figure, but your table won't have them. Check Appendix A for the final markup.

7:00pm	7:30pm	8:00pm
The Sunday Night Movie		
Perry Mason	Candid Camera	What's My Line
Bonanza	The Wackiest Ship in the Army	

Figure 8-7. Practice column spans by writing the markup for this table.

Some hints:

- For simplicity's sake, this table uses all **td** elements.
- The second row shows you that the table has a total of three columns.
- When a cell is spanned over, its **td** element does not appear in the table.

Row spans

Row spans, created with the **rowspan** attribute, work just like column spans, but they cause the cell to span downward over several rows. In this example, the first cell in the table spans down three rows (Figure 8-8).

```
<table>
    <tr>
        <th rowspan="3">Serving Size</th>
        <td>Small (8oz.)</td>
    </tr>
    <tr>
        <td>Medium (16oz.)</td>
    </tr>
    <tr>
        <td>Large (24oz.)</td>
    </tr>
</table>
```

Again, notice that the **td** elements for the cells that were spanned over (the first cells in the remaining rows) do not appear in the source. The **rowspan="3"** implies cells for the subsequent two rows, so no **td** elements are needed.

Serving Size	Small (8oz.)
	Medium (16oz.)
	Large (24oz.)

Figure 8-8. The rowspan *attribute stretches a cell downward to span the specified number of rows.*

exercise 8-3 | Row spans

Try writing the markup for the table shown in Figure 8-9. Remember that cells that are spanned over do not appear in the table code. Rows always span downward, so the "oranges" cell is part of the first row even though its content is vertically centered.

If you're working in a text editor, don't worry if your table doesn't look exactly like the one shown here. The resulting markup is provided in Appendix A.

Some hints:

- Rows always span downward, so the "oranges" cell is part of the first row.
- Cells that are spanned over do not appear in the code.

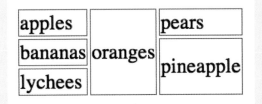

Figure 8-9. Practice row spans by writing the markup for this table.

Space in and Between Cells

By default, cells are sized just large enough to fit their contents, but often you'll want to add a little breathing room around tabular content (Figure 8-10). Because spacing is a matter of presentation, it is a job for style sheets.

Cell padding is the space inside the cell, between the content and the edge of the cell. To add cell padding, apply the CSS **padding** property to the **td** or **th** element.

Cell spacing, the area between cells, is a little more complicated. First, set the **border-collapse** property for the **table** to **separate**, then use the **border-spacing** property to specify the amount of space between borders. Unfortunately, this technique won't work in Internet Explorer 6, but hopefully IE6 usage will be inconsequential by the time you're reading this.

In the past, cell padding and spacing were handled by the **cellpadding** and **cellspacing** attributes in the **table** element, respectively, but they have been made obsolete in HTML5 due to their presentational nature.

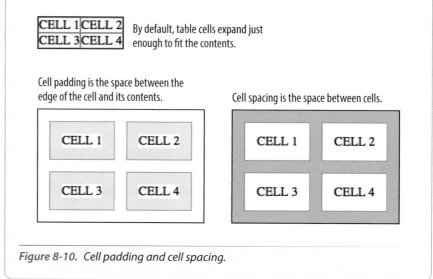

Figure 8-10. Cell padding and cell spacing.

Table Accessibility

As a web designer, it is important that you always keep in mind how your site's content is going to be used by non-sighted visitors. It is especially challenging to make sense of tabular material using a screen reader, but there are measures you can take to improve the experience and make your content more understandable.

Describing table content

The first step is to simply provide a description of your table's contents and perhaps the way it is structured if it is out of the ordinary.

Use the **caption** element to give a table a title or brief description that displays next to the table. You can use it to describe the table's contents or provide hints on how it is structured. When used, the **caption** element must be the first thing within the **table** element, as shown in this example, which adds a caption to the nutritional chart from earlier in the chapter.

```
<table>
    <caption>Nutritional Information</caption>
    <tr>
        <th>Menu item</th>
        <th>Calories</th>
        <th>Fat (g)</th>
    </tr>

    …table continues…
</table>
```

The caption is displayed above the table by default, as shown in Figure 8-11, although you can use a style sheet property (**caption-side**) to move it below the table.

Nutritional Information

Menu item	Calories	Fat (g)
Chicken noodle soup	120	2
Caesar salad	400	26

Figure 8-11. The table caption is displayed above the table by default.

For longer descriptions, you could consider putting the table in a **figure** element and using the **figcaption** element for the description. The HTML5 specification has a number of suggestions for providing table descriptions, which you can find at *www.w3.org/TR/html5/tabular-data.html#table-descriptions-techniques*.

NOTE

HTML 4.01 included a summary *attribute for the* table *element that was used for providing long descriptions to assistive devices while hiding them from visual browsers. However, it was omitted from HTML5 and will trigger validation errors.*

Connecting cells and headers

We discussed headers briefly as a straightforward method for improving the accessibility of table content, but sometimes it may be difficult to know which header applies to which cells. For example, headers may be at the left or right edge of a row rather than at the top of a column. And although it may be easy for sighted users to understand a table structure at a glance, for users hearing the data as text, the overall organization is not as clear. HTML 4.01 introduced a few attributes that allow authors to explicitly associate headers and their respective content.

scope

The **scope** attribute associates a table header with the row, column, group of rows (such as **tbody**), or column group in which it appears using the values **row**, **column**, **rowgroup**, or **colgroup**, respectively. This example uses the **scope** attribute to declare that a header cell applies to the current row.

```
<tr>
    <th scope="row">Mars</th>
    <td>.95</td>
    <td>.62</td>
    <td>0</td>
</tr>
```

headers

For really complicated tables in which **scope** is not sufficient to associate a table data cell with its respective header (such as when the table contains multiple spanned cells), the **headers** attribute is used in the **td** element to explicitly tie it to a header's **id** value. In this example, the cell content ".38" is tied to the header "Diameter measured in earths":

```
<th id="diameter">Diameter measured in earths</th>

…many other cells…
<td headers="diameter">.38</td>
…many other cells…
```

This section is obviously only the tip of the iceberg of table accessibility. In-depth instruction on authoring accessible tables is beyond the scope of this beginner book. If you'd like to learn more, I recommend "Creating Accessible Tables" at WebAIM (*www.webaim.org/techniques/tables*) as an excellent starting point.

Wrapping Up Tables

This chapter gave you a good overview of the components of HTML tables. Exercise 8-4 puts most of what we covered together to give you a little more practice at authoring tables.

After just a few exercises, you're probably getting the sense that writing table markup manually, although not impossible, gets tedious and complicated quickly. Fortunately, web-authoring tools such as Dreamweaver provide interfaces that make the process much easier and time-efficient. Still, you'll be glad that you have a solid understanding of table structure and terminology, as well as the preferred methods for changing a table's appearance.

exercise 8-4 | **The table challenge**

Now it's time to put together the table writing skills you've acquired in this chapter. Your challenge is to write out the source document for the table shown in Figure 8-12.

I'll walk you through it one step at a time.

1. First, open a new document in your text editor and set up its overall structure (**html**, **head**, **title**, and **body** elements). Save the document as *table.html* in the directory of your choice.

2. Next, in order to make the boundaries of the cells and table clearer when you check your work, I'm going to have you add some simple style sheet rules to the document. Don't worry about understanding exactly what's happening here (although it's fairly intuitive); just insert this **style** element in the **head** of the document exactly as you see it here.

```
<head>
  <title>Table Challenge</title>
  <style type="text/css">
    td, th { border: 1px solid #CCC; }
    table {border: 1px solid black; }
  </style>
</head>
```

3. Now it's time to start building the table. I usually start by setting up the table and adding as many empty row elements as I'll need for the final table as placeholders, as shown here (it should be clear that there are five rows in this table).

```
<body>
<table>
  <tr></tr>
  <tr></tr>
  <tr></tr>
  <tr></tr>
  <tr></tr>
</table>
</body>
```

4. Start with the top row, and fill in the **th** and **td** elements from left to right, including any row or column spans as necessary. I'll help with the first row.

The first cell (the one in the top-left corner) spans down the height of two rows, so it gets a **rowspan** attribute. I'll use a **th** here to keep it consistent with the rest of the row. This cell has no content.

```
<table>
  <tr>
    <th rowspan="2"></th>
  </tr>
```

The cell in the second column of the first row spans over the width of two columns, so it gets a **colspan** attribute:

```
<table>
  <tr>
    <th rowspan="2"></th>
    <th colspan="2">A common header for two
    subheads</th>
  </tr>
```

The cell in the third column has been spanned over by the **colspan** we just added, so we don't need to include it in the markup. The cell in the fourth column also spans down two rows.

```
<table>
  <tr>
    <th rowspan="2"></th>
    <th colspan="2">A common header for two
    subheads</th>
    <th rowspan="2">Header 3</th>
  </tr>
```

5. Now it's your turn. Continue filling in the **th** and **td** elements for the remaining four rows of the table. Here's a hint: the first and last cells in the second row have been spanned over. Also, if it's bold in the example, make it a header.

6. To complete the content, add the title over the table using the **caption** element.

7. Finally, use the **scope** attribute to make sure that the Thing A, Thing B, and Thing C headers are associated with their respective rows.

8. Save your work and open the file in a browser. The table should look just like the one on this page. If not, go back and adjust your markup. If you're stumped, the final markup for this exercise is listed in Appendix A.

	A common header for two subheads		Header 3
	Header 1	**Header 2**	
Thing A	data A1	data A2	data A3
Thing B	data B1	data B2	data B3
Thing C	data C1	data C2	data C3

Your Content Here

Figure 8-12. The table challenge.

Test Yourself

The answers to these questions are in Appendix A.

1. What are the parts (elements) of a basic HTML table?

2. Why don't professional web designers use tables for layout anymore?

3. When would you use the `col` (column) element?

4. Find five errors in this table markup.

```
<caption>Primetime Television
    1965</caption>
<table>
  Thursday Night
  <tr></tr>
    <th>7:30</th>
    <th>8:00</th>
    <th>8:30</th>
  <tr>
    <td>Shindig</td>
    <td>Donna Reed Show</td>
    <td>Bewitched</td>
  <tr>
    <colspan>Laredo</colspan>
    <td>Daniel Boone</td>
  </tr>
</table>
```

Element Review: Tables

The following is a summary of the elements we covered in this chapter:

Element and attributes	Description
`table`	Establishes a table element
`td`	Establishes a cell within a table row
`colspan="number"`	Number of columns the cell should span
`rowspan="number"`	Number of rows the cell should span
`headers="header name"`	Associates the data cell with a header
`th`	Table header associated with a row or column
`colspan="number"`	Number of columns the cell should span
`rowspan="number"`	Number of rows the cell should span
`headers="header name"`	Associates a header with another header
`scope="row|col|rowgroup|colgroup"`	Associates the header with a row, row group, column, or column group
`tr`	Establishes a row within a table
`caption`	Gives the table a title that displays in the browser
`col`	Declares a column
`colgroup`	Declares a group of columns
`tbody`	Identifies the table body row group
`tfoot`	Identifies the table footer grow group
`thead`	Identifies the table header row group

FORMS

It didn't take long for the Web to shift from a network of pages to read to a place where you went to get things *done*—making purchases, booking plane tickets, signing petitions, searching a site, posting a tweet...the list goes on! All of these interactions are handled by forms.

In fact, in response to this shift from page to application, HTML5 introduced a bonanza of new form controls and attributes that make it easier for users to fill out forms and for developers to create them. Tasks that have traditionally relied on JavaScript may be handled by markup and native browser behavior alone. HTML5 introduces a number of new form-related elements, 13 new input types, and many new attributes (they are listed in Table 9-1 at the end of this chapter). Some of these features are waiting for browser implementation to catch up, so I will be sure to note which controls may not be universally supported.

This chapter introduces web forms, how they work, and the markup used to create them. I'll also briefly discuss the importance of web form design.

How Forms Work

There are two parts to a working form. The first part is the form that you see on the page itself that is created using HTML markup. Forms are made up of buttons, input fields, and drop-down menus (collectively known as form controls) used to collect information from the user. Forms may also contain text and other elements.

The other component of a web form is an application or script on the server that processes the information collected by the form and returns an appropriate response. It's what makes the form *work*. In other words, posting an HTML document with form elements isn't enough. Web applications and scripts require programming know-how that is beyond the scope of this book, but the "Getting Your Forms to Work" sidebar, later in this chapter, provides some options for getting the scripts you need.

A Word About Encoding

Form data is encoded using the same method used for URLs in which spaces and other characters that are not permitted are translated into their hexadecimal equivalents. For example, each space character in the collected form data is represented by the character string **%20**, and a slash (/) character is replaced with **%2F**. You don't need to worry about this; the browser handles it automatically.

From data entry to response

If you are going to be creating web forms, it is beneficial to understand what is happening behind the scenes. This example traces the steps of a transaction using a simple form that gathers names and email addresses for a mailing list; however, it is typical of the process for many forms.

1. Your visitor, let's call her Sally, opens the page with a web form in the browser window. The browser sees the form control elements in the markup and renders them with the appropriate form controls on the page, including two text entry fields and a submit button (shown in Figure 9-1).

2. Sally would like to sign up for this mailing list, so she enters her name and email address into the fields and submits the form by hitting the "Submit" button.

3. The browser collects the information she entered, encodes it (see the sidebar "A Word About Encoding"), and sends it to the web application on the server.

Figure 9-1. What happens behind the scenes when a web form is submitted.

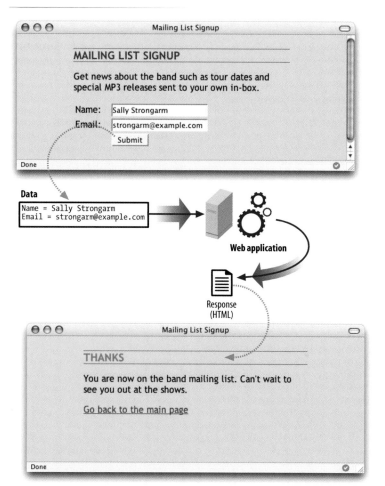

4. The web application accepts the information and processes it (that is, does whatever it is programmed to do with it). In this example, the name and email address are added to a database.

5. The web application also returns a response. The kind of response sent back depends on the content and purpose of the form. Here, the response is a simple web page that contains a thank you for signing up for the mailing list. Other applications might respond by reloading the HTML form page with updated information, by moving the user on to another related form page, or by issuing an error message if the form is not filled out correctly, to name only a few examples.

6. The server sends the web application's response back to the browser where it is displayed. Sally can see that the form worked and that she has been added to the mailing list.

The form Element

`<form>...</form>`

Interactive form

Forms are added to web pages using (no surprise here) the **form** element. The **form** element is a container for all the content of the form, including some number of form controls, such as text entry fields and buttons. It may also contain block elements (**h1**, **p**, and lists, for example). However, it may *not* contain another **form** element.

This sample source document contains a form similar to the one shown in Figure 9-1:

```
<!DOCTYPE html>
<html>
<head>
   <title>Mailing List Signup</title>
   <meta charset="utf-8">
</head>
<body>
   <h1>Mailing List Signup</h1>

   <form action="/mailinglist.php" method="post">
     <fieldset>
     <legend>Join our email list</legend>
     <p>Get news about the band such as tour dates and special MP3
releases sent to your own in-box.</p>
     <ol>
     <li><label for="firstlast">Name:</label>
         <input type="text" name="username" id="firstlast"></li>
     <li><label for="email">Email:</label>
         <input type="text" name="email" id="email"></li>
     </ol>
     <input type="submit" value="Submit">
     </fieldset>
   </form>

</body>
</html>
```

In addition to being a container for form control elements, the **form** element has some attributes that are necessary for interacting with the form-processing program on the server. Let's take a look at each.

The action attribute

The **action** attribute provides the location (URL) of the application or script (sometimes called the action page) that will be used to process the form. The **action** attribute in this example sends the data to a script called *mailinglist. php*.

```
<form action="/mailinglist.php" method="post">...</form>
```

> **TIP**
>
> Be careful not to nest **form** elements or allow them to overlap. A **form** element must be closed before the next one begins.

> **NOTE**
>
> *It is current best practice to wrap form controls in semantic HTML elements such as lists or **divs**. Ordered lists, as shown in this example, are a popular solution, but know that there are often default styles that need to be cleared out before styling them, particularly on mobile browsers.*

The *.php* suffix indicates that this form is processed by a script written in the PHP scripting language, but web forms may be processed using one of the following technologies:

- PHP (*.php*) is an open source scripting language most commonly used with the Apache web server.

- Microsoft's ASP.NET (Active Server Pages) (*.asp*) is a programming environment for the Microsoft Internet Information Server (IIS).

- Ruby on Rails. Ruby is the programming language that is used with the Rails platform. Many popular web applications are built with it.

- JavaServer Pages (*.jsp*) is a Java-based technology similar to ASP.

- Python is a popular scripting language for web and server applications.

There are other forms-processing options that may have their own suffixes or none at all (as is the case for the Ruby on Rails platform). Check with your programmer, server administrator, or script documentation for the proper name and location of the program to be provided by the **action** attribute.

Sometimes there is form-processing code such as PHP embedded right in the HTML file. In that case, leave the action empty and the form will post to the page itself.

The method attribute

The **method** attribute specifies how the information should be sent to the server. Let's use this data gathered from the sample form in Figure 9-1 as an example.

```
username = Sally Strongarm
email = strongarm@example.com
```

When the browser encodes that information for its trip to the server, it looks like this (see the earlier sidebar if you need a refresher on encoding):

```
username=Sally%20Strongarm&email=strongarm%40example.com
```

There are only two methods for sending this encoded data to the server: POST or GET, indicated using the **method** attribute in the **form** element. The method is optional and will default to GET if omitted. We'll look at the difference between the two methods in the following sections. Our example uses the POST method, as shown here:

```
<form action="/mailinglist.php" method="POST">...</form>
```

The POST method

When the form's method is set to POST, the browser sends a separate server request containing some special headers followed by the data. Only the server sees the content of this request, thus it is the best method for sending secure information such as credit card numbers or other personal information.

The POST method is also preferable for sending a lot of data, such as a lengthy text entry, because there is no character limit as there is for GET.

The GET method

With the GET method, the encoded form data gets tacked right onto the URL sent to the server. A question mark character separates the URL from the following data, as shown here:

```
get http://www.bandname.com/mailinglist.php?name=Sally%20Strongarm&email
=strongarm%40example.com
```

The GET method is appropriate if you want users to be able to bookmark the results of a form submission (such as a list of search results). Because the content of the form is in plain sight, GET is not appropriate for forms with private personal or financial information. In addition, GET may not be used when the form is used to upload a file.

In this chapter, we'll stick with the more prevalent POST method. Now that we've gotten through the technical aspects of the **form** element, we can take on the real meat of forms: form controls.

Variables and Content

Web forms use a variety of controls that allow users to enter information or choose options. Control types include various text entry fields, buttons, menus, and a few controls with special functions. They are added to the document using a collection of form control elements that we'll be examining one by one in the upcoming "Great Form Control Roundup" section.

As a web designer, you need to be familiar with control options to make your forms easy and intuitive to use. It is also useful to have an idea of what form controls are doing behind the scenes.

The name attribute

The job of a form control is to collect one bit of information from a user. In the form example a few pages back, text entry fields collect the visitor's name and email address. To use the technical term, "username" and "email" are two variables collected by the form. The data entered by the user ("Sally Strongarm" and "strongarm@example.com") is the value or content of the variable.

The **name** attribute provides the variable name for the control. In this example, the text gathered by a **textarea** element is defined as the "comment" variable:

```
<textarea name="comment" rows="4" cols="45" placeholder="Leave us a
comment."></textarea>
```

NOTE

POST and GET are not case-sensitive and are commonly listed in all upper-case by convention. In XHTML documents, however, the value of the method *attribute (post or get) must be provided in all lowercase letters.*

When a user enters a comment in the field ("This is the best band ever!"), it would be passed to the server as a name/value (variable/content) pair like this:

```
comment=This%20is%20the%20best%20band%20ever%21
```

All form control elements must include a **name** attribute so the form-processing application can sort the information. You may include a **name** attribute for **submit** and **reset** button elements, but they are not required, because they have special functions (submitting or resetting the form) not related to data collection.

Naming your variables

You can't just name controls willy-nilly. The web application that processes the data is programmed to look for specific variable names. If you are designing a form to work with a preexisting application or script, you need to find out the specific variable names to use in the form so they are speaking the same language. You can get the variable names from the developer you are working with, your system administrator, or from the instructions provided with a ready-to-use script on your server.

If the script or application will be created later, be sure to name your variables simply and descriptively and to document them well. In addition, each variable must be named uniquely—that is, the same name may not be used for two variables. You should also avoid putting character spaces in variable names; use an underscore or hyphen instead.

We've covered the basics of the **form** element and how variables are named. Now we can get to the real meat of form markup: the controls.

The Great Form Control Roundup

This is the fun part—playing with the markup that adds form controls to the page. This section introduces the elements used to create:

- Text entry controls
- Specialized text entry controls
- Submit and reset buttons
- Radio and checkbox buttons
- Pull-down and scrolling menus
- File selection and upload control
- Hidden controls
- Dates and times (HTML5)
- Numerical controls (HTML5)
- Color picker control (HTML5)

We'll pause along the way to allow you to try them out by constructing the questionnaire form shown in Figure 9-2.

As you will see, the majority of controls are added to a form using the **input** element. The functionality and appearance of the **input** element changes based on the value of the **type** attribute in the tag. In HTML5, there are *twenty-three* different types of input controls. We'll take a look at them all.

NOTE

The attributes associated with each input type are listed in Table 9-1 at the end of this chapter.

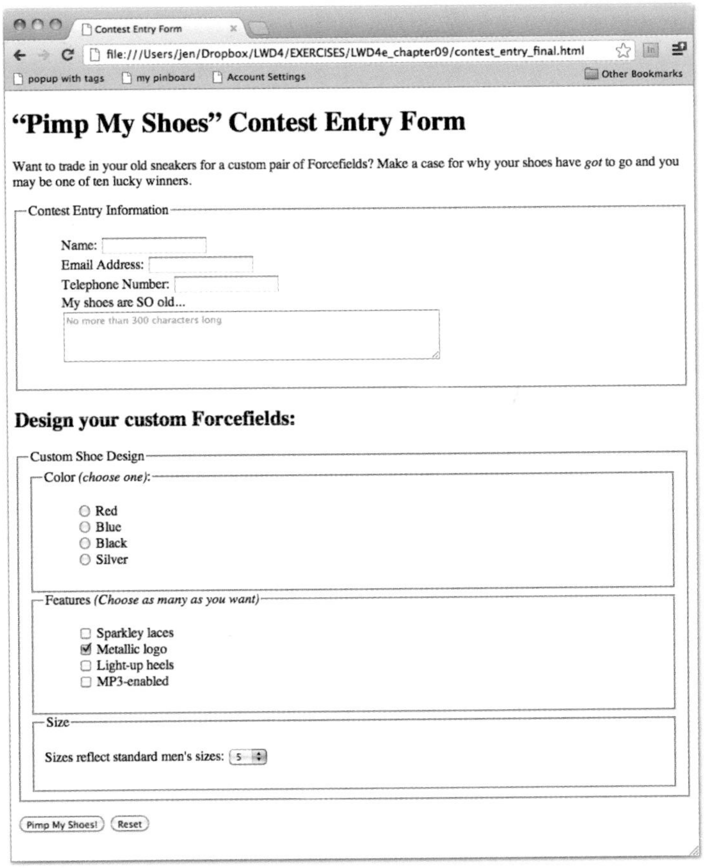

Figure 9-2. The contest entry form we'll be building in the exercises in this chapter.

Text entry controls

One of the most common tasks in a web form is to enter text information. Which element you use depends on whether users are asked to enter a single line of text (**input**) or multiple lines (**textarea**).

NOTE

The markup examples throughout this section include the **label** *element, which is used to improve accessibility. We will discuss* **label** *in more detail in the "Form Accessibility Features" section later in this chapter, but in the meantime, I want you to get used to seeing proper form markup.*

Single-line text field

<input type="text">

Single-line text entry control

One of the most straightforward form input types is the text entry field used for entering a single word or line of text. In fact, it is the default input type, which means it is what you'll get if you forget to include the **type** attribute or include an unrecognized value. Add a text input field to a form with the **input** element with its **type** attribute set to **text**, as shown here and in Figure 9-3.

```
<li><label>City <input type="text" name="city" id="form-city"
value="Your Hometown" maxlength="50"></label></li>
```

There are a few attributes in there I'd like to point out.

name

The **name** attribute is required for indicating the variable name.

value

The **value** attribute specifies default text that appears in the field when the form is loaded. When you reset a form, it returns to this value.

maxlength

By default, users can type an unlimited number of characters in a text field regardless of its size (the display scrolls to the right if the text exceeds the character width of the box). You can set a maximum character limit using the **maxlength** attribute if the forms-processing program you are using requires it.

Multiline text entry field

<textarea>...</textarea>

Multiline text entry control

At times, you'll want your users to be able to enter more than just one line of text. For these instances, use the **textarea** element that is replaced by a multiline, scrollable text entry box when displayed by the browser (Figure 9-3).

NOTE

The specific rendering style of form controls varies by operating system and browser version.

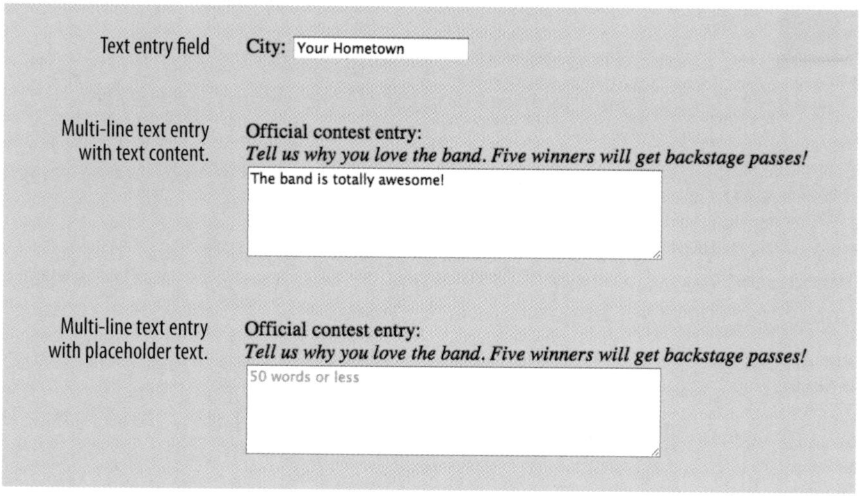

Figure 9-3. Examples of the text entry control options for web forms.

Unlike the empty **input** element, you can put content between the opening and closing tags in the **textarea** element. The content of the **textarea** element will show up in the text box when the form is displayed in the browser. It will also get sent to the server when the form is submitted, so carefully consider what goes there. It is not uncommon for developers to put nothing between the opening and closing tags, and provide a hint of what should go there with a **title** or **placeholder** attribute instead. The new HTML5 **placeholder** attribute can be used with **textarea** and other text-based **input** types and is used to provide a short hint of how to fill in the field. It is not supported on Android, older versions of Firefox (versions earlier than 3.6), or IE as of this writing.

```
<p><label>Official contest entry: <br>
<em>Tell us why you love the band. Five winners will get backstage
passes!</em><br>
<textarea name="contest_entry" rows="5" cols="50">The band is totally
awesome!</textarea></label></p>

<p>Official contest entry:<br>
<em>Tell us why you love the band. Five winners will get backstage
passes!</em><br>
<textarea name="contest_entry" placeholder="50 words or less">
</textarea>
</p>
```

The **rows** and **cols** attributes are a way of specifying the size of the **textarea** using markup, but it is more commonly sized with CSS. **rows** specifies the number of lines the text area should display, and **cols** specifies the width in number of characters. Scrollbars will be provided if the user types more text than fits in the allotted space.

There are also a few attributes not shown in the example. The **wrap** attribute specifies whether the text should keep its line breaks when submitted. A value of **soft** (the default) does not preserve line breaks, and **hard** does. The **maxlength** attribute (new in HTML5) sets a limit on the number of characters that can by typed into the field.

Specialized text entry fields

In addition to the generic single-line text entry, there are a number of input types for entering specific types of information such as passwords, search terms, email addresses, telephone numbers, and URLs.

Password entry field

```
<input type="password">
```
Password text control

A password field works just like a text entry field, except the characters are obscured from view using asterisk (*) or bullet (•) characters, or another character determined by the browser.

disabled and readonly

The **disabled** and **readonly** attributes can be added to any form control element to prevent users from selecting them. When a form element is disabled, it cannot be selected. Visual browsers may render the control as grayed-out by default (which you can change with CSS, of course). The disabled state can only be changed with a script. This is a useful attribute for restricting access to some form fields based on data entered earlier in the form.

The **readonly** attribute prevents the user from changing the value of the form control (although it can be selected). This enables developers to use scripts to set values for controls contingent on other data entered earlier in the form. Inputs that are **readonly** should have strong visual cues that they are somehow different than other inputs, or they could be confusing to users who are trying to change their values.

WARNING

*iOS ignores **disabled** on **option** elements as of this writing (iOS 5 and earlier).*

It's important to note that although the characters entered in the password field are not visible to casual onlookers, the form does not encrypt the information, so it should not be considered a real security measure.

Here is an example of the markup for a password field. Figure 9-4 shows how it might look after the user enters a password in the field.

```
<li><label for="form-pswd">Log in:</label><br>
  <input type="password" name="pswd" maxlength="8" id="form-pswd"></li>
```

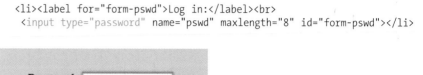

Figure 9-4. Passwords are converted to bullets in the browser display.

HTML5 text inputs

<input type="search">
Search field
NEW IN HTML5

<input type="email">
Email address
NEW IN HTML5

<input type="tel">
Telephone number
NEW IN HTML5

<input type="url">
Location (URL)
NEW IN HTML5

Until HTML5, the only way to collect email addresses, telephone numbers, URLs, or search terms was to insert a generic text input field. In HTML5, the **email**, **tel**, **url**, and **search** input types give the browser a heads-up as to what type of information to expect in the field. These new input types use the same attributes as the generic text input type described earlier (**name**, **maxlength**, **size**, and **value**), as well as a number of new HTML5 attributes.

All of these input types are typically displayed as single-line text inputs. But browsers that support them can do some interesting things with the extra semantic information. For example, Safari on iOS uses the input type to provide a keyboard well suited to the entry task, such as the keyboard featuring a "Search" button for the **search** input type or a ".com" button when the input type is set to **url** (Figure 9-5). Browsers usually add a one-click "clear field" icon (usually a little X) in search fields. A supporting browser could check the user's input to see that it is valid, such as making sure text entered in an **email** input follows standard email address structure (in the past, you needed JavaScript for validation). For example, the Opera (Figure 9-6) and Chrome browsers display a warning if the input does not match the expected format.

Not all browsers support the new HTML5 input types or support them in the same way, but the good news is that if the type isn't recognized, the default generic text input is displayed instead, which works perfectly fine. There is no reason not to start using them right away as a progressive enhancement, even if you can't reap the benefits of easy user input and browser (client-side) validation.

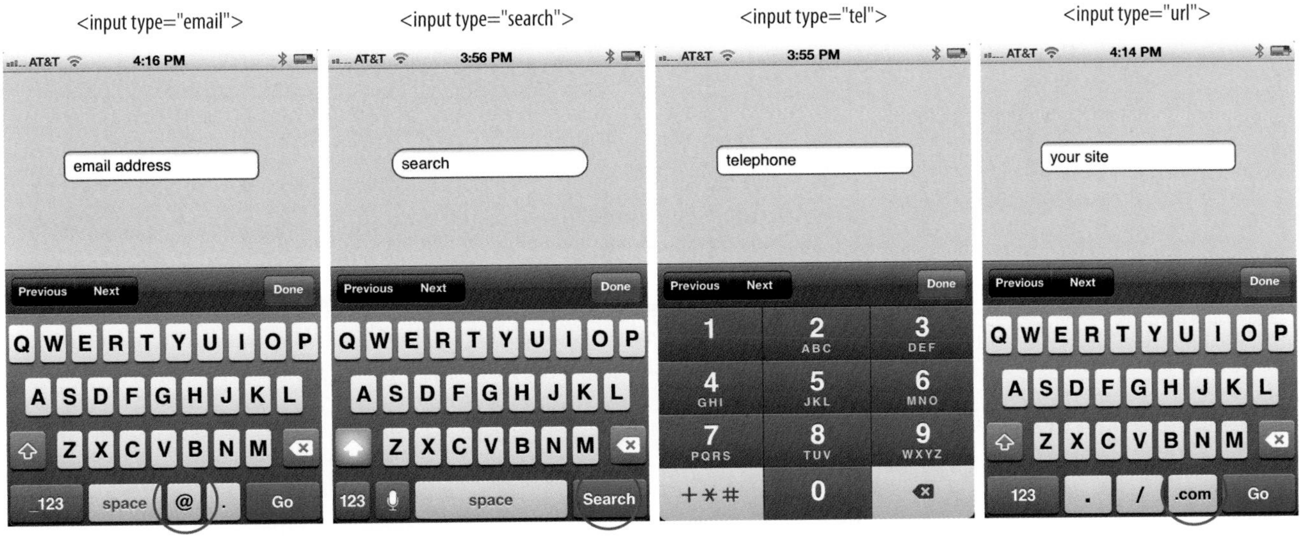

`<input type="email">`   `<input type="search">`   `<input type="tel">`   `<input type="url">`

Figure 9-5. *Safari on iOS provides custom keyboards based on the input type.*

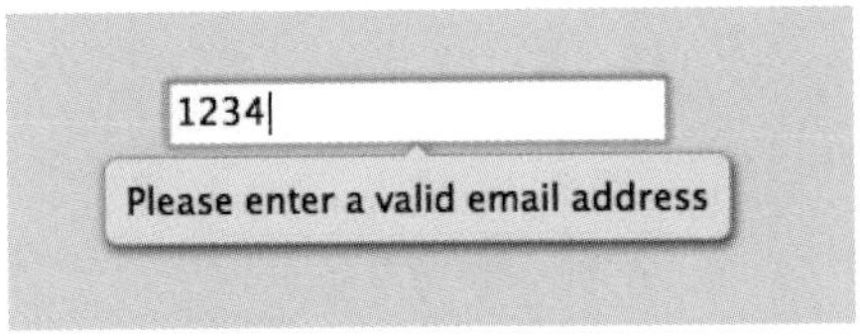

Figure 9-6. *Opera displays a warning when input does not match the expected* `email` *format as part of its client-side validation support.*

The datalist Element

The **datalist** element (new in HTML5) allows the author to provide a drop-down menu of suggested values for any type of text input. It gives the user some shortcuts to select from, but if none are selected, the user can still type in her own text. Within the **datalist** element, suggested values are marked up as option elements. Use the **list** attribute in the **input** element to associate it with the **id** of its respective **datalist**.

In the following example (Figure 9-7), a **datalist** suggests several education level options for a text input.

```
<p>Education completed: <input type="text"
    list="edulevel" name="education">
<datalist id="edulevel">
  <option value="High School">
  <option value="Bachelors Degree">
  <option value="Masters Degree">
  <option value="PhD">
</datalist>
```

As of this writing, only the Opera browser has implemented the **datalist** element. Other browsers will ignore it and present a simple text input, which is a perfectly acceptable fallback. You could also use JavaScript to create **datalist** functionality (i.e., a polyfill).

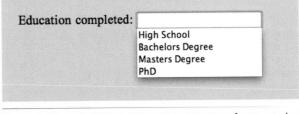

Figure 9-7. *A* datalist *creates a pop-up menu of suggested values for a text entry field.*

Submit and reset buttons

`<input type="submit">`

Submits the form data to the server

`<input type="reset">`

Resets the form controls to their default settings

There are several different kinds of buttons that can be added to web forms. The most fundamental is the submit button. When clicked or tapped, the submit button immediately sends the collected form data to the server for processing. A reset button returns the form controls to the state they were in when the form initially loaded. In other words, resetting the form doesn't simply clear all the fields.

Both submit and reset buttons are added using the **input** element. As mentioned earlier, because these buttons have specific functions that do not include the entry of data, they are the only form control elements that do not require the **name** attribute, although it is OK to add one if you need it.

Submit and reset buttons are straightforward to use. Just place them in the appropriate place in the form, which in most cases is at the very end. By default, the submit button displays with the label "Submit" or "Submit Query" and the reset button is labeled "Reset." Change the text on the button using the **value** attribute, as shown in the reset button in this example (Figure 9-8).

```
<p><input type="submit"> <input type="reset" value="Start over"></p>
```

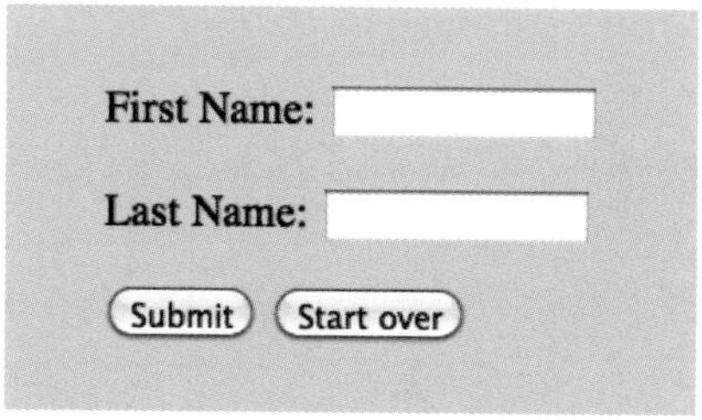

Figure 9-8. Submit and reset buttons.

The reset button is not used in forms as commonly as it used to be. That is because in contemporary form development, we use JavaScript to check the validity of form inputs along the way, so the users get feedback as they go along. With thoughtful design and assistance, fewer users should get to the end of the form and need to reset the whole thing. Still, it is a good function to be aware of.

At this point, you know enough about form markup to start building the questionnaire shown in Figure 9-2. Exercise 9-1 walks you through the first steps.

A Few More Buttons

There are a handful of custom button elements that are a little off the beaten path for beginners, but in the interest of thoroughness, here they are tucked off in a sidebar.

Image buttons

`<input type="image">`

This type of **input** control allows you to replace the submit button with an image of your choice. The image will appear flat, not like a 3-D button. Unfortunately, this type of button has accessibility issues, so be sure to include a carefully chosen **alt** value.

Custom input button

`<input type="button">`

Setting the type of the **input** element to "button" creates a button that can be customized with JavaScript. It has no predefined function on its own, unlike submit and reset buttons.

The button element

`<button>...</button>`

The **button** element is a flexible element for creating custom buttons similar to those created with the **input** element. The content of the button element (text and/or images) is what gets displayed on the button.

For more information on what you can do with the **button** element, read "Push My Button" by Aaron Gustafson at *digital-web.com/articles/push_my_button.*

exercise 9-1 | **Starting the contest form**

Here's the scenario. You are the web designer in charge of creating the entry form for the Forcefield Sneakers "Pimp My Shoes!" Contest. The copy editor has handed you a sketch (Figure 9-9) of the form's content, complete with notes of how some controls should work. There are sticky notes from the programmer with information about the script and variable names you need to use.

Your challenge is to turn the sketch into a functional online form. I've given you a head start by creating a bare-bones document containing the text content and some minimal markup and styles. This document, *contest_entry.html*, is available online at *www.learningwebdesign.com/4e/materials*. The source for the entire finished form is provided in Appendix A if you want to check your work.

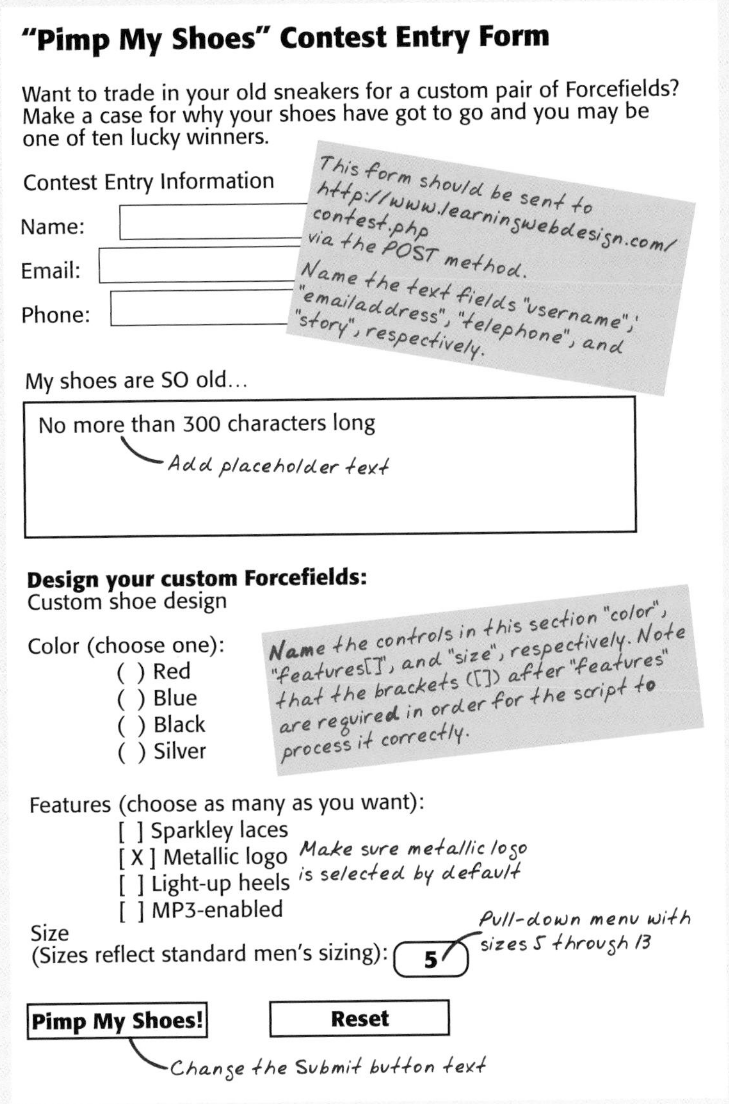

"Pimp My Shoes" Contest Entry Form

Want to trade in your old sneakers for a custom pair of Forcefields? Make a case for why your shoes have got to go and you may be one of ten lucky winners.

Contest Entry Information

This form should be sent to http://www.learningwebdesign.com/contest.php via the POST method.

Name the text fields "username", "emailaddress", "telephone", and "story", respectively.

Name:

Email:

Phone:

My shoes are SO old...

No more than 300 characters long

Add placeholder text

Design your custom Forcefields:
Custom shoe design

Color (choose one):

Name the controls in this section "color", "features[]", and "size", respectively. Note that the brackets ([]) after "features" are required in order for the script to process it correctly.

    ( ) Red
    ( ) Blue
    ( ) Black
    ( ) Silver

Features (choose as many as you want):
    [ ] Sparkley laces
    [X] Metallic logo   *Make sure metallic logo*
    [ ] Light-up heels   *is selected by default*
    [ ] MP3-enabled

Size
(Sizes reflect standard men's sizing):   (5)   *Pull-down menu with sizes 5 through 13*

Pimp My Shoes!   **Reset**

Change the Submit button text

Figure 9-9. A sketch of the contest entry form.

1. Open *contest_entry.html* in a text editor.

2. The first thing we'll do is put everything after the intro paragraph into a **form** element. The programmer has left a note specifying the **action** and the **method** to use for this form. The resulting **form** element should look like this:

```
<form action="http://www.learningwebdesign.com/contest.php"
method="post">
...
</form>
```

3. In this exercise, we'll work on the "Contest Entry Information" section of the form. Start with the first three short text entry form controls that are marked up appropriately as an unordered list. Here's the first one; you insert the other two.

```
<li>Name: <input type="text" name="username"></li>
```

Hints: choose the most appropriate input type for each entry field. Be sure to name the input elements as specified in the programmer's note.

4. Now add a multiline text area for the shoe description on a new line. Because we aren't writing a style sheet for this form, use markup to make it four rows long and 60 characters wide (in the real world, CSS is preferable because it gives you more fine-tuned control).

```
<li>My shoes are SO old...<br>
<textarea name="story" rows="4" cols="60"
maxlength="300" placeholder="No more than 300
characters long"></textarea></li>
```

5. We'll skip the rest of the form for now until we get a few more controls under our belt, but we can add the submit and reset buttons at the end, just before the **</form>** tag. Note that we need to change the text on the submit button.

```
<p><input type="submit" value="Pimp my shoes!">
<input type="reset"></p>
</form>
```

6. Now, save the document and open it in a browser. The parts that are finished should generally match Figure 9-3. If they don't, then you have some more work to do.

Once the document looks right, take it for a spin by entering some information and submitting the form. You should get a response like the one shown in Figure 9-10 (yes, *contest.php* actually works, but sorry, the contest is make-believe).

THANK YOU

Thank you for entering the Forcefield Sneaker "Pimp My Shoe" contest. We have received the following information with your entry:

About you:

Name: Jennifer Robbins
Email Address: jen@oreilly.com
Telephone Number: 555.555.1212
Sad shoe story: My shoes have no soul.

Your shoe design (if you win)

Sorry, we did not receive your information.

Figure 9-10. You should see a response page like this if your form is working.

Radio and checkbox buttons

Both checkbox and radio buttons make it simple for your visitors to choose from a number of provided options. They are similar in that they function like little on/off switches that can be toggled by the user and are added using the **input** element. They serve distinct functions, however.

A form control made up of a collection of radio buttons is appropriate when only one option from the group is permitted—in other words, when the selections are mutually exclusive (such as Yes or No, or Male or Female). When one radio button is "on," all of the others must be "off," sort of the way buttons used to work on old radios: press one button in and the rest pop out.

When checkboxes are grouped together, however, it is possible to select as many or as few from the group as desired. This makes them the right choice for lists in which more than one selection is OK.

Radio buttons

Radio buttons are added to a form using the **input** element with the **type** attribute set to **radio**. Here is the syntax for a minimal radio button:

```
<input type="radio" name="variable" value="value">
```

The **name** attribute is required and plays an important role in binding multiple radio inputs into set. When you give a number of radio button inputs the same **name** value (**age** in the following example), they create a group of mutually exclusive options.

In this example, radio buttons are used as an interface for users to enter their age group (a person can't belong to more than one age group, so radio buttons are the right choice). Figure 9-11 shows how radio buttons are rendered in the browser.

```
<p>How old are you?</p>
<ol>
  <li><input type="radio" name="age" value="under24" checked> under
24</li>
  <li><input type="radio" name="age" value="25-34"> 25 to 34</li>
  <li><input type="radio" name="age" value="35-44"> 35 to 44</li>
  <li><input type="radio" name="age" value="over45"> 45+</li>
</ol>
```

Notice that all of the **input** elements have the same variable name ("age"), but their values are different. Because these are radio buttons, only one button can be checked at a time, and therefore, only one value will be sent to the server for processing when the form is submitted.

NOTE

I have omitted the **fieldset** *and* **label** *elements from the code examples for radio buttons, checkboxes, and menus in order to keep the markup structure as simple and clear as possible. In the upcoming "Form Accessibility Features" section, you will learn why it is important to include them in your markup for all form elements.*

```
<input type="radio">
```
Radio button

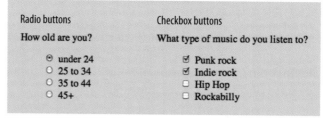

Radio buttons

How old are you?

- ⊙ under 24
- ○ 25 to 34
- ○ 35 to 44
- ○ 45+

Checkbox buttons

What type of music do you listen to?

- ☑ Punk rock
- ☑ Indie rock
- ☐ Hip Hop
- ☐ Rockabilly

Figure 9-11. Radio buttons (left) are appropriate when only one selection is permitted. Checkboxes (right) are best when users may choose any number of choices, from none to all of them.

NOTE

In XHTML syntax, the value of the checked *attribute must be explicitly set to* checked, *as shown in the example.*

```
<input type="radio" name="foo"
checked="checked" />
```

But in HTML syntax, you don't need to write out the value for the checked *attribute. It can be minimized, as shown here:*

```
<input type="radio" name="foo"
checked >
```

You can decide which button is checked when the form loads by adding the **checked** attribute to the **input** element. In this example, the button next to "under 24" will be checked by default (see the note).

Checkbox buttons

```
<input type="checkbox">
```

Checkbox button

Checkboxes are added using the **input** element with its type set to **checkbox**. As with radio buttons, you create groups of checkboxes by assigning them the same **name** value. The difference, as we've already noted, is that more than one checkbox may be checked at a time. The value of every checked button will be sent to the server when the form is submitted. Here is an example of a group of checkbox buttons used to indicate musical interests. Figure 9-11 shows how they look in the browser:

```
<p>What type of music do you listen to?</p>
<ul>
  <li><input type="checkbox" name="genre" value="punk" checked> Punk
rock</li>
  <li><input type="checkbox" name="genre" value="indie" checked> Indie
rock</li>
  <li><input type="checkbox" name="genre" value="hiphop"> Hip Hop</li>
  <li><input type="checkbox" name="genre" value="rockabilly">
Rockabilly</li>
</ul>
```

Checkboxes don't necessarily need to be used in groups, of course. In this example, a single checkbox is used to allow visitors to opt in for special promotions. The value of the control will be passed along to the server only if the user checks the box.

```
<p><input type="checkbox" name="OptIn" value="yes"> Yes, send me news
and special promotions by email.</p>
```

In Exercise 9-2, you'll get a chance to add both radio and checkbox buttons to the contest entry form.

exercise 9-2 | **Adding radio buttons and checkboxes**

The next two questions in the sneaker contest entry form use radio buttons and checkboxes for selecting options. Open the *contest_entry.html* document and follow these steps.

1. In the Custom Shoe Design section, there are lists of color and feature options. The Color options should be radio buttons because shoes can be only one color. Insert a radio button before each option. Follow this example for the remaining color options.

   ```
   <li><input type="radio"
   name="color" value="red">
   Red</li>
   ```

2. Mark up the Features options as you did the Color options, but this time, the **type** should be **checkbox**. Be sure the variable name for each is **features[]**, and that the metallic logo option is preselected, as noted on the sketch.

3. Save the document and check your work by opening it in a browser to make sure it looks right, then submit the form to make sure it's functioning properly.

Menus

Another way to provide a list of choices is to put them in a drop-down or scrolling menu. Menus tend to be more compact than groups of buttons and checkboxes.

You add both drop-down and scrolling menus to a form with the **select** element. Whether the menu pulls down or scrolls is the result of how you specify its size and whether you allow more than one option to be selected. Let's take a look at both menu types.

`<select>...</select>`
Menu control

`<option>...</option>`
An option within a menu

`<optgroup>...</optgroup>`
A logical grouping of options within a menu

Drop-down menus

The **select** element displays as a drop-down menu (also called a pull-down menu) by default when no size is specified or if the **size** attribute is set to 1. In pull-down menus, only one item may be selected. Here's an example (shown in Figure 9-12):

```
<p>What is your favorite 80s band?
<select name="EightiesFave">
    <option>The Cure</option>
    <option>Cocteau Twins</option>
    <option>Tears for Fears</option>
    <option>Thompson Twins</option>
    <option value="EBTG">Everything But the Girl</option>
    <option>Depeche Mode</option>
    <option>The Smiths</option>
    <option>New Order</option>
</select>
</p>
```

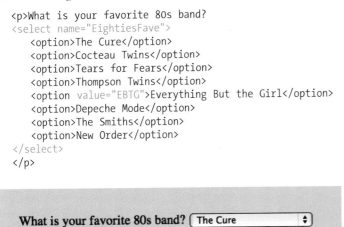

Figure 9-12. Pull-down menus pop open when the user clicks on the arrow or bar.

You can see that the **select** element is just a container for a number of **option** elements. The content of the chosen **option** element is what gets passed to the web application when the form is submitted. If, for some reason, you want to send a different value than what appears in the menu, use the **value** attribute to provide an overriding value. For example, if someone selects "Everything But the Girl" from the sample menu, the form submits the value "EBTG" for the "EightiesFave" variable. For the others, the content between the **option** tags will be sent as the value.

You will make a menu like this one for selecting a shoe size in Exercise 9-3.

Scrolling menus

To make the menu display as a scrolling list, simply specify the number of lines you'd like to be visible using the **size** attribute. This example menu has the same options as the previous one, except it has been set to display as a scrolling list that is six lines tall (Figure 9-13).

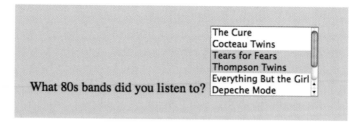

Figure 9-13. A scrolling menu with multiple options selected.

```
<p>What 80s bands did you listen to?
<select name="EightiesBands" size="6" multiple>
    <option>The Cure</option>
    <option>Cocteau Twins</option>
    <option selected>Tears for Fears</option>
    <option selected>Thompson Twins</option>
    <option value="EBTG">Everything But the Girl</option>
    <option>Depeche Mode</option>
    <option>The Smiths</option>
    <option>New Order</option>
</select>
</p>
```

You may notice a few new attributes tucked in there. The **multiple** attribute allows users to make more than one selection from the scrolling list. Note that pull-down menus do not allow multiple selections; when the browser detects the **multiple** attribute, it displays a small scrolling menu automatically by default.

Use the **selected** attribute in an **option** element to make it the default value for the menu control. Selected options are highlighted when the form loads. The **selected** attribute can be used with pull-down menus as well.

Grouping menu options

NOTE

*The **label** attribute in the **option** element is not the same as the **label** element used to improve accessibility (discussed later in this chapter).*

You can use the **optgroup** element to create conceptual groups of options. The required **label** attribute in the **optgroup** element provides the heading for the group. Figure 9-14 shows how option groups are rendered in modern browsers.

```
<select name="icecream" size="7" multiple>
  <optgroup label="traditional">
      <option>vanilla</option>
      <option>chocolate</option>
  </optgroup>
  <optgroup label="fancy">
    <option>Super praline</option>
    <option>Nut surprise</option>
    <option>Candy corn</option>
  </optgroup>
</select>
```

Figure 9-14. Option groups as rendered in a modern browser.

exercise 9-3 | **Adding a menu**

The only other control that needs to be added to the contest entry is a pull-down menu for selecting a shoe size.

1. Insert a **select** menu element with the shoe sizes (5 to 13).

```
<p>Size (sizes reflect men's sizing):
  <select name="size" size="1">
    <option>5</option>
    ...insert more options here...
  </select>
</p>
```

2. Save the document and check it in a browser. You can submit the form, too, to be sure that it's working. You should get the Thank You response page listing all of the information you entered in the form.

Congratulations! You've built your first working web form. In Exercise 9-4, we'll add markup that makes it more accessible to assistive devices. But first, we have a few more control types to cover.

File selection control

Web forms can collect more than just data. They can also be used to transmit external documents from a user's hard drive. For example, a printing company could use a web form to upload artwork for a business card order. A magazine could use a form on its site to collect digital photos for a photo contest.

```
<input type="file">
```
File selection field

The file selection control makes it possible for users to select a document from the hard drive to be submitted with the form data. It is added to the form using our old friend, the **input** element, with its **type** set to **file**.

The markup sample here and Figure 9-15 show a file selection control used for photo submissions.

```
<form action="/client.php" method="POST" enctype="multipart/form-data">
  <label>Send a photo to be used as your online icon
  <em>(optional)</em><br>
  <input type="file" name="photo" size="28"></label>
</form>
```

The file upload widget varies by browser and operating system. It may be a text field with a button to browse the hard drive, as Firefox does (Figure 9-15, top) or it might be just a button, which is how Chrome displays it (bottom).

It is important to note that when a form contains a file selection input element, you must specify the encoding type (**enctype**) of the form as **multipart/form-data** and use the POST method. The **size** attribute in this example sets the character width of the text field (although it could also be controlled with a CSS rule) if the browser displays one.

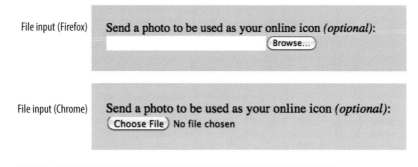

Figure 9-15. A file selection form field.

Hidden controls

<code><input type="hidden"></code>
Hidden control field

There may be times when you need to send information to the form processing application that does not come from the user. In these instances, you can use a hidden form control that sends data when the form is submitted, but is not visible when the form is displayed in a browser.

Hidden controls are added using the **input** element with the **type** set to **hidden**. Its sole purpose is to pass a name/value pair to the server when the form is submitted. In this example, a hidden form element is used to provide the location of the appropriate thank-you document to display when the transaction is complete.

```
<input type="hidden" name="success-link" value="http://www.example.com/
littlechair_thankyou.html">
```

WARNING

It is possible for users to access and manipulate hidden form controls. If you should become a professional web developer, you will learn to program defensively for this sort of thing.

I've worked with forms that have had dozens of hidden controls in the **form** element before getting to the parts that the user actually fills out. This is the kind of information you get from the application programmer, system administrator, or whoever is helping you get your forms processed. If you are using a canned script, be sure to check the accompanying instructions to see if any hidden form variables are required.

Date and time controls (HTML5)

If you've ever booked a hotel or a flight online, you've no doubt used a little calendar widget for choosing the date. Chances are, that little calendar was created using JavaScript. HTML5 introduced six new input types that make date and time selection widgets part of a browser's standard built-in display capabilities (just as they can display checkboxes, pop-up menus, and other widgets today). The date and time pickers are implemented on only a few browsers as of this writing, such as Opera, shown in Figure 9-16, but on non-supporting browsers, the date and time input types display as a perfectly usable text entry field instead.

`<input type="date">`

Date input control

NEW IN HTML5

`<input type="time">`

Time input control

NEW IN HTML5

`<input type="datetime">`

Date/time control with time zone

NEW IN HTML5

`<input type="datetime-local">`

Date/time control with no time zone

NEW IN HTML5

`<input type="month">`

Specifies a month in a year

NEW IN HTML5

`<input type="week">`

Specifies a particular week in a year

NEW IN HTML5

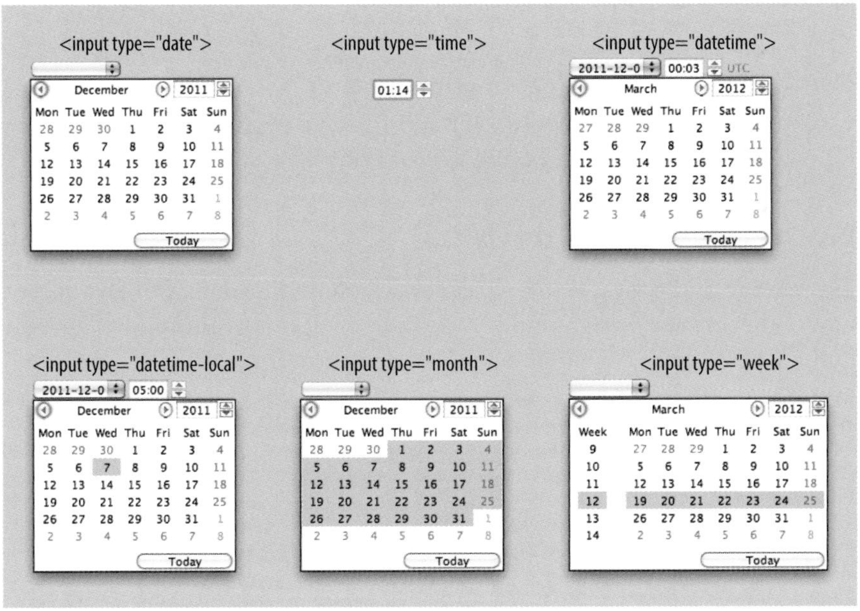

Figure 9-16.   Date and time picker inputs (in Opera 11 on Mac OS X).

The new date- and time-related input types are as follows:

`<input type="date" name="name" value="2004-01-14">`

Creates a date input control, such as a pop-up calendar, for specifying a date (year, month, day). The initial value must be provided in ISO date format (**YYYY-MM-DD**).

`<input type="time" name="name" value="03:13:00">`

Creates a time input control for specifying a time (hour, minute, seconds, fractional sections) with no time zone indicated. The value is provided as **hh:mm:ss**.

```
<input type="datetime" name="name" value="2004-01-14T03:13:00-5:00">
```

Creates a combined date/time input control that includes time zone information. The value is an ISO-formatted date and time with time zone relative to GMT, as we saw for the **time** element in Chapter 5 (**YYYY-MM-DDThh:mm:ssTZD**).

```
<input type="datetime-local" name="name" value="2004-01-14T03:13:00">
```

Creates a combined date/time input control with no time zone information (**YYYY-MM-DDThh:mm:ss**).

```
<input type="month" name="name" value="2004-01">
```

Creates a date input control specifying a particular month in a year (**YYYY-MM**).

```
<input type="week" name="name" value="2004-W2">
```

Creates a date input control for specifying a particular week in a year using an ISO week numbering format (**YYYY-W#**).

Numerical inputs (HTML5)

`<input type="number">`
Number input
NEW IN HTML5

`<input type="range">`
Slider input
NEW IN HTML5

The **number** and **range** input types collect numerical data. For the **number** input, the browser may supply a spinner widget for selecting a specific numerical value (a text input may display in user agents that don't support the input type). The **range** input is typically displayed as a slider (Figure 9-17) that allows the user to select a value within a specified range.

```
<label>Number of guests <input type="number" name="guests" min="1"
max="6"></label>

<label>Satisfaction (0 to 10) <input type="range" name="satis" min="0"
max="10" step="1"></label>
```

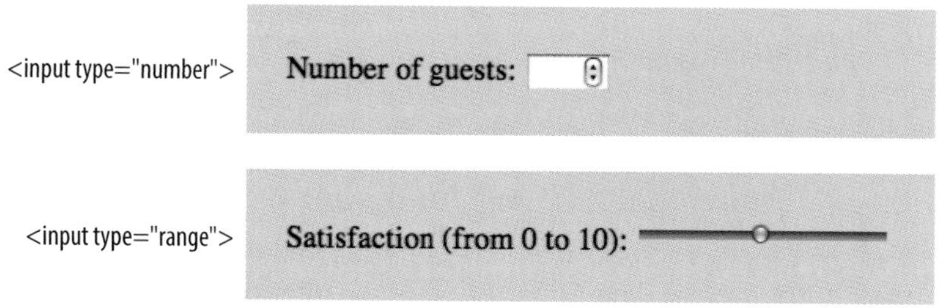

`<input type="number">`   **Number of guests:** [ ][⬍]

`<input type="range">`   **Satisfaction (from 0 to 10):** ───○────

Figure 9-17. The number and range HTML5 input types (in Opera 11 on Mac OS X).

Both the **number** and **range** input types accept the **min** and **max** attributes for specifying the minimum and maximum values allowed for the input (again, the browser could check that the user input complies with the constraint). Both **min** and **max** are optional, and you can also set one without the other.

The **step** attribute allows developers to specify the acceptable increments for numerical input. The default is 1. A value of .5 would permit values 1, 1.5, 2, 2.5, etc.; a value of 100 would permit 100, 200, 300, and so on. You can also set the **step** attribute to **any** to explicitly accept any value increment.

Again, browsers that don't support these new input types display a standard text input field instead, which is a fine fallback.

Color selector (HTML5)

The intent of the color control type is to create a pop-up color picker for visually selecting a color value similar to those used in operating systems or image-editing programs. Values are provided in hexadecimal RGB values (#RRGGBB). Figure 9-18 shows the color picker widget in Opera 11. Non-supporting browsers display the default text input instead.

`<input type="color">`
Color picker
NEW IN HTML5

```
<label>Your favorite color: <input type="color" name="favorite"></label>
```

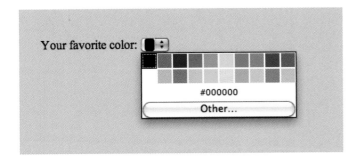

Figure 9-18. The color input type (in Opera 11 on Mac OS X).

That wraps up the form control roundup. Learning how to insert form controls is one part of the forms production process, but any web developer worth her salt will take the time to make sure the form is as accessible as possible. Fortunately, there are a few things we can do in markup to describe the form's structure.

A Few More HTML5 Form Elements

For the sake of completeness, let's look at the remaining form elements that are new in HTML5. As of this writing, they are poorly supported, and are somewhat esoteric anyway, so you may wait a while to add these to your HTML toolbox. We've already covered the **datalist** element for providing suggested values for text inputs. HTML5 also introduced the following elements:

progress

`<progress>...</progress>`

Indicates the state of an ongoing process

`NEW IN HTML5`

The **progress** element gives users feedback on the state of an ongoing process, such as a file download. It can have a specific end value (provided with the **max** attribute) or just indicate that something is happening (such as waiting for a server to respond).

```
Percent downloaded: <progress max="100" name="fave">0</progress>
```

meter

`<meter>...</meter>`

Indicates the state of an ongoing process

`NEW IN HTML5`

meter is similar to **progress**, but it always represents a measurement within a known range of values (also known as a gauge). It has a number of attributes: **min** and **max** indicate the highest and lowest values for the range; **low** and **high** could be used to trigger warnings at undesirable levels; and **optimum** specifies a preferred value. The values would most likely be updated with JavaScript dynamically during the process.

```
<meter min="0" max="100" name="download">50%</meter>
```

output

`<output>...</output>`

Calculated output value

`NEW IN HTML5`

Simply put, the **output** element provides a way to indicate the results of a calculation by a script or program and associate it with inputs that affected the calculation.

keygen

`<keygen>`

Key pair generator

`NEW IN HTML5`

The **keygen** element represents a control for making a key pair (used to ensure privacy). When the form is submitted, the private key is stored locally, and the public key is packaged and sent to the server. Don't worry; I'm a little foggy on what this all means, too. You can read about public-key cryptography (*en.wikipedia.org/wiki/Public-key_cryptography*) and explain it to me when you figure it out.

Form Accessibility Features

It is essential to consider how users without the benefit of visual browsers will be able to understand and navigate through your web forms. The **label**, **fieldset**, and **legend** form elements improve accessibility by making the semantic connections between the components of a form clear. The resulting markup is not only more semantically rich, but there are also more elements available to act as "hooks" for style sheet rules. Everybody wins!

Labels

Although we may see the label "Address" right next to a text field for entering an address in a visual browser, in the source, the label and field input may be separated. The **label** element associates descriptive text with its respective form field. This provides important context for users with speech-based browsers.

Each **label** element is associated with exactly one form control. There are two ways to use it. One method, called implicit association, nests the control and its description within a **label** element. In the following example, **label**s are assigned to individual checkboxes and their related text descriptions. (By the way, this is the way to label radio buttons and checkboxes. You can't assign a label to the entire group.)

```
<ul>
  <li><label><input type="checkbox" name="genre" value="punk"> Punk
rock</label></li>
  <li><label><input type="checkbox" name="genre" value="indie"> Indie
rock</label></li>
  <li><label><input type="checkbox" name="genre" value="hiphop"> Hip
Hop</label></li>
  <li><label><input type="checkbox" name="genre" value="rockabilly">
Rockabilly</label></li>
</ul>
```

The other method, called explicit association, matches the label with the control's **id** reference. The **for** attribute says which control the label is for. This approach is useful when the control is not directly next to its descriptive text in the source. It also offers the potential advantage of keeping the label and the control as two distinct elements, which may come in handy when aligning them with style sheets.

```
<label for="form-login-username">Login account</label>
<input type="text" name="login" id="form-login-username">

<label for="form-login-password">Password</label>
<input type="password" name="password" id="form-login-password">
```

Another advantage to using labels is that users can click or tap anywhere on them to select the form control. Users with touch devices will appreciate the larger tap target.

> **WARNING**
>
> *iOS devices as of this writing do not make implicit labels clickable, so that behavior needs to be created with JavaScript. I know we haven't done any JavaScript yet, but if you are wondering, the fix looks like this:*
>
> ```
> document.getElementsByTagName
> ('label').setAttribute
> ('onclick','');
> ```

> **TIP**
>
> To keep form-related **id**s distinct from other **id**s on the page, consider prefacing them with "form-" as shown in the examples.
>
> Another technique for keeping forms organized is to give the form element an ID name and include it as a prefix in the IDs for the controls it contains as follows:
>
> ```
> <form id="form-login">
>
> <input id="form-login-
> username">
>
> <input id="form-login-
> password">
> ```

fieldset and legend

The **fieldset** element indicates a logical group of form controls. A **fieldset** may also include a **legend** element that provides a caption for the enclosed fields.

Figure 9-19 shows the default rendering of the following example, but you could use style sheets to change the way the **fieldset** and **legend** appear.

```
<fieldset>
  <legend>Mailing List Sign-up</legend>
  <ul>
    <li><label>Add me to your mailing list <input type="radio"
    name="list" value="yes" checked="checked"></label></li>
    <li><label>No thanks <input type="radio" name="list" value="no">
    </label></li>
  </ul>
</fieldset>

<fieldset>
  <legend>Customer Information</legend>
  <ul>
    <li><label>Full name: <input type="text" name="username"></label></
li>
    <li><label>Email: <input type="text" name="email"></label></li>
    <li><label>State: <input type="text" name="state"></label></li>
  </ul>
</fieldset>
```

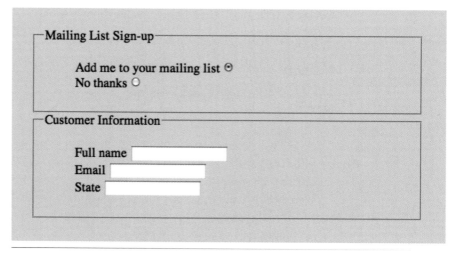

Figure 9-19. The default rendering of fieldsets and legends.

exercise 9-4 | **labels and fieldsets**

Our contest form is working, but we need to label it appropriately and create some **fieldset**s to make it more usable on assistive devices. Once again, open the *contest_entry.html* document and follow these steps.

I like to start with the broad strokes and fill in details later, so we'll begin this exercise by organizing the form controls into fieldsets, and then we'll do all the labeling. You could do it the other way around, and ideally, you'd just mark up the labels and fieldsets as you go along instead of adding them all later.

1. The "Contest Entry Information" at the top of the form is definitely conceptually related, so let's wrap it all in a **fieldset** element. Change the markup of the section title from a paragraph (**p**) to a **legend** for the fieldset.

```
<fieldset>
  <legend>Contest Entry Information</legend>
  <ul>
    <li>Name: <input type="text"
name="username"></li>
    ...
  </ul>
</fieldset>
```

2. Next, group the Color, Features, and Size questions in a big fieldset with the legend "Custom Shoe Design" (the text is there; you just need to change it from a **p** to a **legend**).

```
<h2>Design your custom Forcefields:</h2>
<fieldset>
<legend>Custom Shoe Design</legend>
  Color...
  Features...
  Size...
</fieldset>
```

3. Create another fieldset just for the Color options, again changing the description in a paragraph to a **legend**. Do the same for the Features and Size sections. In the end, you will have three fieldsets contained within the larger "Custom Shoe Design" fieldset. When you are done, save your document and open it in a browser. It should now look very close to the final form shown in Figure 9-2, given the expected browser differences.

```
<fieldset>
<legend>Color <em>(choose one)</em>:</legend>
    <ul>...</ul>
</fieldset>
```

4. OK, now let's get some labels in there. In the Contest Entry Information fieldset, explicitly tie the label to the text input using the **for/id** label method. I've done the first one for you; you do the other three.

```
<li><label for="form-name">Name:</label> <input
type="text" name="username" id="form-name"></li>
```

5. For the radio and checkbox buttons, wrap the **label** element around the **input** and its value label. In this way, the button will be selected when the user clicks or taps anywhere inside the label element. Here is the first one; you do the other seven.

```
<li><label><input type="radio" name="color"
value="red"> Red</label></li>
```

Save your document, and you're done! Labels don't have any effect on how the form looks by default, but you can feel good about the added semantic value you've added and maybe even use them to apply styles at another time.

Form Layout and Design

I can't close this chapter without saying a few words about form design, even though this chapter is about markup, not presentation.

Usable forms

A poorly designed form can ruin a user's experience on your site and negatively impact your business goals. Badly designed forms mean lost customers, so it is critical to get it right—both on the desktop and for small-screen devices with their special requirements. You want the path to a purchase or other action to be as frictionless as possible.

The topic of good web form design is a rich one that could fill a book in itself. In fact, there is such a book: *Web Form Design* (Rosenfeld Media) by web form expert Luke Wroblewski, and I recommend it highly. Luke's subsequent book, *Mobile First* (A Book Apart), includes tips for how to format forms in a mobile context. You can browse over a hundred articles about forms on his site here: *www.lukew.com/ff?tag=forms*.

Here I'll offer just a very small sampling of tips from *Web Form Design* to get you started, but the whole book is worth a read.

Avoid unnecessary questions.

Help your users get through your form as easily as possible by not including questions that are not absolutely necessary to the task at hand. Extra questions, in addition to slowing things down, may make a user wary of your motivations for asking. If you have another way of getting the information (for example, the type of credit card can be determined from the first four numbers of the account), then use alternative means and don't put the burden on the user. If there is information that might be nice to have but is not required, consider asking at a later time, after the form has been submitted and you have built a relationship with the user.

Consider impact of label placement.

The position of the label relative to the input affects the time it takes to fill out the form. The less the user's eye needs to bounce around the page, the quicker the form completion. Putting the labels above their respective fields creates a single alignment for faster scans and completion, particularly when asking for familiar information (username, address, etc.). Top-positioned labels can also accommodate labels of varying lengths and work best on narrow, small-screen devices. They do result in a longer form, however, so if vertical space is a concern, you can position the labels to the left of the inputs. Left alignment of labels results in the slowest form completion, but it may be appropriate if you want the user to slow down or be able to scan and consider the types of information required in the form.

Choose input types carefully.

As you've seen in this chapter, there are quite a few input types to choose from, and sometimes it's not easy to decide which one to use. For example, a list of options could be presented as a pull-down menu or a number of choices with checkboxes. Weigh the pros and cons of each control type carefully, and follow up with user testing.

Group related inputs.

It is easier to parse the many fields, menus, and buttons in a form if they are visually grouped by related topic. For example, a user's contact information could be presented in a compact group so that five or six inputs are perceived as one unit. Usually, all you need is a very subtle indication, such as a fine horizontal rule and some extra space. Don't overdo it.

Clarify primary and secondary actions.

The primary action at the end of the form is usually some form of submit button ("Buy," "Register," etc.) that signals the completion of the form and the readiness to move forward. You want that button to be visually dominant and easy to find (aligning it along the main axis of the form is helpful as well). Secondary actions tend to take you a step back, such as clearing or resetting the form. If you must include a secondary action, make sure that it is styled to look different and less important than the primary action. It is also a good idea to provide an opportunity to undo the action.

Styling Forms

As we've seen in this chapter, the default rendering of form markup is not up to par with the quality we see on most professional web forms today. As for other elements, you can use style sheets to create a clean form layout as well as change the appearance of most form controls. Something as simple as nice alignment and a look that is consistent with the rest of your site can go a long way toward improving the impression you make on a user.

Keep in mind that form widgets are drawn by the browser and are informed by operating system conventions. However, you can still apply dimensions, margins, fonts, colors, borders, and background effects to form elements such as text inputs, select menus, textareas, fieldsets, labels, and legends. Just be sure to test in a variety of browsers to check for unpleasant surprises. Chapter 18, CSS Techniques, in Part III, lists some specific techniques once you have more experience with CSS. For more help, a web search for "CSS for forms" will turn up a number of tutorials.

Test Yourself

Ready to put your web form know-how to the test? Here are a few questions to make sure you've gotten the basics.

1. Decide whether each of these forms should be sent via the GET or POST method:

   a. A form for accessing your bank account online   _____

   b. A form for sending t-shirt artwork to the printer   _____

   c. A form for searching archived articles   _____

   d. A form for collecting long essay entries   _____

2. Which form control element is best suited for the following tasks? When the answer is "input," be sure to also include the type. Some tasks may have more than one correct answer.

   a. Choose your astrological sign from 12 signs.

   b. Indicate whether you have a history of heart disease (yes or no).

   c. Write up a book review.

   d. Select your favorite ice cream flavors from a list of eight flavors.

   e. Select your favorite ice cream flavors from a list of 25 flavors.

3. Each of these markup examples contains an error. Can you spot what it is?

   a. `<input name="country" value="Your country here.">`

   b. `<checkbox name="color" value="teal">`

   c.
   ```
   <select name="popsicle">
      <option value="orange">
      <option value="grape">
      <option value="cherry">
   </select>
   ```

   d. `<input type="password">`

   e. `<textarea name="essay" height="6" width="100">Your story.</textarea>`

Element Review: Forms

We covered this impressive list of elements and attributes related to forms in this chapter. Elements marked with (HTML5) are new in the HTML5 specification.

Element and attributes	Description
`button`	Generic input button
`name="text"`	Supplies a unique variable name for the control
`type="submit｜reset｜button"`	The type of custom button
`value="text"`	Specifies the value to be sent to the server
`datalist` *[HTML5]*	Provides a list of options for text inputs
`fieldset`	Groups related controls and labels
`form`	Form element
`action="url"`	Location of forms processing program (*required*)
`method="get｜post"`	The method used to submit the form data
`enctype="content type"`	The encoding method, generally either **application/x-www-form-urlencoded** (default) or **multipart/form-data**

Element and attributes	Description
input	Creates a variety of controls, based on the **type** value
autofocus	Indicates the control should be ready for input when the document loads

`type="submit|reset|button|text`
`|password|checkbox|radio|image`
`|file|hidden|email|tel|search|`
`url|date|time|datetime|dateti`
`me-local|month|week|number|rang-`
`e|color "`
	The type of input

disabled	Disables the input so it cannot be selected
`form="form id value"`	Associates the control with a specified form
See Table 9-1 for a full list of attributes associated with each input type.	
keygen *[HTML5]*	Generates key pairs for secure transaction certificates
autofocus	Indicates the control should be highlighted and ready for input when the document loads
`challenge="challenge string"`	Provides a challenge string to be submitted with the key
disabled	Disables the control so it cannot be selected
`form="form id value"`	Associates the control with a specified form
`keytype="keyword"`	Identifies the type of key to be generated (e.g., **rsa** or **ec**)
`name="text"`	Gives control an identifying name
label	Attaches information to controls
`for="text"`	Identifies the associated control by its **id** reference
`form="form id value"`	Associates the control with a specified form
legend	Assigns a caption to a **fieldset**
meter *[HTML5]*	Represents a fractional value within a known range
`form="form id value"`	Associates the control with a specified form
`high="number"`	Indicates the range that is considered "high" for the gauge
`low="number"`	Indicates the range that is considered "low" for the gauge
`max="number"`	Specifies the highest value for the range
`min="number"`	Specifies the lowest value for the range
`optimum="number"`	Indicates the number considered to be "optimum"
`value="number"`	Specifies the actual or measured value
optgroup	Defines a group of options
disabled	Disables the **optgroup** so it cannot be selected
`label="text"`	Supplies label for a group of options
option	An option within a select menu control
disabled	Disables the **option** so it cannot be selected
`label="text"`	Supplies an alternate label for the option
selected	Preselects the option
`value="text"`	Supplies an alternate value for the option

Element and attributes	Description
output *[HTML5]*	Represents the results of a calculation
for="*text*"	Creates relationship between output and another element
form="*form id value*"	Associates the control with a specified form
name="*text*"	Supplies a unique variable name for the control
progress *[HTML5]*	Represents the completion progress of a task (can be used even if the maximum value of the task is not known)
form="*form id value*"	Associates the control with a specified form
max="*number*"	Specifies the total value or final size of the task
value="*number*"	Specifies how much of the task has been completed
select	Pull-down menu or scrolling list
autofocus	Indicates the control should be highlighted and ready for input when the document loads
disabled	Indicates the control is nonfunctional; can be activated with a script
form="*form id value*"	Associates the control with a specified form
multiple	Allows multiple selections in a scrolling list
name="*text*"	Supplies a unique variable name for the control
readonly	Makes the control unalterable by the user
required	Indicates the user input is required for this control
size="*number*"	The height of the scrolling list in text lines
textarea	Multiline text entry field
autofocus	Indicates the control should be highlighted and ready for input when the document loads
cols="*number*"	The width of the text area in characters
dirname="*text*"	Allows text directionality to be specified
disabled	Disables the control so it cannot be selected
form="*form id value*"	Associates the control with a specified form
maxlength="*text*"	Specifies the maximum number of characters the user can enter
name="*text*"	Supplies a unique variable name for the control
placeholder="*text*"	Provides a short hint to help the user enter the correct data
readonly	Makes the control unalterable by the user
required	Indicates user input is required for this control
rows="*number*"	The height of the text area in text lines
wrap="hard|soft"	Controls whether line breaks in the text input are returned in the data; **hard** preserves line breaks, while **soft** does not

Table 9-1. Available attributes for each input type

	submit	reset	button	text	password	checkbox	radio	image	file	hidden
accept									•	
alt								•		
checked						•	•			
disabled	•	•	•	•	•	•	•	•	•	•
maxlength				•	•				•	
name	•	•	•	•	•	•	•	•	•	•
readonly				•	•	•	•		•	
size				•	•				•	
src								•		
value	•	•	•	•	•	•	•		•	•
HTML5-only										
autocomplete				•	•					
autofocus	•	•	•	•	•	•	•	•	•	
form	•	•	•	•	•	•	•	•	•	•
formaction	•							•		
formenctype	•							•		
formmethod	•							•		
formnovalidate	•							•		
formtarget	•							•		
height								•		
list				•						
max										
min										
multiple									•	
pattern				•	•					
placeholder				•	•					
required				•	•	•	•		•	
step										
width								•		

	email	telephone, search, url	number	range	date, time, datetime, datetime-local, month, week	color
accept						
alt						
checked						
disabled	•	•	•	•	•	•
maxlength	•	•				
name	•	•	•	•	•	•
readonly	•	•	•		•	
size	•	•				
src						
value	•	•	•	•	•	•
HTML5-only						
autocomplete	•	•	•	•	•	•
autofocus	•	•	•	•	•	•
form	•	•	•	•	•	•
formaction						
formenctype						
formmethod						
formnovalidate						
formtarget						
height						
list	•	•	•	•	•	•
max			•	•	•	
min			•	•	•	
multiple	•					
pattern	•	•				
placeholder	•	•				
required	•	•	•		•	
step			•	•	•	
width						

CHAPTER 10

WHAT'S UP, HTML5?

We've been using HTML5 elements in the past several chapters, but there is a lot more to the HTML5 specification than new markup possibilities (although that is an important part). HTML5 is actually a bundle of new methods for accomplishing tasks that previously required special programming or proprietary plug-in technology such as Flash or Silverlight. It offers a standardized, open source way to put audio, video, and interactive elements on the page as well as the ability to store data locally, work offline, take advantage of location information, and more. With HTML5 for common tasks, developers can rely on built-in browser capabilities and not need to reinvent the wheel for every application.

HTML5 offers so many promising possibilities, in fact, that it has become something of a buzzword with connotations far beyond the spec itself. When marketers and journalists use the term "HTML5," they are sometimes referring to CSS3 techniques or any new web technology that isn't Flash. In this chapter you'll learn what is actually included in the spec, and you can join the rest of us in being slightly irked when the HTML5 label is applied incorrectly. The important thing, however, is that mainstream awareness of web standards is certainly a win and makes our job easier when communicating with clients.

Of course, with any spec in development, browser support is uneven at best. There are some features that can be used right away and some that aren't quite ready for prime time. But this time around, instead of waiting for the entire spec to be "done," browsers are implementing one feature at a time, and developers are encouraged to begin using them (see the "Tracking Browser Support" sidebar). I should also mention that the HTML5 spec is evolving rapidly and parts are likely to have changed by the time you are reading this. I'll do my best to give you a good overview, and you can decide which features to research and follow up on your own.

Much of what's new in HTML5 requires advanced web development skills, so it is unlikely you'll use them right away (if ever), but as always, I think it is beneficial to everyone to have a basic familiarity with what can be done.

IN THIS CHAPTER

What HTML5 is and *isn't*

A brief history of HTML

New elements and attributes

HTML5 APIs

Adding video and audio

The canvas element

And "basic familiarity" is what I'm aiming at with this chapter. For more in-depth discussions of HTML5 features, I recommend the following books:

- *HTML5: Up and Running* by Mark Pilgrim (O'Reilly and Google Press)
- *Introducing HTML5* by Bruce Lawson and Remy Sharp (New Riders)

I feel it's only fair to warn you that this chapter is the cod liver oil of this book. Not pleasant to get down, but good for you. An understanding of the big picture and the context of why we do things the way we do is something any budding web designer should have.

A Funny Thing Happened on the Way to XHTML 2

Understanding where we've been provides useful context for where we are going, so let's kick this off with a quick history lesson. We'll start at the very beginning.

A "don't blink or you'll miss it" history of HTML

The story of HTML, from Tim Berners-Lee's initial draft in 1991 to the HTML5 standard in development today, is both fascinating and tumultuous. Early versions of HTML (HTML+ in 1994 and HTML 2.0 in 1995) built on Tim's early work with the intent of making it a viable publishing option. But when the World Wide Web (as it was adorably called back in the day) took the world by storm, browser developers, most notably Mosaic Netscape and later Microsoft Internet Explorer, didn't wait for any stinkin' standards. They gave the people what they wanted by creating a slew of browser-specific elements for improving the look of pages on their respective browsers. This divisive one-upping is what has come to be known as the Browser Wars. As a result, it became common in the late 1990s to create two separate versions of a site that targeted each of the Big Two browsers.

In 1996, the newly formed W3C put a stake in the ground and released its first Recommendation: HTML 3.2. It is a snapshot of all the HTML elements in common use at the time, and includes many presentational extensions to HTML that were the result of the Netscape/IE feud and the lack of a style sheet alternative. HTML 4.0 (1998) and HTML 4.01 (the slight revision that superseded it in 1999) aimed to get HTML back on track by emphasizing the separation of structure and presentation and improving accessibility. All matters of presentation were handed over to the newly minted Cascading Style Sheets standard that was gaining support.

Tracking Browser Support

There are several nice resources out there to help you know which HTML5 features are ready to use. Most show support for CSS properties and selectors as well.

- When Can I Use… (*caniuse.com*)
- HTML5 Please (*html5please.com*)
- "Comparison of Layout Engines (HTML5)" on Wikipedia (*en. wikipedia.org/wiki/Comparison_ of_layout_engines_(HTML_5)*)

NOTE

For a detailed history of the beginnings of the World Wide Web and HTML, read David Raggett's account from his book Raggett on HTML4 (Addison-Wesley), available on the W3C site (www.w3.org/People/Raggett/book4/ch02.html).

Enter XHTML

Around the same time that HTML 4.01 was in development, folks at the W3C became aware that one limited markup language wasn't going to cut it for describing all the sorts of information (chemical notation, mathematical equations, multimedia presentations, financial information, and so on) that might be shared over the Web. Their solution: XML (eXtensible Markup Language), a metalanguage for creating markup languages. XML was a simplification of SGML (Standardized Generalized Markup Language), the big kahuna of metalanguages that Tim Berners-Lee used to create his original HTML application. But SGML itself proved to be more complex than the Web required.

The W3C had a vision of an XML-based Web with many specialized markup languages working together—even within a single document. Of course, to pull that off, everyone would have to mark up documents very carefully, strictly abiding by XML syntax, to rule out potential confusion.

Their first step was to rewrite HTML according to the rules of XML so that it could play well with others. The result is XHTML (eXtensible HTML). The first version, XHTML 1.0, is nearly identical to HTML 4.01, sharing the same elements and attributes, but with stricter requirements for how markup must be done (see the "XHTML Markup Requirements" sidebar).

HTML 4.01, along with XHTML 1.0, its stricter XML-based sibling, became the cornerstone of the web standards movement (see the sidebar "The Web Standards Project"). They are still the most thoroughly and consistently supported standards as of this writing (although HTML5 is quickly gaining steam).

But the W3C didn't stop there. With a vision of an XML-based Web in mind, they began work on XHTML 2.0, an even bolder attempt to make things work "right" than HTML 4.01 had been. The problem was that it was not backward-compatible with old standards and browser behavior. The writing and approval process dragged on for years with no

XHTML Markup Requirements

- Element and attribute names must be lowercase. In HTML, element and attribute names are not case-sensitive.
- All elements must be closed (terminated). Empty elements are closed by adding a slash before the closing bracket (for example, `<br/>`).
- Attribute values must be in quotation marks. Single or double quotation marks are acceptable as long as they are used consistently. Furthermore, there should be no extra whitespace (character spaces or line returns) before or after the attribute value inside the quotation marks.
- All attributes must have explicit attribute values. XML (and therefore XHTML) does not support attribute minimization, the SGML practice in which certain attributes can be reduced to just the attribute value. So, while in HTML you can write `checked` to indicate that a form button be checked when the form loads, in XHTML you need to explicitly write out `checked="checked"`.
- Proper nesting of elements is strictly enforced. Some elements have new nesting restrictions.
- Special characters must always be represented by character entities (e.g., `&amp;` for the & symbol).
- Use `id` instead of `name` as an identifier.
- Scripts must be contained in a CDATA section so they will be treated as simple text characters and not parsed as XML markup. Here is an example of the syntax:

```
<script type="type/javascript">
  // <![CDATA[
  ... JavaScript goes here...
  // ]]>
</script>
```

The Web Standards Project

In 1998, at the height of the browser wars, a grassroots coalition called the Web Standards Project (WaSP for short) began to put pressure on browser creators (primarily Netscape and Microsoft at the time) to start sticking to the open standards as documented by the W3C. Not stopping there, it educated the web developer community on the many benefits of developing with standards. Its efforts revolutionized the way sites are created and supported. Now browsers (even Microsoft) brag of standards support while continuing to innovate. You can read its mission statement, history, and descriptions of its current efforts on the WaSP site (*webstandards.org*).

browser implementation. Without browser implementation, XHTML 2.0 was stuck.

Hello HTML5!

HTML5 aims to make HTML more useful for creating web applications.

Meanwhile...

In 2004, members of Apple, Mozilla, and Opera formed the Web Hypertext Application Technology Working Group (WHATWG, *whatwg.org*), separate from the W3C. The goal of the WHATWG was to further the development of HTML to meet new demands in a way that was consistent with real-world authoring practices and browser behavior (in contrast to the start-from-scratch ideal that XHTML 2.0 described). Their initial documents, Web Applications 1.0 and Web Forms 1.0, were rolled together into HTML5, which is still in development under the guidance of an editor, Ian Hickson (currently of Google).

The W3C eventually established its own HTML5 Working Group (also led by Hickson) based on the work done by the WHATWG. As of this writing, work on the HTML5 specification is happening in both organizations in tandem, sometimes with conflicting results. It is not yet a formal Recommendation as of this writing, but that isn't stopping browsers from implementing it a little at a time.

NOTE

The WHATWG maintains what it calls the HTML "Living Standard" (meaning the group isn't giving it a version number) at www.whatwg.org. It is nearly identical to HTML5, but it includes a few extra elements and attributes that the W3C isn't quite ready to adopt, and it has a slightly different lineup of APIs.

And XHTML 2.0? At the end of 2009, the W3C officially put it out of its misery, pulling the plug on the working group and putting its resources and efforts into HTML5.

So that's how we got here, and it's a whole lot of prelude to the meat of this chapter, which of course is the new features that HTML5 offers. I also encourage you to read the sidebar "HTML5 Fun Facts" for more juicy information on the specification itself. In this section, I'll introduce what's new in HTML5, including:

- A new DOCTYPE

- New elements and attributes

- Obsolete 4.01 elements

- APIs

HTML5 Fun Facts

HTML5 both builds on previous versions of HTML and introduces some significant departures. Here are some interesting tidbits about the HTML5 specification itself.

- HTML5 is based on HTML 4.01 Strict, the version of HTML that did not include any presentation-based or other deprecated elements and attributes. That means the vast majority of HTML5 is made up of the same elements we've been using for years, and browsers know what to do with them.

- HTML5 does not use a DTD (Document Type Definition), which is a document that defines all of the elements and attributes in a markup language. It is the way you document a language in SGML, and if you'll remember, HTML was originally crafted according to the rules of SGML. HTML 4.01 was defined by three separate DTDs: Transitional (including legacy elements that were marked as "deprecated," or soon to be obsolete), Strict (deprecated features stripped out, as noted earlier), and Frameset (for documents broken into individually scrolling frames, a technique that is now considered obsolete).

- HTML5 is the first HTML specification that includes detailed instructions for how browsers should handle malformed and legacy markup. It bases the instructions on legacy browser behavior, but for once, there is a standard protocol for browser makers to follow when browsers encounter incorrect or non-standard markup.

- HTML5 can also be written according to the stricter syntax of XML (called the XML serialization of HTML5). Some developers have come to prefer the tidiness of well-formed XHTML (lowercase element names, quoted attribute values, closing all elements, and so on), so that way of writing is still an option, although not required. In edge cases, an HTML5 document may be required to be served as XML in order to work with other XML applications, in which case it can use the XML syntax and be ready to go.

- In addition to markup, HTML5 defines a number of APIs (Application Programming Interfaces). APIs make it easier to communicate with web-based applications. They also move some common processes (such as audio and video players) into native browser functionality.

In the Markup Department

We'll start with a look at the markup aspects of HTML5, and then we'll move on to the APIs.

A minimal DOCTYPE

As we saw in Chapter 4, HTML documents should begin with a Document Type Declaration (DOCTYPE declaration) that identifies which version of HTML the document follows. The HTML5 declaration is short and sweet:

```
<!DOCTYPE html>
```

Compare that to a declaration for a Strict HTML 4.01 document:

```
<!DOCTYPE HTML PUBLIC "-//W3C//DTD HTML 4.01//EN"
    "http://www.w3.org/TR/HTML4.01/strict.dtd">
```

Why so complicated? In HTML 4.01 and XHTML 1.0 and 1.1, the declaration must point to the public DTD (Document Type Definition), a document that defines all of the elements in a markup language as well as the rules for using them. HTML 4.01 was defined by three separate DTDs: Transitional (including legacy elements such as font and attributes such as **align** that were marked as "deprecated," or soon to be obsolete), Strict (deprecated features stripped out), and Frameset (for documents broken into individually scrolling frames, a technique that is now considered obsolete). HTML5 does not have a DTD, which is why we have the simple DOCTYPE declaration. DTDs

DTDs are a remnant of SGML and proved to be less helpful on the Web than originally thought, so the authors of HTML5 simply didn't use one.

Validators—software that checks that all the markup in a document is correct (see note)—use the DOCTYPE declaration to make sure the document abides by the rules of the specification it claims to follow. The sidebar "HTML DOCTYPES" lists all declarations in common use, should you need to write documents in HTML 4.01 or XHTML 1.0.

NOTE

To check whether your HTML document is valid, use the online validator at the W3C (validator.w3.org). An HTML5-specific validator is also available at html5.validator.nu. There is also a validator built into Adobe Dreamweaver that allows you to check your document against various specs as you work.

HTML DOCTYPES

The following lists all of the DOCTYPE declarations in common use.

HTML5

```
<!DOCTYPE html>
```

HTML 4.01 Transitional

The Transitional DTD includes deprecated elements and attributes:

```
<!DOCTYPE HTML PUBLIC "-//W3C//DTD HTML 4.01 Transitional//EN"
"http://www.w3.org/TR/HTML4.01/loose.dtd">
```

HTML 4.01 Strict

The Strict DTD omits all deprecated elements and attributes:

```
<!DOCTYPE HTML PUBLIC "-//W3C//DTD HTML 4.01//EN"
"http://www.w3.org/TR/HTML4.01/strict.dtd">
```

HTML 4.01 Frameset

If your document contains frames—that is, it uses **frameset** instead of **body** for its content—then identify the Frameset DTD:

```
<!DOCTYPE HTML PUBLIC "-//W3C//DTD HTML 4.01 Frameset//EN"
"http://www.w3.org/TR/HTML4.01/frameset.dtd">
```

XHTML 1.0 Strict

The same as HTML 4.01 Strict, but reformulated according to the syntax rules of XML:

```
<!DOCTYPE html PUBLIC "-//W3C//DTD XHTML 1.0 Strict//EN"
"http://www.w3.org/TR/xhtml1/DTD/xhtml1-strict.dtd">
```

XHTML 1.0 Transitional

The same as HTML 4.01 Transitional, but reformulated according to the syntax rules of XML:

```
<!DOCTYPE html PUBLIC "-//W3C//DTD XHTML 1.0 Transitional//EN"
"http://www.w3.org/TR/xhtml1/DTD/xhtml1-transitional.dtd">
```

XHTML 1.0 Frameset

The same as HTML 4.01 Frameset, but reformulated according to the syntax rules of XML:

```
<!DOCTYPE html PUBLIC "-//W3C//DTD XHTML 1.0 Frameset//EN"
"http://www.w3.org/TR/xhtml1/DTD/xhtml1-frameset.dtd">
```

Elements and attributes

HTML5 introduced a number of new elements. You'll find them sprinkled throughout this book, but Table 10-1 lists them all in one place.

NOTE

For a detailed list of all the ways HTML5 differs from HTML 4.01, see the W3C official document at www. w3.org/TR/html5-diff/.

Table 10-1. New elements in HTML5

article	datalist	header	output	source
aside	details	hgroup	progress	summary
audio	embed	keygen	rp	time
bdi	figcaption	mark	rt	track
canvas	figure	meter	ruby	video
command	footer	nav	section	wbr

New form input types

We covered the new form input control types in Chapter 9, but here they are at a glance: **color**, **date**, **datetime**, **datetime-local**, **email**, **month**, **number**, **range**, **search**, **tel**, **time**, **url**, and **week**.

New global attributes

Global attributes are attributes that can be applied to any element. The number of global attributes was expanded in HTML5, and many of them are brand new (as noted in Table 10-2). The W3C is still adding and removing attributes as of this writing, so it's worth checking in with the spec for the latest (*dev.w3.org/html5/spec/global-attributes.html#global-attributes*).

Table 10-2. Global attributes in HTML5

Attribute	Values	Description
accesskey	Single text character	Assigns an access key (shortcut key command) to the link. Access keys are also used for form fields. Users may access the element by pressing Alt-<*key*> (PC) or Ctrl-<*key*> (Mac).
aria-*	One of the standardized state or property keywords in WAI-ARIA (*www.w3.org/TR/wai-aria/states_and_properties*)	WAI-ARIA (Accessibile Rich Internet Applications) defines a way to make web content and applications more accessible to users with assistive devices. HTML5 allows any of the ARIA properties and roles to be added to elements. For example, a **div** used for a pop-up menu could include the attribute **aria-haspopup** to make that property clear to a user without a visual browser. See also the related **role** global attribute.
class	Text string	Assigns one or more classification names to the element.
contenteditable	**true** | **false**	NEW IN HTML5 Indicates the user can edit the element. This attribute is already well supported in current browser versions.

Table 10-2. Global attributes in HTML5

Attribute	Values	Description
contextmenu	**id** of the **menu** element	**NEW IN HTML5** Specifies a context menu that applies to the element. The context menu must be requested by the user, for example, by a right-click.
data-*	Text string or numerical data	**NEW IN HTML5** Enables authors to create custom data-related attributes (the "*" is a symbol that means "anything"), for example, **data-length**, **data-duration**, **data-speed**, etc. so that the data can be used by a custom application or scripts.
dir	**ltr** | **rtl**	Specifies the direction of the element ("left to right" or "right to left").
draggable	**true** | **false**	**NEW IN HTML5** A **true** value indicates the element is draggable, meaning it can be moved by clicking and holding on it, then moving it to a new position in the window.
dropzone	**copy** | **link** | **move** | **s:text/plain** | **f:***file-type* (for example, **f:image/jpg**)	**NEW IN HTML5** Indicates the element can accept dragged and dropped text or file data. The values are a space-separated list that includes what type of data it accepts (**s:text/plain** for text strings; **f:***file-type* for file types) and a keyword that indicates what to do with the dropped content: **copy** results in a copy of the dragged data; **move** moves it to the new location; and **link** results in a link to the original data.
hidden	No value for HTML documents In XHTML, set a value **hidden="hidden"**	**NEW IN HTML5** Prevents the element and its descendants from being rendered in the user agent (browser). Any scripts or form controls in hidden sections will still execute, but they will not be presented to the user.
id	Text string (may not begin with an number)	Assigns a unique identifying name to the element.
lang	Two-letter language code (see *www.loc.gov/standards/iso639-2/php/code_list.php*)	Specifies the language for the element by its language code.
role	One of the standard role keywords in WAI-ARIA (see *www.w3.org/TR/wai-aria/roles*)	**NEW IN HTML5** Assigns one of the standardized WAI-ARIA roles to an element to make its purpose clearer to users with disabilities. For example, a **div** with contents that will display as a pop-up menu on visual browsers could be marked with **role="menu"** for clarity on screen readers.
spellcheck	**true** | **false**	**NEW IN HTML5** Indicates the element is to have its spelling and grammar checked.
style	Semicolon-separated list of style rules (**property: value** pairs)	Associates style information with an element. For example: `<h1 style="color: red; border: 1px solid">Heading</h1>`
tabindex	Number	Specifies the position of the current element in the tabbing order for the current document. The value must be between 0 and 32,767. It is used for tabbing through links on a page or fields in a form and is useful for assistive browsing devices. A value of −1 is allowable to remove elements from the tabbing flow and make them focusable only by JavaScript.
title	Text string	Provides a title or advisory information about the element, typically displayed as a tooltip.

Obsolete HTML 4.01 Markup

HTML5 also declared a number of elements in HTML 4.01 to be "obsolete" because they are presentational, antiquated, or poorly supported (Table 10-3). If you use them, browsers will support them, but I strongly recommend leaving them in the dust.

Table 10-3. HTML 4 elements that are now obsolete in HTML5

acronym	dir	noframes
applet	font	strike
basefont	frame	tt
big	frameset	
center	isindex	

Are you still with me? I know, this stuff gets pretty dry. That's why I've included Figure 10-1. It has nothing at all to do with HTML5, but I thought we could all use a little breather before taking on APIs.

Figure 10-1. This adorable baby red panda has nothing to do with HTML5. (Photo by Tara Menne.)

Meet the APIs

HTML specifications prior to HTML5 included only documentation of the elements, attributes, and values permitted in the language. That's fine for simple text documents, but the creators of HTML5 had their minds set on making it easier to create web-based applications that require scripting and programming. For that reason, HTML5 also defines a number of new APIs for making it easier to communicate with an application.

An API (Application Programming Interface) is a documented set of commands, data names, and so on, that lets one software application communicate with another. For example, the developers of Twitter documented the names of each data type (users, tweets, timestamps, and so on) and the methods for accessing them in an API document (*dev.twitter.com/docs*) that lets other developers include Twitter feeds and elements in their programs. That is why there are so many Twitter programs and widgets available. Amazon.com also opens up its product data via an API. In fact, publishers of all ilks are recognizing the power of having their content available via an API. You could say that APIs are hot right now.

But let's bring it back to HTML5, which includes APIs for tasks that traditionally required proprietary plug-ins (like Flash) or custom programming. The idea is that if browsers offer those features natively—with standardized sets of hooks for accessing them—developers can do all sorts of nifty things and count on them working in all browsers, just as we count on the ability to embed an image on a page today. Of course, we have a way to go before there is ubiquitous support of these cutting-edge features, but we're getting there steadily. Some APIs have a markup component, such as embedding multimedia with the new HTML5 **video** and **audio** elements. Others happen entirely behind the scenes with JavaScript or server-side components, such as creating web applications that work even when there is no Internet connection (Offline Web Application API).

The W3C and WHATWG are working on *lots and lots* of APIs for use with web applications, all in varying stages of completion and implementation. Most have their own specifications, separate from the HTML5 spec itself, but they are generally included under the wide HTML5 umbrella that covers web-based applications. HTML5 includes specifications for these APIs:

Media Player API

> For controlling audio and video players embedded on a web page, used with the new **video** and **audio** elements. We will take a closer look at audio and video later in this chapter.

Session History API

> Exposes the browser history for better control over the Back button.

Offline Web Application API

> Makes it possible for a web application to work even when there is no Internet connection. It does it by including a manifest document that lists all of the files and resources that should be downloaded into the browser's cache in order for the application to work. When a connection is available, it checks to see whether any of the documents have changed, then updates those documents.

NOTE

For a list of all the APIs, see the article "HTML Landscape Overview" by Erik Wilde (dret.typepad.com/dretblog/ html5-api-overview.html). The W3C lists all the documents they maintain, many of which are APIs, at www. w3.org/TR/tr-title-all.

Editing API

Provides a set of commands that could be used to create in-browser text editors, allowing users to insert and delete text; format text as bold, italic, or as a hypertext link; and more. In addition, there is a new **contenteditable** attribute that allows any content element to be editable right on the page.

Drag and Drop API

Adds the ability to drag a text selection or file to a target area on the page or another web page. The **draggable** attribute indicates the element can be selected and dragged. The **dropzone** attribute is used on the target area and defines what type of content it can accept (text or file type) and what to do with it when it gets there (**copy**, **link**, **move**).

The following are just a handful of the APIs in development at the W3C with specifications of their own (outside HTML5):

Canvas API

The **canvas** element adds a dynamic, two-dimensional drawing space to a page. We'll take a look at it at the end of this chapter.

Web Storage API

Allows data to be stored in the browser's cache so that an application can use it later. Traditionally, that has been done with "cookies," but the Web Storage API allows more data to be stored. It also controls whether the data is limited to one session (**sessionStorage**: when the window is closed, the data is cleared) or based on domain (**localStorage**: all open windows pointed to that domain have access to the data).

Geolocation API

Lets users share their geographical location (longitude and latitude) so that it is accessible to scripts in a web application. This allows the app to provide location-aware features such as suggesting a nearby restaurant or finding other users in your area.

Web Workers API

Provides a way to run computationally complicated scripts in the background. This allows the browser to keep the web page interface quick and responsive to user actions while working on processor-intensive scripts at the same time. The Web Workers API is part of the HTML5 spec at the WHATWG, but at the W3C, it's been moved into a separate document.

Web Sockets API

Creates a "socket," which is an open connection between the browser client and the server. This allows information to flow between the client and the server in real time, with no lags for the traditional HTTP requests. It is useful for multiplayer games, chat, or data streams that update constantly, such as sports or stock tickers or social media streams.

NOTE

You can think of a web socket as an ongoing telephone call between the browser and server compared to the walkie-talkie, one-at-a-time style of traditional browser/server communication. (A hat tip to Jen Simmons for this analogy.)

Some APIs have correlating HTML elements, such as the **audio** and **video** elements for embedding media players on a page, and the **canvas** element for adding a dynamic drawing area. In the following sections, we'll take a brief look at how those elements are put to use.

Video and Audio

In the earliest days of the World Wide Web (I know, I was there), it was possible to add a MIDI file to a web page for a little beep-boopy soundtrack (think early video games). It wasn't long before better options came along, including RealMedia and Windows Media, that allowed all sorts of audio and video formats to be embedded in a web page. In the end, Flash became the *de facto* embedded multimedia player thanks in part to its use by YouTube and similar video services.

What all of these technologies have in common is that they require third-party, proprietary plug-ins to be downloaded and installed in order to play the media files. Until recently, browsers did not have built-in capabilities for handling sound or video, so the plug-ins filled in the gap. With the development of the Web as an open standards platform, it seemed like time to make multimedia support part of browsers' out-of-the-box capabilities. Enter the new **audio** and **video** elements and their respective APIs.

The good news and the bad news

The good news is that the **audio** and **video** elements are well supported in modern browsers, including IE 9+, Safari 3+, Chrome, Opera, and Firefox 3.5+ for the desktop and iOS Safari 4+, Android 2.3+, and Opera Mobile (however, not Opera Mini).

But lest you envision a perfect world where all browsers are supporting audio and video in perfect harmony, I am afraid that it is not that simple. Although they have all lined up on the markup and JavaScript for embedding and controlling media players, unfortunately they have not agreed on which formats to support. Let's take a brief journey through the land of media file formats. If you want to add audio or video to your page, this stuff is important to understand.

How media formats work

When you prepare audio or video content for web delivery, there are two format decisions to make. The first is how the media is encoded (the algorithms used to convert the source to 1s and 0s and how they are compressed). The method used for encoding is called the codec, which is short for "code/decode" or "compress/decompress." There are a bazillion codecs out there (that's an estimate). Some probably sound familiar, like MP3; others might

Farewell Flash?

Apple's announcement that it would not support Flash on its iOS devices, *ever*, gave HTML5 an enormous push forward and eventually led to Adobe stopping development on its mobile Flash products. Not long after, Microsoft announced that it was discontinuing its Silverlight media player in lieu of HTML5 alternatives. As of this writing, HTML5 is a long way from being able to reproduce the vast features and functionality of Flash, but it's getting there gradually. That means we are likely to see Flash and Silverlight players on the desktop for years to come, but the trajectory away from plug-ins and toward web standards technologies seems clear.

sound new, such as H.264, Vorbis, Theora, VP8, and AAC. Fortunately, only a few are appropriate for the Web, and we'll review them in a moment.

Second, you need to choose the container format for the media...you can think of it as a ZIP file that holds the compressed media and its metadata together in a package. Usually a container format can hold more than one codec type, and the full story is complicated. Because space is limited in this chapter, I'm going to cut to the chase and introduce the most common container/codec combinations for the Web. If you are going to add video or audio to your site, I encourage you to get more familiar with all of these formats. The books in the "For Further Reading: HTML5 Media" sidebar are a great first step.

Meet the video formats

For video, the most common options are:

- **Ogg container + Theora video codec + Vorbis audio codec.** This is typically called "Ogg Theora," and the file should have a *.ogv* suffix. All of the codecs and the container in this option are open source and unencumbered by patents or royalty restrictions, which makes them ideal for web distribution, but some say the quality is inferior to other options.

- **MPEG-4 container + H.264 video codec + AAC audio codec.** This combination is generally referred to as "MPEG-4," and it takes the *.mp4* or *.m4v* file suffix. H.264 is a high-quality and flexible video codec, but it is patented and must be licensed for a fee. The royalty requirement has been a deal-breaker for browsers that refuse to support it.

- **WebM container + VP8 video codec + Vorbis audio codec.** "WebM" is the newest container format and uses the *.webm* file extension. It is designed to work with VP8 and Vorbis exclusively, and has the advantage of being open source and royalty-free.

Of course, the problem that I referred to earlier is that browser makers have not agreed on a single format to support. Some go with open source, royalty-free options like Ogg Theora or WebM. Others are sticking with the better quality of H.264 despite the royalty requirements. What that means is that we web developers need to make multiple versions of videos to ensure support across all browsers. Table 10-4 lists which browsers support the various video options.

> ## For Further Reading: HTML5 Media
>
> I recommend these books when you are ready to learn more about HTML5 media:
>
> - *HTML5 Media*, by Shelley Powers (O'Reilly).
> - *HTML5, Up and Running*, by Mark Pilgrim (O'Reilly) includes a helpful section on HTML5 video.
> - *The Definitive Guide to HTML5 Video*, by Sylvia Pfeiffer (Apress).

Table 10-4. Video support in current browsers (as of mid-2012)

Format	Type	IE	Chrome	Firefox	Safari	Opera Mobile	Mobile Safari	Android
Ogg Theora	video/ogg	–	5.0+	3.5+	–	10.5+	–	–
MP4/H.264	video/mp4	9.0+	–	–	3.1+	–	3.0+	2.0+
WebM	video/webm	9.0+	6.0+	4.0+	–	11+	–	2.3.3+

Meet the audio formats

The landscape looks similar for audio formats: several to choose from, but no format that is supported by all browsers (Table 10-5).

- **MP3.** The MP3 format is a codec and container in one, with the file extension.*mp3*. It has become ubiquitous as a music download format. The MP3 (short for MPEG-1 Audio Layer 3) is patented and requires license fees paid by hardware and software companies (not media creators).

- **WAV.** The WAV format (*.wav*) is also a codec and container in one.

- **Ogg container + Vorbis audio codec.** This is usually referred to as "Ogg Vorbis" and is served with the *.ogg* or *.oga* file extension.

- **MPEG 4 container + AAC audio codec.** "MPEG4 audio" (*.m4a*) is less common than MP3.

- **WebM container + Vorbis audio codec.** The WebM (*.webm*) format can also contain audio only.

Table 10-5. Audio support in current browsers (as of 2012)

Format	Type	IE	Chrome	Firefox	Safari	Opera Mobile	Mobile Safari	Android
MP3	audio/mpeg	9.0+	5.0+	–	4+	–	3.0+	2.0+
WAV	audio/wav or audio/wave	–	5.0+	3.5+	4+	10.5+	3.0+	2.0+
Ogg Vorbis	audio/ogg	–	5.0+	3.5+	–	10.5+	–	2.0+
MPEG-4/AAC	audio/mp4	9.0+	5.0+	–	4+	–	3.0+	2.0+
WebM	audio/webm	9.0+	6.0+	4.0+	–	11+	–	2.3.3+

Video and Audio Encoding Tools

There are scores of options for editing and encoding video and audio files, so I can't cover them all here, but the following tools are free and get the job done.

Video conversion

- Miro Video Converter (*www.mirovideoconverter.com*) is a free tool that converts any video to H.264, Ogg Theora, or WebM format optimized for mobile devices or the desktop with a simple drag-and-drop interface. It is available for OS X and Windows.

- Handbrake (*handbrake.fr*) is a popular open source tool for getting better control over H.264 settings. It is available for Windows, OS X, and Linux.

- Firefogg (*firefogg.org*) is an extension to Firefox for converting video to the Ogg Theora format. Simply install the

Firefogg extension to Firefox 3.5+, then visit the Firefogg site and convert video using its online interface.

Audio conversion

- MP3/WMA/Ogg Converter (*www.freemp3wmaconverter.com*) is a free tool that converts the following audio formats: MP3, WAV, WMA, OGG, AAC, and more. Sorry, Mac users; it is Windows only.

- On the Mac, try Max, an open source audio converter available at *sbooth.org/Max/*. Audacity (*audacity.sourceforge.net/*) also has some basic conversion tools in addition to being a recording tool.

Adding a video to a page

I guess it's about time we got to the markup for adding a video to a web page (this is the HTML part of the book, after all). Let's start with an example that assumes you are designing for an environment where you know exactly what browser your user will be using. When this is the case, you can provide only one video format using the **src** attribute in the **video** tag (just as you do for an **img**). Figure 10-2 shows a movie with the default player in the Chrome browser. We'll look at the other attributes after the example.

```
<video src="highlight_reel.mp4" width="640" height="480"
poster="highlight_still.jpg" controls autoplay>
</video>
```

<video>...</video>

Adds a video player to the page

NEW IN HTML5

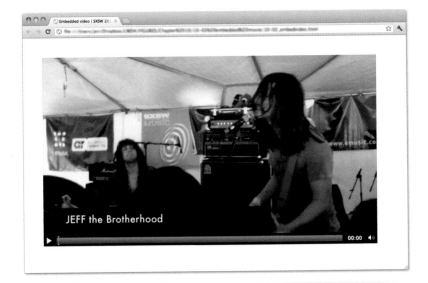

Figure 10-2. An embedded movie using the video *element (shown in Chrome on Mac).*

There are some juicy attributes in that example worth looking at in detail.

width="*pixel measurement***"**
height="*pixel measurement***"**
> Specifies the size of the box the embedded media player takes up on the screen. Generally, it is best to set the dimensions to exactly match the pixel dimensions of the movie. The movie will resize to match the dimensions set here.

poster="*url of image***"**
> Provides the location of a still image to use in place of the video before it plays.

controls
> Adding the **controls** attribute prompts the browser to display its built-in media controls, generally a play/pause button, a "seeker" that lets you move to a position within the video, and volume controls. It is possible

WARNING

iOS 3 devices will not play a video that includes the poster *attribute, so avoid using it if you need to support old iPhones and iPads.*

to create your own custom player interface using CSS and JavaScript if you want more consistency across browsers. How to do that is beyond the scope of this chapter, but is explained in the resources listed in the "For Further Reading: HTML5 Media" sidebar. In many instances, the default controls are just fine.

autoplay

Makes the video start playing automatically once it has downloaded enough of the media file to play through without stopping. In general, use of **autoplay** should be avoided in favor of letting the user decide when the video should start.

In addition, the **video** (and **audio**) element can use the **loop** attribute to make the video play again once it has finished (ad infinitum), **muted** for playing the video track without the audio, **mediagroup** for making a **video** element part of a group of related media elements (such as a **video** and a synced sign language translation), and **preload** for suggesting to the browser whether the video data should be fetched as soon the page loads (**preload="auto"**) or wait until the user presses the play button (**preload="none"**). Setting **preload="metadata"** loads information about the media file, but not the media itself. A device can decide how to best handle the **auto** setting; for example, a browser in a smartphone may protect a user's data usage by not preloading media, even when it is set to **auto**.

Video for all!

But wait a minute! We already know that one video format isn't going to cut it in the real world. At the very least, you need to make two versions of your video: Ogg Theora and MPEG-4 (H.264 video). Some developers prefer WebM instead of Ogg because browser support is nearly as good and the files are smaller. As a fallback for users with browsers that don't support HTML5 video, you can embed a Flash player on the page or use a service like YouTube or Vimeo, in which case you let them handle the conversion, and you just copy the embed code.

In the markup, a series of **source** elements inside the **video** element point to each video file. Browsers look down the list until they find one they support and download only that version. The Flash fallback gets added with the traditional **object** and **embed** elements, so if a browser can't make heads or tails of **video** and **source**, chances are high it can play it in Flash. Finally, to ensure accessibility for all, it is highly recommended that you add some simple links to download the videos so they can be played in whatever media player is available, should all of the above fail.

Without further ado, here is one (very thorough) code example for embedding video that should serve all users, including those on mobile devices. You may choose not to provide all these formats, so adapt it accordingly.

---

object and embed

The **object** element is the generic way to embed media such as a movie, Flash movie, applet, even images in a web page. It contains a number of **param** (for parameters) elements that provide instructions or resources that the object needs to display. You can also put fallback content inside the **object** element that is used if the media is not supported. The attributes and parameters vary by object type and are sometimes specific to the third-party plug-in displaying the media.

The **object**'s poor cousin, **embed**, also embeds media on web pages. It has been a non-standard, but widely supported, element until it was finally made official in HTML5. Some media require the use of **embed**, which is often used as a fallback in an **object** element to appease all browsers.

You can see an example of the **object** and **param** elements in the "Video for Everybody" code example on the following page.

The following example is based on the code in Kroc Camen's article "Video for Everybody" (*camendesign.com/code/video_for_everybody*). I highly recommend checking that page for updates, instructions for modifying the code, and many more technical details. We'll look at each part following the example.

```
<video id="yourmovieid" width="640" height="360" poster="yourmovie_
still.jpg" controls preload="auto">
    <source src="yourmovie-baseline.mp4" type='video/mp4;
codecs="avc1.42E01E, mp4a.40.2"'>
    <source src="yourmovie.webm" type='video/webm; codecs="VP8,
vorbis"'>
    <source src="yourmovie.ogv" type='video/ogg; codecs="theora,
vorbis"'>
<!--Flash fallback -->
    <object width="640" height="360" type="application/x-shockwave-
flash" data="your_flash_player.swf">
        <param name="movie" value="your_flash_player.swf">
        <param name="flashvars" value="controlbar=over&amp;image=poster.
jpg&amp;file=yourmovie-main.mp4">
        <img src="poster.jpg" width="640" height="360" alt=""
        title="No video playback capabilities, please download the video
below">
    </object>
</video>
<p>Download the Highlights Reel:</p>
<ul>
    <li><a href="yourmovie.mp4">MPEG-4 format</a></li>
    <li><a href="yourmovie.ogv">Ogg Theora format</a></li>
</ul>
```

Each **source** element contains the location of the media file (**src**) and information about its file type (**type**). In addition to listing the MIME type of the file container (e.g., **video/ogg**), it is helpful to also list the codecs that were used (see the note). This is especially important for MPEG-4 video because the H.264 codec has a number of different profiles, such as baseline (used by mobile devices), main (used by desktop Safari and IE9+), extended, and high (these two are generally not used for web video). Each profile has its own profile ID, as you see in the first **source** element in the example.

Technically, the order of the **source** elements doesn't matter, but to compensate for a bug on early iPads, it is best to put the baseline MPEG-4 first in the list. iPads running iOS 3 won't find it if it's further down, and it won't hurt any other browsers.

After the **source** elements, an **object** element is used to embed a Flash player that will play the MPEG-4 video for browsers that have the Flash plug-in. There are many Flash players available, but Kroc Camen (of "Video for Everybody" fame) recommends JW Player, which is easy to install (just put a JavaScript *.js* file and the Flash *.swf* file on your server). Download the JW Player and instructions for installing and configuring it at *www.longtailvideo. com/players/jw-flv-player/*. If you use the JW Player, replace *your_flash_player.swf* in the example with **player.swf**.

> **NOTE**
>
> *If you look carefully, you'll see that single quotation marks (') were used to enclose the long string of values for the* **type** *attribute in the* **source** *element. That is because the codecs must be enclosed in double quotation marks, so the whole attribute requires a different quotation mark type.*

> **NOTE**
>
> *In this example, the MPEG-4 video is provided at "baseline" quality in order to play on iOS 3 devices. If iOS 3 is obsolete when you are reading this or does not appear in your traffic data, you can provide the higher-quality "main" profile version instead:*
>
> ```
> <source src="yourmovie-
> main.mp4" type='video/mp4;
> codecs="avc1.4D401E, mp4a.40.2"'>
> ```

It is important to note that the Flash fallback is for browsers that do not recognize the **video** element. If a browser does support **video** but simply does not support one of the media file formats, it will *not* display the Flash version. It shows nothing. That's why it is a good idea to have direct links (a) to the video options outside the **video** element for maximum accessibility.

Finally, if you want the video to start playing automatically, add the **autoplay** attribute to the **video** element and **autostart=true** to the Flash **param** element like this:

```
<video src="movie.mp4" width="640" height="480" autoplay>

<param name="flashvars" value="autostart=true&amp;controlbar=over&amp;
image=poster.jpg&amp; file=yourmovie-main.mp4">
```

Keep in mind that videos will not play automatically on iOS devices, even if you set it in the code. Apple disables **autoplay** on its mobile devices to prevent unintended data transfer.

Adding audio to a page

If you've wrapped your head around the **video** markup example, you already know how to add audio to a page. The **audio** element uses the same attributes as the **video** element, with the exception of **width**, **height**, and **poster** (because there is nothing to display). Just like the **video** element, you can provide a stack of audio format options using the **source** element, as shown in the example here.

```
<audio id="soundtrack" controls preload="auto">
  <source src="soundtrack.mp3" type="audio/mp3">
  <source src="soundtrack.ogg" type="audio/ogg">
  <source src="soundtrack.webm" type="audio/webm">
</audio>
<p>Download the Soundtrack song:</p>
<ul>
  <li><a href="soundtrack.mp3">MP3</a></li>
  <li><a href="soundtrack.ogg">Ogg Vorbis</a></li>
</ul>
```

If you want to be evil, you could embed audio in a page, set it to play automatically and then loop, and not provide any controls to stop it like this:

```
<audio src="soundtrack.mp3" autoplay loop></audio>
```

But you would never, *ever* do something like that, right? *Right?!* Of course you wouldn't.

Canvas

Another cool, "Look Ma, no plug-ins!" addition in HTML5 is the **canvas** element and the associated Canvas API. The **canvas** element creates an area on a web page that you can draw on using a set of JavaScript functions for creating lines, shapes, fills, text, animations, and so on. You could use it to

WARNING

If your server is not configured to properly report the video type (its MIME type) of your video and audio files, some browsers will not play them. The MIME types for each format are listed in the "Type" column in Tables 10-4 and 10-5. So be sure to notify your server administrator or hosting company's technical help if you intend to serve media files and get the MIME types set up correctly.

`<audio>...</audio>`

Adds an audio file to the page

NEW IN HTML5

WARNING

*Firefox versions 7 and earlier do not support the **loop** attribute.*

display an illustration, but what gives the **canvas** element so much potential (and has all the web development world so delighted) is that it's all generated with scripting. That means it is dynamic and can draw things on the fly and respond to user input. This makes it a nifty platform for creating animations, games, and even whole applications...all using the native browser behavior and without proprietary plug-ins like Flash.

The good news is that Canvas is supported by every current browser as of this writing, with the exception of Internet Explorer 8 and earlier. Fortunately, the FlashCanvas JavaScript library (*flashcanvas.net*) can add Canvas support to those browsers using the Flash drawing API. So Canvas is definitely ready for prime time.

Figure 10-3 shows a few examples of the **canvas** element used to create games, drawing programs, an interactive molecule structure tool, and an asteroid animation. You can find more examples at *Canvasdemos.com*.

ie.microsoft.com/testdrive/Performance/AsteroidBelt/#

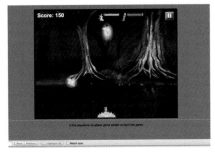

www.relfind.com/game/magician.html

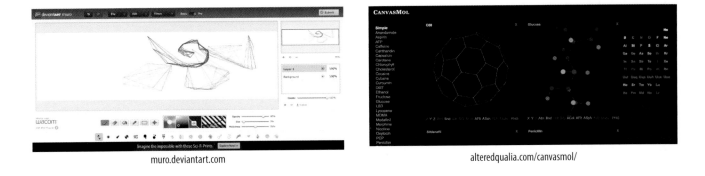

muro.deviantart.com

alteredqualia.com/canvasmol/

Figure 10-3. A few examples of the canvas *element used for games, animations, and applications.*

Mastering the **canvas** element is more than we can take on here, particularly without any JavaScript experience under our belts, but I will give you a taste of what it is like to draw with JavaScript. That should give you a good idea of how it works, and also a new appreciation for the complexity of some of those examples.

The canvas element

<canvas>...</canvas>

Adds a 2-D dynamic drawing area

NEW IN HTML5

You add a canvas space to the page with the **canvas** element and specify the dimensions with the **width** and **height** attributes. And that's really all there is to the markup. For browsers that don't support the **canvas** element, you can provide some fallback content (a message, image, or whatever seems appropriate) inside the tags.

```
<canvas width="600" height="400" id="my_first_canvas">
   Your browser does not support HTML5 canvas. Try using Chrome,
Firefox, Safari or Internet Explorer 9.
</canvas>
```

The markup just clears a space on which the drawing will happen.

Drawing with JavaScript

The Canvas API includes functions for creating basic shapes (such as **strokeRect()** for drawing a rectangular outline and **beginPath()** for starting a line drawing) and moving things around (such as **rotate()** and **scale()**), plus attributes for applying styles (for example, **lineWidth**, **strokeStyle**, **fillStyle**, and **font**).

The following example was created by my O'Reilly Media colleague Sanders Kleinfeld for his book *HTML5 for Publishers* (O'Reilly). He was kind enough to allow me to use it in this book.

Figure 10-4 shows the simple smiley face we'll be creating with the Canvas API.

And here is the script that created it. Don't worry that you don't know any JavaScript yet. Just skim through the script and pay attention to the little notes. I'll also describe some of the functions in use at the end. I bet you'll get the gist of it just fine.

Figure 10-4. The finished product of our "Hello Canvas" canvas example. See the original at examples.oreilly. com/0636920022473/my_first_canvas/ my_first_canvas.html.

```
<script type="text/javascript">
window.addEventListener('load', eventWindowLoaded, false);
function eventWindowLoaded() {
    canvasApp();
}

function canvasApp(){
var theCanvas = document.getElementById('my_first_canvas');
var my_canvas = theCanvas.getContext('2d');
my_canvas.strokeRect(0,0,200,225)
    // to start, draw a border around the canvas

    //draw face
my_canvas.beginPath();
my_canvas.arc(100, 100, 75, (Math.PI/180)*0, (Math.PI/180)*360, false);
    // circle dimensions
my_canvas.strokeStyle = "black"; // circle outline is black
my_canvas.lineWidth = 3; // outline is three pixels wide
my_canvas.fillStyle = "yellow"; // fill circle with yellow
my_canvas.stroke(); // draw circle
my_canvas.fill(); // fill in circle
```

```
my_canvas.closePath();

    // now, draw left eye
my_canvas.fillStyle = "black"; // switch to black for the fill
my_canvas.beginPath();
my_canvas.arc(65, 70, 10, (Math.PI/180)*0, (Math.PI/180)*360, false);
    // circle dimensions
my_canvas.stroke(); // draw circle
my_canvas.fill(); // fill in circle
my_canvas.closePath();

    // now, draw right eye
my_canvas.beginPath();
my_canvas.arc(135, 70, 10, (Math.PI/180)*0, (Math.PI/180)*360, false);
    // circle dimensions
my_canvas.stroke(); // draw circle
my_canvas.fill(); // fill in circle
my_canvas.closePath();

    // draw smile
my_canvas.lineWidth = 6; // switch to six pixels wide for outline
my_canvas.beginPath();
my_canvas.arc(99, 120, 35, (Math.PI/180)*0, (Math.PI/180)*-180, false);
    // semicircle dimensions
my_canvas.stroke();
my_canvas.closePath();

    // Smiley Speaks!
my_canvas.fillStyle = "black"; // switch to black for text fill
my_canvas.font       = '20px _sans'; // use 20 pixel sans serif font
my_canvas.fillText  ("Hello Canvas!", 45, 200); // write text
    }
</script>
```

Finally, here is a little more information on the Canvas API functions used in the example:

strokeRect(*x1, y1, x2, y2***)**
Draws a rectangular outline from the point (x1, y1) to (x2, y2). By default, the origin of the Canvas (0,0) is the top-left corner, and *x* and *y* coordinates are measured to the right and down.

beginPath()
Starts a line drawing.

closePath()
Ends a line drawing that was started with **beginPath()**.

arc(*x, y, arc_radius, angle_radians_beg, angle_radians_end***)**
Draws an arc where (x,y) is the center of the circle, **arc_radius** is the length of the radius of the circle, and **angle_radians_beg** and **_end** indicate the beginning and end of the arc angle.

stroke()
Draws the line defined by the path. If you don't include this, the path won't appear on the canvas.

`fill()`
> Fills in the path specified with **beginPath()** and **endPath()**.

`fillText(your_text, x1, y1)`
> Adds text to the canvas starting at the (x,y) coordinate specified.

In addition, the following attributes were used to specify colors and styles:

`lineWidth`
> Width of the border of the path.

`strokeStyle`
> Color of the border.

`fillStyle`
> Color of the fill (interior) of the shape created with the path.

`font`
> The font and size of the text.

Of course, the Canvas API includes many more functions and attributes than we've used here. For a complete list, see the W3C's HTML5 Canvas 2D Context specification at *dev.w3.org/html5/2dcontext/*. A web search will turn up lots of Canvas tutorials should you be ready to learn more. In addition, I can recommend these resources:

- The book *HTML5 Canvas* by Steve Fulton and Jeff Fulton (O'Reilly)

- If watching a video is more your speed, try this tutorial: *Client-side Graphics with HTML5 Canvases: An O'Reilly Breakdown* (shop.oreilly. com/product/0636920016502.do)

Final Word

By now you should have a good idea of what's up with HTML5. We've looked at new elements for adding improved semantics to documents. You got a whirlwind tour of the various APIs in development that will move some useful functionality into the native browser behavior. You learned how to use the **video** and **audio** elements to embed media on the page (plus a primer on media formats). And finally, you got a peek at the **canvas** element.

In the next part of this book, CSS for Presentation, you'll learn how to write style sheets that customize the look of the page, including text styles, colors, backgrounds, and even page layout. Goodbye, default browser styles!

Test Yourself

Let's see if you were paying attention. These questions should test whether you got the important highlights of this chapter. Good luck! And as always, the answers are in Appendix A.

1. What is the difference between HTML and XHTML?

2. Using the "XHTML Markup Requirements" sidebar as a guide, rewrite these HTML elements in XHTML syntax.

    a. `<H1> … </H1>`

    b. `<img src=image.png>`

    c. `<input type="radio" checked>`

    d. `<hr>`

    e. `<title>Sifl & Olly</title>`

    f.
    ```
    <ul>
      <li>popcorn
      <li>butter
      <li>salt
    </ul>
    ```

3. What is a DTD?

4. Name at least three ways that HTML5 is unique as a specification.

5. What is a "global attribute"?

6. Match the API with its function:

Web Workers _____
Editing API _____
Geolocation API _____
Web Socket _____
Offline Applications _____

a. Makes longitude and latitude information available

b. Holds a line of communication open between the server and browser

c. Makes web apps work even when there is no Internet connection

d. Runs processor-intensive scripts in the background

e. Provides a set of commands for copying, pasting, and text formatting

7. Identify each of the following as a container format, video codec, or audio codec.

Ogg   _____
H.264   _____
VP8   _____
Vorbis   _____
WebM   _____
Theora   _____
AAC   _____
MPEG-4   _____

8. List the two Canvas API functions for drawing a rectangle and filling it with red. You don't need to write the whole script.

CSS FOR PRESENTATION

PART **III**

CHAPTER 11

CASCADING STYLE SHEETS ORIENTATION

You've heard style sheets mentioned quite a bit already, and now we'll finally put them to work and start giving our pages some much needed style. Cascading Style Sheets (CSS) is the W3C standard for defining the presentation of documents written in HTML, and in fact, any XML language. Presentation, again, refers to the way the document is displayed or delivered to the user, whether on a computer screen, a cell phone display, printed on paper, or read aloud by a screen reader. With style sheets handling the presentation, HTML can handle the business of defining document structure and meaning, as intended.

CSS is a separate language with its own syntax. This chapter covers CSS terminology and fundamental concepts that will help you get your bearings for the upcoming chapters, where you'll learn how to change text and font styles, add colors and backgrounds, and even do basic page layout. By the end of Part III, I aim to give you a solid foundation for further reading on your own and lots of practice.

IN THIS CHAPTER

The benefits and power of Cascading Style Sheets (CSS)

How HTML markup creates a document structure

Writing CSS style rules

Attaching styles to the HTML document

The big CSS concepts of inheritance, the cascade, specificity, rule order, and the box model

The Benefits of CSS

Not that you need further convincing that style sheets are the way to go, but here is a quick rundown of the benefits of using style sheets.

- **Precise type and layout controls.** You can achieve print-like precision using CSS. There is even a set of properties aimed specifically at the printed page (but we won't be covering them in this book).

- **Less work.** You can change the appearance of an entire site by editing one style sheet.

- **More accessible sites.** When all matters of presentation are handled by CSS, you can mark up your content meaningfully, making it more accessible for non-visual or mobile devices.

- **Reliable browser support.** Every browser in current use supports CSS Level 2 and many cool parts of CSS Level 3. (See the sidebar "A Quick History of CSS," at the end of this chapter, for what is meant by CSS "levels.")

Come to think of it, there really aren't any disadvantages to using style sheets. There are some lingering hassles from browser inconsistencies, but they can either be avoided or worked around if you know where to look for them.

The power of CSS

We're not talking about minor visual tweaks here, like changing the color of headlines or adding text indents. When used to its full potential, CSS is a robust and powerful design tool. My eyes were first opened to the possibilities of using CSS for design by the variety and richness of the designs at CSS Zen Garden (*www.csszengarden.com*).

In the misty days of yore, when developers were still hesitant to give up their table-based layouts for CSS, David Shea's CSS Zen Garden site demonstrated exactly what could be accomplished using CSS alone. David posted an HTML document and invited designers to contribute their own style sheets that gave the document a visual design. Figure 11-1 shows just a few of my favorites. All of these designs use the *exact same* HTML source document.

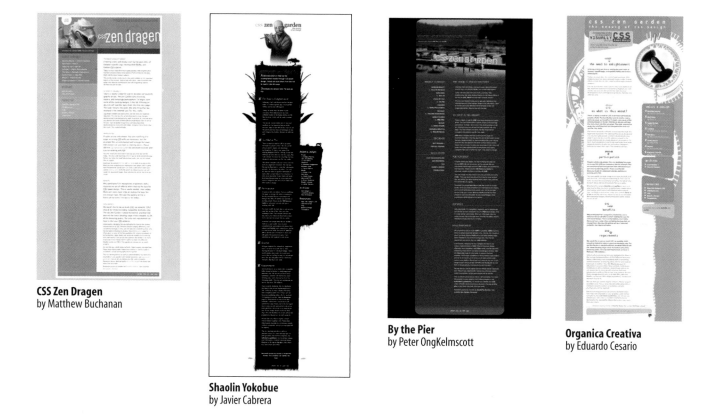

CSS Zen Dragen
by Matthew Buchanan

Shaolin Yokobue
by Javier Cabrera

By the Pier
by Peter OngKelmscott

Organica Creativa
by Eduardo Cesario

Figure 11-1. These pages from the CSS Zen Garden use the same XHTML source document, but the design is changed using exclusively CSS (used with permission of CSS Zen Garden and the individual designers).

Not only that, they don't include a single **img** element (all of the images are used as backgrounds). But look at how different each page looks—and how sophisticated. That's all done with style sheets. It is proof of the power in keeping CSS separate from HTML, and presentation separate from structure.

The CSS Zen Garden is no longer being updated and now is considered a historical document of a turning point in the adoption of web standards. Despite its age, I still find it to be a nice one-stop lesson for demonstrating exactly what CSS can do.

Granted, it takes a lot of practice to be able to create CSS layouts like those shown in Figure 11-1. Killer graphic design skills help too (unfortunately, you won't get those in this book). I'm showing this to you up front because I want you to be aware of the potential of CSS-based design, particularly because the examples in this beginners' book tend to be simple and straight-forward. Take your time learning, but keep your eye on the prize.

How Style Sheets Work

It's as easy as 1-2-3!

1. Start with a document that has been marked up in HTML.

2. Write style rules for how you'd like certain elements to look.

3. Attach the style rules to the document. When the browser displays the document, it follows your rules for rendering elements (unless the user has applied some mandatory styles, but we'll get to that later).

OK, so there's a bit more to it than that, of course. Let's give each of these steps a little more consideration.

1. Marking up the document

You know a lot about marking up content from the previous chapters. For example, you know that it is important to choose elements that accurately describe the meaning of the content. You've also heard me say that the markup creates the structure of the document, sometimes called the structural layer, upon which the presentation layer can be applied.

In this and the upcoming chapters, you'll see that having an understanding of your document's structure and the relationships between elements is central to your work as a style sheet author.

To get a feel for how simple it is to change the look of a document with style sheets, try your hand at Exercise 11-1. The good news is that I've whipped up a little HTML document for you to play with.

exercise 11-1 | Your first style sheet

In this exercise, we'll add a few simple styles to a short article. The document, *twenties.html*, and its associated image, *twenty_20s.jpg*, are available at *www. learningwebdesign.com/4e/materials/*. First, open the document in a browser to see how it looks by default (it should look something like Figure 11-2). You can also open the document in a text editor and get ready to follow along when this exercise continues in the next section.

The Back of the New $20

Have you seen the "Series 2004 $20 Notes"? The U.S. Treasury has rolled out yet another revamp of the U.S. twenty dollar bill in an effort to stop those pesky counterfeiters once and for all. It features high-tech fake-busting elements like a watermark, a security thread, and color-shifting ink. It also features crappy design.

I'm not going to concern myself here with a critique of the front of the bill (my friend Jeff says "it looks like something got spilled on it."). It's the *back* of the note that's driving me crazy.

Too Many 20s

In particular, it's all those little 20s haphazardly sprinkled in the white space. They are nails-on-a-chalkboard to my visual design senses.

Are they supposed to be another security feature? ("They'll *NEVER* be able to duplicate this $20... look at those 20s... they're all *OVER* the place!") Did they let a summer intern at the Bureau of Engraving and Printing design it? ("Hey, let Jimmy try it!") Were they concerned the $20 bill might be confused with a $10? ("What this 20 needs is a LOT more 20s.")

Connect-the-Dots

There must be more to it. My theory: the new 20s contain subliminal connect-the-dots messages, like tiny constellations. So, perhaps the 20s connect to form a secret message designed to stimulate the economy ("SPEND MORE") or boost patriotism ("WE'RE NO.1").

I'm not sure I've successfully cracked the code, so I'm asking for your help. I encourage you all to get a new $20 bill, connect the dots to find the message on the back (pencil is best), and mail it to me for review. Together, we can get to the bottom of this.

Figure 11-2. This is what the article looks like without any style sheet instructions. Although we won't be making it beautiful, you will get a feel for how styles work.

2. Writing the rules

A style sheet is made up of one or more style instructions (called rules or rule sets) that describe how an element or group of elements should be displayed. The first step in learning CSS is to get familiar with the parts of a rule. As you'll see, they're fairly intuitive to follow. Each rule *selects* an element and *declares* how it should look.

The following example contains two rules. The first makes all the **h1** elements in the document green; the second specifies that the paragraphs should be in a small, sans-serif font.

```
h1 { color: green; }
p  { font-size: small; font-family: sans-serif; }
```

In CSS terminology, the two main sections of a rule are the selector that identifies the element or elements to be affected, and the declaration that provides the rendering instructions. The declaration, in turn, is made up of a property (such as **color**) and its value (**green**), separated by a colon and a space. One or more declarations are placed inside curly brackets, as shown in Figure 11-3.

NOTE

Sans-serif fonts do not have a little slab (a serif) at the ends of strokes and tend to look more sleek and modern. We'll talk a lot more about font families in Chapter 12, Formatting Text.

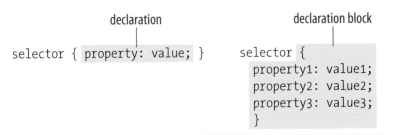

Figure 11-3. The parts of a style sheet rule.

Selectors

In the previous small style sheet example, the **h1** and **p** elements are used as selectors. This is called an element type selector, and it is the most basic type of selector. The properties defined for each rule will apply to every **h1** and **p** element in the document, respectively. In upcoming chapters, I'll introduce you to more sophisticated selectors that you can use to target elements, including ways to select groups of elements and elements that appear in a particular context.

Mastering selectors—that is, choosing the best type of selector and using it strategically—is an important step in becoming a CSS Jedi Master.

Declarations

The declaration is made up of a property/value pair. There can be more than one declaration in a single rule; for example, the rule for the **p** element shown earlier in the code example has both the **font-size** and **font-family** properties. Each declaration must end with a semicolon to keep it separate from the following declaration (see note). If you omit the semicolon, the declaration and the one following it will be ignored. The curly brackets and the declarations they contain are often referred to as the declaration block (Figure 11-3).

Because CSS ignores whitespace and line returns within the declaration block, authors typically write each declaration in the block on its own line, as shown in the following example. This makes it easier to find the properties applied to the selector and to tell when the style rule ends.

```
p  {
   font-size: small;
   font-family: sans-serif;
}
```

Note that nothing has really changed here—there is still one set of curly brackets, semicolons after each declaration, etc. The only difference is the insertion of line returns and some character spaces for alignment.

The heart of style sheets lies in the collection of standard properties that can be applied to selected elements. The complete CSS specification defines dozens of properties for everything from text indents to how table headers

NOTE

Technically, the semicolon is not required after the last declaration in the block, but it is recommended that you get into the habit of always ending declarations with a semicolon. It will make adding declarations to the rule later that much easier.

Providing Measurement Values

When you're providing measurement values, the unit must immediately follow the number, like this:

```
margin: 2em;
```

Adding a space before the unit will cause the property not to work.

INCORRECT: `margin: 2 em;`

It is acceptable to omit the unit of measurement for zero values:

```
margin: 0;
```

should be read aloud. This book covers the most common and best-supported properties that you can begin using right away.

Values are dependent on the property. Some properties take length measurements, some take color values, and others have a predefined list of keywords. When using a property, it is important to know which values it accepts; however, in many cases, simple common sense will serve you well.

Before we move on, why not get a little practice writing style rules yourself in the continuation of Exercise 11-1?

exercise 11-1 | **Your first style sheet (continued)**

Open *twenties.html* in a text editor. In the **head** of the document you will find that I have set up a **style** element for you to type the rules into. The **style** element is used to embed a style sheet in an HTML document.

To begin, we'll simply add the small style sheet that we just looked at in this section. Type the following rules into the document, just as you see them here:

```
<style type="text/css">
h1 {
    color: green;
}
p {
    font-size: small;
    font-family: sans-serif;
}
</style>
```

Save the file, and take a look at it in the browser. You should notice some changes (if your browser already uses a sans-serif font, you may only see a size change). If not, go back and check that you included both the opening and closing curly bracket and semicolons. It's easy to accidentally omit these characters, causing the style sheet not to work.

Now we'll change and add to the style sheet to see how easy it is to write rules and see the effects of the changes. Here are a few things to try (remember that you need to save the document after each change in order for the changes to be visible when you reload it in the browser).

- Make the **h1** element "gray" and take a look at it in the browser. Then make it "blue". Finally, make it "red". (We'll run through the complete list of available color names in Chapter 13, Colors and Backgrounds.)

- Add a new rule that makes the **h2** elements red as well.

- Add a 100-pixel left margin to paragraph (**p**) elements using this declaration:

```
margin-left: 100px;
```

Remember that you can add this new declaration to the existing rule for **p** elements.

- Add a 100-pixel left margin to the **h2** headings as well.

- Add a red, 1-pixel border to the bottom of the **h1** element using this declaration:

```
border-bottom: 1px solid red;
```

- Move the image to the right margin, and allow text to flow around it with the **float** property. The shorthand **margin** property shown in this rule adds zero pixels of space on the top and bottom of the image and 12 pixels of space on the left and right of the image (the values are mirrored in a manner explained in Chapter 14, Thinking Inside the Box).

```
img {
    float: right;
    margin: 0 12px;
}
```

When you are done, the document should look something like the one shown in Figure 11-4.

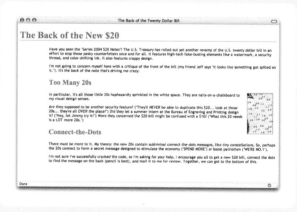

Figure 11-4. The article after adding the small style sheet from the example. As I said, not beautiful—just different.

3. Attaching the styles to the document

In the previous exercise, we embedded the style sheet right in the document using the **style** element. That is just one of three ways that style information can be applied to an HTML document. You'll get to try out each of these soon, but it is helpful to have an overview of the methods and terminology up front.

External style sheets. An external style sheet is a separate, text-only document that contains a number of style rules. It must be named with the *.css* suffix. The *.css* document is then linked to or imported into one or more HTML documents (we'll discuss how in Chapter 13). In this way, all the files in a website may share the same style sheet. This is the most powerful and preferred method for attaching style sheets to content.

Embedded style sheets. This is the type of style sheet we worked with in the exercise. It is placed in a document using the **style** element, and its rules apply only to that document. The **style** element must be placed in the **head** of the document. This example also includes a comment (see the "Comments in Style Sheets" sidebar).

```
<head>
    <title>Required document title here</title>
      <style>
      /* style rules go here */
      </style>
</head>
```

NOTE

In HTML 4.01 and XHTML 1.0/1.1, the **style** *element must contain a* **type** *attribute that identifies the content of the* **style** *element:*

```
<style type="text/css">
```

In HTML5, the **type** *attribute is no longer required.*

The **style** *element may also include the* **media** *attribute used to target specific media such as screen, print, or handheld devices. These are discussed in Chapter 13 as well.*

Comments in Style Sheets

Sometimes it is helpful to leave yourself or your collaborators comments in a style sheet. CSS has its own comment syntax, shown here:

```
/* comment goes here */
```

Content between the **/*** and ***/** will be ignored when the style sheet is parsed, which means you can leave comments anywhere in a style sheet, even within a rule.

```
body {
  font-size: small;
 /* font-size:large; */
}
```

One use for comments is to label sections of the style sheet to make things easier to find later; for example:

```
/* Layout styles */
```

or:

```
/* FOOTER STYLES */
```

CSS comments are also useful for temporarily hiding style declarations in the design process. When I am trying out a number of styles, I can quickly switch styles off by enclosing them in **/*** and ***/**, check it in a browser, then remove the comment characters to make the style appear again. It's much faster than retyping the entire thing.

Inline styles. You can apply properties and values to a single element using the **style** attribute in the element itself, as shown here:

```
<h1 style="color: red">Introduction</h1>
```

To add multiple properties, just separate them with semicolons, like this:

```
<h1 style="color: red; margin-top: 2em">Introduction</h1>
```

Inline styles apply only to the particular element in which they appear. Inline styles should be avoided, unless it is absolutely necessary to override styles from an embedded or external style sheet. Inline styles are problematic in that they intersperse presentation information into the structural markup. They also make it more difficult to make changes because every **style** attribute must be hunted down in the source.

Exercise 11-2 gives you an opportunity to write an inline style and see how it works. We won't be working with inline styles after this point for the reasons listed earlier, so here's your chance.

The Big Concepts

There are a few big ideas that you need to get your head around to be comfortable with how Cascading Style Sheets behave. I'm going to introduce you to these concepts now so we don't have to slow down for a lecture once we're rolling through the style properties. Each of these ideas will certainly be revisited and illustrated in more detail in the upcoming chapters.

Inheritance

Are your eyes the same color as your parents'? Did you inherit their hair color? Your unique smile? Well, just as parents pass down traits to their children, styled HTML elements pass down certain style properties to the elements they contain. Notice in Exercise 11-1, when we styled the **p** elements in a small, sans-serif font, the **em** element in the second paragraph became small and sans-serif as well, even though we didn't write a rule for it specifically (Figure 11-5). That is because it inherited the styles from the paragraph it is in.

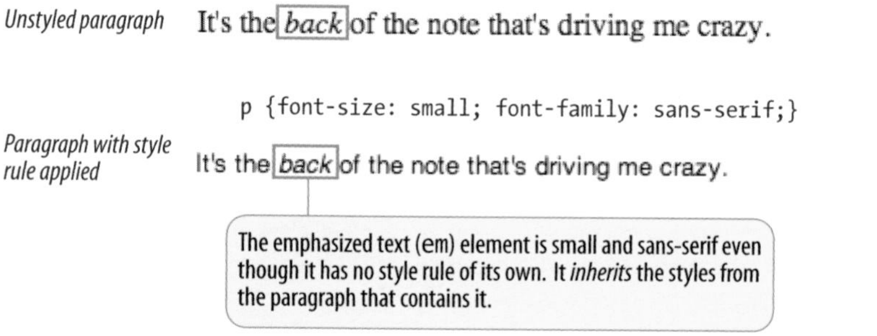

Unstyled paragraph   It's the *back* of the note that's driving me crazy.

```
p {font-size: small; font-family: sans-serif;}
```

Paragraph with style rule applied   It's the *back* of the note that's driving me crazy.

> The emphasized text (em) element is small and sans-serif even though it has no style rule of its own. It *inherits* the styles from the paragraph that contains it.

Figure 11-5. The em *element inherits styles that were applied to the paragraph.*

---

exercise 11-2 |
Applying an inline style

Open the article *twenties.html* in whatever state you last left it in Exercise 11-1. If you worked to the end of the exercise, you will have a rule that makes the **h2** elements red.

Write an inline style that makes the second **h2** gray. We'll do that right in the opening **h2** tag using the **style** attribute, as shown here:

```
<h2 style="color: gray">
Connect-the-Dots</h2>
```

Save the file and open it in a browser. Now the second heading is gray, overriding the red color set in the embedded style sheet. The other **h2** heading is unaffected.

Document structure

This is where an understanding of your document's structure becomes important. As I've noted before, HTML documents have an implicit structure or hierarchy. For example, the sample article we've been playing with has an **html** root element that contains a **head** and a **body**, and the **body** contains heading and paragraph elements. A few of the paragraphs, in turn, contain inline elements such as images (**img**) and emphasized text (**em**). You can visualize the structure as an upside-down tree, branching out from the root, as shown in Figure 11-6.

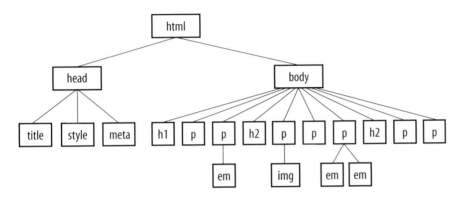

Figure 11-6. The document tree structure of the sample document, twenties.html.

Parents and children

The document tree becomes a family tree when it comes to referring to the relationship between elements. All the elements contained within a given element are said to be its descendants. For example, the **h1**, **h2**, **p**, **em**, and **img** elements in the document in Figure 11-6 are all descendants of the **body** element.

An element that is directly contained within another element (with no intervening hierarchical levels) is said to be the child of that element. Conversely, the containing element is the parent. For example, the **em** element is the child of the **p** element, and the **p** element is its parent.

All of the elements higher than a particular element in the hierarchy are its ancestors. Two elements with the same parent are siblings. We don't refer to "aunts" or "cousins," so the analogy stops there. This may all seem academic, but it will come in handy when writing CSS selectors.

Pass it on

When you write a font-related style rule using the **p** element as a selector, the rule applies to all of the paragraphs in the document as well as the inline text elements they contain. We've seen the evidence of the **em** element inheriting the style properties applied to its parent (**p**) back in Figure 11-5. Figure 11-7 demonstrates what's happening in terms of the document structure diagram. Note that the **img** element is excluded because font-related properties do not apply to images.

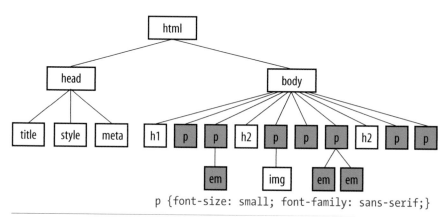

p {font-size: small; font-family: sans-serif;}

*Figure 11-7. Certain properties applied to the **p** element are inherited by their children.*

CSS TIP

When you learn a new property, it is a good idea to note whether it inherits. Inheritance is noted for every property listing in this book. For the most part, inheritance follows your expectations.

WARNING

*The browser's style sheet may override styles set on the **body**, so be on the lookout for unexpected styling.*

Notice that I've been saying "certain" properties are inherited. It's important to note that some style sheet properties inherit and others do not. In general, properties related to the styling of text—font size, color, style, etc.—are passed down. Properties such as borders, margins, backgrounds, and so on that affect the boxed area around the element tend not to be passed down. This makes sense when you think about it. For example, if you put a border around a paragraph, you wouldn't want a border around every inline element (such as **em**, **strong**, or **a**) it contains as well.

You can use inheritance to your advantage when writing style sheets. For example, if you want all text elements to be rendered in the Verdana font face, you could write separate style rules for every element in the document and set the **font-face** to Verdana. A *better* way would be to write a single style rule that applies the **font-face** property to the **body** element, and let all the text elements contained in the **body** inherit that style (Figure 11-8).

Any property applied to a specific element will override the inherited values for that property. Going back to the article example, we could specify that the **em** element should appear in a serif font, and that would override the inherited sans-serif setting.

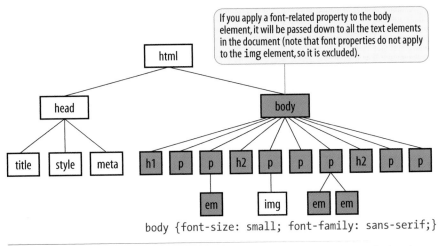

Figure 11-8. *All the elements in the document inherit certain properties applied to the* **body** *element.*

Conflicting styles: the cascade

Ever wonder why they are called "cascading" style sheets? CSS allows you to apply several style sheets to the same document, which means there are bound to be conflicts. For example, what should the browser do if a document's imported style sheet says that **h1** elements should be red, but its embedded style sheet has a rule that makes **h1**s purple?

The folks who wrote the style sheet specification anticipated this problem and devised a hierarchical system that assigns different weights to the various sources of style information. The cascade refers to what happens when several sources of style information vie for control of the elements on a page: style information is passed down ("cascades" down) until it is overridden by a style command with more weight.

For example, if you don't apply any style information to a web page, it will be rendered according to the browser's internal style sheet (we've been calling this the default rendering; the W3C calls it the user agent style sheet). Individual users can apply their own styles as well (the user style sheet), which overrides the default styles in their browser. However, if the author of the web page has attached a style sheet (the author style sheet), that overrides both the user and the user agent styles. The only exception is if the user has identified a style as "important," in which case that style will trump all (see the "Assigning Importance" sidebar).

The style sheet source is one hierarchy that determines which style wins. As we've learned, there are three ways to attach style information to the source document, and they have a cascading order as well. Generally speaking, the closer the style sheet is to the content, the more weight it is given. Embedded style sheets that appear right in the document in the **style** element have more weight than external style sheets. In the example that started this section, the **h1** elements would end up purple as specified in the embedded style sheet, not red as specified in the external *.css* file that has less weight. Inline styles have more weight than embedded style sheets because you can't get any closer to the content than a style right in the element's opening tag. That's the effect we witnessed in Exercise 11-2.

To prevent a specific rule from being overridden, you can assign it "importance" with the **!important** indicator, as explained in the "Assigning Importance" sidebar. The sidebar "Style Sheet Hierarchy" provides an overview of the cascading order from general to specific.

Specificity

Once the applicable style sheet has been chosen, there may still be conflicts; therefore, the cascade continues at the rule level. When two rules in a single style sheet conflict, the type of selector is used to determine the winner. The more specific the selector, the more weight it is given to override conflicting declarations.

When two rules in a single style sheet conflict, the type of selector is used to determine the winner.

It's a little soon to be discussing specificity because we've only looked at one type of selector (and the least specific type, at that). For now, put the term specificity and the concept of some selectors overriding others on your radar. We will revisit it in Chapter 12 when you have more selector types under your belt.

Assigning Importance

If you want a rule not to be overridden by a subsequent conflicting rule, include the **!important** indicator just after the property value and before the semicolon for that rule. For example, to make paragraph text blue always, use the following rule:

```
p {color: blue !important;}
```

Even if the browser encounters an inline style later in the document (which should override a document-wide style sheet), like this one:

```
<p style="color: red">
```

that paragraph will still be blue because the rule with the **!important** indicator cannot be overridden by other styles in the author's style sheet.

The only way an **!important** rule may be overridden is by a conflicting rule in a reader (user) style sheet that has also

been marked **!important**. This is to ensure that special reader requirements, such as large type for the visually impaired, are never overridden.

Based on the previous examples, if the reader's style sheet includes this rule:

```
p {color: black;}
```

the text would still be blue because all author styles (even those not marked **!important**) take precedence over the reader's styles. However, if the conflicting reader's style is marked **!important**, like this:

```
p {color: black !important;}
```

the paragraphs will be black and cannot be overridden by any author-provided style.

> ## Style Sheet Hierarchy
>
> Style information can come from various sources, listed here from general to specific. Items lower in the list will override items above them:
>
> - Browser default settings
> - User style settings (set in a browser as a "reader style sheet")
> - Linked external style sheet (added with the **link** element)
> - Imported style sheets (added with the **@import** function)
> - Embedded style sheets (added with the **style** element)
> - Inline style information (added with the **style** attribute in an opening tag)
> - Any style rule marked **!important** by the author
> - Any style rule marked **!important** by the reader (user)

Rule order

Finally, if there are conflicts within style rules of identical weight, whichever one comes last in the list "wins." Take these three rules, for example:

```
<style>
  p { color: red; }
  p { color: blue; }
  p { color: green; }
</style>
```

In this scenario, paragraph text will be green because the last rule in the style sheet—that is, the one closest to the content in the document—overrides the earlier ones. The same thing happens when conflicting styles occur within a single declaration stack:

```
<style>
  p { color: red;
      color: blue;
      color: green; }
</style>
```

The resulting color will be green because the last declaration overrides the previous two. It is easy to accidentally override previous declarations within a rule when you get into compound properties, so this is an important behavior to keep in mind.

NOTE

This "last one listed wins" rule applies in other contexts in CSS as well. For example, external style sheets listed later in the source will be given precedence over those listed above them.

The box model

As long as we're talking about "big CSS concepts," it is only appropriate to introduce the cornerstone of the CSS visual formatting system: the box model. The easiest way to think of the box model is that browsers see every element on the page (both block and inline) as being contained in a little rectangular box. You can apply properties such as borders, margins, padding, and backgrounds to these boxes, and even reposition them on the page.

We're going to go into a lot more detail about the box model in Chapter 14, but having a general feel for it will benefit you even as we discuss text and backgrounds in the following two chapters.

To see the elements roughly the way the browser sees them, I've written style rules that add borders around every content element in our sample article.

```
h1 { border: 1px solid blue; }
h2 { border: 1px solid blue; }
p { border: 1px solid blue; }
em { border: 1px solid blue; }
img { border: 1px solid blue; }
```

Figure 11-9 shows the results. The borders reveal the shape of each block element box. There are boxes around the inline elements (**em** and **img**) as well. Notice that the block element boxes expand to fill the available width of the browser window, which is the nature of block elements in the normal document flow. Inline boxes encompass just the characters or image they contain.

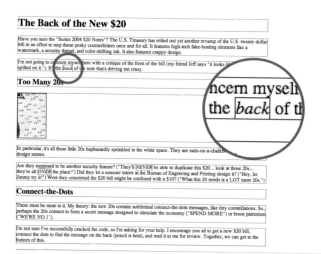

Figure 11-9. Rules around all the elements reveal their element boxes.

Grouped selectors

Hey! This is a good opportunity to show you a handy style rule shortcut. If you ever need to apply the same style property to a number of elements, you can group the selectors into one rule by separating them with commas. This one rule has the same effect as the five rules listed previously. Grouping them makes future edits more efficient and results in a smaller file size.

```
h1, h2, p, em, img { border: 1px solid blue; }
```

Now you have two selector types in your toolbox: a simple element selector and grouped selectors.

A Quick History of CSS

The first official version of CSS (the CSS Level 1 Recommendation, a.k.a CSS1) was officially released in 1996, and included properties for adding font, color, and spacing instructions to page elements. Unfortunately, lack of dependable browser support prevented the widespread adoption of CSS for several years.

CSS Level 2 (CSS2) was released in 1998. It most notably added properties for positioning that allowed CSS to be used for page layout. It also introduced styles for other media types (such as print, handheld, and aural) and more sophisticated methods for selecting elements for styling. CSS Level 2, Revision 1 (CSS2.1) makes some minor adjustments to CSS2 and became a full Recommendation in 2011.

CSS Level 3 (CSS3) is different from prior versions in that it has been divided into many individual modules, each addressing a feature such as animation, multiple column layouts, or borders. While some modules are being standardized, others remain experimental. In that way, browser developers can begin implementing (and we can begin using!) one feature at a time instead of waiting for an entire specification to be "ready." In fact, many developers use enhanced CSS3 features even though they aren't universally supported as long as the fallback is usable and no content is lost. They can be used as "frosting" on an otherwise stable design (or in other words, as an enhancement).

To keep up to date with the various CSS features in the works, see the W3C's CSS Current work page at *www.w3.org/Style/CSS/current-work*.

Moving Forward with CSS

This chapter covered all the fundamentals of Cascading Style Sheets, including rule syntax, ways to apply styles to a document, and the central concepts of inheritance, the cascade, and the box model. Style sheets should no longer be a mystery, and from this point on, we'll merely be building on this foundation by adding properties and selectors to your arsenal as well as expanding on the concepts introduced here.

CSS is a vast topic, well beyond the scope of this book. Bookstores and the Web are loaded with information about style sheets for all skill levels. I've compiled a list of the resources I've found the most useful during my learning process. I've also provided a list of popular tools that assist in writing style sheets.

Books

There is no shortage of good books on CSS out there, but these are the ones that taught me, and I feel good recommending them.

Cascading Style Sheets: The Definitive Guide, by Eric A. Meyer (O'Reilly)

CSS: The Missing Manual, by David Sawyer McFarland (O'Reilly)

Handcrafted CSS: More Bulletproof Web Design, by Dan Cederholm (New Riders)

CSS Cookbook: Quick Solutions to Common CSS Problems, by Christopher Schmitt (O'Reilly)

Online resources

The sites listed here are good starting points for online exploration of style sheets.

World Wide Web Consortium (*www.w3.org/Style/CSS*). The World Wide Web Consortium oversees the development of web technologies, including CSS.

A List Apart (*www.alistapart.com/topics/code/css/*). This online magazine features some of the best thinking and writing on cutting-edge, standards-based web design. It was founded in 1998 by Jeffrey Zeldman and Brian Platz.

CSS-tricks (*css-tricks.com*). The is the blog of CSS whiz kid Chris Coyier. Chris *loves* CSS and enthusiastically shares his research and tinkering on his site.

CSS tools

Here are a couple of tools that I can personally recommend.

Web Developer extension

Web developers are raving about the Web Developer extension written by Chris Pederick. The extension adds a toolbar to the browser with tools that enable you to analyze and manipulate any page in the window. You can edit the style sheet for the page you are viewing as well as get information about the HTML and graphics. It also validates the CSS, HTML, and accessibility of the page. It is available for Chrome and Firefox/Mozilla browsers. Get it at *chrispederick.com/work/web-developer*. Note that Safari has a similar built-in inspector (go to Develop → Show Web Inspector).

Web-authoring programs

Current WYSIWYG authoring programs such as Adobe Dreamweaver and Microsoft Expression Web can be configured to write a style sheet for you automatically as you design the page. The downside is that they are not always written in the most efficient manner (for example, they tend to overuse the `class` attribute to create style rules). Still, they may give you a good head start on the style sheet that you can then edit manually.

Test Yourself

Here are a few questions to test your knowledge of the CSS basics. Answers are provided in Appendix A.

1. Identify the various parts of this style rule:

    ```
    blockquote { line-height: 1.5; }
    ```

    selector: _____   value: _____

    property: _____   declaration: _____

2. What color will paragraphs be when this embedded style sheet is applied to a document? Why?

    ```
    <style type="text/css">
        p { color: purple; }
        p { color: green; }
        p { color: gray; }
    </style>
    ```

3. Rewrite each of these CSS examples. Some of them are completely incorrect, and some could just be written more efficiently.

    a. ```
        p {font-family: sans-serif;}
        p {font-size: 1em;}
        p {line-height: 1.2em;}
        ```

    b.  ```
        blockquote {
            font-size: 1em
            line-height: 150%
            color: gray }
        ```

    c. ```
        body
            {background-color: black;}
            {color: #666;}
            {margin-left: 12em;}
            {margin-right: 12em;}
        ```

    d.  ```
        p {color: white;}
        blockquote {color: white;}
        li {color: white;}
        ```

    e. ```
        Act now!
        ```
        ```

4. Circle all the elements that you would expect to appear in red when the following style rule is applied to a document with the structure diagrammed in Figure 11-10. This rule uses a type of selector you haven't seen yet, but common sense should serve you well.

```
div#intro { color: red;}
```

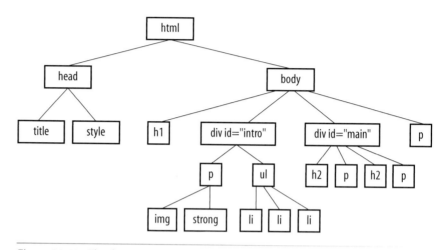

Figure 11-10. The document structure of a sample document.

FORMATTING TEXT
(Plus More Selectors)

Now that you've gotten your feet wet formatting text, are you ready to jump into the deep end? By the end of this chapter, you'll pick up 15 new CSS properties used to manipulate the appearance of text. Along the way, you'll also learn how to use more powerful selectors for targeting elements in a particular context and with a specific **id** or **class** name.

The nature of the Web makes specifying type tricky, if not downright frustrating, particularly if you have experience designing for print (or even formatting text in a word processing program). There is no way to know for sure whether the font you specify will be available or how large or small the type will appear when it hits your users' browsers. We'll address the best practices for dealing with these challenges as we go along.

Throughout this chapter, we'll be sprucing up a Black Goose Bistro online menu similar to the one we marked up back in Chapter 5, "Marking Up Text." I encourage you to work along with the exercises to get a feel for how the properties work. Figure 12-1 shows how the menu looks before and after we're done. It's not a masterpiece, because we're just scratching the surface of CSS here, but at least the text is more refined.

The Font Properties

When I design a text document (for print or the Web), one of the first things I do is specify a font. In CSS, fonts are specified using a little bundle of font-related properties for typeface, size, weight, and font style. There is also a shortcut property that lets you specify all of the font attributes in one fell swoop.

AT A GLANCE

The font-related properties:

    font-family
    font-size
    font-weight
    font-style
    font-variant
    font

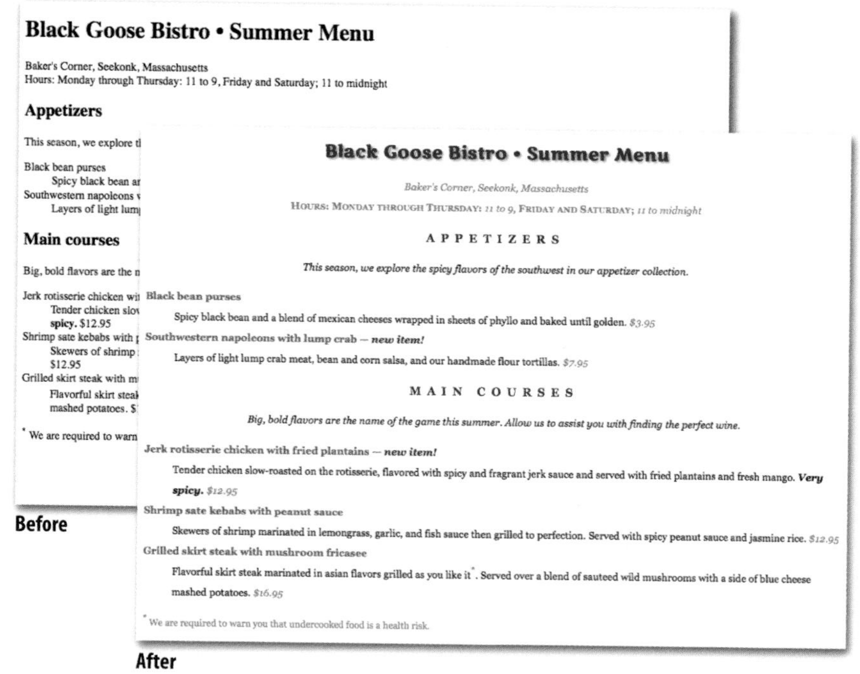

Figure 12-1. Before and after views of the Black Goose Bistro menu that we'll be working on in this chapter.

Specifying the font name

Choosing a typeface, or font family as it is called in CSS, for your text is a good place to start. Let's begin with the **font-family** property and its values.

font-family

Values:	one or more font or generic font family names, separated by commas | inherit
Default:	depends on the browser
Applies to:	all elements
Inherits:	yes

Use the **font-family** property to specify a font or list of fonts (known as a font stack) by name, as shown in these examples.

```
body { font-family: Arial; }
var { font-family: Courier, monospace; }
p { font-family: "Duru Sans", Verdana, sans-serif; }
```

Here are some important syntax requirements:

- All font names, with the exception of generic font families, must be capitalized. For example, use "Arial" instead of "arial".

- Use commas to separate multiple font names, as shown in the second and third examples.

- Notice that font names that contain a character space (such as Duru Sans in the third example) must appear within quotation marks.

A Word About Property Listings

Each new property listing in this book is accompanied by information on how it behaves and how to use it. Here is a quick explanation of each part of property listings.

Values

These are the accepted values for the property. Predefined keyword values appear in code font (for example, `small`, `italic`, or `small-caps`) and must be typed in exactly as shown.

Default

This is the value that will be used for the property by default—that is, if no other value is specified. Note that the default browser style sheet values may vary from the defaults defined in CSS.

Applies to

Some properties apply only to certain types of elements, such as block or table elements.

Inherits

This indicates whether the property will be passed down to the selected element's descendants. See Chapter 11, "Cascading Style Sheets Orientation," for an explanation of inheritance.

You might be asking, "Why specify more than one font?" That's a good question, and it brings us to one of the challenges of specifying fonts for web pages.

Font limitations

Browsers are limited to displaying fonts they have access to. Traditionally, that meant the fonts that were already installed on the user's hard drive. In 2010, however, there was a boom in browser support for embedded web fonts using the CSS `@font-face` rule, so it became possible for designers to provide their own fonts. See the "Say Hello to Web Fonts" sidebar for more information.

But back to our `font-family` rule. Even when you specify that the font should be Futura in a style rule, if the browser can't find it (for example, if that font is not installed on the user's computer or the provided web font fails to load), the browser uses its default font instead.

Fortunately, CSS allows us to provide a list of back-up fonts (that font stack we saw earlier) should our first choice not be available. If the first specified font is not found, the browser tries the next one, and down through the list until it finds one that works. In the third font-family rule shown in the previous code example, if the browser does not find Duru Sans, it will use Verdana, and if Verdana is not available, it will substitute some other sans-serif font.

Say Hello to Web Fonts

The ability to provide your own font for use on a web page has been around since 1998, but it was never feasible due to browser inconsistencies. Fortunately, that story has changed, and now web fonts are a perfectly viable option. The Web has never looked better!

There is a lot to say about web fonts, so this sidebar is merely an introduction to the highlights, starting with the challenges.

What took you so long?

There have been two main hurdles to including fonts with web pages. First, there is the problem that different browsers support different font formats. Most fonts come in OpenType (OTF) or TrueType (TTF) format, but Internet Explorer only accepts its proprietary Embedded Open Type (EOT).

The good news is that there is a new standard for packaging fonts for delivery to web pages that all browser vendors, even IE, are implementing. The new format, WOFF (for Web Open Font Format), is a container that packages font files for web delivery. Now that IE9 is supporting WOFF, one day it may be all we need. As of this writing, however, we still need to provide the same font in a number of different formats (more on that in just a moment).

The other issue with providing fonts on web pages is that the font companies (also called foundries) are concerned (a nice way to say "freaked out") that their fonts will be sitting vulnerably on servers and available for download. Fonts cost a lot to create and are very valuable. Most come with licenses that cover very specific uses by a limited number of machines, and "free to download for whatever" is usually not included.

So, to link to a web font, you need to use the font legally and provide it in a way that all browsers support. There are two general approaches to providing fonts: host them yourself or use a web font service. Let's look at both options.

Host your own

In the "host your own" option, you find the font you want, put it on your server in all the required formats, and link it to your web page using the CSS3 @font-face rule.

Step 1: Find a font. This can be a bit of a challenge because the End User License Agreement (EULA) for virtually all commercial fonts does not cover web usage. Be sure to purchase the additional web license if it is available. However, thanks to demand, some foundries are opening fonts up for web use, and there are a growing number of open source fonts that you can use for free. The service Fontspring (*fontspring.com*), by Ethan Dunham, is a great place to purchase fonts that have a web license that you can use on your site or your own computer. The site Font Squirrel (*fontsquirrel.com*), also by Ethan Dunham, is a great source for open source fonts that can be used for commercial purposes for free.

Step 2: Save it in multiple formats. As of this writing, providing multiple formats is a reality. There are tools that will convert your source font into other formats, but there is a service that will take your font and make everything you need for you—the "@font-face Generator" from Font Squirrel (*www.fontsquirrel.com/fontface/generator*). Go to that page, upload your font, and it gives back the font in TTF, EOT, WOFF, and SVG, as well as the CSS code you need to make it work. Bear in mind that you should use the service only for a font that specifically allows web usage (whether that font is free, open source, or commercial). Note also that you will get better-quality font versions directly from a font vendor than you will using the Generator.

Step 3: Upload to the server. Developers typically keep their font files in the same directory as the CSS files, but that's just a matter of preference. If you download a package from Font Squirrel, be sure to keep the pieces together as you found them.

Step 4: Write the code. Link the font to your site using the @font-face rule in your *.css* document. The rule gives the font a font-family name that you can then reference later in your style sheet. It also lists the locations of the font files in their various formats. This cross-browser code example was developed by Ethan Dunham (yep, him again!) to address a bug in IE. I recommend reading the full article at *www.fontspring.com/blog/the-new-bulletproof-font-face-syntax*. See also Paul Irish's updated version at *paulirish.com/2009/bulletproof-font-face-implementation-syntax/*.

```
@font-face {
font-family: 'Font_name';
  src: url('myfont-webfont.eot?#iefix')
    format('embedded-opentype'),
  url('myfont-webfont.woff') format('woff'),
  url('myfont-webfont.ttf')  format('truetype'),
  url('myfont-webfont.svg#svgFontName')
    format('svg');
}
```

Then you just refer to the established font name in your font rules, like so:

```
p {font-family: Font_name; }
```

Use a font embedding service

If that seems like a lot of work, you may want to sign up with one of the font embedding services that do all the heavy lifting for you. For a fee, you get access to high-quality fonts, and the service handles font licensing and font protection for the foundries. They also generally provide an interface and tools that make embedding a font as easy as copy and paste.

The services have a variety of fee structures. Some charge monthly fees; some charge by the font. Some have a surcharge for bandwidth as well. There are generally tiered plans that range from free to hundreds of dollars per month.

Here are some font embedding services that are popular as of this writing, but it's worth doing a web search to see what's currently offered.

Google Web Fonts (www.google.com/webfonts)

Google Web Fonts is a free service that provides access to hundreds of open source fonts that are free for commercial use. All you have to do is choose a font, then copy and paste the code they generate for you. If you don't have a font budget and you aren't too fussy about fonts, this is a wonderful way to go. We'll use it in the first exercise in this chapter.

Typekit, from Adobe (www.typekit.com)

Typekit was the first web font service and is now part of Adobe. Their service uses JavaScript to link the fonts to your site in a way that improves performance and quality in all browsers. I also recommend their blog for excellent articles on how type works (see blog.typekit.com/category/type-rendering/).

Fonts.com (fonts.com)

Fonts.com boasts the largest font collection from the biggest font foundries. If you need a particular font, they are likely to have it.

Other services include WebINK (www.extensis.com/en/WebINK), Typotheque (www.typotheque.com/webfonts), Fonts Live (www.fontslive.com), and Fontdeck (fontdeck.com). They differ in the number of fonts they offer and their fee structures, so you may want to shop around.

Summing it up

Which method you use to add fonts to your site is up to your discretion. If you like total control, hosting your own font (legally, of course) may be a good way to go. If you need a very particular, well-known font because your client's brand depends on it, you will probably find it on one of the web font services for a price. If you want to experiment with web fonts and are happy to choose from what's freely available, then Google Web Fonts is for you.

You now have a good foundation in providing web fonts. The landscape is likely to change quickly over the next few years, so be sure to do your own research when you are ready to get started.

Generic font families

That last option, "some other sans-serif font," bears more discussion. "Sans-serif" is just one of five generic font families that you can specify with the `font-family` property. When you specify a generic font family, the browser chooses an available font from that stylistic category. Figure 12-2 shows examples from each family. Generic font family names do not need to be capitalized.

serif

> *Examples: Times, Times New Roman, Georgia*
>
> Serif typefaces have decorative slab-like appendages (serifs) on the ends of certain letter strokes.

sans-serif

> *Examples: Arial, Arial Black, Verdana, Trebuchet MS, Helvetica, Geneva*
>
> Sans-serif typefaces have straight letter strokes that do not end in serifs.

monospace

> *Examples: Courier, Courier New, and Andale Mono*
>
> In monospace (also called constant width) typefaces, all characters take up the same amount of space on a line. For example, a capital W will be no wider than a lowercase i. Compare this to proportional typefaces (such as the one you're reading now) that allot different widths to different characters.

Figure 12-2. Examples of the five generic font families.

cursive

> *Examples: Apple Chancery, Zapf-Chancery, and Comic Sans*
>
> Cursive fonts emulate a script or handwritten appearance.

fantasy

> *Examples: Impact, Western, or other decorative font*
>
> Fantasy fonts are purely decorative and would be appropriate for head-
> lines and other display type. Fantasy fonts are rarely used for web text due
> to cross-platform availability and legibility.

Font stack strategies

The best practice for specifying fonts for web pages is to start with your first choice, provide some similar alternatives, and then end with a generic font family that at least gets users in the right stylistic ballpark. For example, if you want an upright, sans-serif font, you might start with your favorite font (Futura), list a few that are more common (Univers, Tahoma, Geneva), and finish with the generic sans-serif. There is no limit to the number of fonts you can include, but many designers strive to keep it under 10.

```
font-family: Futura, Univers, Tahoma, Geneva, sans-serif;
```

A good font stack should include stylistically related fonts that are known to be installed on most computers. Sticking with fonts that come with the Windows, Mac OS, and Linux operating systems as well as fonts that get installed with popular software packages such as Microsoft Office and Adobe Creative Suite gives you a solid list of "web-safe" fonts to choose from. The charts and statistics provided by the following sites are excellent resources for finding what fonts are commonly available.

- Complete Guide to Pre-Installed Fonts in Linux, Mac, and Windows (*www.apaddedcell.com/sites/www.apaddedcell.com/files/fonts-article/final/index.html*)

- Font Matrix (*media.24ways.org/2007/17/fontmatrix.html*)

- Code Style's Web Font Survey and Font Stack Builder (*www.codestyle.org/css/font-family/index.shtml*)

If you are interested in learning more about mastering font stacks, I recommend the following articles, but be sure to do your own web search to find up-to-date recommendations as well.

- "Striking Web Sites with Font Stacks that Inspire" by Vivien (*www.inspirationbit.com/striking-web-sites-with-font-stacks-that-inspire/*)

- "Better CSS Font Stacks" by Nathan Ford (*unitinteractive.com/blog/2008/06/26/better-css-font-stacks/*)

So, as you see, specifying fonts for the Web is more like merely suggesting them. You don't have absolute control over which font your users will see. You might get your first choice; you might get the generic fallback. It's one of those web design quirks you learn to live with.

Now seems like a good time to get started formatting the Black Goose Bistro menu. We'll add new style rules one at a time as we learn each new property.

Best Font Stack Ever

There are loads of articles online touting "best font stacks ever," and the font stack you use will largely be a matter of preference. The following recommendations are inspired by Michael Tuck's "8 Definitive Font Stacks" (*www.sitepoint.com/eight-definitive-font-stacks*) and include fallback fonts for Windows, Mac, and Linux.

Narrow serif (Times-based)

```
Cambria, "Hoefler Text",
"Nimbus Roman No9 L Regular",
Times, "Times New Roman",
serif;
```

Wide serif (Georgia-based)

```
Constantia, "Lucida Bright",
Lucidabright, "Lucida Serif",
Lucida, "DejaVu Serif",
"Liberation Serif", Georgia,
serif;
```

Narrow sans-serif (Arial-based)

```
Univers, Calibri, "Liberation
Sans", "Nimbus Sans L",
Tahoma, Geneva, "Helvetica
Neue", Helvetica, Arial, sans-
serif;
```

Wide sans-serif (Verdana-based)

```
"Lucida Grande", "Lucida Sans
Unicode", "Lucida Sans",
"Liberation Sans", Verdana,
sans-serif;
```

Monospace

```
"Andale Mono WT", "Andale
Mono", "Lucida Console",
"Liberation Mono", "Courier
New", Courier, monospace;
```

exercise 12- 1 | Formatting a menu

In this exercise, we'll add font properties to the Black Goose Bistro menu document, *menu.html*, which is available at *www.learningwebdesign.com/4e/materials*. Open the document in a text editor. You can also open it in a browser to see its "before" state. It should look similar to the page shown in Figure 12-1. Hang onto this document, because this exercise will continue as we pick up additional font properties.

I've included an embedded font in this exercise to show you how easy it is to do with a service like Google Web Fonts.

1. We're going to use an embedded style sheet for this exercise. Start by adding a **style** element in the **head** of the document, like this:

```
<head>
   <title>Black Goose Bistro</title>
   <style>

   </style>
</head>
```

2. I would like the main text to appear in Verdana or some other sans-serif font. Instead of writing a rule for every element in the document, we will write one rule for the **body** element that will be inherited by all the elements it contains. Add this rule to the embedded style sheet.

```
<style>
   body {font-family: Verdana, sans-serif;}
</style>
```

3. I want a fancy font for the "Black Goose Bistro, Summer Menu" headline, so I chose a free display font called Marko One from Google Web Fonts (*www.google.com/webfonts*). Google gave me the code for linking the font file on their server to my HTML file (it's actually a link to an external style sheet). It must be placed in the **head** of the document, so copy it exactly as it appears but keep it on one line.

```
<head>
<title>Black Goose Bistro</title>
<link href="http://fonts.googleapis.com/
css?family=Marko+One" rel="stylesheet">
</head>
```

4. And then write a rule that applies it to the **h1** element. Notice I've specified Georgia or another serif font as fallbacks.

```
<style>
   body {font-family: Verdana, sans-serif;}
   h1 {font-family: "Marko One", Georgia,
serif;}
</style>
```

5. Save the document and reload the page in the browser. It should look like Figure 12-3. Note that you'll need to have an Internet connection and a current browser to view the Marko One headline font. We'll work on the text size in the next exercise.

Figure 12-3. The menu after changing only the fonts.

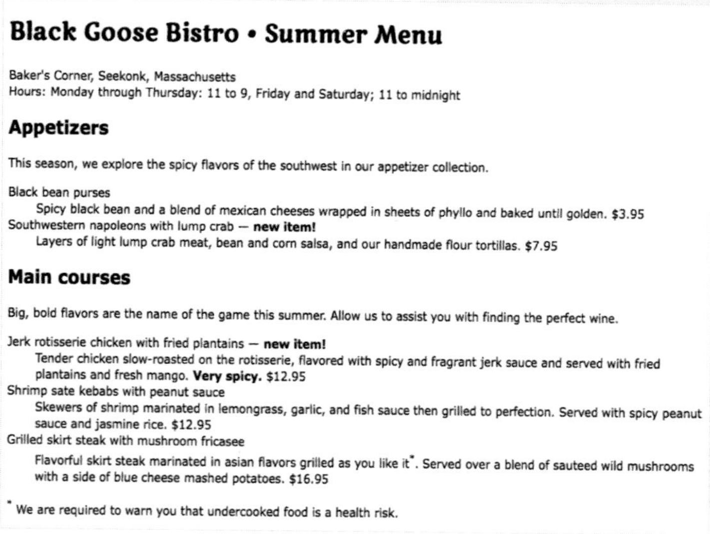

Black Goose Bistro • Summer Menu

Baker's Corner, Seekonk, Massachusetts
Hours: Monday through Thursday: 11 to 9, Friday and Saturday; 11 to midnight

Appetizers

This season, we explore the spicy flavors of the southwest in our appetizer collection.

Black bean purses
   Spicy black bean and a blend of mexican cheeses wrapped in sheets of phyllo and baked until golden. $3.95
Southwestern napoleons with lump crab — **new item!**
   Layers of light lump crab meat, bean and corn salsa, and our handmade flour tortillas. $7.95

Main courses

Big, bold flavors are the name of the game this summer. Allow us to assist you with finding the perfect wine.

Jerk rotisserie chicken with fried plantains — **new item!**
   Tender chicken slow-roasted on the rotisserie, flavored with spicy and fragrant jerk sauce and served with fried plantains and fresh mango. **Very spicy.** $12.95
Shrimp sate kebabs with peanut sauce
   Skewers of shrimp marinated in lemongrass, garlic, and fish sauce then grilled to perfection. Served with spicy peanut sauce and jasmine rice. $12.95
Grilled skirt steak with mushroom fricasee
   Flavorful skirt steak marinated in asian flavors grilled as you like it*. Served over a blend of sauteed wild mushrooms with a side of blue cheese mashed potatoes. $16.95

* We are required to warn you that undercooked food is a health risk.

Specifying font size

Use the aptly named **font-size** property to specify the size of the text.

font-size

Values: length unit | percentage | xx-small | x-small | small | medium | large | x-large | xx-large | smaller | larger | inherit

Default: medium

Applies to: all elements

Inherits: yes

You can specify text size in several ways:

- At a specific size using one of the CSS length units (see the sidebar "CSS Units of Measurement" for a complete list), as shown here:

      h1 { font-size: 1.5em; }

  When specifying a number of units, be sure the unit abbreviation immediately follows the number, with no extra character space in between:

      INCORRECT h1 { font-size: 1.5 em; } /*space before the em*/

- As a percentage value, sized up or down from the element's default or inherited font size:

      h1 { font-size: 150%; }

- Using one of the absolute keywords (**xx-small**, **x-small**, **small**, **medium**, **large**, **x-large**, **xx-large**). On most current browsers, **medium** corresponds to the default font size.

      h1 { font-size: x-large; }

- Using a relative keyword (**larger** or **smaller**) to nudge the text larger or smaller than the surrounding text:

      strong { font-size: larger; }

I'm going to cut to the chase and tell you that, despite all these options, the preferred values for **font-size** in contemporary web design are em measurements and percentage values (or a combination of the two). I'll explain the other **font-size** values in a moment, but let's start our discussion with the most prevalent approach.

Both ems and percentages are relative measurements, which means they are based on another font size, namely the inherited **font-size** of the *parent* element.

Percentage values

In this example, the **font-size** of the **h1**'s parent element (**body**) has been specified as 100% of the default text size (generally 16 pixels). The **h1** inherits the 16px size from the **body** element, and applying the 150% **font-size** value multiplies that *inherited* value, resulting in an **h1** that is 24 pixels. If the user has her font size set to 30 pixels, for example, to read it on a television browser from across the room, the resulting **h1** would be 45 pixels, but would maintain its proportion relative to the main body text, which is the idea of using relative measurements.

```
body { font-size: 100%; }
h1 { font-size: 150%; }   /* 150% of 16 = 24 */
```

CSS Units of Measurement

CSS3 provides a variety of units of measurement. They fall into two broad categories: relative and absolute.

Relative units

Relative units are based on the size of something else, such as the default text size or the size of the parent element.

px   pixel, considered relative in CSS2.1 because it varies with display resolution

em   a unit of measurement equal to the current font size

ex   x-height, approximately the height of a lowercase "x" in the font

The following units are new in CSS3. Browser support may take a while to ramp up.

`rem`   root em, equal to the em size of the root element (`html`)

ch   zero width, equal to the width of a zero (0) in the current font and size

vw   viewport width unit, equal to 1/100 of the current viewport (browser window) width

vh   viewport height unit, equal to 1/100 of the current viewport height

vm   viewport minimum unit, equal to the value of **vw** or **vh**, whichever is smaller

Absolute units

Absolute units have predefined meanings or real-world equivalents.

px   pixel, defined as an absolute measurement equal to 1/96 of an inch in CSS3

pt   points (1/72 inch in CSS2.1)

pc   picas (1 pica = 12 points)

mm   millimeters

cm   centimeters

`in`   inches

Absolute units should be avoided for web page style sheets because they are not relevant on computer screens. However, if you are creating a style sheet to be used when the document is printed, they may be just the ticket.

Did you happen to notice that pixel (**px**) is in both of these lists? That's because the W3C hasn't quite made up its mind. Definitions aside, in practice pixels work as an absolute measurement that is not as flexible as true relative units.

Em measurements

An em is a relative unit of measurement that, in traditional typography, is based on the width of the capital letter M (thus the name "em"). In the CSS specification, an em is calculated as the distance between baselines when the font is set without any extra space between the lines (also known as leading). For text with a font size of 16 pixels, an em measures 16 pixels; for 12-pixel text, an em equals 12 pixels; and so on, as shown in Figure 12-4.

NOTE

Don't confuse the em unit of measurement with the em HTML element used to indicate emphasized text. They are totally different things.

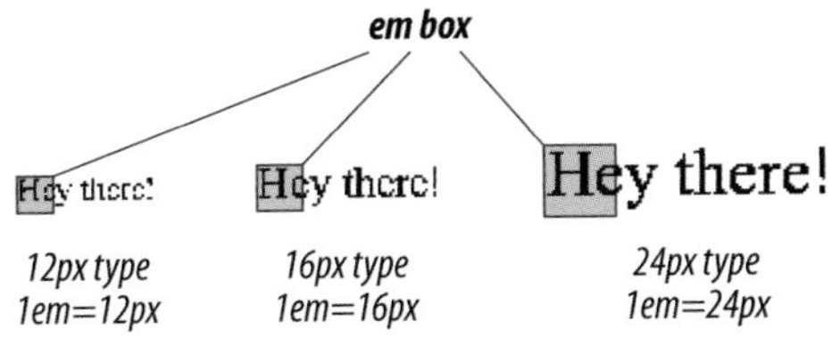

Figure 12-4. An em is based on the size of the text.

Once the dimension of an em for a text element is calculated by the browser, it can be used for all sorts of other measurements, such as indents, margins, the width of the element on the page, and so on.

When setting **font-size** in ems, the em value works like a scaling factor, similar to a percentage. In the following example, the **body** is set at 100% (we'll assume the default of 16 pixels). Setting the **h1** to 1.5 ems makes it one and a half times larger than its inherited size, or 24 pixels.

```
body { font-size: 100%; }
h1 { font-size: 1.5em; }  /* 1.5 x 16 = 24 */
```

Em best practices

As of this writing, the most popular solution for making ems display consistently is to set the size of the **body** element to 100% (keeping it at the default or user's preference), then use ems to size the text elements thereafter, as we've done in the previous example. This preserves the user's preferred text viewing size yet ensures that text elements are sized proportionally.

There are a few snags to working with ems. One is that due to rounding errors, there is some inconsistency among browsers and platforms when text size is set in ems.

The other tricky aspect to using ems is that they are based on the inherited size of the element, which means that their size is based on the context in which they are applied. If you have many nested elements, the size increase or decrease will compound with each nested level. An example will make this clearer.

To calculate % and em values, use this formula:
target size ÷ size of content = result

Say you start with the document's **body** set to 100% (16 pixels), but you want an **article** to be only 14 pixels. Dividing the target (14 pixels) by the context it appears in (16 pixels) gives you .875em for the article **font-size**. Now, let's say you want the **h2** elements in that **article** to be 18 pixels. This time, the em size is not based on the 16-pixel body text size; it is based on the **article** element's 14-pixel size because that is the context of the **h2**. So we divide the target (18px) by the context (14px) to get the final em measurement, 1.28571429. That's quite a value! You can round it down (leave at least four places after the decimal), but there is no need to.

```
body {font-size: 100%;}
article {font-size: .875em;}
    /*based on inherited size of the body text */
article h2 {font-size: 1.28571429em; }
    /*based on the article font size, not body */
```

Ethan Marcotte (of responsive web design fame) has been hammering the "target ÷ context = result" formula into our heads for a few years now, and it comes in handy for building fluid page layouts and other relative sizing tasks. It will certainly come up again in this book.

So pay close attention and write styles rules in a way that compensates for this compounding effect. See the "Introducing the Root Em" sidebar for an up and coming approach that sidesteps this problem.

Pixels and absolute measurements

Although some developers prefer pixel font measurements for the precise control they offer, the predominant attitude is that they are too rigid and that relative measurements (em and %) are more appropriate to the medium. As long as we are kicking **px** to the curb, all of the absolute units—such as **pt**, **pc**, **in**, **mm**, and **cm**—are out because they are irrelevant on screens (although they may be useful for print style sheets).

Another drawback to pixel **font-size** values is that Internet Explorer (all versions) does not allow text-zoom on type sized in pixels. That means users are stuck with your 10- or 11-pixel type, even if they are unable to read it. That's a big no-no in terms of accessibility. IE7 and higher do allow the whole page to be zoomed, which is an improvement, but it is not an ideal user experience.

Introducing the Root Em

There is a new relative measurement in CSS3 called a rem (for root em) that bases font size on the size of the root (**html**) element. If you specify the size of the **html** element (presumably to 100%), all elements that are specified in rem measurements will be relative to that size, not their inherited size. This gets rid of the compounding issue that makes ems potentially aggravating. The drawback is that IE8 and earlier and other older browsers do not support rems, so you need to provide a fallback font size in pixels. Browsers that support rems will use the last declaration in the stack.

```
html {
    font-size: 100%;
}
#main {
    font-size: 12px;
    font-size: .75rem;
}
```

The rem unit is gaining popularity in the web development community. For a more thorough introduction, I recommend the article "Font Sizing with rem" by Jonathan Snook (*snook.ca/archives/html_and_css/font-size-with-rem*).

Working with keywords

The remaining way to specify **font-size** using is one of the predefined absolute keywords: **xx-small**, **x-small**, **small**, **medium**, **large**, **x-large**, and **xx-large**. The keywords do not correspond to particular measurements, but rather are scaled consistently in relation to one another. The default size is **medium** in current browsers. Figure 12-5 shows how each of the absolute keywords renders in a browser when the default text is set at 16 pixels. I've included samples in Verdana and Times to show that, even with the same base size, there is a big difference in legibility at sizes **small** and below.

The benefit of keywords is that current browsers won't let text sized in keywords render smaller than 9 pixels, so they protect against illegible type. On the downside, keywords are imprecise and unpredictable. For example, while most browsers scale each level up by 120%, some browsers use a scaling factor of 150%.

The relative keywords, **larger** and **smaller**, are used to shift the size of text relative to the size of the parent element text. The exact amount of the size change is determined by each browser and is out of your control. Despite that limitation, it is an easy way to nudge type a bit larger or smaller if the exact proportions are not critical.

Figure 12-5. Text sized with absolute keywords.

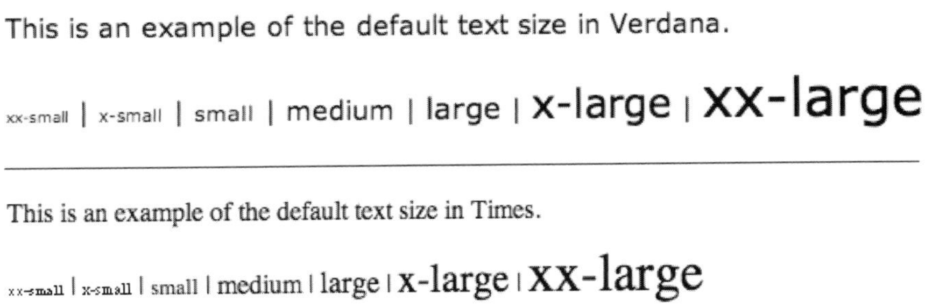

This is an example of the default text size in Verdana.

xx-small | x-small | small | medium | large | x-large | xx-large

This is an example of the default text size in Times.

xx-small | x-small | small | medium | large | x-large | xx-large

exercise 12-2 | **Setting font size**

Let's refine the size of some of the text elements to give the online menu a more sophisticated appearance. Open *menu.html* in a text editor and follow the steps below. You can save the document at any point and take a peek in the browser to see the results of your work. You should also feel free to try out other size values along the way.

1. There are many approaches to sizing text on web pages. In this example, I'll stick with the preferred method of the best web developers I know, which is to start by putting a stake in the ground and setting the **body** element to 100%, thus clearing the way for em measurements thereafter.

```
body {
    font-family: Verdana, sans-serif;
    font-size: 100%;
}
```

2. I'd like the main text elements to be 14 pixels instead of the default 16 pixels (if it's too small for my visitors, they can zoom it larger in the browser). I'll add a new rule with a grouped selector to set the size of **p** and **dl** elements to .875em, using the formula target (14) ÷ context (16) = .875. I could have used 87.5% to achieve the same thing.

```
p, dl {
    font-size: .875em;
}
```

3. Now let's get the size of the headings under control. I'd like the main heading (**h1**) to be one and a half times larger than the body text. The **h2**s can be the default text size (1em).

```
h1 {
    font-family: "Marko One",
Georgia, serif;
    font-size: 1.5em
}
h2 {
    font-size: 1em;
}
```

Figure 12-6 shows the result of our font-sizing efforts.

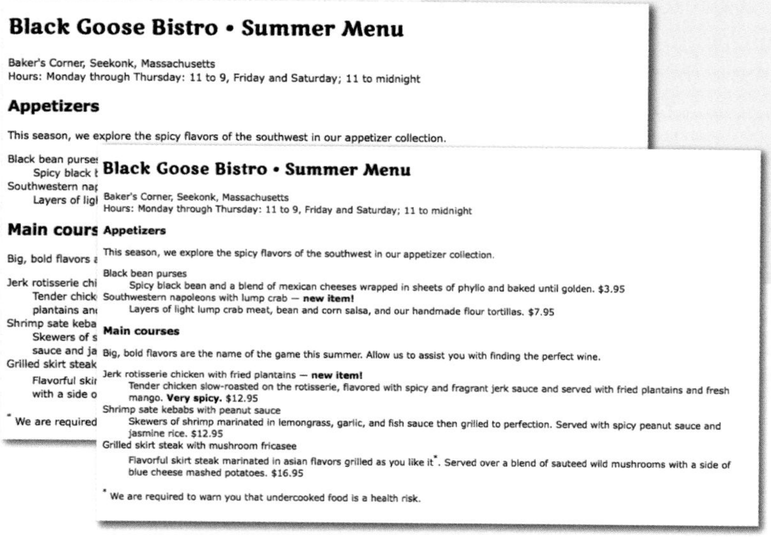

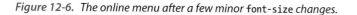

Figure 12-6. The online menu after a few minor font-size *changes.*

Font weight (boldness)

After font families and size, the remaining font properties are straightforward. For example, if you want a text element to appear in bold, use the `font-weight` property to adjust the boldness of type.

font-weight

Values: `normal | bold | bolder | lighter | 100 | 200 | 300 | 400 | 500 | 600 | 700 | 800 | 900 | inherit`

Default: `normal`

Applies to: *all elements*

Inherits: *yes*

As you can see, the `font-weight` property has many predefined values, including descriptive terms (`normal`, `bold`, `bolder`, and `lighter`) and nine numeric values (`100` to `900`) for targeting various weights of a font if they are available. Because most fonts commonly used on the Web have only two weights, normal (or roman) and bold, the only font weight value you will use in most cases is `bold`. You may also use `normal` to make text that would otherwise appear in bold (such as strong text or headlines) appear at a normal weight.

The numeric chart is an interesting idea, but because there aren't many fonts with that range of weights, and because browser support is spotty, they are not often used. In general, numeric settings of 600 and higher result in bold text, although even that can vary by browser, as shown in Figure 12-7.

About inherit

You will see that CSS properties include `inherit` in their list of keyword values. The `inherit` value allows you to explicitly force an element to inherit a style property value from its parent. This may come in handy to override other styles applied to that element and to guarantee that the element always matches its parent.

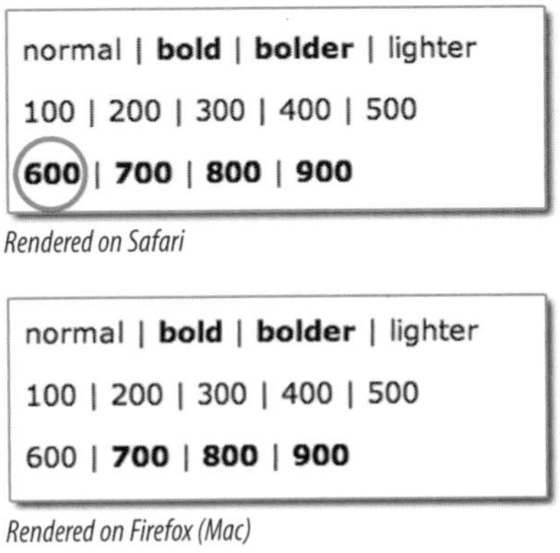
normal | bold | bolder | lighter
100 | 200 | 300 | 400 | 500
600 | 700 | 800 | 900
Rendered on Safari
normal | bold | bolder | lighter
100 | 200 | 300 | 400 | 500
600 | 700 | 800 | 900
Rendered on Firefox (Mac)

Figure 12-7. The effect of `font-weight` values.

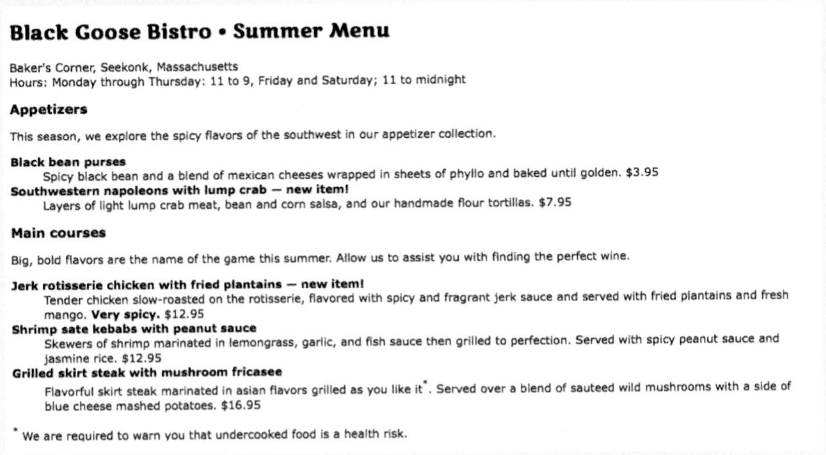
Black Goose Bistro • Summer Menu
Baker's Corner, Seekonk, Massachusetts
Hours: Monday through Thursday: 11 to 9, Friday and Saturday; 11 to midnight
Appetizers
This season, we explore the spicy flavors of the southwest in our appetizer collection.
Black bean purses
Spicy black bean and a blend of mexican cheeses wrapped in sheets of phyllo and baked until golden. $3.95
Southwestern napoleons with lump crab — new item!
Layers of light lump crab meat, bean and corn salsa, and our handmade flour tortillas. $7.95
Main courses
Big, bold flavors are the name of the game this summer. Allow us to assist you with finding the perfect wine.
Jerk rotisserie chicken with fried plantains — new item!
Tender chicken slow-roasted on the rotisserie, flavored with spicy and fragrant jerk sauce and served with fried plantains and fresh mango. Very spicy. $12.95
Shrimp sate kebabs with peanut sauce
Skewers of shrimp marinated in lemongrass, garlic, and fish sauce then grilled to perfection. Served with spicy peanut sauce and jasmine rice. $12.95
Grilled skirt steak with mushroom fricasee
Flavorful skirt steak marinated in asian flavors grilled as you like it*. Served over a blend of sauteed wild mushrooms with a side of blue cheese mashed potatoes. $16.95
* We are required to warn you that undercooked food is a health risk.

Figure 12-8. Applying the `font-weight` property to `dt` elements in the menu.

exercise 12-3 | Making text bold

Back to the menu. I've decided that I'd like all of the menu item names to be in bold text. What I'm *not* going to do is wrap each one in `<b>` tags...that would be so 1996! I'm also not going mark them up as `strong` elements...that is not semantically accurate. Instead, the right thing to do is simply apply a style to the semantically correct `dt` (definition term) elements to make them all bold at once. Add this rule to the end of the style sheet, save the file, and try it out in the browser (Figure 12-8).

```
dt { font-weight: bold; }
```

Font style (italics)

The **font-style** property affects the posture of the text—that is, whether the letter shapes are vertical (**normal**) or slanted (**italic** and **oblique**).

font-style

Values: normal | italic | oblique | inherit

Default: normal

Applies to: all elements

Inherits: yes

Italic and oblique are both slanted versions of the font. The difference is that the italic version is usually a separate typeface design with curved letter forms, whereas oblique text takes the normal font design and just slants it. The truth is that in most browsers, they may look exactly the same (see Figure 12-9). You'll probably only use the **font-style** property to make text **italic** or to make text that is italicized in the browser's default styles (such as emphasized text) display as **normal**.

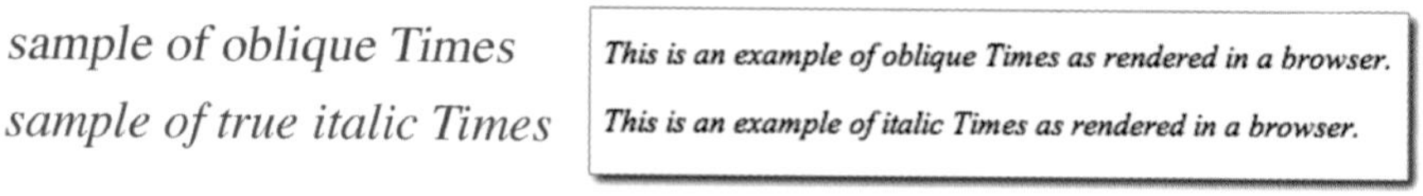

sample of oblique Times   This is an example of oblique Times as rendered in a browser.

sample of true italic Times   This is an example of italic Times as rendered in a browser.

Figure 12-9. Italic and oblique text.

exercise 12-4 |
Making text italic

Now that all the menu item names are bold, some of the text I've marked as **strong** isn't standing out very well, so I think I'll make them italic for further emphasis. To do this, simply apply the **font-style** property to the **strong** element.

```
strong { font-style: italic;}
```

Once again, save and reload. It should look like the detail shown in Figure 12-10.

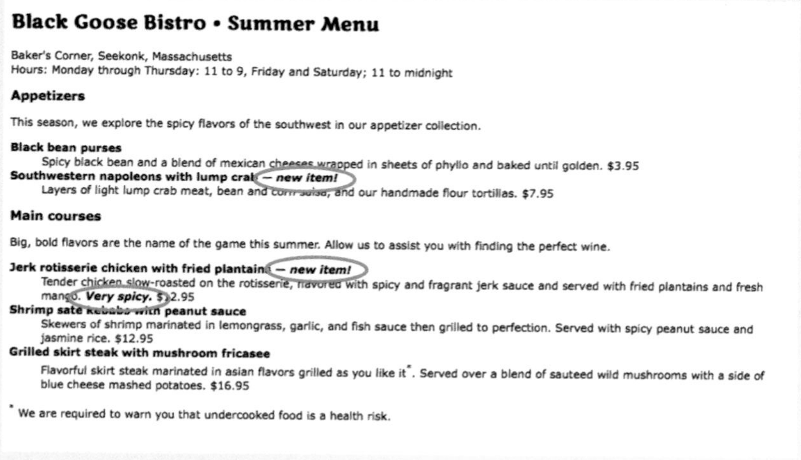

Black Goose Bistro • Summer Menu

Baker's Corner, Seekonk, Massachusetts
Hours: Monday through Thursday: 11 to 9, Friday and Saturday; 11 to midnight

Appetizers

This season, we explore the spicy flavors of the southwest in our appetizer collection.

Black bean purses
Spicy black bean and a blend of mexican cheeses wrapped in sheets of phyllo and baked until golden. $3.95
Southwestern napoleons with lump crab *— new item!*
Layers of light lump crab meat, bean and corn salsa, and our handmade flour tortillas. $7.95

Main courses

Big, bold flavors are the name of the game this summer. Allow us to assist you with finding the perfect wine.

Jerk rotisserie chicken with fried plantains *— new item!*
Tender chicken slow-roasted on the rotisserie, flavored with spicy and fragrant jerk sauce and served with fried plantains and fresh mango. *Very spicy.* $12.95
Shrimp saté kebabs with peanut sauce
Skewers of shrimp marinated in lemongrass, garlic, and fish sauce then grilled to perfection. Served with spicy peanut sauce and jasmine rice. $12.95
Grilled skirt steak with mushroom fricasee
Flavorful skirt steak marinated in asian flavors grilled as you like it*. Served over a blend of sauteed wild mushrooms with a side of blue cheese mashed potatoes. $16.95

* We are required to warn you that undercooked food is a health risk.

Figure 12-10. Applying the font-style property to the strong elements.

Font variant (small caps)

Some typefaces come in a "small caps" variant. This is a separate font design that uses small uppercase-style letters in place of lowercase letter designs. The one-trick-pony **font-variant** property is intended to allow designers to specify such a small-caps font for text elements.

`font-variant`

Values:	normal | small-caps | inherit
Default:	normal
Applies to:	all elements
Inherits:	yes

In most cases, a true small-caps font is not available, so browsers simulate small caps by scaling down uppercase letters in the current font. To typography sticklers, this is less than ideal and results in inconsistent stroke weights, but you may find it an acceptable option for adding variety to small amounts of text. We'll use the **font-variant** property in Exercise 12-6.

The shortcut font property

Specifying multiple font properties for each text element can get repetitive and lengthy, so the creators of CSS provided the shorthand **font** property that compiles all the font-related properties into one rule.

`font`

Values:	*font-style font-weight font-variant font-size/line-height font-family* | inherit
Default:	depends on default value for each property listed
Applies to:	all elements
Inherits:	yes

The value of the **font** property is a list of values for all the font properties we just looked at, separated by character spaces. In this property, the order of the values is important:

```
{ font: style weight variant size/line-height font-family }
```

At minimum, the **font** property *must* include a **font-size** value and a **font-family** value, in that order. Omitting one or putting them in the wrong order causes the entire rule to be invalid. This is an example of a minimal font property value:

```
p { font: 1em sans-serif; }
```

Once you've met the size and family requirements, the other values are optional and may appear in any order *prior* to the **font-size**. When style, weight, or variant are omitted, they revert to **normal**. There is one value in there, **line-height**, that we have not seen before. As it sounds, it adjusts the height of the text line and is used to add space between lines of text. It appears just after **font-size**, separated by a slash, as shown in these examples.

```
h3 { font: oblique bold small-caps 1.5em/1.8em  Verdana, sans-serif; }
h2 { font: bold 1.75em/2 sans-serif; }
```

Let's use the shorthand **font** property to make some changes to the **h2** headings.

---

exercise 12-5 |
Using the shorthand font property

One last tweak to the menu, then we'll take a brief break. To save space, we can combine all the font properties we've specified for the **h1** element in one declaration with the shorthand **font** property.

```
h1 {
    font: bold 1.5em "Marko One", Georgia, serif;
}
```

You might find it redundant that I included the **bold** font weight value in this rule. After all, the **h1** element was already bold by default, right? The thing about shorthand properties is that if you omit a value, it is reset to the default value within that property, not the browser's default value.

In this case, the default **font-weight** value within a **font** declaration is **normal**. Because a style sheet rule we've written overrides the browser's default bold heading rendering, the **h1** would appear in normal-weight text if we don't explicitly make it **bold** in the **font** property. Shorthand properties can be tricky that way…pay attention so you don't leave something out and override a default or inherited value you were counting on.

You can save this and look at in the browser, but if you've done your job right, it should look exactly the same as in the previous step.

Changing Text Color

You got a glimpse of how to change text color in Chapter 11, and to be honest, there's not a lot more to say about it here. You change the color of text with the **color** property.

color

Values: color value (name or numeric) | inherit

Default: depends on the browser and user's preferences

Applies to: all elements

Inherits: yes

Using the **color** property is very straightforward. The value of the **color** property can be a predefined color name (see the "Color Names" sidebar) or a numeric value describing a specific RGB color. Here are a few examples, all of which make the **h1** elements in a document gray:

```
h1 { color: gray; }
h1 { color: #666666; }
h1 { color: #666; }
h1 { color: rgb(102,102,102); }
```

Don't worry about the numeric values for now; I just wanted you to see what they look like. RGB color is discussed in detail in Chapter 13, "Colors and Backgrounds," so in this chapter, we'll just stick with color names for demonstration purposes.

Color is inherited, so you can change the color of all the text in a document by applying the **color** property to the **body** element, as shown here:

```
body { color: fuchsia; }
```

OK, so you probably wouldn't want all your text to be fuchsia, but you get the idea.

For the sake of accuracy, I want to point out that the **color** property is not strictly a text-related property. In fact, according to the CSS specification, it is used to change the foreground (as opposed to the background) color of an element. The foreground of an element consists of both the text it contains as well as its border.

When you apply a color to an element (including image elements), that color will be used for the border as well, unless there is a specific **border-color** property that overrides it. We'll talk more about borders and border color in Chapter 14, "Thinking Inside the Box."

Before we add color to the online menu, I want to take a little side trip and introduce you to a few more types of selectors that will give us more flexibility in targeting elements in the document for styling.

AT A GLANCE

Color Names

CSS2.1 defines 17 standard color names:

black	white	purple
lime	navy	aqua
silver	maroon	fuchsia
olive	blue	orange
gray	red	green
yellow	teal	

The updated CSS3 color module allows names from a larger set of 140 color names to be specified in style sheets. You can see samples of each in Figure 13-2 and at *learningwebdesign. com/colornames.html*.

A Few More Selector Types

So far, we've been using element names as selectors. In the last chapter, you saw how selectors can be grouped together in a comma-separated list so you can apply properties to several elements at once. Here are examples of the selectors you already know.

Element selector	`p { color: navy; }`
Grouped selectors	`p, ul, td, th { color: navy; }`

The disadvantage of selecting elements this way, of course, is that the property (in this case, navy blue text) will apply to every paragraph and other listed elements in the document. Sometimes you want to apply a rule to a particular paragraph or paragraphs. In this section, we'll look at three selector types that allow us to do just that: descendant selectors, ID selectors, and class selectors.

Descendant selectors

A descendant selector targets elements that are contained within (and therefore are descendants of) another element. It is an example of a contextual selector because it selects the element based on its context or relation to another element. The sidebar "Other Contextual Selectors" lists some more.

A character space between element names means that the second element must be contained within the first.

Descendant selectors are indicated in a list separated by a character space. This example targets emphasized text (**em**) elements, but *only* when they appear in list items (**li**). Emphasized text in paragraphs and other elements would be unaffected (Figure 12-11).

```
li em { color: olive; }
```

Here's another example that shows how contextual selectors can be grouped in a comma-separated list, just as we saw earlier. This rule targets **em** elements, but only when they appear in **h1**, **h2**, and **h3** headings.

```
h1 em, h2 em, h3 em { color: red; }
```

It is also possible to nest descendant selectors several layers deep. This example targets **em** elements that appear in anchors (**a**) in ordered lists (**ol**).

```
ol a em { font-variant: small-caps; }
```

Figure 12-11. Only em elements within li elements are selected. The other em elements are unaffected.

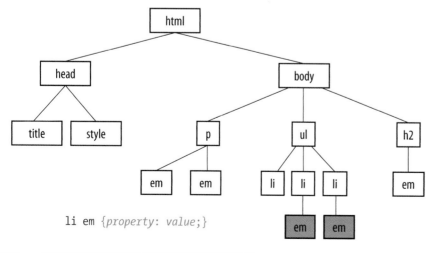

```
li em {property: value;}
```

Other Contextual Selectors

Descendant selectors are one of four types of contextual selectors (called combinators in the CSS3 specification). The other three are child selectors, adjacent sibling selectors, and general sibling selectors.

Child selector

A child selector is similar to a descendant selector, but it targets only the direct children of a given element. There may be no other hierarchical levels in between. They are indicated with the greater-than symbol (>). The following rule affects emphasized text, but only when it is directly contained in a **p** element. An **em** element inside a link (**a**) within the paragraph would not be affected.

```
p > em {font-weight: bold;}
```

Adjacent sibling selector

An adjacent sibling selector targets an element that comes directly after another element with the same parent. It is indicated with a plus (+) sign. This rule gives special treatment to paragraphs that follow an **h1**. Other paragraphs are unaffected.

```
h1 + p {font-style: italic;}
```

General sibling selectors

`NEW IN CSS3`

A general sibling selector selects an element that shares a parent with the specified element and occurs after it in the source order. They do not need to follow one another directly. This type of selector is new in CSS3 and is not supported by Internet Explorer 8 and earlier. The following rule selects any **h2** that both shares a parent element (such as a **section** or **article**) with an **h1** and appears after it in the document.

```
h1 ~ h2 {font-weight: normal;}
```

ID selectors

Way back in Chapter 5, "Marking Up Text," we learned about the **id** attribute that gives an element a unique identifying name (its id reference). The **id** attribute can be used with any HTML element, and it is commonly used to give meaning to the generic **div** and **span** elements.

The # symbol identifies an ID selector.

ID selectors allow you to target elements by their **id** values. The symbol that identifies ID selectors is the octothorpe (**#**), also known as a hash symbol.

Here is an example of a list item with an **id** reference.

```
<li id="catalog1234">Happy Face T-shirt</li>
```

Now you can write a style rule just for that list item using an ID selector, like so (notice the **#** preceding the **id** reference):

```
li#catalog1234 { color: red; }
```

Because **id** values must be unique in the document, it is acceptable to omit the element name. The following rule is equivalent to the last one:

```
#catalog1234 { color: red; }
```

You can also use an ID selector as part of a contextual selector. In this example, a style is applied only to **li** elements that appear within the element identified as "links." In this way, you can treat list items in the element named "links" differently than all the other list items on the page without any additional markup.

```
#links li { margin-left: 10px; }
```

You should be beginning to see the power of selectors and how they can be used strategically along with well-planned semantic markup.

Class selectors

One last selector type, and then we can get back to text style properties. The other element identifier you learned about in Chapter 5 is the **class** identifier, used to classify elements into a conceptual group. Unlike the **id** attribute, multiple elements may share a **class** name. Not only that, but an element may belong to more than one class.

You can target elements belonging to the same class with—you guessed it—a class selector. Class names are indicated with a period (.) at the beginning of the selector. For example, to select all paragraphs with **class="special"**, use this selector (the period indicates the following word is a class selector):

```
p.special { color: orange; }
```

To apply a property to *all* elements of the same class, omit the element name in the selector (be sure to leave the period; it's the character that indicates a class). This would target all paragraphs and any other element that has been marked up with **class="special"**.

```
.special { color: orange; }
```

The period (.) symbol indicates a class selector.

The Universal Selector

CSS2 introduced a universal element selector (*****) that matches any element (like a wildcard in programming languages). The style rule:

```
* {color: gray; }
```

makes the foreground of every element in the document gray. It is also useful as a contextual selector, as shown in this example that selects all elements in an "intro" section:

```
#intro * { color: gray; }
```

The universal selector causes problems with form controls in some browsers. If your page contains form inputs, the safest bet is to avoid the universal selector.

Specificity 101

In Chapter 11, I introduced you to the term specificity, which refers to the fact that more specific selectors have more weight when it comes to handling style rule conflicts. Now that you know a few more selectors, it is a good time to revisit this very important concept.

The actual system CSS uses for calculating selector specificity is quite complicated, but this list of selector types from most to least specific should serve you well in most scenarios.

- ID selectors are more specific than (and will override)
- Class selectors, which are more specific than (and will override)
- Contextual selectors, which are more specific than (and will override)
- Individual element selectors

So, for example, if a style sheet has two conflicting rules for the **strong** element:

```
strong { color: red;}
h1 strong { color: blue; }
```

the contextual selector (**h1 strong**) is more specific and therefore has more weight than the element selector.

You can use specificity strategically to keep your style sheets simple and your markup minimal. For example, it is possible to set a style for an element (**p**, in this example), and then override when necessary by using more specific selectors.

```
p { line-height: 1.2em; }
blockquote p { line-height: 1em; }
p.intro { line-height: 2em; }
```

In these examples, **p** elements that appear within a **blockquote** have a smaller line height than ordinary paragraphs. However, all paragraphs with a **class** of "intro" will have a 2em line height, even if it appears within a **blockquote**, because class selectors are more specific than contextual selectors.

Understanding the concepts of inheritance and specificity are critical to mastering CSS, and there is a lot more to be said about specificity. References are provided in the "More About Specificity" sidebar.

Now, back to the menu. Fortunately, our Black Goose Bistro page has been marked up thoroughly and semantically, so we have a lot of options for selecting specific elements. Give these new selectors a try in Exercise 12-6.

More About Specificity

The specificity overview in this chapter is enough to get you started, but when you get more experienced and your style sheets become more complicated, you may find that you need a more thorough understanding of the inner workings.

For the very technical explanation of exactly how specificity is calculated, see the CSS Recommendation at *www.w3.org/TR/CSS21/cascade. html#specificity*.

Eric Meyer provides a thorough, yet more digestible, description of this system in his book *Cascading Style Sheets: The Definitive Guide* (O'Reilly).

If you are looking for help online, I recommend the *Smashing Magazine* article "CSS Specificity: Things You Should Know" (*coding. smashingmagazine.com/2007/07/27/ css-specificity-things-you-should-know/*) by Vitaly Friedman.

Or if you learn better with *Star Wars* analogies, try Andy Clarke's "CSS: Specificity Wars" (*www. stuffandnonsense.co.uk/archives/ css_specificity_wars.html*).

exercise 12-6 | **Using selectors**

This time, we'll add a few more style rules using descendant, ID, and class selectors combined with the font and color properties we've learned about so far.

1. I'd like to add some color to the "new item!" elements next to certain menu item names. They are marked up as **strong**, so we can apply the color property to the **strong** element. Add this rule to the embedded style sheet, save the file, and reload it in the browser.

```
strong { font-style: italic; color: maroon; }
```

That worked, but now the **strong** element "Very spicy" in the description is maroon, too, and that's not what I want. The solution is to use a contextual selector that targets only the **strong** elements that appear in **dt** elements. Remove the **color** declaration you just wrote from the **strong** rule, and create a new rule that targets only the **strong** elements within definition list terms.

```
dt strong { color: maroon; }
```

2. Look at the document source, and you will see that the content has been divided into three unique **div**s: **info**, **appetizers**, and **entrees**. We can use these to our advantage when it comes to styling. For now, let's do something simple and make all the text in the **header** teal. Because color inherits, we only need to apply the property to the **div** and it will be passed down to the **h1** and **p**.

```
#info { color: teal; }
```

3. Now let's get a little fancier and make the paragraph inside the header italic in a way that doesn't affect the other paragraphs on the page. Again, a contextual selector is the answer. This rule selects only paragraphs contained within the **info** section of the document.

```
#info p { font-style: italic; }
```

4. I want to give special treatment to all of the prices on the menu. Fortunately, they have all been marked up with **span** elements, like this:

```
<span class="price">$3.95</span>
```

So now all we have to do is write a rule using a class selector to change the font to Georgia or some serif font, make them italic, and gray them back.

```
.price {
    font-family: Georgia, serif;
    font-style: italic;
    color: gray;
}
```

5. Similarly, I can change the appearance of the text in the header that has been marked up as belonging to the "label" class to make them stand out.

```
.label {
    font-weight: bold;
    font-variant: small-caps;
    font-style: normal;
}
```

6. Finally, there is a warning at the bottom of the page that I want to make small and red. It has been given the class "warning," so I can use that as a selector to target just that paragraph for styling. While I'm at it, I'm going to apply the same style to the **sup** element (the footnote asterisk) earlier on the page so they match. Note that I've used a grouped selector, so I don't need to write a separate rule.

```
p.warning, sup {
    font-size: x-small;
    color: red;
}
```

Figure 12-12 shows the results of all these changes.

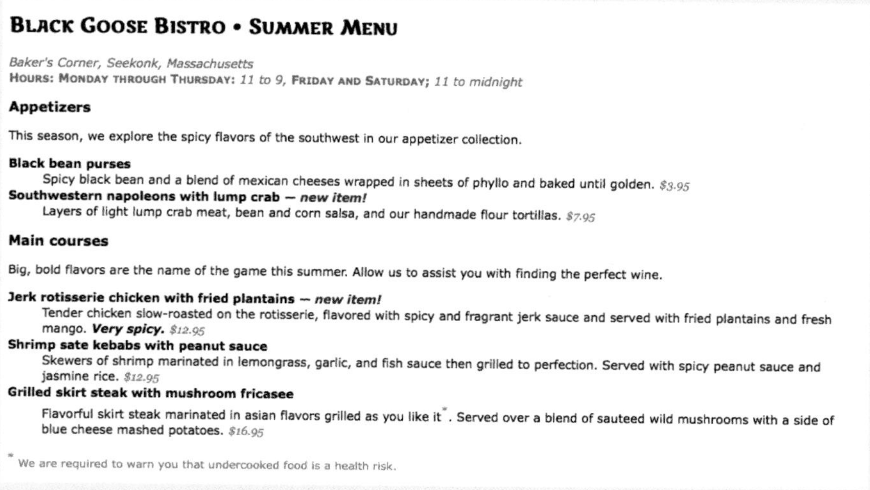

BLACK GOOSE BISTRO • SUMMER MENU

Baker's Corner, Seekonk, Massachusetts
HOURS: MONDAY THROUGH THURSDAY: *11 to 9,* **FRIDAY AND SATURDAY;** *11 to midnight*

Appetizers

This season, we explore the spicy flavors of the southwest in our appetizer collection.

Black bean purses
Spicy black bean and a blend of mexican cheeses wrapped in sheets of phyllo and baked until golden. *$3.95*
Southwestern napoleons with lump crab — *new item!*
Layers of light lump crab meat, bean and corn salsa, and our handmade flour tortillas. *$7.95*

Main courses

Big, bold flavors are the name of the game this summer. Allow us to assist you with finding the perfect wine.

Jerk rotisserie chicken with fried plantains — *new item!*
Tender chicken slow-roasted on the rotisserie, flavored with spicy and fragrant jerk sauce and served with fried plantains and fresh mango. ***Very spicy.*** *$12.95*
Shrimp sate kebabs with peanut sauce
Skewers of shrimp marinated in lemongrass, garlic, and fish sauce then grilled to perfection. Served with spicy peanut sauce and jasmine rice. *$12.95*
Grilled skirt steak with mushroom fricasee
Flavorful skirt steak marinated in asian flavors grilled as you like it*. Served over a blend of sauteed wild mushrooms with a side of blue cheese mashed potatoes. *$16.95*

*We are required to warn you that undercooked food is a health risk.

Figure 12-12. *The current state of the Black Goose Bistro online menu.*

Text Line Adjustments

The next batch of text properties has to do with the treatment of whole lines of text rather than the shapes of characters. They allow web authors to format web text with indents, extra space between lines (leading), and different horizontal alignments, similar to print.

Line height

The **line-height** property defines the minimum distance from baseline to baseline in text. We saw it earlier as part of the shorthand **font** property. A baseline is the imaginary line upon which the bottoms of characters sit. Line height in CSS is similar to leading in traditional typesetting. Although the line height is calculated from baseline to baseline, most browsers split the extra space above and below the text, thus centering it in the overall line height (Figure 12-13).

The **line-height** property is said to specify a "minimum" distance because if you put a tall image or large characters on a line, the height of that line will expand to accommodate it.

line-height

Values:	*number* | *length measurement* | *percentage* | normal | inherit
Default:	normal
Applies to:	*all elements*
Inherits:	*yes*

These examples show three different ways to make the line height twice the height of the font size.

```
p { line-height: 2; }
p { line-height: 2em; }
p { line-height: 200%; }
```

When a number is specified alone, as shown in the first example, it acts as a scaling factor that is multiplied by the current font size to calculate the **line-height** value. Line heights can also be specified in one of the CSS length units, but once again, the relative em unit is your best bet. Ems and percentage values are based on the current font size of the element. In the three examples, if the text size is 16 pixels, the calculated line height would be 32 pixels (see Figure 12-13).

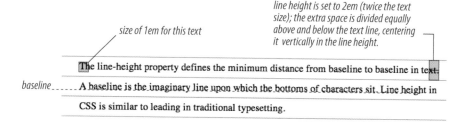

line-height: 2em;

Figure 12-13. In CSS, line height is measured from baseline to baseline, but browsers center the text vertically in the line height.

Indents

The **text-indent** property indents the first line of text by a specified amount (see the note).

text-indent

Values:	*length measurement* | *percentage* | inherit
Default:	*0*
Applies to:	*block-level elements, table cells, and inline blocks*
Inherits:	*yes*

You can specify a length measurement or a percentage value for **text-indent**. Percentage values are calculated based on the width of the *parent* element. Here are a few examples. The results are shown in Figure 12-14.

```
p#1 { text-indent: 2em; }
p#2 { text-indent: 25%; }
p#3 { text-indent: -35px; }
```

2em   Paragraph 1. The text-indent property indents only the first line of text by a specified amount. You can specify a length measurement or a percentage value.

25%   Paragraph 2. The text-indent property indents only the first line of text by a specified amount. You can specify a length measurement or a percentage value.

−35px Paragraph 3. The text-indent property indents only the first line of text by a specified amount. You can specify a length measurement or a percentage value.

Figure 12-14. Examples of the text-indent *property.*

In the third example, notice a negative value was specified, and that's just fine. It will cause the first line of text to hang out to the left of the left text edge (also called a hanging indent).

The **text-indent** property inherits, but it is worth noting that the *calculated* values are passed on to descendant elements. So if a **div** is set to 800 pixels wide with a 10% indent, a **text-indent** of 80 pixels will be passed down (not the 10% value) to elements the **div** contains.

> **DESIGN TIP**
>
> If you use a hanging indent, be sure that there is also a left margin applied to the element. Otherwise, the hanging text may disappear off the left edge of the browser window.

Horizontal alignment

You can align text for web pages just as you would in a word processing or desktop publishing program with the **text-align** property.

text-align

Values:	left | right | center | justify | inherit
Default:	left *for languages that read left to right;* right *for languages that read right to left*
Applies to:	*block-level elements, table cells, and inline blocks*
Inherits:	*yes*

This is a fairly straightforward property to use. The results of the various **text-align** values are shown in Figure 12-15.

text-align: left   aligns text on the left margin

text-align: right   aligns text on the right margin

text-align: center   centers the text in the text block

text-align: justify   aligns text on both right and left margins

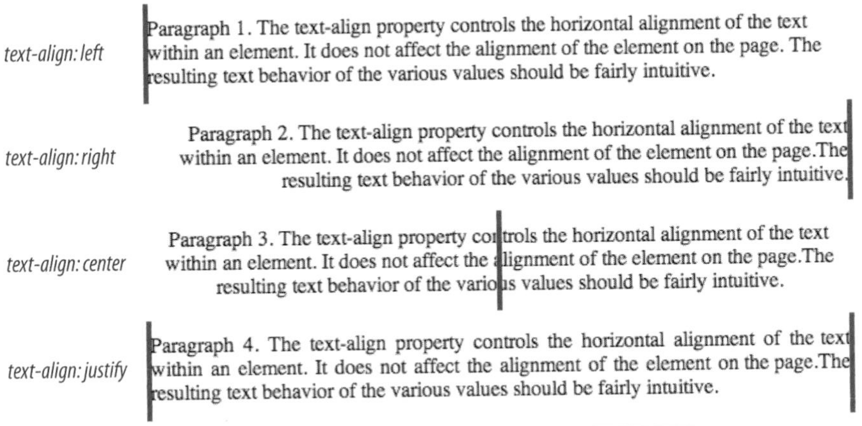

> **NOTE**
>
> *The CSS3 Text Module defines two new related properties—***text-align-last*** (for aligning the last line of text) and* **text-justify** *(for more fine-tuned control over how space is inserted in justified text)—but they are not well supported as of this writing.*

text-align: left

Paragraph 1. The text-align property controls the horizontal alignment of the text within an element. It does not affect the alignment of the element on the page. The resulting text behavior of the various values should be fairly intuitive.

text-align: right

Paragraph 2. The text-align property controls the horizontal alignment of the text within an element. It does not affect the alignment of the element on the page.The resulting text behavior of the various values should be fairly intuitive.

text-align: center

Paragraph 3. The text-align property controls the horizontal alignment of the text within an element. It does not affect the alignment of the element on the page.The resulting text behavior of the various values should be fairly intuitive.

text-align: justify

Paragraph 4. The text-align property controls the horizontal alignment of the text within an element. It does not affect the alignment of the element on the page.The resulting text behavior of the various values should be fairly intuitive.

Figure 12-15. Examples of **text-align** *values.*

Good news—only five more text properties to go! Then we'll be ready to try a few of them out in the Black Goose Bistro menu.

Underlines and Other "Decorations"

If you want to put a line under, over, or through text, or if you'd like to turn the underline off under links, then **text-decoration** is the property for you.

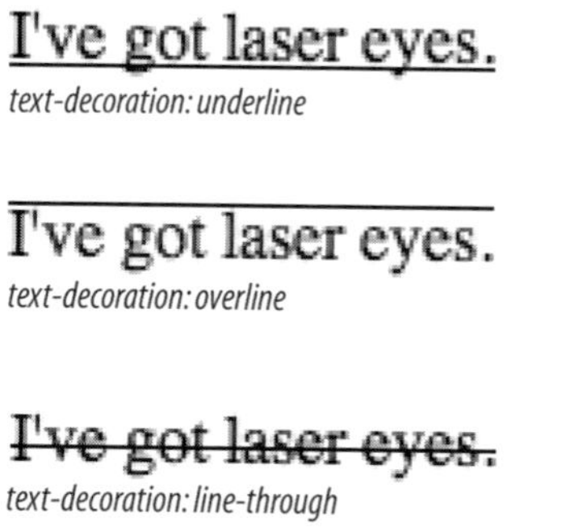

text-decoration

Values:	none | underline | overline | line-through | blink
Default:	none
Applies to:	all elements
Inherits:	no, but since lines are drawn across child elements, they may look like they are "decorated" too

The values for **text-decoration** are intuitive and are shown in Figure 12-16.

text-decoration: underline   underlines the element

text-decoration: overline   draws a line over the text

text-decoration: line-through   draws a line through the text

text-decoration: blink   makes text flash on and off

The most popular use of the **text-decoration** property is turning off the underlines that appear automatically under linked text, as shown here:

    a { text-decoration: none; }

There are a few cautionary words to be said regarding **text-decoration**.

- First, if you get rid of the underlines under links, be sure there are other cues to compensate, such as color and weight.

- On the flip side, because underlines are such a strong visual cue to "click here," underlining text that is *not* a link may be misleading and frustrating. Consider whether italics may be an acceptable alternative.

- Finally, there is no reason to make your text blink. Don't do it. Internet Explorer won't support it anyway.

I've got laser eyes.

text-decoration: underline

I've got laser eyes.

text-decoration: overline

I've got laser eyes.

text-decoration: line-through

Figure 12-16. Examples of text-decoration *values.*

NOTE

The CSS3 Text Module includes enhancements to text-decoration, *including* text-decoration-line, text-decoration-color, text-decoration-style, text-decoration-skip, *and* text-underline-position, *but they are still fairly experimental as of this writing.*

Changing Capitalization

I remember when desktop publishing programs introduced a nifty feature that let me change the capitalization of text on the fly (OK, I'm dating myself here). This made it easy to see how my headlines might look in all capital letters without needing to retype them. CSS includes this feature as well with the **text-transform** property.

text-transform

Values:	none | capitalize | lowercase | uppercase | inherit
Default:	none
Applies to:	all elements
Inherits:	yes

When you apply the **text-transform** property to a text element, it changes its capitalization when it renders without changing the way it is typed in the source. The values are as follows (Figure 12-17):

text-transform: none   as it is typed in the source

text-transform: capitalize   capitalizes the first letter of each word

text-transform: lowercase   makes all letters lowercase

text-transform: uppercase   makes all letters uppercase

And I know what you're thinking.

text-transform: none (as was typed in)

And I Know What You'Re Thinking.

text-transform: capitalize

and i know what you're thinking.

text-transform: lowercase

AND I KNOW WHAT YOU'RE THINKING.

text-transform: uppercase

Figure 12-17. The **text-transform** *property changes the capitalization of characters when they are displayed, regardless of how they are typed in the source.*

Spaced Out

The final two text properties in this chapter are used to insert space between letters (**letter-spacing**) or words (**word-spacing**) when the text is displayed.

letter-spacing

Values:	length measurement | normal | inherit
Default:	normal
Applies to:	all elements
Inherits:	yes

word-spacing

Values:	length measurement | normal | inherit
Default:	normal
Applies to:	all elements
Inherits:	yes

The **letter-spacing** and **word-spacing** properties do what they say: add space between the letters of the text or words in a line, respectively. Figure 12-18 shows the results of these rule examples applied to the simple paragraph shown here.

```
<p>Black Goose Bistro Summer Menu</p>
```

Example 1

```
p { letter-spacing: 8px; }
```

Example 2

```
p { word-spacing: 1.5em; }
```

It is worth noting that when you specify em measurements, the calculated size is passed down to child elements, even if they have a smaller font size than the parent.

In Exercise 12-7, we'll make one last trip back to the Black Goose Bistro menu to add some of these new properties and make a few tweaks.

letter-spacing: 8px;

B l a c k   G o o s e   B i s t r o   S u m m e r   M e n u

word-spacing: 1.5em;

Black   Goose   Bistro   Summer   Menu

Figure 12-18. letter-spacing *(top) and* word-spacing *(bottom).*

Text Shadow

Drop shadows that make text and graphic elements "pop" from the page have become all the rage over the last decade. Now there is a way to add a drop shadow to text using CSS alone with the **text-shadow** property. Text shadows are drawn behind the text but in front of the background and border if there is one.

Text shadows are supported by all current browsers except Internet Explorer (*sad trombone*), but support is rumored in IE10.

text-shadow

NEW IN CSS3

Values:	'horizontal offset' 'vertical offset' 'blur radius' 'color' | none
Default:	none
Applies to:	all elements
Inherits:	yes

The value for the **text-shadow** property is up to three measurements (a horizontal offset, vertical offset, and an optional blur radius) and a color. Figure 12-19 shows an example of a minimal text shadow declaration.

```
h1 {                              h1 {
  color: darkgreen;                 color: darkgreen;
  text-shadow: .2em .2em silver;    text-shadow: -.3em -.3em silver;
}                                 }
```

The Jenville Show   text-shadow: .2em .2em silver;

The Jenville Show   text-shadow: -.3em -.3em silver;

Figure 12-19. A minimal text drop shadow.

The first value is a horizontal offset that positions the shadow to the right of the text (a negative value pulls the shadow to the *left* of the text). The second measurement is a vertical offset that moves the shadow down by the specified amount (a negative value moves the shadow *up*). The declaration ends with the color specification (silver). If the color is omitted, the same color as the text will be used.

That should give you an idea for how the first two measurements work, but that sharp shadow doesn't look very...well...shadowy. What it needs is a blur radius measurement. Zero (0) is no blur, and the blur gets softer with higher values (Figure 12-20). Usually you just have to fiddle with values until you get the effect you want.

The Jenville Show   text-shadow: .2em .2em **.05em** silver;

The Jenville Show   text-shadow: .2em .2em **.15em** silver;

The Jenville Show   text-shadow: .2em .2em **.3em** silver;

Figure 12-20. Adding a blur radius to a text drop shadow.

You can even apply more than one shadow to a single text element. When more than one shadow is listed, the first one in the list is rendered first and subsequent shadows are layered behind it in the defined order. You can also make text appear to glow by positioning a colored shadow directly behind the text. Figure 12-21 demonstrates a few techniques using **text-shadow**.

Multiple shadows

The Jenville Show

```
text-shadow: -.7em -.5em .2em silver,
              .2em .2em .1em gray;
```

Outer glow

The Jenville Show

```
text-shadow: 0 0 .7em purple;
```

Raised look

The Jenville Show

```
body {background-color: thistle;}
h1 {
  color: #ba9eba;
  text-shadow:
      -.05em -.05em .05em white,
      .03em .03em .05em purple;
}
```

For a raised look, position a light shadow above and a dark shadow below the text, using tiny offsets.

Embossed look

The Jenville Show

```
body {background-color: thistle;}
h1 {
  color: #ba9eba;
  text-shadow:
      -.05em -.05em .05em purple,
      .03em .03em .05em white;
}
```

For an embossed look, the light shadow goes below and the dark shadow goes above.

Figure 12-21. Special effects with text shadows.

So go have some fun with text shadows, but be careful not to overdo it. Not only can drop shadows make text difficult to read, but adding a shadow to everything can slow down page performance (scrolling, mouse interactions, etc.), which is particularly problematic for mobile browsers without much processing power. In addition, be careful that your text doesn't require a shadow in order to be visible. Folks with non-supporting browsers won't see a thing. My advice is to use drop shadows as an enhancement in a way that isn't critical if they don't appear.

And speaking of non-supporting browsers, what about Internet Explorer? Versions 9 and earlier won't know what to do with the **text-shadow** property, but there are workarounds. The following articles, both by Zoltan "Du Lac" Hawryluk, discuss workarounds that are beyond the scope of this book but that you may want to explore. I recommend doing a web search for the most current approach.

- "Full CSS Text Shadows—Even in IE" (*www.useragentman.com/blog/2011/06/29/full-css3-text-shadows-even-in-ie/*)

- "CSS3 Text Shadow—Can It Be Done in IE Without JavaScript?" (*www.useragentman.com/blog/2011/04/14/css3-text-shadow-can-it-be-done-in-ie-without-javascript/*)

The Other Text Properties

In the interest of saving space and keeping this an introductory-level book, these properties were not given the full treatment. But being the type of author who doesn't hold anything back, I'm including them here.

vertical-align

Values: baseline | sub | super | top | text-top | middle | textbottom | bottom | *percentage* | *length* | inherit

Specifies the vertical alignment of an inline element's baseline relative to the baseline of the surrounding text. It is also used to set the vertical alignment of content in a table cell (**td**).

white-space

Values: normal | pre | nowrap | pre-wrap | pre-line | inherit

Specifies how whitespace in the element source is handled in layout. For example, the **pre** value preserves the character spaces and returns found in the source, similar to the **pre** HTML element.

visibility

Values: visible | hidden | collapse | inherit

Used to hide the element. When set to **hidden**, the element is invisible, but the space it occupies is maintained, leaving a hole in the content. The element is still there; you just can't see it.

text-direction

Values: ltr | rtl | inherit

Specifies the direction in which the text reads: left to right (**ltr**) or right to left (**rtl**).

unicode-bidi

Values: normal | embed | bidi-override | inherit

Related to bidirectional features of Unicode. The Recommendation states that it allows the author to generate levels of embedding within the Unicode embedding algorithm. If you have no idea what this means, don't worry. Neither do I.

font-size-adjust

NEW IN CSS3

Values: *number* | none

This is a fairly complicated new system for sizing text elements based on x-heights (the height of a lowercase "x") to ensure consistency even when fallback fonts are used. I'll let the W3C explain the rest: *www.w3.org/TR/css3-fonts/#font-size-adjust-prop*.

exercise 12-7 | Finishing touches

Let's add a few finishing touches to the online menu, *menu.html*. It might be useful to save the file and look at it in the browser after each step to see the effect of your edits and to make sure you're on track. The finished style sheet is provided in Appendix A.

1. First, I have a few global changes to the **body** element in mind. I've had a change of heart about the **font-family**. I think that a serif font such as Georgia would be more sophisticated and appropriate for a bistro menu. Let's also use the **line-height** property to open up the text lines and make them easier to read. Make these updates to the **body** style rule, as shown:

```
body {
    font-family: Georgia, serif;
    font-size: small;
    line-height: 1.75em;
}
```

2. I also want to redesign the header section of the document. Remove the teal color setting by deleting that whole rule. Once that is done, make the **h1** purple and the paragraph in the header gray. You can just add color declarations to the existing rules.

```
#info { color: teal; }    /* delete */

h1 {
    font: bold 1.5em "Marko One", Georgia, serif;
    color: purple;}

#info p {
    font-style: italic;
    color: gray;}
```

3. Next, to imitate a fancy print menu, I'm going to center a few key elements on the page using the **text-align** property. Write a rule with a grouped selector to center the headings and the info section.

```
h1, h2, #info {
    text-align: center;}
```

➡

exercise 12-7 | Finishing touches (continued)

DESIGN TIP

Adding letter spacing to small type is one of my favorite heading design tricks. It is a good alternative to large type for drawing attention to the element.

4. I want to make the "Appetizer" and "Main Courses" **h2** headings kind of special. Instead of large, bold type, I'm going to use all uppercase letters, extra letter spacing, and color to call attention to the headings. Here's the new rule for **h2** elements that includes all of these changes.

```
h2 {
    font-size: 1em;
    text-transform: uppercase;
    letter-spacing: .5em;
    color: purple;}
```

5. We're really close now; just a few more tweaks to those paragraphs right after the **h2** headings. Let's center those too and make them italic.

```
h2 + p {
    text-align: center;
    font-style: italic;}
```

Note that I've used an adjacent sibling selector (**h2 + p**) to select "any paragraph that follows an **h2**." This method will not work in Internet Explorer 6, so if that concerns you, you could also select each of them using the contextual selectors **#appetizers p** and **#entrees p**.

6. Next, add a softer color to the menu item names (in **dt** elements). I've chosen "sienna," one of the names from the CSS3 color module. Note that the **strong** elements in those **dt** elements stay maroon because the color applied to the **strong** elements overrides the color inherited by their parents.

```
dt {
    font-weight: bold;
    color: sienna;}
```

Figure 12-22. The formatted Black Goose Bistro menu.

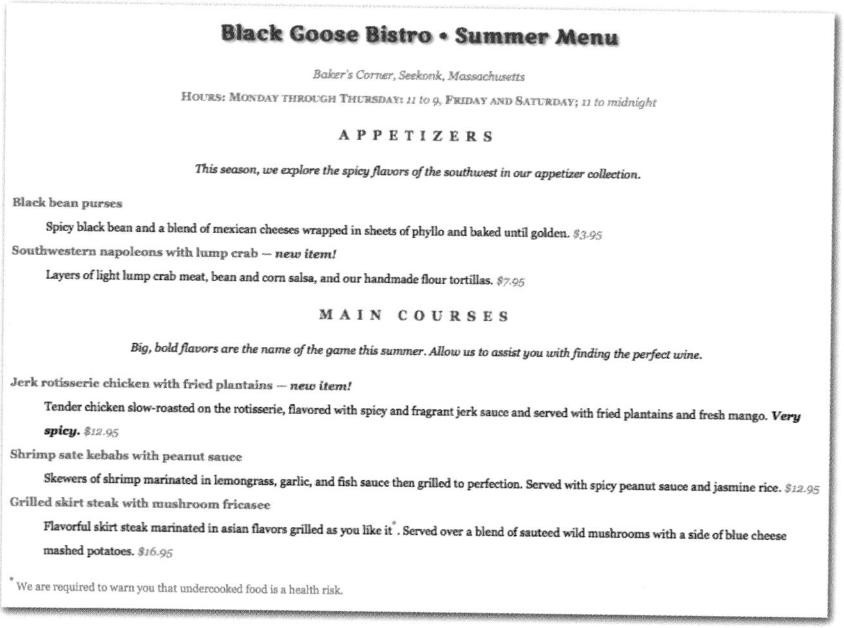

7. Finally, for kicks, let's add a drop shadow under the **h1** heading.

```
h1 {
    font: bold 1.5em "Marko
One", Georgia, serif;
    color: purple;
    text-shadow: .1em .1em .2em
lightslategray;}
```

And we're done! Figure 12-22 shows how the menu looks now…an improvement over the unstyled version, and we used only text properties to do it. Notice that we didn't touch a single character of the document markup in the process. That's the beauty of keeping style separate from structure.

Black Goose Bistro • Summer Menu

Baker's Corner, Seekonk, Massachusetts

HOURS: MONDAY THROUGH THURSDAY: *11 to 9*, FRIDAY AND SATURDAY; *11 to midnight*

A P P E T I Z E R S

This season, we explore the spicy flavors of the southwest in our appetizer collection.

Black bean purses

Spicy black bean and a blend of mexican cheeses wrapped in sheets of phyllo and baked until golden. *$3.95*

Southwestern napoleons with lump crab — *new item!*

Layers of light lump crab meat, bean and corn salsa, and our handmade flour tortillas. *$7.95*

M A I N   C O U R S E S

Big, bold flavors are the name of the game this summer. Allow us to assist you with finding the perfect wine.

Jerk rotisserie chicken with fried plantains — *new item!*

Tender chicken slow-roasted on the rotisserie, flavored with spicy and fragrant jerk sauce and served with fried plantains and fresh mango. **Very spicy.** *$12.95*

Shrimp sate kebabs with peanut sauce

Skewers of shrimp marinated in lemongrass, garlic, and fish sauce then grilled to perfection. Served with spicy peanut sauce and jasmine rice. *$12.95*

Grilled skirt steak with mushroom fricasee

Flavorful skirt steak marinated in asian flavors grilled as you like it*. Served over a blend of sauteed wild mushrooms with a side of blue cheese mashed potatoes. *$16.95*

* We are required to warn you that undercooked food is a health risk.

Changing List Bullets and Numbers

Before we close out this chapter on text properties, I want to show you a few tweaks you can make to bulleted and numbered lists. As you know, browsers automatically insert bullets before unordered list items and numbers before items in ordered lists. For the most part, the rendering of these markers is determined by the browser. However, CSS provides a few properties that allow authors to choose the type and position of the marker, or turn them off entirely.

Choosing a Marker

Use the **list-style-type** property to select the type of marker that appears before each list item.

list-style-type

Values: none | disc | circle | square | decimal | decimal-leading-zero | lower-alpha | upper-alpha | lower-latin | upper-latin | lower-roman | upper-roman | lower-greek | inherit

Default: disc

Applies to: ul, ol, *and* li *(or elements whose display value is* list-item*)*

Inherits: yes

NOTE

This section documents the CSS2.1 list-style *types that are well supported on current browsers. CSS3 extends on the marker functionality shown here, including a method for authors to define their own list styles, allowing for numbering in many languages (*www.w3.org/TR/css3-lists/*).*

More often than not, developers use the **list-style-type** property with its value set to **none** to remove bullets or numbers altogether. This is handy when using list markup as the foundation for a horizontal navigation menu or the entries in a web form. You can keep the semantics but get rid of the pesky markers.

The **disc**, **circle**, and **square** values generate bullet shapes just as browsers have been doing since the beginning (Figure 12-23). Unfortunately, there is no way to change the appearance (size, color, etc.) of generated bullets, so you're basically stuck with the browser's default rendering.

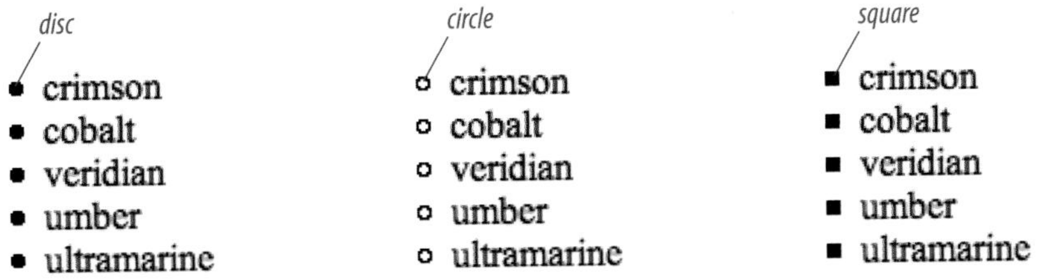

NOTE

CSS3 introduces box, check, diamond, and dash marker types using its new @counter-style *rule. See the spec for details.*

disc
- crimson
- cobalt
- veridian
- umber
- ultramarine

circle
○ crimson
○ cobalt
○ veridian
○ umber
○ ultramarine

square
■ crimson
■ cobalt
■ veridian
■ umber
■ ultramarine

Figure 12-23. The list-style-type *values* disc, circle, *and* square.

List Item Display Role

You may have noticed that the list style properties apply to "elements whose display value is **list-item**." The CSS2.1 specification allows any element to perform like a list item by setting its **display** property to **list-item**. This property can be applied to any HTML element or elements in another XML language. For example, you could automatically bullet or number a series of paragraphs by setting the display property of paragraph (**p**) elements to **list-item**, as shown in this example:

```
p.bulleted {
  display: list-item;
  list-style-type: upper-
alpha;
}
```

NOTE

CSS3 adds the hanging *value for this property. It is similar to* inside, *but the markers would appear outside and abutting the left edge of the shaded area, as shown in Figure 12-24.*

The remaining keywords (Table 12-1) specify various numbering and lettering styles for use with ordered lists.

Table 12-1. Lettering and numbering system (CSS2.1)

Keyword	System
`decimal`	1, 2, 3, 4, 5...
`decimal-leading-zero`	01, 02, 03, 04, 05...
`lower-alpha`	a, b, c, d, e...
`upper-alpha`	A, B, C, D, E...
`lower-latin`	a, b, c, d, e... (same as lower-alpha)
`upper-latin`	A, B, C, D, E... (same as upper-alpha)
`lower-roman`	i, ii, iii, iv, v...
`upper-roman`	I, II, III, IV, V...
`lower-greek`	α, β, γ, δ, ε...

Marker position

By default, the marker hangs outside the content area for the list item, displaying as a hanging indent. The **list-style-position** property allows you to pull the bullet inside the content area so it runs into the list content.

`list-style-position`

Values:	inside | outside | inherit
Default:	outside
Applies to:	ul, ol, and li (or elements whose display value is list-item)
Inherits:	yes

I've applied a background color to the list items in Figure 12-24 to reveal the boundaries of their content area boxes. You can see that when the position is set to **outside** (left), the markers fall outside the content area, and when it is set to **inside**, the content area box extends to include the marker.

```
li {background-color: #F99;}
ul#outside {list-style-position: outside;}
ul#inside {list-style-position: inside;}
```

Make your own bullets

You can also use your own image as a bullet using the **list-style-image** property.

`list-style-image`

Values:	url | none | inherit
Default:	none
Applies to:	ul, ol, and li (or elements whose display value is list-item)
Inherits:	yes

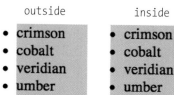

Figure 12-24. The list-style-position *property.*

The value of the **list-style-image** property is the URL of the image you want to use as a marker. The **list-style-type** is set to **disc** as a backup in case the image does not display or the property isn't supported by the browser or other user agent. The result is shown in Figure 12-25.

```
ul {
   list-style-image: url(/images/rainbow.gif);
   list-style-type: circle;
   list-style-position: outside;
}
```

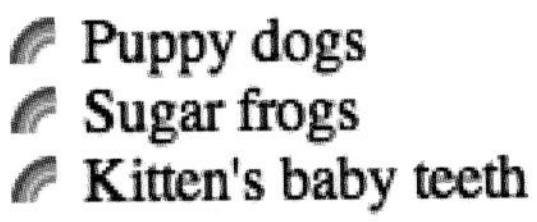
Puppy dogs
Sugar frogs
Kitten's baby teeth

Figure 12-25. Using an image as a marker.

NOTE

There is a `list-style` *shorthand property that combines the values for type, position, and image, in any order. For example:*

```
ul { list-style: url(/images/
     happy.gif) circle outside; }
```

As for all shorthand properties, be careful not to override list style properties set earlier in the style sheet.

Test Yourself

Here are a few questions to see how well you picked up the fundamentals of selectors and text formatting.

1. Here is a chance to get a little practice writing selectors. Using the diagram shown in Figure 12-26, write style rules that make each of the elements described below red (**color: red;**). Write the selector as efficiently as possible. I've done the first one for you.

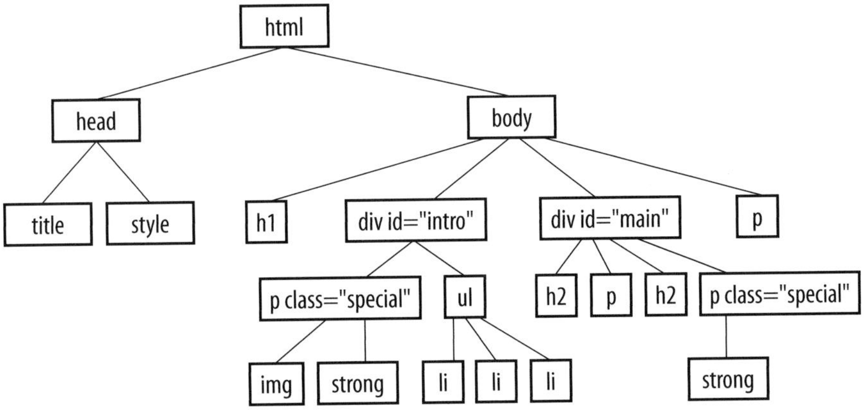
html
head
body
title
style
h1
div id="intro"
div id="main"
p
p class="special"
ul
h2
p
h2
p class="special"
img
strong
li
li
li
strong

Figure 12-26. Sample document structure.

   a. All text elements in the document **body {color: red;}**

   b. **h2** elements

   c. **h1** elements and all paragraphs

   d. Elements belonging to the class "special"

   e. All elements in the "intro" section

   f. **strong** elements in the "main" section

   g. Extra credit: just the paragraph that appears after an **h2** (hint: this selector will not work in Internet Explorer 6)

2. Match the style property with the text samples in Figure 12-27.

a. _____ {font-size: 1.5em;}

b. _____ {text-transform: capitalize;}

c. _____ {text-align: right;}

d. _____ {font-family: Verdana; font-size: 1.5em;}

e. _____ {letter-spacing: 3px;}

f. _____ {font: bold italic 1.2em Verdana;}

g. _____ {text-transform: uppercase;}

h. _____ {text-indent: 2em;}

i. _____ {font-variant: small-caps;}

default font and size

Look for the good in others and they'll see the good in you.

① Look For The Good In Others And They'll See The Good In You.

② Look for the good in others and they'll see the good in you.

❸ **Look for the good in others and they'll see the good in you.**

④ Look for the good in others and they'll see the good in you.

⑤   Look for the good in others and they'll see the good in you.

⑥ LOOK FOR THE GOOD IN OTHERS AND THEY'LL SEE THE GOOD IN YOU.

⑦   Look for the good in others and they'll see the good in you.

⑧ LOOK FOR THE GOOD IN OTHERS AND THEY'LL SEE THE GOOD IN YOU.

⑨ ***Look for the good in others and they'll see the good in you.***

Figure 12-27. Text samples.

CSS Review: Font and Text Properties

In this chapter, we covered the properties used to format text elements. Here is a summary in alphabetical order.

Property	Description
font	A shorthand property that combines font properties
font-family	Specifies a typeface or generic font family
font-size	The size of the font
font-style	Specifies italic or oblique fonts
font-variant	Specifies a small-caps font
font-weight	Specifies the boldness of the font
letter-spacing	Inserts space between letters
line-height	The distance between baselines of neighboring text lines
list-style-image	Specifies an image to be used as a list marker
list-style-position	Puts a list marker inside or outside the content area
list-style-type	Selects marker type for list items
text-align	The horizontal alignment of text
text-decoration	Underlines, overlines, and lines through
text-direction	Whether the text reads left-to-right or right-to-left
text-indent	Amount of indentation of the first line in a block
text-shadow	Adds a drop shadow under the text
text-transform	Changes the capitalization of text when it displays
unicode-bidi	Works with Unicode bidirectional algorithms
vertical-align	Adjusts the vertical position of inline elements relative to the baseline
visibility	Whether the element is rendered or is invisible
white-space	How whitespace in the source is displayed
word-spacing	Inserts space between words

COLORS AND BACKGROUNDS
(Plus Even More Selectors and External Style Sheets)

If you had seen the Web back in 1993, you would have found it to be a fairly dreary affair by today's standards—every background was gray, and all the text was black. Then came Netscape Navigator and, with it, a handful of attributes that allowed rudimentary (but welcome) control over font colors and backgrounds. For years, we made do. But thankfully, we now have style sheet properties that have laid those unmentionable presentational attributes to rest.

We're going to cover a lot of ground in this chapter. Of course, I'll introduce you to all of the properties for specifying colors and backgrounds. This chapter also rounds out your collection of selector types and shows you how to create an external style sheet. Our first order of business, however, is to explore the options for specifying color in CSS, including a primer on the nature of color on computer monitors.

Specifying Color Values

There are two main ways to specify colors in style sheets: with a predefined color name, as we have been doing so far:

```
color: red;        color: olive;        color: blue;
```

or, more commonly, with a numeric value that describes a particular RGB color (the color model on computer monitors). You may have seen color values that look like these:

```
color: #FF0000;        color: #808000;        color: #00F;
```

We'll get to all the ins and outs of RGB color in a moment, but first, a short and sweet section on the standard color names.

Color names

NOTE

The extended color names, also known as the X11 color names, were originally provided with the X Window System for Unix.

The most intuitive way to specify a color is to call it by name. Unfortunately, you can't make up just any color name and expect it to work. It has to be one of the color keywords predefined in the CSS Recommendation. CSS1 and CSS2 adopted the 16 standard color names originally introduced in HTML 4.01. CSS2.1 tossed in **orange** for a total of 17 (Figure 13-1). CSS3 adds support for the extended set of 130 (rather fanciful) color names. Now we can specify names like "burlywood" and my long-time favorite, "papayawhip"! The extended colors are shown in Figure 13-2, but if you want a more accurate view, point your browser at *www.learningwebdesign.com/colornames.html*.

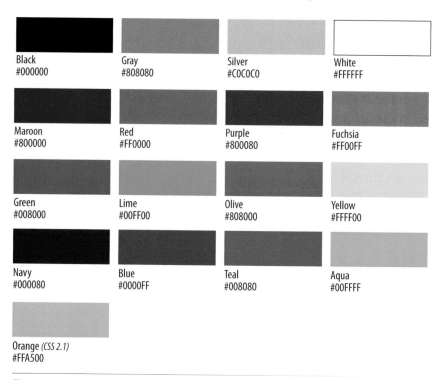

Black
#000000

Gray
#808080

Silver
#C0C0C0

White
#FFFFFF

Maroon
#800000

Red
#FF0000

Purple
#800080

Fuchsia
#FF00FF

Green
#008000

Lime
#00FF00

Olive
#808000

Yellow
#FFFF00

Navy
#000080

Blue
#0000FF

Teal
#008080

Aqua
#00FFFF

Orange *(CSS 2.1)*
#FFA500

Figure 13-1. The 17 standard color names in CSS2.1.

Color names are easy to use—just drop one into place as the value for any color-related property:

```
color: silver;
background-color: gray;
border-bottom-color: teal;
```

aliceblue 240,248,255 F0F8FF	cornsilk 255,248,220 FFF8DC	darkturquoise 0,206,209 00CED1	hotpink 255,105,180 FF69B4	lightskyblue 135,206,250 87CEFA	midnightblue 25,25,112 191970	peru 205,133,63 CD853F	snow 255,250,250 FFFAFA
antiquewhite 250,235,215 FAEBD7	crimson 220,20,60 DC143C	darkviolet 148,0,211 9400D3	indianred 205,92,92 CD5C5C	lightslategray 119,136,153 778899	mintcream 245,255,250 F5FFFA	pink 255,192,203 FFC0CB	springgreen 0,255,127 00FF7F
aqua 0,255,255 00FFFF	cyan 0,255,255 00FFFF	deeppink 255,20,147 FF1493	indigo 75,0,130 4B0082	lightsteelblue 176,196,222 B0C4DE	mistyrose 255,228,225 FFE4E1	plum 221,160,221 DDA0DD	steelblue 70,130,180 46,82,B4
aquamarine 127,255,212 7FFFD4	darkblue 0,0,139 00008B	deepskyblue 0,191,255 00BFFF	ivory 255,240,240 FFF0F0	lightyellow 255,255,224 FFFFE0	moccasin 255,228,181 FFE4B5	powderblue 176,224,230 B0E0E6	tan 210,180,140 D2B48C
azure 240,255,255 F0FFFF	darkcyan 0,139,139 008B8B	dimgray 105,105,105 69,69,69	khaki 240,230,140 F0D58C	lime 0,255,0 00FF00	navajowhite 255,222,173 FFDEAD	purple 128,0,128 800080	teal 0,128,128 008080
beige 245,245,220 F5F5DC	darkgoldenrod 184,134,11 B8860B	dodgerblue 30,144,255 1E90FF	lavender 230,230,250 E6E6FA	limegreen 50,205,50 32CD32	navy 0,0,128 000080	red 225,0,0 FF0000	thistle 216,191,216 D8BFD8
bisque 255,228,196 FFE4C4	darkgray 169,169,169 A9A9A9	firebrick 178,34,34 B22222	lavenderblush 255,240,245 FFF0F5	linen 250,240,230 FAF0E6	oldlace 253,245,230 FDF5E6	rosybrown 188,143,143 BC8F8F	tomato 253,99,71 FF6347
black 0,0,0 000000	darkgreen 0,100,0 006400	floralwhite 255,250,240 FFFAF0	lawngreen 124,252,0 7CFC00	magenta 255,0,255 FF00FF	olive 128,128,0 808000	royalblue 65,105,225 4169E1	turquoise 64,224,208 40E0D0
blanchedalmond 255,255,205 FFFFCD	darkkhaki 189,183,107 BDB76B	forestgreen 34,139,34 228B22	lemonchiffon 255,250,205 FFFACD	maroon 128,0,0 800000	olivedrab 107,142,35 6B8E23	saddlebrown 139,69,19 8B4513	violet 238,130,238 EE82EE
blue 0,0,255 0000FF	darkmagenta 139,0,139 8B008B	fuchsia 255,0,255 FF00FF	lightblue 173,216,230 ADD8E6	mediumaquamarine 102,205,170 66CDAA	orange 255,165,0 FFA500	salmon 250,128,114 FA8072	white 255,255,255 FFFFFF
blueviolet 138,43,226 8A2BE2	darkolivegreen 85,107,47 556B2F	gainsboro 220,220,220 DCDCDC	lightcoral 240,128,128 F08080	mediumblue 0,0,205 0000CD	orchid 218,112,214 DA70D6	sandybrown 244,164,96 F4A460	wheat 245,222,179 F5DEB3
brown 165,42,42 A52A2A	darkorange 255,140,0 FF8C00	ghostwhite 248,248,255 F8F8FF	lightgoldenrodyellow 250,250,210 FAFAD2	mediummorchid 186,85,211 BA55D3	orangered 255,69,0 FF4500	seagreen 46,139,87 2E8B57	whitesmoke 245,245,245 F5F5F5
burlywood 222,184,135 DEB887	darkred 139,0,0 8B0000	gold 255,215,0 FFD700	lightcyan 224,255,255 E0FFFF	mediumpurple 147,112,219 9370DB	palegoldenrod 238,232,170 EEE8AA	seashell 255,245,238 FFF5EE	yellow 255,255,0 FFFF00
cadetblue 95,158,160 5F9EA0	darkorchid 153,50,204 9932CC	goldenrod 218,165,32 DAA520	lightgreen 144,238,144 90EE90	mediumseagreen 60,179,113 3CB371	palegreen 152,251,152 98FB98	sienna 160,82,45 A0522D	yellowgreen 154,205,50 9ACD32
chartreuse 127,255,0 7FFF00	darksalmon 233,150,122 E9967A	gray 128,128,128 808080	lightgrey 211,211,211 D3D3D3	mediumslateblue 123,104,238 7B68EE	paleturquoise 175,238,238 AFEEEE	silver 192,192,192 C0C0C0	
chocolate 210,105,30 D2691E	darkseagreen 143,188,143 8FBC8F	green 0,128,0 008000	lightpink 255,182,193 FFB6C1	mediumspringgreen 0,250,154 00FA9A	palevioletred 219,112,147 DB7093	skyblue 135,206,235 87CEEB	
coral 255,127,80 FF7F50	darkslateblue 72,61,139 483D8B	greenyellow 173,255,47 ADFF2F	lightsalmon 255,160,122 FFA07A	mediumturquoise 72,209,204 48D1CC	papayawhip 255,239,213 FFEFD5	slateblue 106,90,205 6A5ACD	
cornflowerblue 100,149,237 6495ED	darkslategray 47,79,79 2F4F4F	honeydew 240,255,240 F0FFF0	lightseagreen 32,178,170 20B2AA	mediumvioletred 199,21,133 C71385	peachpuff 255,239,213 FFEFD5	slategray 112,128,144 708090	

Figure 13-2. The 140 extended color names in CSS3. Bear in mind that these will look quite different on a screen.

RGB color values

Names are easy, but as you can see, they are limited. By far, the most common way to specify a color is by its RGB value. It also gives you millions of colors to choose from.

For those who are not familiar with how computers deal with color, I'll start with the basics before jumping into the CSS syntax.

A word about RGB color

Computers create the colors you see on a monitor by combining three colors of light: red, green, and blue. This is known as the RGB color model. You can provide recipes (of sorts) for colors by telling the computer how much of each color to mix in. The amount of light in each color "channel" is typically described on a scale from 0 (none) to 255 (full-blast), although it can also be provided as a percent. The closer the three values get to 255 (100%), the closer the resulting color gets to white (Figure 13-3).

Any color you see on your monitor can be described by a series of three numbers: a red value, a green value, and a blue value. This is one of the ways that image editors such as Adobe Photoshop keep track of the colors for every pixel in an image. With the RGB color system, a pleasant lavender can be described as 200, 178, 230.

Figure 13-3. Colors on computer monitors are made by mixing different amounts of red, green, and blue light (thus, RGB). The color in the middle of each diagram shows what happens when the three color channels are combined. The more light there is in each channel (i.e., the higher the number value), the closer the combination is to white.

Picking a color

The easiest way to pick a color and find its RGB color values is to use an image-editing tool such as Adobe Photoshop, Adobe Fireworks, or Corel Paint Shop Pro Photo. Most image tools provide a color picker similar to Photoshop's (Figure 13-4, left). If you don't have an image editor, you can select a color from an online tool like ColorPicker.com (Figure 13-4, right).

The RGB color model

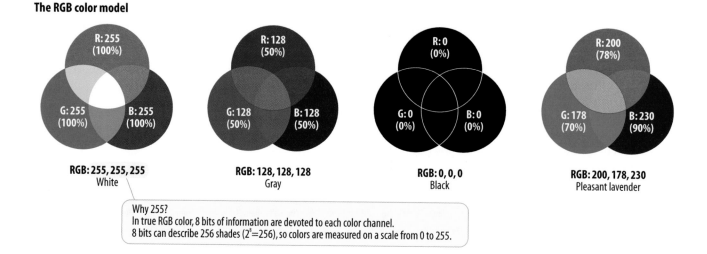

RGB: 255, 255, 255
White

RGB: 128, 128, 128
Gray

RGB: 0, 0, 0
Black

RGB: 200, 178, 230
Pleasant lavender

Why 255?
In true RGB color, 8 bits of information are devoted to each color channel.
8 bits can describe 256 shades ($2^8=256$), so colors are measured on a scale from 0 to 255.

There are several ways to define colors on monitors. The two that are relevant to CSS are RGB (Red, Green, Blue) and HSL (Hue, Saturation, Lightness). RGB is the most commonly used and well supported, so we'll focus on that here, but see the sidebar "HSL Color" for more information on the alternative.

When you select a color from the spectrum in the color picker, the red, green, and blue values are listed, as pointed out in Figure 13-4. And look next to the # symbol—those are the same values, converted to hexadecimal equivalents so they are ready to go in a style sheet. I'll explain the six-digit hex values in a moment.

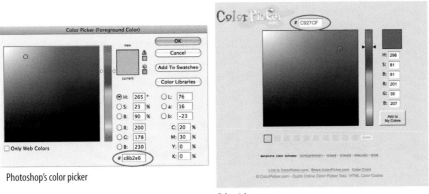

Figure 13-4. *Color pickers such as the one in Photoshop (left) and Colorpicker.com (right) provide the RGB values for a selected pixel color.*

Writing RGB values in style sheets

CSS allows RGB color values to be specified in a number of formats. Going back to that pleasant lavender, we could add it to a style sheet by listing each value on a scale from 0 to 255.

```
color: rgb(200, 178, 230);
```

You can also list them as percentage values, although that is less common.

```
color: rgb(78%, 70%, 90%);
```

Or, you can provide the six-digit hexadecimal version that we saw in the color pickers. These six digits represent the same three RGB values, except they have been converted into hexadecimal (or hex for short) equivalents. I'll explain the hexadecimal system in the next section. Note that hex RGB values are preceded by the # symbol and do not require the **rgb()** notation shown in the previous examples. They may be upper- or lowercase, but it is recommended that you be consistent.

```
color: #C8B2E6;
```

HSL Color

CSS3 introduces the ability to specify colors by their HSL values: Hue (color), Saturation, and Lightness. The color pickers in Figure 13-4 also provide HSL values for the selected color, although they call the last value Brightness (B).

In this system, the colors are spread out around a circle in the order of the rainbow, with red at the top (12 o'clock) position. Hue values are then measured in degrees around the circle: red at 0°, green at 120°, and blue at 240°, with other colors in between. Saturation is a percentage value from 0% (gray) to 100% (color at full blast). Lightness (or brightness) is also a percentage value from 0% (darkest) to 100% (lightest).

Some people find this system more intuitive to use because once you lock into a hue, it is easy to make it stronger, darker, or lighter. RGB values are not intuitive at all, although some practiced designers develop a feel for them.

In CSS, HSL values are provided as the hue value and two percentages. They are never converted to hexadecimal values, as may be done for RGB. Here is that lavender from Figure 13-3 as it would be specified in a style sheet using HSL:

```
color: hsl(265, 23%, 90%);
```

There is one last shorthand way to specify hex color values. If your value happens to be made up of three pairs of doubled digits or letters, such as:

color: #FFCC00; *or* color: #993366;

you can condense each pair down to one digit or letter. The benefit is slightly reducing the file size of your CSS document. These examples are equivalent to the ones listed above:

color: #FC0; *or* color: #936;

About hexadecimal values

It's time to clarify what's going on with that six-digit string of characters. What you're looking at is actually a series of three two-digit numbers, one each for red, green, and blue. But instead of decimal (base-10, the system we're used to), these values are written in hexadecimal, or base-16. Figure 13-5 shows the structure of the hex RGB value.

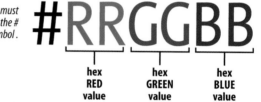

Hexadecimal RGB values must be preceded by the # (octothorpe or hash) symbol.

hex RED value   hex GREEN value   hex BLUE value

Figure 13-5. Hexadecimal RGB values are made up of three two-digit numbers, one for red, one for green, and one for blue.

The hexadecimal numbering system uses 16 digits: 0–9 and A–F (for representing the quantities 10–15). Figure 13-6 shows how this works. The hex system is used widely in computing because it reduces the space it takes to store certain information. For example, the RGB values are reduced from three to two digits once they're converted to hexadecimal.

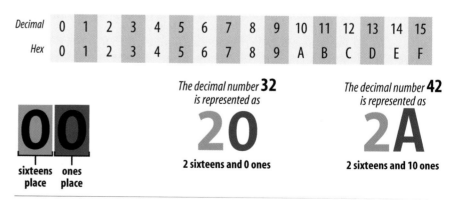

Figure 13-6. The hexadecimal numbering system is base-16.

Now that most graphics and web development software provides easy access to hexadecimal color values (as we saw in Figure 13-4), there isn't much need to translate RGB values to hex yourself, as we needed to do back in the old days. But should you find the need, the "Hexadecimal Calculators" sidebar should help you out.

RGBa color

RGBa color allows you to specify a color and also make it as transparent or as opaque as you like. The "a" in RGBa stands for alpha, which is an additional channel that controls the level of transparency on a scale from 0 (fully transparent) to 1 (fully opaque). Here's how it looks written in a style rule:

```
color: rgba(0, 0, 0, .5);
```

The first three values in the parentheses are regular old RGB values, in this case creating the color black. The fourth value, .5, is the transparency level. So this color is black with 50% transparency. That will allow other colors or background patterns to show through slightly (Figure 13-7).

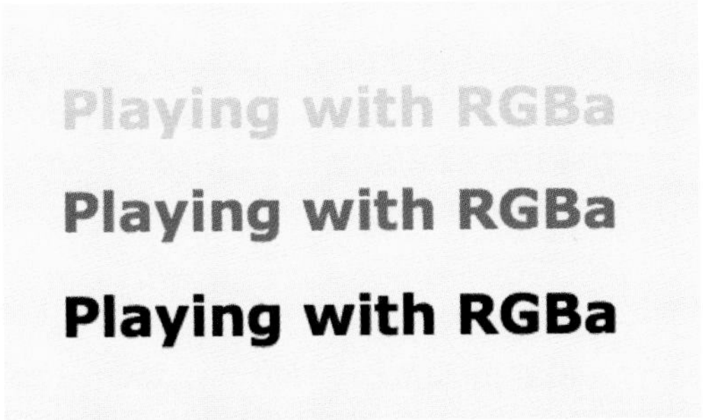

```
h1 {color: rgba(0, 0, 0, .1);}
```

```
h1 {color: rgba(0, 0, 0, .5);}
```

```
h1 {color: rgba(0, 0, 0, 1);}
```

Figure 13-7. Headings with various levels of transparency using RGBa values.

There is a complication, however, and its name is Internet Explorer. IE versions 8 and earlier do not support RGBa color, so you need to provide a fallback for users with those browsers. The easiest is to just pick a fully opaque color that approximates the look you are going for and list it first in the style rule. IE will ignore the RGBa value, and other browsers will override the opaque color when they get to the second declaration.

```
h1 {
   color: rgb(120, 120, 120);
   color: rgba(0, 0, 0, .5);
}
```

But if you simply *must* have true transparency in IE, then you can provide alternatives (a transparent PNG or an IE-proprietary filter) specifically to IE 8, 7, and 6 by wrapping the rules or style element in conditional comments that only IE understands (see the "Targeting IE with Conditional Comments" sidebar). Fortunately, RGBa is supported by IE9 and higher, so as older versions fade into disuse, we won't need to jump through extra hoops.

Hexadecimal Calculators

In Windows, the standard calculator has a hexadecimal converter in the Scientific view. Mac users can download the free "Mac Dec Bin Hex Calculator" for OS X (search for it at *download.com*).

Of course, you could calculate a hex value yourself by dividing your number by 16 to get the first digit, and then using the remainder for the second digit. For example, 200 converts to C8 because 200=(16 × 12) + 8. That's {12,8} in base-16, or C8 in hexadecimal. Whew! I think I'll be sticking with my Color Picker.

NOTE

HSL colors can be given a transparency level as well using the HSLa color format, which has the same syntax as RGBa:

```
color: hsla(0, 0%, 0%, .5);
```

Targeting IE with Conditional Comments

Internet Explorer's conditional comments syntax provides a way to specify styles just for IE or even a particular version of IE. Other browsers ignore whatever is in them, but IE will apply whatever styles it finds there. Conditional comments can go within a style sheet, or as in the examples below, be used to provide a separate embedded style sheet with the **style** element. Be sure to put conditional comments after your regular styles.

Using our RGBa fallback as an example, this conditional comment targets a browser if it is "less than or equal to IE8" (**if lte IE 8**) and applies a PNG that is 50% transparent to the background of **p** elements. (Transparent PNGs are discussed in Chapter 21, "Web Graphics Basics.")

```
<!--[if lte IE 8]>
  <style>
    p {background: transparent url(black-50.
png);}
```

```
  </style>
<![endif]-->
```

Another way to create transparency in IE6 through 8 is to use an Internet Explorer filter rule, which can get a bit tricky, so I'll point you to this helpful article by Eric Ferraiuolo: "RGBA—IE Fallback" (*925html.com/code/rgba-ie-fallback/*). And for the deep dive on conditional comments, go right to the Microsoft Developer Network site for the nitty gritty (*msdn.microsoft.com/en-us/library/ms537512(v=vs.85).aspx*).

You should know that the use of conditional comments is somewhat controversial in the web development community. Some developers avoid them at all costs, choosing JavaScript solutions instead. Others consider them appropriate for the job and don't worry that they aren't strictly valid markup. Hopefully some day, as older versions of IE fade into disuse, this technique will no longer be needed.

Summing up color values

It took us a few pages to get here, but the process for picking and specifying colors in style sheets is actually easy.

- Pick one of the predefined color names,

or

- Use a color picker to select a color and copy down the RGB values (preferably the six-digit hex values). Put those values in the style rule using one of the four RGB value formats, and you're done. Or you could use HSL, if that floats your boat.

There is actually one more colorful way to fill an element, and that's gradients (colors that fade from one hue to another), but that opens up a whole can of worms (namely, vendor prefixes) that I don't want to get into right now, so I'm going to save CSS gradients for the end of this chapter.

Foreground Color

Now that we know how to write color values, let's get to the color-related properties. You can specify the foreground and background colors for any HTML element. There are also **border-color** properties that take color values, but we'll get to those in Chapter 14, "Thinking Inside the Box."

The foreground of an element consists of its text and border (if one is specified). You specify a foreground color with the **color** property, as we saw in the last chapter when we rolled it out to give text a little pizzazz. Here are the details for the **color** property one more time.

color

Values:	*color value (name or numeric)* | inherit
Default:	*depends on the browser and user's preferences*
Applies to:	*all elements*
Inherits:	*yes*

In the following example, the foreground of a **blockquote** element is set to a nice green with the values R:80, G:140, and B:25 (we'll use the hex code **#508C19**). You can see that by applying the **color** property to the **blockquote** element, the color is inherited by the **p** and **em** elements it contains (Figure 13-8). The thick dashed border around the whole blockquote is green as well; however, if we were to apply a **border-color** property to this same element, that color would override the green foreground setting.

The style rule

```
blockquote {
    border: 4px dashed;
    color: #508C19;
}
```

The markup

```
<blockquote>
    <p>I'd recommend Honey Gold cereal to anyone who likes cereal. It's
    the <em>only</em> way to start the day!</p>
    <p>&mdash; Jennifer Robbins, happy consumer</p>
</blockquote>
```

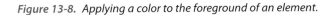

I'd recommend Honey Gold cereal to anyone who likes cereal. It's the *only* way to start the day!

— Jennifer Robbins, happy consumer

Figure 13-8. Applying a color to the foreground of an element.

Background Color

Use the **background-color** property to apply a background color to any element.

background-color

Values:	*color value (name or numeric)* | transparent | inherit
Default:	transparent
Applies to:	*all elements*
Inherits:	*no*

A background color fills the canvas behind the element that includes the content area, and any padding (extra space) added around the content, extending behind the border out to its outer edge. Let's see what happens when we use

Using Color

Here are a few quick tips related to working with color:

- Limit the number of colors you use on a page. Nothing creates visual chaos faster than too many colors. I tend to choose one dominant color and one highlight color. I may also use a couple of shades of each, but I resist adding too many different hues.

- When specifying a foreground and background color, make sure that there is adequate contrast. People tend to prefer reading dark text on very light backgrounds online. My sample in Figure 13-9, although making its point, actually fails the contrast test.

- It is a good idea to specify the foreground color and the background color (particularly for whole pages) in tandem. This will avoid possible color clashes and contrast problems if the user has one or the other set with a user style sheet.

To color the background of the whole page, apply the background-color *property to the* body *element.*

the `background-color` property to make the background of the same sample `blockquote` light blue (Figure 13-9).

```
blockquote {
  border: 4px dashed;
  color: #508C19;
  background-color: #B4DBE6;
}
```

> I'd recommend Honey Gold cereal to anyone who likes cereal. It's the *only* way to start the day!
>
> — Jennifer Robbins, happy consumer

Figure 13-9. Adding a light-blue background color to the sample blockquote.

As expected, the background color fills the area behind the text, all the way to the border. Look closely at the gaps in the border, and you'll see that the background color actually goes all the way to its outer edge. But that's where the background stops; if we apply a margin to this element, the background will not extend into the margin. When we talk about the CSS box model, we'll revisit all these components of an element. For now, just know that if your border has gaps, the background will show through.

It's worth noting that background colors do not inherit, but because the default background setting for all elements is **transparent**, the parent's background color shows through its descendant elements. For example, you can change the background color of a whole page by applying the **background-color** property to the **body** element. The color will show through all the elements on the page.

In addition to setting the color of the whole page, you can change the background color of any element, both block-level (like the **blockquote** shown in the previous example) as well as inline. In this example, I've used the **color** and **background-color** properties to highlight a word marked up as a "glossary" term. You can see in Figure 13-10 that the background color fills the little box created by the inline **dfn** element.

The style rule

```
.glossary {
  color: #7C3306;          /* dark brown */
  background-color: #F2F288;  /* light yellow */
}
```

The markup

```
<p>A <dfn class="glossary">baseline</dfn> is the imaginary line upon
which characters sit.</p>
```

A baseline is the imaginary line upon which characters sit.

Figure 13-10. Applying the background-color *property to an inline element.*

Playing with Opacity

Earlier, we talked about the RGBa color format that adds a level of transparency when it is applied to a color or background. There is another way to make an element slightly see-through, and that's the CSS3 **opacity** property.

opacity

Values:	number (0 to 1)
Default:	1
Applies to:	all elements
Inherits:	no

The value for **opacity** is a number between 0 (completely transparent) and 1 (completely opaque). A value of .5 gives the element an opacity of 50%. The opacity setting applies to the entire element—both the foreground and the background (if one has been set). If you want to just affect one or the other, use an RGBa color value instead.

In the following code example (and Figure 13-11), a heading has been given a color of green and a background color of white. When the **opacity** property is set, it allows the background of the page to show through both the text and the element box.

```
h1 {color: green; background: white; opacity: .25;}
h1 {color: green; background: white; opacity: .5;}
h1 {color: green; background: white; opacity: 1;}
```

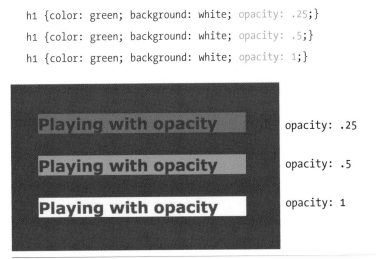

opacity: .25

opacity: .5

opacity: 1

Figure 13-11. Setting the opacity on an element affects both the foreground and background colors.

Oh, but guess what—this very nifty trick won't work if you're using Internet Explorer versions 8 or earlier (you probably saw that coming). To set transparency for those browsers, use the IE-specific filters as shown in the following example. The first declaration works in IE8, and the second works in IE 7 and 6. The **zoom** property ensures that IE recognizes the element in the layout. Ideally, this rule should be served in an IE-specific style sheet with conditional comments.

```
h1 {
  filter:alpha(opacity=50);
  -ms-filter:"progid:DXImageTransform.Microsoft.Alpha(opacity=50)";
  zoom: 1;
}
```

You may be itching to take these color and background properties out for a spin, and we will in a moment, but first, I want to introduce you to some of the fancier CSS selectors and round out your collection. The "At a Glance" sidebar lists the selectors you should feel comfortable with so far.

Introducing…Pseudo-Class Selectors

Have you ever noticed that a link is often one color when you click on it and another color when you go back to that page? That's because, behind the scenes, your browser is keeping track of which links have been clicked (or "visited," to use the lingo). The browser keeps track of other states too, such as whether the user's cursor is over an element (hover state), whether an element is the first of its type, the first or last child of its parent, and whether a form element has been checked or disabled, just to name a few.

In CSS, you can apply styles to elements in these states using a special kind of selector called a *pseudo-class* selector. It's an odd name, but you can think of it as though elements in a certain state belong to the same class. However, the class name isn't in the markup—it's something the browser keeps track of. So it's *kinda* like a class…it's a *pseudo-class*.

The complete list of CSS3 selectors is provided in Appendix B.

Pseudo-class selectors are indicated by the colon (:) character. They typically go immediately after an element name—for example, **li:first-child**.

There are quite a few pseudo-classes in CSS3. In this section I'll introduce you to the most commonly used and the best supported. The full list of CSS3 selectors, with descriptions and examples of each, can be found in Appendix B.

Link pseudo-classes

The most basic pseudo-classes selectors target links (**a** elements) based on whether they have been clicked. Link pseudo-classes are a type of dynamic pseudo-class because they are applied as the result of the user interacting with the page rather than something in the markup.

WARNING

When you alter the appearance of links and visited links, be sure that they still look like links.

:link   Applies a style to unclicked (unvisited) links

:visited   Applies a style to links that have already been clicked

By default, browsers typically display linked text as blue and links that have been clicked as purple, but you can change that with a few style rules.

In these examples, I've changed the color of links to maroon and visited links to gray. It is common for visited links to be a more muted color than unclicked links.

```
a:link {
  color: maroon;
}
a:visited {
  color: gray;
}
```

User action pseudo-classes

Another type of dynamic pseudo-class targets element states that result from direct user actions.

:focus   Applies when the element is selected and ready for input

:hover   Applies when the mouse pointer is over the element

:active   Applies when the element (such a link or button) is in the process of being clicked or tapped

Focus state

If you've ever used a web form, then you should be familiar with how a browser visually emphasizes a form element when you select it. When an element is highlighted and ready for input, it is said to have "focus." The :focus selector lets you apply custom styles to elements when they are in the focused state.

In this example, when a user selects a text input, it gets a yellow background color to make it stand out from the other form inputs.

```
input:focus { background-color: yellow; }
```

Hover state

The :hover selector is an interesting one. It targets elements while the user's mouse pointer is directly over them. Although you can use the hover state with any element, it is most commonly used with links to change their appearance and give the user visual feedback that an action is possible.

This rule gives links a light-pink background color while the mouse hovers over them.

```
a:hover {
  color: maroon;
  background-color: #ffd9d9;
}
```

It is important to note that there is no hover state on touch screen devices such as smartphones and tablets, so this piece of feedback will be lost (see note). That makes it important for links to have clear visual indicators without relying on mouse interactions for discovery.

WARNING

The :focus pseudo-class is not supported in IE6.

NOTE

Although there is no way to hover a finger over an element, iOS Safari and some Android devices may display the :hover state styles after a single tap. To follow the link, a user must tap again. This approach ensures that CSS-driven dropdown menus that expand when hovered over are still accessible on a touch device. On the flip side, it might be confusing or undesirable on other hovered objects. For this reason, some developers choose to create a separate style sheet without :hover styles for mobile devices that might have touch interfaces.

Active state

Finally, the **:active** selector applies styles to an element while it is in the process of being activated. In the case of a link, it is the style that is applied while it is being clicked or while a fingertip is in contact with it on a touch screen. This style may be displayed only for an instant, but it can give a subtle indication that something has happened. In this example, I've brightened up the color for the active state (from maroon to red).

```
a:active {
  color: red;
  background-color: #ffd9d9;
}
```

Putting it all together

Web designers commonly provide styles for all of these link states because it is an easy way to give a nice bit of feedback at every stage of clicking a link (and it usually improves on the browser defaults). In fact, users have come to expect this feedback: that they can see at a glance which links have been followed, that links do something when you point at them, and that they receive confirmation when they are successfully clicked.

When you apply styles to **a** elements with all five pseudo-classes, the order in which they appear is important for them to function properly. For example, if you put **:link** or **:visited** last, they would override the other states, preventing them from appearing. The required order for link pseudo-classes is **:link**, **:visited**, **:focus**, **:hover**, **:active** (LVFHA, which you can remember with LoVe For Hell's Angels, or the mnemonic device of your choice).

It is recommended that you provide a **:focus** style for users who use the keyboard to tab through links on a page rather than clicking with a mouse. Applying the same style used for **:hover** is common, although not required.

To sum things up, the link styles I've shown should look like this in the style sheet. Figure 13-12 shows the results.

```
a { text-decoration: none; }  /* turns underlines off for all links */
a:link { color: maroon; }
a:visited { color: gray; }
a:focus { color: maroon; background-color: #ffd9d9; }
a:hover { color: maroon; background-color: #ffd9d9; }
a:active { color: red; background-color: #ffd9d9; }
```

Samples of my work: **Samples of my work:** **Samples of my work:** **Samples of my work:**

- Pen and Ink Illustrations
- Paintings
- Collage

- Pen and Ink Illustrations
- Paintings
- Collage

- Pen and Ink Illustrations
- Paintings
- Collage

- Pen and Ink Illustrations
- Paintings
- Collage

a:link
Links are maroon and not underlined.

a:focus
a:hover
While the mouse is over the link or when the link has focus, the pink background color appears.

a:active
As the mouse button is being pressed, the link turns bright red.

a:visited
After that page has been visited, the link is gray.

Figure 13-12. Changing the colors and backgrounds of links with pseudo-class selectors.

Other pseudo-class selectors

OK...5 CSS3 pseudo-classes down, only 18 to go! Well, I don't know about you, but that sounds a bit tedious. I want you to know what is possible, so I've tucked them into the "More Pseudo-Classes" sidebar, and we can move on to a few other selector types. In addition, you can find them in Appendix B with descriptions and examples. When you are ready to get more sophisticated with selectors in your documents, you can use that Appendix as a reference.

Pseudo-Element Selectors

Pseudo-classes aren't the only kind of pseudo-selectors. There are also four pseudo-elements that act as though they are inserting fictional elements into the document structure for styling. In CSS3, pseudo-elements are indicated by a double colon (::) symbol, but for better backward compatibility, use a single colon (:) as they were defined in CSS2.

More Pseudo-Classes

In addition to the dynamic pseudo-classes, the CSS3 selector module includes other types of selectors that are based on states the browser keeps track of on the fly.

It should be noted that none of these selector types are supported in Internet Explorer 8 or earlier. To create support using JavaScript, try using Selectivizr (*selectivizr.com*), which is a script you add to the file that emulates support in early IE versions. Selectivizr is an example of a polyfill, a script that adds support for contemporary web functionality in older browsers (polyfills are discussed in Chapter 20, "Using JavaScript").

Structural pseudo-classes

These allow selection based on where the element is in the structure of the document (the document tree). You should find that their names adequately describe what they target.

:root	:only-child	:nth-child()
:empty	:first-of-type	:nth-last-child()
:first-child	:last-of-type	:nth-of-type()
:last-child	:only-of-type	:nth-last-of-type()

UI (user interface) selectors

These selectors apply to states that are typical for form widgets.

:enabled	:disabled	:checked

And more!

Additional pseudo-classes include:

:target (selects elements targeted by a fragment identifier in a URL)

:lang() (selects based on a two-character language code)

:not() (selects every element except what is listed in the parentheses)

First letter and line

The following pseudo-elements are used to select the first line or the first letter of text in an element as displayed in the browser.

:first-line

This selector applies a style rule to the first line of the specified element. The only properties you can apply, however, are:

color	font	background
word-spacing	letter-spacing	text-decoration
vertical-align	text-transform	line-height

:first-letter

This applies a style rule to the first letter of the specified element. The properties you can apply are limited to:

color	font	text-decoration
text-transform	vertical-align	padding
background	margin	line-height
border	float	
letter-spacing	word-spacing	

NOTE

There are a few properties in this list that you haven't seen yet. We'll cover the box-related properties (margin, padding, border) in Chapter 14, "Thinking Inside the Box." The **float** *property is introduced in Chapter 15, "Floating and Positioning."*

Figure 13-13 shows examples of the **:first-line** and **:first-letter** pseudo-element selectors.

```
p:first-line {letter-spacing: 8px;}
```

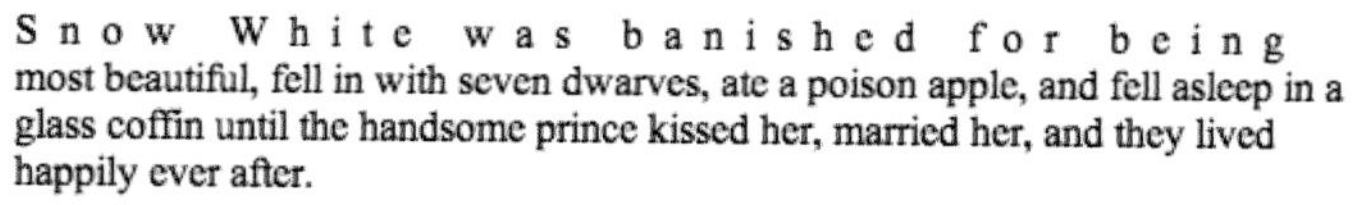

S n o w   W h i t e   w a s   b a n i s h e d   f o r   b e i n g most beautiful, fell in with seven dwarves, ate a poison apple, and fell asleep in a glass coffin until the handsome prince kissed her, married her, and they lived happily ever after.

```
p:first-letter {font-size: 300%; color: orange;}
```

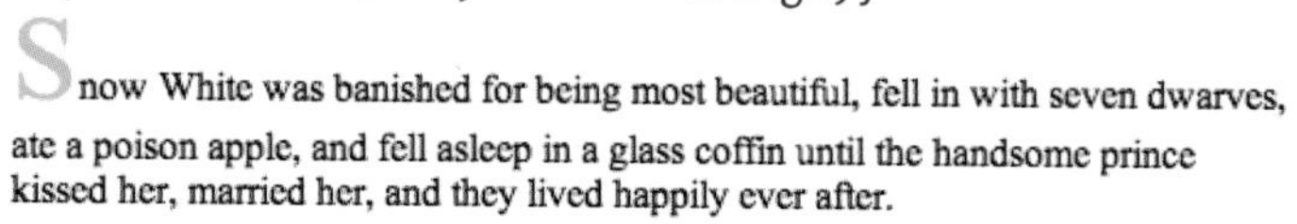

Snow White was banished for being most beautiful, fell in with seven dwarves, ate a poison apple, and fell asleep in a glass coffin until the handsome prince kissed her, married her, and they lived happily ever after.

Figure 13-13. Examples of :first-line *and* :first-letter *pseudo-element selectors.*

Generated content with :before and :after

CSS2 introduced the **:before** and **:after** pseudo-elements that are used to insert content before or after a specified element without actually adding the characters to the source document (this is called generated content in CSS). Generated content can be used to insert language-appropriate quotation marks around a quote, insert automatic counters, or even display URLs next to links when a document is printed.

Here's a simple example that inserts the words "Once upon a time:" before a paragraph and "The End." at the end of the paragraph (Figure 13-14).

The style sheet:

```
p:before {
  content: "Once upon a time: ";
  font-weight: bold;
  color: purple;
}
p:after {
  content: " The End.";
  font-weight: bold;
  color: purple;
}
```

The markup:

```
<p>Snow White was banished for being the most beautiful, ... and they
lived happily ever after.</p>
```

Once upon a time: Snow White was banished for being the most beautiful, fell in with seven dwarves, ate a poison apple, and fell asleep in a glass coffin until the handsome prince kissed her, married her, and they lived happily ever after. **The End.**

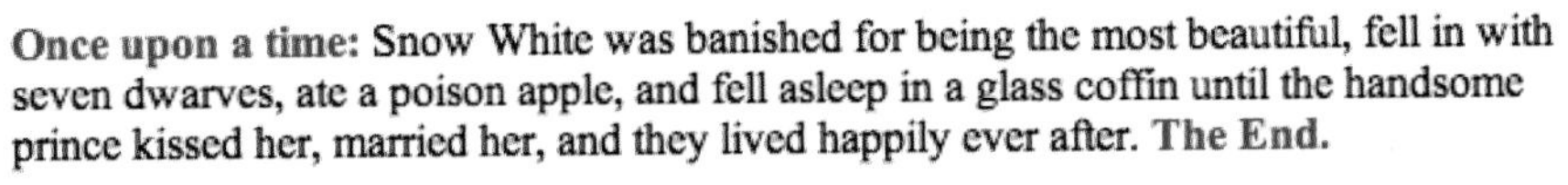

Figure 13-14. Generated content added with the `:before` *and* `:after` *pseudo-selectors, shown in the Firefox browser (Macintosh).*

Generated content is not supported in Internet Explorer 6 and 7, but other browsers handle it just fine. This isn't something you're likely to take on in your first projects, but if you are interested in learning more, I recommend this tutorial from *Smashing Magazine: coding.smashingmagazine.com/2011/07/13/learning-to-use-the-before-and-after-pseudo-elements-in-css/*. And if you want the full technical low-down, read the W3C Generated and Replaced Content Module (*www.w3.org/TR/css3-content/*).

Attribute Selectors

We are finally in the home stretch with selectors. The last type of selector targets elements based on their attributes. You can target attribute names or their values, which provides a lot of flexibility for selecting elements without needing to add a lot of **class** or **id** markup.

The following attribute selectors were introduced in CSS2 and are well supported by browsers, with the exception of IE6.

element[*attribute*]

> The simple attribute selector targets elements with a particular attribute regardless of its value. The following example selects any image that has a **title** attribute.
>
> ```
> img[title] {border: 3px solid;}
> ```

element[*attribute*="*exact value*"]

> The exact attribute value selector selects elements with a specific value for the attribute. In IE7, values are case-sensitive and must be entered correctly in order to be recognized. This selector matches images with exactly the **title** value "first grade".
>
> ```
> img[title="first grade"] {border: 3px solid;}
> ```

element[*attribute*~="*value*"]

> The partial attribute value selector allows you to specify one part of an attribute value. The following example looks for the word "grade" in the title, so images with the title value "first grade" and "second grade" would be selected.
>
> ```
> img[title~="grade"] {border: 3px solid;}
> ```

element[*attribute*|="*value*"]

> The hyphen-separated attribute value selector targets hyphen-separated values. This selector matches any link that points to a document written in a variation on the English language (**en**), whether the attribute value is **en-us** (American English), **en-in** (Indian English), **en-au-tas** (Australian English), and so on. (Remember that the * is the universal selector that selects "any element.")
>
> ```
> *[hreflang|="en"] {border: 3px solid;}
> ```

The following extended attribute selectors are new in CSS3, so they are just gaining steam. They are not supported at all in IE6 or 7, and support in older versions of Safari, Opera, and Firefox is partial or buggy.

element[*attribute*^="*first part of the value*"]

> The beginning substring attribute value selector matches elements whose specified attribute values *start* in the string of characters in the selector. This selector applies the style only to all images that are found in the */images/icons* directory (**<img src="/images/icons…>**).
>
> ```
> img[src^="/images/icons"] {border: 3px solid;}
> ```

element[*attribute*$="*last part of the value*"]

> The ending substring attribute value selector matches elements whose specified attribute values *end* in the string of characters in the selector. In this example, you can apply a style to just the **a** elements that link to PDF files.
>
> ```
> a[href$=".pdf"] {border: 3px solid;}
> ```

element[*attribute***="*any part of the value*"]

> The arbitrary substring attribute value selector looks for the provided text string in any part of the attribute value specified. This rule selects any image that contains the word "February" somewhere in its **title**.
>
> ```
> img[title*="February"] {border: 3px solid;}
> ```

OK, we're done with selectors! All of them. You've been a real trooper. I think it's definitely time to try out foreground and background colors as well as a few of these new selector types in Exercise 13-1.

exercise 13-1 | Adding color to a document

In this exercise, we'll start with a simple black-and-white menu and give it some personality with foreground and background colors (Figure 13-15). You should have enough experience writing style rules by this point that I'm not going hold your hand as much as I have in previous exercises. This time, you write the rules. You can check your work against the finished style sheet provided in Appendix A.

Open the file *bistro.html* (available at *www.learningwebdesign.com/4e/materials*) in a text editor. You will find that there is already an embedded style sheet that provides basic text formatting, including a preview of the **margin** and **padding** properties that we'll be getting to in the next chapter. With the text all set, you'll just need to work on the colors. Feel free to save the document at any step along the way and view your progress in a browser.

1. Make the **h1** heading purple (R:153, G:51, B:153, or **#993399**) by adding a new declaration to the existing **h1** rule. Note that because this value has all double digits, you can (and should) use the condensed version (**#939**) and save a few bytes in the style sheet.

2. Make the **h2** headings light orange-brown (R:204, G:102, B:0, or **#cc6600**).

3. Make the background of the entire page a light green (R:210, G:220, B:157, or **#d2dc9d**). Now might be a nice time to save, have a look in a browser, and troubleshoot if the background and headings do not appear in color.

4. Make the background of the "header" **div** white with 50% transparency (R:255, G:255, B:255, .5) so a hint of the background color shows through.

5. I've already added a rule that turns underlines off under links (**text-decoration:none**), so we'll be relying on color to make the links pop. Write a rule that makes links the same purple as the **h1** (**#993399**).

6. Make visited links a muted purple (**#937393**).

7. When the mouse is placed over links, make the text a brighter purple (**#c700f2**) and add a white background color (**#fff**). This will look a little like the links are lighting up when the mouse is pointing at it. Use these same style rules for when the links are in focus.

8. As the mouse is being clicked (or tapped on a touch device), add a white background color and make the text turn a vibrant purple (**#ff00ff**). Make sure that all of your link pseudo-classes are in the correct order.

When you are done, your page should look like the one in Figure 13-15. We'll be adding background images to this page later, so if you'd like to continue experimenting with different colors on different elements, make a copy of this document and give it a new name.

WARNING

Don't forget the # character before hex values. The rule won't work without it.

Figure 13-15. *The Black Goose Bistro menu page with colors applied.*

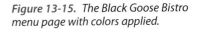

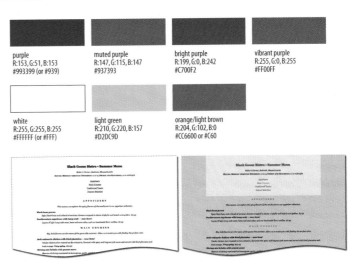

purple
R:153, G:51, B:153
#993399 (or #939)

muted purple
R:147, G:115, B:147
#937393

bright purple
R:199, G:0, B:242
#C700F2

vibrant purple
R:255, G:0, B:255
#FF00FF

white
R:255, G:255, B:255
#FFFFFF (or #FFF)

light green
R:210, G:220, B:157
#D2DC9D

orange/light brown
R:204, G:102, B:0
#CC6600 or #C60

before

after

Background Images

We've seen how to add images to the content of the document using the **img** element, but these days, most decorative images are added to pages and elements as backgrounds using CSS. After all, decorations such as tiling background patterns are firmly part of presentation, not structure. CSS also allows designers to change the look of a site by editing a *.css* file…we've come a long way from the days when sites were giant graphics cut up and held together with tables (*shudder*).

In this section, we'll look at the collection of properties used to place and push around background images, starting with the basic **background-image** property.

Adding a background image

The **background-image** property adds a background image to any element. Its primary job is to provide the location of the image file.

background-image

Values:	url(*location of image*) | none | inherit
Default:	none
Applies to:	all elements
Inherits:	no

NOTE

The proper term for that "URL holder" is a functional notation. It is the same syntax used to list decimal and percentage RGB values.

The value of **background-image** is a sort of URL holder that contains the location of the image (see the note).

The URL is relative to wherever the CSS rule is at the time. If the rule is in an embedded style sheet (a **style** element in the HTML document), then the pathname in the URL should be relative to the location of the HTML file. If the CSS rule is in an external style sheet, then the pathname to the image should be relative to the location of the *.css* file. See the related tip for another approach.

These examples and Figure 13-16 show background images applied behind a whole page (**body**) and a single **blockquote** element with padding and a border applied.

```
body {
   background-image: url(star.gif);
}

blockquote {
   background-image: url(dot.gif);
   padding: 2em;
   border: 4px dashed;
}
```

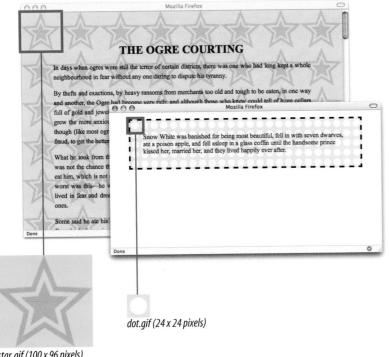

star.gif (100 x 96 pixels)

dot.gif (24 x 24 pixels)

Figure 13-16. *Examples of tiling background images added with the* `background-image` *property.*

RESOURCE

The Standardista site has incredibly detailed browser support charts for every possible background-related property. It's definitely worth a look.

www.standardista.com/css3/css3-background-properties/

Here you can see the default behavior of **background-image**. The image starts in the top-lefthand corner and tiles horizontally and vertically until the entire element is filled (although you'll learn how to change that in a moment). Like background colors, by default tiling background images fill the area behind the content area, the extra padding space around the content, and extend to the outer edge of the border (if there is one).

If you provide both a **background-color** and a **background-image** to an element, the image will be placed on top of the color. In fact, it is recommended that you *do* provide a backup color that is similar in hue, in the event that the image fails to download.

DESIGN TIP

Tiling Background Images

When working with background images, keep these guidelines and tips in mind:

- Use a simple image that won't interfere with the legibility of the text over it.
- Always provide a **background-color** value that matches the primary color of the background image. If the background image fails to display, at least the overall design of the page will be similar. This is particularly important if the text color would be illegible against the browser's default white background.
- As usual for the Web, keep the file size of background images as small as possible.

exercise 13-2 | **Adding a tiling background image**

In this exercise, we're going to add a simple tiling background image to the menu. The images provided for this exercise should be in the *images* directory.

Add a declaration to the **body** style rule that makes the image *bullseye.png* tile in the background of the page. Be sure to include the pathname relative to the style sheet (in this case, the current HTML document).

```
background-image: url(images/bullseye.png);
```

Easy, isn't it? When you save and view the page in the browser, it should look like Figure 13-17.

I want to point out that *bullseye.png* is a slightly transparent PNG graphic, so it will blend into any background color. You'll learn how to make a transparent PNG in Chapter 21, "Image Basics." Try temporarily changing the **background-color** for the **body** element by adding a second **background-color** declaration lower in the stack so it overrides the previous one. Play around with different colors and notice how the circles blend in. When you are done experimenting, delete the second declaration so the background is green again and you're ready to go for upcoming exercises.

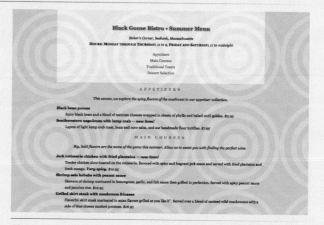

Figure 13-17. *The article with a simple tiling background image.*

Controlling tiling direction

As we saw in Figure 13-16, images tile left and right, up and down, when left to their own devices. You can limit this behavior with the **background-repeat** property.

background-repeat

Values:	repeat | repeat-x | repeat-y | no-repeat | inherit
Default:	repeat
Applies to:	all elements
Inherits:	no

If you want a background image to appear just once, use the **no-repeat** keyword value, like this:

```
body {
  background-image: url(star.gif);
  background-repeat: no-repeat;
}
```

You can also restrict the image to tiling only horizontally (**repeat-x**) or vertically (**repeat-y**), as shown in these examples.

```
body {
    background-image: url(star.gif);
    background-repeat: repeat-x;
}
body {
    background-image: url(star.gif);
    background-repeat: repeat-y;
}
```

Figure 13-18 shows examples of each of the keyword values. Notice that in all the examples, the tiling begins in the top-left corner of the element (or browser window when an image is applied to the **body** element). In the next section, I'll show you how to change that.

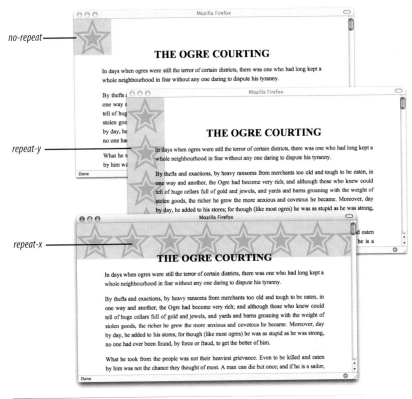

Figure 13-18. *Turning off automatic tiling with* no-repeat *(top), vertical-axis tiling with* repeat-y *(middle), and horizontal-axis tiling with* repeat-x *(bottom).*

exercise 13-3 | **Controlling tile direction**

Now let's try some slightly more sophisticated tiling on the sample article page. This time we'll add a tiling background just along the top edge of the "header" **div**.

1. In the **#header** rule, add the image *purpledot.png* and set it to repeat horizontally only.

```
#header {
    margin-top: 0;
    padding: 3em 1em 2em 1em;
    text-align: center;
    background-color: rgba(255,255,255,.5);
    background-image: url(images/purpledot.png);
    background-repeat: repeat-x;
}
```

2. Save the file and look at it in the browser. It should look something like Figure 13-19. I recommend resizing your browser window to wider and narrower sizes and paying attention to the position of the background pattern. See how

it's always anchored on the left? We're going to learn how to adjust position next.

3. Try changing the style rule to make the dot repeat vertically only, then make it not repeat at all (set it back to **repeat-x** when you're done).

Figure 13-19. *Adding a horizontal tiling image to the* **#header** *div.*

Background position

The **background-position** property specifies the position of the origin image in the background. You can think of the origin image as the first image that is placed in the background from which tiling images extend. Here is the property and its various values.

background-position

Values: length measurement | percentage | left | center | right | top | bottom | inherit

Default: 0% 0% *(same as* left top*)*

Applies to: all elements

Inherits: no

To position the origin image, you provide horizontal and vertical values that describe where to place it. But there are a variety of ways to do it.

Keyword positioning

The keyword values (**left**, **right**, **top**, **bottom**, and **center**) position the origin image relative to the edges of the element's padding. For example, **left** positions the image all the way to the left edge of the background area. The default origin position corresponds to "**left, top**".

Keywords are typically used in pairs, as in these examples:

```
background-position: left bottom;
background-position: right center;
```

If you provide only one keyword, the missing keyword is assumed to be center. Thus, **background-position: right** has the same effect as **background-position: right center**.

Length measurements

You can also specify the position by its distance from the top-left corner of the element using pixel measurements. When providing length values, the horizontal measurement always goes first.

```
background-position: 200px 50px;
```

Percentages

Percentage values are provided in horizontal/vertical pairs, with 0% 0% corresponding to the top-left corner and 100% 100% corresponding to the bottom-right corner. It is important to note that the percentage value applies to both the canvas area and the image itself. For example, the 100% value places the bottom-right corner of the image in the bottom-right corner of the canvas. As with keywords, if you only provide one percentage, the other is assumed to be 50% (centered).

```
background-position: 15% 100%;
```

CSS TIP

To ensure best performance in modern browsers, always supply the horizontal measurement first for all value types.

Figure 13-20 shows the results of each of the aforementioned **background-position** examples with the **background-repeat** set to **no-repeat** for clarity. It is possible to position the origin image and let it tile from there, in both directions or just horizontally or vertically. When the image tiles, the position of the initial image might not be obvious, but you can use **background-position** to make a tile pattern start at a point other than the left edge of the image. This might be used to keep a background pattern centered and symmetrical.

NOTE

Notice in Figure 13-20 that when an origin image is placed in the corner of an element, it is placed inside the border. Only repeated images extend under the border to its outer edge.

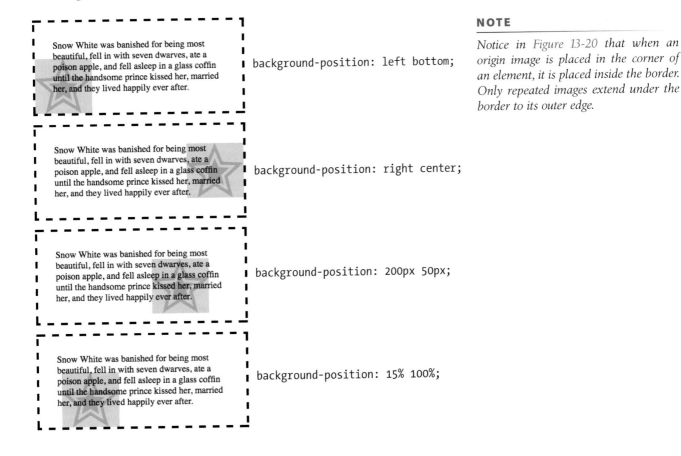

Figure 13-20. Positioning a non-repeating background image.

exercise 13-4 | Positioning background images

Let's have some fun with the position of the background image in the menu. First we're going to make some subtle adjustments to the background images that are already there, and then we'll swap it out for a whole different background and play around some more. We are still working with the *bistro.html* document, which should have repeating tile patterns in the **body** and **#header** elements.

1. I'm thinking that since the main elements of the menu are centered, it would be nice if the background patterns stayed centered, too. Add this declaration to both the **body** and **#header** rules, then save and look at it in the browser. You may not notice the difference until you resize the browser wide and narrow again. Now the pattern is anchored in the center and reveals more or less on both edges, not just the right edge as before.

   ```
   background-position: center top;
   ```

2. For kicks, alter the **background-position** values so that the purple dots are along the bottom edge of the header **div** (**center bottom**). (Doesn't look so good; I'm putting mine back.) Then try moving the *bullseye.png* down 200 pixels (**center 200px**). Notice that the pattern still fills the entire screen—we moved the origin image down, but the background is still set to tile in all directions. Figure 13-21 shows the result of these changes.

3. That looks good, but let's get rid of the background on the **body** for now. I want to show you a little trick. During the design process, I prefer to hide styles in comments instead of deleting them entirely. That way I don't need to remember them or type them in again; I only have to remove the comment indicators and they're back. When the design is done and it's time to publish, I strip unused styles out to keep the file size down. Here is how to hide declarations in comments:

   ```
   body {
       font-family: Georgia, serif;
       font-size: 100%;
       line-height: 175%;
       margin: 0 15%;
       background-color: #d2dc9d;
       /*  background-image: url(images/bullseye.png);
       background-position: center 200px; */
   }
   ```

4. Now, add the *blackgoose.png* images (also a semi-transparent PNG) to the background of the page. Set it to not repeat, and center it in the page.

   ```
   background-image: url(images/blackgoose.png);
   background-repeat: no-repeat;
   background-position: center top;
   ```

   Take a look in the browser window and watch the background scroll up with the content when you scroll the page.

5. I want you to get a feel for the various position keywords and numeric values. Try each of these out and look at them in the browser. Be sure to scroll the page and watch what happens. Note that when you provide a percentage or keyword to the vertical position, it is based on the height of the entire document, not just the browser window. You can try your own variations as well.

   ```
   background-position: right top;
   ```

   ```
   background-position: right bottom;
   ```

   ```
   background-position: left 50%;
   ```

   ```
   background-position: center 100px;
   ```

6. Leave the image positioned at **center 100px** so you are ready to go for the next exercise. Your page should look like the one shown on the right in Figure 13-21.

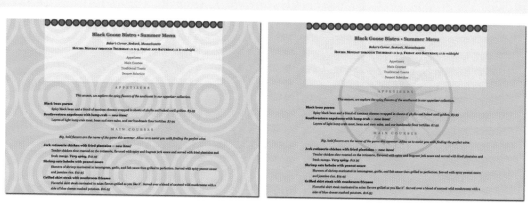

Centered background pattern

Positioned non-repeating image

Figure 13-21. The results of positioning the origin image in the tiling background patterns (left) and positioning a single background logo (right).

Background attachment

In the previous exercise, I asked you to scroll the page and watch what happens to the background image. As expected, it scrolls along with the document and off the top of the browser window, which is its default behavior. However, you can use the **background-attachment** property to free the background from the content and allow it to stay fixed in one position while the rest of the content scrolls.

background-attachment

Values: scroll | fixed | local *(new in CSS3)* | inherit

Default: scroll

Applies to: all elements

Inherits: no

With the **background-attachment** property, you have the choice of whether the background image scrolls with the content or stays in a fixed position. When an image is fixed, it stays in the same position relative to the viewport of the browser (as opposed to being relative to the element it fills). You'll see what I mean in a minute.

In the following example, a large, non-tiling image is placed in the background of the whole document (the **body** element). By default, when the document scrolls, the image scrolls too, moving up and off the page, as shown in Figure 13-22. However, if you set the value of **background-attachment** to **fixed**, it stays where it is initially placed, and the text scrolls up over it.

```
body {
    background-image: url(images/bigstar.gif);
    background-repeat: no-repeat;
    background-position: center 300px;
    background-attachment: fixed;
}
```

The **local** value, which was added in CSS3, makes a background image scroll along with the content inside a scrolling element, independent of the browser viewport scroll. It is not supported in IE6 through 8 or Firefox as of this writing.

NOTE

You can fix the position of a background image for any element, but unfortunately, it won't work for users with Internet Explorer 6 or 7. This is another feature to use as "icing."

Figure 13-22. Preventing the background image from scrolling with the background-attachment *property.*

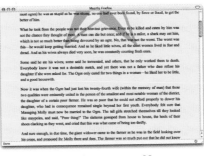

A large non-repeating background image in the body of the document.

background-attachment: scroll;

By default, the background image is attached to the body element and scrolls off the page when the page content scrolls.

background-attachment: fixed;

When background-attachment is set to "fixed," the image stays in its position relative to the browser viewing area and does not scroll with the content.

exercise 13-5 | Fixed position

When we last left the bistro menu, we had applied a large, non-repeating logo image to the background of the page. We'll leave it just like that, but we'll use the **background-attachment** property to keep it in the same place even when the page scrolls.

```
body {
    ...
    background-attachment: fixed;
}
```

Save the document, open it in the browser, and now try scrolling. The background image stays put in the viewing area of the browser. Cool, huh?

For extra credit, see what happens when you fix the attachment of the dot pattern in the **div#header**. (Hint: it stays in the same place, but only within the **div** itself. When the **div** slides out of view, so does its background.)

CSS3 Background Properties

The CSS3 Backgrounds and Borders Module introduced a few more properties for controlling backgrounds. The module is still a working draft, so this information is subject to change. These are not supported in IE6 through 8.

background-clip

NEW IN CSS3

Values: **border-box** | **padding-box** | **content-box**

This specifies exactly how far the background image should extend. We saw that by default, it extends to the edge of the border (**border-box**), but you could also make it end at the padding or the edge of the content box using **padding-box** or **content-box**, respectively. We'll discuss these box model components in the next chapter.

background-size

NEW IN CSS3

Values: [*length* | *percentage* | **auto**] | **cover** | **contain**

This property allows designers to size the background image inside the element. You can provide specific width and height measurements. If you provide only one measurement, the other is presumed to be **auto**. You can also just set the image to **contain**, which resizes the image so that it just fits inside the containing element, even if there is some blank space left over, or **cover**, which resizes the image so that the entire element is covered, even if some of the background image hangs over the edges and out of view.

background-origin

NEW IN CSS3

Values: **border-box** | **padding-box** | **content-box**

This property determines how the **background-position** is calculated, or in other words, where to start counting positioning measurements. You can start from the edge of the border, padding area, or content area.

The Shorthand background Property

You can use the handy **background** property to specify all of your background styles in one declaration.

background

Values:	*background-color background-image background-repeat background-attachment background-position* | inherit
Default:	*see indiviual properties*
Applies to:	*all elements*
Inherits:	*no*

As for the shorthand **font** property, the value of the **background** property is a list of values that would be provided for the individual background properties listed above. For example, this one background rule:

    body { background: white url(arlo.png) no-repeat right top fixed; }

replaces this rule with five separate declarations:

    body {
       background-color: white;
       background-image: url(arlo.png);
       background-repeat: no-repeat;
       background-position: right top;
       background-attachment: fixed;
    }

All of the property values for **background** are optional and may appear in any order. The only restriction is that when providing the coordinates for the **background-position** property, the horizontal value must appear first, immediately followed by the vertical value. Be aware that if a value is omitted, it will be reset to its default (see the sidebar "Watch Out for Overrides").

exercise 13-6 |
Convert to shorthand property

This one is easy. Replace all of the background-related declarations in the **body** of the bistro menu with a single **background** property declaration.

    body {
       font-family: Georgia,
    serif;
       font-size: 100%;
       line-height: 175%;
       margin: 0 15%;
       background: #d2dc9d
    url(images/blackgoose.
    png) no-repeat center 100px
    fixed;
    }

Do the same for the **div** element, and you're done.

Watch Out for Overrides

The **background** property is efficient, but use it carefully. We've addressed this before, but it bears repeating. Because **background** is a shorthand property, when you omit a value, that property will be reset with its default. Be careful that you do not accidentally override style rules earlier in the style sheet with a later shorthand rule that reverts your settings to the defaults.

In this example, the background image *dots.gif* will *not* be applied to **h3** elements because by omitting the value for **background-image**, you essentially set that value to **none**.

    h1, h2, h3 { background: red url(dots.gif) repeat-x;}
    h3 {background: green;}

To override particular properties, use the specific background property you intend to change. For example, if the intent in the above example were to change just the background color of **h3** elements, the **background-color** property would be the correct choice.

Multiple backgrounds

Until recently, you could apply only one background image to an element. To stack up background images in the past, the only solution was to add extra **div**s in the markup and add an image to each one. Thankfully, CSS3 allows multiple background images to be applied to a single element, and browsers are beginning to support them.

NOTE

Although CSS declarations usually work on a "last one wins" rule, for multiple background images, whichever is listed last goes on the bottom and each image higher in the list layers on top of it. You can think of them like Photoshop layers in that they get stacked in the order in which they appear in the list.

To apply multiple values for **background-image**, put them in a list separated by commas. Additional background-related property values also go in comma-separated lists; the first value listed applies to the first image, the second value to the second, and so on. The image defined by the first value will go in front, and others line up behind it, in the order in which they are listed.

```
body {
    background-image: url(image1.png), url(image2.png), url(image3.png);
    background-position: left top, center center, right bottom;
    background-repeat: no-repeat; no-repeat; no-repeat;
    …
}
```

Alternatively, you can take advantage of the **background** shorthand property to make the rule simpler. Now the **background** property has three value series, separated by commas:

```
body {
    background:
      url(image1.png) left top no-repeat,
      url(image2.png) center center no-repeat,
      url(image3.png) right bottom no-repeat;
    …
}
```

Figure 13-23. Three separate background images added to the body *element.*

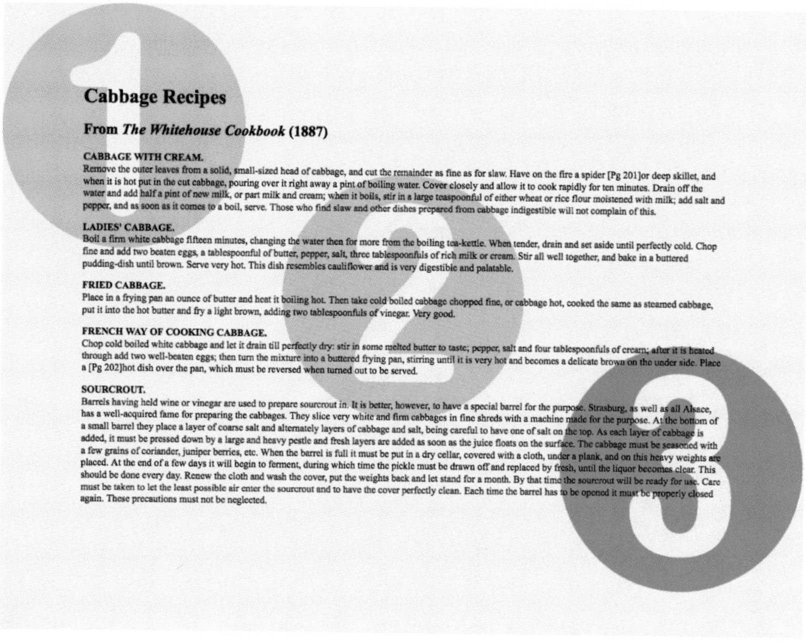

Figure 13-23 shows the result.

As with any new CSS3 technique, support is lacking in Internet Explorer versions 6 through 8, which will completely ignore any **background** declaration with more than one value. The solution is to choose one **background-image** for the element as a fallback for IE and other non-supporting browsers, then specify the multiple **background** rules. Because it comes second, browsers that support them will override the single image with the multiple image rule. As for all background images, it is a good idea to provide a **background-color** should all else fail. Put it last so the shorthand background properties don't override it.

Until support is universal, you can use multiple backgrounds as "icing" for browsers that can show them.

```
body {
   background: url(image_fallback.png) top left no-repeat;
   /* for non-supporting browsers */
   background:
      url(image1.png) left top no-repeat,
      url(image2.png) center center no-repeat,
      url(image3.png) right bottom no-repeat;
   background-color: papayawhip;      /* background color */
}
```

exercise 13-7 | **Multiple background images**

In this exercise, we'll give multiple background images a try. Note that if you are using Internet Explorer 6, 7, or 8, you won't be able to see the multiple images, so use Chrome, Safari, or Firefox instead (they're free!).

I'd like the dot pattern in the **#header div** to run along the left and right sides. I also have a little goose silhouette (*gooseshadow.png*) that might look cute walking along the bottom of the header. Following the current best practice, I've started the rule with a **background-image** fallback (the horizontal row of dots we used before) and ended with the background color.

```
#header {
   ...
   background: url(images/purpledot.png) center top repeat-x;
   background:
      url(images/purpledot.png) left top repeat-y,
      url(images/purpledot.png) right top repeat-y,
      url(images/gooseshadow.png) 90% bottom no-repeat;
   background-color: rgba(255,255,255,.5);
}
```

Figure 13-24 shows the final result. Eh, I liked it better before, but you get the idea.

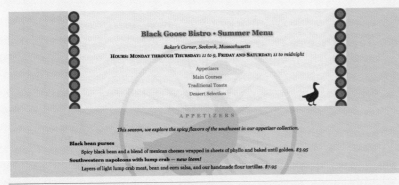

Figure 13-24. *The bistro menu header with two rows of dots and a small goose graphic in the* div#header *element.*

Parallax Scrolling with Multiple Backgrounds

The term parallax motion refers to the visual effect of closer objects seeming to move more quickly than objects farther in the distance. Replicating near, medium, and distance speeds in an animation or motion graphic can give a scene a 3-D effect.

Some designers use multiple background images to create parallax scrolling effects. When you resize the browser window or move a horizontal scrollbar, the staggered way the backgrounds move creates a parallax and 3-D effect. Because you cannot resize or scroll mobile browsers horizontally, this effect will not work on phones and tablets.

A good starting point to learn more is the tutorial "Starry Night: Incredible 3D Background Effect with Parallax," by Chris Coyier (*css-tricks.com/3d-parralax-background-effect/*). See also "How to Recreate Silverback's Parallax Effect," by Paul Annett (*thinkvitamin.com/design/how-to-recreate-silverbacks-parallax-effect/*), which refers to the Silverback app page (*silverbackapp.com*) that got all the cool kids talking.

Like a Rainbow (Gradients)

A gradient is a transition from one color to another, sometimes through multiple colors. In the past, the only way to put a gradient on a web page was to create one in an image-editing program and add the resulting image with CSS.

CSS3 introduced the ability to specify color gradients using CSS notation alone, leaving the task of rendering color blends to the browser. Gradients can be applied anywhere an image may be applied: `background-image`, `border-image`, and `list-style-image`. We'll stick with `background-image` examples in this chapter.

There are two types of gradients:

- Linear gradients change colors along a line, from one edge of the element to the other.

- Radial gradients start at a point and spread outward in a circular or elliptical shape.

Gradients are images that browsers generate on the fly. Use them as you would use a background image.

Linear gradients

The `linear-gradient()` notation provides the angle of the line and one or more points along that line where the pure color is positioned (color stops). You can use color names or any of the numerical color values discussed earlier in the chapter. The angle of the line is specified in degrees (**ndeg**) or using keywords. Using degrees, **0deg** points upward, and positive angles go around clockwise so that **90deg** points to the right. Therefore, if you want to go from yellow on the top edge to green on the bottom edge, set the rotation to **180deg**.

```
#banner
    background-image: linear-gradient(180deg, yellow, green);
}
```

The keywords describe direction in increments of 90° (**to top**, **to right**, **to bottom**, **to left**). Our **180deg** gradient could also be specified with the **to bottom** keyword. The result is shown in Figure 13-25 (top).

```
#banner {
    background-image: linear-gradient(to bottom, yellow, green);
}
```

In this example, the gradient now goes from left to right and includes a third color, orange, which appears 25% of the way across the gradient line (Figure 13-25, middle). You can see that the placement of the color stop is indicated after the color value. The 0% and 100% positions may be omitted.

```
#banner {
    background-image: linear-gradient(90deg, yellow, orange 25%, blue);
}
```

These examples are pretty garish, but if you choose your colors and stops right, gradients are a nice way to give elements subtle shading and a 3-D appearance. The button on the bottom uses a background gradient to achieve a 3D look without graphics (Figure 13-25, bottom).

```
a.button-like {
    background: linear-gradient(to bottom, #e2e2e2 0%, #dbdbdb 50%,
    #d1d1d1 51%, #fefefe 100%);
}
```

`linear-gradient(to bottom, yellow, green);`

`linear-gradient(90deg, yellow, orange 25%, blue);`

`linear-gradient(to bottom, #e2e2e2 0%, #dbdbdb 50%, #d1d1d1 51%, #fefefe 100%);`

Figure 13-25. Examples of linear gradients.

Radial gradients

Radial gradients, like the name says, radiate out from a point in a circle. In the CSS3 spec, the **radial-gradient()** notation describes the shape (**circle** or **ellipse**; circle is the default if no shape is specified), the position of the center of the gradient (following the same syntax as **background-position**), and a size, specified as a radius length or a keyword that describes the side or corner where the last color should stop (**closest-side**, **farthest-side**, **closest-corner**, **farthest-corner**, **cover**, **contain**).

NOTE

For more information on radial gradients, see the very thorough article "CSS3 Radial Gradients," by John Alsopp (www.webdirections.org/blog/css3-radial-gradients/).

This rule fills the box with a radial gradient that will be contained within the element box (Figure 13-26).

```
#banner {
  background-image: radial-gradient(center contain yellow green);
}
```

```
radial-gradient(center, contain, yellow, green);
```

Figure 13-26. Examples of radial gradients.

Introducing vendor prefixes

OK, here's where things get fun, and by "fun," of course, I mean not much fun at all. The CSS gradient examples we've seen so far use the syntax described in the CSS3 specification. But browsers began their own tinkering with gradients before the specification was fully agreed upon. For cutting-edge features like gradients, it is common for browsers to start experimenting with their own solutions and implementing them in shipping browsers before the spec has been fully approved and set in stone.

That's a lot like what browser makers did in the 90s that caused so many incompatibility disasters, but this time around, they've had the good sense to label their proprietary properties with vendor prefixes that clearly indicate proprietary solutions. Table 13-1 lists the browser prefixes in current use.

Table 13-1. Browser vendor prefixes

Prefix	Organization	Most popular browsers
-ms-	Microsoft	Internet Explorer
-moz-	Mozilla Foundation	Firefox, Camino, SeaMonkey
-o-	Opera Software	Opera, Opera Mini, Opera Mobile
-webkit-	Originally Apple; now open source	Safari, Chrome, Android, Silk, BlackBerry, WebOS, many others
-khtml-	Konqueror	Konqueror

What this means for designers and developers is that for some newer CSS3 features, we need to list out the properties for each browser using browser prefixes to accommodate different implementations. Although it means extra work and extra code, it is not a bad thing. It allows browser makers to innovate in a way that does not interfere with the standards process.

Getting back to gradients, the following example shows the yellow-to-green linear gradient as it should be written to address every modern browser (with the Internet Explorer `filter` equivalent thrown in for good measure). Notice that the syntax is slightly different. Where the CSS3 spec uses the `to bottom` keyword, most of the others use `top` and WebKit uses `left top`, `left bottom`.

```
background: #ffff00; /* Old browsers */
background: -moz-linear-gradient(top,  #ffff00 0%, #00ff00 100%);
    /* FF3.6+ */
background: -webkit-gradient(linear, left top, left bottom, color-
    stop(0%,#ffff00), color-stop(100%,#00ff00));
    /* Chrome,Safari4+ */
background: -webkit-linear-gradient(top,  #ffff00 0%,#00ff00 100%);
    /* Chrome10+,Safari5.1+ */
background: -o-linear-gradient(top,  #ffff00 0%,#00ff00 100%);
    /* Opera 11.10+ */
background: -ms-linear-gradient(top,  #ffff00 0%,#00ff00 100%);
    /* IE10+ */
background: linear-gradient(to bottom,  #ffff00 0%,#00ff00 100%);
    /* W3C */
filter: progid:DXImageTransform.Microsoft.gradient(
    startColorstr='#ffff00', endColorstr='#00ff00',GradientType=0 );
    /* IE6-9 */
```

The good news is that as newer standards-compliant browsers emerge and old versions go away, some properties, such as **text-shadow**, that once required browser prefixes no longer do. It could be that by the time you are reading this, browser prefixes will be a quaint stop-gap method from the past (and I hope that is the case). But more likely, it will still be useful to be familiar with vendor prefixes and which properties require them.

In upcoming chapters, whenever a property requires vendor prefixes, I will be sure to note it. Otherwise, you can assume that the standard CSS is all you need.

Designing gradients

That last code example was a doozy! Vendor prefixes aside, just the task of describing gradients can be daunting. Although it is not impossible to write the code by hand, I recommend you do what I do—use an online gradient tool! My favorite is The Ultimate CSS Gradient Generator from Colorzilla (*www.colorzilla.com/gradient-editor/*), shown in Figure 13-27. Simply enter as many color stops as you'd like, slide the sliders around until you get the look you want, and then copy the code. That's exactly what I did to get the example we just looked at.

FOR FURTHER READING

For an excellent explanation of browser prefixes, I highly recommend the article "Prefix or Posthack" by my buddy Eric A. Meyer: *www.alistapart. com/articles/prefix-or-posthack/*.

For an overview of all the browser-prefixed properties, some of which will never make it into the standard, see this dizzying chart compiled by Peter Beverloo: *peter.sh/experiments/ vendor-prefixed-css-property-overview*.

NOTE

For more information on gradient syntax for various browsers as well as the advantages gradients have over graphics, read "Speed Up with CSS3 Gradients" by Chris Coyier (css-tricks.com/css3-gradients/).

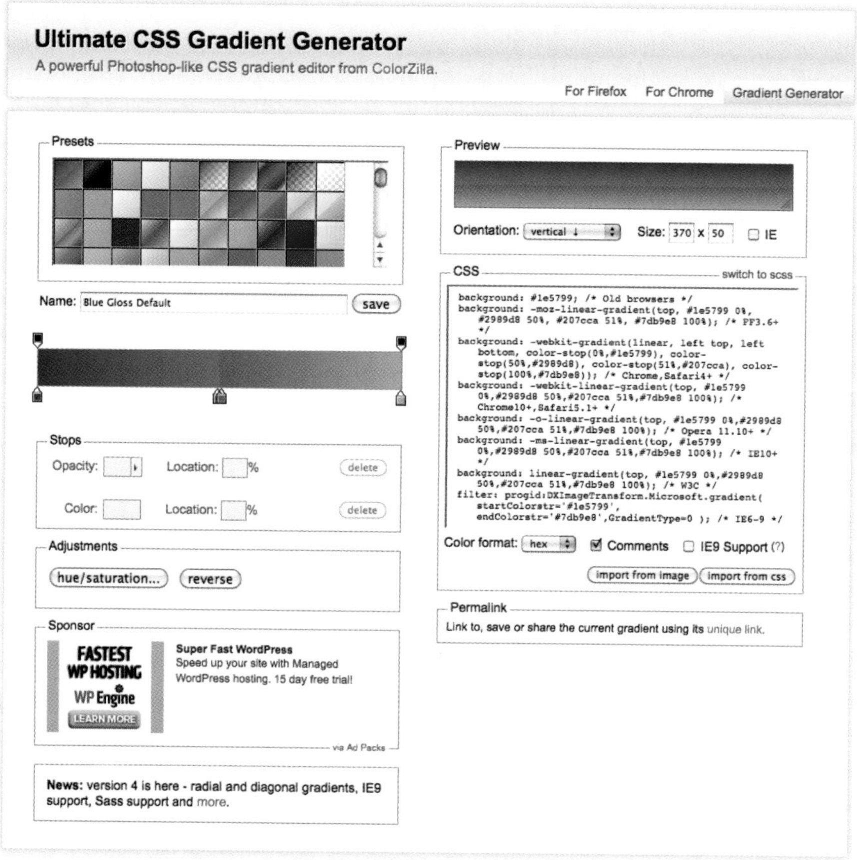

Figure 13-27. The Ultimate CSS Gradient Generator (www.colorzilla.com/gradient-editor) makes creating CSS gradients a breeze.

Finally, External Style Sheets

Back in Chapter 11, "Cascading Style Sheets Orientation," I told you that there are three ways to connect style sheets to a HTML document: inline with the **style** attribute, embedded with the **style** element, and as an external *.css* document linked to or imported into the document. In this section, we finally get to that third option.

External style sheets are by far the most powerful way to use CSS because you can make style changes across an entire site simply by editing a single style sheet document. That is the advantage to having all the style information in one place, and not mixed in with the document source.

First, a little bit about the style sheet document itself. An external style sheet is a plain-text document with at least one style sheet rule. It may *not* include any HTML tags (there's no reason to, anyway). It may contain comments, but they must use the CSS comment syntax that you've seen already:

```
/* This is the end of the section */
```

The style sheet should be named with the *.css* suffix (there are some exceptions to this rule, but you're unlikely to encounter them as a beginner). Figure 13-28 shows how a short style sheet document looks in my text editor.

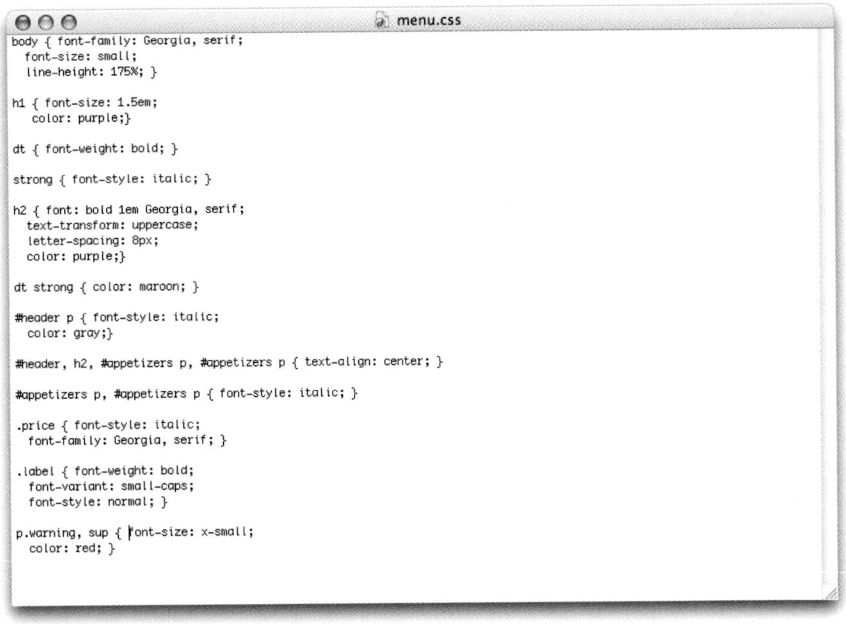

```
                                  menu.css
body { font-family: Georgia, serif;
  font-size: small;
  line-height: 175%; }

h1 { font-size: 1.5em;
  color: purple;}

dt { font-weight: bold; }

strong { font-style: italic; }

h2 { font: bold 1em Georgia, serif;
  text-transform: uppercase;
  letter-spacing: 8px;
  color: purple;}

dt strong { color: maroon; }

#header p { font-style: italic;
  color: gray;}

#header, h2, #appetizers p, #appetizers p { text-align: center; }

#appetizers p, #appetizers p { font-style: italic; }

.price { font-style: italic;
  font-family: Georgia, serif; }

.label { font-weight: bold;
  font-variant: small-caps;
  font-style: normal; }

p.warning, sup { font-size: x-small;
  color: red; }
```

Figure 13-28. External style sheets contain only CSS rules and comments in a plain-text document.

There are two ways to refer to an external style sheet: the **link** element and an **@import** rule. Let's look at both of these attachment methods.

Using the link element

The best-supported method is to create a link to the *.css* document using the **link** element in the **head** of the document, as shown here:

```
<head>
  <title>Titles are required.</title>
  <link rel="stylesheet" href="/path/stylesheet.css">
</head>
```

You need to include two attributes in the **link** element (see note):

rel="stylesheet"

Defines the linked document's relation to the current document. The value of the **rel** attribute is always **stylesheet** when linking to a style sheet.

href="url"

Provides the location of the *.css* file.

NOTE

The **link** *element is empty, so you need to terminate it with a trailing slash in XHTML documents (* **<link />** *). Omit the trailing slash in HTML documents.*

NOTE

In HTML4.01 and XHTML1.0, the **link** *element must include the* **type** *attribute set to text/css:*

type="text/css"

The type attribute is no longer required in HTML5.

You can include multiple **link** elements to different style sheets and they'll all apply. If there are conflicts, whichever one is listed last will override previous settings, due to the rule order and the cascade.

Importing with @import

The other method for attaching an external style sheet to a document is to import it with an **@import** rule. The **@import** rule is another type of rule you can add to a style sheet, either in an external *.css* style sheet document, or right in the **style** element, as shown in the following example.

```
<head>
  <style>
    @import url("/path/stylesheet.css");
    p { font-face: Verdana;}
  </style>
  <title>Titles are required.</title>
</head>
```

In this example, a relative URL is shown, but it could also be an absolute URL (beginning with **http://**). The **@import** rule must go in the beginning of the style sheet *before any selectors*. You can import more than one style sheet and they all will apply, but rules from the last style sheet listed take precedence over earlier ones.

You can try both the **link** and **@import** methods in Exercise 13-8.

N O T E

You can also supply the URL without the **url( )** *notation:*

```
@import "/path/style.css";
```

Again, absolute pathnames, beginning at the root, will ensure that the .css document will always be found.

Modular Style Sheets

Because you can compile information from multiple external style sheets, modular style sheets have become a popular technique for style management. Many developers keep styles they frequently reuse, such as typography treatments, layout rules, or form-related styles, in separate style sheets, then combine them in mix-and-match fashion using **@import** rules. Again, the **@import** rules need to go before rules that use selectors.

Content of clientsite.css:

```
/* basic typography */
@import url("type.css");

/* form inputs */
@import url("forms.css");

/* navigation */
@import url("list-nav.css");
```

---

exercise 13-8 |
Making an external style sheet

It is OK to use an embedded style sheet while designing a page, but it is probably best moved to an external style sheet once the design is finished so it can be reused by multiple documents in the site. We'll do just that for the bistro menu style sheet.

1. Open the latest version of *bistro. html*. Select and cut all of the rules within the **style** element, but leave the **<style>...</style>** tags because we'll be using them in a moment.

2. Create a new plain ASCII text document and paste all of the style rules. Make sure that no markup got in there by accident.

3. Save this document as *menustyles.css* in the same directory as the *bistro.html* document.

4. Now, back in *bistro.html*, add an **@import** rule to attach the external style sheet:

```
<style>
@import url(menustyles.css);
</style>
```

Save the file and reload it in the browser. It should look exactly the same as it did when the style sheet was embedded. If not, go back and make sure that everything matches the examples.

5. Delete the whole style element, and this time we'll add the style sheet with a **link** element in the **head** of the document.

```
<link rel="stylesheet"
href="menustyles.css" >
```

Again, test your work by saving the document and viewing it in the browser.

```
/* site-specific styles */
body { background: orange; }
```

   ...*more style rules*...

This is a good technique to keep in mind as you build experience in creating sites. You'll find that there are some solutions that just work for you, and it is nice not to have to reinvent the wheel for every new site. Modular style sheets are a good time-saving and organizational device (see note for a caveat).

Test Yourself

This time we'll test your background prowess entirely with matching and multiple-choice questions.

1. Which of these areas gets filled with a background color?

   a. The area behind the content

   b. Any padding added around the content

   c. The area under the border

   d. The margin space around the element

   e. All of the above

   f. a and b

   g. a, b, and c

2. Which of these is *not* a way to specify the color white in CSS?

   a. #FFFFFF   b. #FFF   c. rgb(255, 255, 255)

   d. rgb(FF, FF, FF)   e. white   f. rgb(100%, 100%, 100%)

3. Match the pseudo-class with the elements it targets.

   a. `a:link`   1. Links that have already been clicked

   b. `a:visited`   2. An element that is highlighted and ready for input

   c. `a:hover`   3. An element that is the first child element of its parent

   d. `a:active`   4. A link with the mouse pointer over it

   e. `:focus`   5. Links that have not yet been visited

   f. `:first-child`   6. A link that is in the process of being clicked

4. Match the following rules with their respective samples shown in Figure 13-29. All of the samples in the figure use the same source document,

NOTE

Although modular style sheets are useful, they can be a problem for performance and caching. If you use this method, it is recommended that you compile all of the styles into a single document before delivering them to a browser. Not to worry, you don't need to do it manually; there are tools out there that will do it for you. The LESS and Sass CSS frameworks (which will be formally introduced in Chapter 18, "CSS Techniques") are two tools that offer compiling functionality.

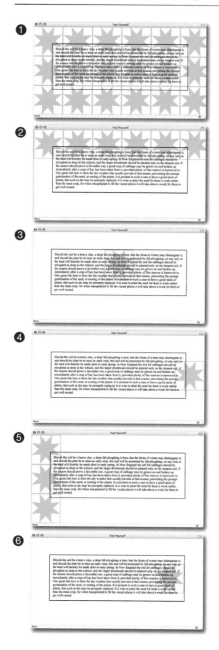

Figure 13-29. *Samples for Question 4.*

consisting of one paragraph element to which some padding and a border have been applied.

a. `body {background-image: url(graphic.gif);}`

b. `p {background-image: url(graphic.gif); background-repeat: no-repeat; background-position: 50% 0%;}`

c. `body {background-image: url(graphic.gif); background-repeat: repeat-x;}`

d. `p {background: url(graphic.gif) no-repeat right center;}`

e. `body {background-image: url(graphic.gif); background-repeat: repeat-y;}`

f. `body { background: url(graphic.gif) no-repeat right center;}`

CSS Review: Color and Background Properties

Here is a summary of the properties covered in this chapter, in alphabetical order.

Property	Description
background	A shorthand property that combines background properties
background-attachment	Specifies whether the background image scrolls or is fixed
background-clip	Specifies how far the background image should extend
background-color	Specifies the background color for an element
background-image	Provides the location of an image to use as a background
background-origin	Determines how the **background-position** is calculated (from edge of border, padding, or content box)
background-position	Specifies the location of the origin background image
background-repeat	Whether and how a background image repeats (tiles)
background-size	Specifies the size of the background image
color	Specifies the foreground (text and border) color
opacity	Specifies the transparency level of the foreground and background

CHAPTER 14

THINKING INSIDE THE BOX

(Padding, Borders, and Margins)

In Chapter 11, "Cascading Style Sheets Orientation," I introduced the box model as one of the fundamental concepts of CSS. According to the box model, every element in a document generates a box to which properties such as width, height, padding, borders, and margins can be applied. You probably already have a feel for how element boxes work, from adding backgrounds to elements. This chapter covers all the box-related properties. Once we've covered the basics, we will be ready to move boxes around in Chapter 15, "Floating and Positioning."

We'll begin with an overview of the components of an element box, then take on the box properties from the inside out: content dimensions, padding, borders, and margins.

IN THIS CHAPTER

The components of an element box

Setting box dimensions

Adding padding around content

Adding borders

Adding margins

Assigning display roles

Adding a drop shadow

The Element Box

As we've seen, every element in a document, both block-level and inline, generates a rectangular element box. The components of an element box are diagrammed in Figure 14-1. Pay attention to the new terminology—it will be helpful in keeping things straight later in the chapter.

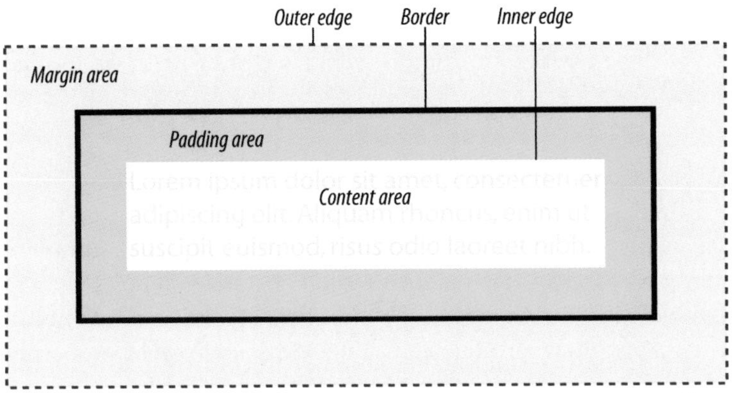

Figure 14-1. The parts of an element box according to the CSS box model.

Content area

At the core of the element box is the content itself. In Figure 14-1, the content area is indicated by text in a white box.

Inner edges

The edges of the content area are referred to as the inner edges of the element box. Although the inner edges are made distinct by a color change in Figure 14-1, in real pages, the edge of the content area would be invisible.

Padding

The padding is the area held between the content area and an optional border. In the diagram, the padding area is indicated by a yellow-orange color. Padding is optional.

Border

The border is a line (or stylized line) that surrounds the element and its padding. Borders are also optional.

Margin

The margin is an optional amount of space added on the *outside* of the border. In the diagram, the margin is indicated with light-blue shading, but in reality, margins are always transparent, allowing the background of the parent element to show through.

Outer edge

The outside edges of the margin area make up the outer edges of the element box. This is the total area the element takes up on the page, and it includes the width of the content area plus the total amount of padding, border, and margins applied to the element. The outer edge in the diagram is indicated with a dotted line, but in real web pages, the edge of the margin is invisible.

All elements have these box components; however, as you will see, some properties behave differently based on whether the element is block or inline. In fact, we'll see some of those differences right away as we look at box dimensions.

Specifying Box Dimensions

By default, the width and height of a block element are calculated automatically by the browser (thus the default **auto** value). The box will be as wide as the browser window or other containing block element, and as tall as necessary to fit the content. However, you can use the **width** and **height** properties to make the content area of an element a specific width or height.

NOTE

The total size of an element box includes the content plus the total amount of padding, borders, and margins applied to the element.

Unfortunately, setting box dimensions is not as simple as just dropping those properties in your style sheet. You have to know exactly which part of the element box you are sizing.

CSS3 provides two ways to specify the size of an element. The default method—introduced way back in CSS1—applies the width and height values to the *content box*. That means that the resulting size of the element will be the dimensions you specify *plus* the amount of padding and borders that have been added to the element. The other method—introduced as part of the new **box-sizing** property in CSS3—applies the width and height values to the *border box*, which includes the content, padding, and border. With this method, the resulting visible element box, including padding and borders, will be exactly the dimensions you specify. Some find this a more intuitive method for sizing. We are going to get familiar with both methods in this section.

Regardless of the method you choose, you can only specify the width and height for block-level elements and non-text inline elements such as images. The **width** and **height** properties do not apply to inline text (a.k.a. non-replaced) elements and will be ignored by the browser. In other words, you cannot specify the width and height of an anchor (**a**) or **strong** element (see note).

NOTE

Actually, there is a way to apply **width** *and* **height** *properties to inline elements such as anchors (**a**) by forcing them to behave as block elements with the* **display** *property, covered at the end of this chapter.*

box-sizing
NEW IN CSS3

Values:	content-box | border-box
Default:	content-box
Applies to:	all elements
Inherits:	no

width

Values:	length measurement | percentage | auto | inherit
Default:	auto
Applies to:	block-level elements and replaced inline elements (such as images)
Inherits:	no

height

Values:	length measurement | percentage | auto | inherit
Default:	auto
Applies to:	block-level elements and replaced inline elements (such as images)
Inherits:	no

Sizing the content box (default)

By default (that is, if you do not include a **box-sizing** rule in your styles), the **width** and **height** properties are applied to the content box. That is the way all current browsers interpret width and height values, but you can explicitly specify this behavior by setting **box-sizing: content-box**.

In the following example and in Figure 14-2, a simple box is given a width of 500 pixels, a height of 150 pixels, with 20 pixels of padding, a 2-pixel border, and a 20-pixel margin all around. Using the content box model, the **width** and **height** values are applied to the *content area only*.

```
p {
  background: #c2f670;
  width: 500px;
  height: 150px;
  padding: 20px;
  border: 2px solid gray;
  margin: 20px;
}
```

The resulting width of the *visible* element box ends up being 544 pixels (the content plus 40px padding and 4px of border). When you throw in 40 pixels of margin, the width of the entire element box is 584 pixels. Knowing the resulting size of your elements is critical to getting layouts to behave predictably.

20px + 2px + 20px + 500px width **+ 20px + 2px + 20px = 584 pixels**

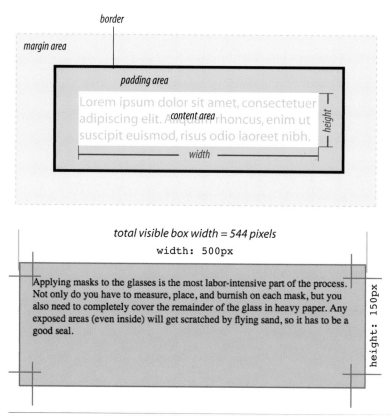

Figure 14-2. Specifying the width *and* height *with the* content-box *model.*

The border-box model

The other way to specify the size of an element is to apply width and height dimensions to the entire visible box, including the padding and border. Because this is not the default browser behavior, you'll need to explicitly set `box-sizing: border-box` in the style sheet.

Let's look at the same paragraph example from the previous section and see what happens when we make it 500 pixels using the `border-box` method (Figure 14-3). Notice that (as of this writing) you need to provide `-webkit-` and `-moz-` vendor prefixes to get this to work in Safari, Chrome, and Firefox. Opera and Internet Explorer 8 and higher support it without a suffix (see note).

```
p {
    …
    -webkit-box-sizing: border-box;
    -moz-box-sizing: border-box;
    box-sizing: border-box;
    width: 500px;
    height: 150px;
}
```

NOTE

Internet Explorer 6 and 7 do not support the `box-sizing` *property at all, but there are workarounds. You could use conditional comments to serve a separate style sheet to IE versions less than 8 that has alternative widths for the elements in question. A cleaner method is to use the Box-sizing Polyfill (a script that makes non-supporting browsers mimic feature support) by Christian Shaefer, available here: github.com/Schepp/box-sizing-polyfill. Put the script on your server and follow the instructions on the GitHub page.*

Maximum and Minimum Dimensions

CSS2 introduced properties for setting minimum and maximum heights and widths for block elements. They may be useful if you want to put limits on the size of an element.

```
max-height, max-width,
min-height, min-width
```

Values: *percentage* | *length* | **none** | **inherit**

These properties work with block-level and replaced elements (like images) only. When the **content-box** model is used, the value applies to the content area only, so if you apply padding, borders, or margins, it will make the overall element box larger, even if a **max-width** or **max-height** property has been specified. These properties are not supported by Internet Explorer 6 and earlier.

WARNING

Avoid using `max-` *and* `min-` *widths and heights with the* `border-box` *model. They are known to cause browser problems.*

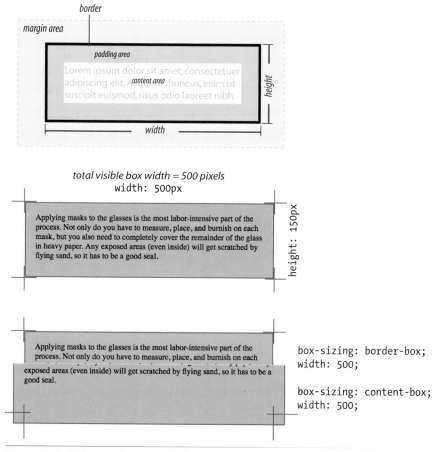

Figure 14-3. Sizing an element with the border-box method. The bottom diagram compares the resulting boxes from each sizing method.

Many developers find the **border-box** model to be a more intuitive way to size elements. It is particularly helpful for specifying widths in percentages, which is a cornerstone of responsive design. For example, you can make two columns 50% wide and know that they will fit next to each other without having to mess around with adding calculated padding and border widths to the mix. In fact, some designers simply set *everything* in the document to use the **border-box** model using the universal selector:

```
* {box-sizing: border-box;}
```

Read this article by Paul Irish for more information about the technique: *paulirish.com/2012/box-sizing-border-box-ftw/*.

The Internet Explorer Box Model "Bug"

Web design old-timers remember when the **border-box** sizing method was known as an Internet Explorer "bug." In 1996, the CSS1 specification described the **content-box** model as the standard way for browsers to calculate element dimensions. But that didn't stop Microsoft from implementing its own **border-box** model in IE5, causing discrepancies that created headaches for developers for years.

IE eventually switched to the standard **content-box** model in IE6, but only when in Standards Mode. When documents don't start with a valid DOCTYPE declaration, IE 6 and 7 still revert to Quirks Mode and use the old IE **border-box** model—a good reason to always include the DOCTYPE. Thankfully, the days are numbered for these browsers.

For a detailed history of the development of the box model, read "The Revenge of the IE Box Model" by Jeff Kaufmann (*www.jefftk.com/news/2012-02-18.html*).

Specifying height

In general practice, it is less common to specify the height of elements. It is more in keeping with the nature of the medium to allow the height to be calculated automatically, allowing the element box to change based on the font size, user settings, or other factors. If you do specify a height for an element containing text, be sure to also consider what happens should the content not fit. Fortunately, CSS gives you some options, as we'll see in the next section.

Handling overflow

When an element is set to a size that is too small for its contents, it is possible to specify what to do with the content that doesn't fit, using the **overflow** property.

overflow

Values: visible | hidden | scroll | auto | inherit
Default: visible
Applies to: *block-level elements and replaced inline elements (such as images)*
Inherits: no

Figure 14-4 demonstrates the predefined values for **overflow**. In the figure, the various values are applied to an element that is 150 pixels square. The background color makes the edges of the content area apparent.

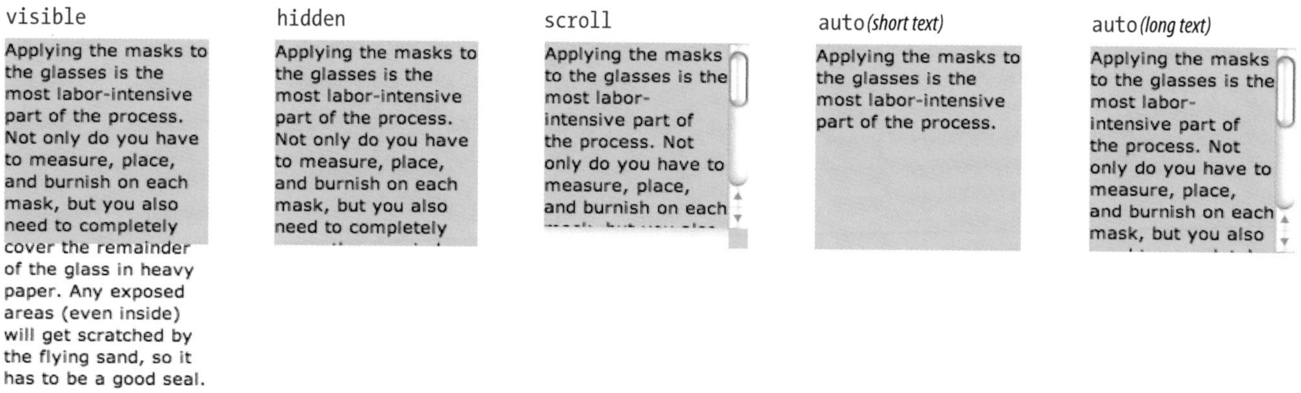

visible

Applying the masks to the glasses is the most labor-intensive part of the process. Not only do you have to measure, place, and burnish on each mask, but you also need to completely cover the remainder of the glass in heavy paper. Any exposed areas (even inside) will get scratched by the flying sand, so it has to be a good seal.

hidden

Applying the masks to the glasses is the most labor-intensive part of the process. Not only do you have to measure, place, and burnish on each mask, but you also need to completely

scroll

Applying the masks to the glasses is the most labor-intensive part of the process. Not only do you have to measure, place, and burnish on each

auto *(short text)*

Applying the masks to the glasses is the most labor-intensive part of the process.

auto *(long text)*

Applying the masks to the glasses is the most labor-intensive part of the process. Not only do you have to measure, place, and burnish on each mask, but you also

Figure 14-4. Options for handling content overflow.

> **WARNING**
>
> ## Scrolling Regions on Mobile Devices
>
> As of this writing, the **overflow** property is known to cause problems on some (mostly older) mobile devices, which is a shame because having a small scrollable area within a page is a nice space-saver for some content. Some mobile browsers simply hide the overflow text. Others add a scrollbar, but require a difficult-to-discover two-finger scroll motion to control it.
>
> One solution is to use Scott Jehl's "Overthrow" script to simulate support in problematic browsers. Learn about Overthrow at *filamentgroup.com/lab/overthrow*.

visible

The default value is **visible**, which allows the content to hang out over the element box so that it all can be seen.

hidden

When **overflow** is set to **hidden**, the content that does not fit gets clipped off and does not appear beyond the edges of the element's content area.

scroll

When **scroll** is specified, scrollbars are added to the element box to let users scroll through the content. Be aware that when you set the value to **scroll**, the scrollbars will always be there, even if the content fits in the specified height just fine.

auto

The **auto** value allows the browser to decide how to handle overflow. In most cases, scrollbars are added only when the content doesn't fit and they are needed.

Padding

Padding is the space between the content area and the border (or the place the border would be if one isn't specified). I find it helpful to add padding to elements when using a background color or a border. It gives the content a little breathing room, and prevents the border or edge of the background from bumping right up against the text.

You can add padding to the individual sides of any element (block-level or inline). There is also a shorthand **padding** property that lets you add padding on all sides at once.

padding-top, padding-right, padding-bottom, padding-left

Values:	*length measurement* | *percentage* | inherit
Default:	0
Applies to:	*all elements except table-row, table-row-group, table-header-group, table-footer-group, table-column, and table-column-group*
Inherits:	*no*

padding

Values:	*length measurement* | *percentage* | inherit
Default:	0
Applies to:	*all elements*
Inherits:	*no*

The **padding-top**, **padding-right**, **padding-bottom**, and **padding-left** properties specify an amount of padding for each side of an element, as shown in this example and Figure 14-5 (note that I've also added a background color to make the edges of the padding area apparent).

```
blockquote {
  padding-top: 1em;
  padding-right: 3em;
  padding-bottom: 1em;
  padding-left: 3em;
  background-color: #D098D4;
}
```

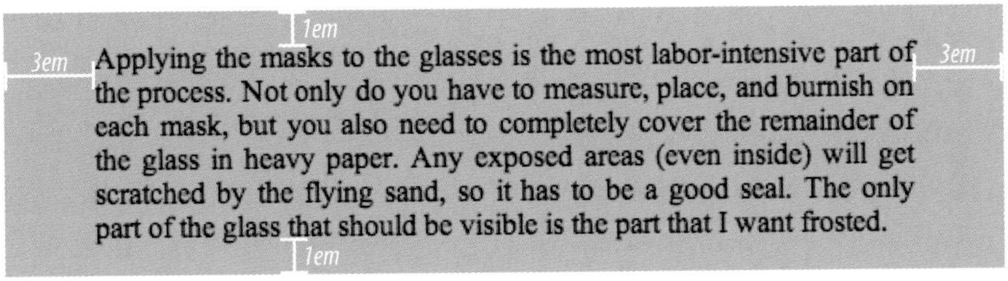

Figure 14-5. Adding padding around the content of an element.

Specify padding in any of the CSS length units (**em** and **px** are the most common) or as a percentage of the *width* of the parent element. Yes, the parent's width is used as the basis, even for top and bottom padding. If the width of the parent element changes, so will the padding values on all sides of the child element, which makes percentage values somewhat tricky to manage.

The shorthand padding property

As an alternative to setting padding one side at a time, you can use the shorthand **padding** property to add padding all around the element. The syntax is interesting; you can specify four, three, two, or one value for a single **padding** property. Let's see how that works, starting with four values.

When you supply four **padding** values, they are applied to each side in *clockwise* order, starting at the top. Some people use the mnemonic device

"TRouBLe" for the order *Top Right Bottom Left*. This is a common syntax for applying shorthand values in CSS, so take a careful look.

```
padding: top right bottom left;
```

Using the **padding** property, we could reproduce the padding specified with the four individual properties in the previous example like this:

```
blockquote {
    padding: 1em 3em 1em 3em;
    background-color: #D098D4;
}
```

If the left and right padding are the same, you can shorten it by supplying only three values. The value for "right" (the second value in the string) will be mirrored and used for "left" as well. It is as though the browser assumes the "left" value is missing, so it just uses the "right" value on both sides. The syntax for three values is as follows:

```
padding: top right/left bottom;
```

This rule would be equivalent to the previous example because the padding on the left and right edges of the element should be set to 3em.

```
blockquote {
    padding: 1em 3em 1em;
    background-color: #D098D4;
}
```

Continuing with this pattern, if you provide only two values, the first one is used for the top and the bottom edges, and the second one is used for the left and right edges:

```
padding: top/bottom right/left;
```

Again, the same effect achieved by the previous two examples could be accomplished with this rule.

```
blockquote {
    padding: 1em 3em;
    background-color: #D098D4;
}
```

Note that all of the previous examples have the same visual effect as shown in Figure 14-5.

Finally, if you provide just one value, it will be applied to all four sides of the element. This declaration applies 15 pixels of padding on all sides of a **div** element.

```
div#announcement {
    padding: 15px;
    border: 1px solid;
}
```

AT A GLANCE

Shorthand Values

1 value

```
padding: 10px;
```

Applied to all sides.

2 values

```
padding: 10px 6px;
```

First is top and bottom; second is left and right.

3 values

```
padding: 10px 6px 4px;
```

First is top; second is left and right; third is bottom.

4 values

```
padding: 10px 6px 4px 10px;
```

Applied clockwise to top, right, bottom, and left edges consecutively (TRBL).

---

exercise 14-1 | **Adding a little padding**

In this exercise, we'll use basic box properties to improve the appearance of a fictional shopping site, Jenware.com. I've given you a big head start by marking up the source document and creating a style sheet that handles text formatting, colors, and backgrounds. The document, *jenware.html*, is available at *www.learningwebdesign. com/4e/materials*.

Figure 14-6 shows before and after shots of the Jenware home page. It's going to take a few exercises to get this page into presentable shape, and padding is just the beginning.

Whoa! That navigation section is ugly! But don't worry; we'll turn it into a nice horizontal navigation menu in Chapter 15.

Start by opening *jenware.html* in a browser and a text editor to see what you've got to work with. The document has been divided into two main **div** elements ("intro" and "content"), and the **#content div** is divided again into "products" and "testimonials". The background colors have been added to the **body, #nav, #products**, and **#testimonials** divisions. I've also added a gradient at the top of the page and an exclamation point image to the background of the "testimonials" **div**. The remaining rules are for formatting text.

Figure 14-6. *Before and after shots of the Jenware home page.*

1. The first thing we'll do is add padding to the "products" **div**. One em of padding all around ought to be fine. Find the **#products** selector and add the **padding** declaration.

   ```
   #products {
      background-color: #FFF;
      line-height: 1.5em;
         padding: 1em;
   }
   ```

2. Next, we'll get a little fancier with the "testimonials" section. I want to clear some space in the left side of the **div** so that my nifty exclamation-point background image is visible. There are several approaches to applying different padding amounts to each side, but I'm going to do it in a way that gives you experience deliberately overriding earlier declarations.

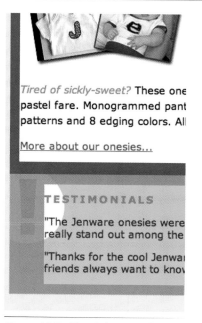

Tired of sickly-sweet? **These one**
pastel fare. Monogrammed pant
patterns and 8 edging colors. All

More about our onesies...

TESTIMONIALS

"The Jenware onesies were
really stand out among the

"Thanks for the cool Jenwar
friends always want to knov

*Figure 14-7. The pink area indicates
padding added to the testimonials section.
Blue indicates the products section
padding.*

Use the **padding** shorthand property to add 1em of padding on all sides of the
testimonials **div**. Then write a second declaration that adds 55 pixels of padding
to the left side only. Because the **padding-left** declaration comes second, it will
override the 1em setting applied with the **padding** shorthand property.

```
#testimonials {
    background: #FFBC53 url(images/ex-circle-corner.gif) no-repeat
left top;
    color: #633;
    font-size: .875em;
    line-height: 1.5em;
    padding: 1em;
    padding-left: 55px;
}
```

3. Save your work and look at it in the browser. The testimonials and product
descriptions should look a little more comfortable in their boxes. Figure 14-7
highlights the padding additions.

Borders

A border is simply a line drawn around the content area and its (optional)
padding. You can choose from eight border styles and make them any width
and color you like. You can apply the border all around the element or just a
particular side or sides. CSS3 introduces properties for rounding the corners
or applying images to borders. We'll start our border exploration with the
various border styles.

Border style

The style is the most important of the border properties because, according
to the CSS specification, if there is no border style specified, the border does
not exist. In other words, you must always declare the style of the border, or
the other border properties will be ignored.

Border styles can be applied one side at a time or by using the shorthand
border-style property.

border-top-style, border-right-style,
border-bottom-style, border-left-style

Values: none | dotted | dashed | solid | double | groove | ridge | inset | outset | inherit
Default: none
Applies to: all elements
Inherits: no

`border-style`

Values:	none | dotted | dashed | solid | double | groove | ridge | inset | outset | inherit
Default:	none
Applies to:	all elements
Inherits:	no

The value of the **border-style** property is one of 10 keywords describing the available border styles, as shown in Figure 14-8.

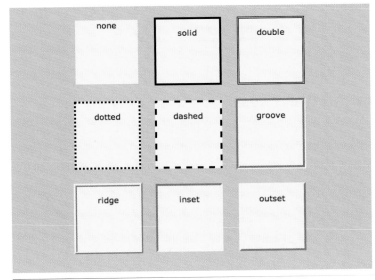

Figure 14-8. The available border styles (shown at the default medium width).

Use the side-specific border style properties (**border-top-style**, **border-right-style**, **border-bottom-style**, and **border-left-style**) to apply a style to one side of the element. If you do not specify a width, the default medium width will be used. If there is no color specified, the border uses the foreground color of the element (same as the text).

In the following example, I've applied a different style to each side of an element to show the single-side border properties in action (Figure 14-9).

```
div#silly {
    border-top-style: solid;
    border-right-style: dashed;
    border-bottom-style: double;
    border-left-style: dotted;
    width: 300px;
    height: 100px;
}
```

The **border-style** shorthand property works on the clockwise (TRouBLe) system described for **padding** earlier. You can supply four values for all four sides or fewer values when the left/right and top/bottom borders are the same. The silly border effect in the previous example could also be specified using the **border-style** property as shown here, and the result would be the same as shown in Figure 14-9.

```
border-style: solid dashed double dotted;
```

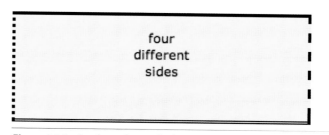

Figure 14-9. Border styles applied to individual sides of an element.

Border width (thickness)

Use one of the border width properties to specify the thickness of the border. Once again, you can target each side of the element with a single-side property, or specify several sides at once in clockwise order with the shorthand **border-width** property.

border-top-width, border-right-width, border-bottom-width, border-left-width

Values:	length units | thin | medium | thick | inherit
Default:	medium
Applies to:	all elements
Inherits:	no

border-width

Values:	length units | thin | medium | thick | inherit
Default:	medium
Applies to:	all elements
Inherits:	no

The most common way to specify the width of borders is using a pixel or em measurement; however, you can also specify one of the keywords (**thin**, **medium**, or **thick**) and leave the rendering up to the browser.

I've included a mix of values in this example (Figure 14-10). Notice that I've also included the **border-style** property because if I didn't, the border would not render at all.

```
div#help {
  border-top-width: thin;
  border-right-width: medium;
  border-bottom-width: thick;
  border-left-width: 12px;
  border-style: solid;
  width: 300px;
  height: 100px;
}
```

or:

```
div#help {
    border-width: thin medium thick 12px;
    border-style: solid;
    width: 300px;
    height: 100px;
}
```

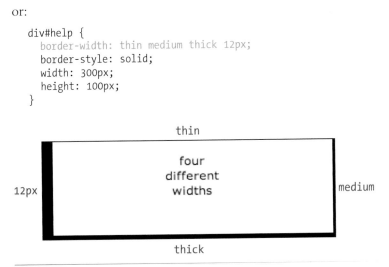

Figure 14-10. Specifying the width of borders.

Border color

Border colors are specified in the same way: using the side-specific properties or the **border-color** shorthand property. When you specify a border color, it overrides the foreground color as set by the **color** property for the element.

`border-top-color`, `border-right-color`, `border-bottom-color`, `border-left-color`

Values:	color name or RGB value | transparent | inherit
Default:	the value of the color property for the element
Applies to:	all elements
Inherits:	no

`border-color`

Values:	color name or RGB value | transparent | inherit
Default:	the value of the color property for the element
Applies to:	all elements
Inherits:	no

You know all about specifying color values, and you should be getting used to the shorthand properties as well, so I'll keep this example short and sweet (Figure 14-11). Here, I've provided two values for the shorthand **border-color** property to make the top and bottom of a **div** maroon and the left and right sides aqua.

```
div#special {
    border-color: maroon aqua;
    border-style: solid;
    border-width: 6px;
    width: 300px;
    height: 100px;
}
```

NOTE

CSS2 added the **transparent** *keyword value for border colors that allows the background of the parent to show through the border, yet holds the width of the border as specified. This may be useful when creating rollover (*:hover*) effects with CSS because the space where the border will appear is maintained when the mouse is not over the element. Transparent borders are not supported by Internet Explorer 6.*

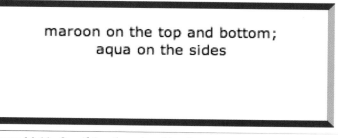

Figure 14-11. Specifying the color of borders.

Combining style, width, and color

The authors of CSS didn't skimp when it came to border shortcuts. They also created properties for providing style, width, and color values in one declaration, one side at a time. Again, you can specify the appearance of specific sides, or use the **border** property to change all four sides at once.

border-top, border-right, border-bottom, border-left

Values:	*border-style border-width border-color* | inherit
Default:	*defaults for each property*
Applies to:	*all elements*
Inherits:	*no*

border

Values:	*border-style border-width border-color* | inherit
Default:	*defaults for each property*
Applies to:	*all elements*
Inherits:	*no*

The values for **border** and the side-specific border properties may include style, width, and color values in any order. You do not need to declare all three, but keep in mind that if the border style value is omitted, no border will render.

The **border** shorthand property works a bit differently than the other shorthand properties that we covered in that it takes one set of values and always applies them to all four sides of the element. In other words, it does not use the clockwise TRBL system that we've seen with other shorthand properties.

Here is a smattering of valid border shortcut examples to get an idea for how they work.

```
h1 { border-left: red .5em solid; }      /* left border only */
h2 { border-bottom: 1px solid; }         /* bottom border only */
p.example { border: 2px dotted #663; }   /* all four sides */
```

Rounded corners with border-radius

Boxes with rounded corners have become a trendy style element over recent years. Originally, rounded corners on web pages could only be made with images and extra markup. Now, thankfully, all current browser versions can put rounded corners on elements using the CSS **border-radius** property alone. That means fewer calls to the server to grab graphics and less Photoshop work for designers. In this section, we'll start with the code as it appears in the CSS3 spec, look at some examples, and then finish with a few words about browser support.

As we've seen for other properties, there are individual corner properties as well as a **border-radius** shorthand.

border-top-left-radius, border-top-right-radius, border-bottom-right-radius, border-bottom-left-radius

NEW IN CSS3

Values:	*length measurement	percentage*
Default:	*0*
Applies to:	*all elements*
Inherits:	*no*

border-radius

NEW IN CSS3

Values:	*1, 2, 3, or 4 length or percentage values*
Default:	*0*
Applies to:	*all elements*
Inherits:	*no*

To round off the corner of an element, simply apply one of the **border-radius** properties, but keep in mind that you will see the result only if the element has a border or a different background color than the background of the page. Values are typically provided in ems or pixels. Percentages are allowed and are nice for keeping the curve proportional to the box should it resize, but you may run into some browser inconsistencies.

You can target the corners individually or use the shorthand **border-radius** property. If you provide one value for **border-radius**, it is applied to all four corners. Four values are applied clockwise starting in the top-left corner (top-left, top-right, bottom-right, bottom-left). When you supply two values, the first one is used for top-left and bottom-right, and the second is for the other two corners.

Compare the various **border-radius** values to the resulting boxes in Figure 14-12. You can achieve many different effects, from slightly softened corners to a long lozenge shape, depending how you set the values.

p { width: 200px; height: 100px; background: darkorange; }

border-top-right-radius: 50px;

border-top-left-radius: 1em;
border-top-right-radius: 2em;
border-bottom-right-radius: 1em;
border-bottom-left-radius: 2em;
~or~
border-radius: 1 em 2em;

border-radius: 5px 20px; 40px 60px;

border-radius: 1em;

border-radius: 50px;

Figure 14-12. Make the corners of element boxes rounded with the border-radius *properties.*

Elliptical corners

So far, the corners we've made are sections of perfect circles, but you can also make a corner elliptical by specifying two values: the first for the horizontal radius and the second for the vertical radius (see Figure 14-13, A and B).

A border-top-right-radius: 100px 50px;

B border-top-right-radius: 50px 20px;
border-top-left-radius: 50px 20px;

If you want to use the shorthand property, the horizontal and vertical radii get separated by a slash (otherwise, they'd be confused for different corner values). The following example sets the horizontal radius on all corners to 60px and the vertical radius to 40px (Figure 14-13, C).

C border-radius: 60px / 40px;

If you want to see something really nutty, take a look at a **border-radius** shorthand property that specifies a different ellipse for each of the four corners. All of the horizontal values are lined up on the left of the slash in clockwise order (top-left, top-right, bottom-right, bottom-left), and all of the corresponding vertical values are lined up on the right (Figure 14-13, D).

D border-radius: 36px 40px 60px 20px / 12px 10px 30px 36px;

Browser support

As I mentioned earlier, the current versions of all major browsers now support **border-radius** using the CSS3 specification syntax. That's good news! The longer story is that earlier versions of Safari, Chrome, and Firefox have been supporting rounded corners for a while now, but they had their own syntax with browser prefixes (see the sidebar "Ye Olde Radius Prefixes"). And then there's Internet Explorer, which has no **border-radius** support at all prior to version 9.

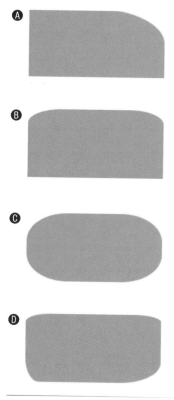

Figure 14-13. Applying elliptical corners to boxes.

So what to do about IE6 through 8? Chances are, the success and usability of your site doesn't depend on rounded corners, so this is a good opportunity to practice progressive enhancement: IE gets perfectly OK square boxes, and better browsers get a little something extra. If for some reason it is mandatory for your boxes to be rounded in older versions of IE as well, you need to resort to a JavaScript patch such as Curvy Corners (*www.curvycorners.net*).

Ye Olde Radius Prefixes

Older versions of Firefox and WebKit browsers only support **border-radius** with their own vendor-prefixed properties. Unlike Internet Explorer versions that stick around for a decade, other browsers get upgraded automatically or at least more regularly. For that reason, many developers have already stopped using prefixes for **border-radius**. The area where they still might come in handy is on some older mobile browsers, so if rounded corners on early Android versions are important to your product, you may want to include the **-webkit-** prefixes.

WebKit browsers
(Safari <5, Chrome <10.5, Android <2.2, iOS < 4)

```
-webkit-border-top-left-radius
-webkit-border-top-right-radius
-webkit-border-bottom-left-radius
-webkit-border-bottom-right-radius
-webkit-border-radius
```

Firefox (Mozilla)
(Firefox <4)

```
-moz-border-radius-topleft
-moz-border-radius-topright
-moz-border-radius-bottomleft
-moz-border-radius-bottomright
-moz-border-radius
```

Picture-perfect borders

Here we are, eight pages into a discussion on CSS borders...who knew there could be so much to say about lines around boxes? I've saved the fanciest and trickiest border treatment for last. In this section, we'll look at using the **border-image** property to fill the sides and corners of a border box with an image of your choice. This property eliminates the need to cut up separate image files and add a bunch of useless markup to contain them. Now a single image can be applied around an element using CSS.

It should be noted that as of this writing, no version of Internet Explorer (not even 9 or 10) supports border images, so the best you can do is provide a pleasant and functional fallback color and border style. The browsers that do support browser images (Safari, Chrome, Firefox, and Opera) require their respective vendor prefixes to get them to work.

border-image
NEW IN CSS3

Values:	`border-image-source border-image-slice border-image-width` `border-image-outset border-image-repeat`
Default:	*defaults for each property*
Applies to:	*all elements except table elements where* `border-collapse` *is* `collapse`
Inherits:	*no*

Let's kick off this discussion with a visual to give you an idea of what I'm talking about here. Figure 14-14 shows two elements and the respective images used to fill their borders. Notice that the corners of the image fill the corners of the element exactly. The sides of the element can be set to stretch (as shown on the top) or tile (bottom).

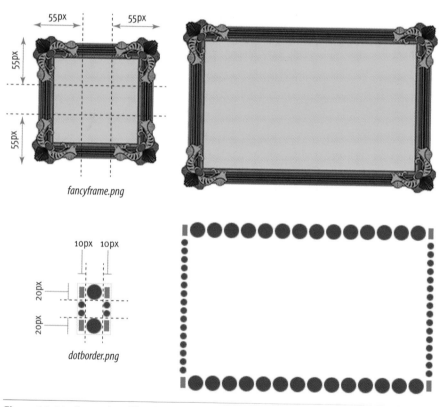

Figure 14-14. *Examples of border images with stretched sides and repeated sides.*

OK, now the code. The **border-image** shorthand property as it is supported as of this writing includes three parts (Figure 14-15). See the sidebar "The Border Image Spec" for further details.

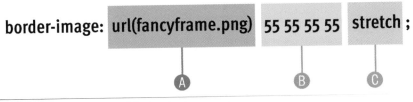

Figure 14-15. *The parts of the border-image rule.*

The URL notation Ⓐ contains the location of the border image file.

The next value indicates the positions of slice lines that divide the image into nine sections Ⓑ. The measurements are offsets from each edge of the image, listed clockwise (top, right, bottom, left) in the same TRouBLe pattern we learned for the padding shorthand value. Value shortcuts can be used, such as providing one value to move the slice lines the same distance from all four edges. When specifying pixel measurements, you can omit the "px" unit. Percentages also may be specified.

The final keyword describes how to fill in the sides of the border Ⓒ. The values are **stretch** (which stretches the image to fit, naturally), **repeat** (which tiles the image), and **round** (which repeats the image but stretches or squooshes it a little to make it fit exactly without any partial bits left over). The **round** value is not currently supported by Safari or Chrome—**repeat** is used instead—although that may change in future versions.

Here is the style rule that creates the fancy frame border image in Figure 14-14 (top). I'm leaving off the vendor-prefixed properties for now to keep it simple.

```
.framed {
    ...
    background-color: #fec227;   /* bright yellow-orange */
    border-color: #fec227;       /* bright yellow-orange */
    border-style: solid;
    border-width: 55px;
    border-image: url(fancyframe.png) 55 stretch;
}
```

The source of the border image is *fancyframe.png*. Because the slice points are the same on all four sides (55 pixels), I only need to specify the value 55 once (note that no unit is required for pixels). Finally, the **stretch** keyword indicates that the sides of the box are to be filled by stretching the sides of the graphic. As a fallback, I've specified the background color and border color to be the same bright yellow-orange from the center of the border image. Internet Explorer images will get a box the same size and color, but without the frame image (see note).

NOTE

Different types of border images may suggest other fallback solutions, but since this one was so thick, I felt the best thing to do was fill it with solid color.

Here's how the rule looks with all its browser prefixes. If you venture into border images, your rules will look like this too. Be sure to put the standard, non-prefixed property last.

```
.framed {
    …
  background-color: #fec227;  /* bright yellow-orange */
  border-color: #fec227;      /* bright yellow-orange */
  border-style: solid;
  border-width: 55px;
  -moz-border-image: url(fancyframe.png) 55 stretch;
  -webkit-border-image: url(fancyframe.png) 55 stretch;
  -o-border-image: url(fancyframe.png) 55 stretch;
  border-image: url(fancyframe.png) 55 stretch;
}
```

Here is the style rule for the dotted border image. It differs in that the top and sides are different widths (thus, two **border-image-slice** and **border-width** values), and I've set the repeat to **round**, to fill the space with repeating tiles resized to fit exactly. Note that WebKit browsers currently display **round** as a simple **repeat**.

```
.dotted {
  background-color: white;
  border-color: #0063a4;
  border-style: dotted;
  border-width: 20px 10px;
  -moz-border-image: url(dotborder.png) 20 10 round;
  -webkit-border-image: url(dotborder.png) 20 10 round;
  -o-border-image: url(dotborder.png) 20 10 round;
  border-image: url(dotborder.png) 20 10 round;
}
```

Now it is time to try your hand at borders. Exercise 14-2 will not only give you some practice, but it should also give you some ideas on the ways borders can be used to add visual interest to designs.

NOTE

According to the CSS3 spec, browsers should not render the center of the image by default, but all browsers today display the center of the image in the center of the element. The center area stretches or repeats as specified for the borders. If you want to provide a different background color or image in the background of the content box, create the border-image graphic with a transparent center so the background shows through.

---

exercise 14-2 | **Border tricks**

In this exercise, we'll have some fun with borders on the Jenware home page. In addition to putting subtle borders around content sections on the page, we'll use borders to beef up the product headlines and as an alternative to underlines under links.

1. Open *jenware.html* in a text editor if it isn't already. We'll start with the basics by using the shorthand **border** property to add a light-orange (#FFBC53) double rule around the "products" area. The shade should be light enough as to not call too much attention to itself. Add the new declaration to the rule for the "products" **div**.

```
#products {
    …
    border: double #FFBC53;
}
```

➡

---

2. Next, let's give the "testimonials" section rounded corners. They won't show up for Internet Explorer 6–8 and some other old browser versions, but that doesn't really hurt anything.

```
#testimonials {
   …
   border-radius: 20px;
}
```

3. Just for fun (and practice), we'll add a decorative border on two sides of the product category headings (**h3**). I want the borders to be the same color as the text, so we don't need to specify the **border-color**. Find the existing rule for **h3** elements in the "products" **div**, and add a declaration that adds a 1-pixel solid rule on the top of the headline. Add another declaration that adds a thicker, 3-pixel solid rule on the left side. Finally, to prevent the text from bumping into that left border, we can add a little bit of padding (1em) to the left of the headline content.

```
#products h3 {
   font-size: 1em;
   text-transform: uppercase;
   color: #F26521;
   border-top: 1px solid;
   border-left: 3px solid;
   padding-left: 1em;
}
```

4. The last thing we'll do is replace the standard text underline under links with a decorative bottom border. Start by turning the underline off for all links by setting the **text-decoration** to **none** for the **a** element. Add this rule in the "link styles" section of the style sheet.

```
a {
   text-decoration: none;
}
```

5. Next, add a 1-pixel dotted border to the bottom edge of links by adding this declaration to the **a** rule.

```
a {
   text-decoration: none;
   border-bottom: 1px dotted;
}
```

Notice that because we want the border to have the same color as the links, we do not need to specify a color. However, if you try this on your own pages, you can easily change the color and style of the bottom border.

As is often the case when you add a border to an element, it is a good idea to also add a little padding to keep things from bumping together. Add some padding to the bottom edges only, like so:

```
a {
   text-decoration: none;
   border-bottom: 1px dotted;
   padding-bottom: .1em;
}
```

See Figure 14-16 for what the page looks like.

Figure 14-16. The results of our border additions.

More about custom barware...

BABYWARE

Tired of sickly-sweet? **These onesies with oversize**
fare. **Monogrammed pants and baby shoes are als**
and 8 edging colors. Allow 2 to 4 weeks for delive

More about our onesies...

TESTIMONIALS

"The Jenware onesies were the hit of the baby showe
cookie-cutter clothes from the department store."

"Thanks for the cool Jenware barware. I couldn't wait
know where I got them so I send them to your site."

Margins

The last remaining component of the element box is its margin, which is an optional amount of space that you can add on the outside of the border. Margins keep elements from bumping into one another or the edge of the browser window. You can even use margins to make space for another column of content (we'll see how that works in Chapter 16, "Page Layout with CSS"). In this way, margins are an important tool in CSS-based page layout.

The side-specific and shorthand **margin** properties work much like the **padding** properties we've looked at already; however, margins have some special behaviors to be aware of.

`margin-top`, `margin-right`, `margin-bottom`, `margin-left`

Values:	length measurement | percentage | auto | inherit
Default:	auto
Applies to:	all elements
Inherits:	no

`margin`

Values:	length measurement | percentage | auto | inherit
Default:	auto
Applies to:	all elements except elements with table display types other than table-caption, table, and inline-table
Inherits:	no

The margin properties are very straightforward to use. You can either specify an amount of margin to appear on each side of the element or use the **margin** property to specify all sides at once.

The shorthand **margin** property works the same as the **padding** shorthand. When you supply four values, they are applied in clockwise order (top, right, bottom, left) to the sides of the element. If you supply three values, the middle value applies to both the left and right sides. When two values are provided, the first is used for the top and bottom, and the second applies to the left and right edges. Finally, one value will be applied to all four sides of the element.

As for most web measurements, ems, pixels, and percentages are the most common ways to specify margins. Be aware, however, that if you specify a percentage value, the percentage value is calculated based on the *width* of the parent element. If the parent's width changes, so will the margins on all four sides of the child element (padding has this behavior as well). The **auto** keyword allows the browser to fill in the amount of margin necessary to fit or fill the available space.

Figure 14-17 shows the results of the following margin examples. Note that I've added a light dotted rule to indicate the outside edge of the margin for clarity purposes only, but they would not appear on a real web page.

Ⓐ
```
p#A {
    margin: 4em;
    border: 1px solid red;
    background: #FCF2BE;
}
```
Ⓑ
```
p#B {
    margin-top: 2em;
    margin-right: 250px;
    margin-bottom: 1em;
    margin-left: 4em;
    border: 1px solid red;
    background: #FCF2BE
}
```
Ⓒ
```
body {
    margin: 0 15%;
    border: 1px solid red;
    background-color: #;
}
```

NOTE

Adding a margin to the body element adds space between the page content and the edges of the browser window.

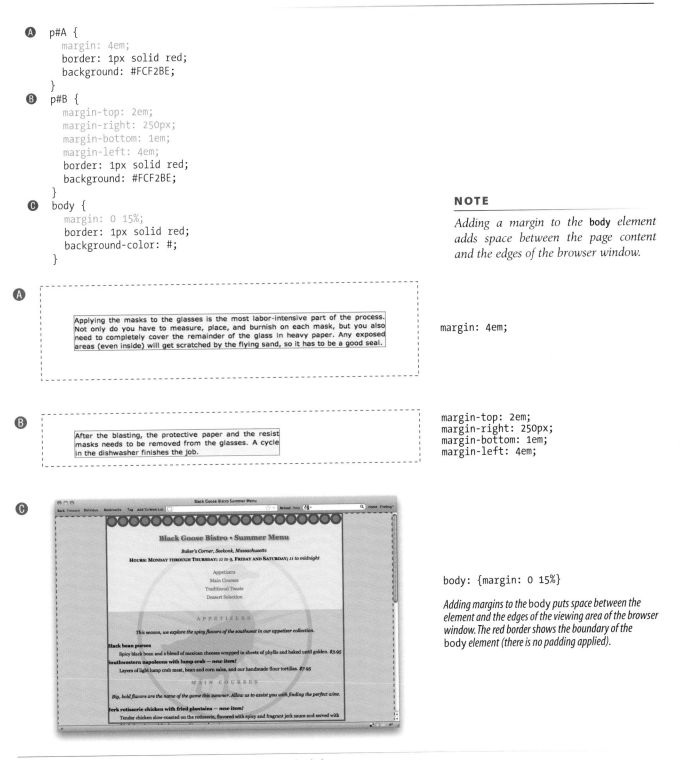

margin: 4em;

margin-top: 2em;
margin-right: 250px;
margin-bottom: 1em;
margin-left: 4em;

body: {margin: 0 15%}

Adding margins to the body puts space between the element and the edges of the viewing area of the browser window. The red border shows the boundary of the body element (there is no padding applied).

Figure 14-17. Applying margins to the body and to individual elements.

Margin behavior

Although it is easy to write rules that apply margin amounts around HTML elements, it is important to be familiar with some of the quirks of margin behavior.

Collapsing margins

The most significant margin behavior to be aware of is that the top and bottom margins of neighboring elements collapse. This means that instead of accumulating, adjacent margins overlap, and only the largest value will be used.

Using the two paragraphs from the previous figure as an example, if the top element has a bottom margin of 4 ems, and the following element has a top margin of 2 ems, the resulting margin space between elements does not add up to 6 ems. Rather, the margins collapse and the resulting margin between the paragraphs will be 4 ems, the largest specified value. This is demonstrated in Figure 14-18.

FURTHER READING

Collapsing Margins

When spacing between and around elements behaves unpredictably, collapsing margins are often to blame. Here are a few articles that dig deep into collapsing margin behavior. They were written nearly a decade ago, but the information is still solid and may help you understand what is happening behind the scenes in your layouts.

- "No Margin for Error" by Andy Budd (*www.andybudd.com/archives/2003/11/no_margin_for_error/*)

- "Uncollapsing Margins" by Eric A. Meyer (*www.complexspiral.com/publications/uncollapsing-margins/*)

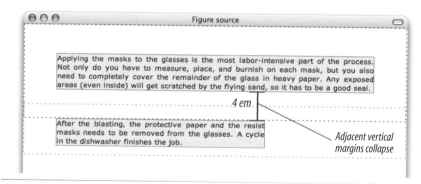

Figure 14-18. Vertical margins of neighboring elements collapse so that only the larger value is used.

The only time top and bottom margins *don't* collapse is for floated or absolutely positioned elements (we'll get to that in Chapter 15). Margins on the left and right sides never collapse, so they're nice and predictable.

Margins on inline elements

You can apply top and bottom margins to inline text elements (or "non-replaced inline elements," to use the proper CSS terminology), but it won't add vertical space above and below the element, and the height of the line will not change. However, when you apply left and right margins to inline text elements, margin space *will* be held clear before and after the text in the flow of the element, even if that element breaks over several lines.

Just to keep things interesting, margins on replaced elements, such as images, do render on all sides, and therefore do affect the height of the line. See Figure 14-19 for examples of each.

```
em { margin: 2em;}
```
Only horizontal margins are rendered on non-replaced (text) elements.

Applying the masks to the glasses is the most labor-intensive part of the process. Not only do you have to measure, place, and burnish on each mask, but you also need to   *completely*   cover the remainder of the glass in heavy paper. Any exposed areas (even inside) will get scratched by the flying sand, so it has to be a good seal.

```
img { margin: 2em;}
```
Margins are rendered on all sides of replaced elements, such as images.

Applying the masks to the glasses is the most labor-intensive part of the process. Not only do you have to measure, place, and burnish on each

mask, but you also need to completely cover the remainder of the glass in heavy paper. Any exposed areas (even inside) will get scratched by the flying sand, so it has to be a good seal.

Figure 14-19. Margins applied to inline text and image elements.

Negative margins

It is worth noting that it is possible to specify negative values for margins. When you apply a negative margin, the content, padding, and border are moved in the opposite direction that would have resulted from a positive margin value.

This should be made clear with an example. Figure 14-20 shows two neighboring paragraphs with different colored borders applied to show their boundaries. In the left view, I've added a 4em bottom margin to the top paragraph, and it has the effect of pushing the following paragraph *down* by that amount. If I specify a negative value (–4em), the following element moves *up* by that amount and overlaps the element with the negative margin.

```
p.top { margin-bottom: 4em;}
```
Pushes the following paragraph element away by 4 ems

Applying the masks to the glasses is the most labor-intensive part of the process. Not only do you have to measure, place, and burnish on each mask, but you also need to *completely* cover the remainder of the glass in heavy paper. Any exposed areas (even inside) will get scratched by the flying sand, so it has to be a good seal.

Applying the masks to the glasses is the most labor-intensive part of the process. Not only do you have to measure, place, and burnish on each mask, but you also need dot to completely cover the remainder of the glass in heavy paper. Any exposed areas (even inside) will get scratched by the flying sand, so it has to be a good seal.

```
p.top { margin-bottom: -4em;}
```
The following element moves back by 4 ems

Applying the masks to the glasses is the most labor-intensive part of the process. Not only do you have to measure, place, and burnish on each mask, but you also need to *completely* cover the remainder of the glass in

Applying the masks to the glasses is the most labor-intensive part of the process. Not only do you have to measure, place, and burnish on each mask, but you also need dot to completely cover the remainder of the glass in heavy paper. Any exposed areas (even inside) will get scratched by the flying sand, so it has to be a good seal.

Figure 14-20. Using negative margins.

This may seem like a strange thing to do, and in fact, you probably wouldn't make blocks of text overlap as shown. The point here is that you can use margins with both positive and negative values to move elements around on the page. This is the basis of many CSS layout techniques.

Now let's use margins to add some space between parts of the Jenware home page in Exercise 14-3.

---

exercise 14-3 |
Adding margin space around elements

Open *jenware.html* in your text editor if it isn't open already, and we'll adjust the margins. We'll start by adjusting the margins on the whole document, and then make tweaks to each section from top to bottom.

1. It is common practice to set the margin for the **body** element to zero, thus clearing out the browser's default margin setting and creating a starting point for setting our own margins on elements throughout the page.

   ```
   body {
       …
       margin: 0;
   }
   ```

   Save the file and take a look in the browser. I like the way the purple navigation bar stretches from edge to edge of the browser window, but I think we need to tweak our other content areas.

2. Start with the **#intro div**, and add a 2em margin on the top and 1em below. I also want to close up the space between the logo and the tagline, so set the bottom margin on the **h1** to zero and the top margin on the **h2** to –10px to move the tagline up nice and close to the logo. Finally, put a 1em margin all around the introductory paragraph (**p**).

   ```
   #intro {
       …
       margin: 2em 0 1em;
   }
   #intro h1 {
       margin-bottom: 0;
   }
   #intro h2 {
       …
       margin-top: -10px;
   }
   #intro p {
       …
       margin: 1em;
   }
   ```

3. Give the **#products** section a 1em margin all around.

   ```
   #products {
       …
       margin: 1em;
   }
   ```

➔

---

4. Now add a 2.5em space above the products subsection headings (**h3**). By this point, I bet you could write this one without my help, but for the sake of thoroughness, here is the new declaration added to **h3**s in the "products" section. You can try different amounts of space and see what you like best.

```
#products h3 {
    …
    margin-top: 2.5em;
}
```

5. Finally, we'll set apart the Testimonials box by adding 1em of space above and 10% on the left and right edges. This time, see if you can figure it out on your own.

6. Save the document again, and it should look something like the one in Figure 14-21. This isn't the most beautiful design, particularly if your browser window is set wide. However, if you resize your browser window very narrow, you'll find that it wouldn't be too bad as the small-screen version in a responsive web design. (Consider this foreshadowing for the work we'll do in Chapter 18.) The final style sheet for this page is available in Appendix A.

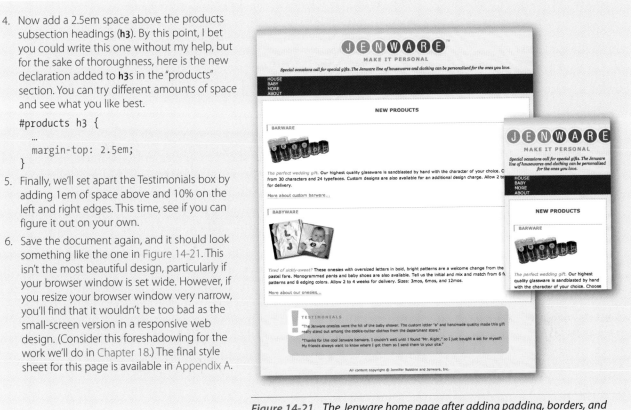

Figure 14-21. *The Jenware home page after adding padding, borders, and margins.*

A good understanding of padding, borders, and margins is the first step to mastering CSS layouts. In the next chapter, we'll learn about the properties used to float and position elements on the page. We'll even turn the Jenware page into a two-column layout. But before we move on, there are a couple more box-related properties to get out of the way.

Assigning Display Roles

As long as we're talking about boxes and the CSS layout model, this is a good time to introduce the **display** property. You should already be familiar with the display behavior of block and inline elements. However, not all XML languages assign default display behaviors (or display roles, to use the proper term from the CSS specification) to the elements they contain. For this reason, the **display** property was created to allow authors to specify how elements should behave in layouts.

display

Values: inline|block|list-item|inline-block|table|inline-table|
table-row-group|table-header-group|table-footer-group|table-row|
table-column-group|table-column|table-cell|table-caption|none
The following are new in CSS3: run-in|compact|ruby|ruby-base|ruby-text|
ruby-base-container|ruby-text-container

Default: inline

Applies to: *all elements*

Inherits: *yes*

The **display** property defines the type of element box an element generates in the layout. In addition to the familiar **inline** and **block** display roles, you can also make elements display as list items or the various parts of a table. As you can see from the list of values, there are a lot of roles an element can play, but there are only a handful that are used in everyday practice.

In general, the W3C discourages the random reassigning of display roles for HTML elements. However, in certain scenarios, it is benign and has even become commonplace. For example, it is common practice to make **li** elements (which usually display with the characteristics of block elements) display as inline elements to turn a list into a horizontal navigation bar. You may also make an otherwise inline **a** (anchor) element display as a block in order to give it a specific width and height.

```
ul.navigation li { display: inline; }
ul.navigation li a { display: block; }
```

Another useful value for the display property is **none**, which removes the content from the normal flow entirely. Unlike **visibility: hidden**, which just makes the element invisible but holds the space it would have occupied blank, **display: none** removes the content, and the space it would have occupied is closed up.

One popular use of **display: none** is to prevent certain content in the source document from displaying in specific media, such as when the page is printed or displayed on devices with small screens. For example, you could have a paragraph that appears when the document is printed, but is not part of the page when it is displayed on a computer screen.

WARNING

Bear in mind that changing the presentation of an HTML element with the CSS display *property does not change the definition of that element as block-level or inline in HTML. Putting a block-level element within an inline element will always be invalid, regardless of its display role.*

WARNING

Be aware that content that has its display *set to* none *still downloads with the document. Setting some content to* display:none *for devices with small screens may keep the page shorter, but it is not doing anything to reduce data usage or download times.*

Adding Drop Shadows to Boxes

We've arrived at the last stop on the element box tour. In Chapter 12, "Formatting Text," you learned about the **text-shadow** property, which adds a drop shadow to text. The **box-shadow** property (new in CSS3) applies a drop shadow around the entire visible element box (excluding the margin).

box-shadow
NEW IN CSS3

Values:	*'horizontal offset' 'vertical offset' 'blur distance' 'spread distance' color* inset	none
Default:	none
Applies to:	all elements
Inherits:	no

The value of the **box-shadow** property should seem familiar after working with **text-shadow**: specify the horizontal and vertical offset distances, the amount the shadow should blur, and a color. For box shadows, you can also specify a spread amount, which increases (or decreases with negative values) the size of the shadow. By default, the shadow color is the same as the foreground color of the element, but specifying a color overrides it.

Figure 14-22 shows the results of the following code examples. The first **A** adds a simple box shadow six pixels to the right and six pixels down, without blur or spread. The second **B** adds a blur value of 5 pixels, and the third **C** shows the effect of a 10-pixel spread value. Box shadows are always applied to the area *outside* the border of the element (or the place it would be if a border isn't specified). If the element has a transparent or translucent background, you will not see the box shadow in the area behind the element.

```
A -webkit-box-shadow: 6px 6px #666;
  -moz-box-shadow: 6px 6px #666;
  box-shadow: 6px 6px #666;
```

```
B -webkit-box-shadow: 6px 6px 5px #666;
  -moz-box-shadow: 6px 6px 5px #666;
  box-shadow: 6px 6px 5px #666;/* 5 pixel blur */
```

```
C -webkit-box-shadow: 6px 6px 5px 10px #666;
  -moz-box-shadow: 6px 6px 5px 10px #666;
  box-shadow: 6px 6px 5px 10px #666;/* 5px blur, 10px spread */
```

Figure 14-22. Adding drop shadows around an element with the box-shadow property.

Figure 14-23. An inset box shadow renders on the inside of the element box.

WARNING

Box shadows, text shadows, and gradients take a lot of processor power because you are shifting the burden of interpreting and rendering them onto the browser. The more you use, the slower performance will be, and as we all know, performance is everything on the Web. So go easy on them.

You can make the shadow render inside the edges of the visible element box by adding the **inset** keyword to the rule. This makes it look like the element is pressed into the screen (Figure 14-23).

```
-webkit-box-shadow: inset 6px 6px 5px #666;
-moz-box-shadow: inset 6px 6px 5px #666;
box-shadow: inset 6px 6px 5px #666;
```

As for **text-shadow**, you can specify multiple box shadows on an element by providing the values in a comma-separated list. The values that come first get placed on top, and subsequent shadows are placed behind it in the order in which they appear in the list.

The **box-shadow** property is supported by all current version browsers, with the exception of Opera Mini for mobile. To accommodate recent WebKit browsers (Safari and Mobile Safari, Chrome, and Android) and older versions of Firefox, as of this writing, it is recommended that you include the vendor-prefixed properties as shown in the previous examples.

Internet Explorer 9 and higher support the standard property, but IE6 through 8 don't support it at all. My opinion is that it isn't the end of the world if users of those old browsers don't see a nifty little drop shadow. If you must have shadows in old IE versions, you will need to use the proprietary IE filter property, as explained in the article "How to Simulate CSS3 box-shadow in IE6-8 without JavaScript" by Zoltan "Du Lac" Hawryluk (*www.useragent-man.com/blog/2011/08/24/how-to-simulate-css3-box-shadow-in-ie7-8-without-javascript/*).

Test Yourself

At this point you should have a good feel for element boxes and how to manipulate the space within and around them. These are the raw tools you'll need to do real CSS-based layouts. In the next chapter, we'll start moving the boxes around on the page, but first, why not get some practice at writing rules for padding, borders, and margins in the following test?

In this test, your task is to write the declarations that create the effects shown in each example in Figure 14-24. All the paragraphs shown here share a rule that sets the dimensions and the background color for each paragraph. You need only provide the box-related property declarations. Answers, as always, appear in Appendix A.

Some useful hints: outer margin edges are indicated by dotted blue lines. All necessary measurements are provided in red. Borders use one of the 17 standard color names.

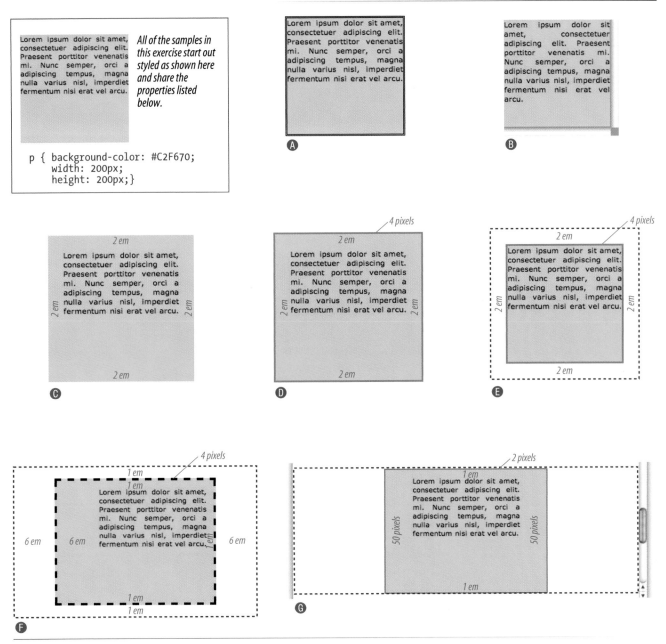

Figure 14-24. *Write the declarations for these examples.*

CSS Review: Basic Box Properties

Property	Description
`border`	A shorthand property that combines border properties

`border-top,`
`border-right,`
`border-bottom,`
`border-left`
	Combine border properties for each side of the element

`border-color`	Shorthand property for specifying the color of borders

`border-top-color,`
`border-right-color,`
`border-bottom-color,`
`border-left-color`
	Specify the border color for each side of the element

`border-image` *(CSS3)*	Adds an image inside the border area
`border-radius` *(CSS3)*	Shorthand property for rounding the corners of the visible element box

`border-top-left-radius,`
`border-top-right-radius,`
`border-bottom-right-radius,`
`border-bottom-left-radius`
	Specifies the radius curve for each individual corner

`border-style`	Shorthand property for specifying the style of borders

`border-top-style,`
`border-right-style,`
`border-bottom-style,`
`border-left-style`
	Specifies the border style for each side of the element

`border-width`	Shorthand property for specifying the width of borders

`border-top-width,`
`border-right-width,`
`border-bottom-width,`
`border-left-width`
	Specifies the border width for each side of the element

`box-sizing`	Specifies whether width and height dimensions apply to the content box or the border box
`box-shadow` *(CSS3)*	Adds a drop shadow around the visible element box
`display`	Defines the type of element box an element generates
`height`	Specifies the height of the element's content area
`margin`	Shorthand property for specifying margin space around an element

`margin-top,`
`margin-right,`
`margin-bottom,`
`margin-left`
	Specifies the margin amount for each side of the element

Property	Description
max-height	Specifies the maximum height of an element
max-width	Specifies the maximum width of an element
min-height	Specifies the minimum height of an element
min-width	Specifies the minimum width of an element
overflow	How to handle content that doesn't fit in the content area
padding	Shorthand property for specifying space between the content area and the border
padding-top, padding-right, padding-bottom, padding-left	Specify the padding amount for each side of the element
width	Specifies the width of an element's content area

FLOATING AND POSITIONING

At this point, you've learned dozens of CSS properties that allow you to change the appearance of text elements and the boxes they generate. But so far, we've merely been decorating elements as they appear in the flow of the document.

In this chapter, we'll look at floating and positioning, the CSS methods for breaking out of the normal flow and arranging elements on the page. Floating an element moves it to the left or right, and allows the following text to wrap around it. Positioning is a way to specify the location of an element anywhere on the page with pixel precision.

We'll start by examining the properties responsible for floating and positioning, so you'll get a good feel for how the CSS layout tools work. In Chapter 16, "Page Layout with CSS," we'll broaden the scope and see how these properties are used to create common multicolumn page layouts.

Before we start moving elements around, let's be sure we are well acquainted with how they behave in the normal flow.

Normal Flow

We've covered the normal flow in previous chapters, but it's worth a refresher. In the CSS layout model, text elements are laid out from top to bottom in the order in which they appear in the source, and from left to right (in left-to-right reading languages*). Block elements stack up on top of one another and fill the available width of the browser window or other containing element. Inline elements and text characters line up next to one another to fill the block elements.

When the window or containing element is resized, the block elements expand or contract to the new width, and the inline content reflows to fit (Figure 15-1).

---

* For right-to-left reading languages such as Arabic and Hebrew, the normal flow is top to bottom and right to left.

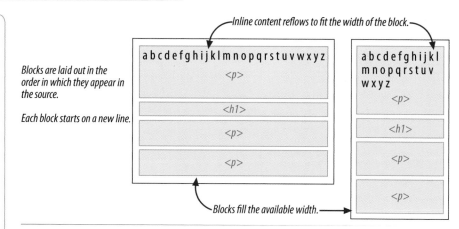

Figure 15-1. One more example of the normal flow behavior.

Objects in the normal flow affect the layout of the objects around them. This is the behavior you've come to expect in web pages—elements don't overlap or bunch up. They make room for one another.

We've seen all of this before, but in this chapter we'll be paying attention to whether elements are in the flow or removed from the flow. Floating and positioning change the relationship of elements to the normal flow in different ways. Let's first look at the special behavior of floated elements (or "floats" for short).

Floating

Simply stated, the **float** property moves an element as far as possible to the left or right, allowing the following content to wrap around it. It is not a positioning scheme *per se*, but a unique feature built into CSS with some interesting behaviors. Floats are one of the primary tools of modern CSS-based web design, used to create multicolumn layouts, navigation toolbars from lists, and table-like alignment without tables. Let's start with the **float** property itself.

float

Values:	left | right | none | inherit
Default:	none
Applies to:	all elements
Inherits:	no

The best way to explain floating is to demonstrate it. In this example, the **float** property is applied to an **img** element to float it to the right. Figure 15-2 shows how the paragraph and the contained image are rendered by default (top) and how it looks when the **float** property is applied (bottom).

The markup

```
<p><img src="crown.gif" alt="">They went down, down,...</p>
```

The style sheet

```
img {
   float: right;
}
p {
   padding: 15px;
   background-color: #FFF799;
   border: 2px solid #6C4788;
}
```

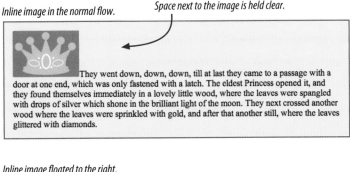

Inline image in the normal flow.

Space next to the image is held clear.

Inline image floated to the right.

Image moves over and text wraps around it.

Figure 15-2. The layout of an image in the normal flow (top), and with the `float` *property applied (bottom).*

That's a nice effect...we've gotten rid of a lot of wasted space on the page, but now the text is bumping right up against the image. How do you think you would add some space between the image element and the surrounding text? If you guessed "add a margin," you're absolutely right. I'll add 10 pixels of space on all sides of the image using the **margin** property (Figure 15-3). You can begin to see how all the box properties work together in page layout.

Figure 15-3. Adding a 10-pixel margin around the floated image.

```
img {
   float: right;
   margin: 10px;
}
```

Indicates outer margin edge
(this rule would not appear in the actual web page)

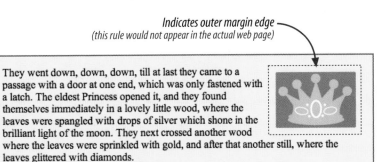

Some key behaviors of floated elements are apparent in the previous two figures:

A floated element is like an island in a stream.

First and foremost, you can see that the image is removed from its position in the normal flow yet continues to influence the surrounding content. The subsequent paragraph text reflows to make room for the floated **img** element. One popular analogy compares floats to islands in a stream—they are not in the flow, but the stream has to flow around them. This behavior is unique to floated elements.

Floats stay in the content area of the containing element.

It is also important to note that the floated image is placed within the content area (the inner edges) of the paragraph that contains it. It does not extend into the padding area of the paragraph.

Margins are maintained.

In addition, margins are held on all sides of the floated image, as indicated in Figure 15-3 by the dotted line. In other words, the entire element box, from outer edge to outer edge, is floated.

Floating inline and block elements

Those are the basics...let's look at more examples and explore additional floating behaviors. Before style sheets, the only thing you could float was an image by using the obsolete **align** attribute. With CSS, it is possible to float any HTML element, both inline and block-level, as we'll see in the following examples.

Floating an inline text element

In the previous example, we floated an inline image element. This time, let's look at what happens when you float an inline text (non-replaced) element (Figure 15-4).

The markup

```
<p><span class="disclaimer">Disclaimer: The existence of silver,
gold, and diamond trees is not confirmed.</span> They went down,
down, down, till at last they came to a passage... </p>
```

The style sheet

```
span.disclaimer {
  float: right;
  margin: 10px;
  width: 200px;
  color: #FFF;
  background-color: #9D080D;
  padding: 4px;
}
```

```
p {
    padding: 15px;
    background-color: #FFF799;
    border: 2px solid #6C4788;
}
```

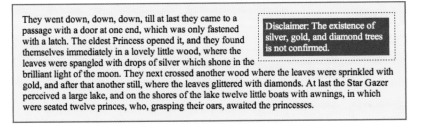

Figure 15-4. Floating an inline text (non-replaced) element.

From the look of things, it is behaving the same as the floated image, which is what we'd expect. But there are some subtle things at work here that bear pointing out.

Always provide a width for floated text elements.

First, you'll notice that the style rule that floats the **span** includes the **width** property. In fact, it is necessary to specify a width for floated text elements because without one, the content area of the box expands to its widest possible width (or, on some browsers, it may collapse to its narrowest possible width). Images have an inherent width, so we didn't need to specify a width in the previous example (although we certainly could have).

It is necessary to specify the width for floated text elements.

Floated inline elements behave as block elements.

Notice that the margin is held on all four sides of the floated **span** text, even though top and bottom margins are usually not rendered on inline elements (see Figure 14-18 in the previous chapter). That is because all floated elements behave like block elements. Once you float an inline element, it follows the display rules for block-level elements, and margins are rendered on all four sides.

Margins on floated elements do *not* collapse.

In the normal flow, abutting top and bottom margins collapse (overlap), but for floated elements, the margins are maintained on all sides as specified.

Floating block elements

Let's look at what happens when you float a block within the normal flow. In this example, a whole paragraph element is floated to the left (Figure 15-5).

The markup

```
<p>ONCE upon a time....</p>
<p id="float">As he had a white skin, blue eyes,...</p>
<p>The fact was he thought them very ugly...</p>
```

The style sheet

```
p#float {
   float: left;
   width: 200px;
   margin-top: 0px;
   background: #A5D3DE;
}
p {
   border: 1px solid red;
}
```

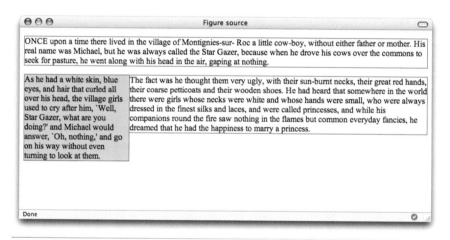

Figure 15-5. Floating a block-level element.

I've added a red rule around all **p** elements to show their boundaries. In addition, I set the top margin on the float to 0 (zero) to override the browser's default margin settings on paragraphs. This allows the floated paragraph to align with the top of the following paragraph.

Just as we saw with the image, the paragraph moves off to the side (left this time) and the following content wraps around it, even though blocks normally stack on top of one another. There are two things I want to point out in this example:

You must provide a width for floated block elements.

If you do not provide a **width** value, the width of the floated block will be set to **auto**, which fills the available width of the browser window or other containing element. There's not much sense in having a full-width floated box, because the idea is to wrap text next to the float, not start below it.

Elements do not float higher than their reference in the source.

A floated block will float to the left or right relative to where it occurs in the source, allowing the following elements in the flow to wrap around it. It will stay below any block elements that precede it in the flow (in effect, it is "blocked" by them). That means you can't float an element up to the top corner of a page, even if its nearest ancestor is the **body** element. If you want a floated element to start at the top of the page, it must appear first in the document source.

NOTE

Absolute positioning is the CSS method for placing elements on a page regardless of how they appear in the source. We'll get to absolute positioning in a few sections.

Clearing floated elements

If you're going to be floating elements around, it's important to know how to turn the text wrapping *off* and get back to layout as usual. You do this by clearing the element that you want to start below the float. Applying the **clear** property to an element prevents it from appearing next to a floated element and forces it to start against the next available "clear" space below the float.

clear

Values:	left | right | both | none | inherit
Default:	none
Applies to:	block-level elements only
Inherits:	no

Keep in mind that you apply the **clear** property to the element you want to start below the floated element, not the floated element itself. The **left** value starts the element below any elements that have been floated to the left. Similarly, the **right** value makes the element clear all floats on the right edge of the containing block. If there are multiple floated elements, and you want to be sure an element starts below all of them, use the **both** value to clear floats on both sides.

Figure 15-6. Clearing a left-floated element

In this example, the **clear** property has been used to make **h2** elements start below left-floated elements. Figure 15-6 shows how the **h2** heading starts at the next available clear edge below the float.

```
img {
    float: left;
    margin-right: 10px;
}
h2 {
    clear: left;
    margin-top: 2em;
}
```

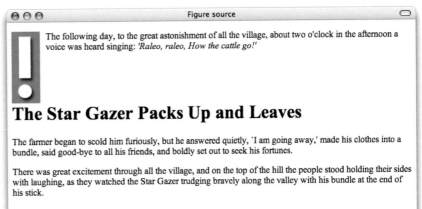

Notice in Figure 15-6 that although there is a 2em top margin applied to the **h2** element, it is not rendered between the heading and the floated image. That's the result of collapsing vertical margins in the flow. If you want to make sure space is held between a float and the following text, apply a bottom margin to the floated element itself.

I think by now you have enough float know-how to give it a try in Exercise 15-1.

---

exercise 15-1 | **Floating images**

In the exercises in this chapter, we'll make further improvements to the Jenware home page that we worked on in Chapter 14. If you did not follow along with the exercises in the previous chapter, or if you'd just like a fresh start, there is a copy of the document in its most recent state, *jenware_ch15.html*, in the Chapter 15 materials (*www.learningwebdesign.com/4e/materials*).

1. Open the Jenware home page document in a text editor and browser (it should look like Figure 14-21 in the previous chapter).

   We'll start by removing wasted vertical space next to the product images by floating the images to the left. We'll use a contextual selector to make sure that we float only those images in the "products" section of the page. While we're at it, let's add a little margin on the right and bottom sides using the **margin** shorthand property.

   ```
   #products img {
       float: left;
       margin: 0 6px 6px 0;
   }
   ```

   Save the document and take a look at it in the browser. You should see the product descriptions wrapping to the right of the images.

2. Next, I'd like the "More about…" links to always appear below the images so they are clearly visible and consistently on the left side of the products section. This change is going to require a little extra markup because we need a way to target just the paragraphs that contain "more about" links. Add the class name "more" to each of the paragraphs that contain links. Here is the first one:

   ```
   <p class="more"><a href="#">More about custom
       barware...</a></p>
   ```

   Now we can use a class selector to make those paragraphs clear the floated images.

   ```
   #products .more {
       clear: left;
   }
   ```

Figure 15-7 shows the new and improved Products section.

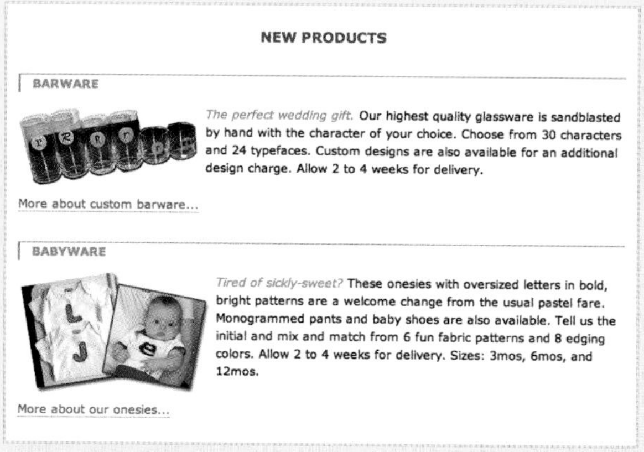

Figure 15-7. The product section with floated images and wrapped text has less wasted space.

NEW PRODUCTS

BARWARE

The perfect wedding gift. **Our highest quality glassware is sandblasted by hand with the character of your choice. Choose from 30 characters and 24 typefaces. Custom designs are also available for an additional design charge. Allow 2 to 4 weeks for delivery.**

More about custom barware...

BABYWARE

Tired of sickly-sweet? **These onesies with oversized letters in bold, bright patterns are a welcome change from the usual pastel fare. Monogrammed pants and baby shoes are also available. Tell us the initial and mix and match from 6 fun fabric patterns and 8 edging colors. Allow 2 to 4 weeks for delivery. Sizes: 3mos, 6mos, and 12mos.**

More about our onesies...

Floating multiple elements

It's perfectly fine to float multiple elements on a page or even within a single element. In fact, it is one way to turn a list of links into a horizontal menu, as we'll see in a moment.

When you float multiple elements, there is a complex system of behind-the-scenes rendering rules that ensures floated elements do not overlap. You can consult the CSS specification for the details, but the upshot of it is that floated elements will be placed as far left or right (as specified) and as high up as space allows.

Figure 15-8 shows what happens when a series of sequential paragraphs is floated to the same side. The first three floats start stacking up from the left edge, but when there isn't enough room for the fourth, it moves down and to the left until it bumps into something—in this case, the edge of the browser window. However, if one of the floats, such as "P2," had been very long, it would have bumped up against the edge of the long float instead.

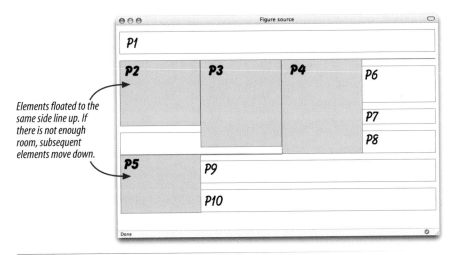

Elements floated to the same side line up. If there is not enough room, subsequent elements move down.

Figure 15-8. Multiple floated elements line up and do not overlap.

The source

```
<p>P1</p>
<p class="float">P2</p>
<p class="float">P3</p>
<p class="float">P4</p>
<p class="float">P5</p>
<p>P6</p>
<p>P7</p>
<p>P8</p>
<p>P9</p>
<p>P10</p>
```

The style sheet

```
p.float {
    float: left;
    width: 200px;
    margin: 0px;
    background: #CCC;
}
p
    {border: 1px solid red;
}
```

That's the underlying behavior, but let's apply it to something more practical, like a navigation menu. It makes sense semantically to mark up navigation as an unordered list, as shown here. I've omitted real URL values in the **a** elements to simplify the markup.

```
<ul>
    <li><a href="#">serif</a></li>
    <li><a href="#">sans-serif</a></li>
    <li><a href="#">script</a></li>
    <li><a href="#">display</a></li>
    <li><a href="#">dingbats</a></li>
</ul>
```

There are various approaches to converting the list to a horizontal bar (see note) but the primary steps in our floating example are as follows.

1. Turn off the bullets, and set padding and margins to zero.

```
ul {
    list-style-type: none;
    margin: 0;
    padding: 0;
}
```

2. Float each list item to the left so they line up, taking advantage of the multiple float behavior described earlier.

```
ul li {
    float: left;
}
```

NOTE

The other way to make list items line up is to make them display as inline elements instead of as block elements (li `{display: inline;}`*). From there, you can make the anchor elements display as blocks and apply styles. This method makes it more difficult to precisely control the spacing between navigation items, however, because the browser sizes the whitespace between list items in the source according to the* `font-size` *of the container.*

3. Make the anchor elements in the list items (**a**) display as block elements so you can set the dimensions, padding, margins, and other visual styles. You could set the styles for the other link states as well (such as **a:hover**), but I'll keep this example short.

```
ul li a {
    display: block;
    /*  more styles */
}
```

4. Clear the element that comes after the menu in the document so it starts below the menu.

At the very least, you will want to add some padding and/or margins to the anchor elements to give the links a little breathing room, but you can add any of the styles we've seen so far—colors, borders, rounded corners, background images—to give the navigation the look you want. The following styles turn the earlier list example into the tab-like menu shown in Figure 15-9.

```
ul li a {
    display: block;
    width: 100px;
    text-align: center;
    text-decoration: none;
    padding: 10px 10px;
    margin: 5px;
    color: white;
    background-color: lightslategray;
    border-top-left-radius: 15px;
    border-top-right-radius: 15px;
}
```

Figure 15-9. The unordered list is transformed into a tab-like menu using CSS alone and no images.

Containing floats

As long as we're talking about multiple floats, this is a good time to address another float quirk, and that's float containment. By default, floats are designed to hang out of the element they are contained in. That's just fine for allowing text to flow around a floated image, but sometimes this behavior can cause some unwanted behaviors.

For instance, take the example in Figure 15-10. Clearly, it would be nicer if the border stretched to contain all the content, but the floated image hangs right out the bottom.

Hand-stitched iPhone motif
More info

Figure 15-10. The containing element does not stretch to accommodate the floated image.

And if you float all the elements in a container element—as you might do to create a multicolumn layout—there will be no elements remaining in the flow to hold the containing element open. This phenomenon is illustrated in Figure 15-11. The **#container div** contains two paragraphs. The view of the normal flow (left) shows that the **#container** has a background color and border that wraps around the content. However, when both paragraphs are floated, the element box for the **#container** closes up to have a height of zero, leaving the floats hanging down below (you can still see the empty border at the top). This clearly is not the effect we are after.

In the normal flow, the container div encloses the paragraphs.

Etiam convallis, nulla ut ullamcorper mollis, ipsum purus imperdiet tellus, ut ultrices massa tortor vitae nulla. Fusce non arcu quam. Nullam lacinia facilisis lacus, et varius ligula imperdiet ut. Morbi molestie auctor magna, quis venenatis felis adipiscing sed. Aliquam ipsum nibh, dapibus sit amet tristique at, tincidunt in leo. Quisque accumsan lobortis lacus, id gravida tortor luctus et. Donec quis diam et odio volutpat blandit nec nec enim. Nam vitae vestibulum risus. Cras in adipiscing odio. Nam vel dolor id purus pretium suscipit quis in quam. Proin varius tincidunt facilisis. Maecenas eget felis ut nisi ullamcorper pretium non at nulla. Etiam suscipit aliquet velit ac facilisis. Etiam egestas ante eu velit ullamcorper ornare. Suspendisse vestibulum leo sed lectus posuere eget convallis nisi placerat. Vestibulum porttitor egestas ornare.

Cras id ipsum dui. Donec semper congue lectus quis vulputate. Ut felis leo, bibendum at blandit non, luctus ac lorem. Nunc vitae ligula ut neque convallis sagittis. Quisque consequat orci sed arcu tincidunt et volutpat tellus tempor. Nulla vulputate ante nec felis elementum auctor. Duis magna neque, posuere eu hendrerit sit amet, dapibus quis quam. Pellentesque habitant morbi tristique senectus et netus et malesuada fames ac turpis egestas. Class aptent taciti sociosqu ad litora torquent per conubia nostra, per inceptos himenaeos. Nunc dapibus dui dignissim dolor rutrum vel consequat nibh sagittis. Morbi non dolor diam, nec iaculis neque. Aenean at eros sit amet velit iaculis porttitor. Nam lobortis sodales augue, sit amet tincidunt erat sagittis eu. Class aptent taciti sociosqu ad litora torquent per conubia nostra, per inceptos himenaeos. Donec ut ultricies velit. Quisque tempor fermentum ante, quis tempus est fringilla eu.

When both paragraphs are floated, the container does not stretch around them.

Etiam convallis, nulla ut ullamcorper mollis, ipsum purus imperdiet tellus, ut ultrices massa tortor vitae nulla. Fusce non arcu quam. Nullam lacinia facilisis lacus, et varius ligula imperdiet ut. Morbi molestie auctor magna, quis venenatis felis adipiscing sed. Aliquam ipsum nibh, dapibus sit amet tristique at, tincidunt in leo. Quisque accumsan lobortis lacus, id gravida tortor luctus et. Donec quis diam et odio volutpat blandit nec nec enim. Nam vitae vestibulum risus. Cras in adipiscing odio. Nam vel dolor id purus pretium suscipit quis in quam. Proin varius tincidunt facilisis. Maecenas eget felis ut nisi ullamcorper pretium non at nulla. Etiam suscipit aliquet velit ac facilisis. Etiam egestas ante eu velit ullamcorper ornare. Suspendisse vestibulum leo sed lectus posuere eget convallis nisi placerat. Vestibulum porttitor egestas ornare.

Cras id ipsum dui. Donec semper congue lectus quis vulputate. Ut felis leo, bibendum at blandit non, luctus ac lorem. Nunc vitae ligula ut neque convallis sagittis. Quisque consequat orci sed arcu tincidunt et volutpat tellus tempor. Nulla vulputate ante nec felis elementum auctor. Duis magna neque, posuere eu hendrerit sit amet, dapibus quis quam. Pellentesque habitant morbi tristique senectus et netus et malesuada fames ac turpis egestas. Class aptent taciti sociosqu ad litora torquent per conubia nostra, per inceptos himenaeos. Nunc dapibus dui dignissim dolor rutrum vel consequat nibh sagittis. Morbi non dolor diam, nec iaculis neque. Aenean at eros sit amet velit iaculis porttitor. Nam lobortis sodales augue, sit amet tincidunt erat sagittis eu. Class aptent taciti sociosqu ad litora torquent per conubia nostra, per inceptos himenaeos. Donec ut ultricies velit. Quisque tempor fermentum ante, quis tempus est fringilla eu.

Figure 15-11. The container box disappears entirely when all its contents are floated.

Fortunately, there are a few fixes to this problem, and they are pretty straightforward. One option is to float the containing element as well and give it a width of 100%.

```
#container {
  float: left;
  width: 100%;
  background-color: #GGG;
  padding: 1em;
}
```

The other common solution is to take advantage of the behavior of the **overflow** property. Setting the overflow of the containing element to **auto** or **hidden** will also make it stretch to contain the floated elements. I've also added an explicit width value to address bugs in old IE versions, but note that if your container element has a border, the 100% width will make the border hang outside of the browser window.

```
#container {
  overflow: auto;
  width: 100%;
  background-color: #GGG;
  padding: 1em;
}
```

Figure 15-12. Our hanging floats are now contained.

Hand-stitched iPhone motif
More info

Etiam convallis, nulla ut ullamcorper mollis, ipsum purus imperdiet tellus, ut ultrices massa tortor vitae nulla. Fusce non arcu quam. Nullam lacinia facilisis lacus, et varius ligula imperdiet ut. Morbi molestie auctor magna, quis venenatis felis adipiscing sed. Aliquam ipsum nibh, dapibus sit amet tristique at, tincidunt in leo. Quisque accumsan lobortis lacus, id gravida tortor luctus et. Donec quis diam et odio volutpat blandit nec nec enim. Nam vitae vestibulum risus. Cras in adipiscing odio. Nam vel dolor id purus pretium suscipit quis in quam. Proin varius tincidunt facilisis. Maecenas eget felis ut nisi ullamcorper pretium non at nulla. Etiam suscipit aliquet velit ac facilisis. Etiam egestas ante eu velit ullamcorper ornare. Suspendisse vestibulum leo sed lectus posuere eget convallis nisi placerat. Vestibulum porttitor egestas ornare.

Cras id ipsum dui. Donec semper congue lectus quis vulputate. Ut felis leo, bibendum at blandit non, luctus ac lorem. Nunc vitae ligula ut neque convallis sagittis. Quisque consequat orci sed arcu tincidunt et volutpat tellus tempor. Nulla vulputate ante nec felis elementum auctor. Duis magna neque, posuere eu hendrerit sit amet, dapibus quis quam. Pellentesque habitant morbi tristique senectus et netus et malesuada fames ac turpis egestas. Class aptent taciti sociosqu ad litora torquent per conubia nostra, per inceptos himenaeos. Nunc dapibus dui dignissim dolor rutrum vel consequat nibh sagittis. Morbi non dolor diam, nec iaculis neque. Aenean at eros sit amet velit iaculis porttitor. Nam lobortis sodales augue, sit amet tincidunt erat sagittis eu. Class aptent taciti sociosqu ad litora torquent per conubia nostra, per inceptos himenaeos. Donec ut ultricies velit. Quisque tempor fermentum ante, quis tempus est fringilla eu.

Figure 15-12 shows the result of applying a containment technique to the previous examples. Either one will do the trick.

Now it is time to spiff up that navigation section on the Jenware page in Exercise 15-2.

exercise 15-2 | Making a navigation bar

Open your copy of *jenware.html* (or *jenware_ch15.html*) if it isn't already.

1. Start by making the **ul** element as neutral as possible. The bullets have already been turned off, but we should clear out any padding and margin that might be happening in there.

```
#nav ul {
    list-style-type: none;
    padding: 0;
    margin: 0;
}
```

Next float the list items to the left, and clear the following **#products div**.

```
#nav ul li {
    ...
    float: left;
}
```

```
#products {
    ...
    clear: both;
}
```

Save the document and take a look at it in a browser. You should see that the links are now lined up pretty tightly, but also that the purple navigation bar has shrunk to nothing—float containment fail! Let's fix it with the overflow technique. And while we're at it, let's do the same for the **#products div** so it is sure to contain the floated images.

```
#nav {
    ...
    overflow: hidden;
    width: 100%;
}
#products {
    ...
    overflow: hidden;
}
```

2. Now we can work on the appearance of the links. Start by making the **a** elements display as block elements instead of inline. Instead of setting specific dimensions for each link, we'll use padding (.5em) to give them a little breathing room inside the border and use margins (.25em) to add space between links. I've added a lavender border as the default, but I brighten it up to white for the **:focus** and **:hover** states.

```
#nav ul li a {
    display: block;
    padding: .5em;
    border: 1px solid #ba89a8;
    border-radius: .5em;
    margin: .25em;
}
```

```
#nav ul a:focus {
    color:#fc6;
    border-color: #fff;
}
```

```
#nav ul a:hover {
    color: #fc6;
    border-color: #fff;
}
```

3. Finally, let's center the list in the width of the **nav** section. We can do this by applying a width to the **ul** element and setting its side margins to **auto**. I confess that I had to fiddle around with a few width measurements to arrive at one that fit the entire menu just right (19.5em). If it's too wide, the menu won't be truly centered.

```
#nav ul {
    list-style: none;
    padding: 0;
    margin: 0 auto;
    width: 19.5em;
}
```

Figure 15-13 shows the way your navigation should look when you view it in the browser.

Figure 15-13. The list of links is now styled as a horizontal menu bar.

Using floats to create columns

So far, we've floated small parts of a page, but as mentioned earlier, you can also float whole sections of the page to create columns. In fact, that's the way the pros do it! There are a couple of solutions, and they mostly come down to a matter of preference.

For a two-column float, you can do the following:

- Float one **div** and add a wide margin on the side of the text element that wraps around it.

- Float both **div**s to the left or right.

- Float one **div** to the left and the second **div** to the right (or vice versa).

Three-column floats work basically the same way; there's just more calculating to do.

Regardless of which method works best for your content or suits your fancy, there are a few things you need to keep in mind. First, every float needs to have a specified width. Thereafter, you need to be very careful that you have calculated the widths of each column correctly, factoring in padding, borders, and margins. If the total width of all the columns exceeds the available width of the browser or other containing element, you'll get what is known as "float drop." That is, the final floated column will run out of room and get bumped down below the column next to it. Bummer.

The limitation to using floats for columns is that it is dependent on the order of the elements in the source document. The floated element must appear *before* the content that wraps around it, and your source may not always be ordered conveniently.

Now, get a feel for making a two-column layout with floats in Exercise 15-3 using the "one float plus a margin" technique listed above.

NOTE

There are ways to break free of the source order using negative margins, as you'll learn in Chapter 16.

exercise 15-3 | Creating columns with floats

The layout we've been using for the Jenware site might be a good starting point for a small-screen device, but it gets awkward in larger browser windows. In this exercise, we'll write styles to give the page a fluid two-column layout using floats. I recommend making a copy of your current Jenware file and renaming it *jenware-float.html*. That will keep a copy fresh for the next exercise, and you won't need to undo what you've done here.

What we're going to do is give the **#products div** a width, float it to the left, and allow the Testimonials box to flow around it on the right side, creating a second column. I want this layout to resize proportionally to always fill the width of the screen, so I'm going to use percentages for all the horizontal measurements (that means making a few changes to our prior code).

1. Start by setting the width of the **#products div** to 55% and floating it to the left. Currently the padding and margins are set at 1em all around, but change the left and right padding and margins to 2% for this fluid layout. That means the Products box is now taking up roughly 63% of the width of the screen (2% + 2% + 55% + 2% + 2%), plus a few pixels more for the borders. Figure 15-14 shows the results of these changes. In addition, set the top margin of **#products** to zero.

```css
#products {
    background-color: #FFF;
    line-height: 1.5em;
    padding: 1em 2%;
    border: double #FFBC53;
    margin: 0 2% 1em;
    clear: both;
    float: left;
    width: 55%;
}
```

There are some interesting behaviors to observe here. The Testimonials text has moved up to the right of the Products box, which is expected, but the Testimonials box (with the exclamation point graphic) is hidden behind the Products box. Only the content wraps; the element box just moves up and does not resize.

2. Time to get that Testimonials box into shape. What we need to do is adjust the margins, specifically to make the left margin on the Testimonials box wide enough that it clears the Products box. The Products box is taking up a hair more than 63% of the width of the page, so let's give the Testimonials box a left margin of 64% to accommodate it and add a little space between. I've also set a narrow right margin of 2% (remember the order of the declaration values is Top, Right, Bottom, Left). Reload the page, and the Testimonials box should be centered in the right column.

```css
#testimonials {
    ...
    margin: 1em 10%;/* delete */
    margin: 1em 2% 1em 64%;
}
```

3. Just a few more tweaks here. Clear the copyright paragraph so it appears at the bottom of the page. Finally, I think the "New Products" **h2** would look better left-aligned in this layout, so let's adjust that too.

```css
p#copyright {
    ...
    clear: left;
}
#products h2 {
    ...
    text-align: center left;
}
```

The results are shown in Figure 15-15. Hey, look at that! Your first two-column layout, created with a float and a wide margin. This is the basic concept behind many CSS-based layout templates, as you'll see in Chapter 16.

Figure 15-14. *The results of floating the products* **div**.

Figure 15-15. *A new two-column layout for the Jenware home page, created with a float and a wide margin on the following content. This layout would work well for tablet devices or desktop browser windows.*

Be careful mixing fluid columns with borders. It is usually best if your percentages add up to less then 100%, to accommodate the border widths (if they are used) and to accommodate rounding errors that browsers sometimes make. If too many column widths are rounded up, the columns may be calculated as too wide for the browser and you'll get the dreaded float drop.

Mixing % and Ems

In Exercise 15-2, we specified margins in a combination of percentage values and ems. This is actually common in contemporary web development, particularly for creating fluid layouts that respond to the size of the viewport. Some developers use percentages for all horizontal measurements so they are relative to the viewport size, but use ems for all vertical measurements because it is in keeping with the scale and the rhythm of lines of text. This technique is a preference, not a requirement, but it is something to keep in mind.

That covers the fundamentals of floating. Let's move on to the other approach to moving elements around on the page—positioning.

Positioning Basics

CSS provides several methods for positioning elements on the page. They can be positioned relative to where they would normally appear in the flow, or removed from the flow altogether and placed at a particular spot on the page. You can also position an element relative to the browser window (technically known as the viewport in the CSS Recommendations), and it will stay put while the rest of the page scrolls.

Types of positioning

`position`

Values: static | relative | absolute | fixed | inherit

Default: static

Applies to: *all elements*

Inherits: *no*

The **position** property indicates that an element is to be positioned and specifies which positioning method to use. I'll introduce each keyword value briefly here, and then we'll take a more detailed look at each method in the remainder of this chapter.

static

This is the normal positioning scheme in which elements are positioned as they occur in the normal document flow.

relative

Relative positioning moves the box relative to its original position in the flow. The distinctive behavior of relative positioning is that the space the element would have occupied in the normal flow is preserved as an empty space.

absolute

Absolutely positioned elements are removed from the document flow entirely and positioned with respect to the browser window or a containing element (we'll talk more about this later). Unlike relatively positioned elements, the space they would have occupied is closed up. In fact, they have no influence at all on the layout of surrounding elements.

fixed

The distinguishing characteristic of fixed positioning is that the element stays in one position in the window even when the document scrolls. Fixed elements are removed from the document flow and positioned relative to the browser window (or other viewport) rather than another element in the document. It currently causes some hiccups on mobile devices, as discussed later in this chapter.

Each positioning method has its purpose, but absolute positioning is the most versatile. With absolute positioning, you can place an object anywhere in the viewport or within another element. Absolute positioning can even be used to create multicolumn layouts, but it is more commonly used for small tasks, like positioning a search box in the top corner of a header. You can also use absolute positioning to break an image or chunk out of its containing box, creating hanging indents or overlap effects. It's a handy tool when used carefully and sparingly.

Specifying position

Once you've established the positioning method, the actual position is specified with four offset properties.

top, right, bottom, left

Values: length measurement | percentage | auto | inherit

Default: auto

Applies to: positioned elements (where position value is relative, absolute, or fixed)

Inherits: no

The value provided for each of the offset properties defines the distance the element should be moved *away* from that respective edge. For example, the value of **top** defines the distance the top outer edge of the positioned element should be offset from the top edge of the browser or other containing element. A positive value for **top** results in the element box moving *down* by that amount. Similarly, a positive value for **left** would move the positioned element to the right (toward the center of the containing block) by that amount.

NOTE

Negative values are acceptable and move the element in the opposite direction of positive values. For example, a negative value for **top** *would have the effect of moving the element up.*

Further explanations and examples of the offset properties will be provided in the discussions of each positioning method. We'll start our exploration of positioning with the fairly straightforward **relative** method.

Relative Positioning

As mentioned previously, relative positioning moves an element relative to its original spot in the flow. The space it would have occupied is preserved and continues to influence the layout of surrounding content. This is easier to understand with a simple example.

Here I've positioned an inline **em** element (a background color makes its boundaries apparent). First, I used the **position** property to set the method to **relative**, and then I used the **top** offset property to move the element 30 pixels down from its initial position and the **left** property to move it 60 pixels to the right. Remember, offset property values move the element away from the specified edge, so if you want something to move to the right, as I did here, you use the **left** offset property. The results are shown in Figure 15-16.

```
em {
    position: relative;
    top: 30px;
    left: 60px;
    background-color: fuchsia;
}
```

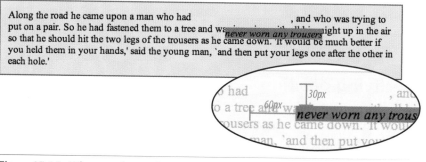

Figure 15-16. *When an element is positioned with the relative method, the space it would have occupied is preserved.*

I want to point out a few things that are happening here.

The original space in the document flow is preserved.

> You can see that there is a blank space where the emphasized text would have been if the element had not been positioned. The surrounding content is laid out as though the element were still there, and therefore we say that the element still "influences" the surrounding content.

Overlap happens.

> Because this is a positioned element, it can potentially overlap other elements, as shown in Figure 15-16.

The empty space left behind by relatively positioned objects can be a little awkward, so this method is not used as often as absolute positioning. However, relative positioning is commonly used to create a "positioning context" for an absolutely positioned element, as I'll explain in the next section.

Absolute Positioning

Absolute positioning works a bit differently and is actually a more flexible method for accurately placing items on the page than relative positioning. Now that you've seen how relative positioning works, let's take the same example as shown in Figure 15-16, only this time we'll change the value of the **position** property to **absolute**.

```
em {
    position: absolute;
    top: 30px;
    left: 60px;
    background-color: fuchsia;
}
```

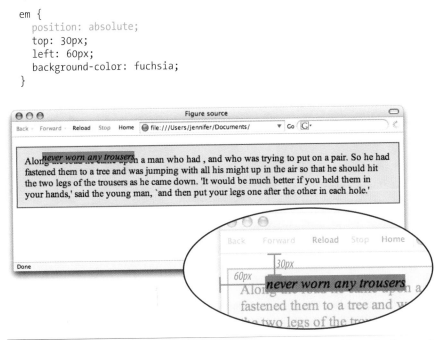

Figure 15-17. When an element is absolutely positioned, it is removed from the flow and the space is closed up.

As you can see in Figure 15-17, the space once occupied by the **em** element is now closed up, as is the case for all absolutely positioned elements. In its new position, the element box overlaps the surrounding content. In the end, absolutely positioned elements have no influence whatsoever on the layout of surrounding elements.

The most significant difference here, however, is the location of the positioned element. This time, the offset values position the **em** element 30 pixels down and 60 pixels to the right of the top-left corner of the browser window.

But wait. Before you start thinking that absolutely positioned elements are always placed relative to the browser window, I'm afraid that there's more to it than that.

What actually happens in absolute positioning is that the element is positioned relative to its nearest *containing block*. It just so happens that the nearest containing block in Figure 15-17 is the root (**html**) element, also known as the initial containing block, so the offset values position the **em** element relative to the whole document.

NOTE

*Some browsers base the initial containing block on the **body** element. The net result is the same in that it fills the browser window.*

Getting a handle on the containing block concept is the first step to tackling absolute positioning.

Containing blocks

The CSS2.1 Recommendation states, "The position and size of an element's box(es) are sometimes calculated relative to a certain rectangle, called the containing block of the element." It is critical to have an awareness of the containing block of the element you want to position. We sometimes refer to this as the positioning context.

The recommendation lays out a number of intricate rules for determining the containing block of an element, but it basically boils down to this:

- If the positioned element is *not* contained within another positioned element, then it will be placed relative to the initial containing block (created by the `html` element).

- But if the element has an ancestor (i.e., is contained within an element) that has its position set to **relative**, **absolute**, or **fixed**, the element will be positioned relative to the edges of *that* element instead.

Figure 15-17 is an example of the first case: the **p** element that contains the absolutely positioned **em** element is *not* positioned itself, and there are no other positioned elements higher in the hierarchy. Therefore the **em** element is positioned relative to the initial containing block, which is equivalent to the browser window area.

Let's deliberately turn the **p** element into a containing block and see what happens. All we have to do is apply the **position** property to it; we don't have to actually move it. The most common way to make an element into a containing block is to set the **position** to **relative**, but don't move it with offset values. (By the way, this is what I was talking about earlier when I said that relative positioning is most often used to create a context for an absolutely positioned element.)

We'll keep the style rule for the **em** element the same, but we'll add a **position** property to the **p** element, thus making it the containing block for the positioned **em** element. Figure 15-18 shows the results.

```
p {
    position: relative;
    padding: 15px;
    background-color: #DBFDBA;
    border: 2px solid #6C4788;
}
```

Or, to Put It Another Way...

The containing block for an absolutely positioned element is the nearest *positioned* ancestor element (that is, any element with a value for **position** other than **static**).

If there is no containing block present (in other words, if the positioned element is *not* contained within another positioned element), then the initial containing block (created by the `html` element) will be used instead.

Figure 15-18. The relatively positioned p element acts as a containing block for the em element.

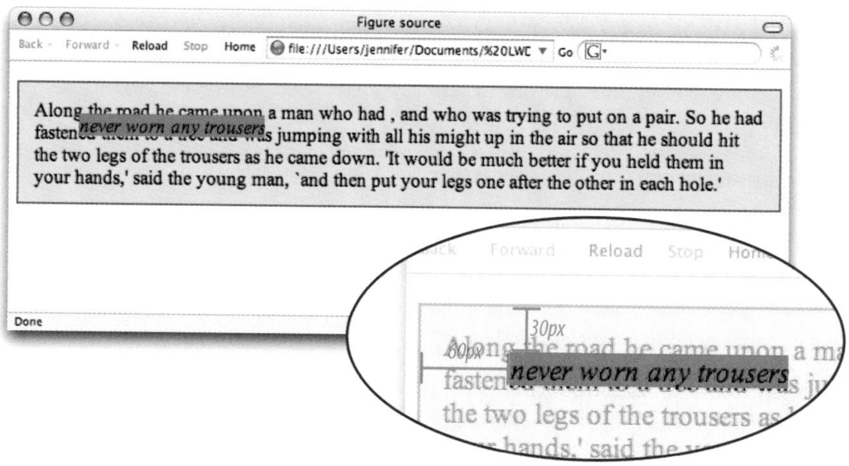

You can see that the **em** element is now positioned 30 pixels down and 60 pixels from the top-left corner of the paragraph box, not the browser window. Notice also that it is positioned relative to the *padding edge* of the paragraph (just inside the border), not the content area edge. This is the normal behavior when block elements are used as containing blocks (see note).

I'm going to poke around at this some more to reveal additional aspects of absolutely positioned objects. This time, I've added **width** and **margin** properties to the positioned **em** element (Figure 15-19).

```
em {
    width: 200px;
    margin: 25px;
    position: absolute;
    top: 30px;
    left: 60px;
    background-color: fuchsia;
}
```

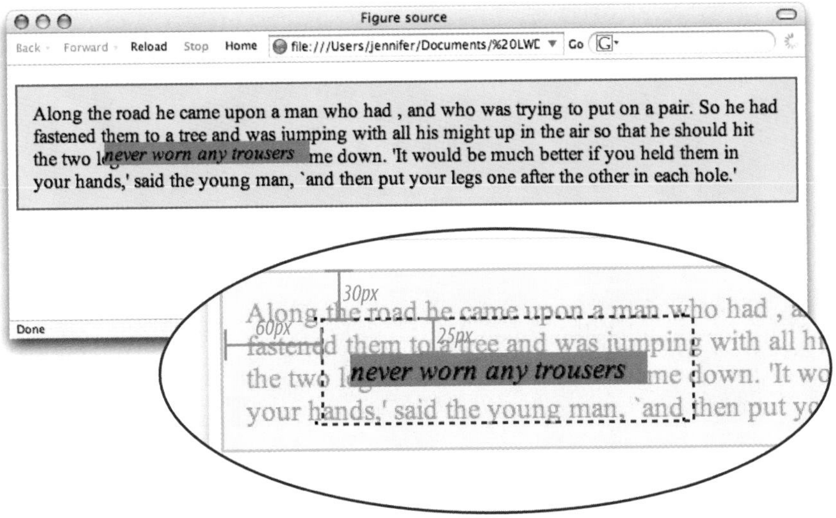

NOTE

When inline elements are used as containing blocks (and they can be), the positioned element is placed relative to the content area edge, not the padding edge.

Figure 15-19. Adding a width and margins to the positioned element.

Here we can see that:

- The offset values apply to the outer edges of the element box (from margin edge to margin edge), and

- Absolutely positioned elements always behave as block-level elements. For example, the margins on all sides are maintained, even though this is an inline element. It also permits a width to be set for the element.

It is important to keep in mind that once you've positioned an element, it becomes the new containing block for all the elements it contains. Consider this example in which a **div** named "content" is positioned in the top-left corner of the page. When a positioned list item within that **div** is given offset values that place it in the top-right corner, it appears in the top-right corner of the contents **div**, not the entire page (Figure 15-20). That is because once the **div** is positioned, it acts as the containing block for the **li** element.

The markup

```
<div id="preface">
...
</div>

<div id="contents">
<h2>Contents</h2>
<ul>
    <li>The Nix in Mischief</li>
    <li id="special">The Ogre Courting</li>
    <li>Murdoch's Wrath</li>
    <li>The Little Darner</li>
    <li>The Magic Jar</li>
</ul>
</div>
```

The style sheet

```
div#contents {
  width: 200px;
  position: absolute;
  top: 0;     /* positioned in the top-left corner */
  left: 0;
  background-color: #AFD479;
  padding: 10px;
}

li#special {
  position: absolute;
  top: 0;      /* positioned in the top-right corner */
  right: 0;
  background-color: fuchsia;
}
```

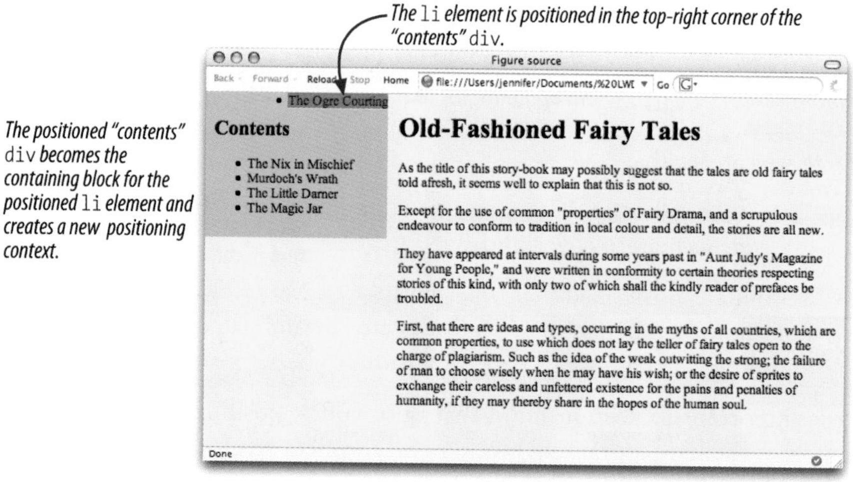

The **li** element is positioned in the top-right corner of the "contents" div.

The positioned "contents" div becomes the containing block for the positioned **li** element and creates a new positioning context.

Figure 15-20. Positioned elements become the containing block for the elements they contain. In this example, the list item is positioned relative to the containing div element, not the whole page.

Specifying position

Now that you have a better feel for the containing block concept, let's take some time to get better acquainted with the offset properties. So far, we've only seen an element moved a few pixels down and to the right, but that's not all you can do, of course.

Pixel measurements

As mentioned previously, positive offset values push the positioned element box *away* from the specified edge and toward the center of the containing block. If there is no value provided for a side, it is set to **auto**, and the browser adds enough space to make the layout work. In this example, I've used pixel lengths for all four offset properties to place the positioned element at a particular spot in its containing element (Figure 15-21).

```
div#a {
    position: relative;      /* creates the containing block */
    height: 120px;
    width: 300px;
    border: 1px solid;
    background-color: #CCC;
}

div#b {
    position: absolute;
    top: 20px;
    right: 30px;
    bottom: 40px;
    left: 50px;
    border: 1px solid;
    background-color: teal;
}
```

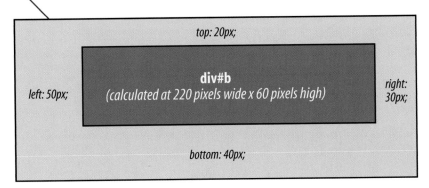

Figure 15-21. Setting offset values for all four sides of a positioned element.

Notice that by setting offsets on all four sides, I have indirectly set the dimensions of the positioned **div#b** (it fills the 220 × 60 pixel space that is left over within the containing block after the offset values are applied). If I had also specified a width and other box properties for **div#b**, there is the potential for conflicts if the total of the values for the positioned box and its offsets does not match the available space within the containing block.

The CSS specification provides a daunting set of rules for handling conflicts, but the upshot is that you should just be careful not to over-specify box properties and offsets. In general, a width (factoring in optional padding, border, and margin) and one or two offset properties are all that are necessary to achieve the layout you're looking for. Let the browser take care of the remaining calculations.

Percentage values

You can also specify positions with percentage values. In the first example in Figure 15-22, the image is positioned halfway down the left edge of the containing block. In the second example on the right, the **img** element is positioned so that it always appears in the bottom-right corner of the containing block.

```
img#A {
    position: absolute;
    top: 50%;
    left: 0%;   /* the % symbol could be omitted for a 0 value */
}
img#B {
    position: absolute;
    bottom: 0%;   /* the % symbol could be omitted for a 0 value */
    right: 0%;   /* the % symbol could be omitted for a 0 value */
}
```

WARNING

Be careful when positioning elements at the bottom of the initial containing block (the html *element). Although you may expect it to be positioned at the bottom of the whole page, browsers actually place the element in the bottom corner of the browser window. Results may be unpredictable. If you want something positioned in a bottom corner of your page, put it in a containing block element at the end of the document source, and go from there.*

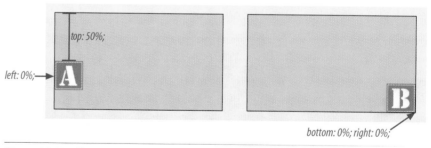

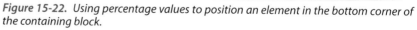

Figure 15-22. Using percentage values to position an element in the bottom corner of the containing block.

Although the examples here specify both a vertical and horizontal offset, it is common to provide just one offset for a positioned element, for example, to move it left or right into a margin using either **left** or **right** properties.

In Exercise 15-4, we'll make further changes to the Jenware home page, this time using absolute positioning.

exercise 15-4 | **Absolute positioning**

In this exercise, we'll use absolute positioning to add an award graphic to the site and to create a two-column layout. Open the pre-Exercise 15-3 version of *jenware.html* (or *jenware_ch15.html*) in a text editor. You should be starting with the single-column layout with floated images and a horizontal menu.

1. Let's pretend that Jenware.com won the "Awesome Site of the Week" award, and now we have the privilege of displaying a little award banner on the home page. Because it is new content, we'll need to add it to the markup. Because it is non-essential information, we'll add the image in a new **div** at the very end of the document, after the copyright paragraph.

```
<div id="award">
    <img src="images/awesomesite.gif" alt="awesome
site of the week">
</div>
```

Just because it is at the end of the document source doesn't mean it needs to display at the bottom of the page. We can use absolute positioning to place the **#award div** in the top-left corner of the browser window for all to see by adding a new rule to the style sheet that positions the **div**, like so:

```
#award {
    position: absolute;
    top: 35px;
    left: 25px;
}
```

Save the document and take a look (Figure 15-23). Resize the browser window very narrow, and you will see that the positioned award image overlaps the header content. Notice also that when you scroll the document, the image scrolls with the rest of the page. Try playing around with other offset properties and values to get a feel for positioning in the browser window (or the "initial containing block" to use the correct term).

Figure 15-23. An absolutely positioned award graphic.

2. In Exercise 15-3 we created two columns with a float. Now let's do the same thing with absolute positioning. This time we'll make the Testimonials box a fixed width and allow the Products box to flex to fill the remaining space. This is just another common layout approach that I want you to get a feel for.

As the document stands now, if we position the Testimonials **div**, it will be relative to the browser window, which is not what we want. We want it to always appear under the **#nav div**, so we'll start by creating a new containing block after **#nav** that holds the products and testimonial **div**s and will serve as the new positioning context.

This is going to require some changes to the markup. Wrap **#products** and **#testimonials** in a new **div** with an **id** of "content." The structure of the document should look like this:

```
<div id="content">
    <div id="products"> ... </div>
    <div id="testimonials">... </div>
</div>
<p class="copyright">...</p>
```

3. Now we can turn the "content" **div** into a containing block simply by positioning it with the "unmoved-relative-position" trick:

```
#content {
    position: relative;
}
```

4. With that in place, we can position the **#testimonials** box in the top-right corner of the **#content div**. Add the position as well as top and right properties to the **#testimonials** rule as shown next. In addition, make the content 14 ems wide. Adjust the top margin to 0, and change the left and right margins from 10% to just 1em.

```
#testimonials {
    ...
    margin: 1em 10%; 0 1em;
    position: absolute;
    top: 0;
    right: 0;
    width: 14em; }
```

5. If you save the file and take a look in the browser, you should see the Testimonials box in the right corner, plopped right on top of the Products box. The next step is to put a right margin on the Products box to make a space for the Testimonials. But how much space? Let's calculate like web geeks do.

6. The Testimonials box has approximately 3.5 ems of left padding (55px), 14em-wide content, 1em of right padding, and a 1em right margin, for a total of 19.5em. If we make the right margin on **#products** 20.5em, that will make space for the Testimonials box plus a little space in between the columns. We'll do it using the TRBL shorthand, as shown here.

```
#products {
  …
  margin:  1em 20.5em 1em 1em;
  …
}
```

Save the document and look at it in the browser (Figure 15-24). Resize the window and compare how the boxes behave compared to the previous floated column example.

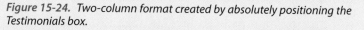

Figure 15-24. Two-column format created by absolutely positioning the Testimonials box.

Reality check

Before you get too excited about the ease of creating multicolumn layouts with absolute positioning, let me point out that this exercise represents a best-case scenario in which the positioned sidebar column is pretty much guaranteed to be shorter than the main content. There is also no significant footer to worry about. If the sidebar were to grow longer with more testimonials, it would overlap any full-width footer that might be on the page, which is not ideal. Consider this a heads-up that there's more to the story, as we'll see in Chapter 16.

Stacking order

Before we close the book on absolute positioning, there is one last related concept that I want to introduce. As we've seen, absolutely positioned elements overlap other elements, so it follows that multiple positioned elements have the potential to stack up on one another.

By default, elements stack up in the order in which they appear in the document, but you can change the stacking order with the **z-index** property. Picture the z-axis as a line that runs perpendicular to the page, as though from the tip of your nose, through this page, and out the other side.

```
z-index
```

Values:	number | auto | inherit
Default:	auto
Applies to:	positioned elements
Inherits:	no

The value of the **z-index** property is a number (positive or negative). The higher the number, the higher the element will appear in the stack. Lower numbers and negative values move the element lower in the stack. Let's look at an example to make this clear (Figure 15-25).

Here are three paragraph elements, each containing a letter image (A, B, and C, respectively) that have been positioned in such a way that they overlap on the page. By default, paragraph "C" would appear on top because it appears last in the source. However, by assigning higher **z-index** values to paragraphs "A" and "B," we can force them to stack in our preferred order.

Note that the values of **z-index** do not need to be sequential, and they do not relate to anything in particular. All that matters is that higher number values position the element higher in the stack.

The markup

```
<p id="A"><img src="A.gif" alt="A" /></p>
<p id="B"><img src="B.gif" alt="B" /></p>
<p id="C"><img src="C.gif" alt="C" /></p>
```

The style sheet

```
#A {
    z-index: 10;
    position: absolute;
    top: 200px;
    left: 200px;
}

#B {
    z-index: 5;
    position: absolute;
    top: 225px;
    left: 175px;
}
```

```
#C {
  z-index: 1;
  position: absolute;
  top: 250px;
  left: 225px;
}
```

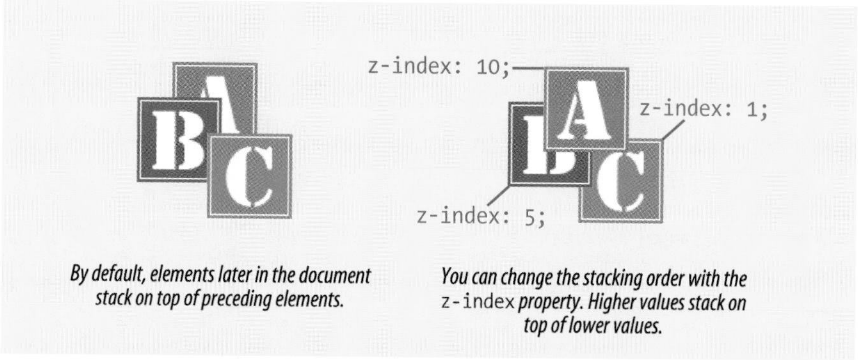

By default, elements later in the document stack on top of preceding elements.

You can change the stacking order with the z-index property. Higher values stack on top of lower values.

Figure 15-25. Changing the stacking order with the z-index *property.*

To be honest, the **z-index** property is not often required for most page layouts, but you should know it's there if you need it. If you want to guarantee that a positioned element always ends up on top, assign it a very high **z-index** value, such as:

```
img#essential {
  z-index: 100;
  position: absolute;
  top: 0px;
  left: 0px;
}
```

Fixed Positioning

We've covered relative and absolute positioning, so now it's time to take on the remaining method: fixed positioning.

WARNING

Fixed positioning is not supported in Internet Explorer 6.

For the most part, fixed positioning works just like absolute positioning. The significant difference is that the offset values for fixed elements are *always* relative to the viewport, which means the positioned element stays put even when the rest of the page scrolls. By contrast, you may remember that when you scrolled the Jenware page in Exercise 15-4, the award graphic scrolled along with the document—even though it was positioned relative to the initial containing block (equivalent to the browser window). Not so with fixed positioning, where the position is, well, *fixed*.

Fixed elements are often used for menus that stay in the same place at the top, bottom, or side of a screen so they are always available, even when the content scrolls. Please take a moment to read the sidebar "Watch Out for position:fixed on Mobile" for a heads-up on potential problems.

Let's switch the award graphic on the Jenware page to fixed positioning in Exercise 15-5 to see the difference.

exercise 15-5 | **Fixed positioning**

This should be simple. Open the Jenware page and edit the style rule for the **#award div** to make it **fixed** rather than **absolute**.

```
#award {
    position: fixed;
    top: 35px;
    left: 25px;
}
```

Save the document and open it in a browser. However, when you scroll the page, you will see that the award now stays put where we positioned it in the browser window (Figure 15-26).

Figure 15-26. The award graphic stays in the same place in the top-left corner of the browser window when the document scrolls.

Now you've been introduced to all the tools of the trade for CSS-based layout: floating and three types of positioning (relative, absolute, and fixed). You should have a good feel for how they work when we start putting them to use in the various design approaches and templates in Chapter 16.

Watch Out for position:fixed on Mobile

The **position: fixed** property causes some quirky behaviors on many mobile browsers as of this writing. Some treat it as merely static, letting it scroll with the rest of the content. Some "supporting" browsers scroll the fixed element off the screen but snap it back into place when the scrolling stops (at least one browser then miscalculates where it should land), resulting in an awkward user experience. Others cause everything to be jittery.

There are some fixes, but they have drawbacks. One solution is to disable the ability for the user to zoom the page, but that removes a useful usability feature. The other is to use a JavaScript solution to create the correct fixed positioning behavior, but that introduces a new level of complexity and potential for incompatible support. The best option is to consider whether you need a fixed element at all for good usability, then explore the JavaScript options as needed.

For a good description of the problem and links to JavaScript solutions, I recommend Brad Frost's article "Fixed Positioning in Mobile Browsers," located at *bradfrostweb. com/blog/mobile/fixed-position/*. Because device support issues change quickly, be sure to search for the latest recommendations.

Test Yourself

Before we move on, take a moment to see how well you absorbed the principles in this chapter.

1. Which of the following is *not* true of floated elements?

   a. All floated elements behave as block elements.

   b. Floats are positioned against the padding edge of the containing element.

   c. The contents of inline elements flow around a float, but the element box is unchanged.

   d. You must provide a **width** property for floated block elements.

2. Which of these style rules is incorrect? Why?

   a. `img { float: left; margin: 20px;}`

   b. `img { float: right; width: 120px; height: 80px; }`

   c. `img { float: right; right: 30px; }`

   d. `img { float: left; margin-bottom: 2em; }`

3. How do you make sure a "footer" **div** starts below a floated sidebar?

4. Write the name of the positioning method or methods (static, relative, absolute, or fixed) that best matches each of the following descriptions.

   a. Positions the element relative to a containing block.

   b. Removes the element from the normal flow.

   c. Always positions the element relative to the viewport.

   d. The positioned element may overlap other content.

   e. Positions the element in the normal flow.

   f. The space the element would have occupied in the normal flow is preserved.

g. The space the element would have occupied in the normal flow is closed up.

h. You can change the stacking order with `z-index`.

i. Positions the element relative to its original position in the normal flow.

CSS Review: Floating and Positioning Properties

Here is a summary of the properties covered in this chapter.

Property	Description
clear	Prevents an element from being laid out next to a float
float	Moves the element to the right or left and allows the following text to flow around it
position	Specifies the positioning method to be applied to the element
top, bottom, right, left	Specifies the offset amount from each respective edge
z-index	Specifies the order of appearance within a stack of overlapping positioned elements

PAGE LAYOUT WITH CSS

Now that you understand the principles of moving elements around on the page using CSS floats and positioning, we can put these tools to use in some standard page layouts. This chapter looks at the various approaches to CSS-driven web design and provides some simple templates that will get you on your way to building basic two- and three-column web pages.

Before we get started, it must be said that there are seemingly endless variations on creating multicolumn layouts with CSS. This chapter is intended to be a "starter kit." The templates presented here are simplified and may not work for every situation, although I've tried to point out the relevant shortcomings of each.

Page Layout Strategies

Before we start dissecting CSS layouts, let's talk about the various options for structuring a web page. As you know, web pages appear on browsers of all sizes, from tiny phone screens to cinema displays. In addition, users can resize their text, which has an impact on the layout of the page. Over time, several standard page layout approaches have emerged that address these issues in various ways:

- Fixed layouts stay put at a specific pixel width regardless of the size of the browser window or text size.

- Fluid (or liquid) layouts resize proportionally when the browser window resizes.

- Elastic layouts resize proportionally based on the size of the text.

- Hybrid layouts combine fixed and scalable areas.

Let's examine how each strategy works, as well as the reasons for and against using each of them.

Fixed layouts

Fixed layouts, as the name implies, are created at a specific pixel width as determined by the designer. Akin to print, they allow the designer to control the relationship of page elements, alignment, and line lengths (see the sidebar "Optimal Line Length"). This layout approach became popular due to the fact that folks have traditionally viewed the Web primarily on desktop monitors with ample real estate, and web designers were keen on reproducing designs that looked exactly the same on every screen. But as you know, times are a'changin', and we no longer make those assumptions or strive for pixel perfection.

When you design a page to be a specific width, you need to decide a couple of things. First, you need to pick the width, usually based on common monitor resolutions. As of this writing, most sites are designed to be 960 pixels wide or thereabouts to fit nicely in the most common 1,024 × 768 monitor resolution. Some designers keep their layouts narrower; some venture even larger as monitor resolution increases. Either way, it is a design decision.

You also need to decide where the fixed-width layout should be positioned in the browser window. By default, it stays on the left edge of the browser, with the extra space to the right of it. You can also center the page, splitting the extra space over left and right margins, which may make the page look as though it better fills the browser window. Figure 16-1 shows two fixed-width layouts, positioned differently in the browser window.

One of the main concerns with using fixed layouts is that if the user's browser window is not as wide as the page, the content on the right edge of the page will be hidden. Although it is possible to scroll horizontally, it may not always be clear that there is more content there in the first place. In addition, although the structure of the page doesn't change, if a user has text set to a very large size to make it easier to read, there may be very few words on a line and the layout may look awkward or break altogether.

Optimal Line Length

Line length is a measure of the number of words or characters in a line of text. The rule of thumb is that the optimal line length is 10 to 12 words or between 60 and 75 characters.

When line lengths grow too long, the text becomes more difficult to read. Not only is it hard to focus long enough to get to the end of a long line, but it also requires extra effort to find the beginning of the next.

Line length is at the heart of the debate over which layout technique is superior. In fluid layouts, line lengths might get too long when the browser is sized very wide. In fixed-width designs, line lengths may become awkwardly short if the text is sized large within narrow and rigid column widths. The elastic layout introduced later in this chapter, however, offers predictable line lengths even when the text is sized larger. This makes it a popular option for balancing design and accessibility priorities.

Figure 16-1. Examples of fixed layouts (left-aligned and centered).

```
#wrapper {width: 750px;
  position: absolute;
  margin-left: auto;
  margin-right: auto;
  border: 1px solid black;
  padding: 0px;}

#extras {position: absolute;
  top: 0px;
  left: 0px;
  width: 200px;
  background: orange; }

#main {margin-left: 225px;
  background-color: yellow;}
```

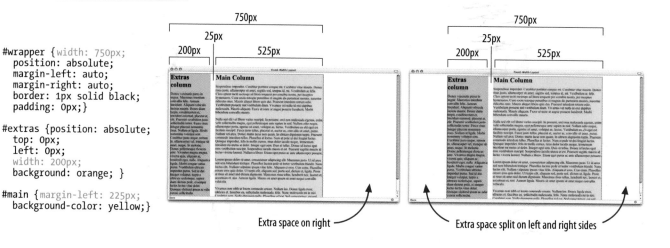

Let's review the pros and cons of the fixed-width strategy.

Advantages

The layout is predictable and offers better control over line length.

It is easier to design and produce.

It behaves the way the majority of web pages behave as of this writing, but that may change as users visit the web primarily on devices other than the desktop.

Disadvantages

Content on the right edge will be hidden if the browser window is smaller than the page.

There may be an awkward amount of leftover space on large screens.

Line lengths may grow awkwardly short at very large text sizes.

Takes control away from the user.

How to create fixed-width layouts

Fixed-width layouts are created by specifying width values in pixel units. Typically, the content of the entire page is put into a `div` (often named "content," "container," "wrapper," or "page") that can then be set to a specific pixel width. This `div` may also be centered in the browser window. Widths of column elements, and even margins and padding, are also specified in pixels. We will see examples of this technique later in this chapter.

CSS Grid Frameworks

Designers have been using grids for alignment and content organization since the early days of graphic design, and grid systems have become a useful tool for web designers as well. A grid is an invisible foundation that divides the page into equal units that can be used to determine where columns, headlines, images, and so on should fall (Figure 16-2). Sticking to grid units not only ensures that your content will be proportional, but it can also make design decisions go more quickly.

Many CSS grid frameworks (think of them as "kits") have emerged to help streamline the design and development process. Perhaps the most well known is the 960 Grid System (*960.gs*), which divides a 960-pixel-wide page into either 12- or 16-column units. Blueprint (*www.blueprintcss.org*) and BlueTrip (*bluetrip.org*) are based on similar fixed-width grids. For a fluid two- or three-column grid, there is YUI12 from Yahoo! (*developer.yahoo.com/yui/grids/*).

With the emergence of mobile, we are beginning to see responsive grid systems hit the scenes, including the 1140 CSS Grid (*cssgrid.net*), Skeleton (*getskeleton.com*), and Bootstrap from Twitter (*twitter.github.com/bootstrap*).

Of course, this is just a snapshot of the CSS framework scene as of this writing, and this list barely scratches the surface. By all means do a web search to find the latest and greatest. Using a framework requires solid HTML and CSS chops, but once you get up to speed, they may save you time. The downside is that the code tends to be more bloated than if it were handcrafted, and you may be forcing unnecessary data to download. For this reason, some designers use frameworks to speed up the design process but create custom code for the final site production.

If you are interested in learning more about grid systems and their benefits, I recommend the book *Ordering Disorder, Grid Principles for Web Design*, by Khoi Vinh (*grids.subtraction.com/*).

Figure 16-2. An example of a web page design using a 16-column grid system.

Fluid page design

In fluid page layouts (also called liquid layouts), the page area and columns within the page get wider or narrower to fill the available space in the browser window. In other words, they follow the default behavior of the normal flow. There is no attempt to control the width of the content or line breaks; the text is permitted to reflow as required and as is natural to the medium. Figure 16-3 shows the W3C site (*W3.org*), which is a good example of a liquid layout.

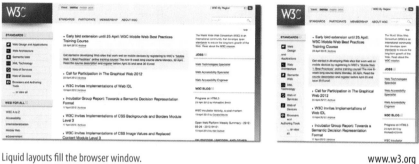

Liquid layouts fill the browser window.
Content reflows when the browser window and columns resize.

www.w3.org

Figure 16-3. Example of a fluid (liquid) layout.

NOTE

Ethan Marcotte (coiner of the term "responsive web design") talks about designing the W3C site with a fluid grid in his article "Fluid Grids" on A List Apart (www.alistapart.com/articles/fluidgrids/). It is evidence that using fluid layouts doesn't mean giving up all control.

Fluid layouts are a cornerstone of the responsive web design technique. Now that web designers are coming to terms with the vast variety of browser window and screen sizes, particularly those smaller than the traditional desktop monitor, many are moving to designs that flex to fill the browser width, whatever that might be. Because it is futile to try to build a fixed-width design for every screen size, I think fluid layouts will see a resurgence.

Of course, fluid layouts have both advantages and disadvantages.

Advantages	Disadvantages
Fluid layouts keep with the spirit and nature of the medium.	On large monitors, line lengths can get very long and uncomfortable to read.
They avoid potentially awkward empty space because the text fills the window.	They are less predictable. Elements may be too spread out or too cramped at extreme browser dimensions.
On desktop browsers, users can control the width of the window and content.	It may be more difficult to achieve whitespace.
No horizontal scrollbars.	There is more math involved in calculating measurements.

How to create fluid layouts

Create a fluid layout by specifying widths in percentage values. You may also simply omit the **width** attribute, in which case the width will be set to the default **auto** setting and the element will fill the available width of the window or other containing element.

In this two-column layout (Figure 16-4), the width of each **div** has been specified as a percentage of the available page width. The main column will always be 70% of the width of the window, and the right column fills 25% (the remaining 5% is used for the margin between the columns), regardless of the window size. You've already gotten a taste for this approach when you created a column with a float in Exercise 15-3 in the previous chapter.

One potential drawback to fluid layouts is overly long line lengths, but you can prevent the layout from becoming ridiculously wide by specifying a maximum width for the page (see the "Say 'Enough Is Enough' with max-width" sidebar later in this chapter). You can also use **min-width** to keep the page from getting crazy skinny. That gives you some of the advantages of a fixed layout while still providing flexibility at sizes in between.

Create a liquid layout by specifying widths in percentages.

NOTE

min-width and max-width are not supported by Internet Explorer 6, but there is an IE-specific CSS patch you can use if you really need to support that old dinosaur. Read about it on Cameron Moll's site here: www.cameronmoll.com/archives/000892.html.

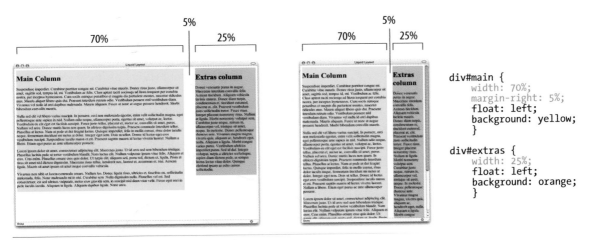

```
div#main {
    width: 70%;
    margin-right: 5%;
    float: left;
    background: yellow;
}

div#extras {
    width: 25%;
    float: left;
    background: orange;
}
```

Figure 16-4. Fluid layout using percentage values.

Elastic layouts

A third layout approach marries resizable text with predictable line lengths. Elastic layouts expand or contract with the size of the text. If the user makes the text larger, the box that contains it expands proportionally. Likewise, if the user likes her text size very small, the containing box shrinks to fit. The result is that line lengths (in terms of words or characters per line) stay the same regardless of the text size. This is an advantage over liquid layouts, where line lengths can get too long, and fixed layouts, where very large text may result in awkwardly few characters per line.

NOTE

Patrick Griffiths, the creator of Elastic Lawn, wrote about elastic layouts in the "Elastic Designs" article at A List Apart (alistapart.com/articles/elastic). It's getting on in years, but still provides good details on his method.

Figure 16-5 shows the Elastic Lawn design by Patrick Griffiths at CSS Zen Garden (*www.csszengarden.com/?cssfile=/063/063.css*), an oldie-but-goodie for showing elastic layout at work. Notice that when the text size gets bigger in each sample, so does the content area of the page. However, instead of rewrapping in the larger layout space, the linebreaks are the same.

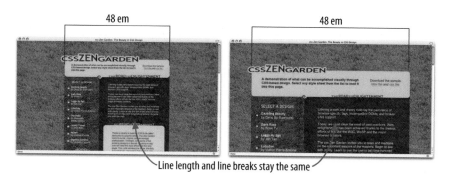

Figure 16-5. The Elastic Lawn design by Patrick Griffiths at CSS Zen Garden is a classic example of elastic page layout.

The full-page zoom feature offered by most current browsers has stolen some of elastic design's thunder. Now, all web pages appear to scale up proportionally, but elastic layouts can still address issues caused by users making changes to their default browser font size.

Proponents of elastic designs like that the proportions of the page are tied to the typographic content. In these days of unknown screen dimensions, it makes sense to design with our content elements as the core. However, elastic layouts have the same issues as fixed-width layouts at large sizes (although you can control that with a `max-width` property) and are generally not as useful as fluid layout in the mobile context. Another drawback is that although the page grid scales with the text, embedded media such as images and movies do not (there are solutions to that as well, but those are beyond the scope of this chapter).

It's time to review the pros and cons of elastic layouts:

Advantages	Disadvantages
Provide a consistent layout experience while allowing flexibility in text size. Tighter control over line lengths than liquid and fixed layouts.	Images and videos don't lend themselves to automatic rescaling along with the text and the rest of the layout (but there are methods to achieve this).
	The width of the layout might exceed the width of the browser window at largest text sizes.
	Not as useful for addressing device and browser size variety.
	More complicated to create than fixed-width layouts.

How to create elastic layouts

The key to elastic layouts is the em, the unit of measurement that is based on the size of the text. For example, for an element with 16-pixel text, an em is 16 pixels. It is common to specify **font-size** in ems. In elastic layouts, the dimensions of containing elements are specified in ems as well. That is how the widths can respond to the text size. For example, if the body text size is set to 16 pixels (the default size on most browsers), and the page is set to 40em, the resulting page width would be 640 pixels (40em × 16px/em). If the user resizes the text up to 20 pixels, the page grows to 800 pixels.

You create elastic layouts by specifying widths in em units.

Hybrid layouts

Layouts that use a combination of pixel, percentage, and em measurements are sometimes called hybrid layouts. In many scenarios, it makes sense to mix fixed and scalable content areas. For example, you might have a sidebar that contains a stack of ad banners that must stay a particular size. You could specify that sidebar at a particular pixel width and allow the column next to it to resize to fill the remaining space. You may remember that we created a page like that in Exercise 15-4.

Figure 16-6 illustrates a hybrid layout. The secondary column on the left is set to a specific pixel width, and the main content area is set to auto and fills the remaining space in the window. A word of warning: when you mix length units (px, %, and em), it becomes much more complicated to calculate page and element widths. But it's possible if there is a good reason to do so.

Which one should I use?

As you can see, each layout approach has its own advantages and drawbacks. And as layout trends come and go, we're seeing a shift from fixed, desktop-appropriate sites to fluid designs that are better suited to work well across all devices. You may find that a fluid layout works best for the smaller screen sizes in a responsive site, but a fixed layout gives you the control you

Figure 16-6. Hybrid layout combining fixed-width and auto sized columns.

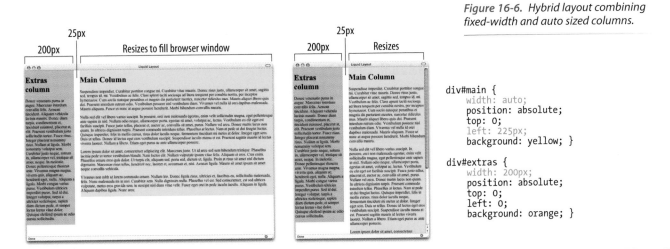

```
div#main {
    width: auto;
    position: absolute;
    top: 0;
    left: 225px;
    background: yellow; }

div#extras {
    width: 200px;
    position: absolute;
    top: 0;
    left: 0;
    background: orange; }
```

want when the page is viewed on very large monitors. Or perhaps your site is a complex intranet application that requires a fixed design and is likely to be used only on a desktop browser. So there is no "right" way, and it is important that you be familiar with all the options to make the best decision for your site or application based on its content, purpose, and primary use.

Page Layout Techniques

Here it is...the section you've been waiting for: how to create two- and three-column layouts using CSS. The examples in this section should give you a good head start toward understanding how layout works, but they are not universal solutions. Your content may dictate more complicated approaches.

This section provides templates and techniques for the following:

- Two- and three-column layouts using floats
- A source-independent layout using floats and negative margins
- A multicolumn layout using positioning

Using the examples

The sample pages in this section aren't pretty. In fact, I've stripped them down to their bare minimum to help make the structure and strategy as clear as possible. Here are a few notes regarding the templates and how to use them.

Simplified markup and styles

I've included only the bare minimum markup and styles in the examples— just enough to follow how each layout is created. All style rules not related to layout have been omitted to save space and to focus on what is needed to move elements around.

Color coding

I've added outlines (see the "CSS Outlines" sidebar) around each column so you can see the edges of the floated or positioned elements in the layout. The outlines are color coded with the markup and the styles that create them in an effort to make the connections more clear.

Headers and footers

I've included a header and footer on many of these examples, but either one or both could easily be omitted for a minimal two- or three-column layout.

Make it yours

There is obviously a lot more that could be done with text, backgrounds, margins, padding, and borders to make these pages more appealing. Once you've laid a framework with these templates, you should feel free to change the measurements and add your own styles.

NOTE

The HTML and CSS for all of the templates in this section are available in the materials folder for this chapter on learningwebdesign.com.

CSS Outlines

In the examples in this section, I've taken advantage of the **outline** property to reveal the edges of the floated and positioned columns. Outlines look like borders and the syntax is the same, but there is an important difference. Outlines, unlike borders, are not calculated in the width of the element box. They just lay on top, not interfering with anything. This makes outlines a great tool for checking your layout work because you can turn them on and off without affecting your width measurements.

The **outline** shorthand property combines values for width (**outline-width**), style (**outline-style**), and color (**outline-color**) properties, just like **border**.

```
div#links { outline: 2px
    dashed red; }
```

Multicolumn Layouts Using Floats

Floats are the primary tool for creating columns on web pages. As a tool, it is flawed, but it's the best that we've got as of this writing. See the sidebar "The Future of CSS Layout" for more sophisticated solutions that are just on the horizon.

The advantages that floats have over absolute positioning for layout are that they prevent content from overlapping other content, and they make it easier to keep footer content at the bottom of the page. The drawback is that they are dependent on the order in which the elements appear in the source, although there is a workaround using negative margins, as we'll see later in this section.

The following examples reveal the general strategy for approaching two- and three-column layouts using floats and should serve as a good head start toward implementing your own layouts.

The Future of CSS Layout

Cascading style sheets are constantly evolving to meet the needs of designers and developers, and there are some new layout technologies in the works that may free us from hacking together columns with floats and positioned elements.

Columns

The most straightforward layout improvement that is already being implemented in browsers is the ability to divide an element into honest-to-goodness columns. Thank heavens! You can specify a number of columns (`column-count`) or a specific column width that will repeat until it runs out of room (`column-width`). There's a lot more to it, of course, which you can read for yourself in the W3C CSS3 Multi-column Layout Module (*www.w3.org/TR/css3-multicol*). CSS columns are currently supported in Safari and Chrome with the `-webkit-` prefix, Firefox with the `-moz-` prefix, and in Opera and IE10 with no prefix.

Flexbox

The CSS Flexible Box Layout Model (known as Flexbox, for short) provides a much simpler way to arrange element boxes in relation to one another. For example, you can line children elements up within a parent, select where extra space appears, center things horizontally or vertically, and even change the order of appearance—all without resorting to floats and margin offsets and the tricky calculations that come with them. With Flexbox, you can basically just say, "Make this a box and center its child element horizontally and vertically within it." There's too much to the spec to even dabble in here, but

I recommend Stephen Hay's introductory article (*www.the-haystack.com/2012/01/04/learn-you-a-flexbox/*), as well as the Recommendation itself. Flexbox is currently supported on the very latest browser versions with vendor prefixes.

Grid layout system

Microsoft has begun implementing a collection of CSS properties that allow you to establish a grid of rows and columns for an element and then position other elements along that grid. This is in its very early stages as of this writing, but it is worth keeping an eye on. Read more about it at the W3C (*dev.w3.org/csswg/css3-grid-layout*) and the Microsoft Developer Network (*msdn.microsoft.com/library/ie/hh673536.aspx#_CSSGrid*).

Regions and Exclusions

Adobe, the company that brings you Photoshop and other designerly products, is making contributions to the CSS canon in the form of layout modules that duplicate some of the functionality of its page layout products. CSS Regions allow content to flow from one element into another, similar to the way text flows from text box to text box in InDesign. CSS Exclusions are a method for making text wrap around an irregular shape, such as you'd see in a magazine layout. You can read more about the development of these cutting-edge features at the W3C (*dev.w3.org/csswg/css3-regions* and *dev.w3.org/csswg/css3-exclusions*), as well as at the Adobe + HTML site (*html.adobe.com*).

NOTE

All of the layout examples in this section use margins to maintain space between columns. If you want to add padding and borders to the floated elements, remember to adjust the width values to accommodate them. Alternatively, you could set the box-sizing property to box-model (remembering vendor prefixes), and you won't need to figure paddings and borders into your calculations.

Two columns, fluid layout

In Exercise 15-3 in the previous chapter, we created a two-column layout by floating one element and using a margin on the second to make room for it. In the following examples, we'll float all the elements to one side. You can float columns to the left or right depending on the source order in your document and where you want each column to appear on the page. We'll start with a very simple two-column layout.

The strategy

Set widths on both column elements and float them to the left. Clear the footer to keep it at the bottom of the page. The underlying structure and resulting layout is shown in Figure 16-7.

The markup

```
<div id="header">Masthead and headline</div>

<div id="main">Main article</div>

<div id="extras">List of links and news</div>

<div id="footer">Copyright information</div>
```

The styles

```
#main {
   float: left;
   width: 60%;
   margin: 0 5%;
}
#extras {
   float: left;
   width: 25%;
   margin: 0 5% 0 0;
}
#footer {
   clear: left;
}
```

Remember the TRouBLe value order for margin: Top, Right, Bottom, Left.

Notes

This one is pretty straightforward, but because this is our first one, I'll point a few things out:

- Remember that I've omitted the header, footer, and text styles to keep the examples as simple as possible. Keep in mind that there is a bit more at work in here than what is listed under "The styles" (nothing you couldn't figure out, though: background colors, padding, stuff like that).

- The source document has been divided into four **div**s, one each for the header, main content, extras, and footer. The markup shows the order in which they appear in the source.

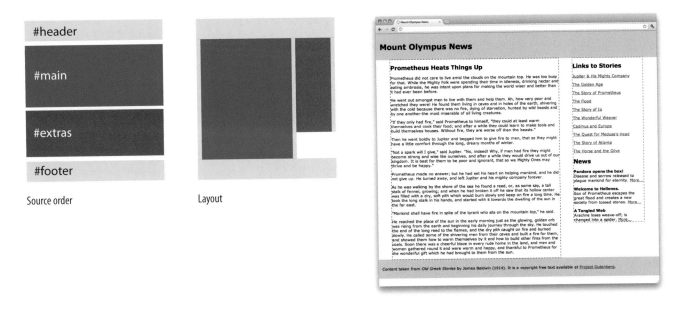

Figure 16-7. *Floating two columns.*

- Both #main and #extras have been floated to the left. Because they are floats, widths were specified for each. You can make your columns as wide as you like.

- The #main element has a 5% margin applied on the left and right sides. The #extras element only needs a margin on the right. The margins on the top have been set to zero so they vertically align.

- The #footer is cleared so it starts below the floated content.

NOTE

You could also float one column to the left and the other to the right for the same effect.

Say "Enough Is Enough" with max-width

Fluid layouts are great because they can adapt themselves to the screen or browser window size on which they are displayed. We spend a lot of time considering how our pages fare in small spaces, but don't forget that at the other end of the spectrum are high-resolution monitors approaching or exceeding 2,000 pixels in width. Users may not maximize their browser windows to fill the whole screen, but there is the potential for the browser window to be so wide that the text in your flexible columns becomes difficult to read.

You can put a stop to the madness with the `max-width` property. Apply it to the column element you are most concerned about becoming unreadable (like the #main column in the "two columns, fluid layout" example), or put the the whole page in a wrapper element and put the the brakes on the width of whole page.

Similarly, the `min-width` property is available if you want to prevent your page from looking too scrunched. Remember that neither property is supported in IE6.

Two columns, fixed-width layout

This time, let's make the layout fixed width instead of fluid.

The strategy

Wrap the content in a **div** to which we can set a specific pixel width. We'll specify pixel values for the floated elements as well, but the floating and clearing method is the same. The resulting layout is shown in Figure 16-8.

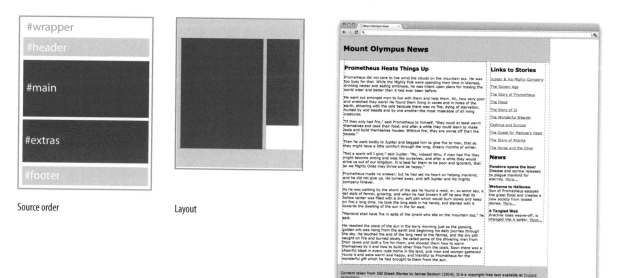

Source order   Layout

Figure 16-8. *A fixed width, two-column layout using floats.*

The styles

```css
#wrapper {
  width: 960px;
}
#main {
  float: left;
  width: 650px;
  margin: 0 20px;
}
#extras {
  float: left;
  width: 250px;
  margin: 0 20px 0 0;
}
#footer {
  clear: left;
}
```

The markup

```html
<div id="wrapper">

  <div id="header">Masthead and headline</div>

  <div id="main">Main article</div>

  <div id="extras">List of links and news</div>

  <div id="footer">Copyright information</div>

</div>
```

Notes

- All of the content is contained in a **#wrapper div** that has been set to the very popular 960-pixel width.

- The widths and margins have been changed to pixel measurements as well, taking care not to exceed a total of 960. If they added up to more than the width of the **#wrapper** container, we'd get the dreaded float drop. Keep in mind that if you add padding or borders, the total of their widths would need to be subtracted from the width values to keep the total width the same.

Two columns, fixed width, centered

At this point, it's really easy to center the fixed-width layout.

The strategy

Set the left and right margins on the **#wrapper** container to **auto**, which will keep the whole page centered. The markup is exactly the same as in the previous example. We only need to add a **margin** declaration to the styles. Easy as pie. The resulting layout is shown in Figure 16-9.

The styles

```
#wrapper {
  width: 960px;
  margin: 0 auto;
}
```

Notes

- The **auto** margin setting on the left and right sides keeps the **#wrapper** centered in the browser window.

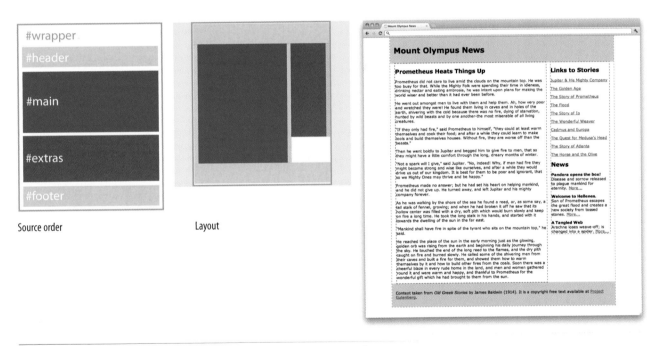

Figure 16-9. Our fixed-width layout is now centered in the browser window.

Full-Width Headers and Footers

If you wanted the **#header** and **#footer** to be the full browser width, but also wanted to keep the content between them fixed width and centered (Figure 16-10), change the markup so that only **#main** and **#extras** are inside the **#wrapper**. Everything else stays the same as the "two columns, fixed width, centered" example.

```
<div id="header">Masthead and headline</div>
<div id="wrapper">
  <div id="main">Main article</div>
  <div id="extras">List of links and news</div>
</div>
<div id="footer">Copyright information</div>
```

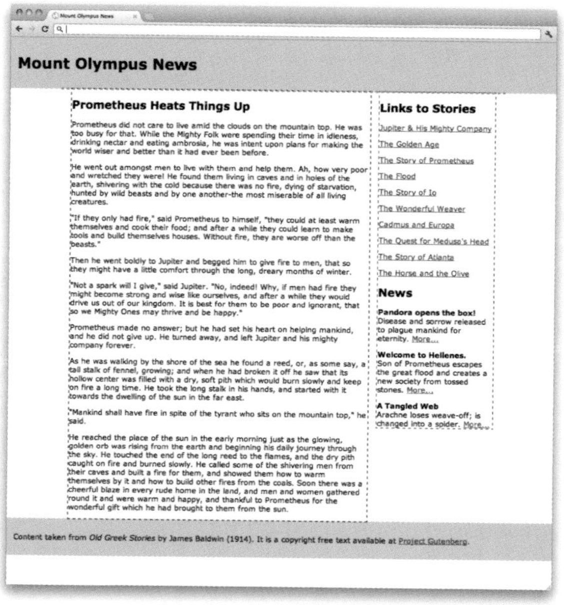

Figure 16-10. The header and footer fill the width of the browser, but the content between them remains a fixed width.

Three columns, fluid layout

I suspect you're getting the hang of it so far. Now we'll tackle three-column layouts, which use the same principles but take a little extra finagling. In this example, we'll float all of the elements to the left. Using simple floats, you will see that we are quite tied to the order in which the three floated elements appear in the source.

The strategy

Set widths on all three-column elements and float them to the left. Clear the footer to keep it at the bottom of the page. The underlying structure and resulting layout is shown in Figure 16-11.

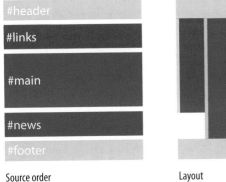

Source order   Layout

Figure 16-11. *A fluid-width, three-column layout using three floats.*

The markup

```
<div id="header">Masthead and headline</div>

<div id="links">List of links</div>

<div id="main">Main article</div>

<div id="news">News items</div>

<div id="footer">Copyright information</div>
```

The styles

```
#links {
    float: left;
    width: 22.5%;
    margin: 0 0 0 2.5%;
}
#main {
    float: left;
    width: 45%;
    margin: 0 2.5%;
}
#news {
    float: left;
    width: 22.5%;
    margin: 0 2.5% 0 0;
}
#footer {
    clear: left;
}
```

Notes

- The markup shows that we now have a total of five **div**s in the document: **#header**, **#links**, **#main**, **#news**, and **#footer**.

- Using simple floats alone, if we want the main content column to appear in the middle between the links and news columns, then the **#main div** needs to appear between the **#link**s and **#news div**s in the source. (We'll break free of source order in the upcoming "Any order columns using negative margins" example.)

- All three columns are given widths and floated to the left. Care must be taken to ensure that the total of the **width** and **margin** measurements is not greater than 100%.

exercise 16-1 | **You try it**

We've seen a lot of examples so far of two- and three-column layouts using floats, in both fluid and fixed-width layouts. I think it is time you try some of these techniques out using the three-column fluid layout we just looked at as a starting point. The file for this exercise, *mountolympus-ex1.html*, is in the *materials* folder for this chapter on *learningwebdesign.com*. The resulting styles are listed in Appendix A. The outline styles are included, but you can "comment them out" (wrap them in /* and */ to hide them) if you want to turn the outlines off and see the layout without them.

First, rearrange the side columns so that **#links** is on the right and **#news** is on the left. You don't need to change the markup, only a few style values. (Hint: think float direction.) Be sure to adjust the left and right margins on the side columns and clear the **#footer**.

Next, convert this fluid design into a centered, fixed-width design. This time you will need to add some markup (see the two-column fixed example if you need help). The resulting page is shown in Figure 16-12.

Figure 16-12. The resulting fixed-width layout with swapped side columns.

Any order columns using negative margins

When float-based layouts were beginning to gain steam, many designers wondered, "Is there a way to do three-column floats that is independent from the source order?" Turns out the answer was "Yes!" The trick is to use the magic of negative margin values and a heaping tablespoon of math (a little bit of math never hurt anyone, right?). The technique was first brought to light by Alex Robinson in his classic 2005 article "The Search for One True Layout" (*positioniseverything.net/articles/onetruelayout/*).

The strategy

Apply widths and floats to all three column elements, and use a negative margin to "drag" the left column across the page into the left position. The underlying structure and resulting layout is shown in Figure 16-13. Notice that although **#main** comes first in the source, it is in the second column position. In addition, the **#links div** (last in the source) is in the first column position on the left. This example is fixed, but you can do the same thing with a fluid layout using percentage values.

The markup

```
<div id="wrapper">

    <div id="header">Masthead and headline</div>

    <div id="main">Main article</div>

    <div id="news">News items</div>

    <div id="links">List of links</div>

    <div id="footer">Copyright information</div>

</div>
```

The styles

```
#wrapper {
  width: 960px;
  margin: 0 auto;
}
#main {
  float: left;
  width: 520px;
  margin-top: 0;
  margin-left: 220px;
  margin-right: 20px;
}
#news {
  float: left;
  width: 200px;
  margin: 0;
}
```

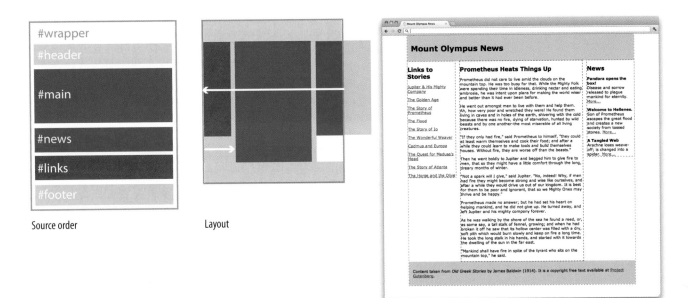

Figure 16-13. A fixed-width, three-column layout using three floats. It looks like the previous example, but it is special in that the column order is not the same as the source order.

```
#links {
    float: left;
    width: 200px;
    margin-top: 0;
    margin-left: -960px;
}
#footer {
    clear: left;
}
```

Notes

This one requires a bit more explanation, so we'll look at how it's done one step at a time.

In the markup, we see that **#main** comes first, presumably because it is the most important content, and **#links** comes last. The whole page is wrapped in a **#wrapper** so that it can be set to a specific width (960px). In the layout, however, the order of the columns from left to right is **#links** (200px wide), **#main** (520px wide), then **#news** (200px wide). This layout has 20 pixels of space between columns.

The first step to getting there is moving the **#main** content to the middle position by applying a left margin that pushes it over enough to make room for the left column (200px) plus the space between (20px). So, **margin-left: 220px**. While we're at it, we'll add a 20px right margin on **#main** as well to make room on its right side. Figure 16-14 shows how it looks after applying styles to **#main**.

NOTE

If you are required to support Internet Explorer 6, add a `display: inline;` *declaration to #main as well to fix a problem IE6 has with doubling left margins. It won't hurt anything on other browsers.*

Next—and this is the cool part—pull the content that you want to go in the left column (#links, in this case) to the left using a *negative* margin value. The trick is figuring out how far to the left it needs to be moved. If you look at Figure 16-14, you can see a ghostly version of #links that shows where it *wants* to be if the #wrapper were wide enough. I find it useful to look at the layout in that way because it makes it clear that we need to pull #links to the left by the widths of all the element boxes ahead of it in the source.

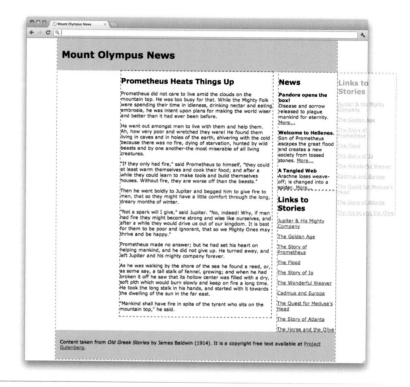

Figure 16-14. The layout after margins are applied to the middle (#main) column element. The shaded box on the right shows where #links would like to be if it weren't forced under #news.

In this example, the element box width for #main is 520px + 220px for the left margin + 20px for the right margin, for a total of 760 pixels. The total width of #news is 200px (no margins are applied). That means that the #links div needs to be pulled a total of 960 pixels to the left to land in the left column slot (margin-left: -960px;). When the negative margin is applied, #links slides into place and we have the final layout shown in Figure 16-13.

The negative margins technique can be used to position any number of columns in any order. In Exercise 16-2, you'll get a chance to rearrange the columns so that #news is on the left.

exercise 16-2 | **Using negative margins**

Now that you know the strategy, you should be able to write the styles that position the **#news** content in the left column and the **#links** on the right. This exercise is based on the same HTML source order as the previous example. Note, however, that the column width values have changed (to make things interesting). As before, put 20 pixels of space between columns.

If you'd like to play around with the actual files in a text editor, the *mountolympus-ex2.html* document is in the *materials* folder for this chapter. Otherwise, you can grab a pencil and write in the style rules below. The final styles are provided in Appendix A.

Remember, the key is to move **#news** to the left, using a negative margin, by the total width of the elements that precede it in the source.

```
#main {
   float: left;
   width: 400px;
   /* write your margin declarations below */


}
#news {
   float: left;
   width: 300px;
   /* write your margin declarations below */


}
#links {
   float: left;
   width: 220px;
   /* write your margin declarations below */


}
```

The resulting layout should look like the one shown in Figure 16-15.

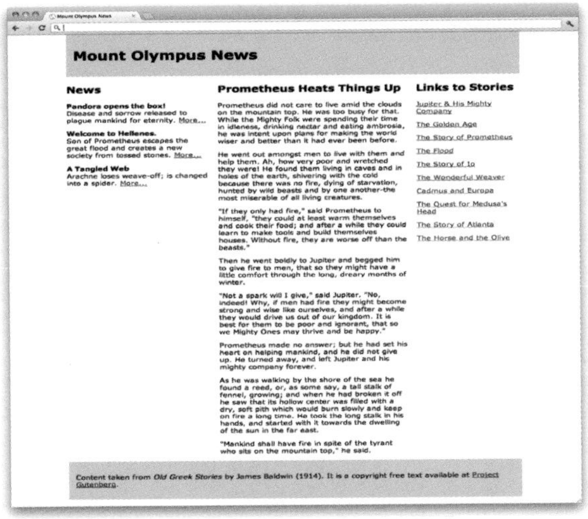

Figure 16-15. The final three-column layout in Exercise 16-2.

Positioned Layout

I think we've got floated columns covered. The other way to create columns in a layout is to use absolute positioning. Back in Exercise 15-4, we created a hybrid two-column layout with a positioned, fixed-width column. In this section, we'll use positioning to arrange three columns in both fluid and fixed-width pages.

Note that in both examples, I have omitted the **#footer** element. I've done this for a couple of reasons. First, when you position all of the elements in a layout, as we will in these examples, they no longer "participate in the layout," which means there is nothing to hold a footer at the bottom of the page. It will rise right up to the top. There are solutions to this problem using JavaScript, but they are beyond the scope of this chapter.

But say we position only the two side columns and let the main center column stay in the flow to hold the footer down. This is certainly a possibility, but if either of the side columns grows longer than the center column, it will overlap the footer content. Between leaping footers and potential overlaps, it's just kind of messy, which is why I've chosen to omit the footer here (and why floats are the more popular layout technique).

Three columns, positioned, fluid layout

Figure 16-16. Three positioned, fluid columns

This layout uses percentage values to create three flexible columns. The resulting layout is shown in Figure 16-16.

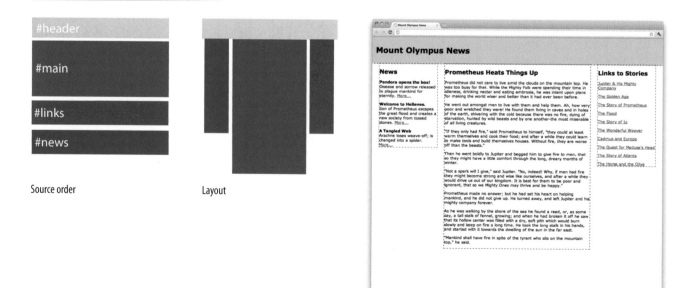

Source order   Layout

The strategy

Wrap the three content divs (#main, #news, #links) in a div (#content) to serve as a containing block for the three positioned columns. Then give the column elements widths and position them in the containing #content element.

The markup

```
<div id="header">Masthead and headline</div>

<div id="content">
  <div id="main">Main article</div>

  <div id="news">News items</div>

  <div id="links">List of links</div>
</div>
```

Notes

I think that you'll find the styles for this layout to be fairly straightforward.

- I created the **#content** containing block to position the columns because we want the columns to always start below the **#header**. If we positioned them relative to the browser window (the initial containing block), they may be in the wrong spot if the height of the header should change, such as the result of the **h1** text changing size. Make the **#content div** a containing block by applying the declaration **position: relative**.

- The **#main div** is given a width of 50%, and absolute positioning is used to place it at the top of the **#content div** and 25% from the left edge. This will accommodate the 20% width of the left column plus the 2.5% margin to the left and right of it.

- The **#news div** is positioned at the top of the **#content div** and 2.5% from the left edge (top: 0; left: 2.5%;).

- The **#links div** is positioned at the top of the **#content div** (**top: 0; right: 2.5%;**) and 2.5% from the right edge. No need to calculate the position from the left edge...just put it on the right! Note that we could have positioned the **#news** and **#links** columns flush against their respective edges and used padding to make a little space on the sides. There are usually multiple ways to approach layout goals.

- The only trick to getting this right is making sure your **width** and **margin** measurements do not exceed 100%. Remember to factor in padding and borders as well.

The styles

```
#content {
  position: relative;
  margin: 0;
}
#main {
  width: 50%;
  position: absolute;
  top: 0;
  left: 25%;
  margin: 0;
}
#news {
  width: 20%;
  position: absolute;
  top: 0;
  left: 2.5%;
  margin: 0;
}
#links {
  width: 20%;
  position: absolute;
  top: 0;
  right: 2.5%;
  margin: 0;
}
```

Three columns, positioned, fixed

If you prefer to have pixel-level control over your positioned layout, that's pretty easy to do, as we'll see in this example (Figure 16-17). It differs from the previous fluid example in that the whole page is contained in a **#wrapper** so it can be fixed and centered, and pixel values are used for the measurements. To save space, I'll just show you the resulting styles here. The positioning strategy is the same.

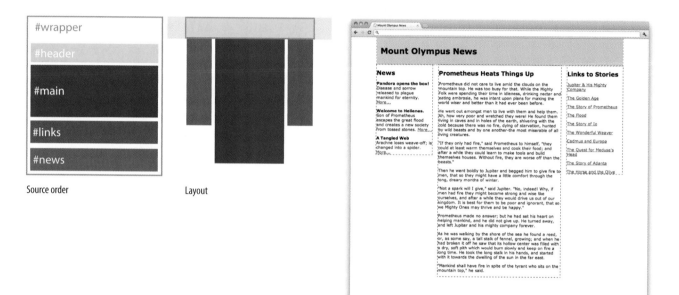

Figure 16-17. *Three positioned columns in a centered, fixed-width page.*

The styles

```
#wrapper {
  width: 960px;
  margin: 0 auto;
}
#content {
  margin: 0;
  position: relative;
}
#main {
  width: 520px;
  position: absolute;
  top: 0;
  left: 220px;
  margin: 0;
}
```

```
#news {
  width: 200px;
  position: absolute;
  top: 0;
  left: 0;
  margin: 0;
}
#links {
  width: 200px;
  position: absolute;
  top: 0;
  right: 0;
  margin: 0;
}
```

Top-to-Bottom Column Backgrounds

Adding color to columns is an effective way to further emphasize the division of information and bring a little color to the page. But if you take a look at the dashed borders in all the screenshot examples we've seen so far, you'll see that the column element often stops well before the bottom of the page. This means we need to get fancy if we want to apply backgrounds from top to bottom.

Unfortunately, there is no supported way of setting the height of an element to 100% of the page height, and although there are JavaScript workarounds and the emerging Flexbox spec that produce full-height column elements, they are beyond the scope of this chapter.

But don't fret. There is a reliable solution known affectionately as the "faux columns" trick that will work with any of the fixed-width templates in this chapter. In this technique, you create a graphic with the column colors in their proper positions and apply it as a vertically tiling background image to the page or containing element (such as **#wrapper** in the examples). The Faux Columns method was first introduced by Dan Cederholm in his 2004 article for *A List Apart*, and in his book *Web Standards Solutions*.

Here's how it works. The column shading in Figure 16-18 is the result of a horizontal image with bands of color that match the width of the columns. When the image is set to tile vertically in the background, the result is vertical stripes over which a multicolumn layout may be positioned. This method works only when the width of the column or page is set in a specific pixel measurement. We'll get to fluid column backgrounds in a moment.

You may recognize the layout in Figure 16-18 as the two-column, fixed-centered layout we made earlier in Figure 16-9. This time, it has the *two_columns.png* graphic tiling vertically in the **#wrapper** element.

```
#wrapper {
    width: 960px;
    margin: 0 auto;
    background-image: url(two_columns.png);
    background-repeat: repeat-y;
}
```

NOTE

If your layout lacks a footer *element to hold the container element open after the columns are floated, apply* overflow: hidden; *to the* #wrapper *to make it stretch around the floats.*

Figure 16-18. A tiling background image is used to create colored columns.

two_columns.png

Faux columns for fluid layouts

Now that you understand the basic technique, you may be wondering how to make it work for columns of varying widths. The secret is a *really, really* wide background graphic and the `background-position` property.

We may not know the exact width of the columns in a fluid layout, but we *do* know the point at which the columns are divided. Let's use the twocolumn fluid example from Figure 16-7 as an example. The column division occurs 67.5% from the left edge (5% left margin + 60% `#main` column width + 2.5%, which is half of the 5% space between margins).

Over in Photoshop (or your image editor of choice), create a horizontal image that is wider than any monitor is likely to go—3,000 pixels ought to do it. Because the graphic needs to be only a few pixels high and is likely to be made up of a few flat colors, the file size should stay pretty small. When you create the column colors, make sure they match the proportion of your columns. In our example, the left column background should fill 67.5% of the width of the graphic (67.5% × 3,000 = 2,025 pixels).

Apply the wide image as a background pattern to the **body** element, and use `background-position` to align the point where the color changes in the graphic (67.5%) with the point where the columns divide on the page (also 67.5%). In that way, the column break in the image will always be centered in the space between the columns. And there you have it—faux columns that expand and contract with the column widths.

```
body {
    background-image: url(two_cols_3000px.png);
    background-repeat: repeat-y;
    background-position: 67.5%;
}
```

two_cols_3000px.png

Figure 16-19. The background image is anchored at the point between the two columns, so when the browser window gets larger or smaller, it is always in the right place. The graphic file is wide enough that there will be enough image to fill both columns, even on the widest of browsers.

Three faux columns

Well, that works for two columns, but what about three? It is possible, thanks to the "Liquid Bleach" technique introduced by Doug Bowman. It's called Liquid Bleach because that's the name Doug gave his "Bleach" blog template after he converted it to a fluid layout.

Fundamentally, the process is the same as the one we just saw: position a really wide background graphic proportionally in a container **div**. But for three columns, you position two background images. One image provides the color band for the left column, and the remaining right portion is transparent. A second image provides the color for the right column, with its left portion remaining transparent (Figure 16-20). The background color of the page shows through the transparent areas and provides the color for the middle column.

The markup requires two containers. I've named them **#wrapper** and **#inner** in this example:

```
<div id="wrapper">
  <div id="inner">
        <div id="main"></div>
        <div id="news"></div>
        <div id="links"></div>
        </div> <!-- end inner div -->
</div>    <!-- end wrapper div -->
```

The left column graphic goes in **#wrapper**, positioned at the point between the left and center columns (26.25% for the example in Figure 16-20). The right column graphic goes in **#inner**, positioned between the center and right columns (73.75%). When the browser window resizes, the background images stay put at their proper point between columns and the background color fills in the space in between.

NOTE

Transparent GIFs and PNGs are discussed in Chapter 21, "Web Graphics Basics."

NOTE

You could achieve the same effect by placing multiple background images in the #wrapper, which does away with the need for the extra markup. Simply position one image to tile vertically on the left side and another to tile down the right side. The images should be wide enough to extend from the percentage point of the column division well beyond the edges of the browser window. The downside is that it won't work on IE6 through 8 or on really old versions of Firefox.

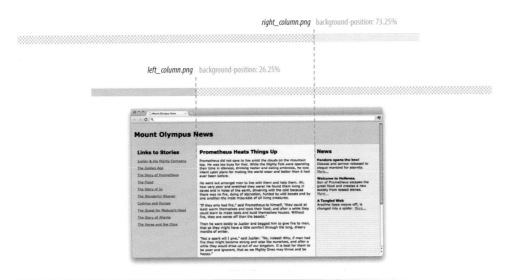

Figure 16-20. Faux columns for a fluid, three-column layout.

Test Yourself

If you successfully created multiple-column layouts in the exercises, then you've gotten the main point of this chapter. Here are a few questions to make sure you got the finer details of layout strategy.

1. Match each layout type with the factor that determines the final size of the page area.

   Fixed-width layouts   a. The browser window

   Fluid layouts   b. Font size

   Elastic layouts   c. The designer

2. Match each layout type with the unit of measurement used to create it.

   Fixed-width layouts   a. Ems

   Fluid layouts   b. Pixels

   Elastic layouts   c. Percentages and/or **auto**

3. Match each layout type with its primary potential advantage.

   Fixed-width layouts   a. Predictable line lengths

   Fluid layouts   b. No awkward "leftover" space

   Elastic layouts   c. Pixel-perfect layout grid

4. Match each layout type with its potential disadvantage.

   Fixed-width layouts   a. Uncomfortably long line lengths

   Fluid layouts   b. Images don't scale with the page

   Elastic layouts   c. Right side of the page gets cut off on narrow browser windows

TRANSITIONS, TRANSFORMS, AND ANIMATION

We've seen CSS used for visual effects like rounded corners, color gradients, and drop shadows that previously had to be created with graphics. In this chapter, we'll look at some CSS3 properties for producing animated interactive effects that were previously only possible with Flash or JavaScript.

We'll start with CSS Transitions, a nifty way to make style changes fade smoothly from one to another. Then we'll discuss CSS Transforms for repositioning, scaling, rotating, and skewing elements and look at how you can animate them with transitions. I'm going to close out the chapter with brief introductions to 3D Transforms and CSS Animation, which are important to know about but are too vast a topic to cover here, so I'll give you just a taste.

The problem with this chapter is that animation and time-based effects don't work on paper, so I can't show them off right here. I did the next best thing, though, and you can interact with most of the figures in this chapter online at *www.learningwebdesign.com/4e/chapter17/figures.html*.

Ease-y Does It (CSS Transitions)

Picture in your mind, if you will, a link in a navigation menu that changes from blue to red when the mouse hovers over it. The background is blue... mouse passes over it...BAM! Red! It goes from state to state instantly, with no states in between. Now imagine putting your mouse over the link and the background gradually changes from blue to red, passing through several shades of purple on the way. It's smoooooth. And when you remove the mouse, it fades back down to blue again.

That's what CSS Transitions do. They smooth out otherwise abrupt changes from state to state over time by filling in the frames in between. Animators call that tweening. When used subtly and with reserve, they can add sophistication and polish to your interface and make them more pleasing to use.

CSS Transitions were originally developed by the WebKit team for the Safari browser, but they are now a Working Draft at the W3C. As of this writing, the set of transition properties is still pretty cutting-edge and the specification is

IN THIS CHAPTER

Creating smooth transitions

Moving, rotating, and scaling elements

Combining transitions and transforms

A few words about 3D transforms

A few words about keyframe animations

NOTE

You can read CSS Transitions Module for yourself at ww.w3.org/TR/css3-transitions/.

WARNING

The CSS Transitions module is going through some transitions itself. This is a snapshot as it was as of this writing, but you should be sure to check the W3C site for the latest developments.

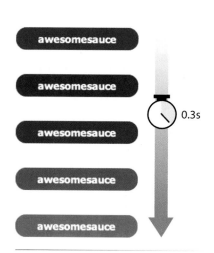

Figure 17-1. The background color of this link gradually fades from blue to red when ~~awesome sauce~~ a transition is applied.

likely to change, so all browsers that support transitions require their respective browser prefixes. They have good support (with prefixes) on iOS, Android, and Opera mobile browsers as well.

The only browser versions that do *not* support transitions at all are Internet Explorer 9 and earlier, Firefox 3.6 and earlier, and Opera 10.1 and earlier. But if you use transitions for progressive enhancement, it shouldn't matter too much that users of those browsers won't see the effects. For those folks, snapping directly from blue to red is not a big deal.

Transition basics

Transitions are a lot of fun, so let's give them a whirl. When applying a transition, you have a few decisions to make, each of which is set with a CSS property:

- Which CSS property to change (**transition-property**)
- How long it should take (**transition-duration**)
- The manner in which the transition accelerates (**transition-timing-function**)
- Whether there should be a pause before it starts (**transition-delay**)

You also need something to trigger the transition. A state change such as **:hover**, **:focus**, or **:active** makes a good trigger, and that's what we'll be using for the examples in this chapter. You could use JavaScript to change the element (such as adding a **class** attribute) and use that as a transition trigger as well.

Let's put that all together with a simple example. Here is that blue-to-red link you imagined earlier (Figure 17-1). There's nothing special about the markup. I added a **class** name so I could be specific about which links receive transitions.

The transition properties are applied to the **a** element in its normal state. You'll see them in the set of other declarations for **a.smooth**, like **padding** and **background-color**. This allows them to be reused for other state changes in the document. I've changed the background color of the link to red by declaring the **background-color** for the **:hover** state (and **:focus** too, in case someone is tabbing through links on a keyboard).

The markup

```
<a href="" class="smooth">awesomesauce</a>
```

The styles

```
a.smooth {
  display: block;
  text-decoration:none;
  text-align: center;
  padding: 1em 2em;
```

```
      width: 10em;
      border-radius: 1.5em;
      color: #fff;
      background-color: mediumblue;
      transition-property: background-color;
      transition-duration: 0.3s;
    }
    a.smooth:hover, a.smooth:focus {
      background-color: red;
    }
```

Specifying the property

transition-property

`NEW IN CSS3`

Values: *property-name* | all | none

Default: all

Applies to: *all elements,* :before *and* :after *pseudo-elements*

Inherits: *no*

transition-property identifies the CSS property that we want to transition smoothly. In our example, it's the **background-color**. You can also change the foreground color, borders, dimensions, font- and text-related attributes, and many more. The complete list (as of this writing) is listed in Table 17-1. More properties are likely to be added to this list as browsers implement them, so check the spec for updates.

How long should it take?

transition-duration

`NEW IN CSS3`

Values: *time*

Default: 0s

Applies to: *all elements,* :before *and* :after *pseudo-elements*

Inherits: *no*

transition-duration sets the amount of time it will take for the animation to complete in seconds (**s**) or milliseconds (**ms**). I've chosen .3 seconds, which is just enough to notice something happened but not so long that the transition feels sluggish or slows the user down. There is no correct duration, of course, but my travels I've found that .2s seems to be a popular transition time for UI elements. Experiment to find the duration that makes sense for your application.

Table 17-1.
Animatable CSS properties

Backgrounds
- background-color
- background-position

Borders and outlines
- border-bottom-color
- border-bottom-width
- border-left-color
- border-left-width
- border-right-color
- border-right-width
- border-top-color
- border-top-width
- border-spacing
- outline-color
- outline-offset
- outline-width

Color and opacity
- color
- opacity
- visibility

Font and text
- font-size
- font-weight
- letter-spacing
- line-height
- text-indent
- text-shadow
- word-spacing
- vertical-align

Element box measurements
- height
- width
- max-height
- max-width
- min-height
- min-width
- margin-bottom
- margin-left

Continued on following page.

margin-right

margin-top

padding-bottom

padding-left

padding-right

padding-top

crop

Position

top

right

bottom

left

z-index

clip

**Transforms
(not in the spec as of this writing,
but supported)**

transform

transform-origin

Timing functions

transition-timing-function
NEW IN CSS3

Values:	ease | linear | ease-in | ease-out | ease-in-out | step-start | step-end | steps | cubic-bezier(*#,#,#,#*)
Default:	ease
Applies to:	*all elements,* :before *and* :after *pseudo-elements*
Inherits:	*no*

The property and the duration form the foundation of a transition, but you can refine it further. There are a number of ways a transition can roll out over time. For example, it could start out fast and then slow down, start out slow and speed up, or it could stay the same speed all the way through, just to name a few. I think of it as the transition "style," but in the spec, it is known as the timing function.

I can set the **transition-timing-function** to ease-in-out to make the link change from blue to red more gently. To be honest, at very short durations, the differences are barely noticeable.

```
a.smooth {
    …
    transition-property: background-color;
    transition-duration: 0.3s;
    transition-timing-function: ease-in-out;
}
```

The **transition-timing-function** property takes one of the following keyword values:

ease

> Starts slowly, accelerates quickly, and then slows down at the end. This is the default value and works just fine for most short transitions.

linear

> Speed stays consistent from the transition's beginning to end.

ease-in

> Starts slowly, then speeds up.

`ease-out`

Starts out fast, then slows down.

`ease-in-out`

Starts slowly, speeds up, and then slows down again at the very end. It is similar to **ease**, but with less pronounced acceleration in the middle.

`cubic-bezier(#,#,#,#)`

This is a function for defining a Bezier curve that describes the transition acceleration. It's super math-y and I can't explain it all here. You can read how to do it in the spec (*www.w3.org/TR/css3-transitions/#transition-timing-function-property*) if none of the keywords suit you.

`steps(#, start|end)`

Divides the transitions into a number of steps as defined by a stepping function. The first value is the number of steps, and the **start** and **end** keywords define whether the change in state happens at the beginning (**start**) or end of each step. See the spec for details.

`step-start`

This changes states in one step, at the beginning of the duration time (the same as **steps(1,start)**). The result is a sudden state change, the same as if no transition had been applied at all.

`step-end`

This changes states in one step, at the end of the duration time (the same as **steps(1,end)**).

I can't demonstrate the various options on the page, but I have put together a little demo online (Figure 17-2). The width of each labeled element (white with an orange border) transitions over the course of four seconds when you hover over the blue box. They all arrive at their full width at exactly the same time, but they get there in different manners.

NOTE

As of this writing, only the Chrome browser has implemented stepping functions, so start with Chrome if you want the full effect.

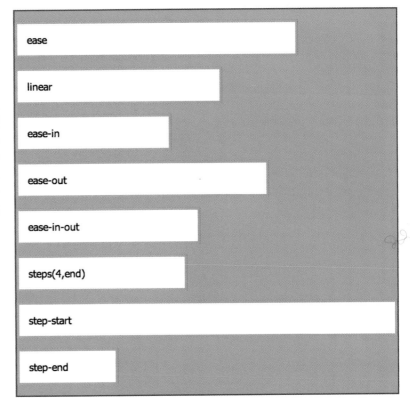

Figure 17-2. In this `transition-timing-function` *demo, the elements reach full width at the same time but vary in the manner in which they get there.*

Setting a delay

`transition-delay`

NEW IN CSS3

Values:　time

Default:　0s

Applies to:　all elements, `:before` and `:after` pseudo elements

Inherits:　no

The **transition-delay** property, as you might guess, delays the start of the animation by a specified amount of time. In the following example, the background color transition will start .2 seconds after the pointer moves over the link.

```
a.smooth {
  ...
  transition-property: background-color;
  transition-duration: 0.3s;
  transition-timing-function: ease-in-out;
  transition-delay: 0.2s;
}
```

If you were especially dastardly, you could make a button disappear (**opacity: 0;**) after a person has held his finger or pointer down on it (**:active**) for two seconds (**transition-delay; 2s;**) as shown in the following example and Figure 17-3. That'll teach him to be indecisive! Of course, **transition-delay** has useful and less nefarious applications.

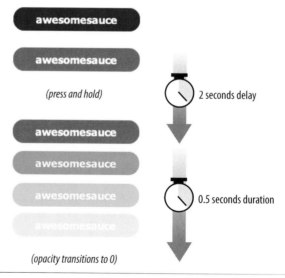

Figure 17-3. The transition-delay *property starts the animation effect (in this case making the button disappear using the* opacity *property) after two seconds.*

```
a.smooth {
  …
  transition-property: opacity;         -
  transition-duration: .05s;
  transition-timing-function: ease-out;
  transition-delay: 2s;
}
a.smooth:hover, a.smooth:focus {
  background-color: red;
}
a.smooth:active {
  opacity: 0;
}
```

I want to note that I've been using the non-prefixed properties throughout my examples to make them easier to follow, but remember that you must include vendor prefixes for all browsers if you use transitions in your pages. Always include the non-prefixed version last for forward-compatibility with supporting browsers of the future. This is how that blue-to-red link transition we've been working on would be written out in the real world:

```
a.smooth {
  …
  -webkit-transition-property: background-color;
  -webkit-transition-duration: 0.3s;
  -webkit-transition-timing-function: ease-in-out;
  -webkit-transition-delay: 0.2s;

  -moz-transition-property: background-color;
  -moz-transition-duration: 0.3s;
  -moz-transition-timing-function: ease-in-out;
  -moz-transition-delay: 0.2s;

  -o-transition-property: background-color;
  -o-transition-duration: 0.3s;
  -o-transition-timing-function: ease-in-out;
  -o-transition-delay: 0.2s;

  -ms-transition-property: background-color;
  -ms-transition-duration: 0.3s;
  -ms-transition-timing-function: ease-in-out;
  -ms-transition-delay: 0.2s;

  transition-property: background-color;
  transition-duration: 0.3s;
  transition-timing-function: ease-in-out;
  transition-delay: 0.2s;
}
```

It's extra work, but that's the way it is for the foreseeable future until all the old browsers fade away and the spec is stable and implemented consistently. Fortunately, there is a shortcut that helps cut down on all that code.

The shorthand transition property

Thankfully, the authors of the CSS3 spec had the good sense to give us the shorthand **transition** property to combine all of these properties into one declaration. You've seen this sort of thing with the shorthand **border** property. Here is the syntax:

```
transition: property duration timing-function delay;
```

The values for each of the **transition-*** properties are listed out, separated by character spaces. If you provide only one time value, it will be assumed to be the duration. If you provide two time values, make sure that the duration is listed first.

Using the blue-to-red link example, the four transition properties we've applied so far could be combined into this one line:

```
a.smooth {
    …
    transition: background-color 0.3s ease-in-out 0.2s;
}
```

And the full prefixed version is reduced from 20 lines to 5.

```
a.smooth {
    …
    -webkit-transition: background-color 0.3s ease-in-out 0.2s;
    -moz-transition: background-color 0.3s ease-in-out 0.2s;
    -o-transition: background-color 0.3s ease-in-out 0.2s;
    -ms-transition: background-color 0.3s ease-in-out 0.2s;
    transition: background-color 0.3s ease-in-out 0.2s;
}
```

Definitely an improvement.

Applying multiple transitions

So far, we've changed only one property at a time, but it is possible to transition several properties at once. Let's go back to the "awesomesauce" link example. This time, in addition from changing from blue to red, I'd like the **letter-spacing** to increase a bit. I also want the text color to change to black, but more slowly than the other animations. Figure 17-4 attempts to show these transitions on a printed page.

One way to do this is to list all of the values for each property separated by commas, as shown in this example.

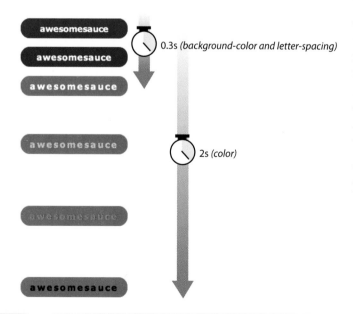

Figure 17-4. The color, background-color, *and* letter-spacing *change at different paces.*

```
a.smooth {
  …
  transition-property: background-color, color, letter-spacing;
  transition-duration: 0.3s, 2s, 0.3s;
  transition-timing-function: ease-out, ease-in, ease-out;

}
a:hover, a:focus {
    background-color: red;
    letter-spacing: 3px;
    color: black;
}
```

The values are matched up according to their positions in the list. For example, the transition on the **color** property (second in the list) has a duration of two seconds (2s) and uses the **ease-in** timing function. If one list has fewer values than the others, the browser repeats the values in the list, starting over at the beginning. In the previous example, if I had omitted the third value (.3s) for **transition-duration**, the browser would loop back to the beginning of the list and use the first value (.3s) for **letter-spacing**. In this case, the effect would be the same.

You can line up values for the shorthand **transition** property as well. The same set of styles we just saw could also be written as:

```
a.smooth {
  …
  transition: background-color 0.3s ease-out,
    color 2s ease-in,
    letter-spacing 0.3s ease-out;
}
```

That seems like a nice way to go, especially when you consider you have four vendor-prefixed versions to add to each transition declaration.

A transition for all occasions

But what if you just want to add a little bit of smoothness to all your state changes, regardless of which property might change? For cases when you want the same duration, timing function, and delay to apply to all transitions that might occur on an element, use the **all** value for **transition-property**. In the following example, I've specified that any property that might change for the **a.smooth** element should last .2 seconds and animate using the **ease-in-out** function.

```
a.smooth {
  …
  -webkit-transition: all 0.2s ease-in-out;
  -moz-transition: all 0.2s ease-in-out;
  -o-transition: all 0.2s ease-in-out;
  -ms-transition: all 0.2s ease-in-out;
  transition: all 0.2s ease-in-out;
}
```

For user interface changes, a short, subtle transition is often all you need for all your transitions, so the **all** value will come in handy.

Well, that wraps up our lesson on CSS3 Transitions. Now you give it a try in Exercise 17-1.

exercise 17-1 | **Trying out transitions**

In this exercise, we're going to create the rollover and active states for a menu link (Figure 17-5) with animated transitions. I've put together a starter document (*exercise1.html*) for you in the *materials* folder for this chapter. The resulting code is in Appendix A. I recommend that you use a current version of a WebKit-based browser (Chrome or Safari) to view your work.

1. First, take a look at the styles that are already applied. The list has been converted to a horizontal menu using floats. The **a** element has been set to display as a block element, underlines are turned off, dimensions and padding are applied, and the color, background color, and border are established. I used the **box-shadow** property to make it look as though the links are floating off the page.

2. Now we'll define the styles for the hover and focus states. When the user puts the pointer over or tabs to the link, make the background color change to gold (**#fdca00**) and the border color change to orange (**#fda700**).

    ```
    a:hover, a:focus {
      background-color: #fdca00;
      border-color: #fda700;
    }
    ```

3. While the user clicks or taps the link (**:active**), make it move down by three pixels as though it is being pressed. Do this by setting the **a** element's position to relative, then change the value the **top** property for the active state. This moves the link three pixels away from the top edge (in other words, down).

    ```
    a {
      …
      position: relative;
    }
    a:active {
      top: 3px;
    }
    ```

4. Logically, if the button were pressed down, there would be less room for the shadow, so we'll reduce the **box-shadow** distance as well.

    ```
    a:active {
      top: 3px;
      box-shadow: 0 1px 2px rgba(0,0,0,.5);
    }
    ```

5. Save the file and give it a try in the browser. The links should turn yellow and move down when you click or tap them. I'd say it's pretty good just like that. Even without the box shadows, which is how users of IE8 and earlier will see them, they look and work just fine. Now we can enhance the experience by adding some smooth transitions.

6. Make the background and border color transition ease in over .2 seconds, and see how that changes the experience of using the menu. I'm using the shorthand **transition** property to keep the code simple. I'm also using the default **ease** timing function at first so we can omit that from the style as well.

I'm going to show all browser prefixes on this first example, but if you are using Chrome or Safari, you can just use **-webkit-** to save time typing. In upcoming examples, I'll show only the standard, prefix-free property to save space (but the prefixed versions will be there in spirit).

```
a {
  -webkit-transition: background-color 0.2s, border-color 0.2s;
  -moz-transition:  background-color 0.2s, border-color 0.2s;
  -o-transition:  background-color 0.2s, border-color 0.2s;
  -ms-transition:  background-color 0.2s, border-color 0.2s;
  transition:  background-color 0.2s, border-color 0.2s;
}
```

7. Save your document, open it in the browser, and try moving your mouse over the links (see the note). Do you agree it feels nicer? Now I'd like you to try some other duration values. See if you can still see the difference with a .1s duration. Now try a full second (1s). I think you'll find that one second is surprisingly slow. I'd worry that people would miss it. Try setting it to several seconds and trying out various **timing-function** values (just add them after the duration times). Can you tell the difference? Do you have a preference? When you are done experimenting, set the duration back to .2 seconds.

8. Now let's see what happens when we add a transition to the downward motion of the link when it is clicked or tapped. Transition both the **top** and **box-shadow** properties because they should move in tandem. Let's start with a **0.2s** duration like the others.

```
a {
  transition: background-color 0.2s, border-color 0.2s, top 0.2s,
box-shadow 0.2s;
}
```

Save the file, open it in the browser, and try clicking the links. That transition really changes the experience of using the menu, doesn't it? The buttons feel more difficult to press. Try increasing the duration. Do they feel even more difficult? I find it interesting to see the effect that timing has on the experience of a user interface. It is important to get it right and not make things feel sluggish. I'd say that a very short transition such as .1 second—or even no transition at all—would keep these buttons feeling snappy and responsive.

9. If you thought increasing the duration made the menu uncomfortable to use, try adding a short .5-second delay to the **top** and **box-shadow** properties.

```
a {
  transition: background-color 0.2s, border-color 0.2s, top 0.2s
0.5s, box-shadow 0.2s 0.5s;
}
```

I think you'll find that little bit of extra time makes the whole thing feel broken. Timing is everything!

NOTE

If you're using a touch device for this exercise, you'll miss out on this effect because there is no hover state on touch screens.

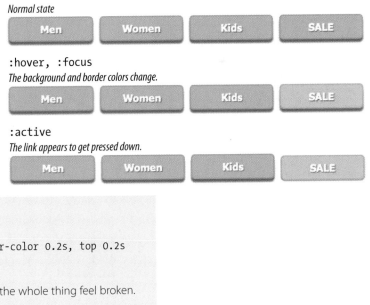

Figure 17-5. In this exercise, we'll create transitions between these link states.

CSS Transforms

`transform`

NEW IN CSS3

Values:	*transform function(s)* | none
Default:	*none*
Applies to:	*transformable elements (see sidebar)*
Inherits:	*no*

The CSS3 Transforms module gives authors a way to rotate, relocate, resize, and skew HTML elements in both two- and three-dimensional space. This chapter, however, focuses on the more straightforward 2-D varieties because they have more practical uses. Transforms are supported on all major browser versions with vendor prefixes. They are not supported at all on IE8 and earlier, Firefox 3 and earlier, and Opera 10.1 and earlier.

You can apply a transform to the normal state of an element and it will appear in its transformed state when the page loads. Just be sure that the page is still usable on browsers that don't support transforms. It is common to pull out the transforms only when users interact with the element via a rollover or JavaScript event (on the "experience layer" as CSS master Dan Cederholm phrases it in *CSS for Web Designers*). Either way, transforms are a good candidate for progressive enhancement—if an IE8 user sees an element straight instead of at a jaunty angle, it's probably no biggie.

Figure 17-6 shows a representation of four types of two-dimensional transforms: **rotate**, **translate**, **scale**, and **skew**. The dashed outline shows the element's original position.

NOTE

The 2D Transforms, 3D Transforms, and SVG Transforms modules were rolled into one CSS Transforms draft document in 2012. The spec is available at www.w3.org/TR/css3-transforms/.

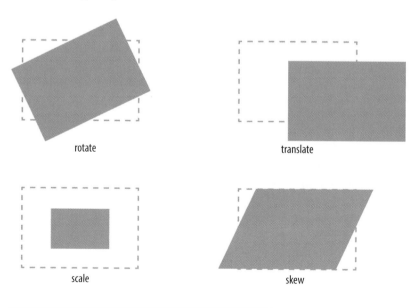

Figure 17-6. Four types of transforms: rotate, translate, scale, *and* skew.

When an element transforms, its element box keeps its original position and influences the layout around it, in the same way that space is left behind by a relatively positioned element. It is as though the transformation magically picks up the pixels of the rendered element, messes around with them, and lays them back down on top of the page. So if you move an element with transform, you're only moving a picture of it. That picture has no effect on the surrounding layout.

Let's go through the transform functions one by one, starting with **rotate**.

Transforming the angle (rotate)

If you'd like an element to appear on a bit of an angle, use the **rotate** transform function. The value of the **rotate** function is an angle specified in positive or negative degrees. The image in Figure 17-7 has been rotated −10 degrees (350 degrees) using the following style rule. The tinted image shows the element's original position for reference.

```
img {
  width: 300px;
  height: 400px;
  transform: rotate(-10deg);
}
```

Figure 17-7. Rotating an img *element using* transform: rotate()*.*

Notice that the image rotates around its center point, which is the default point around which all transformations happen. But you can change that easily with the **transform-origin** property.

transform-origin

NEW IN CSS3

Values:	*percentage* | *length* | left | center | right | top | bottom
Default:	50% 50%
Applies to:	*transformable elements*
Inherits:	*no*

NOTE

There are actually five 2-D transform functions in the CSS spec. The fifth, matrix, allows you to craft your own transformation using six values and some badass trigonometry. Fascinating in theory, but more than I'm willing to take on personally. If you are interested and remember your trig, the transformation matrix is defined at www.w3.org/TR/SVG/coords.html#InterfaceSVGMatrix.

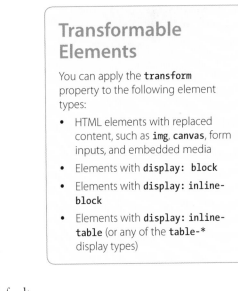

Transformable Elements

You can apply the **transform** property to the following element types:

- HTML elements with replaced content, such as **img**, **canvas**, form inputs, and embedded media
- Elements with **display: block**
- Elements with **display: inline-block**
- Elements with **display: inline-table** (or any of the **table-*** display types)

The value for **transform-origin** is either two keywords, length measurements, or percentage values. The first value is the horizontal offset, and the second is the vertical offset. If only one value is provided, it will be used for both. If we wanted to rotate the redwood forest image around a point at the center of its top edge, we could write it in any of the following ways:

```
transform-origin: center top;

transform-origin: 50%, 0%;

transform-origin: 150px, 0;
```

The images in Figure 17-8 have all been rotated 25 degrees, but from different origin points.

transform-origin: center top;

transform-origin: 100% 100%;

transform-origin: 400px 0;

Figure 17-8. Changing the point around which the image rotates using transform-origin.

It is easy to demonstrate the origin point with the rotate function, but keep in mind that you can set an origin point for any of the transform functions.

Transforming the position (translate)

Another thing you can do with the **transform** property is give the element's rendering a new location on the page using one of three **translate** functions, as shown in the examples in Figure 17-9. The **translateX** function allows you to move an element on a horizontal axis; **translateY** is for moving along the vertical axis; and **translate** is a shorthand for combining both X and Y values (**translate(***translateX, translateY***)**).

```
transform: translateX(50px);

transform: translateY(25px);

transform: translate(50px, 25px);
```

transform: translate(90px, 60px);   transform: translate(-5%, -25%);

Figure 17-9. Moving an element around with the translate *function.*

You can provide a length value in any of the CSS units or as a percentage value. Percentages are calculated on the width of the bounding box—that is, from border edge to border edge (which, incidentally, is how percentages are calculated in SVG, from which transforms were adapted). As shown in Figure 17-9, you can provide positive or negative values.

If you provide only one value for the shorthand **translate** function, it will be presumed to be the **translateX** value, and **translateY** will be set to zero. So **translate(20px)** would be equivalent to applying both **translateX(20px)** and **translateY(0)**.

How do you like the **transform** property so far? We have two more functions to go.

Transforming the size (scale)

Make an element appear larger or smaller using one of three scale functions: **scaleX** (horizontal), **scaleY** (vertical), and the shorthand **scale**. The value is a unitless number that specifies a size ratio. This example makes an image 150% its original width:

```
a img {
  transform: scaleX(1.5);
}
```

The **scale** shorthand lists a value for **scaleX** and a value for **scaleY**. This example makes an element twice as wide but half as tall as the original.

```
a img {
  transform: scale(2, .5);
}
```

Unlike **translate**, however, if you provide only one value for **scale**, it will be used as the scaling factor in both directions. So specifying **scale(2)** is the same as applying **scaleX(2)** and **scaleY(2)**, which is intuitively the way you'd want it to be.

Figure 17-10 shows the results of all our scaling endeavors.

transform: scale(1.25);

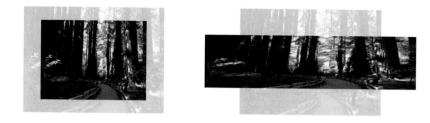

transform: scale(.75);

transform: scale(1.5, .5);

Figure 17-10. *Changing the size of an element with the* scale *function.*

Making it slanty (skew)

The quirky collection of skew properties (**skewX**, **skewY**, and the shorthand **skew**) changes the angle of either the horizontal or vertical axis (or both axes) by a specified number of degrees. As for **translate**, if you provide only one value, it is used for **skewX**, and **skewY** will be set to zero.

The best way to get an idea of how skewing works is to take a look at some examples (Figure 17-11).

```
a img {
    transform: skewX(15deg);
}

a img {
    transform: skewY(30deg);
}

a img {
    transform: skew(15deg, 30deg);
}
```

Figure 17-11. *Slanting an element using the* skew *function.*

transform: skewX(15deg);

transform: skewY(30deg);

transform: skew(15deg, 30deg);

Applying multiple transforms

Of course it is possible to apply more than one transform to a single element. Just list out the functions and their values, separated by spaces, like this:

```
transform: function(value) function(value);
```

In the example in Figure 17-12, I've made the forest image get larger, tilt a little, and move down and to the right when the mouse is over it or when it is in focus.

```
img:hover, img:focus {
    transform: scale(1.5) rotate(-5deg) translate(50px,30px);
}
```

Normal state

:hover, :focus
(rotate, translate, and scale applied)

Figure 17-12. Applying scale, rotate, *and* translate *to a single element.*

It is important to note that transforms are applied in the order in which they are listed. For example, if you apply a **translate** and then **rotate**, you get a different result than a **rotate** and then a **translate**.

Another thing to watch out for is that if you want to apply an additional transform on a different state (such as **hover**, **focus**, or **active**), you need to repeat all of the transforms already applied to the element. For example, this **a** element is rotated 45 degrees in its normal state. If I apply a **scale** transform on the **hover** state, I would lose the rotation unless I explicitly declare it again.

```
a {
    transform: rotate(45deg);
}
a:hover {
    transform: scale(1.25);   /* rotate on a element would be lost */
}
```

To achieve both the rotation and the scale, provide both transform values:

```
a:hover {
    transform: rotate(45deg) scale(1.25);   /* rotates and scales */
}
```

Don't Forget Your Prefixes

For the sake of clarity, I've been presenting the **transform** examples using only the standard syntax. The reality is, however, that the **transform** property requires vendor prefixes in all browsers that support it. Here's that multiple transform example again as it should appear on a published site.

```
a:hover img, a:focus img{
   -webkit-transform: scale(1.5) rotate(-5deg) translate(50px,30px);
   -moz-transform: scale(1.5) rotate(-5deg) translate(50px,30px);
   -o-transform: scale(1.5) rotate(-5deg) translate(50px,30px);
   -ms-transform: scale(1.5) rotate(-5deg) translate(50px,30px);
   transform: scale(1.5) rotate(-5deg) translate(50px,30px);
}
```

Smooooooth transforms

The multiple transforms applied to the redwood forest image look interesting, but it might *feel* better if we got there with a smooth animation instead of just BAM! Now that you know about transitions and transforms, let's put them together and make some magic happen. And by "magic," of course I mean some basic animation effects between two states. We'll do that together, step by step, in Exercise 17-2.

Figure 17-13. Photos get larger and tilt on :hover and :focus. A transition is used to help make it flow. You can see how it works when you are finished with this exercise (or check it out at learningwebdesign.com/4e/chapter17/figures.html).

exercise 17-2 | Transitioning transforms

In this exercise, we'll make the travel photos in the gallery shown in Figure 17-13 grow and spin out to an angle when the user mouses over them—and we'll make it smooooooth with a transition. A starter document (*aquarium.html*) and all of the images are available in the *materials* folder for this chapter.

1. Open *aquarium.html* in a text editor, and you will see that there are already styles that arrange the list items horizontally and apply a slight drop shadow to each image. (Note that if you're not seeing the drop shadow, you're not using a current browser). The first thing we are going to do is add the **transform** property for each image.

2. We want the transforms to take effect only when the mouse is over the image or when the image has focus, so the **transform** property should be applied to the :**hover** and :**focus** states. Because I want each image to tilt a little differently, we'll need to write a rule for each one, using its unique id as the selector. You can save and check your work when you're done.

```
a:hover #img1, a:focus #img1 {
   transform: rotate(-3deg);
}
a:hover #img2, a:focus #img2 {
   transform: rotate(5deg);
}
a:hover #img3, a:focus #img3 {
   transform: rotate(-7deg);
}
a:hover #img4, a:focus #img4 {
   transform: rotate(2deg);
}
```

3. Now let's make them a little larger as well, to give visitors a better view. Add **scale(1.5)** to each of the **transform** values. Here is the first one; you do the rest.

```
a:hover #img1 {
   transform: rotate(-3deg) scale(1.5);
}
```

It is important to note that my image files are created at the larger size and then scaled down for the thumbnail view. If we started with small images and scaled them larger, they would look crummy.

4. As long as we are giving the appearance of lifting the photos off the screen, let's make the drop shadow appear to be a little farther away by increasing the offset and blur and lightening the shade of gray. All images should have the same effect, so add one rule using **a:hover img** as the selector.

```
a:hover img {
   box-shadow: 6px 6px 6px rgba(0,0,0,.3);
}
```

Save your file and check it out in a browser. The images should tilt and look larger when you mouse over them. But the action is kind of jarring. Let's fix that with a transition.

5. Add the **transition** shorthand property to the normal **img** state (i.e., not on **:hover** or **:focus**). The property we want to transition in this case is **transform**. Set the duration to .3 seconds and use the **linear** timing function.

```
img {
   …
   transition: transform 0.3s linear;
}
```

Note that in the prefixed versions, the **transform** property needs to be prefixed as well. For example, the WebKit version would be:

```
-webkit-transition: -webkit-transform .3s linear;
```

And that's all there is to it! You can try playing around with different durations and timing functions or try altering the transforms or their origin points to see what other effects you can come up with.

NOTE

Note that I'm omitting the prefixed versions, but you will need the `-webkit-` *prefix to view the changes in Chrome or Safari.*

3-D transforms

In addition to the two-dimensional transform functions, the CSS Transforms spec also describes a system for creating a sense of space and perspective. Combined with transitions, you can use 3-D transforms to create rich interactive interfaces, such as image carousels, flippable cards, or *spinning cubes*! (There is no shortage of CSS cubes on the Web right now; it must be a good project to learn on.) Figure 17-14 shows a few examples of interfaces created with 3-D transforms. In the past, if you saw 3-D interfaces like these, you would assume it was Flash. Now it is native browser capabilities and good old CSS3.

Figure 17-14. Some examples of 3-D transforms.

Paul Hayes' 3D cube
(www.paulhayes.com/experiments/cube-3d/touch.html)

Safari Technology Demos: Web Gallery
(developer.apple.com/safaridemos/showcase/gallery/)

Snow Stack by Charles Ying
(www.satine.org/research/webkit/snowleopard/snowstack.html)

3-D transforms are not a need-to-know skill for folks just starting out in web design, so I'm not going to go into full detail here, but I will give you a taste of what it takes to add a third dimension to a design. If you'd like to learn more, the following tutorials are good places to start:

- "Adventures In The Third Dimension: CSS 3D Transforms," by Peter Gasston (*coding.smashingmagazine.com/2012/01/06/adventures-in-the-third-dimension-css-3-d-transforms/*)

- "Intro to 3D Transforms," by David DeSandro (*desandro.github.com/3dtransforms/*)

To give you a very basic example, I'm going to use the images from Exercise 17-2 and arrange them as though they are in a 3-D carousel-style gallery (Figure 17-15).

Figure 17-15. Our aquarium images arranged in space...space...space...

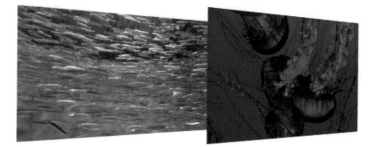

The markup is the same unordered list used in the previous exercise.

```
<ul>
   <li><a href=""><img src="anchovies.jpg" id="img1" alt=""></a></li>
   <li><a href=""><img src="jellyfish1.jpg" id="img2" alt=""></a></li>
   <li><a href=""><img src="bluejellyfish.jpg" id="img3" alt=""></a>
   </li>
   <li><a href=""><img src="seadragon.jpg" id="img4"alt=""></a></li>
</ul>
```

The first step is to add some amount of "perspective" to the containing element using the **perspective** property. This tells the browser that the child elements should behave as though they are in 3-D space. The value of the **perspective** property is some integer larger than zero that specifies a distance from the element's origin on the z-axis. The lower the value, the more extreme the perspective. I have found that values between 300 and 1500 are reasonable, but this is something you need to fuss around with until you get the desired effect.

```
ul {
   width: 1000px;
   height: 100px;
   list-style-type: none;
   padding: 0;
   margin: 0;
   -webkit-perspective: 600;
   -moz-perspective: 600;
   perspective: 600;
}
```

The **perspective-origin** property (not shown) describes the position of your eyes relative to the transformed items. The values are a horizontal position (**left**, **center**, **right**, or a length or percentage) and a vertical position (**top**, **bottom**, **center**, or a length or percentage value). The default (shown in Figure 17-15) is centered vertically and horizontally (**perspective-origin: 50% 50%**). The final transform-related property is **backface-visibility**, which controls whether the reverse side of the element is visible when it spins around.

With the 3-D space established, apply one of the 3-D transform functions to each **li** within the **ul**. The 3-D functions include: **translate3d**, **translateZ**, **scale3d**, **scaleZ**, **rotate3d**, **rotateX**, **rotateY**, **rotateZ**, and **matrix3d**. You should recognize some terms in there. The ***Z** functions define the object's orientation relative to the z-axis (picture it running from your nose to this page, where the x- and y-axes lie flat on the page).

In our example in Figure 17-15, each **li** is rotated 45 degrees around its y-axis (vertical axis) using the **rotateY** function.

Compare the result to Figure 17-16 in which each **li** is rotated on its x-axis (horizontal axis) using **rotateX**.

```
li {
  float: left;
  margin-right: 10px;
  -webkit-transform: rotateX(45deg);
  -moz-transform: rotateX(45deg);
  transform: rotateX(45deg);
}
```

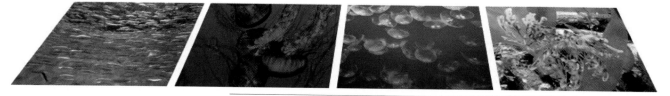

Figure 17-16. The same list of images rotated on their horizontal axes with `rotateX`.

Obviously, I'm barely scratching the surface of what can be done with 3-D transforms, but it should give you a decent mental model for how it works. Next up, I'll introduce you to a more sophisticated way to set your web pages in motion.

Keyframe Animation

The CSS Animations module allows authors to create real, honest-to-goodness keyframe animation. Unlike transitions that go from one state to another, keyframe animation allows you to explicitly specify other states at points along the way, allowing for more granular control of the action.

Those "points along the way" are established by keyframes that define the beginning or end of a segment of animation. CSS transitions are animations with two keyframes: a start state and an end state. More complex animations require many keyframes to control property changes in the sequence.

Creating keyframe animations is complex, and more than I can cover here. But I would like for you to have some idea of how it works, so I'll sketch out the minimal details. The following resources are good starting points for learning more:

- "A Masterclass in CSS Animations," by Estelle Weyl (*www.netmagazine.com/tutorials/masterclass-css-animations*)

- "The Guide to CSS Animation: Principles and Examples" (*coding.smashingmagazine.com/2011/09/14/the-guide-to-css-animation-principles-and-examples/*)

- Rich Bradshaw's tutorial "Using CSS3 Transitions, Transforms, Animations, Filters and More!" (*css3.bradshawenterprises.com*)

- *Anthonycalzadilla.com*. My friend Anthony Calzadilla has done groundbreaking work in CSS animation, including the walking At-At and CSS3-Man animations (Figure 17-17), which were ahead of their time. His site has links to animation examples and general news from the CSS world. He runs an occasional CSS Animations tutorial as well.

Pure CSS3 AT-AT Walker
by Anthony Calzadilla
(www.anthonycalzadilla.com/css3-ATAT/)

CSS3-Man
by Anthony Calzadilla
(www.optimum7.com/css3-man/)

How I Learned to Walk
by Andrew Hoyer
(andrew-hoyer.com/blog/2010/10/21/walking/)

Star Wars Intro recreation in CSS3
by Guillermo Esteves
(www.gesteves.com/experiments/starwars.html)

Figure 17-17. Examples of animations using only CSS.

Animation Tools

If you want to use CSS Animations but lack the wherewithal to learn to code it all yourself, there are tools that give you a timeline interface for creating your animations and generate the HTML and CSS for you. Here are a few as of this writing:

- Tumult Hype, *tumultco.com/hype/* (Mac only)
- Sencha Animator, *www.sencha.com/products/animator/*
- Adobe Edge, *labs.adobe.com/technologies/edge/*

Establishing the keyframes

The animation process has two parts: first, establish the keyframes with a **@keyframes** rule, and then add animation properties to the elements that will be animated.

Here is a very simplistic set of keyframes that changes the background color of an element over time. It's not a very action-packed animation, but it should give you a basic understanding of what a **@keyframes** rule does.

```
@keyframes colors {
  0% { background-color: red; }
  20% { background-color: orange; }
  40% { background-color: yellow; }
  60% { background-color: green; }
  80% { background-color: blue; }
  100% { background-color: purple; }
}
```

NOTE

The @keyframes rule needs vendor prefixes as well, like this:

```
@-webkit-keyframes
```

What that **@keyframes** rule says is this: create an animation sequence called "colors." At the beginning of the animation, the **background-color** of the element should be red, at 20% through the animation runtime the background color should be orange, and so on, until it reaches the end of the animation.

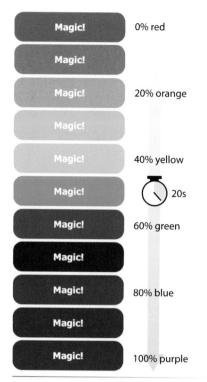

0% red

20% orange

40% yellow

20s

60% green

80% blue

100% purple

Figure 17-18. Animating through the colors of the rainbow using keyframes.

The browser fills in all the shades of color in between each keyframe (or *tweens* it, to use the lingo). This is represented the best I could in Figure 17-18.

Each percentage value and the property/value declaration defines a keyframe in the animation sequence. In addition to percentages, you could also use the keyword **from** at the start of an animation sequence and to denote the end. Here's what a **@keyframes** rule looks like abstracted down to its syntax.

```
@keyframes animation-name {
    keyframe { property: value; }
    keyframe { property: value; }
}
```

Adding animation properties

Now we can apply this animation sequence to an element or multiple elements in the document using a collection of animation properties that are very similar to the set of transition properties that you already know.

I am going to apply the rainbow animation to the **#magic div** in my document.

```
<div id="magic">Magic!</div>
```

In the CSS rule for **#magic**, I can make some decisions about the animation I want to apply:

- Which animation to use (**animation-name**)
- How long it should take (**animation-duration**)
- The manner in which it should accelerate (**animation-timing-function**)
- Whether to pause before it starts (**animation-delay**)

Looking familiar? There are a few other animation-specific properties as well.

- How many times it should repeat (**animation-iteration-count**).
- Whether it plays forward, in reverse, or alternates back and forth (**animation-direction**).
- Whether it should be running or paused. The play-state can be toggled on and off with JavaScript or on hover (**animation-play-state**).
- Whether to override defaults that prevent properties from applying outside runtime (**animation-fill-mode**).

The **animation-name** property tells the browser which keyframes sequence to apply to the **#magic div**. I've also set the duration and timing function, and used **animation-iteration-count** to make it repeat for infinity. I could have provided a specific number value, like 2 to play it twice, but how fun is only two rainbows? And for fun, I've set the **animation-direction** to **alternate**, which makes the animation play in reverse after it has played forward. The other options are simply **forward** or **reverse**. Here is the resulting rule for the animated **div**.

```
#magic {
  ...
  animation-name: colors;
  animation-duration: 5s;
  animation-timing-function: linear;
  animation-iteration-count: infinite;
  animation-direction: alternate;
}
```

That gets a bit verbose, especially when you consider that each one would need to be repeated with vendor prefixes for a published site. You can also use the **animation** shorthand property to combine the values, just as we did for **transition**.

```
#magic {
  animation: colors 5s linear infinite alternate;
}
```

Those are the bare bones of creating keyframes and applying animations to an element on the page. To make elements move around (what we typically think of as "animation"), use keyframes to change the position of an element on the screen with the **translate** transform or **top**, **right**, **bottom**, **left** properties. When the keyframes are tweened, the object will move smoothly from position to position. You can also animate the other transform methods.

I hope I've helped you to wrap your head around how CSS can be used to add a little motion and smoothness to your pages. It's cool stuff, but remember that it is important to use it with restraint and only as an enhancement on normal sites. If you are showcasing your animation, it might be fine to ask your visitors to upgrade to a supporting browser.

Now let's see if you were paying attention with the upcoming little quiz!

NOTE

In the spec, the value of **animation-name** *should appear in single quotation marks in the* **@keyframe** *rule and the* **animation** *property. The shorthand declaration would be written as follows:*

```
animation: 'colors' 5s linear
    infinite reverse;
```

However, developers currently omit the quotation marks to get around a buggy implementation in Firefox.

Test Yourself

Think you know your way around transitions, transforms, and keyframe animations? Here are a few questions to find out.

1. What is "tweening"?

2. If a transition had keyframes, how many would it have?

3. Write out the transition declaration (property and value) you would use to accomplish the following:

   a. Wait .5 seconds before the transition starts.

   b. Make the transition happen at a constant speed.

   c. Make the transition last .5 seconds.

   d. Make the lines of text slowly grow farther apart.

4. Which of the following can you *not* animate?

   a. `width`

   b. `padding`

   c. `text-transform`

   d. `word-spacing`

5. Which timing function will be used if you omit the **transition-timing-function** property? Describe its action.

6. In the following transition, what does .2s describe?

   `transition: color .2s linear;`

7. Which transition will finish first?

   a. `transition: width 300ms ease-in;`

   b. `transition: width 300ms ease-out;`

8. Write the transform declaration you would use to accomplish the following:

    a. Tilt the element seven degrees.

    b. Reposition the element 25 pixels up and 50 pixels to the left.

    c. Rotate the element from its bottom-right corner.

    d. Make a 400-pixel-wide image display at 500 pixels wide.

9. In the following transform declaration, what does the 3 value describe?

    ```
    transform: scale(2, 3)
    ```

10. Which 3-D transform would look more angled and dramatic?

    a. `perspective: 250;`

    b. `perspective: 1250;`

11. What happens halfway through this animation?

    ```
    @keyframes border-bulge {
        from { border-width: 1px; }
        25% { border-width: 10px; }
        50% { border-width: 3px; }
        to { border-width: 5px; }
    }
    ```

12. Write the animation declaration you would use to accomplish the following:

    a. Make the animation play in reverse.

    b. Make the entire animation last five seconds.

    c. Wait two seconds before running the animation.

    d. Repeat the animation three times and then stop.

CSS Review: Transitions, Transforms, and Animation

Here is a summary of the properties covered in this chapter.

Property	Description
animation	A shorthand property that combines animation properties
animation-name	Specifies a name for the animation sequence
animation-duration	The amount of time the animation lasts
animation-timing-function	Describes the acceleration of the animation
animation-iteration-count	The number of times the animation repeats
animation-direction	Whether the animation plays forward, in reverse, or alternates back and forth
animation-play-state	Whether the animation is running or paused
animation-delay	The amount of time before the animation starts running
animation-fill-mode	Overrides limits to when animation properties can be applied
backface-visibility	Determines whether the reverse side of an element may be visible in 3-D transforms
perspective	Establishes an element as a 3-D space and specifies the perceived depth
perspective-origin	Specifies the position of your viewpoint in a 3-D space
transform	Specifies that the rendering of an element should be altered using one of the 2-D or 3-D transform functions
transform-origin	The point around which an element is transformed
transform-style	Used to preserve a 3-D context when transformed elements are nested
transition	A shorthand property that combines transition properties
transition-property	Defines which CSS property will be transitioned
transition-duration	The amount of time the transition animation lasts
transition-timing-function	Describes the manner in which the transition happens (changes in acceleration rates)
transition-delay	The amount of time before the transition starts

CSS TECHNIQUES

By now you have a solid foundation in writing style sheets. You can style text and element boxes, create page layouts using floats, and even add subtle animation effects to your designs. But there are a few common CSS techniques that I want you to know about before we move on to learning about JavaScript in Part IV.

This chapter is a grab bag of sorts. It starts with some techniques that are part of the web developer's basic toolkit: clearing out browser styles with a CSS reset, using images in place of text (only when necessary!), and reducing the number of server requests with CSS sprites. It moves on to general approaches and special properties for styling forms and tables. Finally—and I've saved the best for last—you'll get to use media queries to create a responsive site in step-by-step exercises.

A Clean Slate (CSS Reset)

As you know, browsers have their own built-in style sheets (called user agent style sheets) for rendering HTML elements. If you don't supply styles for an **h1**, you can be certain that it will display as large, bold text with space above and below. But just how much larger and how much space may vary from browser to browser, giving inconsistent results. Furthermore, even if you do provide your own style sheet, elements in your document may be inheriting certain styles from the user agent style sheets, causing unexpected results.

For that reason, many designers use what is known as a CSS reset, a collection of style rules that overrides all user agent styles and creates a starting point that is as neutral as possible. From there, you must explicitly specify font, text, margin, and padding styles for every element in your document, but you can be certain that no styles from the browser will interfere with them.

The most popular reset was written by Eric Meyer (the author of too many CSS books to list). It is presented here, and I've also included a copy of it in the *materials* folder for this chapter for your copy-and-paste pleasure.

```
/* http://meyerweb.com/eric/tools/css/reset/
     v2.0 | 20110126 License: none (public domain)*/
html, body, div, span, applet, object, iframe,
h1, h2, h3, h4, h5, h6, p, blockquote, pre,
a, abbr, acronym, address, big, cite, code,
del, dfn, em, img, ins, kbd, q, s, samp,
small, strike, strong, sub, sup, tt, var,
b, u, i, center, dl, dt, dd, ol, ul, li,
fieldset, form, label, legend,
table, caption, tbody, tfoot, thead, tr, th, td,
article, aside, canvas, details, embed,
figure, figcaption, footer, header, hgroup,
menu, nav, output, ruby, section, summary,
time, mark, audio, video {
    margin: 0;
    padding: 0;
    border: 0;
    font-size: 100%;
    font: inherit;
    vertical-align: baseline;
}
/* HTML5 display-role reset for older browsers */
article, aside, details, figcaption, figure,
footer, header, hgroup, menu, nav, section {
    display: block;
}
body {
    line-height: 1;
}
ol, ul {
    list-style: none;
}
blockquote, q {
    quotes: none;
}
blockquote:before, blockquote:after,
 q:before, q:after {
    content: '';
    content: none;
}
table {
    border-collapse: collapse;
    border-spacing: 0;
}
```

NOTE

There is another reset made available by the developers at Yahoo!. To use it, simply paste the following line into the **head** *of your HTML document:*

```
<link rel="stylesheet"
    type="text/css" href="http://
    yui.yahooapis.com/3.5.1/
    build/cssreset/cssreset-min.
    css">
```

Before you do, however, be sure to read about what it does here: yuilibrary.com/yui/docs/cssreset/.

To use the reset, place these styles at the top of your own style sheet. You can use them exactly as you see them here or customize them as your project requires. I also recommend that you read Eric's posts about the thinking that went into his settings (*meyerweb.com/eric/tools/css/reset/* and *meyerweb.com/eric/thoughts/2007/04/18/reset-reasoning/*).

CSS resets aren't for everyone. You may decide that you want to lean on the browser for some basic styling and not be required to write styles for every little thing. But if you want to be sure that all the styles showing up are yours, a reset may be the way to go.

Image Replacement Techniques

Before web fonts were a viable option, we needed to use an image anytime we wanted text in a font fancier than Times or Helvetica. Fortunately, that is no longer the case, and we can have very stylish headlines and text treatments without the added burden of images. Every now and then, however, even a web font won't do, and it is necessary to use an image in place of a few words of text. For example, you may want to use a stylized logo for your company name or use familiar icons in place of text links.

Removing the text altogether and replacing it with an **img** element is a bad idea because valuable content would be gone forever. The solution is to use a CSS-based image replacement technique that uses the image as a background in the element, then shifts the text out of the way so that it is not rendered on the page. Visual browsers see the background image, while the text content stays in the file for the benefit of search engines, screen readers, and other assistive devices. Everybody wins!

One elegant image replacement technique comes from Scott Kellum (Jeffrey Zeldman christened it "The Kellum Technique"). It uses the **text-indent** property to push the text content all the way to the right and out of the visible element box (Figure 18-1).

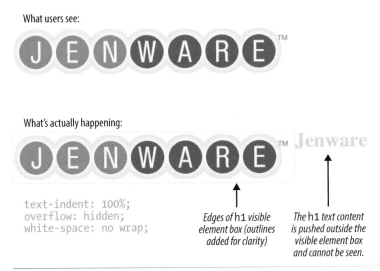

Figure 18-1. The Kellum image replacement technique hides the HTML text by pushing it out of the visible element box with a text indent.

In this example, I'll use the fancy Jenware logo in place of the **h1** "Jenware" HTML text. The markup is simple:

```
<h1 id="logo">Jenware</h1>
```

The style rule is as follows:

```
h1#logo {
  width: 450px;
  height: 80px
  background: url(jenware.png) no-repeat;
  text-indent: 100%;
  white-space: no-wrap;
  overflow: hidden;
}
```

There are a few things of note here. First, the **h1** element displays as a block by default, so we can just specify its **width** and **height** to match the dimensions of the image used as a background. The **text-indent** property pushes the word "Jenware" over to the right by the full width (100%) of the element. The **white-space** property is set to **no-wrap**, which ensures that long strings of text won't wrap around and show up again in the element box. Finally, **overflow: hidden** instructs the browser that anything that falls outside of the element box (like our **h1** text) should not be displayed.

There are actually a dozen or so image replacement techniques that have emerged over the years. One of the most popular is the Phark technique, which uses an extremely large negative **text-indent** value (typically **-9999px**) to pull the HTML text all the way out to the left of the viewport area.

```
h1#logo {
  width: 450px;
  height: 100px
  background: url(jenware.png) no-repeat;
  text-indent: -9999px;
}
```

The downside to this approach is that browsers are forced to calculate and draw the wide element box even though it won't be rendered, which slows down performance. But if you come across an example of text with a background image and a –9999px indent, you'll know what's going on.

The downside to any image replacement approach is that it means an extra request to the server for every image used. In the next section, we'll look at a way to curb unnecessary requests.

NOTE

You can replace images with image replacement techniques as well, for example, to replace a standard web image with a high-resolution image when the page is printed or displayed on high-density (Retina) screens. Aaron Gustafson documents the approach on his blog at v2.easy-designs.net/articles/iIR and blog.easy-designs.net/archives/2012/04/16/iir-redux.

CSS Sprites

When I talked about performance back in Chapter 3, I noted that you can improve site performance by reducing the number of requests your page makes to the server (a.k.a. HTTP requests). One strategy for reducing the number of image requests is to combine all your little images into one big image file so that only one image gets requested. The large image that contains multiple images is known as a sprite, a term coined by the early computer graphic and video game industry. That image gets positioned in the element using the **background-position** property in such a way that only the relevant portion of it is visible. An example should make this clear.

O'Reilly Media's Velocity Conference site featured nine commonly found social media icons, as shown in Figure 18-2. In an effort to improve the site's performance, one of the strategies employed by Tony Quartorolo and Zebulon Young was to turn those nine icon graphics into one sprite and reduce the number of HTTP requests accordingly. They organized the icons into one stack with two pixels of space between icons.

NOTE

For more CSS sprite goodness, please read the Smashing Magazine article "The Mystery of CSS Sprites: Techniques, Tools, and Tutorials," by Sven Lennartz (coding.smashingmagazine.com/2009/04/27/the-mystery-of-css-sprites-techniques-tools-and-tutorials/). It includes excellent examples of sprites in the wild, including sprites used by Amazon, Facebook, and the like.

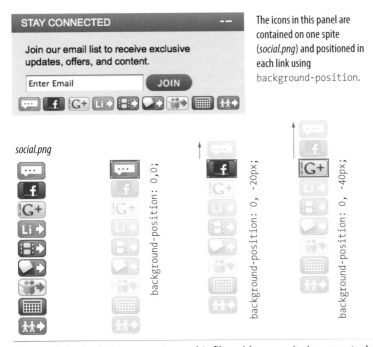

The icons in this panel are contained on one sprite (*social.png*) and positioned in each link using `background-position`.

NOTE

Read the article about Tony and Zeb's optimization process online at radar. oreilly.com/2012/05/velocity-performance-makeover.html.

Figure 18-2. *Replacing separate graphic files with one sprite image cuts down on the number of HTTP requests to the server and improves site performance.*

The styles and markup shown here are a simplification of the code used on the Velocity site, but the result is the same.

The markup

```
<ul>
  <li><a href="" class="hide twitter">Twitter</a></li>
  <li><a href="" class="hide fb">Facebook</a></li>
  <li><a href="" class="hide gplus">Google+</a></li>
  <li><a href="" class="hide linkedin">LinkedIn</a></li>
  <li><a href="" class="hide blip">BlipTV</a></li>
  <li><a href="" class="hide lanyrd">Lanyrd</a></li>
  <li><a href="" class="hide slides">Slideshare</a></li>
  <li><a href="" class="hide sched">Schedule</a></li>
  <li><a href="" class="hide attendees">Attendee List</a></li>
</ul>
```

Sprite Generators

There are several tools that create sprite files and their respective styles automatically. Here are just a few:

- SpriteMe (*spriteme.org*). SpriteMe is a tool for converting images on an existing site into a sprite and style rules. Just go to your website, click the SpriteMe bookmarklet button, and SpriteMe analyzes the page, making suggestions for what images can be combined into a sprite.

- CSS Sprite Generator (*spritegen. website-performance.org*). CSS Sprite Generator is an online service that allows you to upload your individual images to be turned into a sprite and the CSS that controls it.

WARNING

CSS Sprites cannot be used for images that tile in a background (well, not without some finagling anyway). Use them for single background images.

The styles

```css
.hide {
    text-indent: 100%;
    white-space: nowrap;
    overflow: hidden;
}
li a {
    display: block;
    width: 29px;
    height: 18px;
    background-image: url(social.png);
}
li a.twitter { background-position: 0 0;}
li a.fb { background-position: 0 -20px;}
li a.gplus { background-position: 0 -40px;}
li a.linkedin { background-position: 0 -60px; }
li a.blip { background-position: 0 -80px; }
li a.lanyrd { background-position: 0 -100px; }
li a.slides { background-position: 0 -120px; }
li a.sched { background-position: 0 -140px; }
li a.attendees { background-position: 0 -160px; }
```

In the markup, each item has two **class** values. The **hide** class is used as a selector to apply the image replacement technique I covered in the previous section. The other **class** name is particular to each social network link. The unique **class** values allow us to position the sprite appropriately for each link.

At the top of the style sheet you should recognize the image replacement styles. Notice in the next rule that all link (**a**) elements use *social.png* as their background image.

Finally, we get to the styles that do the heavy lifting. The **background-position** is set differently for each link in the list, and the visible element box works like a little window revealing a portion of the background image. The first item has the value "0,0"; this positions the top-left corner of the image in the top-left corner of the element box. To make the Facebook icon visible, we need to move the image *up* by 20 pixels, so its vertical position is set to –20px (its horizontal position of 0 is fine). The image is moved up by 20-pixel increments for each link, revealing image areas farther and farther down the sprite stack.

In this example, all of the icons have the same dimensions and stack up nicely, but that is not a requirement. You can combine images with a variety of dimensions on one sprite. The process of setting a size for the element and then lining the sprite up perfectly with the **background-position** property is the same.

Sass and LESS

I know you are just getting used to writing CSS rules the regular way, but there are some super-charged alternatives I want you to know about. Finding the normal CSS syntax repetitive, developers Hampton Catlin and Nathan Weizenbaum created a new style sheet syntax that takes advantage of the time-saving power tools of scripting languages. They called their new syntax Sass ("Syntactically awesome style sheets"). A later release known as SCSS (for "Sassy CSS") is based on original indented Sass syntax but also allows normal CSS syntax to be mixed in.

In Sass style documents, you can do things that you would do in scripting, such as setting a variable name for a value you plan to use frequently. For example, O'Reilly uses the same shade of red repeatedly on its site, so it could create a variable named "oreilly-red" and use the variable name for color values. That way, if it needed to tweak the shade later, it only needs to change the variable value in one place. Here's what setting up and using a variable looks like in Sass:

```
$oreilly-red: #900;

a { border-color: $oreilly-red; }
```

You can even reuse whole sets of styles using a convention called mixins. The following example saves a combination of background, color, and border styles as a mixin named "special." To apply that combination of styles, **@include** it in the declaration and call it by name.

```
@mixin special {
    color: #fff;
    background-color: #befc6d;
    border: 1px dotted #59950c;
}
a.nav {
    @include special;
}
```

In addition, Sass allows nested rules, handles math operations, and adjusts colors mathematically, just to name a few functions borrowed from scripting languages.

Browsers do not know how to interpret the syntax of a *.sass* or *.scss* file, so you need to use the Sass compiler (written in Ruby), which runs on the server. The compiler converts the Sass file to standard CSS syntax before it is delivered to the browser.

LESS is another CSS syntax with scripting-like abilities. It is very similar to Sass, but it lacks a few features and has minor differences in syntax (for instance, variables in LESS are indicated by the **@** symbol instead of **$**, so it's **@oreilly-red**. The other major difference is that a LESS file is processed into regular CSS syntax by JavaScript (*less. js*) instead of Ruby. Note that compiling a LESS file into CSS is processor-intensive and would bog down a browser. For that reason, it is best to do the conversion to CSS before sending it to the server. One recommended tool for doing so is CodeKit (*incident57.com/less/*), but there are others out there.

Once you get some practice under your belt and feel that you are ready to take your style sheets to the next level, explore some of these Sass and LESS articles and resources:

- The Sass site (*sass-lang.com*)
- The LESS site (*lesscss.org*)
- Compass, a full-featured CSS authoring framework that uses Sass (*compass-style.org*)
- "Getting Started with Sass," by David Demaree (*alistapart.com/articles/getting-started-with-sass*)
- "An Introduction to LESS, and Comparison to Sass," by David Hixon (*coding.smashing magazine.com/2011/09/09/an-introduction-to-less-and-comparison-to-sass*)

Styling Forms

Web forms can look a bit hodge-podge right out of the box with no styles applied (Figure 18-3), so you'll certainly want to give them a more professional appearance using CSS. Not only do they look better, but studies show that forms are much easier and faster to use when the labels and inputs are lined up nicely. In this section, we'll look at how various form elements can be styled and how to align form elements without using tables.

Now, I'm not going to lie: styling forms is somewhat of a dark art due to the variety of ways in which browsers handle form elements. But the efforts are well worth it to make your forms look as professional as the rest of your site.

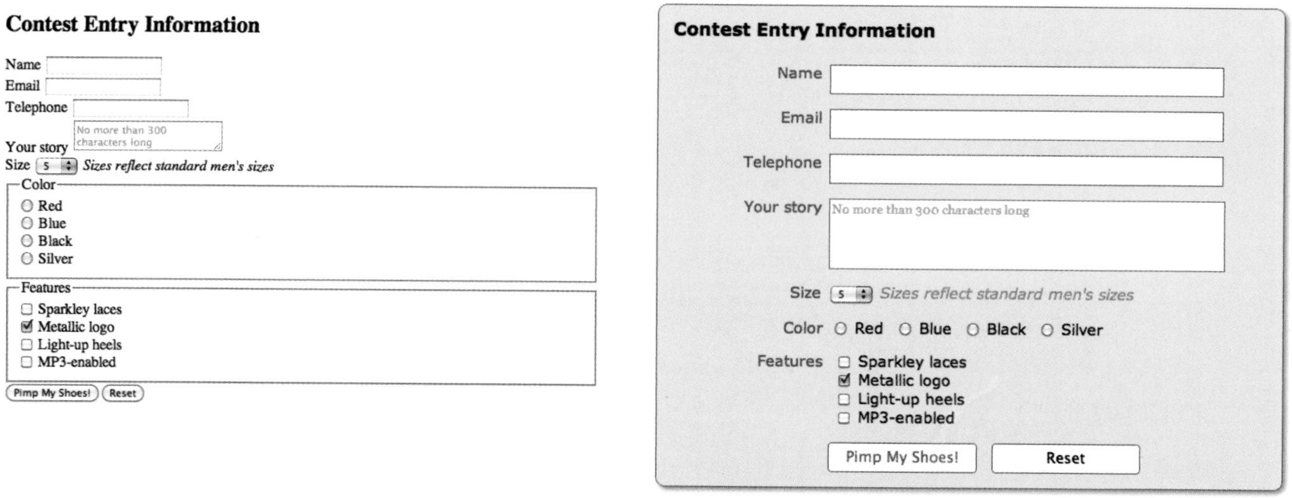

Figure 18-3. Forms tend to be ugly and difficult to use with HTML alone (left). A little CSS can make a big difference (right). This section walks you through the styling of this form step by step.

There aren't any special properties for styling forms; just use the standard color, background, font, border, margin, and padding properties that you've learned in the previous chapters. The following is a quick rundown of the types of things you can do for each form control type.

Text inputs (`text`, `password`, `email`, `search`, `tel`, `url`)

Change the appearance of the box itself with `width`, `height`, `background-color`, `background-image`, `border`, `border-radius`, `margin`, `padding`, and `box-shadow`. You can also style the text inside the entry field with `color` and the various font properties.

The `textarea` element

This can be styled in the same way as text-entry fields. `textarea` elements use a monospace font by default, so you will need to change that to match your other text-entry fields. Because there are multiple lines, you may also specify a `line-height`. Note that some browsers display a handle on the lower-right corner of the `textarea` box that makes it resizable, but you can turn it off by adding the style `resize: none;`.

Button inputs (`submit`, `reset`, `button`)

Apply any of the box properties to submit and reset buttons (`width`, `height`, `border`, `background`, `margin`, `padding`, and `box-shadow`). Note however, that buttons are set to the `border-box` sizing model by default, so `width` and `height` values apply border to border. Most browsers also add a bit of padding by default, which can be overridden by your own `padding` value. You can also style the text that appears on the buttons.

Radio and checkbox buttons

The best practice for radio and checkbox buttons is to leave them alone. At best, Internet Explorer will show a little color around the box, which looks awkward. If you are tenacious, you could use JavaScript to change the buttons altogether.

Drop-down and select menus

You can specify the `width` and `height` for a `select` element, but note that it uses the `border-box` box-sizing model by default. Some browsers allow you to apply `color`, `background-color`, and font properties to `option`s, but it's probably best to leave them alone to be rendered by the browser and operating system.

Fieldsets and legends

You can treat a `fieldset` as any other element box, adjusting the `border`, `background`, `margin`, and `padding`. Turning the border off entirely is one way to keep your form looking tidy while preserving semantics and accessibility. By default, `legend` elements are positioned on an indent, centered vertically with the top border of the `fieldset`, and unfortunately browsers make them difficult to change. Some developers use a `span` or **b** element within the `legend` and apply styles to the contained element for more predictable results.

Now we know what we can do to style individual controls, but the grander goal is to make the form more organized and easier to use. In the past, we used tables for the task, but it is preferable to stick with CSS for matters of presentation, such as alignment. I'm going to walk you through writing the styles for the form shown in Figure 18-3 and take you step by step from point A to point B.

The markup

Here is the markup for the contest entry form. Each question in the form is contained in a list item, and labels are provided for all controls. There are also two **fieldset**s, grouping the radio buttons and checkboxes.

```
<form action="" method="">

<h2>Contest Entry Information</h2>

<ul>
  <li>
    <label for="form-name">Name</label>
    <input type="text" name="username" id="form-name" class="textinput">
  </li>
  <li>
    <label for="form-email">Email</label>
    <input type="email" name="emailaddress" id="form-email"
    class="textinput">
  </li>
  <li>
    <label for="form-tel">Telephone</label>
    <input type="tel" name="telephone" id="form-tel"class="textinput">
  </li>
  <li>
    <label for="form-story">Your story</label>
    <textarea name="story" maxlength="300" id="form-story" rows="3"
    cols="30" placeholder="No more than 300 characters long"></textarea>
  </li>
  <li>
    <label for="sizes">Size</label>
    <select name="size">
      <option>5</option>
      <option>6</option>
      <option>7</option>
      <option>8</option>
      <option>9</option>
      <option>10</option>
      <option>11</option>
      <option>12</option>
      <option>13</option>
    </select>
    <em>Sizes reflect standard men's sizes</em>
  </li>
  <li>
    <fieldset id="colors">
      <legend>Color</legend>
      <ul>
        <li><label><input type="radio" name="color" value="red"> Red
        </label> </li>
        <li><label><input type="radio" name="color" value="blue">
        Blue</label> </li>
        <li><label>input type="radio" name="color" value="black">
        Black</label></li>
        <li><label><input type="radio" name="color" value="silver">
        Silver</label></li>
      </ul>
    </fieldset>
  </li>
  <li>
```

```
<fieldset id="features">
<legend>Features</legend>
  <ul>
    <li>
      <label><input type="checkbox" name="feature" value="laces">
      Sparkley laces</label>
    </li>
    <li>
      <label><input type="checkbox" name="feature" value="logo"
checked>
        Metallic logo</label>
    </li>
    <li>
      <label><input type="checkbox" name="feature" value="heels">
      Light-up heels</label>
    </li>
    <li>
      <label><input type="checkbox" name="feature" value="mp3">
      MP3-enabled</label>
    </li>
  </ul>
</fieldset>
</li>
<li class="buttons">
  <input type="submit" value="Pimp My Shoes!">
  <input type="reset">
</li>
</ul>
</form>
```

Step 1: Adding basic styles

The first set of styles takes care of some basic document styling, including the **body**, **h2**, and some standard **ul** styles to remove the bullets. I've also created a rule for the **form** element, giving it a width, background color, rounded corners, a shadow, and some padding. Because I know I'm going to be floating a lot of its contents, I've added **overflow:hidden;** as a float container. Similarly, the **ul li** rule includes a **clear:both;** declaration in anticipation of floats. To save a little space, only the form-related styles are presented here. The result is shown in Figure 18-4.

```
ul { list-style-type: none;
  … }
ul li { clear: both;
  … }
form {
  width: 40em;
  border: 1px solid #666;
  border-radius: 10px;
  box-shadow: .2em .2em .5em #999;
  background-color:#d0e9f6;
  padding: 1em;
  overflow: hidden;
}
```

Figure 18-4. After adding styles to the form *element.*

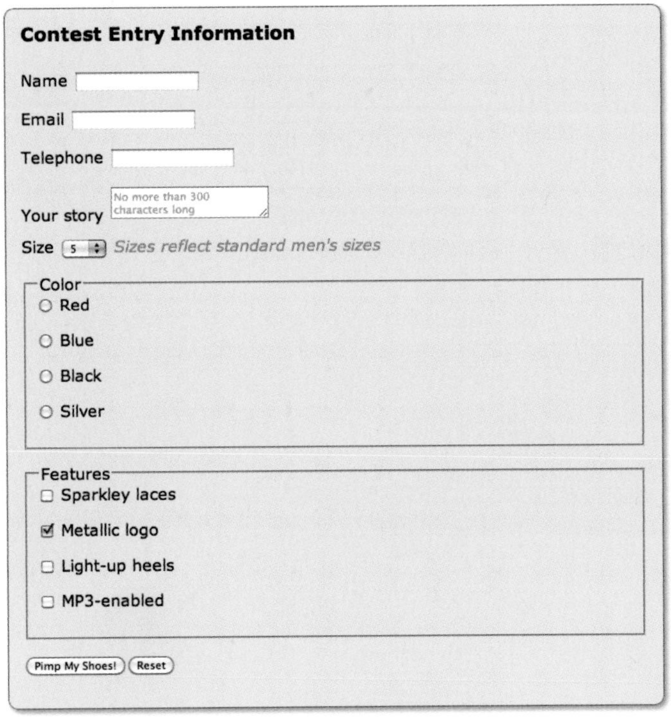

Step 2: Aligning labels and inputs

Now we're getting to the good stuff! Notice in the "after" shot in Figure 18-3 that all of the labels and inputs are aligned in neat columns. To make that happen, give the **label** elements a specific width, float them to the left, and then align the label text to the right so they are near their respective inputs. A little margin on the right of the **label** elements creates a nice gutter between the columns. You should be able to see all these styles at work in the **label** style rule shown here.

```
label {
    display: block;
    float: left;
    width: 10em;
    text-align: right;
    margin-right: .5em;
    color: #04699d;
}
```

The text inputs and the **textarea** are given **width** and **height** values as well as a simple 1-pixel border. In addition, similar font properties are applied to both. I've removed the ability to resize the **textarea** element by setting **resize** to **none**. The form in Figure 18-5 is starting to look a little better, but now we have some problems with the radio button and checkbox labels that we need to fix.

```
input.textinput {
    width: 30em;
    height: 2em;
    border: 1px solid #666;
}
textarea {
    display: block;
    width: 30em;
    height: 5em;
    border: 1px solid #666;
    margin-bottom: 1em;
    line-height: 1.25;
    overflow: auto;
    resize: none;
}
input.textinput, textarea {
    font-family: Georgia, "Times New Roman", Times, serif;
    font-size: .875em;
}
```

NOTE

I've added a `class="textinput"` *attribute to the various text input types (*`text`*,* `tel`*, etc.) so I can select just the text-entry inputs. I also could have used attribute selectors (for example,* `input[type="tel"]`*) for each one, but they are not supported by some versions of Internet Explorer. I chose the more bulletproof* `class` *method because I want everyone to see these styles.*

Figure 18-5. *After aligning the labels and inputs.*

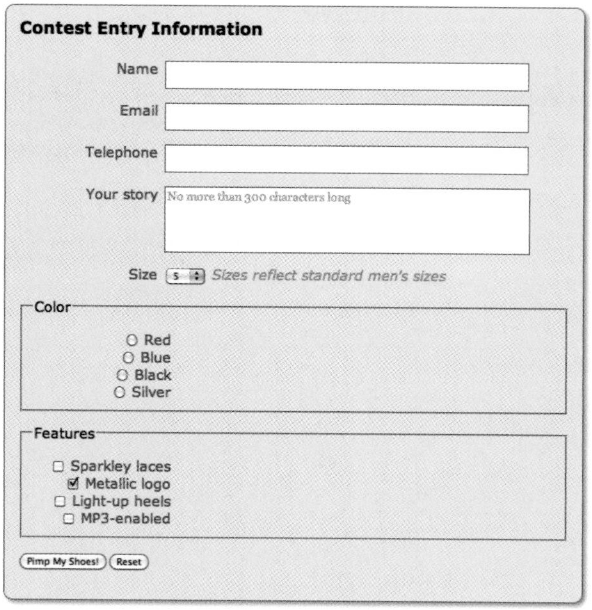

Step 3: Fixing fieldsets and minor labels

The next thing I'm going to do is override the default styles on the **fieldset** elements so they are not so prominent. I'm also going to treat the **legend** for each **fieldset** with the same styles I've applied to the **label**s.

As a result of the styles added in Step 2, the **label** elements for the radio buttons and checkboxes inside the **fieldset**s are styled the same as the main labels, which is not what I want. I've written styles especially for **label** elements inside the Colors and Features **fieldset**s that get rid of the color, dimensions, and floats. Finally, I displayed the list items in the Colors section as inline so they would appear on one line and save some space. The Features checkbox list needed a few little tweaks such as adding a left margin so the checkboxes line up with the other form controls (**margin-left:11em**) and resetting the **clear** property so the first checkbox list item does not start below the floated legend (**clear:none**). The result is shown in Figure 18-6.

```
fieldset {
  margin: 0;
  padding: 0;
  border: none;
}
legend {
  display: block;
  width: 10em;
  float: left;
  margin-right: .5em;
  text-align: right;
  color: #04699d;
}
#features label, #colors label {
  color: #000;
  display: inline;
  float: none;
  text-align: inherit;
  width: auto;
  font-weight: normal;
  background-color: inherit;
}
#colors ul li {
  display: inline;
  margin-bottom: 0;
}
#features ul {
  margin-left: 11em;
}
#features ul li {
  margin-bottom: 0;
  clear: none;
}
```

Figure 18-6. Fixing the labels next to checkboxes and radio buttons.

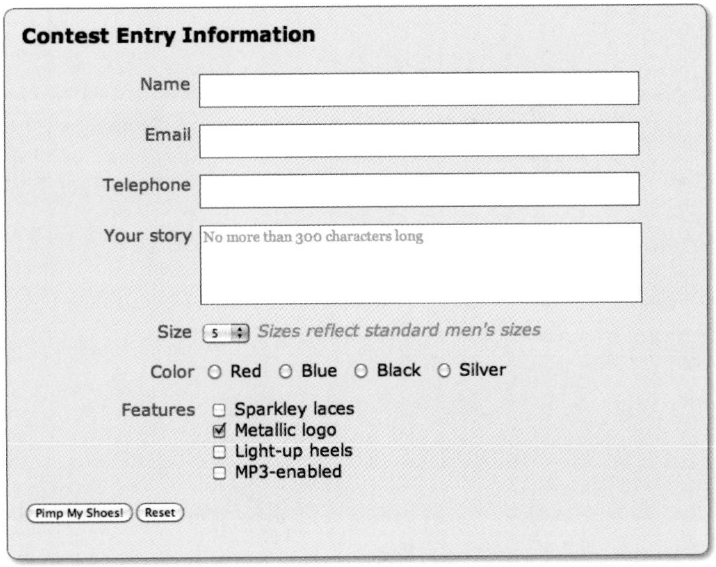

Step 4: Adjusting the buttons

All that is left to do now is fix the alignment and styling of the submit and reset buttons (Figure 18-7). I've aligned the buttons with the other form controls by applying a left margin to the submit button. I've also given the buttons new dimensions, a background color, a rounded border, and a slight drop shadow. The **font-size:inherit;** declaration ensures that the buttons use the same font size as the rest of the form (overriding the browser defaults), making the em measurements predictable.

```
input[type="submit"], input[type="reset"] {
    display: block;
    width: 10em;
    height: 2em;
    float: left;
    background: white;
    font-size: inherit;
    border: 1px solid #04699d;
    border-radius: 4px;
    box-shadow: 2px 2px 3px rgba(0,0,0,.5);
}

input[type="submit"] {
    margin-left: 10.5em;
    margin-right: 1em;
    color: #C00; /* the submit button text is attention-getting red */
}
```

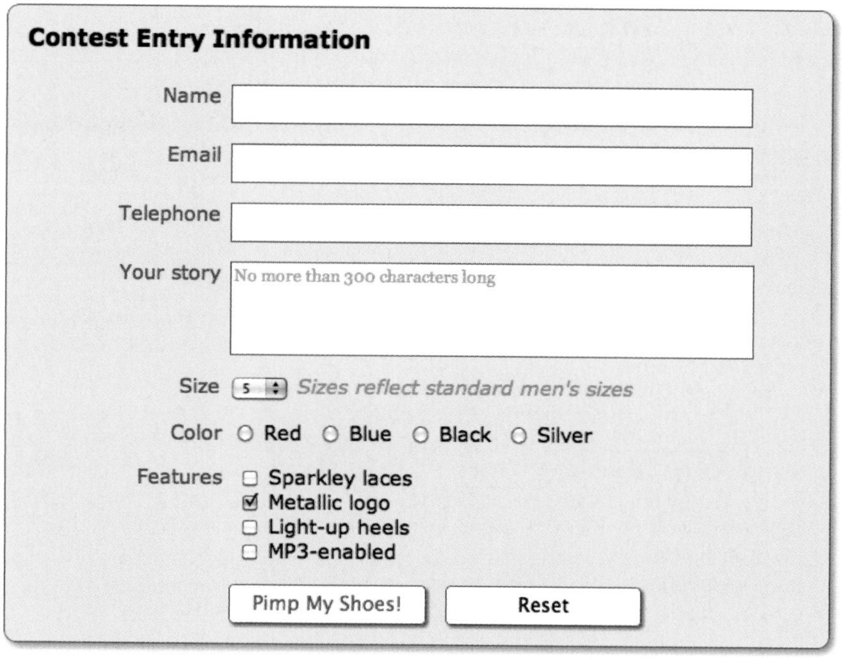

Figure 18-7. The finished form with styled and aligned buttons.

And there you have it! I've concentrated on the styles used for alignment, colors, and text treatments in this example. For your forms, you'll probably want to add styles for interactivity, such as `:hover` styles on the buttons and `:focus` styles for the text inputs when they are selected.

Styling Tables

We've already covered the majority of style properties you'll need to style content in tables. You can change the appearance and alignment of the content within the cells with the various font, text, and background properties as you would for any other text element. In addition, you can treat the table and cells themselves with padding, margins, and borders.

There are a few CSS properties, however, that were created specifically for tables. Some of them are fairly esoteric and are briefly introduced in the sidebar "Advanced Table Properties." This section focuses on properties that directly affect table display—specifically, the treatment of borders.

Separated and collapsed borders

CSS provides two methods for displaying borders between table cells: separated or collapsed. When borders are separated, a border is drawn on all four sides of each cell and you can specify the space between the borders. In the collapsing border model, the borders of adjacent borders "collapse" so that only one of the borders is visible and the space is removed (Figure 18-8).

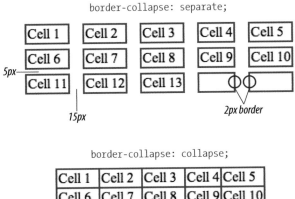

Figure 18-8.   Separated borders (top) and collapsed borders (bottom).

The `border-collapse` property allows authors to choose which of these border-rendering methods to use.

Advanced Table Properties

There are a few more properties related to the CSS table model.

Table layout

The `table-layout` property allows authors to specify one of two methods of calculating the width of a table. The `fixed` value bases the table width on `width` values provided for the table, columns, or cells. The `auto` value bases the width of the table on the minimum width of the contents of the table. Auto layout may display nominally more slowly because the browser must calculate the default width of every cell before arriving at the width of the table.

Table display values

Chapter 14 introduced the `display` property used to specify what kind of box an element generates in the layout. CSS is designed to work with all XML languages, not just HTML and XHTML. It is likely that other languages will have the need for tabular layouts, but will not have elements like `table`, `tr`, or `td` in their vocabularies.

To this end, there are a variety of table-related `display` values that allow authors of XML languages to assign table layout behavior to any element. The table-related `display` values are: `table`, `inline-table`, `table-row-group`, `table-header-group`, `table-footer-group`, `table-row`, `table-column-group`, `table-column`, `table-cell`, and `table-caption`. You could assign these display roles to other HTML elements, but it is generally discouraged.

---

border-collapse

Values:	separate | collapse | inherit
Default:	separate
Applies to:	*table and inline-table elements*
Inherits:	*yes*

Separated border model

Tables render with separated borders by default, as shown in the top table in Figure 18-8. You can specify the amount of space you'd like to appear between cells using the **border-spacing** property.

border-spacing

Values:	*length length* | inherit
Default:	0
Applies to:	*table and inline-table elements*
Inherits:	*yes*

The values for **border-spacing** are two length measurements. The horizontal value comes first and applies between columns. The second measurement is applied between rows. If you provide one value, it will be used both horizontally and vertically. The default setting is 0, causing the borders to double up on the inside grid of the table.

These are the style rules used to create the custom border spacing shown in the top table in Figure 18-8.

```
table {
  border-collapse: separate;
  border-spacing: 15px 5px;
  border: none;   /* no border around the table itself */
}
td {
  border: 2px solid purple;   /* borders around the cells */
}
```

NOTE

Although the **border-spacing** *default is zero, browsers add two pixels of space for the* **cellspacing** *attribute by default. If you want to see the doubling-up effect, you need to set the* **cellspacing** *attribute to 0 in the* **table** *element.*

Collapsed border model

When the collapsed border model is chosen, only one border appears between table cells. This is the style sheet that created the bottom table in Figure 18-8.

```
table {
  border-collapse: collapse;
  border: none;   /* no border around the table itself */
}
td {
  border: 2px solid purple;   /* borders around the cells */
}
```

Notice that although each table cell has a 2-pixel border, the borders between cells measure a total of two pixels, not four. Borders between cells are centered on the grid between cells, so if cells are given a 4-pixel border, two pixels will fall in one cell and two pixels in another. For odd numbers of pixels, the browser decides where the extra pixel falls.

In instances where neighboring cells have different border styles, a complicated pecking order is called in to determine which border will display. If the **border-style** is set to **hidden** for either of the cells, then no border will display. Next, border width is considered: wider borders take precedence over narrower ones. Finally, if all else is equal, it comes down to a matter of style. The creators of CSS rated the border styles from most to least precedence as follows: **double**, **solid**, **dashed**, **dotted**, **ridge**, **outset**, **groove**, and (the lowest) **inset**.

Empty cells

For tables with separated borders, you can decide whether you want empty cells to display their backgrounds and borders using the **empty-cells** property.

empty-cells

Values: show | hide | inherit

Default: show

Applies to: table cell elements

Inherits: yes

For a cell to be "empty," it may not contain any text, images, or non-breaking spaces. It may contain carriage returns and space characters.

Figure 18-9 shows the previous separated table border example with its empty cells (what would be Cell 14 and Cell 15) set to **hide**.

```
table {
    border-collapse: separate;
    border-spacing: 15px 5px;
    empty-cells: hide;
    border: none;
}
td {
    border: 1px solid purple;
}
```

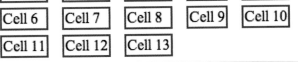
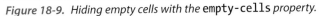

Figure 18-9. Hiding empty cells with the empty-cells *property.*

Basic Responsive Web Design

Responsive web design is a technique that uses CSS to adapt a page's layout based on screen size. It is just one strategy we are employing to cope with the mind-blowing variety of screen sizes.

Of course, responsive design is a big, fat, gnarly topic that could fill (and has filled) whole books. What I'm going to do here is introduce you to the basic ingredients of a responsive site so you get a feel for building one. The approach presented here is based closely on the method of responsive design described by Ethan Marcotte in his landmark book *Responsive Web Design* (A Book Apart). By the time you read this, I'm sure there will be many more marvelous books on the topic, not to mention a mountain of information online (see also the "For Further Reading" sidebar at the end of this chapter). Which is all to say that after you finish the exercises in this section, your journey toward mastering responsive web design will have just begun.

A simple example

In this section, we'll work together on making the Jenware page responsive. Figure 18-10 shows how the same Jenware HTML page will look on a narrow screen, a tablet screen in portrait and landscape orientations, and a large desktop monitor by the time we are finished.

320px (iPhone)   768px (iPad portrait)   1024px (iPad landscape)   > 1024px (Chrome/desktop)

Figure 18-10. The newly responsive Jenware site. You can look at it on your own mobile devices at www.learningwebdesign.com/rwd/.

On the smartphone-sized screen, the page has a one-column layout and very narrow side margins. On tablets in portrait mode, there is room for slightly more generous margins and wrapped text. At 1,024 pixels wide, there is room for a second column, and in very wide browser windows, the width of the content is limited with the `max-width` property to make sure the line lengths don't get out of control. These are very modest adjustments compared to professionally designed responsive sites, but they should be enough to show you how it works.

NOTE

For more inspired responsive adaptations, see the Media Queries gallery site (mediaqueri.es).

How it works

Responsive design as first proposed by Mr. Marcotte has three core components:

A fluid layout

> You learned all about fluid layouts in Chapter 16, "CSS Layouts," and fortunately, the Jenware site has already been designed to be fluid. (Gee, how did I know?!)

Flexible images

> When the layout scales down, the images and other embedded media need to scale with it; otherwise, they would hang out of view. We'll make sure the Jenware images scale down to fit.

CSS media queries

> Media queries are a method for applying styles based on the medium via which the document is displayed. Queries start with questions, such as, "Is the document being printed? Then use these print-appropriate styles." Or, "Is the document on a screen, and is that screen at least 1,024 pixels wide and in landscape mode? Then use *these* styles." I'll show you how that looks in CSS syntax in a moment.

To this list of ingredients, I would add the viewport **meta** element that makes the width of the web page match the width of the screen, and that's where we'll begin our responsive project.

Setting the viewport

To fit standard websites onto small screens, mobile browsers render the page on a canvas called the viewport and then shrink that viewport down to fit the width of the screen (device width). For example, on iPhones, Mobile Safari sets the viewport width to 980 pixels, so a web page is rendered as though it were on a desktop browser window set to 980 pixels wide. But that rendering gets shrunk down to 320 pixels wide when the iPhone is in portrait orientation, cramming a lot of information into a tiny space.

Mobile Safari introduced the viewport **meta** tag that allows developers to control the size of that initial viewport. Soon other mobile browsers followed suit, and this is an essential first step to a responsive design. Simply add the following **meta** element to the **head** of the HTML document:

```
<meta name="viewport" content="width=device-width, initial-scale=1">
```

This line tells the browser to set the width of the viewport equal to the width of the device screen (**width=device-width**), whatever that happens to be. The **initial-scale** sets the zoom level to 1 (100%).

Now seems like a good time to start giving the Jenware site the responsive treatment. We'll do it one step at a time, starting in Exercise 18-1.

> **NOTE**
>
> *The viewport* **meta** *element also allows the* **maximum-scale** *attribute. Setting it to 1 (***maximum-scale=1***) prevents users from zooming the page, but it is strongly recommended that you avoid doing so because resizing is important for accessibility and usability.*

NOTE

Use Chrome, Firefox, Safari, or Internet Explorer 9 or higher for the exercises in this chapter. IE8 and earlier do not support the media queries we'll be using later.

Exercise 18-1 | Set the viewport size

In this exercise you'll get familiar with the Jenware site materials and set the viewport before we move on to editing the style sheet. The files *jenware-rwd.html* and *jenware.css* are available in the *materials* folder for this chapter. You may recognize the page from previous exercises, but I have made some small style changes to give you a cleaner starting point.

1. Start by opening the file *jenware-rwd.html* in the browser. The style sheet, *jenware.css*, takes care of the basic styling such as backgrounds, colors, borders, and text styles, providing a good baseline styled experience. Resize the browser window very narrow to approximate the width of a smartphone. You should see something similar to the iPhone screenshot in Figure 18-10, except that the Jenware logo graphic hangs out the right edge of the screen. Scroll down and see that the **#products** and **#testimonials** boxes go right to the edges of the window.

2. Now resize the window as wide as you can. You should find that the page stretches uncomfortably wide and that the text does not wrap around the product images. This design clearly needs some love to look better at wide browser widths.

3. Let's get that viewport **meta** element in there. Open *jenware-rwd.html* in a text editor and add the standard **meta** element as shown here:

```
<meta name="viewport" content="width=device-width,
    initial-scale=1">
```

Save the file, and you're done. Because this is a mobile thing, you won't notice any changes when you look at the page again in your desktop browser, but the foundation has been laid for improvements.

Fluid layouts

Because fluid layouts are fundamental to responsive design, I think it bears a quick recap. Fluid layouts are created using percentage width measurements so that elements resize proportionally to fill the available width of the screen or window.

It's not feasible to create a design for all the possible device widths on which your page might be viewed. Web designers generally create two or three designs (sometimes a few more) targeted at major device classes, such as smartphones, tablets, and desktop browsers. They rely on fluid layouts to take care of all the possible sizes in between. Fluid layouts avoid awkward amounts of leftover space and prevent the right side of the page from getting cut off.

Because I've picked up the fluid layout styles from the previous exercises for this project, there is nothing we need to do to the Jenware styles. For your own projects, however, be sure to design flexibly. And speaking of flexible, let's do something about that logo image!

Adaptive Layout

As an alternative approach—especially when there is no time or budget for a true responsive site redesign—some designers choose to create an adaptive layout instead. Adaptive layouts feature two or three different *fixed* layout designs that target the most common device breakpoints. They may be quicker and less disruptive to produce, but the advantages of fluid layouts are lost. Some consider adaptive layouts to be more of a stopgap solution than a long-term mobile design strategy.

Making images flexible

Every now and then a solution is simple. Take, for example, the style rule required to make images scale down to fit the size of their container:

```
img {
  max-width: 100%;
}
```

That's it! When the layout gets smaller, the images in it will scale down to fit the width of the container they are in. If the container is larger than the image—for example, in the tablet or desktop layouts—the image does not scale larger; it stops at 100% of its original size. When you apply the `max-width` property, be sure that there are no `width` and `height` attributes in the `img` elements in the HTML document, or the image won't scale proportionally.

But wait, things are never that simple, right? I'm afraid that although the style rule is simple, the larger issue of images on the mobile display is more complicated. Even in our modest example, we are serving an image to the smartphone that is larger than it needs, which means unnecessary data is transferred. I'm going to revisit this conundrum again in the "Responsive Images" section later in this chapter. For now, just bear it in mind.

Before we move on to the exercise, I should also note that you can scale down other embedded media, such as an `object`, `embed`, or `video` (see note), using `max-width` as well.

NOTE

To preserve the aspect ratio of a scaled-down video, you need to jump through a few more hoops. Thierry Koblentz documents the strategy nicely in his article "Creating Intrinsic Ratios for Video" at www.alistapart.com/articles/creating-intrinsic-ratios-for-video. There is also a JavaScript solution at fitvidsjs.com.

WARNING

IE6 does not support the `max-width` property.

Figure 18-11. The `max-width` property makes the image shrink proportionally when its container gets smaller.

exercise 18-2 |
Flex those images

This is another quick one. Open *jenware.css* and add the image resizer to the style sheet right after the **body** rule set.

```
img { max-width: 100%; }
```

Save the file and reload the page in the browser. Now when you resize the window very narrow, the logo resizes down with it (Figure 18-11). The product images do the same thing, but you may not be able to get the viewport narrow enough to see it.

Media query magic

Now we get to the real meat of responsive design: media queries.

Media queries allow designers to deliver styles based on media type. The defined media types are **print**, **speech**, **handheld**, **braille**, **projection**, **screen**, **tty**, and **tv**. The keyword **all** indicates that the styles apply to all media types. Media queries can also evaluate specific media features, such as the **device-width**, **orientation**, and **resolution**. Most properties can be tested for a minimum or maximum value using the **min-** and **max-** prefixes, respectively. For example, **min-width: 480px** tests whether the display is at least 480 pixels wide. 768-pixel-wide displays pass the test and get the styles; a 320-pixel display would not.

The complete list of device features you can detect with media queries appears in Table 18-1.

You can add media queries to a style sheet along with your other styles. Here is an example of a style sheet media query that determines whether the media type is a screen and whether it is at least 480 pixels wide:

```
@media screen and (min-width: 480px;) {

    /* put styles for devices & browsers that pass this test inside the
       curly braces */

}
```

The query starts with **@media** followed by the target media type keyword (**screen** in this case). The media feature and the value that is being tested are

Table 18-1. Media features you can evaluate with media queries

Feature	Description
width	The width of the display area (viewport).
height	The height of the display area (viewport).
device-width	The width of the devices rendering surface (the whole screen).
device-height	The height of the devices rendering surface (the whole screen).
orientation	Whether the device is in portrait or landscape orientation. (Does not accept min-/max- prefixes.)
aspect-ratio	Ratio of the viewport's width divided by height (width/height).
device-aspect-ratio	Ratio of the whole screen's (rendering surface) width to height.
color	The bit depth of the display; for example, color: 8 tests for whether the device has at least 8-bit color.
color-index	The number of colors in the color lookup table.
monochrome	The number of bits per pixel in a monochrome device.
resolution	The density of pixels in the device. This is increasingly relevant for detecting high-resolution displays.
scan	Whether a tv media type uses progressive or interlace scanning. (Does not accept min-/max- prefixes.)
grid	Whether the device uses a grid-based display, such as a fixed-width font. (Does not accept min-/max-prefixes.)

contained within parentheses. The style rules for browsers meeting those conditions get put between the curly braces.

Here is another example that tests for two feature values: whether the screen is under 700 pixels wide *and* is in landscape orientation. Notice that each feature and value pair is placed inside parentheses. The word "and" strings the various requirements together. The device must pass all of the requirements in order to deliver the enclosed styles.

```
@media screen and (max-width: 700px;) and (orientation: landscape;) {

   /* put styles for devices & browsers that pass this test here */

}
```

Finally, in this example, the media query looks to see whether the device has a high-density display like the Retina iPhone, iPad, and newer MacBook Pro. This example includes vendor-prefixed queries as well as a standard query. Here the separate queries are in a comma-separated list. The enclosed styles are applied when either of the query conditions is met.

```
@media screen and (-webkit-min-device-pixel-ratio: 2),
       screen and (-moz-min-device-pixel-ratio: 2),
       screen and (-o-min-device-pixel-ratio: 2),
       screen and (-ms-min-device-pixel-ratio: 2),
       screen and (min-device-pixel-ratio: 2) {

   /* styles referencing high-resolution images here */

}
```

Media queries in the document head

The `@media` queries we've been looking at so far go in the style sheet itself. Media queries can also be carried out with the `media` attribute in the `link` element to conditionally load separate *.css* files when the conditions are met.

In this example, the basic styles for a site are requested first, followed by a style sheet that will be used only if the device is more than 780 pixels wide (and if the browser supports media queries).

```
<head>
  <link rel="stylesheet" href="styles.css">
  <link rel="stylesheet" href="2column-styles.css" media="screen and
    (min-width:780px)">
</head>
```

Some developers find this method helpful for managing modular style sheets, but it comes with the disadvantage of requiring extra HTTP requests for each additional *.css* file. Be sure to provide only as many links as necessary (perhaps one for each major breakpoint), and rely on `@media` rules within style sheets to make minor adjustments for sizes in between.*

WARNING

Internet Explorer 8 and earlier do not support media queries at all. I will show you a workaround in Exercise 18-3.

---

* This technique was suggested by Stephanie Rieger in her presentation "Pragmatic Responsive Design." You can see the slides for her very thorough case study here: *www.slideshare.net/yiibu/ pragmatic-responsive-design.*

NOTE

For a good summary of the mobile-first design approach, see Brad Frost's article "Creating a Mobile-First Responsive Web Design" (www.html5rocks.com/en/mobile/responsivedesign/) and his related post "Anatomy of a Mobile-First Responsive Web Design" (bradfrostweb.com/blog/mobile/anatomy-of-a-mobile-first-responsive-web-design/), which describes the thinking that went into every component in the demo. It's a great peek into a mobile web designer's mind.

WARNING

Be sure that you nest and close your curly braces properly. It is easy to forget that last curly brace that ends the media query.

"Mobile first" media queries

That takes care of the mechanics, but let's talk a little about strategy. A best practice for responsive sites is to adopt a "mobile first" mentality. That means that you take care of the styles for the smallest, simplest devices first, and use media queries to bring in overriding styles that adapt the design as more display real estate and features become available. (If this sounds like a form of progressive enhancement to you, you are right.)

Mobile-first media queries tend to begin with the **min-** prefix, bringing in new styles when the width is *at least* the specified width or larger. That allows developers to layer up styles based on the more simple styles already applied.

Remember that styles lower in a stack override the styles that precede them, whether it's rules in a single style sheet or a list of **link** elements. It should follow that our baseline styles should come first, followed by the small device styles, followed by the enhanced styles for larger browsers. That's exactly what we'll be doing in Exercise 18-3.

Figure 18-12. *The Jenware site after the tablet styles have been applied.*

exercise 18-3 | Adding media queries

Now we can get to work adding the styles that will change the layout based on the width of the display area. I've done the design busywork for you. You can copy the finished styles as you see them here or grab a copy of them from the *jenware-final.css* document in the *materials* folder.

1. Open *jenware.css* in a text editor. The current style sheet creates that edge-to-edge, one-column design that works great for narrow screens but looks miserable when it gets wide. I've decided that it will do just fine for smartphones in portrait and landscape mode (up to 480 pixels wide), but after that, I want to give everything a little more breathing room.

2. I start by adding styles for devices that are at least 481 pixels wide. With a little extra space, I can float the product images to the left and clear the following "More about…" links. I've also put margins around the white **#products** box and applied the rounded corners and margins to the **#testimonials** box, as we did in the exercises in Chapters 14 and 15 (Figure 18-12). The resulting media query shown here goes at the end of the style sheet so it can selectively override properties set before it.

```
@media screen and (min-width: 481px) {
    #products img {
        float: left;
        margin: 0 6px 6px 0;
    }
    #products .more {
        clear: left;
    }
    #products {
        margin: 1em;
    }
    #testimonials {
        margin: 1em 5%;
        border-radius: 16px;
    }
}
```

Note that we are testing for the width of the display area (`width`), not the width of the whole screen (`device-width`), because there is often app chrome around web pages when they are viewed on mobile devices. Testing for the `width` will give us more accurate results.

3. The next set of styles kick in when the display area is at least 780 pixels wide. The styles in this media query create a two-column layout by floating the `#products div` to the left and applying a wide left margin to the `#testimonials` box. The copyright paragraph is cleared so it appears at the bottom of the page. Finally, I've set a `max-width` on the `#content div` so the content will never appear wider than 1,024 pixels, even if the browser is expanded much wider (Figure 18-13).

This media query should go below the one we just added in the style sheet document.

```
@media screen and (min-width: 780px) {
  #products {
    float: left;
    margin: 0 2% 1em;
    clear: both;
    width: 55%;
    overflow: auto;
  }
  #testimonials {
    margin: 1em 2% 1em 64%;
  }
  p#copyright {
    clear: both;
  }
  #content {
    max-width: 1024px;
    margin: 0 auto;
  }
}
```

Figure 18-13. The Jenware site on wide screens.

4. Now you can save the document and open it in a browser (use Chrome, Safari, Firefox, or IE9). Try resizing the window and watch as the layout adapts on the fly. What you're looking at is your first responsive web page!

But what about Internet Explorer 8 and earlier?

As I mentioned in a note earlier, Internet Explorer versions 8 and earlier do not support media queries, so the styles within them would be ignored. That means a user with IE8 on a big desktop monitor would get the single-column, lowest-common-denominator version of the page. Not cool.

The solution is to take the styles appropriate for the desktop and put them in a separate style sheet served only to non-mobile versions of Internet Explorer less than version 9 (`(lt IE 9)&(!IEMobile)`).

If you want to play along, copy the styles from inside the media queries (but *not* the media query notation) and paste them into a new file called *ie-layout.css*. From the first media query, take the styles for floating the images and rounding the corners of the Testimonials box. All of the styles from the second media query apply to the desktop, so paste in all of those too.

An IE-specific conditional comment provides a link to the special style sheet and must come after the other style sheet links. You can add this to the **head** of *jenware-rwd.html*.

```
<link rel="stylesheet" href="jenware.css">
<!--[if (lt IE 9)&(!IEMobile)]>
  <link rel="stylesheet" href="ie-layout.css">
<![endif]-->
```

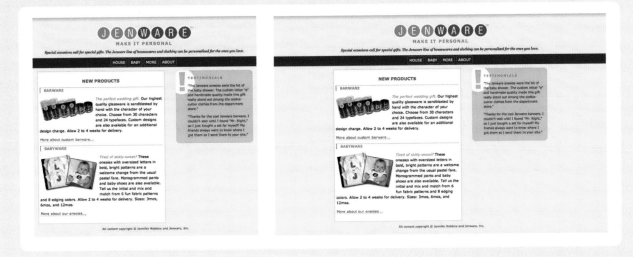

The tricky bits

The Jenware site qualifies as a responsive design, but it is clearly simplified and represents some best-case scenarios. Getting responsive right takes some planning and work. Because the mobile Web is relatively new, the development community is still encountering and working through the challenges of mobile design. I'd like to bring you up to speed on some of the trickier aspects and limitations of RWD and mobile design in general.

Choosing breakpoints

One of the primary design decisions in creating a responsive design is deciding at which widths to introduce a significant design change. The point at which the media query delivers a new set of styles is known as a breakpoint. Some sites have just two layouts triggered at a single breakpoint. More commonly, responsive sites use three designs targeted at typical phone, tablet, and desktop widths, and I've seen as many as five. How many you choose depends on the nature of your site's design.

But how do you choose your breakpoints? One way is to use the pixel dimensions of popular devices, as we did in the Jenware exercise. Figure 18-14 shows a breakpoint chart that lists the dimensions of the most popular device classes in both portrait and landscape mode as of this writing.

The reality is that new device widths are bubbling up all the time, and we can't be expected to create a separate design for all of them. For that reason, there has been a move away from pixel values in media queries toward that web development darling, the em. Many developers let their content determine where the breakpoints should happen, which is, in short, the point at

Figure 18-14. This breakpoint chart shows the pixel widths of some popular devices.

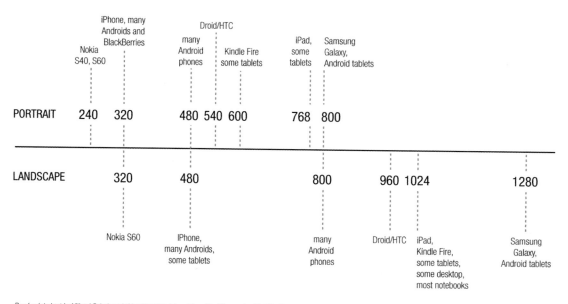

Breakpoint chart by Viljami Salminen (with adaptations) from his article "Responsive Workflow" (viljamis.com/blog/2012/responsive-workflow/).

which things start looking really bad! Thinking in terms of single column, wide single column, and multiple columns, and then defining the logical breakpoints points in ems, is a more future-friendly approach. To learn more, I refer you to the article "The Ems have it: Proportional Media Queries FTW!" by Lyza Gardner (*blog.cloudfour.com/the-ems-have-it-proportional-media-queries-ftw/*).

Responsive images

One of the most vexing problems facing mobile web developers as of this writing is how to get images right. Ideally, a device should download only the image size that is appropriate for its dimensions and network speed. The goal is to avoid downloading unnecessary data, whether that comes in the form of an image that is larger than it needs to be for a small screen or downloading two versions of an image (low-res and high-res) when only one is needed.

What makes images so complicated is that knowing the device size does not necessarily tell you anything about the network speed. Small phones may be using slow EDGE networks or speedy WiFi. Retina iPads are hungry for large images, but may be downloading them over 3G. In addition, you might not want to simply scale down an image for a small display. In some cases, it may be preferable to use a different image entirely that has been cropped to reveal important details at smaller dimensions.

As of this writing, there seems to be more debate than solutions. Some have proposed new HTML markup that makes it easier to specify image files based on dimensions and screen resolution. Some feel the server needs to play a larger role, particularly to negotiate network speeds. Others think that a new image format that can contain multiple versions of the same image is the answer. The sudden explosion of mobile web use caught our web technologies off-guard.

A web search for "responsive images" should help you get up to speed with where things stand currently. Jason Grigsby has written several high-profile articles that effectively describe the dilemma as of 2012. They should serve as a good starting place for understanding the challenge and possible solutions.

- "Responsive IMGs—Part 1" (*blog.cloudfour.com/responsive-imgs/*)

- "Responsive IMGs Part 2—In-depth Look at Techniques" (*blog.cloudfour.com/responsive-imgs-part-2/*)

- "Responsive IMGs Part 3—Future of the IMG" (*blog.cloudfour.com/responsive-imgs-part-3-future-of-the-img-tag/*)

- "The Real Conflict Behind <picture> and @srcset" (*blog.cloudfour.com/the-real-conflict-behind-picture-and-srcset/*)

Resizing Images on the Server

Sencha.io Src is a service that shrinks your images down on the fly and delivers them at the appropriate size to the device doing the asking. All you need to do is add a bit of extra markup to your **img** tag that points the image to the Sencha.io server.

The Sencha.io server uses the user agent string (a bit of text that browsers use to identify themselves) to look up that device in a database. Once its width is determined, Sencha.io Src scales the image down to that width and sends back the smaller file.

Learn more about it here: *docs.sencha.io/0.1.3/index.html#!/guide/src*.

One size doesn't fit all

CSS works fine for swapping out styles and moving elements around on the screen (or even hiding them). But in many cases, smaller devices are better served with different content or the same content in a different order. JavaScript can handle a certain amount of rearranging and offers a way to conditionally load content. Customizing content with JavaScript is beyond the scope of this section, but you should know that content tweaks are possible and ought to be considered when designing for the mobile context.

Responsive limitations

For some websites, particularly text-heavy sites like blogs, a responsive redesign is all that is needed to make them pleasant to use on small screens. For other sites, however, simply adjusting the styles is not enough. When the mobile use case for a site or service is significantly different from desktop use (based on user testing, of course), then it may be necessary to build a separate mobile site.

But even separate mobile sites can benefit from the basic ingredients of responsive design we covered here. Responsive techniques are proving themselves to be an essential skill for every web designer.

Wrapping Up Style Sheets

We've come to the end of our style sheet exploration. By now, you should be comfortable formatting text and even doing basic page layout using CSS. The trick to mastering style sheets, of course, is lots of practice and testing. If you get stuck, you will find that there are many resources online to help you find the answers you need.

In Part IV, I hand over the keyboard to JavaScript master Mat Marquis, who will introduce you to JavaScript and its syntax (also somehow managing to make it very entertaining). I'll be back in Part V to talk about web graphics.

Test Yourself

See how well you picked up the CSS techniques in this chapter with these questions. As always, the answers are available in Appendix A.

1. What is the purpose of a CSS reset?

    a. To override browser defaults

    b. To make presentation more predictable across browsers

    c. To prevent elements from inheriting unexpected styles

    d. All of the above

For Further Reading

The Web is the best place to keep up with developments in responsive design because this stuff is changing at a furious pace. For one-stop shopping, I recommend Brad Frost's Mobile Web Best Practices site (*mobilewebbestpractices.com*). On the Resources page, Brad has assembled lists of the best articles, books, galleries, presentations, scripts, and more related to developing websites for the mobile context.

There are many books on the topic, but the ones I found most useful were *Head First Mobile Web* (O'Reilly) by Lyza Danger Gardner and Jason Grigsby as well as *Implementing Responsive Design* (Peachpit/New Riders) by Tim Kadlec.

2. What is the purpose of a CSS sprite?

    a. To improve site performance

    b. To use small images in place of large ones, reducing file size

    c. To reduce the number of HTTP requests

    d. a. and c.

    e. All of the above

3. Name two differences between LESS and Sass.

4. What is the purpose of an image replacement technique?

    a. To achieve really big text indents

    b. To use a decorative graphic in place of text

    c. To remove the text from the document and replace it with a decorative image

    d. To maintain the semantic content of the document

    e. b. and d.

    f. All of the above

5. What is the secret to aligning form controls and their respective labels without tables? A general description will do here.

6. Why is it important to set the viewport size?

7. Match the media query with its meaning.

    a. `@media screen and (max-width: 800px) { }`

    b. `@media screen and (min-device-width: 800px) { }`

    c. `@media print and (orientation: portrait) { }`

    d. `<link rel="stylesheet" href="special.css" media="screen and (min-width: 800px)">`

    e. `@media all and (monochrome) { }`

    _____ Apply these styles when printing in portrait mode

    _____ Apply these styles to all black and white media

    _____ Apply this external style sheet when the display area is at least 800 pixels wide

    _____ Apply these styles when the display area is under 800 pixels wide

    _____ Apply these styles when the whole device screen is at least 800 pixels wide.

8. Match the style rules with their respective tables in Figure 18-15.

```
1.  table { border-collapse: collapse;}
    td { border: 2px black solid; }

2.  table { border-collapse: separate; }
    td { border: 2px black solid; }

3.  table {
       border-collapse: separate;
       border-spacing: 2px 12px; }
    td { border: 2px black solid; }

4.  table {
       border-collapse: separate;
       border-spacing: 5px;
       border: 2px black solid; }
    td { background-color: #99f; }

5.  table {
       border-collapse: separate;
       border-spacing: 5px; }
    td {
       background-color: #99f;
       border: 2px black solid; }
```

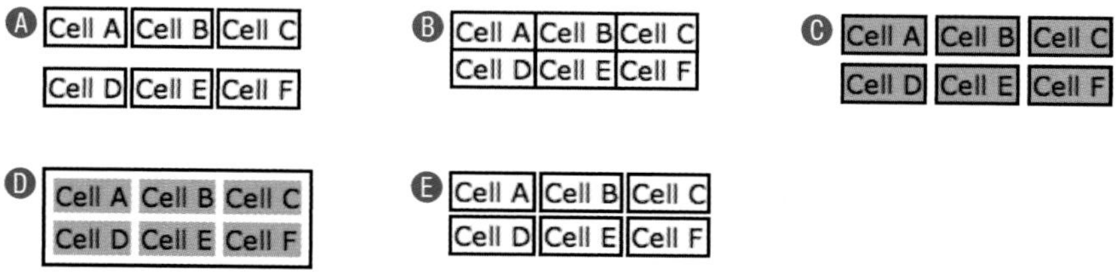

Figure 18-15. Match these tables with the code examples in Question 8.

CSS Review: Table Properties

The following is a summary of the properties covered in this chapter.

Property	Description
border-collapse	Whether borders between cells are separate or collapsed
border-spacing	The space between cells set to render as separate
empty-cells	Whether borders and backgrounds should render for empty cells

JAVASCRIPT FOR BEHAVIORS

PART **IV**

INTRODUCTION TO JAVASCRIPT

by Mat Marquis

In this chapter, I'm going to introduce you to JavaScript. Now, it's possible you've just recoiled a little bit, and I understand. We're into full-blown "programming language" territory now, and that can be a little intimidating. I promise, it's not so bad!

We'll start by going over what JavaScript is—and what it isn't—and discuss some of the ways it is used. The majority of the chapter is made up of an introduction to JavaScript syntax—variables, functions, operators, loops, stuff like that. Will you be coding by the end of the chapter? Probably not. But you will have a good head start toward understanding what's going on in a script when you see one. I'll finish up with a look at some of the ways you can manipulate the browser window and tie scripts to user actions such as clicking or submitting a form.

What Is JavaScript?

If you've made it this far in the book, you no doubt already know that JavaScript is the programming language that adds interactivity and custom behaviors to our sites. It is a client-side scripting language, which means it runs on the user's machine and not on the server, as other web programming languages such as PHP and Ruby do. That means JavaScript (and the way we use it) is reliant on the browser's capabilities and settings. It may not even be available at all, either because the user has chosen to turn it off or because the device doesn't support it, which good developers keep in mind and plan for. JavaScript is also what is known as a dynamic and loosely typed programming language. Don't sweat this description too much; I'll explain what all that means later.

First, I want to establish that JavaScript is kind of misunderstood.

What it isn't

Right off the bat, the name is pretty confusing. Despite its name, JavaScript has nothing to do with Java. It was created by Brendan Eich at Netscape in 1995 and originally named "LiveScript." But Java was all the rage around that time, so for the sake of marketing, "LiveScript" became "JavaScript." Or just "JS," if you want to sound as cool as one possibly can while talking about JavaScript.

JS also has something of a bad reputation. For a while it was synonymous with all sorts of unscrupulous Internet shenanigans—unwanted redirects, obnoxious pop-up windows, and a host of nebulous "security vulnerabilities," just to name a few. There was a time when JavaScript allowed less reputable developers to do all these things (and worse), but modern browsers have largely caught on to the darker side of JavaScript development and locked it down. We shouldn't fault JavaScript itself for that era, though. As the not-so-old cliché goes: "with great power comes great responsibility." JavaScript has always allowed developers a tremendous amount of control over how pages are rendered and how our browsers behave, and it's up to us to use that control in responsible ways.

What it is

NOTE

JavaScript was standardized in 1996 by the European Computer Manufacturer's Association (ECMA), which is why you sometimes hear it called ECMAScript.

Now we know what JavaScript isn't: it isn't related to Java, and it isn't a mustachioed villain lurking within your browser, wringing its hands and waiting to alert you to "hot singles in your area." Let's talk more about what JavaScript *is*.

JavaScript is a lightweight but incredibly powerful scripting language. We most frequently encounter it through our browsers, but JavaScript has snuck into everything from native applications to PDFs to ebooks. Even web servers themselves can be powered by JavaScript.

As a dynamic programming language, JavaScript doesn't need to be run through any form of compiler that interprets our human-readable code into something the browser can understand. The browser effectively reads the code the same way we do and interprets it on the fly.

JavaScript is also loosely typed. All this means is that we don't necessarily have to tell JavaScript what a variable is. If we're setting a variable to a value of 5, we don't have to programmatically specify that variable as a number. As you may have noted, 5 is already a number, and JavaScript recognizes it as such.

Now, you don't necessarily need to memorize these terms to get started writing JS, mind you—to be honest, I didn't. Even now my eyes gloss over a little as I read them. This is just to introduce you to a few of the terms you'll hear often while you're learning JavaScript, and they'll start making more and more sense as you go along. This is also to provide you with conversation material for your next cocktail party! "Oh, me? Well, I've been really into loosely typed dynamic scripting languages lately." People will just nod silently at you, which I think means you're doing well conversationally. I don't go to a lot of cocktail parties.

What JavaScript can do

Most commonly we'll encounter JavaScript as a way to add interactivity to a page. Where the "structural" layer of a page is our markup and the "presentational" layer of a page is made up of CSS, the third "behavioral" layer is made up of our JavaScript. All of the elements, attributes, and text on a web page can be accessed by scripts using the DOM (Document Object Model), which we'll be looking at in Chapter 20, "Using JavaScript." We can also write scripts that react to user input, altering either the contents of the page, the CSS styles, or the browser's behavior on the fly.

You've likely seen this in action if you've ever attempted to register for a website, entered a username, and immediately received feedback that the username you've entered is already taken by someone else (Figure 19-1). The red border around the text input and the appearance of the "sorry, this username is already in use" message are examples of JavaScript altering the contents of the page. Blocking the form submission is an example of JavaScript altering the browser's default behavior.

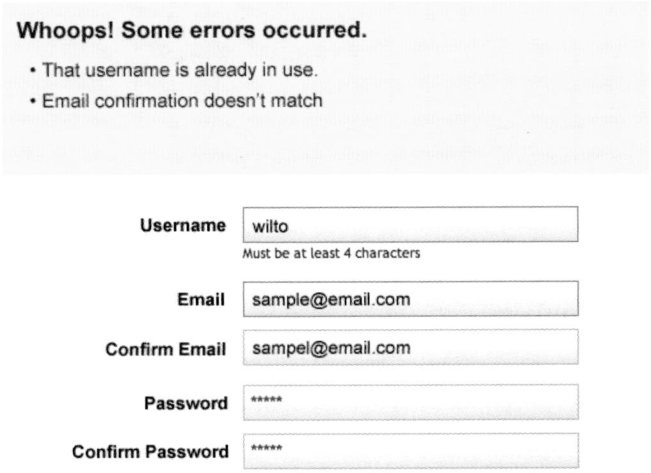

Whoops! Some errors occurred.

- That username is already in use.
- Email confirmation doesn't match

Username	wilto
	Must be at least 4 characters
Email	sample@email.com
Confirm Email	sampel@email.com
Password	*****
Confirm Password	*****

Figure 19-1. JavaScript detects that a username is not available and then inserts a message and alters styles to make the problem apparent.

In short, JavaScript allows you to create highly responsive interfaces that improve the user experience and provide dynamic functionality, without waiting for the server to load up a new page. For example, we can use JavaScript to do any of the following:

- Suggest the complete term a user might be entering in a search box as he types. You can see this in action on Google.com (Figure 19-2).

what can javascript do

what can javascript **do**
what can javascript **be used for**
what can javascript **do for a website**
what can javascript **programs do**

Figure 19-2. Google.com uses JavaScript to automatically complete a search term as it is typed in.

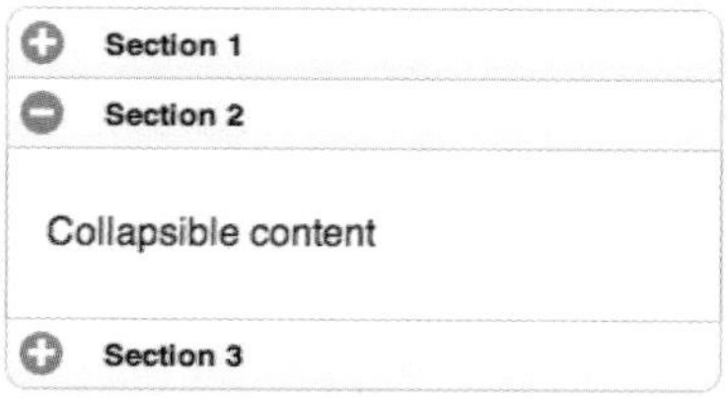

- Request content and information from the server and inject it into the current document as needed, without reloading the entire page—this is commonly referred to as "Ajax."

- Show and hide content based on a user clicking on a link or heading, to create a "collapsible" content area (Figure 19-3).

Section 1

Section 2

Collapsible content

Section 3

Figure 19-3. JavaScript can be used to reveal and hide portions of content.

- Test for browsers' individual features and capabilities. For example, one can test for the presence of "touch events," indicating that the user is interacting with the page through a mobile device's browser, and add more touch-friendly styles and interaction methods.

- Fill in gaps where a browser's built-in functionality falls short, or add some of the features found in newer browsers to older browsers. These kinds of scripts are usually called shims or polyfills.

Figure 19-4. JavaScript can be used to load images into a lightbox-style gallery.

- Load an image or content in a custom styled "lightbox"—isolated on the page using CSS—after a user clicks on a thumbnail version of the image (Figure 19-4).

This list is nowhere near exhaustive!

Adding JavaScript to a Page

Like CSS, you can embed a script right in a document or keep it in an external file and link it to the page. Both methods use the **script** element.

Embedded script

To embed a script on a page, just add the code as the content of a **script** element:

```
<script>
    … JavaScript code goes here
</script>
```

External scripts

The other method uses the **src** attribute to point to a script file (with a *.js* suffix) by its URL. In this case, the **script** element has no content.

```
<script src="my_script.js"></script>
```

The advantage to external scripts is that you can apply the same script to multiple pages (the same benefit external style sheets offer). The downside, of course, is that each external script requires an additional HTTP request of the server, which slows down performance.

Script placement

The **script** element can go anywhere in the document, but the most common places for scripts are in the **head** of the document and at the very end of the **body**. It is recommended that you don't sprinkle them throughout the document, because they would be difficult to find and maintain.

For most scripts, the end of the document, just before the **</body>** tag, is the preferred placement because the browser will be done parsing the document and its DOM structure. Consequently, that information will be ready and available by the time it gets to the scripts and they can execute faster. In addition, the script download and execution blocks the rendering of the page, so moving the script to the bottom improves the perceived performance. However, in some cases, you might want your script to do something before the body completely loads, so putting it in the **head** will result in better performance.

The Anatomy of a Script

There's a reason why the book *JavaScript: The Definitive Guide* by David Flanagan (O'Reilly) is 1,100 pages long. There's a *lot* to say about JavaScript! In this section, we have only a few pages to make you familiar with the basic building blocks of JavaScript so you can begin to understand scripts when you encounter them. Many developers have taught themselves to program

> **NOTE**
>
> *In HTML 4.01 the* **script** *tag must include the* **type** *attribute in order to be valid:*
>
> ```
> <script type="text/
>     javascript">…</script>
> ```
>
> *For XHTML documents, you must identify the content of the* **script** *element as CDATA by wrapping the code in the following wrapper:*
>
> ```
> <script type="text/javascript">
>    // <![CDATA[
>    …JavaScript code goes here
>    // ]]>
> </script>
> ```

by finding existing scripts and adapting them for their own needs. After some practice, they are ready to start writing their own from scratch. You may want to learn to write JavaScript yourself as well to round out your web designer skill set. Recognizing the parts of a script is the first step, so that's where we'll start.

Originally, JavaScript's functionality was mostly limited to crude methods of interaction with the user. We could use a few of JavaScript's built-in functions (Figure 19-5) to provide user feedback, such as **alert()** to push a notification to a user and **confirm()** to ask a user to approve or decline an action. To request the user's input, we were more or less limited to the built-in **prompt()** function. Although these methods still have their time and place today, they're jarring, obtrusive, and—in common opinion, at least—fairly obnoxious ways of interacting with users. As JavaScript has evolved over time, we've been afforded much more graceful ways of adding behavior to our pages, creating a more seamless experience for our users.

In order to take advantage of these interaction methods, we have to first understand the underlying logic that goes into scripting. These are logic patterns common to all manner of programming languages, although the syntax may vary. To draw a parallel between programming languages and spoken languages, although the vocabulary may vary from one language to another, many grammar patterns are shared by the majority of them.

By the end of this section, you're going to know about variables, arrays, comparison operators, if/else statements, loops, functions, and more. Ready?

```
alert("Hi there");
```

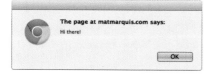

```
confirm("I'm gonna do something, okay?");
```

```
prompt("What should I do?");
```

Figure 19-5. Built-in JavaScript functions: `alert()` *(top),* `confirm()` *(middle), and* `prompt()` *(bottom).*

JavaScript is case-sensitive.

The basics

There are a few common syntactical rules that wind their way though all of JavaScript.

It is important to know that JavaScript is case-sensitive. A variable named "myVariable", a variable named "myvariable", and a variable named "MYVariable" will be treated as three different objects. Also, whitespace such as tabs and spaces are ignored, unless they're part of a string of text and enclosed in quotes.

Statements

A script is made up of a series of statements. A statement is a command that tells the browser what to do. Here is a simple statement that makes the browser display an alert with the phrase "Thank you."

```
alert("Thank you.");
```

The semicolon at the end of the statement tells JavaScript that it's the end of the command, just as a period ends a sentence. According to the JavaScript standard, a line break will also trigger the end of a command, but it is a best practice to end each statement with a semicolon.

Comments

JavaScript allows you to leave comments that will be ignored at the time the script is executed, so you can leave reminders and explanations throughout your code. This is especially helpful if this code is likely to be edited by another developer in the future.

There are two methods of using comments. For single-line comments, use two slash characters (**//**) at the beginning of the line. You can put single-line comments on the same line as a statement, as long as it comes after the statement. It does not need to be closed, as a line break effectively closes it.

```
// This is a single-line comment.
```

Multiple-line comments use the same syntax that you've seen in CSS. Everything within the **/* */** characters is ignored by the browser. You can use it to "comment out" notes and even chunks of the script when trouble-shooting.

```
/* This is a multi-line comment.
Anything between these sets of characters will be
completely ignored when the script is executed.
This form of comment needs to be closed. */
```

I'll be using the single-line comment notation to add short explanations to example code, and we'll make use of the **alert()** function we saw earlier (Figure 19-5) so we can quickly view the results of our work.

Variables

If you're anything like me, the very term "variables" triggers nightmarish flashbacks to eighth-grade math class. The premise is pretty much the same, though your teacher doesn't have a bad comb-over this time around.

A variable is like an information container.

A variable is like an information container. You give it a name and then assign it a value, which can be a number, text string, an element in the DOM, or a function—anything, really. This gives us a convenient way to reference that value later by name. The value itself can be modified and reassigned in what-ever way our scripts' logic dictates.

The following declaration creates a variable with the name "foo" and assigns it the value 5:

```
var foo = 5;
```

We start by declaring the variable using the **var** keyword. The single equals sign (=) indicates that we are assigning it a value. Because that's the end of our statement, we end the line with a semicolon. Variables can also be declared without the **var** keyword, which impacts what part of your script will have access to the information they contain. We'll discuss that further in the "Variable scope and the var keyword" section later on in this chapter.

You can use anything you like as a variable name, but make sure it's a name that will make sense to you later on. You wouldn't want to name a variable something like "data"; it should describe the information it contains. In our earlier very specific example, "numberFive" might be a more useful name than "foo." There are a few rules around variable naming:

- It must start with a letter or an underscore.

- It may contain letters, digits, and underscores in any combination.

- It may not contain character spaces. As an alternative, use underscores in place of spaces or close up the space and use camel case instead (for example, `my_variable` or `myVariable`).

- It may not contain special characters (`!` `.` `,` `/` `\` `+` `*` `=` etc.).

You can change the value of a variable at any time by redeclaring it anywhere in your script. Remember: JavaScript is case-sensitive, and so are those variable names.

Data types

The values we assign to variables fall under a few distinct data types.

Undefined

The simplest of these data types is likely "undefined." If we declare a variable by giving it a name but no value, that variable contains a value of "undefined."

```
var foo;

alert(foo); // This will open a dialog containing "undefined".
```

Odds are you won't find a lot of use for this right away, but it's worth knowing for the sake of troubleshooting some of the errors you're likely to encounter early on in your JavaScript career. If a variable has a value of "undefined" when it shouldn't, you may want to double-check that it has been declared correctly or that there isn't a typo in the variable name. (We've all been there.)

Null

Similar to the above, assigning a variable of "null" (again, case-sensitive) simply says, "Define this variable, but give it no inherent value."

```
var foo = null;
alert(foo); // This will open a dialog containing "null".
```

Numbers

You can assign variables numeric values.

```
var foo = 5;
alert(foo); // This will open a dialog containing "5".
```

The word "foo" now means the exact same thing as the number five as far as JavaScript is concerned. Because JavaScript is "loosely typed," we don't have to tell our script to treat the variable **foo** as the *number* five.

The variable behaves the same as the number itself, so you can do things to it that you would do to any other number using classic mathematical notation: **+**, **-**, *****, and **/** for plus, minus, multiply, and divide, respectively. In this example, we use the plus sign (**+**) to add **foo** to itself (**foo + foo**).

```
var foo = 5;
alert(foo + foo); // This will alert "10".
```

Strings

Another type of data that can be saved to a variable is a string, which is basically a line of text. Enclosing characters in a set of single or double quotes indicates that it's a string, as shown here:

```
var foo = "five";
alert( foo ); // This will alert "five"
```

The variable **foo** is now treated exactly the same as the word "five". This applies to any combination of characters: letters, numbers, spaces, and so on. If the value is wrapped in quotation marks, it will be treated as a string of text. If we were to wrap the number five (5) in quotes and assign it to a variable, that variable wouldn't behave as a number; instead, it would behave as a string of text containing the character "5."

Earlier we saw the plus (**+**) sign used to add numbers. When the plus sign is used with strings, it sticks the strings together (called concatenation) into one long string, as shown in this example.

```
var foo = "bye"
alert (foo + foo);  // This will alert "byebye"
```

Notice what the alert returns in the following example when we define the value 5 in quotation marks, treating it as a string instead of a number.

```
var foo = "5";
alert( foo + foo ); // This will alert "55"
```

If we concatenate a string and a number, JavaScript will assume that the number should be treated as a string as well, since the math would be impossible.

```
var foo = "five";
var bar = 5;
alert( foo + bar ); // This will alert "five5"
```

Booleans

We can also assign a variable a "true" or "false" value. This is called a Boolean value, and it is the lynchpin for all manner of advanced logic. Boolean values use the **true** and **false** keywords built into JavaScript, so quotation marks are not necessary.

```
var foo = true; // The variable "foo" is now true
```

Just as with numbers, if we were to wrap the value above in quotation marks, we'd be saving the *word* "true" to our variable instead of the inherent value of "true" (i.e., "not false").

In a sense, everything in JavaScript has either an inherently "true" or "false" value. "null", "undefined", "0", and empty strings ("") are all inherently false, while every other value is inherently true. These values, although not identical to the Booleans "true" and "false", are commonly referred to as being "truthy" and "falsy." I promise I didn't make that up.

Arrays

An array is a group of multiple values (called members) that can be assigned to a single variable. The values in an array are said to be indexed, meaning you can refer to them by number according to the order in which they appear in the list. The first member is given the index number 0, the second is 1, and so on, which is why one almost invariably hears us nerds start counting things at zero—because that's how JavaScript counts things, and many other programming languages do the same. We can avoid a lot of future coding headaches by keeping this in mind.

So, let's say our script needs all of the variables we defined earlier. We could define them three times and name them something like **foo1**, **foo2**, and so on, or we can store them in an array, indicated by square brackets ([ ]).

```
var foo = [5, "five", "5"];
```

Now anytime you need to access any of those values, you can grab them from the single **foo** array by referencing their index number:

```
alert( foo[0] ); // Alerts "5"

alert( foo[1] ); // Alerts "five"

alert( foo[2] ); // Also alerts "5"
```

Comparison operators

Now that we know how to save values to variables and arrays, the next logical step is knowing how to compare those values. There is a set of special characters called comparison operators that evaluate and compare values in different ways:

==	Is equal to
!=	Is not equal to
===	Is identical to (equal to and of the same data type)
!==	Is not identical to
>	Is greater than
>=	Is greater than or equal to
<	Is less than
<=	Is less than or equal to

There's a reason all of these definitions read as parts of a statement. In comparing values, we're making an assertion, and the goal is to obtain a result that is either inherently true or inherently false. When we compare two values, JavaScript evaluates the statement and gives us back a Boolean value depending on whether the statement is true or false.

```
alert( 5 == 5 ); // This will alert "true"

alert( 5 != 6 ); // This will alert "true"

alert( 5 < 1 ); // This will alert "false"
```

Equal versus identical

The tricky part is understanding the difference between "equal to" (==) and "identical to" (===). We already learned that all of these values fall under a certain data type. For example, a string of "5" and a number 5 are similar, but they're not quite the same thing.

Well, that's exactly what === is meant to check.

```
alert( "5" == 5 ); // This will alert "true". They're both "5".

alert( "5" === 5 ); // This will alert "false". They're both "5", but
they're not the same data type.

alert( "5" !== 5 ); // This will alert "true", since they're not the
same data type.
```

Even if you have to read it a couple of times, understanding the preceding sentence means you've already begun to adopt the special kind of crazy one needs to be a programmer. Welcome! You're in good company.

Mathematical operators

The other type of operator is a mathematical operator, which performs mathematical functions on numeric values. We touched briefly on the straightforward mathematical operators for add (+), subtract (-), multiply (*), and divide (/). There are also some useful shortcuts you should be aware of:

+=   Adds the value to itself

++   Increases the value of a number (or a variable containing a number value) by 1

--   Decreases the value of a number (or a variable containing a number value) by 1

WARNING

Be careful not to accidentally use a single equals sign, or you'll be reassigning the value of the first variable to the value of the second variable!

If/else statements

If/else statements are how we get JavaScript to ask itself a true/false question. They are more or less the foundation for all the advanced logic that can be written in JavaScript, and they're about as simple as programming gets. In fact, they're almost written in plain English. The structure of a conditional statement is as follows.

```
if( true ) {
    // Do something.
}
```

It tells the browser "if this condition is met, then execute the commands listed between the curly braces ({ })." JavaScript doesn't care about whitespace in our code, remember, so the spaces on either side of the (true) are purely for the sake of more readable code.

Here is a simple example using the array we declared earlier:

```
var foo = [5, "five", "5"];

if( foo[1] === "five" ) {
  alert("This is the word five, written in plain English.");
}
```

Since we're making a comparison, JavaScript is going to give us a value of either "true" or "false". The highlighted line of code breaks says "true or false: the value of the **foo** variable with an index of **1** is identical to the word 'five'?"

In this case, the alert would fire because the **foo** variable with an index of **1** (the second in the list, if you'll remember) is identical to "five". In this case, it is indeed true, and the alert fires.

We can also explicitly check if something is false, by using the != comparison operator that reads as "not equal to."

```
if( 1 != 2 ) {
  alert("If you're not seeing this, we have bigger problems than
    JavaScript.");
  // 1 is never equal to 2, so we should always see this alert.
}
```

I'm not much good at math, but near as I can tell, 1 will never be equal to 2. JavaScript says, "That '1 is not equal to 2' line is a true statement, so I'll run this code."

If the statement doesn't evaluate to "true", the code inside of the curly braces will be skipped over completely:

```
if( 1 == 2 ) {
  alert("If you're seeing this, we have bigger problems than
    JavaScript.");
// 1 is not equal to 2, so this code will never run.
}
```

Idiomatic JavaScript

There is an effort in the JavaScript community to create a style guide for writing JavaScript code. The document "Principles of Writing Consistent, Idiomatic JavaScript" states the following: "All code in any code-base should look like a single person typed it, no matter how many people contributed." To achieve that goal, a group of developers has written an Idiomatic Style Manifesto that describes how whitespace, line breaks, quotation marks, functions, variables, and more should be written to achieve "beautiful code." Learn more about it at *github.com/rwldrn/idiomatic.js/*.

That covers "if," but what about "else"?

Lastly—and I promise we're almost done here—what if we want to do one thing if something is true and something *else* if that thing is false? We could write two if statements, but that's a little clunky. Instead, we can just say, "else, do something…else."

```
var test = "testing";
if( test == "testing" ) {
        alert( "You haven't changed anything." );
} else {
    alert( "You've changed something!" );
}
```

Changing the value of the **testing** variable to something else—anything other than the word "testing"—will trigger the alert "You've changed something!"

Loops

There are cases in which we'll want to go through every item in an array and do something with it, but we won't want to write out the entire list of items and repeat ourselves a dozen or more times. You are about to learn a technique of *devastating power*, readers: loops.

I know. Maybe I made loops sound a little more exciting than they seem, but they *are* incredibly useful. With what we've covered already, we're getting good at dealing with single variables, but that can get us only so far. Loops allow us to easily deal with huge sets of data.

Say we have a form that requires none of the fields to be left blank. If we use the DOM to fetch every text input on the page, the DOM provides an array of every text input element. (I'll tell you more about how the DOM does this in the next chapter.) We could check every value stored in that array one item at a time, sure, but that's a lot of code and a maintenance nightmare. If we use a loop to check each value, we won't have to modify our script, regardless of how many fields are added to or removed from the page. Loops allow us to act on every item in an array, regardless of that array's size.

There are several ways to write a loop, but the **for** method is one of the most popular. The basic structure of a **for** loop is as follows:

```
for( initialize the variable;  test the condition;  alter the value; )
{
    // do something
}
```

Here is an example of a **for** loop in action.

```
for( var i = 0; i <= 2; i++ ) {
    alert( i ); // This loop will trigger three alerts, reading "0", "1",
      and "2" respectively.
}
```

That's a little dense, so let's break it down part-by-part:

for()

First, we're calling the **for** statement, which is built into JavaScript. It says, "For every time this is true, do this." Next we need to supply that statement with some information.

var i = 0;

This creates a new variable, **i**, with its value set to zero. You can tell it's a variable by the single equals sign. More often than not, you'll see coders using the letter "i" (short for "index") as the variable name, but keep in mind that you could use any variable name in its place. It's a common convention, not a rule.

We set that initial value to "0" because we want to stay in the habit of counting from zero up. That's where JavaScript starts counting, after all.

i <= 2;

With **i <= 2;**, we're saying, "for as long as **i** is less than or equal to 2, keep on looping." Since we're counting from zero, that means the loop will run three times.

i++

Finally, **i++** is shorthand for "every time this loop runs, add one to the value of **i** (**++** is one of the mathematical shortcut operators we saw earlier). Without this step, **i** would always equal zero, and the loop would run forever! Fortunately, modern browsers are smart enough not to let this happen. If one of these three pieces is missing, the loop simply won't run at all.

{ *script* }

Anything inside of those curly braces is executed once for each time the loop runs, which is three times in this case. That **i** variable is available for use in the code the loop executes as well, as we'll see next.

Let's go back to the "check each item in an array" example. How would we write a loop to do that for us?

```
var items = ["foo", "bar", "baz"]; // First we create an array.
for( var i = 0; i <= items.length; i++ ) {
  alert( items[i] ); // This will alert each item in the array.
}
```

This example differs from our first loop in two key ways:

items.length

Instead of using a number to limit the number of times the loop runs, we're using a property built right into JavaScript to determine the "length" of our array, which is the number of items it contains. **.length** is just one of the standard properties and methods of the **Array** object in JavaScript.

`items[i]`

> Remember how I mentioned that we can use that **i** variable inside of the loop? Well, we can use it to reference each index of the array. Good thing we started counting from zero; if we had set the initial value of **i** to 1, the first item in the array would have been skipped.

Now no matter how large or small that array should become, the loop will execute only as many times as there are items in the array, and will always hold a convenient reference to each item in the array.

There are literally dozens of ways to write a loop, but this is one of the more common patterns you're going to encounter out there in the wild. Developers use loops to perform a number of tasks, such as:

- Looping through a list of elements on the page and checking the value of each, applying a style to each, or adding/removing/changing an attribute on each. For example, we could loop through each element in a form and ensure that users have entered a valid value for each before they proceed.

- Creating a new array of items in an original array that have a certain value. We check the value of each item in the original array within the loop, and if the value matches the one we're looking for, we populate a new array with only those items. This turns the loop into a filter, of sorts.

Functions

I've introduced you to a few functions already in a sneaky way. Here's an example of a function that you might recognize:

```
alert("I've been a function all along!");
```

A function is a bit of code that doesn't run until it is referenced or called. **alert()** is a function built into our browser. It's a block of code that runs only when we explicitly tell it to. In a way, we can think of a function as a variable that contains *logic*, in that referencing that variable will run all the code stored inside it.

All functions share a common pattern (Figure 19-6). The function name is always immediately followed by a set of parentheses (no space), then a pair of curly braces that contains their associated code. The parentheses sometimes contain additional information used by the function called arguments. Arguments are data that can influence how the function behaves. For example, the **alert** function we know so well accepts a string of text as an argument, and uses that information to populate the resulting dialog.

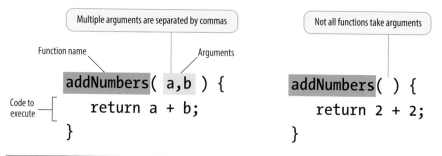

Figure 19-6. The structure of a function.

There are two types of functions: those that come "out of the box" (native JavaScript functions) and those that you make up yourself (custom functions). Let's look at each.

Native functions

There are hundreds of predefined functions built into JavaScript, including:

`alert()`, `confirm()`, and `prompt()`

These functions trigger browser-level dialog boxes.

`Date()`

Returns the current date and time.

`parseInt("123")`

This function will, among other things, take a string data type containing numbers and turn it into a number data type. The string is passed to the function as an argument.

`setTimeout(functionName, 5000)`

Will execute a function after a delay. The function is specified in the first argument, and the delay is specified in milliseconds in the second (in the example, 5,000 milliseconds equals 5 seconds).

There are scores more beyond this, as well.

Custom functions

To create a custom function, we type the **function** keyword followed by a name for the function, followed by opening and closing parentheses, followed by opening and closing curly brackets.

```
function name() {
    // Our function code goes here.
}
```

Just as with variables and arrays, the function's name can be anything you want, but all the same naming syntax rules apply.

If we were to create a function that just alerts some text (which is a little redundant, I know), it would look like this:

```
function foo() {
    alert("Our function just ran!");
        // This code won't run until we call the function 'foo()'
}
```

We can then call that function and execute the code inside it anywhere in our script by writing the following:

```
foo(); // Alerts "Our function just ran!"
```

We can call this function any number of times throughout our code. It saves a lot of time and redundant coding.

Arguments

Having a function that executes the exact same code throughout your script isn't likely to be all that useful. We can "pass arguments" (provide data) to native and custom functions in order to apply a function's logic to different sets of data at different times.

An argument is a value or data that a function uses when it runs.

To hold a place for the arguments, add one or more comma-separated variables in the parentheses at the time the function is defined. Then, when we call that function, anything we include between the parentheses will be passed into that variable as the function executes. This might sound a little confusing, but it's not so bad once you see it in action.

For example, let's say we wanted to create a very simple function that alerts the number of items contained in an array. We've already learned that we can use `.length` to get the number of items in an array, so we just need a way to pass the array to be measured into our function. We do that by supplying the array to be measured as an argument. In order to do that, we specify a variable name in the parentheses when we define our custom function. That variable will then be available inside of the function and will contain whatever argument we pass when we call the function.

```
function alertArraySize(arr) {
        alert(arr.length);
}
```

Now any array we specify between the parentheses when we call the function will be passed to the function with the variable name **arr**. All we need to do is get its length.

```
var test = [1,2,3,4,5];
alertArraySize(test); // Alerts "5"
```

Returning a value

This part is particularly wild, and incredibly useful.

It's pretty common to use a function to calculate something and then give you a value that you can use elsewhere in your script. We could accomplish this using what we know now, through clever application of variables, but there's a much easier way.

The **return** keyword inside a function effectively turns that function into a variable with a dynamic value! This one is a little easier to show than it is to tell, so bear with me while we consider this example.

```
function addNumbers(a,b) {
    return a + b;
}
```

We now have a function that accepts two arguments and adds them together. That wouldn't be much use if the result always lived inside that function, because we wouldn't be able to use the result anywhere else in our script. Here we use the **return** keyword to pass the result out of the function. Now any reference you make to that function gives you the result of the function—just like a variable would.

```
alert( addNumbers(2,5) ); // Alerts "7"
```

In a way, the **addNumbers** function is now a variable that contains a dynamic value: the value of our calculation. If we didn't return a value inside of our function, the preceding script would alert "undefined", just like a variable that we haven't given a value.

The **return** keyword has one catch. As soon as JavaScript sees that it's time to return a value, the function ends. Consider the following:

```
function bar() {
    return 3;
    alert("We'll never see this alert.");
}
```

When you call this function using **bar()**, the alert on the second line never runs. The function ends as soon as it sees it's time to return a value.

Variable scope and the var keyword

There are times when you'll want a variable that you've defined within a function to be available anywhere throughout your script. Other times, you may want to restrict it and make it available *only* to the function it lives in. This notion of the availability of the variable is known as its scope. A variable that can be used by any of the scripts on your page is globally scoped, and a variable that's available only within its parent function is locally scoped.

JavaScript variables use functions to manage their scope. If a variable is defined outside of a function, it will be globally scoped and available to all scripts. When you define a variable within a function and you want it to be used only by that function, you can flag it as locally scoped by preceding the variable name with the **var** keyword.

```
var foo = "value";
```

To expose a variable within a function to the global scope, we omit the **var** keyword and simply define the variable:

```
foo = "value";
```

You need to be careful about how you define variables within functions, or you could end up with unexpected results. Take the following JavaScript snippet, for example:

```
function double( num ){
  total = num + num;
  return total;
}
var total = 10;
var number = double( 20 );
alert( total ); // Alerts 40.
```

You may expect that because you specifically assigned a value of 10 to the variable **total,** the **alert(total)** function at the end of the script would return 10. But because we didn't scope the **total** variable in the function with the **var** keyword, it bleeds into the global scope. Therefore, although the variable **total** is set to 10, the following statement runs the function and grabs the value for **total** defined there. Without the **var**, the variable "leaked out."

As you can see, the trouble with global variables is that they'll be shared throughout all the scripting on a page. The more variables that bleed into the global scope, the better the chances you'll run into a "collision" in which a variable named elsewhere (in another script altogether, even) matches one of yours. This can lead to variables being inadvertently redefined with unexpected values, which can lead to errors in your script.

Remember that we can't always control all the code in play on our page. It's very common for pages to include code written by third parties, for example:

- Scripts to render advertisements
- User-tracking and analytics scripts
- Social media "share" buttons

It's best not to take any chances on variable collisions, so when you start writing scripts on your own, locally scope your variables whenever you can (see sidebar).

This concludes our little (OK, not so little) introductory tour of JavaScript syntax. There's a lot more to it, but this should give you a decent foundation for learning more on your own and being able to interpret scripts when you see them. We have just a few more JavaScript-related features to tackle before we look at a few examples.

Keeping variables out of the global scope

If you want to be sure that all of your variables stay out of the global scope, you can put all of your JavaScript in the following wrapper:

```
<script>
(function() {
    //All your code here!
})();
<script>
```

This little quarantining solution is called an IIFE (Independently Invoked Functional Expression), and we owe this method and the associated catchy term to Ben Alman.

The Browser Object

In addition to being able to control elements on a web page, JavaScript also gives you access to and the ability to manipulate the parts of the browser window itself. For example, you might want to get or replace the URL that is in the browser's address bar, or open or close a browser window.

In JavaScript, the browser is known as the **window** object. The **window** object has a number of properties and methods that we can use to interact with it. In fact, our old friend **alert()** is actually one of the standard browser object methods. Table 19-1 lists just a few of the properties and methods that can be used with **window** to give you an idea of what's possible.

Table 19-1. Browser properties and methods

Property/method	Description
event	Represents the state of an event
history	Contains the URLs the user has visited within a browser window
location	Gives read/write access to the URI in the address bar
status	Sets or returns the text in the status bar of the window
alert()	Displays an alert box with a specified message and an OK button
close()	Closes the current window
confirm()	Displays a dialog box with a specified message and an OK and a Cancel button
focus()	Sets focus on the current window

Events

JavaScript can access objects in the page and the browser window, but did you know it's also "listening" for certain events to happen? An event is an action that can be detected with JavaScript, such as when the document loads or when the user clicks on an element or just moves her mouse over it. HTML 4.0 made it possible for a script to be tied to events on the page whether initiated by the user, the browser itself, or other scripts. This is known as event binding.

Event handlers "listen" for certain document, browser, or user actions and bind scripts to those actions.

In scripts, an event is identified by an event handler. For example, the **onload** event handler triggers a script when the document loads, and the **onclick** and **onmouseover** handlers trigger a script when the user clicks or mouses over an element, respectively. Table 19-2 lists some of the most common event handlers.

Table 19-2. Common events

Event handler	Event description
onblur	An element loses focus
onchange	The content of a form field changes
onclick	The mouse clicks an object
onerror	An error occurs when the document or an image loads
onfocus	An element gets focus
onkeydown	A key on the keyboard is pressed
onkeypress	A key on the keyboard is pressed or held down
onkeyup	A key on the keyboard is released
onload	A page or an image is finished loading
onmousedown	A mouse button is pressed
onmousemove	The mouse is moved
onmouseout	The mouse is moved off an element
onmouseover	The mouse is moved over an element
onmouseup	A mouse button is released
onsubmit	The submit button is clicked in a form

There are three common methods for applying event handlers to items within our pages:

- As an HTML attribute

- As a method attached to the element

- Using `addEventListener`

In the examples of the latter two approaches, we'll use the **window** object. Any events we attach to **window** apply to the entire document. We'll be using the **onclick** event in all of these as well.

As an HTML attribute

You can specify the function to be run in an attribute in the markup as shown in the following example.

```
<body onclick="myFunction();"> /* myFunction will now run when the user
clicks anything within 'body' */
```

Although still functional, this is an antiquated way of attaching events to elements within the page. It should be avoided for the same reason we avoid using **style** attributes in our markup to apply styles to individual elements. In this case, it blurs the line between the semantic layer and behavioral layers of our pages, and can quickly lead to a maintenance nightmare.

As a method

This is another somewhat dated approach to attaching events, though it does keep things strictly within our scripts. We can also attach functions using helpers already built into JavaScript.

```
window.onclick = myFunction; /* myFunction will run when the user
clicks anything within the browser window */
```

We can also use an anonymous function rather than a predefined one:

```
window.onclick = function() {
    /* Any code placed here will run when the user clicks anything
    within the browser window */
};
```

This approach has the benefit of both simplicity and ease of maintenance, but does have a fairly major drawback: we can bind only one event at a time with this method.

```
window.onclick = myFunction;
```

```
window.onclick = myOtherFunction;
```

In the example just shown, the second binding overwrites the first, so when the user clicks inside the browser window, only **myOtherFunction** will run. The reference to **myFunction** is thrown away.

addEventListener

NOTE

For more information on **addEventListener***, see the "element.addEventListener" page on the Mozilla Developer Network* (*developer.mozilla.org/en/DOM/element.addEventListener*).

Although a little more complex at first glance, this approach allows us to keep our logic within our scripts and allows us to perform multiple bindings on a single object. The syntax is a bit more verbose. We start by calling the **addEventListener** method of the target object, and then specify the event in question and the function to be executed as two arguments.

```
window.addEventListener("click", myFunction);
```

Notice that we omit the preceding "on" from the event handler with this syntax.

Like the previous method, **addEventListener** can be used with an anonymous function as well:

```
window.addEventListener("click", function(e) {

});
```

Putting It All Together

Now you have been introduced to many of the important building blocks of JavaScript. You've seen variables, data types, and arrays. You've met if/else statements, loops, and functions. You know your browser objects from your event handlers. That's a lot of bits and pieces. Let's walk through a few simple script examples to see how they get put together.

Example 1: A tale of two arguments

Here's a simple function that accepts two arguments and returns the greater of the two values.

```
greatestOfTwo( first, second ) {
  if( first > second ) {
    return first;
  } else {
    return second;
  }
}
```

We start by naming our function: "greatestOfTwo". We set it up to accept two arguments, which we'll just call "first" and "second" for want of more descriptive words. The function contains an if/else statement that returns "first" if the first argument is greater than the second, and returns "second" if it isn't.

Example 2: The longest word

Here's a function that accepts an array of strings as a single argument and returns the longest string in the array.

```
longestWord( strings ) {
  var longest = strings[0];

  for( i = 1; i < strings.length; i++ ) {
    if ( strings[i].length > longest.length ) {
      longest = strings[i];
    }
  }
  return longest;
}
```

First, we name the function and allow it to accept a single argument. Then, we set the **longest** variable to an initial value of the first item in the array: **strings[0]**. We start our loop at 1 instead of 0 since we already have the first value in the array captured. Each time we iterate through the loop, we compare the length of the current item in the array to the length of the value saved in the **longest** variable. If the current item in the array contains more characters than the current value of the **longest** variable, we change the value of **longest** to that item. If not, we do nothing. After the loop is complete we return the value of **longest**, which will now contain the longest string in the array.

exercise 19-2 | **You try it**

In this exercise you will write a script that updates the page's title in the browser window with a "new messages" count. You may have encountered this sort of script in the wild from time to time. We're going to assume for the sake of the exercise that this is going to become part of a larger web app some day, and we're tasked only with updating the page title with the current "unread messages" count.

I've created a document for you already (*title.html*), which is available in the *materials* folder for this chapter on *learningwebdesign.com*.

1. Start by opening *title.html* in a browser. You'll see a blank page, with the **title** element already filled out. If you look up at the top of your browser window, you'll notice it reads "Million Dollar WebApp".

2. Now open the document in a text editor. You'll find a **script** element containing a comment just before the closing **</body>** tag. Feel free to delete the comment.

3. If we're going to be changing the page's title, we should save the original first. Create a variable named **originalTitle**. For its value, we'll have the browser get the title of the document using the DOM method **document.title**. Now we have a saved reference to the page title at the time the page is loaded. This variable should be global, so we'll declare it outside any functions.

   ```
   var originalTitle = document.title;
   ```

4. Next, we'll define a function so we can reuse the script whenever it's needed. Let's call the function something easy to remember, so we know at a glance what it does when we encounter it in our code later. "showUnreadCount" works for me, but you can name it whatever you'd like.

   ```
   var originalTitle = document.title;

   function showUnreadCount() {
   }
   ```

5. We need to think about what the function needs to make it useful. This function does something with the unread message count, so its argument is a single number referred to as "unread" in this example.

   ```
   var originalTitle = document.title;

   function showUnreadCount( unread ) {
   }
   ```

6. Now let's add the code that runs for this function. We want the document title for the page to display the title of the document plus the count of unread messages. Sounds like a job for concatenation (**+**)! Here we set the **document.title** to be (**=**) whatever string was saved for **originalTitle** plus the number in **showUnreadCount**. As we learned earlier, JavaScript combines a string and a number as though they are both strings.

   ```
   var originalTitle = document.title;

   function showUnreadCount( unread ) {
     document.title = originalTitle + unread;
   }
   ```

7. Let's try out our script before we go too much further. Below where you defined the function and the **originalTitle** variable, enter **showUnreadCount(3);**. Now save the page and reload it in your browser (Figure 19-7).

   ```
   var originalTitle = document.title;

   function showUnreadCount( unread ) {
     document.title = originalTitle + unread;
   }
   showUnreadCount(3);
   ```

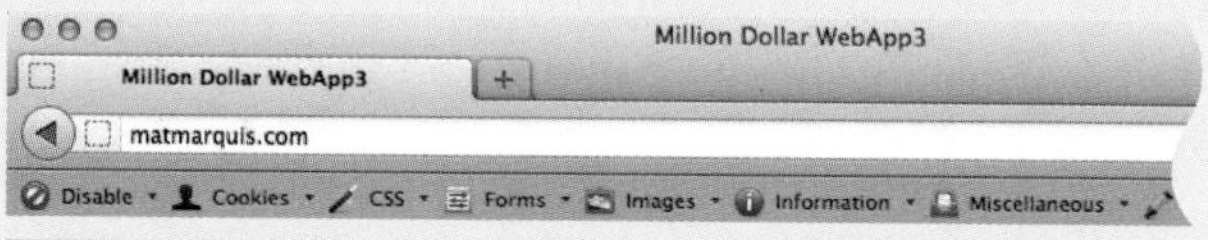

   Figure 19-7. Our title tag has changed! It's not quite right yet, though.

8. Our script is working, but it's not very easy to read. Fortunately, there's no limit on the number of strings we can combine at once. Here we're adding additional strings that wrap the count value and the words "new messages" in parentheses (Figure 19-8).

   ```
   var originalTitle = document.title;

   function showUnreadCount( unread ) {
     document.title = originalTitle + " (" + unread
   + " new messages!) ";
   }
   showUnreadCount(3);
   ```

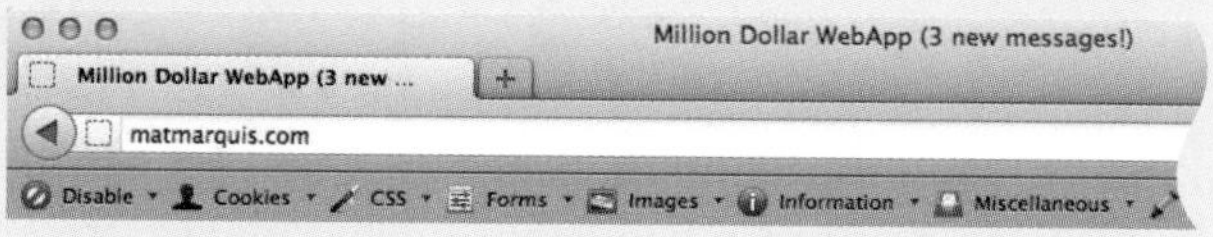

   Figure 19-8. Much better!

Test Yourself

We covered a lot of new material in this chapter. Here's a chance to test what sunk in.

1. Name one good thing and one bad thing about linking to an external *.js* file.

2. Given the following array:

    ```
    var myArray = [1, "two", 3, "4"]
    ```

    write what the alert message will say for each of these examples:

    a. alert(myArray[0]);

    b. alert(myArray[0] + myArray[1]);

    c. alert(myArray[2] + myArray[3]);

    d. alert(myArray[2] – myArray[0]);

3. What will each of these alert messages say?

    a.
    ```
    var foo = 5;
    foo += 5;
    alert( foo );
    ```

    b.
    ```
    i = 5;
    i++;
    alert( i );
    ```

    c.
    ```
    var foo = 2;
    alert( foo + " " + "remaining");
    ```

    d.
    ```
    var foo = "Mat";
    var bar = "Jennifer";
    if( foo.length > bar.length ) {
      alert( foo  + " is longer." );
    } else {
      alert( bar + " is longer." );
    }
    ```

    e.
    ```
    alert( 10 === "10" );
    ```

4. Describe what this does:
    ```
    for( var i = 0; i <= items.length;  i++ ) {  }
    ```

5. What is the problem with globally scoped variables?

6. Match what's happening with its event handler.

   a. onload

   b. onchange

   c. onfocus

   d. onmouseover

   e. onsubmit

   1. The user finishes a form and hits the submit button.

   2. The page finishes loading.

   3. The pointer hovers over a link.

   4. A text entry field is selected and ready for typing.

   5. A user changes her name in a form field.

USING JAVASCRIPT

by Mat Marquis

Now that you have a sense for the language of JavaScript, let's look at some of the ways we can put it to use in modern web design. First, we'll explore DOM scripting, which allows us to manipulate the elements, attributes, and text on a page. I'll introduce you to some ready-made JavaScript and DOM scripting resources, so you don't have to go it alone. You'll learn about "polyfills," which provide older browsers with modern features and normalize functionality. I'll also introduce you to JavaScript libraries that make developers' lives easier with collections of polyfills and shortcuts for common tasks.

Meet the DOM

You've seen references to the Document Object Model (DOM for short) several times throughout this book, but now is the time to give it the attention it deserves. The DOM gives us a way to access and manipulate the contents of a document. We commonly use it for HTML, but the DOM can be used with any XML language as well. And although we're focusing on its relationship with JavaScript, it is worth noting that the DOM can be accessed by other languages too, such as PHP, Ruby, Python, C++, Java, Perl, and more. Although DOM Level 1 was released by the W3C in 1998, it was nearly five years later that DOM scripting began to gain steam.

The DOM is a programming interface (an API) for HTML and XML pages. It provides a structured map of the document, as well as a set of methods to interface with the elements contained therein. Effectively, it translates our markup into a format that JavaScript (and other languages) can understand. It sounds pretty dry, I know, but the basic gist is that the DOM serves as a map to all the elements on a page. We can use it to find elements by their names or attributes, and then add, modify, or delete elements and their content.

Without the DOM, JavaScript wouldn't have any sense of a document's contents—and by that, I mean the *entirety* of the document's contents. Everything from the page's **doctype** to each individual letter in the text can be accessed via the DOM and manipulated with JavaScript.

IN THIS CHAPTER

Using the DOM to access and change elements, attributes, and contents

Using polyfills to make browser versions work consistently

Using JavaScript libraries

A brief introduction to Ajax

The DOM gives us a way to access and manipulate the contents of a document.

485

The node tree

A simple way to think of the DOM is in terms of the document tree (Figure 20-1). You saw documents diagrammed in this way when you were learning about CSS selectors.

```
<html>
<head>
  <title>Document title</title>
  <meta charset="utf-8">
</head>
<body>
  <div>
    <h2>Subhead</h2>
    <p>Paragraph text with a <a href="foo.html">link</a> here.</p>
  </div>
  <div>
    <p>More text here.</p>
  </div>
</body>
</html>
```

> **AT A GLANCE**
>
> The DOM is a collection of nodes:
> - Element nodes
> - Attribute nodes
> - Text nodes

Figure 20-1. A simple document tree

Figure 20-2. The nodes within the first p element in our sample document.

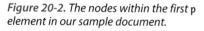

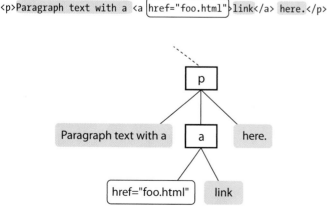

Each element within the page is referred to as a node. If you think of the DOM as a tree, each node is an individual branch that can contain further branches. But the DOM allows deeper access to the content than CSS because it treats the actual content as a node as well. Figure 20-2 shows the structure of the first **p** element. The element, its attributes, and its contents are all nodes in the DOM's node tree.

It also provides a standardized set of methods and functions through which JavaScript can interact with the elements on our page. Most DOM scripting involves reading from and writing to the document.

There are several ways to use the DOM to find what you want in a document. Let's go over some of the specific methods we can use for accessing objects defined by the DOM (we JS folks call this "crawling the DOM" or "traversing the DOM"), as well as some of the methods for manipulating those elements.

Accessing DOM nodes

The **document** object in the DOM identifies the page itself, and more often than not will serve as the starting point for our DOM crawling. The **document** object comes with a number of standard properties and methods for accessing collections of elements. This is reminiscent of the **length** property we learned about in Chapter 19, "Introduction to JavaScript." Just as **length** is a standard property of all arrays, the **document** object comes with a number of built-in properties containing information about the document. We then wind our way to the element we're after by chaining those properties and methods together, separated by periods, to form a sort of route through the document.

To give you a general idea of what I mean, the statement in this example says to look on the page (**document**), find the element that has the **id** value "beginner", find the HTML content within that element (**innerHTML**), and save those contents to a variable (**foo**).

```
var foo = document.getElementById( "beginner" ).innerHTML;
```

Because the chains tend to get long, it is also common to see each property or method broken onto its own line to make it easier to read at a glance. Remember, whitespace in JavaScript is ignored, so this has no effect on how the statement is parsed.

```
var foo = document
  .getElementById( "beginner" )
    .innerHTML;
```

There are several methods for accessing nodes in the document.

By element name

getElementsByTagName()

We can access individual elements by the tags themselves using **document.getElementsByTagName()**. This method retrieves any element or elements you specify as an argument.

For example, **document.getElementsByTagName("p")** returns every paragraph on the page, wrapped in something called a collection or nodeList, in the order they appear in the document from top to bottom. nodeLists behave much like arrays. To access specific paragraphs in the nodeList, we reference them by their index, just like an array.

```
var paragraphs = document.getElementsByTagName("p");
```

Based on this variable statement, **paragraphs[0]** is a reference to the first paragraph in the document, **paragraph[1]** refers to the second, and so on.

NOTE

nodeLists are living collections. If you manipulate the document in a nodeList loop—for example, looping through all paragraphs and appending new ones along the way—you can end up in an infinite loop. Good times!

If we had to access each element in the nodeList separately, one at a time... well, it's a good thing we learned about looping through arrays earlier. Loops work the exact same way with a nodeList.

```
var paragraphs = document.getElementsByTagName("p");
for( var i = 0; i < paragraphs.length; i++ ) {
 // do something
}
```

Now we can access each paragraph on the page individually by referencing **paragraphs[i]** inside the loop, just as with an array, but with elements on the page instead of values.

By id attribute value

getElementById()

This method returns a single element based on that element's ID (the value of its **id** attribute), which we provide to the method as an argument. For example, to access this particular image:

```
<img src="photo.jpg" alt="" id="lead-photo">'
```

we include the **id** value as an argument for the **getElementById()** method:

```
var photo = document.getElementById("lead-photo");
```

By class attribute value

getElementsByClassName()

Just as it says on the tin, this allows you to access nodes in the document based on the value of a **class** attribute. This statement assigns any element with a **class** value of "column-a" to the variable **firstColumn** so it can be accessed easily from within a script.

```
var firstColumn = document.getElementsByClassName("column-a");
```

Like **getElementsByTagName**, this returns a nodeList that we can reference by index or loop through one at a time.

By selector

querySelectorAll()

querySelectorAll allows you to access nodes of the DOM based on a CSS-style selector. The syntax of the arguments in the following examples should look familiar to you. It can be as simple as accessing the child elements of a specific element:

```
var sidebarPara = document.querySelectorAll(".sidebar p");
```

or as complex as selecting an element based on an attribute:

```
var textInput = document.querySelectorAll("input[type='text']");
```

Like **getElementsByTagName** and **getElementsByClassName**, **querySelectorAll** returns a nodeList (even if the selector matches only a single element).

Accessing an attribute value

`getAttribute()`

As I mentioned earlier, elements aren't the only thing you can access with the DOM. To get the value of an attribute attached to an element node, we call **getAttribute()** with a single argument: the attribute name. Let's assume we have an image, *stratocaster.jpg*, marked up like this:

```
<img src="stratocaster.jpg" alt="electric guitar" id="lead-image">
```

In the following example, we access that specific image (**getElementbyId**) and save a reference to it in a variable (**bigImage**). At that point, we could access any of the element's attributes (**alt**, **src**, or **id**) by specifying it as an argument in the **getAttribute** method. In the example, we get the value of the **src** attribute and use it as the content in an alert message. (I'm not sure *why* we would ever do that, but it does demonstrate the method.)

```
var bigImage = document.getElementById("lead-image");

alert( bigImage.getAttribute("src") ); // Alerts "stratocaster.jpg".
```

Manipulating nodes

Once we've accessed a node using one of the methods discussed previously, the DOM gives us several built-in methods for manipulating those elements, their attributes, and their contents.

`setAttribute()`

To continue with the previous example, we saw how we *get* the attribute value, but what if we wanted to *set* the value of that **src** attribute to a new pathname altogether? Use **setAttribute()**! This method requires two arguments: the attribute to be changed and the new value for that attribute.

In this example, we use a bit of JavaScript to swap out the image by changing the value of the **src** attribute.

```
var bigImage = document.getElementById("lead-image");

bigImage.setAttribute("src", "lespaul.jpg");
```

Just think of all the things you could do with a document by changing the values of attributes. Here we swapped out an image, but this same method could be used to make a number of changes throughout our document:

- Update the **checked** attributes of checkboxes and radio buttons based on user interaction elsewhere on the page.

- Find the **link** element for our *.css* file and point the **href** value to a different style sheet, changing all the page's styles.

- Update a **title** attribute with information on an element's state ("this element is currently selected," for example).

innerHTML

innerHTML gives us a simple method for accessing and changing the text and markup inside an element. It behaves differently from the methods we've covered so far. Let's say we need a quick way of adding a paragraph of text to the first element on our page with a class of **intro**:

```
var introDiv = document.getElementsByClassName("intro");
introDiv[0].innerHTML = "<p>This is our intro text</p>";
```

The second statement here adds the content of the string to **introDiv** (an element with the **class** value "intro") as a *real live element* because **innerHTML** tells JavaScript to parse the strings "<p>" and "</p>" as markup.

style

The DOM also allows you to add, modify, or remove a CSS style from an element using the **style** property. It works similarly to applying a style with the inline **style** attribute. The individual CSS properties are available as properties of the **style** property. I bet you can figure out what these statements are doing using your new CSS and DOM know-how:

```
document.getElementById("intro").style.color = "#fff";
document.getElementById("intro").style.backgroundColor = "#f58220";
    //orange
```

In JavaScript and the DOM, property names that are hyphenated in CSS (such as **background-color** and **border-top-width**) become camel case (**backgroundColor** and **borderTopWidth**, respectively) so the **-** character isn't mistaken for an operator.

In the examples you've just seen, the **style** property is used to set the styles for the node. It can also be used to get a style value for use elsewhere in the script. This statement gets the background color of the **#intro** element and assigns it to the **brandColor** variable:

```
var brandColor = document.getElementById("intro").style.backgroundColor;
```

Adding and removing elements

So far, we've seen examples of getting and setting nodes in the existing document. The DOM also allows developers to change the document structure itself by adding and removing nodes on the fly. We'll start out by creating new nodes, which is fairly straightforward, and then we'll see how we add the nodes we've created to the page. The methods shown here are more surgical and precise than adding content with **innerHTML**. While we're at it, we'll remove nodes, too.

createElement()

To create a new element, use the aptly named **createElement()** method. This function accepts a single argument: the element to be created. Using this method is a little counterintuitive at first because the new element doesn't appear on the page right away. Once we create an element in this way, that new element remains floating in the JavaScript ether until we add it to the document. Think of it as creating a *reference* to a new element that lives purely in memory—something that we can manipulate in JavaScript as we see fit, then add to the page once we're ready.

```
var newDiv = document.createElement("div");
```

createTextNode()

If we want to enter text into either an element we've created or an existing element on the page, we can call the **createTextNode()** method. To use it, provide a string of text as an argument, and the method creates a DOM-friendly version of that text, ready for inclusion on the page. Much like **createElement**, this creates a reference to the new text node that we can store in a variable and add to the page when the time comes.

```
var ourText = document.createTextNode("This is our text.");
```

appendChild()

So we've created a new element and a new string of text, but how do we make them part of the document? Enter the **appendChild** method. This method takes a single argument: the node you want to add to the DOM. You call it on the existing element that will be its *parent* in the document structure. Time for an example.

Here we have a simple **div** on the page with the **id** "our-div":

```
<div id="our-div"></div>
```

Let's say we want to add a paragraph to **#our-div** that contains the text "Hello, world". We start by creating the **p** element (**document.createElement()**) as well as a text node for the content that will go inside it (**createTextNode()**).

```
var ourDiv = document.getElementById("our-div");
var newParagraph = document.createElement("p");
var copy = document.createTextNode("Hello, world!");
```

Now we have our element and some text, and we can use **appendChild()** to put the pieces together.

```
newParagraph.appendChild( copy );
ourDiv.appendChild( newParagraph );
```

The first statement appends **copy** (that's our "Hello, world" text node) to the new paragraph we created (**newParagraph**), so now that element has some content. The second line appends the **newParagraph** to the original **div** (**ourDiv**). Now **ourDiv** isn't sitting there all empty in the DOM, and it will display on the page with the content "Hello, world."

You should be getting the idea of how it works. How about a couple more?

insertBefore()

The **insertBefore()** method, as you might guess, inserts an element before another element. It takes two arguments: the first is the node that gets inserted, and the second is the element it gets inserted in front of. You also need to know the parent to which the element will be added.

So, for example, to insert a new heading before the paragraph in this markup:

```
<div id="our-div">
  <p id="our-paragraph">Our paragraph text</p>
</div>
```

we start by assigning variable names to the **div** and the **p** it contains, then create the **h1** element and its text node and put them together, just as we saw in the last example.

```
var ourDiv = document.getElementById("our-div");
var para = document.getElementById("our-paragraph");

var newHeading = document.createElement("h1");
var headingText = document.createTextNode("A new heading");
newHeading.appendChild( headingText );
// Add our new text node to the new heading
```

Finally, in the last statement shown here, the **insertBefore()** method places the **newHeading h1** element before the **para** element inside **ourDiv**.

```
ourDiv.insertBefore( newHeading, para );
```

replaceChild()

The **replaceChild()** method replaces one node with another and takes two arguments. The first argument is the new child (i.e., the node you want to end up with). The second is the node that gets replaced by the first. Like **insertBefore()**, you also need to identify the parent element in which the swap happens. For the sake of simplicity, let's say we start with the following markup:

```
<div id="our-div">
  <div id="swap-me"></div>
</div>
```

and we want to replace the **div** with the **id** "swap-me" with an image. We start by creating a new **img** element and setting the **src** attribute to the pathname to the image file. In the final statement, we use **replaceChild()** to put **newImg** in place of **swapMe**.

```
var ourDiv = document.getElementById("our-div");
var swapMe = document.getElementById("swap-me");
var newImg = document.createElement("img");
// Create a new image element

newImg.setAttribute( "src", "path/to/image.jpg" );
// Give the new image a "src" attribute
ourDiv.replaceChild( newImg, swapMe );
```

`removeChild()`

To paraphrase my mother, "We brought these elements into this world, and we can take them out again." You remove a node or an entire branch from the document tree with the **removeChild()** method. The method takes one argument, which is the node you want to remove. Remember that the DOM thinks in terms of *nodes*, not just elements, so the child of an element may be the text (node) it contains, not just other elements.

Like **appendChild**, the **removeChild** method is always called on the parent element of the element to be removed (hence, "remove *child*"). That means we'll need a reference to both the parent node and the node we're looking to remove. Let's assume the following markup pattern:

```html
<div id="parent">
  <div id="remove-me">
    <p>Pssh, I never liked it here anyway.</p>
  </div>
</div>
```

Our script would look something like this:

```javascript
var parentDiv = document.getElementById("parent");
var removeMe = document.getElementById("remove-me");

parentDiv.removeChild( removeMe );
    // Removes the div with the id "remove-me" from the page.
```

For further reading

That should give you a good idea of what DOM Scripting is all about. Of course, I've just barely scratched the surface of what can be done with the DOM, but if you'd like to learn more, definitely check out the book *DOM Scripting: Web Design with JavaScript and the Document Object Model, Second Edition*, by Jeremy Keith and Jeffrey Sambells (Friends of Ed).

Polyfills

You've gotten familiar with a lot of new technologies in this book so far: new HTML5 elements, new ways of doing things with CSS3, using JavaScript to manipulate the DOM, and more. In a perfect world, all browsers would be in lockstep, keeping up with the cutting-edge technologies and getting the established ones right along the way (see the "Browser Wars" sidebar). In that perfect world, browsers that couldn't keep up (I'm looking at you, IE6) would just vanish completely. Sadly, that is not the world we live in, and browser inadequacies remain the thorn in every developer's side.

I'll be the first to admit that I enjoy a good wheel-reinvention. It's a great way to learn, for one thing. For another, it's the reason our cars aren't rolling around on roundish rocks and sections of tree trunk. But when it comes to dealing with every strange browser quirk out there, we don't have to start from scratch. Tons of people smarter than I have run into these issues before

The Browser Wars

JavaScript came about during a dark and lawless time, before the web standards movement, when all the major players in the browser world were—for want of a better term—winging it. It likely won't come as a major surprise to anyone that Netscape and Microsoft implemented radically different versions of the DOM, with the prevailing sentiment being "may the best browser win."

I'll spare you the gory details of the Battle for JavaScript Hill, but the two competing implementations were so different that they were both largely useless, unless you wanted to either maintain two separate code bases or add a "best viewed in Internet Explorer/Netscape" warning label to your sites.

Enter the web standards movement! During this cutthroat time, the W3C was putting together the foundations for the modern-day standardized DOM that we've all come to know and love. Fortunately for us, Netscape and Microsoft got on board with the standards movement. The standardized DOM is supported all the way back to Internet Explorer 5 and Netscape Navigator 6. Unfortunately, Internet Explorer's advancements in this area stagnated for quite some time following IE6. As a result, older versions of IE have a few significant differences from the modern-day DOM. Fortunately with Internet Explorer 9, and soon with 10, they're catching right back up.

Trouble is, your project likely still needs to support those users with older versions of IE. It's a pain, but we're up for it. We have an amazing set of tools at our disposal, such as polyfills and JavaScript libraries full of helper functions, that normalize the strange little quirks we're apt to encounter from browser to browser.

and have already found clever ways to work around them and fix the parts of JavaScript and the DOM where some browsers may fall short. We can use JavaScript to fix JavaScript.

Polyfill is a term coined by Remy Sharp to describe a JavaScript "shim" that normalizes differing behavior from browser to browser.

> *"A shim that mimics a future API providing fallback functionality to older browsers."* —Paul Irish

There's a lot of time travel going on in that quote, but basically what he's saying is that we're making something new work in browsers that don't natively support it—whether that's brand-new technology like detecting a user's physical location or fixing something that one of the browsers just plain got wrong.

There are tons of polyfills out there targeted to specific tasks, such as making old browsers recognize new HTML5 elements or CSS3 Selectors, and new ones are popping up all the time as new problems arise. I'm going to fill you in on the most commonly used polyfills in the modern developer's toolbox as of the release of this book. You may find that new ones are necessary by the time you hit the web design trenches.

HTML5 shiv (or shim)

You may remember seeing this one back in Chapter 5, "Marking Up Text," but let's give it a little more attention now that you have some JavaScript under your belt.

An HTML5 shiv/shim is used to enable Internet Explorer 8 and earlier to recognize and style newer HTML5 elements such as **article**, **section**, and **nav**.

How it works

> There are several variations on the HTML5 shim/shiv, but they all work in much the same way: crawl the DOM looking for elements that IE doesn't recognize, and then immediately replace them with the same element so they are visible to IE in the DOM. Now any styles we write against those elements work as expected.

Who made it

> Sjoerd Visscher originally discovered this technique, and many, many variations of these scripts exist now. Remy Sharp's version is the one likely in widest use today.

How to use it

> Every variation on this script has the same requirement: it must be referenced in the **head** of the document, in order to "tell" Internet Explorer about these new elements before it finishes rendering the page.

```
<!--[if lt IE 9]>
    <script src="html5shim.js"></script>
<![endif]-->
```

Potential drawbacks

The major caveat here is that older versions of Internet Explorer that have JavaScript disabled or unavailable will receive unstyled elements.

Where to get it and learn more

- The Wikipedia entry for HTML Shiv (*en.wikipedia.org/wiki/HTML5_Shiv*)

- Remy Sharp's original post (*remysharp.com/2009/01/07/html5-enabling-script*)

Modernizr

Modernizr isn't a polyfill in and of itself, but rather a test suite that can be used to detect the presence of browser features and load polyfills as needed. The Modernizr team also curates a massive repository of polyfills for a huge number of features (see note).

How it works

Modernizr looks for the presence of methods and functions used by the JavaScript APIs of newer HTML5 and CSS3 features, and uses their presence to determine whether the browser natively supports the feature or should receive a polyfill. For example, if the browser contains built-in methods for interacting with the HTML5 **canvas** element, we can assume that that browser supports **canvas**. This is known as "feature detection," and it stands in stark contrast to the more outdated practice of UA (User Agent, or browser) detection. Modernizr also includes, right out of the box, an HTML5 shim similar to the one detailed previously.

Who made it

Modernizr was created by Faruk Ateş, and is actively developed by Paul Irish, Alex Sexton, Ryan Seddon, and Alexander Farkas.

How to use it

Modernizr.com has a builder tool that will allow you to include only the tests that are relevant to your project, as well as a "development" build that contains the entire library of tests. Once you've downloaded a custom build, simply include it as you would any other external script.

Where to get it and learn more

The Modernizr site (*modernizr.com*)

NOTE

The polyfill archive maintained by the Modernizr team is available at github.com/Modernizr/Modernizr/wiki/HTML5-Cross-Browser-Polyfills.

Selectivizr

Selectivizr allows older versions of Internet Explorer to understand complex CSS3 selectors such as `:nth-child` and `::first-letter`.

How it works

Selectivizr uses JavaScript to fetch and parse the contents of your style sheet and patch holes where the browser's native CSS parser falls short.

Who made it

Selectivizr was created and is maintained by Keith Clark.

How to use it

Selectivizr must be used with a JavaScript library (I talk about them in the next section). The link to the script goes in an IE conditional comment after the link to the library *.js* file, like so:

```
<script type="text/javascript" src="[JS library]"></script>
<!--[if (gte IE 6)&(lte IE 8)]>
  <script type="text/javascript" src="selectivizr.js"></script>
  <noscript><link rel="stylesheet" href="[fallback css]" /></noscript>
<![endif]-->
```

Potential drawbacks

Because we're forgoing the native CSS parser here, we may see a slight performance hit in applicable browsers.

Where to get it and learn more

*   The Selectivizr site (*selectivizr.com*)

Respond.js

Respond.js is a fast and lightweight polyfill that allows older browsers (again, most commonly Internet Explorer 8 and below) to understand `min-width` and `max-width` media queries, which are commonly used in responsive designs.

How it works

Like Selectivizr, Respond.js looks through style sheets independent of the browser's built-in parser, and upon finding a `min-width` or `max-width` media query, manually applies those styles to elements on the page through JavaScript, depending on the browser window's width.

Who made it

Respond.js was created by my fellow Filament Group and jQuery Mobile team member Scott Jehl. It was originally developed for use on the responsive BostonGlobe.com site, and was later released as an open source project.

How to use it

Unsurprisingly, one need only download Respond.js and reference it in a `script` tag within the `head` of the document (after the style sheets).

Potential drawbacks

Again, like Selectivizr, we may see a slight performance hit when using this script, but only in browsers where it ends up being used.

Where to get it and learn more

Scott Jehl's Respond page on GitHub (*github.com/scottjehl/Respond*)

JavaScript Libraries

Continuing on the "you don't have to write everything from scratch yourself" theme, it's time to take on JavaScript libraries. A JavaScript library is a collection of prewritten functions and methods that you can use in your scripts to accomplish common tasks or simplify complex ones.

There are many, many JS libraries out there. Some are large frameworks that include all of the most common polyfills, shortcuts, and widgets you'd ever need to build full-blown Ajax web applications (see the sidebar "What Is Ajax?"). Some are targeted at specific tasks, such as handling forms, animation, charts, or math functions. For seasoned JavaScript-writing pros, starting with a library is an awesome time-saver. And for folks like you who are just getting started, a library can handle tasks that might be beyond the reach of your own skills.

What Is Ajax?

Ajax (sometimes written AJAX) stands for Asynchronous JavaScript And XML. The "XML" part isn't that important—you don't have to use XML to use Ajax (more on that in a moment). The "asynchronous" part is what matters.

Traditionally, when a user interacted with a web page in a way that required data to be delivered from the server, everything had to stop and wait for the data, and the whole page needed to reload when it was available. This made for a not especially smooth user experience.

But with Ajax, because the page can get data from the server in the background, you can make updates to the page based on user interaction smoothly and in real time. This makes web applications feel more like "real" applications.

You see this on a number of modern websites, although sometimes it's subtle. On Twitter, for example, scrolling to the bottom of a page loads in a set of new tweets. Those aren't hardcoded in the page's markup; they're loaded dynamically as needed. Google's image search uses a similar approach. When you reach the bottom of the current page, you're presented with a button that allows you to load more, but you never navigate away from the current page.

The term "Ajax" was first coined by Jesse James Garrett in an article entitled "Ajax: A New Approach to Web Applications." Ajax is not a single technology, but rather a combination of HTML, CSS, the DOM, and JavaScript, including the `XMLHttpRequest` object that allows data to be transferred asynchronously. Ajax may use XML for data, but it has become more common to use JSON (JavaScript Object Notation), a JavaScript-based and human-readable format, for data exchange.

Writing web applications with Ajax isn't the type of thing you would do right out of the gate, but many of the JavaScript libraries discussed in this chapter have built-in Ajax helpers and methods that let you get started with significantly less effort.

The disadvantage of libraries is that because they generally contain all of their functionality in one big *.js* file, you may end up forcing your users to download a lot of code that never gets used. But the library authors are aware of this and have made many of their libraries modular, and they continue to make efforts to optimize their code. In some cases, it's also possible to customize the script and use just the parts you need.

A few libraries you ought to know

Some of the most popular JS libraries as of this writing include:

- **jQuery** (*jquery.com*). jQuery, written in 2005 by John Resig, is by far the most popular JavaScript library today, finding its way onto more than half of the 10,000 most-visited websites. It is free, open source, and employs a syntax that makes it easy to use if you are already handy with CSS, JavaScript, and the DOM. You can supplement jQuery with the jQuery UI library, which adds cool interface elements such as calendar widgets, drag-and-drop functionality, expanding accordion lists, and simple animation effects. I mentioned earlier that I work on jQuery Mobile. That's another jQuery-based library that provides UI elements and polyfills designed to account for the variety of mobile browsers and their notorious quirks.

- **Dojo** (*dojotoolkit.org*). Dojo is an open source, modular toolkit that is particularly helpful for developing web applications with Ajax.

- **Prototype** (*prototypejs.org*). The Prototype JavaScript Framework, written by Sam Stephenson, was developed to add Ajax support to Ruby on Rails.

- **MooTools** (*mootools.net*). MooTools (which stands for My Object-Oriented Tools) is another open source, modular library written by Valerio Proietti.

- **YUI** (*yuilibrary.com*). The Yahoo! User Interface Library is another free, open source JS library for building rich web applications. It is part of the YUI Library project at Yahoo!, founded by Thomas Sha.

As for smaller JS libraries that handle specialized functions, because they are being created and made obsolete all the time, I recommend doing a web search for "JavaScript libraries for _____" and see what is available. Some library categories include:

- Forms

- Animation

- Games

- Information graphics

- Image and 3-D effects in **canvas**

NOTE

For a comparison of over 20 JavaScript libraries and their sizes and features, see the "Comparison of JavaScript frameworks" entry on Wikipedia: en.wikipedia.org/wiki/Comparison_of_ JavaScript_frameworks.

The Google Developers site also maintains a list of the more popular open source JavaScript libraries, available here: developers.google.com/speed/ libraries/.

- String and math functions
- Database handling

How to use a JS library (jQuery)

It's easy to implement any of the libraries I just listed. All you do is download the JavaScript (*.js*) file, put it on your server, point to it in your **script** tag, and you're good to go. It's the *.js* file that does all the heavy lifting, providing prewritten functions and syntax shortcuts. Once you've included it, you can write your own scripts that leverage the features built into the framework. Of course, what you actually do with it is the interesting part (and largely beyond the scope of this chapter, unfortunately).

As a member of the jQuery Mobile team, I have a pretty obvious bias here, so we're going to stick with jQuery in the upcoming examples. Not only is it the most popular library anyway, but they said they'd give me a dollar every time I say "jQuery."

Download the jQuery .js file

To get started with jQuery (*cha-ching*), go to *jQuery.com* and hit the big Download button to get your own copy of *jquery.js*. You have a choice between a "production" version that has all the extra whitespace removed for a smaller file size, or a "development" version that is easier to read but nearly eight times larger in file size. The production version should be just fine if you are not going to edit it yourself.

Copy the code, paste it into a new plain-text document, and save it with the same filename that you see in the address bar in the browser window. As of this writing, the latest version of jQuery is 1.7.2, and the filename of the production version is *jquery-1.7.2.min.js* (the *min* stands for "minimized"). Put the file in the directory with the other files for your site. Some developers keep their scripts in a *js* directory for the sake of organization, or they may simply keep them in the root directory for the site. Wherever you decide put it, be sure to note the pathname to the file because you'll need it in the markup.

Add it to your document

Include the jQuery script the same way you'd include any other script in the document: with a **script** element.

```
<script src="pathtoyourjs/jquery-1.7.2.min.js"></script>
```

And that's pretty much it. There is an alternative worth mentioning, however. If you don't want to host the file yourself, you can point to one of the publically hosted versions and use it that way. The jQuery Download page lists a few options, including the following link to the code on Google's server. Simply copy this code exactly as you see it here, paste it into the **head** of the document or before the **</body>** tag, and you've got yourself some jQuery!

```
<script src="https://ajax.googleapis.com/ajax/libs/jquery/1.7.2/jquery.
min.js"></script>
```

Get "ready"

You don't want to go firing scripts before the document and the DOM are ready for them, do you? Well, jQuery has a statement known as the ready event that checks the document and waits until it's ready to be manipulated. Not all scripts require this (for example, if you were only firing a browser alert), but if you are doing anything with the DOM, it is a good idea to start by setting the stage for your scripts by including this function in your custom **script** or *.js* file:

```
<script src="pathtoyourjs/jquery-1.7.2.min.js"></script>

<script>
$(document).ready(function(){

    // Your code here

});
</script>
```

Scripting with jQuery

Once you're set up, you can begin writing your own scripts using jQuery. The shortcuts jQuery offers break down into two general categories:

- A giant set of built-in feature detection scripts and polyfills

- A shorter, more intuitive syntax for targeting elements (jQuery's selector engine)

You should have a decent sense of what the polyfills do after making your way through that last section, so let's take a look at what the selector engine does for you.

One of the things that jQuery simplifies is moving around through the DOM because you can use the selector syntax that you learned for CSS. Here is an example of getting an element by its **id** value *without* a library:

```
var paragraph = document.getElementById( "status" );
```

The statement finds the element with the ID "status" and saves a reference to the element in a variable (**paragraph**). That's a lot of characters for a simple task. You can probably imagine how things get a little verbose when you're accessing lots of elements on the page. Now that we have jQuery in play, however, we can use this shorthand.

```
var paragraph = $("#status");
```

That's right—that's the **id** selector you know and love from writing CSS. And it doesn't just stop there. *Any* selector you'd use in CSS will work within that special helper function.

You want to find everything with a class of "header"? Use **$(".header");**.

By the element's name? Sure: **$("div");**.

Every subhead in your sidebar? Easy-peasy: **$("#sidebar .sub");**.

You can even target elements based on the value of attributes: **$("[href='http://google.com']");**.

But it doesn't stop with selectors. We can use a huge number of helper functions built into jQuery and libraries like it to crawl the DOM like so many, uh, Spider-men. Spider-persons. Web-slingers.

jQuery also allows us to chain objects together in a way that can target things even CSS can't (an element's parent element, for example). Let's say we have a paragraph and we want to add a **class** to that paragraph's parent element. We don't necessarily know what that parent element will be, so we're unable to target the parent element directly. In jQuery we can use the **parent()** object to get to it.

```
$("p.error").parent().addClass("error-dialog");
```

Another major benefit is that this is highly readable at a glance: "find any paragraph(s) with the class 'error' and add the class 'error-dialog' to their parent(s)."

But what if I don't know how to write scripts?

It takes time to learn JavaScript, and it may be a while before you can write scripts on your own. But not to worry. If you do a web search for what you need (for example, "jQuery image carousel" or "jQuery accordion list"), there is a very good chance you will find lots of scripts that people have created and shared, complete with documentation on how to use them. Because jQuery uses a selector syntax very similar to CSS, it makes it easier to customize jQuery scripts for use with your own markup.

Big Finish

In all of two chapters, we've gone from learning the very basics of variables to manipulating the DOM to leveraging a JavaScript library. Even with all we've covered here, we've just barely begun to cover all the things JavaScript can do.

The next time you're looking at a website and it does something cool, view the source in your browser and have a look around for the JavaScript. You can learn a lot from reading and even taking apart someone else's code. And remember, there's nothing you can break with JavaScript that can't be undone with a few strokes of the Delete key.

Better still, JavaScript comes with an entire community of passionate developers who are eager to learn and just as eager to teach. Seek out like-minded developers and share the things you've learned along the way. If you're stuck on a tricky problem, don't hesitate to seek out help and ask questions. It's rare that you'll encounter a problem that nobody else has, and the open source developer community is always excited to share the things they've learned. That's why you've had to put up with me for two chapters, as a matter of fact.

Test Yourself

Just a couple of questions for those of you playing along at home.

1. Ajax is a combination of what technologies?

2. What does this do?

    ```
    document.getElementById("main")
    ```

3. What does this do?

    ```
    document.getElementById("main").getElementsByTagName("section");
    ```

4. What does this do?

    ```
    document.body.style.backgroundColor = "papayawhip"
    ```

5. What does this do? This one is a little tricky because it nests functions, but you should be able to piece it together.

    ```
    document
      .getElementById("main")
        .appendChild(
          document.createElement("p")
            .appendChild(
              documentCreateTextNode("Hey, I'm walking here!")
            )
        );
    ```

6. Match the polyfill with the tasks on the right.

a. HTML5 Shim   1. Add support for `::first-letter`.

b. Respond.js   2. Add support for `min-width` and `max-width` media queries.

c. Modernizr   3. Add support for `nav` and `aside`.

d. Selectivizr   4. Check browser for `canvas` support.

7. What is the benefit of using a JavaScript library such as jQuery?

a. Access to a packaged collection of polyfills

b. Possibly shorter syntax

c. Simplified Ajax support

d. All of the above

CREATING WEB GRAPHICS

PART

WEB GRAPHICS BASICS

Unless you plan to publish text-only sites, chances are you'll need to know how to create web graphics. For many of you, that might mean getting your hands on an image-editing program for the first time and acquiring some basic graphics production skills. If you are a seasoned designer accustomed to print, you may need to adapt your style and process to make graphics that are appropriate for web delivery.

This chapter covers the fundamentals of web graphics production, beginning with some options for finding and creating images. From there, it introduces the file formats available for web graphics and helps you decide which to use. You'll also learn the basics of image resolution, resizing, and transparency.

As always, there are step-by-step exercises along the way. I want to point out, however, that I write with the assumption that you have some familiarity with an image-editing program. I use Adobe Photoshop (the industry standard) in the examples and exercises, but you can follow along with most steps using other tools listed in this chapter. If you are starting at square one, I recommend spending time with the manual or other books about your graphics software.

Image Sources

You have to *have* an image to save an image, so before we jump into the nitty-gritty of file formats, let's look at some ways to get images in the first place. There are many options: from scanning, shooting, or illustrating them yourself, to using available stock photos and clip art, to just hiring someone to create images for you.

Creating your own images

In most cases, the most cost-effective way to generate images for your site is to make your own from scratch. The added bonus is that you know you have full rights to use the images (we'll address copyright again in a moment). Designers may generate imagery with scanners, digital cameras, or a drawing program.

Digital cameras

You can capture the world around you and pipe it right into an image-editing program with a digital camera. Depending on the type of imagery you're after, you may get sufficient quality with a standard consumer digital camera or even the camera in your phone.

Electronic illustration

If you have illustration skills, you can make your own image in a drawing or photo-editing application. The sidebar "Tools of the Trade" introduces some of the most popular graphics programs available today. Every designer has her own favorite tools and techniques. For logos and line drawings, I recommend starting with a vector drawing program like Adobe Illustrator or Fireworks, then saving to a web-appropriate copy as needed. You will find it is useful to have a high-quality, resolution-independent version around for print and other high-resolution applications. For photos, textures, and other bitmapped (raster) image types, Adobe Photoshop is the professional's tool of choice. Again, it's always a good idea to create a high-resolution version of your images and save smaller copies as needed.

Scanning

Scanning is a great way to collect source material. You can scan almost anything, from flat art to 3-D objects. Beware, however, the temptation to scan and use found images. Keep in mind that most images you find are probably copyright-protected and may not be used without permission, even if you modify them considerably. See the "Scanning Tips" sidebar for some how-to information.

Stock photography and illustrations

If you aren't confident in your design skills, or you just want a head start with some fresh imagery, there are plenty of collections of ready-made photos, illustrations, buttons, animations, and textures available for sale or for free. Stock photos and illustrations generally fall into two broad categories: rights-managed and royalty-free.

Rights-managed means that the copyright holder (or a company representing them) controls who may reproduce the image. In order to use a rights-managed image, you must obtain a license to reproduce it for a particular use and for a particular period of time. One of the advantages to licensing images is that you can arrange to have exclusive rights to an image within a particular medium (such as the Web) or a particular business sector (such as the health care industry or banking). On the downside, rights-managed images get quite pricey. Depending on the breadth and length of the license, the price tag may be many thousands of dollars for a single image. If you don't want exclusive rights and you want to use the image only on the Web, the cost is more likely to be a few hundred dollars, depending on the source.

If that still sounds too steep, consider using royalty-free artwork for which you don't need to pay a licensing fee. Royalty-free artwork is available for a one-time fee that gives you unlimited use of the image, but you have no control over who else is using the image. Royalty-free images are available from the top-notch professional stock houses such as Getty Images for as little as 30 bucks an image, and from other sites for less (or even for free).

Another way to get free images is to find photos and drawings released by the artist under a Creative Commons license by the artists who created them. There are a few types of Creative Commons licenses, so be sure to check the terms. Some artists make their work free to use however you want; some artists ask only that you give them credit (attribution-only); some limit the image use to non-commercial purposes.

Following is a list of a few of my favorite resources for finding high-quality stock photography and illustrations, but it is by no means exhaustive. A web search will turn up plenty more sites with images for sale.

Flickr Creative Commons (*www.flickr.com/creativecommons/*)

The photo-sharing service Flickr is my first stop for finding photos released on a Creative Commons license. The quality varies, but I can usually find what I need (such as the red panda in Chapter 10) for the cost of a photo credit. Try using the Flickr search tool Compfight (*compfight.com*) to find images based on "interestingness."

iStockPhoto (*www.istockphoto.com*)

If you're on a tight budget (and even if you're not), there's no better place to find images than iStockPhoto. Prices start at about three bucks a pop. It's my personal favorite image resource.

Getty Images (*www.gettyimages.com*)

Getty is the largest stock image house, having acquired most of its competitors over recent years. It offers both rights-managed and royalty-free photographs and illustrations at a variety of price ranges.

Veer (*www.veer.com*)

I like Veer because it tends to be a little more hip and edgy than its competitors. It offers both rights-managed and royalty-free photographs, illustrations, fonts, and stock video.

Clip art and icons

Clip art refers to collections of royalty-free illustrations, animations, buttons, and other doo-dads that you can copy and paste into a wide range of uses. There are a number of resources online, and the good news is that some of these sites give graphics away for free, although you may have to suffer through a barrage of pop-up ads. Others charge a membership fee, anywhere from $10 to $200 a year. The drawback is that a lot of them are poor

NOTE

For more information about Creative Commons licenses, go to creativecommons.org/licenses/.

SCANNING TIPS

When scanning images for use on the Web, these tips will help you create images with better quality.

- Because it is easier to maintain image quality when resizing smaller than resizing larger, scan the image larger than you actually need. This gives you more flexibility for creating other sizes later. Issues of image size are discussed in more detail in the "Image Size and Resolution" section later in this chapter.

- Scan black-and-white images in grayscale (8-bit) mode, not in black-and-white (1-bit, or bitmap) mode. This enables you to make adjustments in the midtone areas once you have sized the image to its final dimensions and resolution. If you really want only black-and-white pixels, convert the image as the last step.

- If you are scanning an image that has been printed, you need to eliminate the dot pattern that results from the printing process. The best way to do this is to apply a slight blur to the image (in Photoshop, use the Gaussian Blur filter), resize the image slightly smaller, and then apply a sharpening filter. This will eliminate those pesky dots. Make sure you have the rights to use the printed image, too, of course.

quality or kind of hokey (but then, "hokey" is in the eye of the beholder). The following are just a few sites to get you started.

Clipart.com (*www.clipart.com*)

> This service charges a membership fee, but is well organized and tends to provide higher-quality artwork than the free sites.

#1 Free Clip Art (*www.1clipart.com*)

> Another no-frills free clip art site.

It is also easy to find icons for web pages and applications for free or for a low price (a simple search for "free icons" will do the trick). Here are two resources to start you off.

The Noun Project (*thenounproject.com*)

> The Noun Project collects and organizes classic, one-color icons from around the world and makes them available for free. How cool is that?

Icon Finder (*www.iconfinder.com*)

> This is a vast resource for free full-color icons of all styles. Be sure to check the terms of the Creative Commons license, which varies by icon set.

Hire a designer

Finding and creating images takes time and particular talents. If you have more money than either of those things, consider hiring a graphic designer, photographer, or illustrator to generate the imagery for your site for you. If you start with good original images, you can still use the skills you learn in this book to produce web versions of the images as you need them.

Meet the Formats

Once you have your hands on some images, you need to get them into a format that will work on a web page. There are dozens of graphics file formats out in the world. For example, if you use Windows, you may be familiar with BMP graphics, or if you are a print designer, you may commonly use images in TIFF and EPS format. On the Web, bitmapped (pixel-based) images need to be saved in one of three formats: GIF (pronounced "jiff" or "giff"), JPEG ("jay-peg"), and PNG ("ping" or "Pee-en-gee").

There is a fourth format I want you to know about, SVG (Scalable Vector Graphics), which is a bit of an oddball in that it is a vector drawing format generated by an XML text file, so I'm going to save that for the end of this chapter. In the meantime, we'll focus on the universally supported bitmapped image formats GIF, JPEG, and PNG.

If this sounds like alphabet soup to you, don't worry. By the end of this section, you'll know a GIF from a JPEG and when to use each one. Here is a quick rundown:

GIF images are most appropriate for images with flat colors and hard edges or when transparency or animation is required.

JPEGs work best for photographs or images with smooth color blends.

PNG files can contain any image type, but they are especially efficient for storing images with flat colors. PNG is the only format that allows multiple levels of transparency.

This section tackles terminology and digs deep into the features and functions of each format. Understanding the technical details will help you make the highest-quality web graphics at the smallest sizes.

The ubiquitous GIF

The GIF (Graphic Interchange Format) file was the first image format supported by web browsers. Although not designed specifically for the Web, it was adopted for its versatility, small file sizes, and cross-platform compatibility. GIF also offers transparency and the ability to contain simple animations. Over 20 years later, it is arguably still the most widely used web graphics format.

Because the GIF compression scheme excels at compressing flat colors, it is the best file format to use for logos, line art, icons, etc. (Figure 21-1). You can save photographs or textured images as GIFs, too, but they won't be saved as efficiently, resulting in larger file sizes. However, GIF does work nicely for images with a combination of small amounts of photographic imagery and large, flat areas of color.

To make really great GIFs, it's important to be familiar with how they work under the hood and what they can do.

8-bit indexed color

In technical terms, GIF files are indexed color images that contain 8-bit color information (they can also be saved at lower bit depths). Let's decipher that statement one term at a time. 8-bit means GIFs can contain up to 256 colors—the maximum number that 8 bits of information can define (2^8=256). Lower bit depths result in fewer colors and also reduce file size.

> ### Name Files Properly
>
> Be sure to use the proper file extensions for your image files. GIF files must be named with the *.gif* suffix. JPEG files must have *.jpg* (or the less common *.jpeg*) as a suffix. PNG files must end in *.png*. Browsers look at the suffix to determine how to handle various media types, so it is best to stick with the standardized suffixes for image file formats.

Figure 21-1. The GIF format is great for graphical images comprised mainly of flat colors and hard edges.

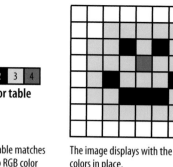

The pixels in an indexed color image contain numerical references to the color table for the image.

The color table matches numbers to RGB color values. This is the map for a 2-bit image with only 4 colors.

The image displays with the colors in place.

Figure 21-2. A 2-bit image and its color table.

Indexed color means that the set of colors in the image, its palette, is stored in a color table (also called a color map). Each pixel in the image contains a numeric reference (or "index") to a position in the color table. This should be made clear with a simple demonstration. Figure 21-2 shows how a 2-bit (4-color) indexed color image references its color table for display. For 8-bit images, there are 256 slots in the color table.

When you open an existing GIF in Photoshop, you can view (and even edit) its color table by selecting Image → Mode → Color Table (Figure 21-3). You also get a preview of the color table for an image when you use Photoshop's Save for Web function to export an image in GIF format, as we'll do later in this chapter. In Fireworks, the color table is displayed in the Optimize panel.

Most source images (scans, illustrations, photos, etc.) start out in RGB format, so they need to be converted to indexed color in order to be saved as a GIF. When an image goes from RGB to indexed mode, the colors in the image are reduced to a palette of 256 colors or fewer. In Photoshop and Fireworks, the conversion takes place when you save or export the GIF. Other image-editing programs may require you to convert the image to indexed color manually first, then export the GIF as a second step.

Figure 21-3. The Color Table in Photoshop and Fireworks displays the 64 pixel colors used in the image.

In either case, you will be asked to select a palette for the indexed color image. The sidebar "Common Color Palettes" outlines the various palette options available in the most popular image tools. It is recommended that you use Selective or Perceptual in Photoshop, Adaptive in Fireworks, and Optimized Median Cut in Paint Shop Pro for the best results for most image types.

Photoshop

Fireworks

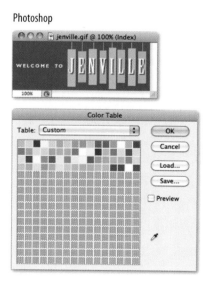

Common Color Palettes

All 8-bit indexed color images, including GIF and PNG, use palettes to define the colors in the image, and there are several standard palettes to choose from. Some are methods for producing a custom palette based on the colors in the image. Others apply a preexisting palette to the image.

Exact. Creates a custom palette out of the actual colors in the image if the image already contains fewer than 256 colors.

Adaptive. Creates a custom palette using the most frequently used pixel colors in the image. It allows for color-depth reduction while preserving the original character of the image.

Perceptual (Photoshop only). Creates a custom color table by giving priority to colors for which the human eye has greater sensitivity. Unlike Adaptive, it is based on algorithms, not just a pixel count. It generally results in images with better color integrity than Adaptive palette images.

Selective (Photoshop only). This is similar to Perceptual, but it gives preference to areas of broad color.

Web Adaptive, Restrictive, or Web216. Creates a palette of colors exclusively from a palette of 216 colors that do not dither on 8-bit monitors. Eight-bit monitors are a thing of the past, so the web-safe palette is no longer relevant or recommended.

Custom. This allows you to load a palette that was previously saved and apply it to the current image. Otherwise, it preserves the current colors in the palette.

System (Windows or Macintosh). Uses the colors in the specified system's default palette.

Optimized Median Cut (Paint Shop Pro Photo only). This reduces the image to a few colors using something similar to an Adaptive palette.

Optimized Octree (Paint Shop Pro Photo only). Use this palette if the original image has just a few colors and you want to keep those exact colors.

GIF compression

GIF compression is "lossless," which means that no image information is sacrificed in order to compress the indexed image (although some image information may be lost when the RGB image is converted to a limited color palette). It uses a compression scheme (called "LZW" for Lempel-Ziv-Welch) that takes advantage of repetition in data. When it encounters a string of pixels of identical color, it can compress that into one data description. This is why images with large areas of flat color condense better than images with textures.

To use an extremely simplified example, when the compression scheme encounters a row of 14 identical blue pixels, it makes up a shorthand notation that means "14 blue pixels." The next time it encounters 14 blue pixels, it uses only the code shorthand (Figure 21-4). By contrast, when it encounters a row that has a gentle gradation from blue to aqua to green, it needs to store a description for every pixel along the way, requiring more data. What actually happens in technical terms is more complicated, of course, but this example is a good mental model to keep in mind when designing GIF images for maximum compression.

GIF compression stores repetitive pixel colors as a single description.

"14 blue"

In an image with gradations of color, it has to store information for every pixel in the row. The longer description means a larger file size.

"1 blue, 1 aqua, 2 light aqua..." (and so on)

Figure 21-4. A simplified demonstration of LZW compression used by GIF images.

Transparency

You can make parts of GIF images transparent so that the background image or color shows through. Although all bitmapped graphics are rectangular by nature, with transparency, you can create the illusion that your image has

Figure 21-5. Transparency allows the striped background to show through the image on the bottom.

Figure 21-6. Interlaced GIFs display in a series of passes, each clearer than the pass before.

a more interesting shape (Figure 21-5). Transparency is discussed in detail later in this chapter.

Interlacing

Interlacing makes a GIF display in a series of passes. Each pass is clearer than the pass before, until the image is fully rendered in the browser window (Figure 21-6). Without interlacing, some browsers may wait until the entire image is downloaded before displaying the image. Others may display the image a few rows at a time, from top to bottom, until the entire picture is complete.

Over a fast connection, these effects (interlacing or image delays) may not even be perceptible. However, over slow connections (modem or mobile carrier network), interlacing large images may be a way to provide a hint of the image to come while the entire image downloads. Whether you interlace or not is your design decision. I never do, but if you have a large image and an audience with a significant percentage of slow connections, interlacing may be worthwhile.

Animation

Another feature built into the GIF file format is the ability to display simple animations (Figure 21-7). Many of the spinning, blinking, fading, or otherwise moving ad banners you see are animated GIFs (although Flash movies have also been popular for web advertising).

Figure 21-7. All the frames of this simple animation are contained within one GIF file.

Animated GIFs contain a number of animation frames, which are separate images that, when viewed together quickly, give the illusion of motion or change over time, kind of like a flip-book. All of the frames are stored within a single GIF file, along with settings that describe how they should be played. Settings include whether and how many times the sequence repeats, how long each frame stays visible (frame delay), the manner in which one frame replaces another (disposal method), whether the image is transparent, and whether it is interlaced.

Adobe Fireworks and Photoshop have interfaces for creating animated GIFs. In Photoshop CS5 and earlier, use the Animation window. In CS6, use the Timeline window and select "Create Frame Animation." A web search will turn up many dedicated animated GIF tools, many of them free.

Animated GIFs

If you would like to learn how to make an animated GIF, you can download a PDF of the Animated GIFs chapter from a previous edition of this book at *www.learningwebdesign.com*. The chapter includes detailed explanations of the animation settings and step-by-step instructions for creating animations.

The photogenic JPEG

Another popular graphic format on the Web is JPEG, which stands for Joint Photographic Experts Group, the standards body that created it.

Unlike GIFs, JPEGs use a compression scheme that *loves* gradient and blended colors, but doesn't work especially well on flat colors or hard edges. JPEG's full-color capacity and compression scheme make it the ideal choice for photographic images (Figure 21-8).

Figure 21-8. The JPEG format is ideal for photographs (color or grayscale) or any image with subtle color gradations.

24-bit Truecolor images

Unlike GIFs, JPEGs don't use color palettes. Instead, they are 24-bit images, capable of displaying colors from the millions of colors in the RGB color space (also referred to as the Truecolor space; see note). This is one aspect that makes them ideal for photographs—they have all the colors you'll ever need. With JPEGs, you don't have to worry about limiting yourself to 256 colors the way you do with GIFs. JPEGs are much more straightforward.

NOTE

RGB color is explained in Chapter 14, "Colors and Backgrounds."

Cumulative Image Quality Loss

Be aware that once image quality is lost in JPEG compression, you can never get it back again. For this reason, you should avoid resaving a JPEG as a JPEG. You lose image quality every time.

It is better to hang on to the original image and make JPEG copies as needed. That way, if you need to make a change to the JPEG version, you can go back to the original and do a fresh save or export. Fortunately, Photoshop's Save for Web feature does exactly that. Fireworks also preserves the original and lets you save or export copies.

Lossy compression

The JPEG compression scheme is lossy, which means that some of the image information is thrown out in the compression process. Fortunately, this loss is not discernible for most images at most compression levels. When an image is compressed with high levels of JPEG compression, you begin to see color blotches and squares (usually referred to as artifacts) that result from the way the compression scheme samples the image (Figure 21-9).

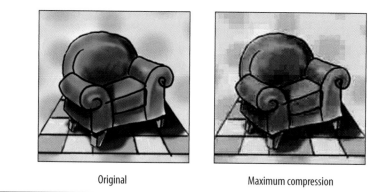

Original   Maximum compression

Figure 21-9. JPEG compression discards image detail to achieve smaller file sizes. At high compression rates, image quality suffers, as shown in the image on the right.

You can control how aggressively you want the image to be compressed. This involves a trade-off between file size and image quality. The more you compress the image (for a smaller file size), the more the image quality suffers. Conversely, when you maximize quality, you also end up with larger files. The best compression level is based on the particular image and your objectives for the site. Compression strategies are discussed in more detail in Chapter 22, "Lean and Mean Web Graphics."

Progressive JPEGs

Progressive JPEGs display in a series of passes (like interlaced GIFs), starting with a low-resolution version that gets clearer with each pass, as shown in Figure 21-10. In some graphics programs, you can specify the number of passes it takes to fill in the final image (3, 4, or 5).

The advantage to using progressive JPEGs is that viewers can get an idea of the image before it downloads completely. Also, making a JPEG progressive usually reduces its file size slightly. The disadvantage is that they take more processing power (which can make them problematic for low-end mobile devices) and can slow down final display.

Figure 21-10. Progressive JPEGs render in a series of passes.

Decompression

JPEGs need to be decompressed before they can be displayed; therefore, it takes a browser longer to decode and assemble a JPEG than a GIF of the same file size. It's usually not a perceptible difference, however, so this is not a reason to avoid the JPEG format. It's just something to know.

The powerful PNG

The last bitmapped format to join the web graphics roster is the versatile PNG (Portable Network Graphic). Despite getting off to a slow start, PNGs are now supported by all browsers in current use and are becoming many developers' first choice in web graphics formats.

PNGs offer an impressive lineup of features:

- The ability to contain 8-bit indexed, 24-bit RGB, 16-bit grayscale, and even 48-bit color images

- A lossless compression scheme

- Simple on/off transparency (like GIF) or multiple levels of transparency

- Progressive display (similar to GIF interlacing)

- Gamma (brightness) adjustment information

- Embedded text for attaching information about the author, copyright, and so on

This section takes a closer look at each of these features and helps you decide when the PNG format is the best choice for your image.

Multiple image formats

The PNG format was designed to replace GIF for online purposes and TIFF for image storage and printing. A PNG can be used to save many image types: 8-bit indexed color, 24- and 48-bit RGB color, and 16-bit grayscale.

8-bit indexed color images

Like GIFs, PNGs can store 8-bit indexed images with a maximum of 256 colors. They may be saved at 1-, 2-, and 4-bit depths as well. Indexed color PNGs are generally referred to as PNG-8.

RGB/Truecolor (24- and 48-bit)

In PNGs, each channel (red, green, and blue) can be defined by 8- or 16-bit information, resulting in 24- or 48-bit RGB images, respectively. In graphics programs, 24-bit RGB PNGs are identified as PNG-24. It should be noted that 48-bit images are useless for the Web, and even 24-bit images should be used with care. Because it is lossless, 24-bit PNGs are nearly always significantly larger than a lossy JPEG of the same image.

> ## Use Progressive JPEGs for Retina Displays
>
> In general, it is not necessary to save a JPEG as progressive. The exception to this rule (as of this writing) is when you are creating double-sized JPEGs targeted at iOS devices with Retina displays. In this case, you should save in progressive format to get around a byte limit issue in Mobile Safari. This workaround may no longer be necessary in future versions of Safari and as Retina screens become more widespread. Other special considerations are discussed in the "Dealing with High-Density Displays" sidebar later in this chapter.

Grayscale

PNGs can also support 16-bit grayscale images—that's as many as 65,536 shades of gray (216), enabling black-and-white photographs and illustrations to be stored with enormous subtlety of detail, although they are not appropriate for the Web.

Transparency

PNGs can contain transparent areas that let the background image or color show through. The killer feature that PNG has over GIF, however, is the ability to contain multiple levels of transparency, commonly referred to as alpha-channel (or just alpha) transparency.

Figure 21-11 shows the same PNG against two different background images. The orange circle is entirely opaque, but the drop shadow contains multiple levels of transparency, ranging from nearly opaque to entirely transparent. The multiple transparency levels stored in the PNG allow the drop shadow to blend seamlessly with any background. The ins and outs of PNG transparency will be addressed in the upcoming "Working with Transparency" section.

Figure 21-11. Alpha-channel transparency allows multiple levels of transparency, as shown in the drop shadow around the orange circle PNG.

Progressive display (interlacing)

PNGs can also be coded for interlaced display. When this option is selected, the image displays in a series of seven passes. Unlike interlaced GIFs, which fill in horizontal rows, PNGs fill in both horizontally and vertically. Interlacing adds to the file size and is usually not necessary, so to keep files as small as possible, turn interlacing display off.

Gamma correction

Gamma refers to the brightness setting of a monitor. Because gamma settings vary by platform, the graphics you create may not look the way you intend for the end user. PNGs can be tagged with information regarding the gamma setting of the environment in which they were created. This can then be interpreted by the software displaying the PNG to make appropriate gamma compensations. When this is implemented on both the creator and end user's sides, the PNG retains its intended brightness and color intensity.

Unfortunately, as of this writing, this feature doesn't work as intended in the real world. Internet Explorer (all versions) displayed gamma incorrectly, and PNGs ended up darker than intended. Photoshop stopped embedding gamma information in PNGs starting with CS3. Be aware that it may be difficult to get a PNG to match a background color in some browsers, even if the RGB values are the same. The solution is to make the edges of the PNG transparent so the background shows through or to use a GIF.

Embedded text

PNGs also have the ability to store strings of text. This is useful for permanently attaching text to an image, such as copyright information or a description of what is in the image. The only tools that accommodate text annotations to PNG graphics are Corel Paint Shop Pro Photo and GIMP. Ideally, the meta-information in the PNG would be accessible via right-clicking on the graphic in a browser, but this feature is not yet implemented in current browsers.

When to use PNGs

PNGs pack a lot of powerful options, but competition among web graphic formats nearly always comes down to file size.

For images that would typically be saved as GIFs, 8-bit PNG is often a better option. You may find that a PNG version of an image has a smaller file size than a GIF of the same image, but that depends on how efficiently your image program handles PNG compression.

Although PNG does support 24-bit color images, its lossless compression scheme nearly always results in a dramatically larger file than JPEG compression applied to the same image. For web purposes, JPEG is still the best choice for photographic and continuous tone images.

The exception to the "smallest file wins" rule is if you want to take advantage of multiple levels of transparency. In that case, PNG is your only option and may be worth a slightly heftier file size.

The following section takes a broader look at finding the best graphic format for the job.

Choosing the best format

Part of the trick to making quality web graphics that maintain quality and download quickly is choosing the right format. Table 21-1 provides a good starting point.

NOTE

If you are dedicated to PNG and hardcore about quality, you could remove the gamma (gAMA) information from the PNG using a utility like PNGcrush, as detailed in this article by Trevor Morris (morris-photographics.com/photoshop/articles/png-gamma.html).

Work in RGB Mode

Regardless of the final format of your file, you should always do your image-editing work in RGB mode (grayscale is fine for non-color images). To check the color mode of the image in Photoshop, select Image → Mode and make sure there is a checkmark next to RGB Color.

JPEG and PNG-24 files compress the RGB color image directly. If you are saving the file as a GIF or PNG-8, the RGB image must be converted to indexed color mode, either manually or as part of the Save for Web or Export process.

If you need to edit an existing GIF or PNG-8, convert the image to RGB as the first step before editing. This enables the editing tool to use colors from the full RGB spectrum when adjusting the image. If you resize the original indexed color image, you'll get lousy results because the new image is limited to the colors from the existing color table.

If you have experience creating graphics for print, you may be accustomed to working in CMYK mode (printed colors are made up of Cyan, Magenta, Yellow, and blacK ink). CMYK mode is irrelevant and inappropriate for web graphics, so convert to RGB mode at the beginning of the image-editing process.

Table 21-1. Choosing the best bitmapped (raster) file format

If your image...	use...	because...
Is graphical, with flat colors	GIF or 8-bit PNG	GIF and PNG excel at compressing flat color.
Is a photograph or contains graduated color	JPEG	JPEG compression works best on images with blended color. Because it is lossy, it generally results in smaller file sizes than 24-bit PNG.
Is a combination of flat and photographic imagery	GIF or 8-bit PNG	Indexed color formats are best at preserving and compressing flat color areas. The dithering that appears in the photographic areas as a result of reducing to a palette is usually not problematic.
Requires transparency	GIF or PNG	Both GIF and PNG allow on/off transparency in images.
Requires multiple levels of transparency	PNG	PNG is the only format that supports alpha-channel transparency.
Requires animation	GIF	GIF is the only format that can contain animation frames.

Saving an image in your chosen format

Virtually every up-to-date graphics program allows you to save images in GIF, JPEG, and PNG format, but some give you more options than others. If you use Photoshop, Fireworks, or Corel Paint Shop Pro, be sure to take advantage of their special web graphics features.

Start with an RGB image at the highest quality available—you never know in which other contexts you will need to use it. After you are done adjusting the image (cropping, color correction, etc.), save the image at full size so you are sure to have a good original. Then you can resize the image so that it is appropriate to a web page. In fact, these days it is common to make a number of images targeted to different device sizes, which is all the more reason to keep a clean, high-quality original. When you are finished resizing (I'll show one resizing technique later in this chapter), follow these instructions for saving it as GIF, JPEG, or PNG.

Adobe Photoshop

Open Photoshop's Save for Web dialog box (File → Save for Web; see Figure 21-12) and select the file type from the pop-up menu. When you choose a format, the panel displays settings appropriate to that format. The Save for Web window also shows you a preview of the resulting image and its file size. You can even do side-by-side comparisons of different settings, for example, GIF and PNG-8 version of the same image and their resulting file sizes. Once you have selected the file type and made your settings, click Save and give the file a name.

We'll see the Save for Web dialog box again later in this chapter when we resize images and work with transparency. It also pops up in Chapter 22, "Lean and Mean Web Graphics" when we discuss the various settings related to optimization.

Photoshop

Select the file type in the **Save for Web Devices** dialog box. You can change the settings and compare resulting images before you save.

Figure 21-12. Selecting a file type in Photoshop's handy Save for Web dialog box.

Fireworks

With the image open and the Preview tab selected, the file type can be selected from the Optimize panel (Figure 21-13). When you are finished with your settings, select Export from the File menu and give the image file a name.

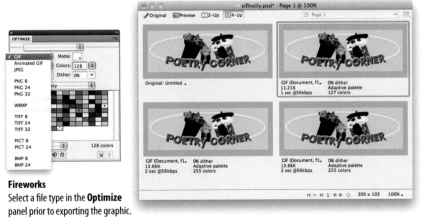

Fireworks

Select a file type in the **Optimize** panel prior to exporting the graphic.

Figure 21-13. Selecting a file type in the Fireworks Optimize panel.

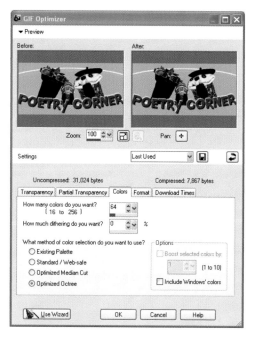

Figure 21-14. Web optimization options in Corel Paint Shop Pro.

Paint Shop Pro

The GIF Optimizer, JPEG Optimizer, and PNG Optimizer are accessed from the Export option in the File menu. Each opens a multipanel dialog box with all the settings for the respective file type and a preview of a portion of the compressed image. The Colors panel of the GIF optimizer is shown in Figure 21-14. When you have made all your settings, click OK. Note that you need to choose your file type *before* accessing the settings, and unlike Photoshop and Fireworks, there is no way to compare image type previews in Paint Shop Pro.

Image Size and Resolution

One thing that GIF, JPEG, and PNG images have in common is that they are all bitmapped (also called raster) images. When you zoom in on a bitmapped image, you can see that it is like a mosaic made up of many pixels (tiny, single-colored squares). These are different from vector graphics, which are made up of smooth lines and filled areas, all based on mathematical formulas. Figure 21-15 illustrates the difference between bitmapped and vector graphics.

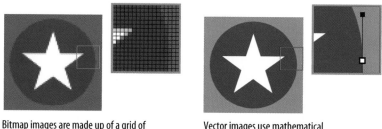

Bitmap images are made up of a grid of variously colored pixels, like a mosaic.

Vector images use mathematical equations to define shapes.

Figure 21-15. Bitmapped and vector graphics.

Goodbye inches, hello pixels!

If you've used bitmapped images for print or the Web, you may be familiar with the term resolution, the number of pixels per inch. In the print world, image resolutions of 300 and 600 pixels per inch (ppi) are common.

On the Web, however, the notion of "inches" is irrelevant. Although I may have created an image at 72 pixels per inch, it's unlikely that it will measure precisely one inch when it is displayed (Figure 21-16). In fact, with the emergence of high-density screens such as the Apple Retina display, even the notion of a "pixel" has gotten a lot more complicated, as discussed in the upcoming "Pixel madness" section and in the "Dealing with High-Density Displays" sidebar.

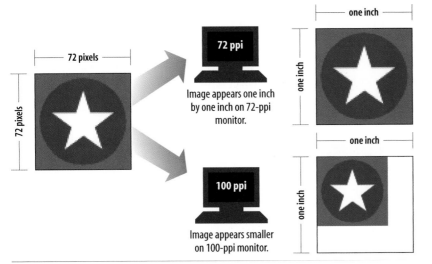

Figure 21-16. Inches, and therefore "pixels per inch," are not relevant for digital media, where the size of in image is dependent on monitor resolution.

Dots Per Inch

Because web graphics exist solely on the screen, it is correct to measure their resolutions in pixels per inch (ppi).

When it comes to print, however, devices and printed pages are measured in dots per inch (dpi), which describes the number of printed dots in each inch of the image. The dpi may or may not be the same as the ppi for an image.

In your travels, you may hear the terms dpi and ppi used interchangeably (albeit incorrectly so). It is important to understand the difference.

If you're tossing out inches, you have to toss out "pixels per inch" as well. The only thing we know for sure is that the graphic in Figure 21-16 is 72 pixels across, and it will be twice as wide as a graphic that is 36 pixels across. Web designers measure their images in total number of pixels, so the resolution of the image is technically not relevant.

That said, however, most designers I know create their images at 72ppi just to get in the ballpark. I find that when I create all my images at 72ppi and view them at 100% in Photoshop, it keeps them in proportion to one another and displays them at roughly the size they'll appear on a desktop monitor. 72ppi is a good starting resolution when creating images targeted at high-density displays (like the Apple Retina display) as well; just double the pixel dimensions.

Pixel madness

Not so long ago, we could count on the pixels in an image mapping one-to-one with the hardware pixels in the desktop monitor. For the most part, that is still true, but there have been developments in technology that break that rule.

First, many browsers now automatically scale large images to fit inside the browser window regardless of its size and allow users to zoom web pages, thus the 1:1 mapping is lost. Images are obviously scaled down to fit small handheld devices as well.

Manufacturers have been pushing the resolution of displays higher and higher. As a result, an actual hardware pixel is so small that images and text would be illegibly tiny if they were mapped one to one. To compensate, devices use a measurement called a reference pixel to which pixels in images,

NOTE

For a more in-depth explanation, I recommend the article "A Pixel Identity Crisis" by Scott Kellum (www.alistapart.com/articles/a-pixel-identity-crisis/).

text, and CSS rules are mapped. On Apple Retina displays on newer iPhones, iPads, and MacBook Pros, the width of a reference pixel is equivalent to two hardware pixels. On some Android tablets, a reference pixel is 1.5 hardware pixels. It adds a new layer of complexity to our jobs as web designers (see the "Dealing with High-Density Displays" sidebar).

Dealing with High-Density Displays

Imagine a device that requires enormous images to take advantage of its full potential, but that may be accessing those images on the slowest 3G networks. That's exactly what we have with the iPad 3 released in the spring of 2012. The new iPad sports a Retina display with a resolution of 2,048 × 1,536—that's a whopping 3.1 million or so pixels. The Retina MacBook Pro with a resolution of 2,800 × 1,800 was released soon after, and I'm sure this is only the beginning of a trend toward high-density displays.

It's exciting for consumers because images can appear with the clarity and precision of print. But the new Retina display temporarily knocked us web developers for a loop. On Retina displays, regular web images look fuzzy and slightly pixelated. In order to get images to look crisp, you have to double the dimensions of the graphic and let the browser size them down to the intended dimensions in the layout. Figure 21-17 compares a standard web graphic to the same image created at 2× size especially for the Retina display.

Unfortunately, when you double the dimensions of a web image, you end up with four times the number of pixels, and as much as four times the file size. And as we know, on the Web, performance is everything. Devices with high-density displays may prefer to display high-resolution images, but that doesn't mean the networks have magically grown faster to deal with them.

So, what to do? To be honest, we're still figuring out strategies for dealing with the inevitable onslaught of high-resolution devices. Addressing the requirements of our sites in hi-res will become another aspect of our jobs as web designers.

Here are a few things we do know:

- Doubling the dimensions of images makes them look crisp at high resolutions, as shown in Figure 21-17.
- Apple's Safari browser has a limit on how many megabytes of JPEG image can display on a page. For images over two megapixels (2.1 million pixels), it automatically degrades the

image and the crisp quality is lost. To get around the Safari JPEG limit, save your JPEGs in Progressive format.

- You don't need to super-size every image. Consider creating 2× images only for the most important image or images on the page (known in the biz as hero images). This might include a singular mood-setting image, your logo, or product shots where detail is important, such as indicating the texture of fabric.

- You can use a CSS media query to test whether the device has a 2× resolution and serve appropriately large images to just those devices, preventing small devices from getting unnecessarily large images. You could also use JavaScript to replace a standard image with a 2× image.

- Unfortunately, knowing that the user has a Retina or other high-density display doesn't tell you anything about the user's network speed, so you risk sending giant images over slow connections that can't display them quickly. Strategies for discovering the user's current connection speed are under development and are beyond the scope of this graphics chapter. Because these techniques are developing rapidly, I recommend you do your own web search for the latest thinking.

Standard web images look fuzzy on Retina displays. The PNG is 350 pixels wide in an img *element set to 350px wide.*

Images look sharp on Retina displays when they are created at twice the final layout size. This PNG is 700 pixels wide in an img *element set to 350px wide.*

Figure 21-17. Typical web graphics look slightly pixel-y on the Retina iPad display.

Resizing images

Because source images generally are not appropriate for the Web, sizing images smaller makes up a large portion of the time I spend doing graphics production, so image resizing is a good basic skill to have.

In Exercise 21-1, I'll show you an easy way to resize an image using Photoshop's Save for Web feature. With this method, the exported web graphic is resized, but the original remains unaltered. This makes it easy to save the same image at a number of sizes appropriate for different devices in just a few steps. For other programs, or if you want more control over the final image quality, see the "Using Image Size" sidebar following the exercise.

NOTE

If you don't have Photoshop, you can download a free trial version at www. adobe.com/downloads and follow along.

exercise 21-1 | **Resizing an image smaller in Photoshop**

In this exercise, we'll take a high-resolution photo and size it to fit on a web page. The source image, *ninja.tif*, is available with the materials for this chapter at *www.learningwebdesign. com/4e/materials/*.

Open the file *ninja.tif* in Photoshop. Select all the pixels in the image (Select → All), and then check the pixel dimensions in the Info panel (Figure 21-18 **A**). If the Info panel is not open, select Window → Info. If the measurements are listed in inches or some other unit, change it to pixels in the Preferences (Photoshop → Preferences → Units & Rulers). Our ninja image is 1,600 × 1,600 pixels, which is too big for a web page. For this example, let's imagine the space in the page layout is 400 pixels square.

Now we'll resize the image and save it as a JPEG in one fell swoop. Select Save for Web from the File menu. Select JPEG **B** from the Formats pop-up menu.

Using the Image Size settings on the bottom half of the Settings column **C**, enter the dimensions that you'd like the final JPEG to be when it is saved, in this case 400 pixels. When the link icon is checked, the height changes automatically when you enter the new width.

Next, select the Quality **D**. Bicubic or Bicubic Sharper give the best results when sizing smaller. You will see the resized image in the Optimized Image view (select the tab at the top if it isn't already displayed).

Click Save **E**, give the file a name, and select a directory in which to save it. When the Save for Web dialog box closes, you will see that the original *ninja.tif* file is unchanged, so you can make additional images at different sizes in this same manner. Saving the file saves the most recent export settings.

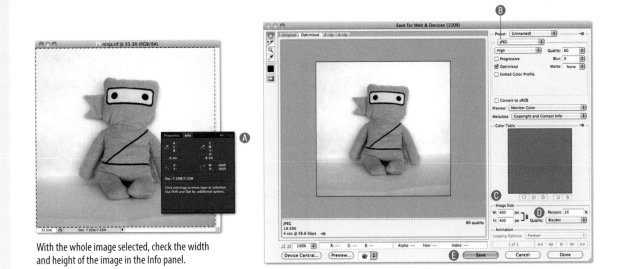

With the whole image selected, check the width and height of the image in the Info panel.

Figure 21-18. Using the Save for Web dialog box to resize an image.

Using Image Size

The disadvantage to the method shown in Exercise 21-1 is that you give up control over the quality of the image. If you are an image quality control freak (like me), you may prefer resizing the image using the Image Size dialog box (Figure 21-19). In Fireworks, Modify → Canvas… → Image Size… gives you a similar set of options.

Be sure that Resample Image and Constrain Proportions are checked at the bottom, and select Bicubic (or Bicubic Sharper) as the Quality setting. The resolution is not important for web graphics, as we previously discussed.

Then enter the desired final pixel dimensions at the top of the box and click OK. Double-clicking on the magnifying glass tool (not shown) displays the resized image at 100%.

Now you can apply sharpening filters and other effects, and once you are happy with the image, use Save For Web to create the web version.

I find that resizing an extremely large image in a couple of steps helps preserve quality. First, I resize it to an in-between dimension and sharpen it with a sharpening filter. Then I resize it to its final dimensions and sharpen again. You can't do that with the Save for Web method.

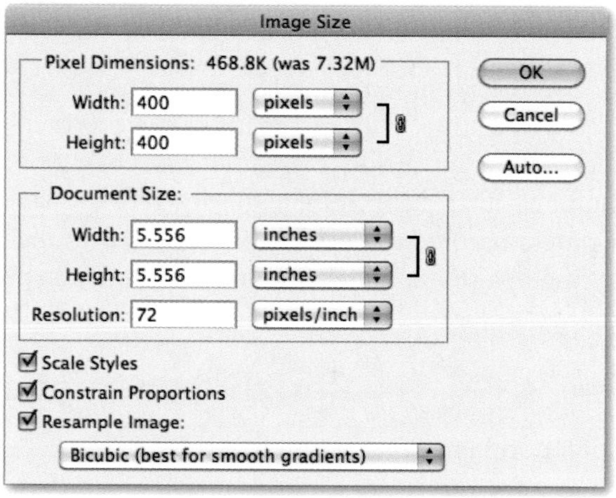

Figure 21-19. The Image Size dialog box in Photoshop.

WARNING

Remember that the Image Size settings resize the original image. Be careful not to save it, or you'll lose your high-quality version!

Working with Transparency

Both GIF and PNG formats allow parts of an image to be transparent, allowing the background color or image to show through. In this section, we'll take a closer look at transparent graphics, including tips on how to make them.

Remember that there are two types of transparency. In binary transparency, pixels are either entirely transparent or entirely opaque, like an on/off switch. Both GIF and PNG files support binary transparency.

In alpha (or alpha-channel) transparency, a pixel may be totally transparent, totally opaque, or up to 254 levels of opaqueness in between (a total of 256 opacity levels). Only PNGs support alpha transparency. The advantage of PNGs with alpha transparency is that they blend seamlessly with any background color or pattern, as shown back in Figure 21-11.

In this section, you'll become familiar with how each type of transparency works, and learn how to make transparent images using Photoshop.

How binary transparency works

Remember that the pixel colors for GIFs and PNG-8s are stored in an indexed color table. Transparency is simply treated as a separate color, occupying a position in the color table. Figure 21-20 shows the color table in Photoshop for a simple transparent GIF. The slot in the color table that is set to transparent is indicated by a checker pattern. Pixels that correspond to that position will be completely transparent when the image displays in the browser. Note that only one slot is transparent—all the other pixel colors are opaque.

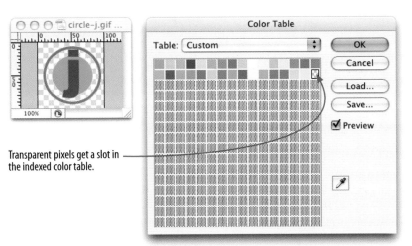

Transparent pixels get a slot in the indexed color table.

Figure 21-20. Transparency is treated as a color in the indexed color table.

How alpha transparency works

RGB images, such as JPEGs and PNG-24s, store color in separate channels: one for red, one for green, and one for blue. PNG-24 files add another channel, called the alpha channel, to store transparency information. In that channel, each pixel may display one of 256 values, which correspond to 256 levels of transparency when the image is displayed. The black areas of the alpha channel mask are transparent, the white areas are opaque, and the grays are on a scale in between. I think of it as a blanket laid over the image that tells each pixel below it how transparent it is (Figure 21-21).

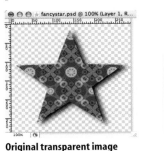

Original transparent image

Black areas in the alpha channel correspond to transparent image areas; white areas are opaque; and grays are variable levels of transparency in between.

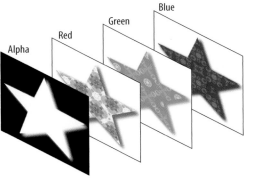

Figure 21-21. Transparency information is stored as a separate (alpha) channel in 24-bit PNGs.

Internet Explorer 6 and Alpha Transparency

It is worth noting that Internet Explorer 6 and earlier will show PNGs with alpha transparency as entirely opaque. If you have reason to support IE6, there is a complicated workaround using Microsoft's proprietary AlphaImageLoader filter, which is documented by Michael Lovitt here: *www.alistapart.com/ articles/pngopacity*.

Making transparent GIFs and PNGs

The easiest way to make parts of an image transparent is to design them that way from the start and preserve the transparent areas when you create the GIF or PNG version of the image. Once again, Photoshop's Save for Web feature or Firework's Optimize panel are perfect tools for the job.

It is possible to add transparent areas to a flattened opaque image, but it may be difficult to get a seamless blend with a background. We'll look at the process for making portions of an existing image transparent later in this section.

NOTE

The principles and settings outlined in Exercise 21-2 are nearly identical in Fireworks, so the same general instructions apply, although the interface is slightly different.

But first, follow along with the steps in Exercise 21-2 that demonstrate how to preserve transparent areas and guarantee a good match with the background using Photoshop's Save for Web dialog box. There are some new concepts tucked in there, so even if you don't do the exercise, I recommend giving it a read, particularly steps 5, 6, and 7.

---

exercise 21-2 | Creating transparent images

In this exercise, we're going to start from scratch, so you'll get the experience of creating a layered image with transparent areas. I'm going to keep it simple, but you can apply these techniques to fancier designs, of course.

1. Launch Photoshop and create a new file (File → New...). There are a few settings in the New dialog box (Figure 21-22) that will set you off in the right direction for creating transparent web graphics.

   • First, make your new graphic 500 pixels wide and 100 pixels high to match the example in this exercise **A**.

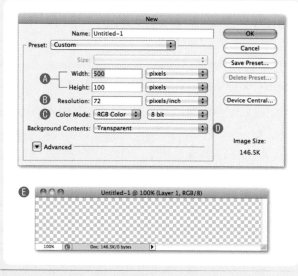

Figure 21-22. Creating a new image with a transparent background.

   • Set the resolution to 72 pixels/inch **B**, which is what I use when making web graphics (although, as you learned, it doesn't really matter).

   • Make sure the color mode is RGB Color, 8-bit **C**.

   • Finally, and most importantly for this exercise, select Transparent from the Background Contents options **D**. This option creates a layered Photoshop file with a transparent background. It is much easier to preserve transparent areas in an image than to add it later. The transparent areas (in this case, the whole area, since we haven't added any image content yet) are indicated by a gray checkerboard pattern **E**.

2. Now we'll add some text and give it a drop shadow (Figure 21-23).

   • Use the type tool **F** and type your name. Open the Character window **G** (Window → Character) to change the look of the font. With the text selected, choose a bold typeface (something chunky) and set the size large enough to fill the space, as shown in the example. Click the swatch next to Color, and use the Color Picker to choose a color for the text that is not too light and not too dark. I'm using a medium pink.

   • Next, add a soft drop shadow to the text. Open the Layers window **H** (Window → Layers) if it isn't open already. You will see the layer containing your text in the list. Add a drop shadow by clicking the Layer Style button (it looks like an FX) at the bottom of the Layers window and select "Drop Shadow..." **I**. In the Layer Style dialog box **J**, you can play around with the settings, but I recommend setting the Distance and Size to at least 5 to get the most out of the rest of the exercise. When you are done, click OK.

---

3. Save the image as a Photoshop file to preserve the layers for easier editing later, if necessary. I'm naming mine *jennifer.psd* (use the *.psd* suffix). With a nice source image saved, we are ready to start making the web versions.

Figure 21-23. Adding text with a soft drop shadow.

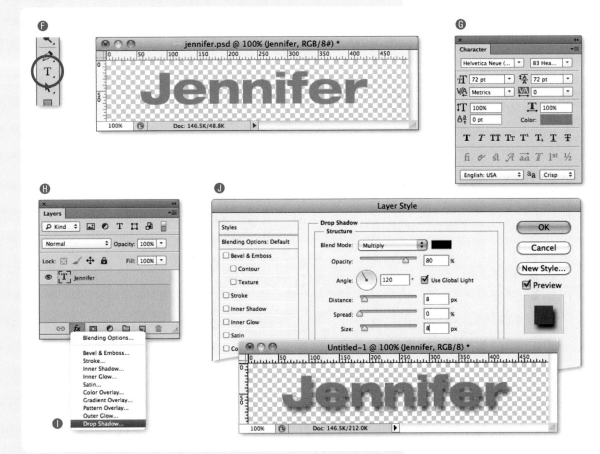

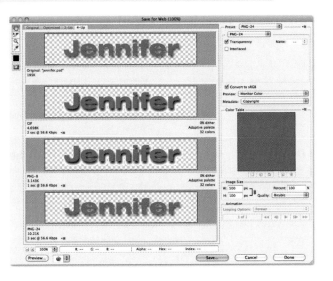

4. With the new file still open, select Save for Web from the File menu. Click on the 4-Up tab at the top to compare the original image to several other versions (Figure 21-24). Your previews may display in a grid instead of a stack.

Figure 21-24. The "4-Up" tab in the Save for Web dialog box allows you to compare four different versions of the same image.

5. Let's see how the image looks as a GIF with and without transparency. Click on the second preview to select it, then set the file type to GIF and set the number of colors to 32. Now, toggle the checkmark next to Transparency off and on (Figure 21-25).

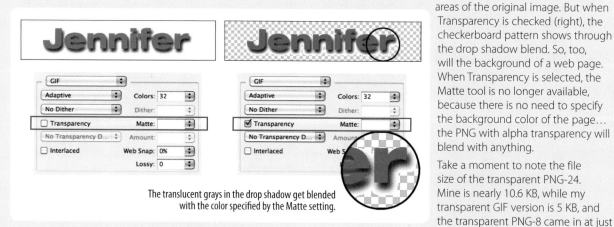

The translucent grays in the drop shadow get blended with the color specified by the Matte setting.

Figure 21-25. Previews of transparency turned off (left) and on (right) in a GIF.

- When Transparency is off (not checked, as shown on the left), the Matte color is used to fill in the transparent areas of the original image. Set the Matte color to white to match my example.

- When Transparency is on (checked, as shown on the right), a checkerboard pattern appears in the transparent areas of the image, indicating where the background color or pattern of the web page will show through. If you look carefully at the drop shadow area, you will see that the shades of gray are blended with the white Matte color. Try changing the Matte color and watch what happens in the drop shadow area.

6. Leave the GIF preview alone for a moment and select the next preview. Set the file type to PNG-8 and try toggling the Transparency checkbox. As expected, it behaves exactly the same as the GIF because both formats use binary transparency. The previews should look like those shown in Figure 21-25.

7. Now select the fourth preview, make it a PNG-24, and toggle the Transparency checkbox (Figure 21-26). When it is unchecked (left), the Matte color fills in the transparent areas of the original image. But when Transparency is checked (right), the checkerboard pattern shows through the drop shadow blend. So, too, will the background of a web page. When Transparency is selected, the Matte tool is no longer available, because there is no need to specify the background color of the page… the PNG with alpha transparency will blend with anything.

Take a moment to note the file size of the transparent PNG-24. Mine is nearly 10.6 KB, while my transparent GIF version is 5 KB, and the transparent PNG-8 came in at just 3.3 KB. The significantly larger file size is the price you pay for the versatility of the alpha transparency.

8. Save the PNG-24 with Transparency turned on, and name the file with the *.png* suffix (mine is *jennifer.png*). Open the Save for Web dialog box again and save a GIF version of the image with Transparency turned on (make sure that Matte is set to white). Name the file with the *.gif* suffix. We'll be using these graphics again in the next section.

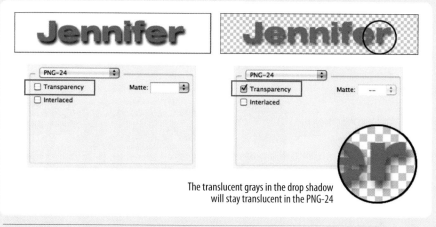

The translucent grays in the drop shadow will stay translucent in the PNG-24

Figure 21-26. Previews of Transparency turned off (left) and on (right) in a PNG-24.

DESIGN TIP

The trick to getting a transparent GIF to blend seamlessly with a background is to use the RGB values from the web page's background color (or the dominant color from a background image) for the Matte color. If your page background is a multicolored pattern or is otherwise difficult to match, opt for a Matte color that is slightly darker than the predominant background color.

PNG-8 "Alpha" Transparency

Technically, variable levels of transparency are *not* limited to 24-bit PNGs. PNG-8 files can do it too. Instead of using an alpha channel, they store different transparency levels in multiple slots in the index color table. The resulting file size is potentially smaller than the same image saved as a PNG-24 with an alpha channel.

As of this writing, only Fireworks allows you to create PNG-8s with multiple levels of transparency, and browser support is poor. Most browsers display them as though they have simple binary transparency. For now, this is another cool PNG feature that remains untapped due to lagging software support.

Avoiding "halos"

Now that I have some transparent graphics, I'm going to try them out on a minimal web page with a white background. If you want to work along, open a text editor and create an HTML document like the one shown here:

```
<!DOCTYPE html>
<html>
<head>
  <title>Transparency test</title>
  <style>
    body {background-color: white;}
  </style>
</head>
<body>
  <p><img src="jennifer.png" alt=""></p>
  <p><img src="jennifer.gif" alt=""></p>
</body>
</html>
```

When I open the file in a browser, the graphics look more or less the same against the white background (Figure 21-27, left). But if I change the background color of the web page to teal (`background-color: teal;`), the difference between the alpha and binary transparency becomes very clear (right).

Anti-aliasing

Anti-aliasing is a slight blur applied to rounded edges of bitmapped graphics to make smoother transitions between colors. Aliased edges, by contrast, have stair-stepped edges. Anti-aliasing text and graphics can give your graphics a more professional appearance.

PNG-24
(Alpha)

GIF
(Binary)

Figure 21-27. The difference between binary and alpha transparency becomes very clear when the background color of the page changes.

When the background color changes, the GIF no longer matches the background, resulting in an ugly fringe commonly called a halo. Halos are the result of anti-aliased edges that have been blended with a color other than the background color of a page. They are a potential hazard of binary transparency, whether GIF or PNG-8.

Matte Alternative

If you are using a graphics tool that doesn't have the Matte feature, create a new layer at the bottom of the layer "stack" and fill it with the background color of your page. When the image is flattened as a result of changing it to Indexed Color, the anti-aliased edges blend with the proper background color. Just select that background color to be transparent during export to GIF or PNG format and your image should be halo-free.

Prevention is the name of the game when it comes to dealing with binary transparency and halos. As you've just seen, the Matte color feature in Photoshop and Fireworks makes it easy to blend the edges of the graphic to a target background color. If the background color changes, you can re-export the GIF or PNG-8 with the new Matte color. See the "Matte Alternative" sidebar for options if your tool doesn't have a Matte setting.

Another option is to save your image as a PNG-24 with variable transparency. That way, you don't have to worry about the background color or pattern, and it will be no problem if it changes in the future. The trade-off, of course, is the larger file size to download and the lack of support in IE6, as noted earlier.

Adding transparency to flattened images

It is possible to add transparent areas to images that have already been flattened and saved as a GIF or PNG. The GIF containing a yellow circle on a purple background in Figure 21-28 blends in fine against a solid purple background, but would be an obvious square if the background were changed to a pattern. The solution is to make the purple areas transparent to let the background show through. Fortunately, most graphics tools make it easy to do so by selecting a pixel color in the image, usually an eyedropper tool, that you'd like to be transparent.

Figure 21-28. Making a color transparent in Photoshop.

In Photoshop, the transparency eyedropper is found on the Color Table dialog box (Image → Mode → Color Table). Click on the eyedropper, and then on a pixel color in the image, and it magically turns transparent (Figure 21-28). To save the new transparent graphic, use the Save for Web feature as demonstrated earlier.

If you look closely, you can see that there is a fringe of pixels still anti-aliased to purple, which means that this graphic will work well only against purple backgrounds. On other background colors, there will be a pesky halo. Unfortunately, the only way to fix a halo in an image that has already been flattened is to get in there and erase the anti-aliased edges, pixel by pixel. Even if you get rid of the fringe, you may be left with unattractive stair-

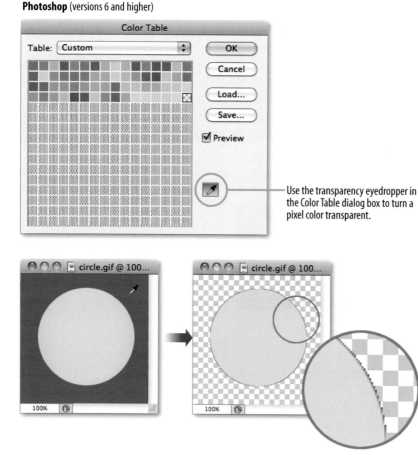

Photoshop (versions 6 and higher)

Use the transparency eyedropper in the Color Table dialog box to turn a pixel color transparent.

stepped edges. You could also use a layer mask to erase the areas that you want to be transparent, making sure to erase the blended edges in the original image.

If you are concerned with the professional appearance of your site, I'd say it's better to re-create the graphic from scratch, taking care to prevent halos, than to waste time trying to fix them. This is another reason to always save your layered files.

Introduction to SVG

So far this chapter has focused on the tried-and-true bitmapped web graphic formats, but there is another up-and-coming option that I'd like you to be familiar with. It's somewhat misleading to call Scalable Vector Graphics (SVG) "up-and-coming" because the specification has been in development since 1999 and it became a Recommendation in 2003, but thanks to improving browser support, we may finally be able to take advantage of the benefits it has to offer.

As I mentioned at the beginning of this chapter, SVG is a bit of an oddball. Unlike other web image formats, SVG is a vector image format, meaning that it contains instructions for drawing shapes rather than grids of pixels. This makes SVG a good choice for icons, logos, charts, and other line drawings (Figure 21-29). It is not appropriate for photographic imagery, although bitmapped images and even videos can be embedded in SVG.

NOTE

In Fireworks, the eyedropper is at the bottom of the Optimize panel. The Add to Transparency tool allows you to select more than one pixel color to make transparent. This can be useful for removing unwanted colors around the edge of the image.

NOTE

Two good sources for free SVG artwork are the Noun Project (thenounproject. com) and the Open Clip Art library (openclipart.org).

The Noun Project

"ben", Open Clip Art

Ozer Kavak, Open Clip Art

Ghostscript tiger

Figure 21-29. SVG format is appropriate for line-style illustrations.

NOTE

Fireworks gives you a choice of Index or Alpha Transparency for PNG-8 graphics. See the "PNG-8 'Alpha' Transparency" sidebar for details.

Vector images can scale very large or very small without any change in quality (Figure 21-30). Lines and text stay sharp, regardless of whether the image is viewed at 100 pixels or 10,000 pixels—try doing that with a bitmapped image! Now that our web designs and interfaces must work on all devices of all scales, from smartphones to high-density monitors and large-screen televisions, the ability to create a single image that looks great in all contexts is an epic win. Ubiquitous SVG support would certainly solve some of the issues we are facing with maintaining image resolution on high-density displays.

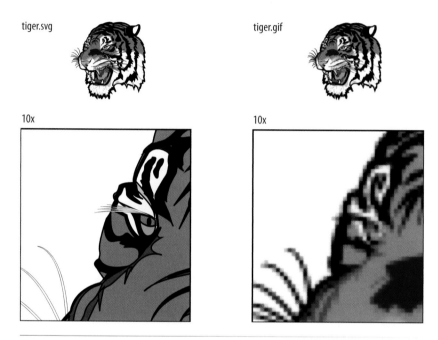

tiger.svg   tiger.gif

10x   10x

Figure 21-30. Vector SVG images scale without loss of quality.

Drawing with XML

What really sets SVG apart is that it is an XML language for providing drawing instructions. Bitmapped graphics are stored as largely unintelligible code (should you care to peek inside), but SVG images are created by text files that are generally human-readable.

Figure 21-31. A basic SVG image, svg4u.svg.

Let's look at a simple example and the XML text file behind the scenes. Figure 21-31 shows an SVG image, *svg4u.svg*, that contains a blue square, an ellipse with a gradient fill, and some text (not pretty, I know, but it gets the point across).

Here is the file that generates that image. If you read through it closely, I think you'll find it's fairly intuitive.

```
<?xml version="1.0" encoding="utf-8"?>
<svg version="1.1"
  xmlns="http://www.w3.org/2000/svg"
```

```
    xmlns:xlink="http://www.w3.org/1999/xlink"
    width="450px" height="200px">
  <linearGradient id="yellowgrad">
    <stop  offset="0" stop-color="#FFF200"/>
    <stop  offset="1" stop-color="#F15A29"/>
  </linearGradient>

  <rect x="50" y="50" width="100" height="100" fill="#4F5AA8"
      stroke="#000000" stroke-width="4" />

  <ellipse cx="100" cy="100" rx="50" ry="25" fill="url(#yellowgrad)" />

  <text x="175" y="150" fill="rgb(200,0,0)" font-family="Verdana"
      font-weight="bold" font-size="50">SVG 4 U!</text>
  </svg>
```

Let's take a closer look at what is going on in *svg4ru.svg*. Because it is an XML file, it starts with an XML declaration. It also needs to follow the XML syntax, so you'll notice that all elements are lowercase, all attributes are in quotation marks, and all elements are closed (for example, **<rect />**). The **svg** element establishes a drawing area that is 450 × 200 pixels. Pixels are the default measurement unit in SVG, so you don't need to include the "px". The **xmlns** attribute stands for "XML namespace," and it simply identifies the XML languages used in the document.

OK, here is the drawing part. The square is created using the **rect** (for rectangle) element with its width and height set to 100 pixels. You can see that attributes are used to provide the position, dimensions, fill color, stroke style, and so on. In addition to **rect**, SVG includes the elements **circle**, **ellipse**, **line**, **polygon**, and **polyline** for drawing lines and shapes.

In our example, the **ellipse** element is positioned to appear centered over the square, and it is filled with the "yellowgrad" gradient that was created by the **linearGradient** element earlier in the document. The text in the image is contained in a **text** element and styled with attributes that take their syntax from CSS. Although it is not shown in this example, it is also possible to place bitmapped images in SVG graphics using the **image** tag.

Of course, there is a *lot* more to the SVG language than I can cover here, but by now you should have a general understanding of how it works.

SVG tools

Technically, all you need to create SVG graphics is a text editor (and genius visualization skills, as well as heroic patience!), but you'll be much happier having a graphics program doing it for you. Fortunately, in Adobe Illustrator, you can choose "SVG (svg)" from the Format menu when saving a drawing and *ta da*—SVG file! If you don't have Illustrator, try downloading the Inkscape (Figure 21-31) image editor, which is made specifically for SVG (*inkscape.org*). It is available for Windows, Mac, and Linux. It takes a little getting used to, but you can't beat the price (free).

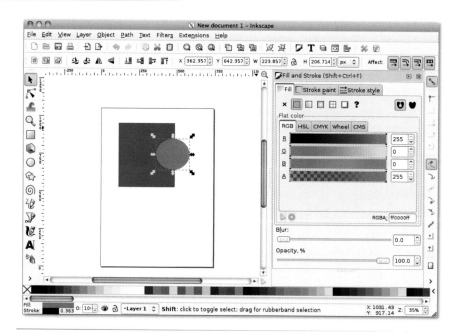

Figure 21-32. Inkscape, an open source SVG editor.

Adding SVG to a page

An SVG image can be added to a web page using the **object**, **embed**, or **iframe** elements. HTML5 allows an **svg** element to be added directly inline as part of the HTML document with no containing element. This W3Schools page has a nice little summary of the various SVG embedding options and their respective advantages and disadvantages: *www.w3schools.com/svg/svg_inhtml.asp*. This stuff is changing quickly, so I recommend you do a little research to see the latest best practices.

As of this writing, the **object** element pointing to an external *.svg* file has the best browser support, so I'm using that method in this example.

```
<!DOCTYPE html>
<html>
<head><title>SVG 4 U</title></head>
<body>
  <object width="450" height="200" type="image/svg+xml"
    data="svg4u.svg"></object>
  <p>Give SVG a try and see what it can do.</p>
</body>
</html>
```

The **width** and **height** attributes are required for the **object** to hold the proper amount of space for the image. If it is too small, the image will be clipped. And to prevent confusion, it is recommended that you include the file type (**image/svg+xml**) so browsers know what to do. Finally, the **data** attribute points to the *.svg* file itself.

But wait…there's more!

Our "SVG 4 U" example demonstrated SVG used for a static illustration, but SVG has more to offer.

Animation

SVG includes transform and transition features (the same used in CSS3), so any part of an SVG image can be animated using SVG syntax alone. This code causes a black rectangle to contract and expand by 50% in a two-second loop.

```
<rect width="150" height="150" fill="black">
  <animate attributeName="width" values="0%;50%;0%" dur="2s"
    repeatCount="indefinite" />
  <animate attributeName="height" values="0%;50%;0%" dur="2s"
    repeatCount="indefinite" />
</rect>
```

Scriptable

Because all of the parts of an SVG file are in XML and are part of the DOM (the structured collection of objects in the document), you can use JavaScript to add behaviors like animation to SVG drawings. You could also use JavaScript to dynamically draw images based on user input in real time, such as generating a chart or graph that reflects values entered into a form. Cool stuff, and certainly beyond the scope of this chapter.

Style-able (if that's a word)

I didn't cover it in this chapter, but you can also use CSS to affect the appearance of elements in SVG images.

Accessible

The content of an SVG image is available in an XML file, so it is potentially more accessible than the **canvas** element, which exists as an abstract grid of pixels. You can also add a **title** and **description** in the **svg** element.

> ## SVG vs. Canvas
>
> In Chapter 10, "What's Up, HTML5?" we looked at the HTML5 **canvas** element and API that creates a space for two-dimensional, dynamic drawing on a web page. The difference is that an SVG image is drawn with a structural markup language and a canvas is drawn with JavaScript commands. Both can contain images, videos, animation, and dynamic updates in real time.
>
> **canvas** is better for quick redraws on the fly (it's only pixels, after all), making it better suited for games, image editing, and saving images to bitmapped formats. SVG offers advantages in the ease of scripting, animation, and accessibility; however, complicated documents require more processing power than **canvas** elements.

Browser support

Man, just when we were having so much fun, I had to go and mention "browser support"! Actually, the news isn't all bad. As I write this, the current version of every major browser, both desktop and mobile, has basic support for SVG images. And the situation has probably already improved by the time you are reading this. For updated statistics, take a look at the *Can I Use* site's SVG listing (*caniuse.com/#cats=SVG*).

So the future is looking bright for SVG, but we still have past browser versions to reckon with, most notably Internet Explorer 8 and earlier. Fortunately there are workarounds, such as the SVGWeb JavaScript library (*code.google. com/p/svgweb/*), which allows scriptable SVG on 95% of browsers.

exercise 21-3 |
Playing around with SVG

SVG files are kind of fun to play around with. I've included the file *svg4u.svg* and its corresponding HTML file in the exercise materials for this chapter so you can get a feel for how it works.

1. Open the *svgtest.html* file in a browser that supports SVG (the latest version of Chrome, Safari, or Firefox will work). You should see the (sadly ugly) SVG 4 U! graphic from Figure 21-31.

2. Open the SVG file in a text editor. Notepad or TextEdit is fine, as long as the file stays in ASCII format and is not styled.

3. Try moving the pieces around by adjusting the x and y coordinates. Try changing the dimensions. Change the fill color. Reload the *svgtest.html* in the browser each time to view your changes. I got a kick out of doing this my first time.

4. If you are feeling more adventurous, open the "SVG Primer for Today's Browsers" (listed in the For further reading section) and try making other shapes and lines. Or you could try creating a simple graphic in Illustrator, save it as an *.svg* file, open it in a text editor, and poke around in the code. There will be a lot of extra stuff to sift through, but you should be able to recognize and edit basic shapes.

In the mobile space, SVG support is trickier to predict because device manufacturers can turn off otherwise supported features for specific devices, but phones and tablets running Android 2.3 and earlier are certain to lack SVG support.

If you do choose to explore SVG for certain types of graphics, be sure to test on a wide variety of devices (not just your iPhone) and be sure to provide useful fallbacks, even if it is just descriptive text, should they not display.

For further reading

Obviously, I could only scratch the surface of Scalable Vector Graphics in this chapter. If you find the motivation and opportunity to use them on your site, you'll have a lot more brushing up to do. In addition to your own web search for up-to-date SVG information, I recommend these resources to get better acquainted.

- *HTML5 Graphics with SVG & CSS*, by Kurt Cagle (O'Reilly).

- *Painting the Web*, by Shelley Powers (O'Reilly). Although this book is getting on in years (it was written in 2008), the chapter on SVG provides a good overview of what the format can do. It also has great in-depth information on other image formats, CSS, and all things visual on the Web.

- "An SVG Primer for Today's Browsers" (*www.w3.org/Graphics/SVG/IG/resources/svgprimer.html*). This article gives you a thorough tutorial on SVG graphics, but it is not exactly a quick read.

- "SVG Examples" (*www.w3schools.com/svg/svg_examples.asp*) shows the code for a lot of shapes and special effects.

Summing Up Images

We've covered a lot of ground in this chapter! If I've done my job, you should now have a good foundation in web graphics, including where to find an image, what file format to save it in, and how to resize it so it is appropriate for the Web. You also know the difference between binary and alpha transparency, and how to make graphics that blend well with the background of a web page. You even have a smattering of SVG vocabulary under your belt.

In the next chapter, we'll take graphics production to the next level and explore all the ways to make images as small as possible for faster downloads. But first, a little quiz.

Test Yourself

Answer the following questions to see if you got the big picture on web graphics. The answers appear in Appendix A.

1. What is the primary advantage to using rights-managed images?

2. What does ppi stand for?

3. What is "indexed color"? What file formats use it?

4. How many colors are in the color table for an 8-bit graphic? If you are up for a bit of math, figure out the maximum number of colors in a 5-bit graphic.

5. Name two things you can do with a GIF that you can't do with a JPEG.

6. Name one thing you can do with a GIF that you can't do with a PNG.

7. Name one thing you can do with a PNG that you can't do with a GIF.

8. JPEG's lossy compression is cumulative. What does that mean? Why is it important to know?

9. What is the difference between binary and alpha transparency?

10. Pick the best graphic file format for each of the images in Figure 21-33. You should be able to make the decision just by looking at the images as they're printed here and explain your choice. Some images may have more than one option.

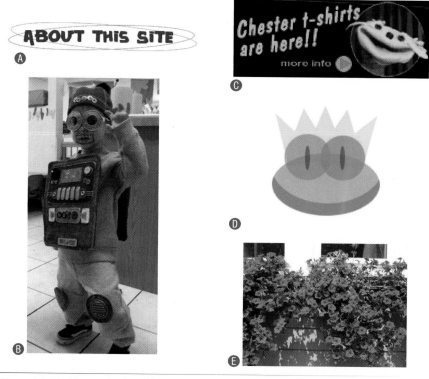

Figure 21-33. Choose the best file format for each image.

LEAN AND MEAN WEB GRAPHICS

Because a web page is published over a network, it needs to zip through the lines as little packets of data in order to reach the end user. It is fairly intuitive, then, that larger amounts of data will require a longer time to arrive. And guess which part of a standard web page packs a whole lotta bytes— that's right, the graphics.

Thus is born the conflicted relationship with graphics on the Web. On the one hand, images make a web page more interesting than text alone, and the ability to display graphics is one of the factors contributing to the Web's success. On the other hand, graphics also try the patience of users with slow Internet connections and gobble the data plans of mobile devices (see the note).

This chapter covers the strategies and tools available for making web graphic file sizes as small as possible (a process known as optimizing) while maintaining acceptable image quality. I hope that I impressed upon you the importance of optimizing site performance back in Chapter 3, "Some Big Concepts You Need to Know." In addition to cutting down on the number of requests your page makes to the server, reducing the total file size of images is the next powerful tool for making pages display as quickly as possible. It is well worth the extra effort to learn how to squeeze every unnecessary byte out of the images you create.

NOTE

One strategy to lighten the load for mobile devices is to serve a separate, smaller image targeted to small-screen devices. That process, known as responsive images, is addressed briefly in Chapter 18, "CSS Techniques."

General Image Optimization Strategies

Imagine you are designing banner ads for a big client and they tell you that all banner graphics have a 15K limit (the file cannot exceed 15 kilobytes in size). This scenario is fairly common in the biz, so you're going to need a few tricks up your sleeve for making the target. That's what this chapter is about.

Regardless of the image or file type, there are a few basic strategies to keep in mind for limiting file size. In the broadest of terms, they are:

Limit dimensions

Although fairly obvious, the easiest way to keep file size down is to limit the dimensions of the image itself. There aren't any magic numbers; just don't make images any larger than they need to be. By simply eliminating extra space in the graphic in Figure 22-1, I was able to reduce the file size by 3K (23%).

Reuse and recycle

If you use the same image repeatedly in a site, it is best to create only one image file and point to it repeatedly wherever it is needed. This allows the browser to take advantage of the cached image and avoid additional downloads. Caching is explained in the "Take Advantage of Caching" sidebar in Chapter 7, "Adding Images."

Design for compression

One of the best strategies for making files as small as possible is to design for efficient compression. For example, because you know that GIF compression likes flat colors, don't design GIF images with gradient color blends when a flat color will suffice. Similarly, because JPEG likes soft transitions and no hard edges, you can try strategically blurring images that will be saved in JPEG format. These strategies are discussed in more detail later in this chapter.

Use web graphics tools

If you know you will be doing a lot of web production work, it is worth investing in image-editing software such as Adobe Photoshop or Fireworks. In the previous chapter, we saw how the Save for Web dialog box in Photoshop and the Optimize and Preview panels in Fireworks provided useful shortcuts for making web graphics. In this chapter, we'll take full advantage of the settings that pertain to keeping file sizes as small as possible.

Figure 22-1. You can reduce the size of your files simply by cropping out extra space.

600 x 200 pixels (**13 KB**)

500 x 136 pixels (**10 KB**)

Both tools allow you to preview the final image and its respective file size as you make your optimization settings, so you can tweak settings and see the results instantly. The set of options varies by file type, so I'll explain them one format at a time, starting with that old favorite, GIF.

Online Image Optimizers

If you don't have Fireworks or Photoshop, you can use one of the free online image-optimizing tools listed here. They do not give you control over settings that you find in web image tools, but they are effective and certainly better than no optimization at all.

Smush.it (*www.smushit.com*). Smush.it uses optimization techniques specific to image format to remove unnecessary bytes from image files. It is a lossless tool, which means it optimizes images without changing their look or visual quality. I've personally found that it finds a way to slightly reduce the file size of images I've already optimized myself in Photoshop. This is a great resource.

Dynamic Drive Online Image Optimizer (*tools.dynamicdrive.com/imageoptimizer*). This is another online tool that takes your files and returns optimized versions based on more aggressive optimization settings. It is not a lossless tool, so you need to choose from the optimized images to find the one that maintains acceptable quality.

And if those aren't enough for you, check out PunyPNG (*punypng.com*) and ImageOptim (*imageoptim.com*) as well.

Optimizing GIFs

When optimizing GIF images, it is useful to keep in mind that GIF compression works by condensing bands of repetitive pixel colors. Many optimization strategies work by creating more areas of solid color for the compression scheme to sink its teeth into.

The general methods for keeping GIF file sizes in check are:

* Reducing the number of colors (the bit depth) of the image

* Reducing dithering in the image

* Applying a "lossy" filter

* Designing with flat colors

This section looks at each of these options using Photoshop's Save for Web and Fireworks' Optimize panels as springboards (Figure 22-2). When a feature is specific to these tools, I will note it; otherwise, the approaches shown here should be achievable with most image-editing software.

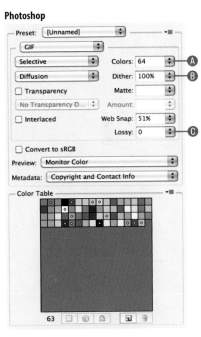

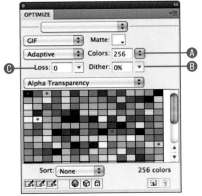

Figure 22-2. GIF optimization options in Photoshop and Fireworks.

Reducing the number of colors

The most effective way to reduce the size of a GIF file, and therefore the first stop in your optimization journey, is to reduce the number of colors in the image.

Although GIFs can contain up to 256 colors, there's no rule that says they have to. In fact, by reducing the number of colors (the bit depth), you can significantly reduce the file size of an image. One reason for this is that files with lower bit depths contain less data. Another byproduct of the color reduction is that more areas of flat color are created by combining similar, abutting pixel colors. More flat color areas mean more efficient compression.

Nearly all graphics programs that allow you to save or export to GIF format will also allow you to specify the number of colors or bit depth. In Photoshop and Fireworks, the color count and the color table are revealed in the settings panel. Click on the Colors pop-up menu (Figure 22-2, ⒶＡ)to select from a standard list of numbers of colors. Some tools give you a list of bit depths instead. See the "Bit Depth" sidebar for how bit depths match up to numbers of colors. When you select smaller numbers, the resulting file size shrinks as well.

If you reduce the number of colors too far, of course, the image begins to fall apart or may cease to communicate effectively. For example, in Figure 22-3, once I reduced the number of colors to eight, I lost the rainbow, which was the whole point of the image. This "meltdown" point is different from image to image.

Bit Depth

Bit depth is a way to refer to the maximum number of colors a graphic can contain. This chart shows the number of colors each bit depth can represent:

1-bit	2 colors
2-bit	4 colors
3-bit	8 colors
4-bit	16 colors
5-bit	32 colors
6-bit	64 colors
7-bit	128 colors
8-bit	256 colors

256 colors: 21 KB

64 colors: 13 KB

8 colors: 6 KB

Figure 22-3. Reducing the number of colors in an image reduces the file size.

You'll be surprised to find how many images look perfectly fine with only 32-pixel colors (5-bit). That is usually my starting point for color reduction, and I go higher only if necessary. Some image types fare better than others with reduced color palettes, but as a general rule, the fewer the colors, the smaller the file.

Reducing dithering

When the colors in an image are reduced to a specific palette, the colors that are *not* in that palette get approximated by dithering. Dithering is a speckle pattern that results when palette colors are mixed to simulate an unavailable color.

In photographic images, dithering is not a problem and can even be beneficial; however, dithering in flat color areas is usually distracting and undesirable. In terms of optimization, dithering is undesirable because the speckles disrupt otherwise smooth areas of color. Those stray speckles stand in the way of GIF compression and result in larger files.

One way to shave extra bytes off a GIF is to limit the amount of dithering. Again, nearly all GIF creation tools allow you to turn dithering on and off. Photoshop and Fireworks go one step further by allowing you to set the specific amount of dithering on a sliding scale (Figure 22-2 **B**). You can even preview the results of the dither setting, so you can decide at which point the degradation in image quality is not worth the file size savings (Figure 22-4). In images with smooth color gradients, turning dithering off results in unacceptable banding and blotches.

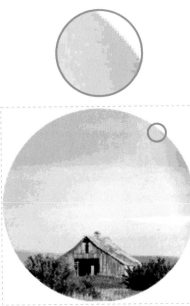

Dithering: 9.6 KB   **No dithering: 7.8 KB**

GRAPHICS TIP

Finding the "Sweet Spot"

You will see that finding the best optimization for a given image requires adjusting all of these attributes (bit depth, dithering, lossiness) in turn until the best image quality at the smallest file size is achieved. It takes time and practice, but eventually, you will find the "sweet spot" for each image.

Figure 22-4. Turning off or reducing the amount of dithering reduces the file size. Both images have 32-pixel colors and use an adaptive palette.

Lossy set to 0%: 13.2 KB

Lossy set to 25%: 7.5 KB

Figure 22-5. File size without and with the Lossy setting applied in Photoshop.

280 bytes

585 bytes

Figure 22-7. GIFs designed with horizontal bands of color will compress more efficiently than those with vertical bands.

Using the Lossy filter

The final optimization setting in the Save for Web dialog box is Lossy (Figure 22-2 ❻). In Fireworks, it is called Loss. This setting allows the program to selectively throw away data in order to reduce the file size. The higher the setting, the more data is discarded. Depending on the image, you can apply a loss value of 5% to 20% without seriously degrading the image. Figure 22-5 shows the results of applying Photoshop's Lossy setting to the barn image. At higher settings, images tend to look windswept and blown apart.

This technique works best for continuous tone art (but then, images that are all continuous tone should probably be saved as JPEGs anyway). You might try playing with loss settings on an image with a combination of flat and photographic content.

Designing for GIF compression

Now that you've seen how high bit depths and dithering bloat GIF file sizes, you have a good context for my next tip. Before you even get to the point of making optimization settings, you can be proactive about optimizing your graphics by designing them to compress well in the first place.

Keep it flat

I've found that as a web designer, I've changed my illustration style to match the medium. In graphics where I might have used a gradient blend, I now opt for a flat color. In most cases, it works just as well, and it doesn't introduce unflattering banding and dithering or drive up the file size (Figure 22-6). You may also choose to replace areas of photos with subtle blends, such as a blue sky, with flat colors if you need to save them as GIFs (otherwise, the JPEG format may be better).

This GIF has gradient blends and 256 colors. Its file size is **19 KB**.

Even when I reduce the number of colors to 8, the file size is **7.6 KB**.

When I create the same image with flat colors, the size is only **3.2 KB**.

Figure 22-6. You can keep file sizes small by designing in a way that takes advantage of the GIF compression scheme.

Horizontal stripes

Here's an esoteric little tip. When designing web graphics, keep in mind that GIF compression works best on horizontal bands of color. If you want to make something striped, it's better to make the stripes horizontal rather than vertical (Figure 22-7). Silly, but true.

Summing up GIF optimization

The GIF format offers many opportunities for optimization. Designing with flat colors in the first place is a good strategy for creating small GIFs. The next tactic is to save the GIF with the fewest number of colors possible to keep the image intact. Adjusting the amount of dithering and applying a loss filter are additional ways to squeeze out even more bytes.

Exercise 22-1 gives you a chance to try out some of these techniques.

Optimizing JPEGs

JPEG optimization is slightly more straightforward than GIF. The general strategies for reducing the file size of JPEGs are:

- Be aggressive with compression

- Use Weighted (Selective) Optimization if available

- Choose Optimized if available

- Soften the image (Blur/Smoothing)

This section explains each approach, again using Photoshop's and Fireworks' optimization tools, shown in Figure 22-9. Notice that there is no color table for JPEGs because they do not use palettes.

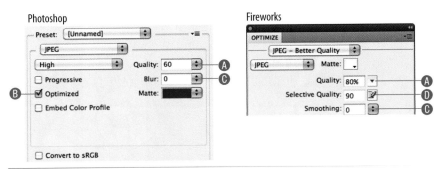

Figure 22-9. JPEG optimization options in Photoshop's Save for Web dialog box (left) and Fireworks' Optimize panel (right).

Before we get to specific settings, let's take a look at what JPEG compression is good at. This will provide some perspective for later techniques in this section.

Getting to know JPEG compression

The JPEG compression scheme loves images with subtle gradations, few details, and no hard edges. One way you can keep JPEGs small is to start with the kind of image it likes.

asian.psd; target: **4 to 5 KB**

info.psd; target: **<300 bytes**

bunny.psd; target: **5 to 6 KB**

Figure 22-8. Create GIFs that are optimized to the target file sizes.

Avoid detail

JPEGs compress areas of smooth, blended colors more efficiently than areas with high contrast and sharp detail. In fact, the blurrier your image, the smaller the resulting JPEG. Figure 22-10 shows two similar graphics with blended colors. You can see that the image with contrast and detail is more than four times larger at the same compression/quality setting.

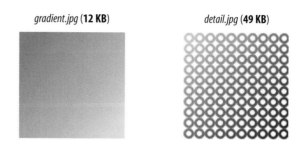

gradient.jpg (**12 KB**) detail.jpg (**49 KB**)

Figure 22-10. JPEG compression works better on smooth, blended colors than hard edges and detail.

Avoid flat colors

It's useful to know that totally flat colors don't fare well in JPEG format, because the colors tend to shift and get mottled as a result of the compression, particularly at higher rates of compression (Figure 22-11). In general, flat graphical images should be saved as GIFs because the image quality will be better and the file size smaller.

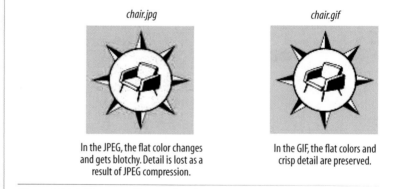

chair.jpg chair.gif

In the JPEG, the flat color changes and gets blotchy. Detail is lost as a result of JPEG compression.

In the GIF, the flat colors and crisp detail are preserved.

Figure 22-11. The same flat graphical image saved as both a JPEG and a GIF.

Unpredictable Color in JPEGs

In GIF images, you have total control over the colors that appear in the image, making it easy to match RGB colors in adjoining GIFs or in an inline GIF and a background image or color.

Unfortunately, flat colors shift around and get somewhat blotchy with JPEG compression, so there is no way to control the colors precisely. Even pure white can get distorted in a JPEG.

This means there is no guaranteed way to create a perfect, seamless match between a JPEG and another color, whether in a GIF, PNG, another JPEG, or even an RGB background color. If you need a seamless match between the foreground and background image, consider switching formats to GIF or PNG to take advantage of transparency and let the background show through.

Be aggressive with compression

The primary tool for optimizing JPEGs is the Quality setting (Figure 22-9 Ⓐ). The Quality setting allows you to set the rate of compression; lower quality means higher compression and smaller files. Figure 22-12 shows the results of different quality (compression) rates as applied in Photoshop and Fireworks.

Notice that the image holds up reasonably well, even at very low quality settings. Notice also that the same settings in each program produce different results. This is because the quality rating scale is not objective—it varies from program to program. For example, 1% in Photoshop is similar to 30% in Fireworks and other programs. Furthermore, different images can withstand different amounts of compression. It is best to go by the way the image looks rather than a specific number setting.

Figure 22-12. A comparison of various compression levels in Photoshop and Fireworks.

Photoshop

100% (42.2 KB)

80% (22.3 KB)

60% (13.6 KB)

40% (8.5 KB)

20% (6.3 KB)

1% (3.7 KB)

Fireworks

100% (51.5 KB)

80% (12.3 KB)

60% (7.7 KB)

40% (5 KB)

20% (1.8 KB)

1% (1.2 KB)

Quality: 20; Blur: 0 (9.3 KB)

This JPEG was saved at low quality (20% in Photoshop) with no Blur applied.

Quality: 20; Blur: .5 (7.2 KB)

With a Blur setting of only .5, the resulting file size is 22% smaller. In Fireworks, use Smoothing for similar results.

Figure 22-13. Blurring the image slightly before exporting as a JPEG results in smaller file sizes.

Choose optimized JPEGs

Optimized JPEGs have slightly smaller file sizes and better color fidelity (although I've never been able to see the difference) than standard JPEGs. For this reason, you should select the Optimized option if your image software offers it (Figure 22-9 **B**). Look for the Optimized option in Photoshop and third-party JPEG compression utilities. Fireworks does not offer the option as of this writing.

Blurring or smoothing the image

Because soft images compress smaller than sharp ones, Photoshop and Fireworks make it easy to blur the image slightly as part of the optimization process. In Photoshop, the tool is called Blur; in Fireworks, it's Smoothing (Figure 22-9 **C**). Blurring makes the JPEG compression work better, resulting in a smaller file (Figure 22-13). If you don't have these tools, you can soften the whole image yourself by applying a slight blur to the image with the Gaussian Blur filter (or similar) manually prior to export.

The downside of Blur and Smoothing filters is that they are applied evenly to the entire image. If you want to preserve detail in certain areas of the image, you can apply a blur filter just to the areas you don't mind being blurry. When you're done, export the JPEG as usual. The blurred areas will take full advantage of the JPEG compression, and your crisp areas will stay crisp.

Selective quality (Fireworks)

Not all image areas are created equal. You may wish to preserve detail in one area, such as a person's face, but compress the heck out of the rest of the image. To this end, Fireworks gives us Selective Quality—a method for applying different amounts of JPEG compression within a single image: one setting for a selected area and another setting for the rest of the image.

NOTE

Photoshop included a similar Weighted Optimization feature in versions CS3 and earlier, but it was removed in version CS4.

To use the Selective Quality setting (Figure 22-9 **D**), select the areas of the image you want to preserve (Figure 22-14 **A**), then select Modify → Selective JPEG → Save Selection as JPEG Mask **B**. In the Optimize panel, you can set the Selective Quality for your selection or click the adjacent icon **C** to access the Selective JPEG dialog box **D** with a full set of options, such as preserving type and button quality and selecting a color for the masked area. The regular Quality setting will be used for all other areas of the image.

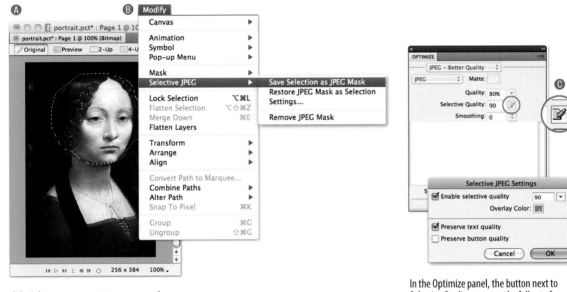

Select the area you want to preserve and save it as a Selective JPEG Mask.

In the Optimize panel, the button next to Selective Quality accesses the full set of quality options for the selection.

Figure 22-14. Using Selective Quality in Fireworks.

Summing up JPEG optimization

Your primary tool for optimizing JPEGs is the Quality (compression) setting. If your tools offer them, making the JPEG Optimized or applying Blur or Smoothing will make them smaller.

Now it's your turn to play around with JPEGs in Exercise 22-2.

falcon.tif
target: 35–40 KB

Imagine that this image is going on a site that sells posters where it would be important to preserve the type and painting detail throughout the image. The result is you can't compress it as far as other images.

boats.psd
target: 24–30 KB

Watch for JPEG artifacts around the lines and masts of the boats. Try to keep those lines clean.

penny.tif
target: 12–18 KB

This image is a good candidate for some manual blurring of the background prior to compression.

Figure 22-15. Match the file sizes.

Optimizing PNGs

As discussed in the previous chapter, there are two types of PNG files: 24-bit PNGs (PNG-24), which contain colors from the millions of colors in the RGB color space, and 8-bit indexed PNGs (PNG-8) with a palette limited to 256 colors. This section looks at what you can (and can't) do to affect the file size of both kinds of PNG files.

PNG-24

PNG's lossless compression makes PNG-24 a wonderful format for preserving quality in images, but unfortunately, it makes it a poor option for web graphics. A PNG-24 will always be significantly larger than a JPEG of the same image because no pixels are sacrificed in the compression process. Therefore, your first "lean and mean" strategy is to avoid PNG-24 for photographic images and choose JPEG instead.

The exception to this rule, of course, is if you want to use multiple levels of transparency (alpha transparency). In that case, given today's tools and browsers, PNG-24 is your only option.

There aren't any tricks for reducing the file size of a PNG-24, as evidenced by the lack of options on the PNG-24 export panels (Figure 22-16). You'll have to accept the file size that your image-editing tool cranks out, although you may try running it through the online image optimization tool Smush.it (*www.smush.it*) to see if it can make any improvements.

PNG-8

Indexed color PNGs work similarly to GIFs, and in fact, usually result in smaller file sizes for the same images, making them a good byte-saving option. The general strategies for optimizing GIFs also apply to PNG-8s:

- Reduce the number of colors

- Reduce dithering

- Design with flat colors

You can see that the list of export options for PNG-8s is more or less the same as for GIF (Figure 22-16). The notable exception is that there is no "lossy" filter for PNGs as there is for GIFs. Otherwise, all of the techniques listed in the Optimizing GIFs section apply to PNGs as well.

It is worth noting that making a PNG interlaced significantly increases its file size, by as much as 20 or 30 percent. It is best to avoid this option unless you deem it absolutely necessary to have the image appear in a series of passes.

For an in-depth look at PNG compression and optimization, I recommend the *Smashing Magazine* article "Clever PNG Optimization Techniques," by Sergey Chikuyonok (*www.smashingmagazine.com/2009/07/15/clever-png-optimization-techniques/*).

Optimize to File Size

There is one last optimizing technique that is good to know about if you use Photoshop or Fireworks.

In some instances, you may need to optimize a graphic to hit a specific file size—for example, when designing an ad banner with a strict K-limit. Both Photoshop and Fireworks offer an Optimize to File Size function. You just set the desired file size and let the program figure out the best settings to use to get there, saving you lots of time.

Photoshop

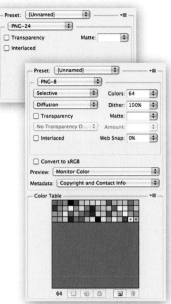

Fireworks

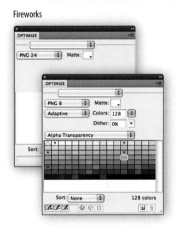

Figure 22-16. PNG-24 and PNG-8 settings in Photoshop and Fireworks.

This feature is pretty straightforward to use. In Photoshop, choose Optimize to File Size from the Options pop-up menu in the Save for Web dialog box. In Fireworks, choose Optimize to Size from the Options pop-up menu in the Optimize panel (Figure 22-17). All you need to do is type in your desired target size and click OK. The tool does the rest.

Photoshop also asks if you'd like to start with your own optimization settings or let Photoshop select GIF or JPEG automatically. Curiously, PNG is not an option for automatic selection, so start with your own settings if you want to save as PNG.

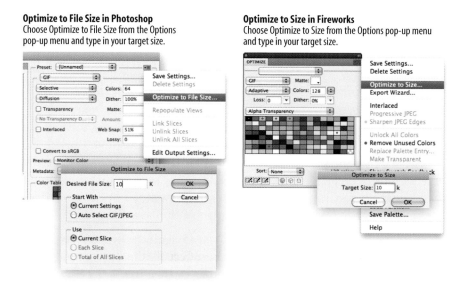

Optimize to File Size in Photoshop
Choose Optimize to File Size from the Options pop-up menu and type in your target size.

Optimize to Size in Fireworks
Choose Optimize to Size from the Options pop-up menu and type in your target size.

Figure 22-17. Optimizing to a specific file size (in Photoshop and Fireworks).

Optimization in Review

If this collection of optimization techniques feels daunting, don't worry. After a while, they'll become part of your standard production process. You'll find it's easy to keep your eye on the file size and make a few setting tweaks to bring that number down. Now that you have the added advantage of understanding what the various settings are doing behind the scenes, you can make informed and efficient optimization decisions.

Test Yourself

Now that you're acquainted with the world of graphics optimization, it's time to take a little test. I know you'll ace it.

1. Why do professional web designers optimize their graphics?

2. How does dithering affect the file size of a GIF?

3. How does the number of pixel colors affect the file size of a GIF?

4. What is the most effective setting for optimizing a JPEG?

5. How does the Blur or Smoothing setting affect JPEG size?

6. What is the best way to optimize a PNG-8? A PNG-24?

ANSWERS

Chapter 1: Where Do I Start?

1. B, D, A, C

2. The W3C guides the development of web-related technologies.

3. C, D, A, E, B

4. Frontend design is concerned with aspects of a site that appear in or are related to the browser. Backend development involves the programming required on the server for site functionality.

5. A web-authoring tool provides a visual interface for creating entire web pages, including the necessary HTML, CSS, and scripts. HTML editors provide only shortcuts to writing HTML documents manually.

Chapter 2: How the Web Works

1. c; 2. j; 3. h; 4. g; 5. f; 6. i; 7. b; 8. a; 9. d; 10. e

Chapter 3: Some Big Concepts You Need to Know

1. There are a number of unknown factors when you're developing a site:

   - The size of the screen or browser window

   - The user's Internet connection speed

   - Whether the user is at a desk or on the go (context and attention span)

2. 1. c; 2. d; 3. e; 4. a; 5. b

3. The four general disability categories include:

   - Sight impairment: make sure the content is semantic and in logical order for when it is read by a screen reader.

   - Hearing impairment: provide transcripts for audio and video content.

   - Mobility impairment: use measures that help users without a mouse or keyboard.

   - Cognitive impairment: content should be simple and clearly organized.

4. You would use a waterfall chart to evaluate your site's performance in the optimization process.

5. Responsive design takes care of the layout, but does not in itself provide alternate content that may be appropriate for the mobile context. Servers are able to detect more features than CSS media queries and can make better decisions about what content to serve.

Chapter 4: Creating a Simple Page (HTML Overview)

1. A tag is part of the markup (brackets and element name) used to delimit an element. An element consists of the content and its tags.

2. The minimal markup of an HTML document is as follows:

```
<!DOCTYPE html>
<html>
<head>
    <meta charset="utf8">
    <title>Title</title>
</head>
<body>
</body>
</html>
```

3. a. *Sunflower.html*—Yes

    b. *index.doc*—No, it must end in *.html* or *.htm*

    c. *cooking home page.html*—No, there may be no character spaces

    d. *Song_Lyrics.html*—Yes

    e. *games/rubix.html*—No, there may be no slashes in the name

    f. *%whatever.html*—No, there may be no percent symbols

4. All of the following markup examples are incorrect. Describe what is wrong with each one, and then write it correctly.

    a. It is missing the **src** attribute: `<img src="birthday.jpg">`

    b. The slash in the end tag is missing: `<i>Congratulations!</i>`

    c. There should be no attribute in the end tag: `<a href="file.html">linked text</a>`

    d. The slash should be a forward slash: `<p>This is a new paragraph</p>`

5. Make it a comment: `<!-- product list begins here -->`

Chapter 5: Marking Up Text

1. `<p>People who know me know that I love to cook.</p>`
   `<hr>`
   `<p>I've created this site to share some of my favorite recipes.</p>`

2. A `blockquote` is a block-level element used for long quotations or quoted material that may consist of other block elements. The `q` (quote) element is for short quotations that go in the flow of text and do not cause line breaks.

3. `pre`

4. The `ul` element is an unordered list for lists that don't need to appear in a particular order. They display with bullets by default. The `ol` element is an ordered list in which sequence matters. The browser automatically inserts numbers for ordered lists.

5. Use a style sheet to remove bullets from an unordered list.

6. `<abbr title="World Wide Web Consortium">W3C</abbr>`

7. A `dl` is the element used to identify an entire description list. The `dt` element is used to identify just one term within that list.

8. The `id` attribute is used to identify a unique element in a document, and the name in its value may appear only once in a document. `class` is used to classify multiple elements into conceptual groups.

9. An `article` element is intended for a self-contained body of content that would be appropriate for syndication or might appear in a different context. A `section` divides content into thematically related chunks.

10.

`&mdash;`	em dash (—)
`&amp;`	ampersand (&)
` `	non-breaking space
`&copy;`	copyright (©)
`&bull;`	bullet (•)
`&trade;`	trademark symbol (™)

Exercise 5-1

```
<!DOCTYPE html>
<html>
<head>
  <meta charset="utf-8">
  <title>Tapenade Recipe</title>
</head>
<body>

<h1>Tapenade (Olive Spread)</h1>

<p>This is a really simple dish to prepare and it's always a big hit
at parties. My father recommends:</p>

<blockquote><p>"Make this the night before so that the flavors have
time to blend. Just bring it up to room temperature before you serve it.
 In the winter, try serving it warm."</p></blockquote>

<h2>Ingredients</h2>

<ul>
  <li>1 8oz. jar sundried tomatoes</li>
  <li>2 large garlic cloves</li>
  <li>2/3 c. kalamata olives</li>
  <li>1 t. capers</li>
</ul>

<h2>Instructions</h2>
```

```
<ol>
  <li>Combine tomatoes and garlic in a food processor. Blend until
as smooth as possible.</li>

  <li>Add capers and olives. Pulse the motor a few times until they are incorporated, but still retain some
    texture.</li>

  <li>Serve on thin toast rounds with goat cheese and fresh basil garnish (optional).</li>
</ol>

</body>
</html>
```

Exercise 5-2

```
<article>
  <header>
    <p>posted by BGB, <time datetime="2012-11-15" pubdate>November 15, 2012</time></p>
  </header>
  <h1>Low and Slow</h1>
  <p>This week I am <em>extremely</em> excited about a new cooking technique
    called <dfn><i>sous vide</i></dfn>. In <i>sous vide</i> cooking, you submerge the food (usually vacuum-
    sealed in plastic) into a water bath that is precisely set to the target temperature you want the food
    to be cooked to. In his book, <cite>Cooking for Geeks</cite>, Jeff Potter describes it as <q>ultra-low-
    temperature poaching</q>.</p>
  <p>Next month, we will be serving <b>Sous Vide Salmon with Dill Hollandaise</b>. To reserve a seat at the
    chef table, contact us before November 30.</p>
  <p>blackgoose@example.com<br> 555-336-1800</p>
  <p><small>Warning: Sous vide cooked salmon is not pasteurized. Avoid it if you are pregnant or have
    immunity issues.</small></p>
</article>
```

Exercise 5-3

```
<!DOCTYPE html>
<html>
<head>
  <meta charset="utf-8">
  <title>Black Goose Bistro: Blog</title>
</head>
<body>
<header>
  <h1>The Black Goose Blog</h1>
  <nav>
    <ul>
      <li>Home</li>
      <li>Menu</li>
      <li>Blog</li>
      <li>Contact</li>
    </ul>
  </nav>
</header>

<article>
  <header>
    <h2>Summer Menu Items</h2>
    <p>posted by BGB, <time datetime="2013-06-15" pubdate>June 15, 2013</time></p>
  </header>
  <p>Our chef has been busy putting together the perfect menu for the
```

```html
summer months. Stop by to try these appetizers and main courses while
the days are still long.</p>

      <section id="appetizers">
        <h3>Appetizers</h3>
        <dl>
          <dt>Black bean purses</dt>
          <dd>Spicy black bean and a blend of mexican cheeses wrapped in sheets
of phyllo and baked until golden. <span class="price">$3.95</span></dd>
          <dt class="newitem">Southwestern napoleons with lump crab &mdash;
<strong>new item!</strong><dt>
          <dd>Layers of light lump crab meat, bean and corn salsa, and our
handmade flour tortillas. <span class="price">$7.95</span></dd>
        </dl>
      </section>
      <section id="maincourses">
        <h3>Main courses</h3>
        <dl>
          <dt>Shrimp sate kebabs with peanut sauce</dt>
          <dd>Skewers of shrimp marinated in lemongrass, garlic, and fish sauce then grilled to perfection.
      Served with spicy peanut sauce and jasmine rice. <span class="price">$12.95</span></dd>

          <dt class="newitem">Jerk rotisserie chicken with fried plantains &mdash; <strong>new item!</strong></dt>
          <dd>Tender chicken slow-roasted on the rotisserie, flavored with spicy and fragrant jerk sauce and
      served with fried plantains and fresh mango. <span class="price">$12.95</span></dd>
        </dl>
      </section>
    </article>

    <article>
      <header>
        <h2>Low and Slow</h2>
        <p>posted by BGB, <time datetime="2012-11-15" pubdate>November 15, 2012</time></p>
      </header>
      <p>This week I am <em>extremely</em> excited about a new cooking technique called <dfn><i>sous vide</i>
        </dfn>. In <i>sous vide</i> cooking, you submerge the food (usually vacuum-sealed in plastic) into a
        water bath that is precisely set to the target temperature of the food. In his book, <cite>Cooking for
        Geeks</cite>, Jeff Potter describes it as <q>ultra-low-temperature poaching</q>.</p>
      <p>Next month, we will be serving <b>Sous Vide Salmon with Dill Hollandaise</b>. To reserve a seat at the
        chef table, contact us before November 30.</p>
    </article>

    <footer>
      <div id="about">
        <p>Location:<br>Baker's Corner, Seekonk, MA</p>
        <p>Hours:<br>Tuesday to Saturday, <time datetime="11:00">11am</time> to <time datetime="00:00">midnight</
        time></p>
      </div>
      <p><small>All content copyright &copy; 2012, Black Goose Bistro and Jennifer Robbins</small><p>
    </footer>

  </body>
</html>
```

Chapter 6: Adding Links

1. `<a href="tutorial.html">...</a>`

2. `<a href="examples/instructions.html">...</a>`

3. `<a href="examples/french/family.html">...</a>`

4. `<a href="/examples/german/numbers.html">...</a>`

5. `<a href="../index.html">...</a>`

6. `<a href="http://www.learningwebdesign.com">...</a>`

7. `<a href="../instructions.html">...</a>`

8. `<a href="../../index.html">...</a>`

9. `<img src="images/arrow.gif" alt="" >`

10. `<img src="../images/arrow.gif" alt="" >`

11. `<img src="../../images/bullet.gif" alt="" >`

Exercise 6-1

```
<li><a href="http://www.epicurious.com">Epicurious</a></li>
```

Exercise 6-2

```
<p><a href="index.html">Back to the home page</a></p>
```

Exercise 6-3

```
<li><a href="recipes/tapenade.html">Tapenade (Olive Spread)</a></li>
```

Exercise 6-4

```
<li><a href="recipes/pasta/linguine.html">Linguine with Clam Sauce</a></li>
```

Exercise 6-5

```
<p><a href="../index.html">[Back to the home page]</a></p>
```

Exercise 6-6

```
<p><a href="../../index.html">[Back to the home page]</a></p>
```

Exercise 6-7

1. `<p><a href="tapenade.html">Go to the Tapenade recipe</a></p>`

2. `<p><a href="../salmon.html">Try this with Garlic Salmon</a></p>`

3. `<p><a href="pasta/linguine.html">Try the Linguine with Clam Sauce</a></p>`

4. `<p><a href="../../about.html">About Jen's Kitchen</a></p>`

5. `<p><a href="http://www.allrecipes.com">Go to AllRecipes.com</a></p>`

Chapter 7: Adding Images

1. The `src` and `alt` attributes are required for the document to be valid. If the `src` attribute is omitted, the browser won't know which image to use. You may leave the value of the `alt` attribute empty if alternative text would be meaningless or clumsy when read in context.

2. `<img src="furry.jpg" alt="">`

3. a. It improves accessibility by providing a description of the image if it is not available or not viewable, and b. because HTML documents are not valid if the `alt` attribute is omitted.

4. It allows the browser to render the rest of the content while the image is being retrieved from the server, which can speed up the display of the page. Leave `width` and `height` attributes out if you are doing a responsive site design where image sizes need to stay flexible.

5. The three likely causes for a missing image are: a. the URL is incorrect, so the browser is looking in the wrong place or for the wrong filename (names are case-sensitive); b. the image file is not in an acceptable format; and c. the image file is not named with the proper suffix (*.gif*, *.jpg*, or *.png*, as appropriate).

Exercise 7-1

In *index.html*:

```
<h2>The Tuscan Countryside</h2>

<p><a href="countryside.html"><img src="thumbnails/countryside_thumb.jpg" alt="view of the rolling tuscan hills"
width="100" height="75"></a> This is …</p>

<h2>Sienna</h2>

<p><a href="sienna.html"><img src="thumbnails/sienna_thumb.jpg" alt="view from the bedroom window" width="75"
height="100"></a> The closest city …</p>
```

In *countryside.html*:

```
<p><img src="photos/countryside.jpg" alt="rolling hills in greens and golds" width="500" height="375"></p>
```

In *sienna.html*:

```
<p><img src="photos/sienna.jpg" alt="a narrow, steep street in Sienna" width="375" height="500"></p>
```

Chapter 8: Basic Table Markup

1. The table itself (`table`), rows (`tr`), header cells (`th`), data cells (`td`), and an optional caption (`caption`).

2. Because they use Cascading Style Sheets (CSS) for layout.

3. If you want to add more information about the structure of a table, to specify widths to speed up display, or to add certain style properties to a column of cells.

4. a. The `caption` should be the first element inside the `table` element; b. there can't be text directly in the `table` element; it must go in a `th` or `td`; c. the `th` elements must go inside the `tr` element; d. there is no `colspan` element; this should be a `td` with a `colspan` attribute; e. the second `tr` element is missing a closing tag.

Exercise 8-1

```
<table>
<tr>
  <th>Album</th>
  <th>Year</th>
</tr>
<tr>
  <td>Rubber Soul</td>
  <td>1968</td>
</tr>
<tr>
  <td>Revolver</td>
  <td>1966</td>
</tr>
<tr>
  <td>Sgt. Pepper's</td>
  <td>1967</td>
</tr>
<tr>
  <td>The White Album</td>
  <td>1968</td>
</tr>
<tr>
  <td>Abbey Road</td>
  <td>1969</td>
<tr>
</table>
```

Exercise 8-2

```
<table>
  <tr>
    <th>7:00pm</th><th>7:30pm</th><th>8:00pm</th>
  </tr>
  <tr>
    <td colspan="3">The Sunday Night Movie</td>
  </tr>
  <tr>
    <td>Perry Mason</td>
    <td>Candid Camera</td>
    <td>What's My Line</td>
  </tr>
  <tr>
    <td>Bonanza</td>
    <td colspan="2">The Wackiest Ship in the Army</td>
  </tr>
</table>
```

Exercise 8-3

```
<table>
  <tr>
    <td>apples</td>
    <td rowspan="3">oranges</td>
    <td>pears</td>
  </tr>
  <tr>
    <td>bananas</td>
    <td rowspan="2">pineapple</td>
  </tr>
  <tr>
    <td>lychees</td>
  </tr>
</table>
```

Exercise 8-4

```
<table>
  <caption>Your Content Here</caption>
  <tr>
    <th rowspan="2"> </th>
    <th colspan="2">A common header for two subheads</th>
    <th rowspan="2">Header 3</th>
  </tr>
  <tr>
    <th>Header 1</th>
    <th>Header 2</th>
  </tr>
  <tr>
    <th scope="row">Thing A</th>
    <td>data A1</td>
    <td>data A2</td>
    <td>data A3</td>
  </tr>
  <tr>
    <th scope="row">Thing B </th>
    <td>data B1</td>
    <td>data B2</td>
    <td>data B3</td>
  </tr>
  <tr>
    <th scope="row">Thing C</th>
    <td>data C1</td>
    <td>data C2</td>
    <td>data C3</td>
  </tr>
</table>
```

Chapter 9: Forms

1. a. POST (because of security issues)

    b. POST (because it uses the file selection input type)

    c. GET (because you may want to bookmark search results)

    d. POST (because it is likely to have a length text entry)

2. a. Pull-down menu: `<select>`

   b. Radio buttons: `<input type="radio">`

   c. `<textarea>`

   d. Eight checkboxes: `<input type="checkbox">`

   e. Scrolling menu: `<select multiple="multiple">`

3. Each of these markup examples contains an error. Can you spot what it is?

   a. The `type` attribute is missing.

   b. Checkbox is not an element name; it is a value of the `type` attribute in the `input` element.

   c. The `option` element is not empty. It should contain the value for each option (for example, `<option>Orange </option>`).

   d. The required `name` attribute is missing.

   e. The width and height of a text area are specified with the `cols` and `rows` attributes, respectively.

Exercises 9-1 through 9-4: Final source document

```
<!DOCTYPE html >
<html>
<head>
  <meta charset="utf-8" >
    <title>Contest Entry Form</title>
    <style type="text/css">
       ol, ul {
       list-style-type: none;
       }
    </style>
</head>

<body>

<h1>&ldquo;Pimp My Shoes&rdquo; Contest Entry Form</h1>

<p>Want to trade in your old sneakers for a custom pair of Forcefields? Make a case for why your shoes have
    <em>got</em> to go and you may be one of ten lucky winners.</p>


<form action="http://www.learningwebdesign.com/contest.php" method="post">

<fieldset>
<legend>Contest Entry Information</legend>

<ul>
<li><label for="form-name">Name:</label> <input type="text" name="username" id="form-name"></li>
<li><label for="form-email">Email Address:</label> <input type="email" name="emailaddress" id="form-email">
    </li>
<li><label for="form-tel">Telephone Number:</label> <input type="tel" name="telephone" id="form-tel"></li>
<li><label for="form-story">My shoes are SO old...</label><br>
<textarea name="story" rows="4" cols="60" maxlength="300" id="form-story" placeholder="No more than 300
    characters long"></textarea></li>
</ul>
</fieldset>
```

```
<h2>Design your custom Forcefields:</h2>

<fieldset>
<legend>Custom Shoe Design</legend>

<fieldset>
<legend>Color <em>(choose one)</em>:</legend>
  <ul>
  <li><label><input type="radio" name="color" value="red"> Red</label></li>
  <li><label><input type="radio" name="color" value="blue"> Blue</label></li>
  <li><label><input type="radio" name="color" value="black"> Black</label></li>
  <li><label><input type="radio" name="color" value="silver"> Silver</label></li>
  </ul>
</fieldset>

<fieldset>
<legend>Features <em>(Choose as many as you want)</em></legend>
  <ul>
  <li><label><input type="checkbox" name="feature" value="laces"> Sparkley laces</label></li>
  <li><label><input type="checkbox" name="feature" value="logo" checked> Metallic logo</label></li>
  <li><label><input type="checkbox" name="feature" value="heels"> Light-up heels</label></li>
  <li><label><input type="checkbox" name="feature" value="mp3"> MP3-enabled</label></li>
  </ul>
</fieldset>

<fieldset>
<legend>Size</legend>
<p><label for="form-size">Sizes reflect standard men's sizes:</label>
<select id="form-size" name="size" size="1">
  <option>5</option>
  <option>6</option>
  <option>7</option>
  <option>8</option>
  <option>9</option>
  <option>10</option>
  <option>11</option>
  <option>12</option>
  <option>13</option>
</select>
</p>
</fieldset>

</fieldset>

<p><input type="submit" value="Pimp My Shoes!"><input type="reset"></p>
</form>
</body>
</html>
```

Chapter 10: What's Up, HTML5?

1. XHTML is defined by and requires the stricter syntax rules of XML. HTML has a looser syntax based on SGML.

2. a. `<h1>` … `</h1>`

   b. `<img src="image.png" />`

   c. `<input type="radio" checked="checked">`

d. `<hr />`

e. `<title>Sifl &amp; Olly</title>`

f. `<ul>`
    `<li>popcorn</li>`
    `<li>butter</li>`
    `<li>salt</li>`
  `</ul>`

3. A DTD stands for Document Type Definition and is a document that defines all the elements, attributes, and values in a language and their rules for use.

4. HTML5 is unique among HTML specs in that:

   - It includes APIs, not just element and attribute definitions.

   - It includes instructions for how browsers should render elements and handle errors.

   - It does not use a DTD.

   - It can be written in either HTML or XHTML syntax.

5. A global attribute can be used with any HTML element.

6. Web Workers, d; Editing API, e; Geolocation API, a; Web Socket, b; Offline Applications, c

7. Ogg, container; H.264, video; VP8, video; Vorbis, audio; WebM, container; Theora, video; AAC, audio; MPEG-4, container

8. `strokeRect()` and `fill()`

Chapter 11: CSS Orientation

1. selector: `blockquote`; property: `line-height`; value: `1.5`; declaration: `line-height: 1.5`

2. The paragraph text will be gray because when there are conflicting rules of identical weight, the last one listed in the style sheet will be used.

3. a. Use one rule with multiple declarations applied to the p element.
```
p {font-family: sans-serif;
   font-size: 1em;
   line-height: 1.2em;}
```

   b. The semicolons are missing.
```
blockquote {
    font-size: 1em;
    line-height: 150%;
    color: gray;
}
```

   c. There should not be curly braces around every declaration, only around the entire declaration block.
```
body {background-color: black;
   color: #666;
   margin-left: 12em;
   margin-right: 12em;}
```

   d. This could be handled with a single rule with a grouped element type selector.
```
p, blockquote, li {color: white;}
```

e. This inline style is missing the property name.

```
<strong style="color: red">Act now!</strong>
```

4. `div#intro { color: red; }`

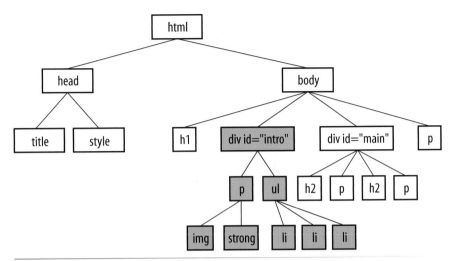

Figure A-1. The highlighted elements would be red as a result of the style rule: `div#intro {color: red;}`.

Exercise 11-1

```
h1 {
  color: red;
  border-bottom: 1px solid red;
}
p {
  font-size: small;
  font-family: sans-serif;
  margin-left: 100px;
}
h2 {
  color: red;
  margin-left: 100px;
}
img {
  float: right;
  margin: 0 12px;
}
```

Chapter 12: Formatting Text

1. a. All text elements in the document: `body {color: red;}`

   b. `h2` elements: `h2 {color: red;}`

   c. `h1` elements and all paragraphs: `h1, p {color: red;}`

   d. Elements belonging to the `class` "special": `.special {color: red; }`

   e. All elements in the "intro" section: `#intro {color: red;}`

f. **strong** elements in the "main" section: `#main strong {color: red;}`

g. Extra credit: just the paragraph that appears after an **h2** (hint: this selector will not work in Internet Explorer 6): `h2 + p {color: red;}`

2. a. ❹, b. ❶, c. ❼, d. ❸, e. ❷, f. ❾, g. ❽, h. ❺, i. ❻

Exercises 12-1 through 12-3

```
<head>
<meta charset="utf-8">
<title>Black Goose Bistro Summer Menu</title>
<link href='http://fonts.googleapis.com/css?family=Marko+One' rel='stylesheet'>
<style>

body {
   font-family: Georgia, serif;
   font-size: 100%;
   line-height: 1.75em;
}
p, dl {
   font-size: .875em;
}
h1 {
   font: bold 1.5em "Marko One", Georgia, serif;
   color: purple;
   text-shadow: .1em .1em .2em lightslategray;
}
h2 {
   font-size: 1em;
   text-transform: uppercase;
   letter-spacing: .5em;
   color: purple;
}
dt {
   font-weight: bold;
   color: sienna;
}
strong {
   font-style: italic;
}
dt strong {
   color: maroon;
}
#info p {
   font-style: italic;
   color: gray;
}
.price {
   font-family: Georgia, serif;
   font-style: italic;
   color: gray;
}
p.warning, sup {
   font-size: small;
   color: red;
}
.label {
   font-weight: bold;
   font-variant: small-caps;
```

```
    font-style: normal;
  }
h1, h2, #info {
  text-align: center;
}
h2 + p {
  text-align: center;
  font-style: italic;
}

</style>
</head>
```

Chapter 13: Colors and Backgrounds

1. g.   a, b, and c

2. d.   rgb(FF, FF, FF)

3. a. −5; b. −1; c. −4; d. −6; e. −2; f. −3

4. a. −1; b. −3; c. −2; d. −6; e. −5; f. −4

Exercise 13-1

```
body {
  …
  background-color: #d2dc9d;
}
#header {
  …
  background-color: rgba(255,255,255,.5);
}
a:link {
  color: #939;
}
a:visited {
  color: #937393;
}
a:focus {
  background-color: #fff;
  color: #c700f2;
}
a:hover {
  background-color: #fff;
  color: #c700f2;
}
a:active {
  background-color: #fff;
  color: #f0f;
}
h1 {
  …
  color: #939;
}
h2 {
  …
  color: #c60;
}
```

Exercise 13-2

```
body {
    …
    background-color: #d2dc9d;
    background-image: url(images/bullseye.png);
}
```

Exercise 13-3

```
#header {
    …
    background-color: rgba(255,255,255,.5);
    background-image: url(images/purpledot.png);
    background-repeat: repeat-x;
}
```

Exercise 13-4

```
body {
    …
    background-color: #d2dc9d;
    /* background-image: url(images/bullseye.png);
    background-position: center 200px; */
    background-image: url(images/blackgoose.png);
    background-repeat: no-repeat;
    background-position: center 100px;
}
#header {
    …
    background-color: rgba(255,255,255,.5);
    background-image: url(images/purpledot.png);
    background-repeat: repeat-x;
    background-position: center top;
}
```

Exercise 13-5

```
body {
    …
    background-color: #d2dc9d;
    background-image: url(images/blackgoose.png);
    background-repeate: no-repeat;
    background-position: center 100px;
    background-attachment: fixed;
}
```

Exercise 13-6

```
body {
    …
    background: #d2dc9d url(images/blackgoose.png) no-repeat center 100px fixed;
}
#header {
    …
    background: rgba(255,255,255,.5) url(images/purpledot.png) repeat-x center top;
}
```

Exercise 13-7

```
#header {
  …
  background-image: url(images/purpledot.png) center top repeat-x;}
  background:
   url(images/purpledot.png) left top repeat-y,
   url(images/purpledot.png) right top repeat-y,
   url(images/gooseshadow.png) 90% bottom no-repeat;
  background-color: rgba(255,255,255,.5);
}
```

Exercise 13-8

```
<head>
  …
  <link rel="stylesheet" href="menustyles.css">
</head>
```

Chapter 14: Thinking Inside the Box

a. `border: double black medium;`

b. `overflow: scroll;`

c. `padding: 2em;`

d. `padding: 2em; border: 4px solid red;`

e. `margin: 2em; border: 4px solid red;`

f. `padding: 1em 1em 1em 6em; border: 4px dashed; margin: 1em 6em;`

   or

   `padding: 1em; padding-left: 6em; border: 4px dashed; margin: 1em 6em;`

g. `padding: 1em 50px; border: 2px solid teal; margin: 0 auto;`

Exercise 14-1

```
#products {
  …
  padding: 1em;
}
#testimonials {
  …
  padding: 1em;
  padding-left: 55px;
}
```

Exercise 14-2

```
#products {
  …
  padding: 1em;
  border: double #FFBC53;
}
```

```
#products h3 {
    ...
  border-top: 1px solid;
  border-left: 3px solid;
  padding-left: 1em;
}
#testimonials {
    ...
  padding: 1em;
  padding-left: 55px;
  border-radius: 20px;
}
a {
  text-decoration: none;
  border-bottom: 1px dotted;
  padding-bottom: .1em;
}
```

Exercise 14-3

```
body {
  margin: 0;
}
a {
  text-decoration: none;
  border-bottom: 1px dotted;
  padding-bottom: .1em;
}
/* link styles omitted to save space */

/* styles for the intro section */
#intro {
  text-align: center;
  margin: 2em 0 1em;
}
#intro h1 {
  margin-bottom: 0;
}
#intro h2 {
    ...
  margin-top: -10px;
}
#intro p {
    ...
  margin: 1em;
}
/* styles for navigation omitted to save space */

/* styles for the products section */
#products {
    ...
  padding: 1em;
  border: double #FFBC53;
  margin: 1em;
}
...
#products h3 {
    ...
  border-top: 1px solid;
  border-left: 3px solid;
```

```
    padding-left: 1em;
    margin-top: 2.5em;
}

/* styles for the testimonials box */
#testimonials {
    ...
    padding: 1em;
    padding-left: 55px;
    border-radius: 20px;
    margin: 1em 10%;
    }
/* remaining styles omitted to save space */
```

Chapter 15: Floating and Positioning

1. b is not true. Floats are positioned against the content edge, not the padding edge.

2. c is incorrect. Floats do not use offset properties, so there is no reason to include `right`.

3. Clear the footer `div` to make it start below a floated sidebar: `div#footer { clear: both; }`.

4. a. absolute; b. absolute, fixed; c. fixed; d. relative, absolute, fixed; e. static; f. relative; g. absolute, fixed; h. relative, absolute, fixed; i. relative

Exercise 15-1

```
#products img {
    float: left;
    margin: 0 6px 6px 0;
}
#products .more {
    clear: left;
}
```

Exercise 15-2

```
#nav ul {
    ...
    margin: 0 auto;
    width: 19.5em;
}
#nav ul li {
    ...
    float: left;
}
#nav ul li a {
    display: block;
    padding: .5em;
    border: 1px solid #ba89a8;
    border-radius: .5em;
    margin: .25em;
}
...
#nav ul a:focus {
    color: #fc6
    border-color: #fff;
}
```

```
#nav ul a:hover {
  color: #fc6;
  border-color: #fff;
}
…
#products {
  …
  clear: both;
}
```

Exercise 15-3

```
#products {
  …
  width: 55%;
  float: left;
}
#products h2 {
  …
  text-align: left;
}
#testimonials {
  …
  margin: 1em 2% 1em 64%;
}
p#copyright {
  …
  clear: left;
}
```

Exercise 15-4

```
…
#content {
  position: relative;
}
#testimonials {
  …
  margin: 0 1em;
  position: absolute;
  top: 0;
  right: 0;
  width: 14em;
}
#products {
  …
  margin: 1em 20.5em 1em 1em;
  clear: both;
}
#award {
  position: absolute;
  top: 35px;
  left: 25px;
}
```

Exercise 15-5

```
...
#award {
  position: fixed;
  top: 35px;
  left: 25px;
}
```

Chapter 16: Page Layout with CSS

1. Fixed, c.; Fluid, a.; Elastic, b.

2. Fixed, b.; Fluid, c.; Elastic, a.

3. Fixed, c.; Fluid, b.; Elastic, a.

4. Fixed, c.; Fluid, a.; Elastic, b.

Exercise 16-1

```
<style>
#wrapper {
  width: 960px;
  margin: 0 auto;
}
#header {
  background-color: #CCC;
  padding: 15px;
}
#links {
  float: right;
  width: 22.5%;
  margin: 0 2.5% 0 0 ;
  outline: 2px dashed #dd0009;
}
#main {
  float: right;
  width: 45%;
  margin: 0 2.5%;
  outline: 2px dashed #0053ae;
}
#news {
  float: right;
  width: 22.5%;
  margin: 0 0 0 2.5% ;
  outline: 2px dashed #009554;
}
#footer {
  clear: right;
  padding: 15px;
  background: #CCC;
}
/* remaining unchanged styles omitted to save space */
</style>

<body>
<div id="wrapper">
  ... contents of page here...
</div>
</body>
```

Exercise 16-2

```
#main {
  float: left;
  width: 400px;
  margin-top: 0;
  margin-left: 320px;
  margin-right: 20px;
}

#news {
  float: left;
  width: 300px;
  margin-top: 0;
  margin-left: -740px;
}

#links {
  float: left;
  width: 220px;
  margin: 0;
}
```

Chapter 17: Transitions, Transforms, and Animation

1. Tweening is the process in animation in which frames are generated between two end point states.

2. A transition would have two keyframes, one for the beginning state and one for the end.

3. a. `transition-delay: 0.5s;` b. `transition-timing-function: linear;` c. `transition-duration: .5s;` d. `transition-property: line-height;`

4. c. `text-transform` is not an animatable property.

5. Ease is the default timing function. It starts out slowly, speeds up quickly, and then slows down again at the very end.

6. .2s is the `transition-duration` value.

7. Trick question! They will arrive at the same time, 300ms after the transition begins. The timing function has no effect on the total amount of time it takes.

8. a. `transform: rotate(7deg);` b. `translate(-50px, -25px);` c. `transform-origin: bottom right;` d. `transform: scale(1.2);`

9. The 3 value indicates that the element should be resized three times larger than its original *height*.

10. a. `perspective: 250;` because lower number values are more dramatic.

11. The border is 3 pixels wide at 50% through the animation.

12. a. `animation-direction: reverse;` b. `animation-duration: 5s;` c. `animation-delay: 2s;` d. `animation-iteration-count: 3;`

Exercise 17-1

```css
a {
  /* non-transition styles omitted to save space */
  position: relative;
  -webkit-transition: background-color 0.2s ease-in, border-color 0.2s, top 0.2s, box-shadow 0.2s;
  -moz-transition:  background-color 0.2s, border-color 0.2s, top 0.2s, box-shadow 0.2s;
  -o-transition:  background-color 0.2s, border-color 0.2, top 0.2s, box-shadow 0.2s;
  -ms-transition:  background-color 0.2s, border-color 0.2s, top 0.2s, box-shadow 0.2s;
  transition:  background-color 0.2s, border-color 0.2s, top 0.2s, box-shadow 0.2s;
}
a:hover, a:focus {
  background-color: #fdca00;
  border-color: #fda700;
}
a:active {
  top: 3px;
  box-shadow: 0 1px 2px rgba(0,0,0,.5);
}
```

Exercise 17-2

Vendor-prefixed properties have been omitted to save space.

```css
img {
  width: 200px;
  height: 150px;
  box-shadow: 2px 2px 2px rgba(0,0,0,.4);
  transition: transform .3s ease-in-out;
}
a:hover img {
  box-shadow: 6px 6px 6px rgba(0,0,0,.3);
}
a:hover #img1, a:focus #img1  {
  transform: scale(1.5) rotate(-3deg);
}
a:hover #img2, a:focus #img2  {
  transform: scale(1.5) rotate(5deg);
}
a:hover #img3, a:focus #img3  {
  transform: scale(1.5) rotate(-7deg);
}
a:hover #img4, a:focus #img4  {
  transform: scale(1.5) rotate(2deg);
}
```

Chapter 18: CSS Techniques

1. d. All of the above

2. d. a. and c.

3. The differences between LESS and Sass include:

    *   LESS lacks some of the functionality of Sass.

    *   They use a slightly different syntax (**$variable** versus **@variable**).

    *   Sass is compiled into standard CSS by a Ruby program on the server; LESS uses JavaScript.

4. e. b. and d.

5. Give the label elements the same width and float them to the left, then align the text right so it appears next to the control it describes.

6. If you do not set the viewport size, the mobile browser will scale down the page, even if it is designed to be 320 pixels wide.

7. c., e., d., a., b.

8. b., e., a., d., c.

Exercises 18-1 through 18-3

```css
img {
  max-width: 100%;
}

@media screen and (min-width: 481px) {
  #products img {
    float: left;
    margin: 0 6px 6px 0;
  }
  #products .more {
    clear: left;
  }
  #products {
    margin: 1em;
  }
  #testimonials {
    margin: 1em 5%;
    border-radius: 16px;
  }
}

@media screen and (min-width: 780px) {
  #products {
    float: left;
    margin: 0 2% 1em;
    clear: both;
    width: 55%;
    overflow: auto;
  }
  #testimonials {
    margin: 1em 2% 1em 64%;
  }
  p#copyright {
    clear: both;
  }
  #content {
    max-width: 1024px;
    margin: 0 auto;
  }
}
```

Chapter 19: Introduction to JavaScript

1. When you link to an external *.js* file, you can reuse the same scripts for multiple documents. The downside is that it requires an additional HTTP request.

2. a. 1; b. 1two; c. 34; d. 2

3. a. 10; b. 6; c. "2 remaining"; d. "Jennifer is longer."; e. false

4. It loops through a number of items by starting at the first one in the array and ending when there are no more left.

5. Globally scoped variables may "collide" with variables with the same names in other scripts. It is best to use the **var** keyword in functions to keep your variables scoped locally.

6. a. 2; b. 5; c. 4; d. 3; e. 1

Exercise 19-1

1. `var friends = ["name", "othername", "thirdname", "lastname"];`

2. `alert(friends[2]);`

3. `var name = "`*yourName*`";`

4. `if( name === Jennifer) { alert("That's my name too!"); }`

5.
```
var myVariable = #;
if( myVariable > 5) {
  alert("upper");
} else {
  alert ("lower");
}
```

Exercise 19-2
```
<script>
var originalTitle = document.title;
function showUnreadCount( unread ) {
  document.title = originalTitle + " (" + unread + "new message!");
}
showUnreadCount(3);
</script>
```

Chapter 20: Using JavaScript

1. Ajax is a combination of HTML, CSS, and JavaScript (with the **XMLHttpRequest** JavaScript method used to get data in the background).

2. It accesses the element that has the **id** value "main".

3. It creates a **nodeList** of all the **section** elements in the element with the **id** of "main".

4. It sets the background color of the page (**body** element) to "papayawhip".

5. It creates a new text node that says, "Hey, I'm walking here!", inserts it in a newly created **p** element, and puts the new **p** element in the element with the **id** "main".

6. a. 3; b. 2; c. 4; d. 1

7. d. All of the above.

Chapter 21: Web Graphics Basics

1. You can get a license to have exclusive rights to an image so that your competitor doesn't use the same photo on her site.

2. ppi stands for "pixels per inch" and is a measure of resolution.

3. Indexed color is a mode for storing color information in an image that stores each pixel color in a color table. GIF and 8-bit PNG formats are indexed color images.

4. There are 256 colors in an 8-bit graphic and 32 colors in a 5-bit graphic.

5. GIF can contain animation and transparency. JPEG cannot.

6. GIF can contain animation. PNGs cannot.

7. PNGs can have multiple levels of transparency. GIF has only binary (on/off) transparency.

8. Lossy compression is cumulative, which means you lose image data every time you save an image as a JPEG. If you open a JPEG and save it as a JPEG again, even more image information is thrown out than the first time you saved it. Be sure to keep your full-quality original and save JPEG copies as needed.

9. In binary transparency, a pixel is either entirely transparent or entirely opaque. Alpha transparency allows up to 256 levels of transparency.

10. Ⓐ GIF or PNG-8 because it is text, flat colors, and hard edges. Ⓑ JPEG because it is a photograph. Ⓒ GIF or PNG-8 because although it has some photographic areas, most of the image is flat colors with hard edges. Ⓓ GIF or PNG-8 because it is a flat graphical image. Ⓔ JPEG because it is a photograph.

Chapter 22: Lean and Mean Web Graphics

1. Smaller graphic files means shorter download and display times. Every second counts toward creating a favorable user experience of your site.

2. Dithering introduces a speckle pattern that interrupts strings of identical pixels, and therefore the GIF compression scheme can't compress areas with dithering as efficiently as flat colors.

3. The fewer pixel colors in the image, the smaller the resulting GIF, both because the image can be stored at a lower bit depth and because there are more areas of similar color for the GIF to compress.

4. The Quality (compression) setting is the most effective tool for controlling the size of a JPEG.

5. JPEG compression works effectively on smooth or blurred areas, so introducing a slight blur allows the JPEG compression to work more efficiently, resulting in smaller files.

6. Just as you would do for an indexed GIF, optimize a PNG-8 by designing with flat colors, reducing the number of colors, and avoiding dithering. There are no strategies for optimizing a PNG-24 because they are designed to store images with lossless compression.

CSS3 SELECTORS

Selector	Type of selector	Description
Simple selectors and combinators		
*	Universal selector	Matches any element. `* {font-family: serif;}`
A	Type selector	Matches the name of an element. `div {font-style: italic;}`
A, B	Grouped selectors	Matches elements A and B. `h1, h2, h3 {color: blue;}`
A B	Descendant selector	Matches element B only if it is a descendant of element A. `blockquote em {color: red;}`
A>B	Child selector	Matches any element B that is a child of element A. `div.main>p {line-height: 1.5;}`
A+B	Adjacent sibling selector	Matches any element B that immediately follows any element A, where A and B share the same parent. `p+ul {margin-top: 0;}`
A~B	General sibling selector	Matches any element B that is preceded by A, where A and B share the same parent. `blockquote~cite {margin-top: 0;}`
Class and ID selectors		
.classname A.classname	Class selector	Matches the value of the **class** attribute in all elements or in a specified element. `p.credits {font-size: 80%;}`
#idname A#idname	ID selector	Matches the value of the id attribute in an element. `#intro {font-weight: bold;}`
Attribute selectors		
A[att]	Simple attribute selector	Matches any element A that has the given attribute defined, whatever its value. `table[border] {background: white;}`
A[att="val"]	Exact attribute value selector	Matches any element A that has the specified attribute set to the specified value. `table[border="3"] {background: yellow;}`

Selector	Type of selector	Description
`A[att~="val"]`	Partial attribute value selector	Matches any element A that has the specified value as one of the values in a list given to the specified attribute. `table[class~="example"] {background: yellow;}`
`A[att|="val"]`	Hyphenated prefix attribute selector	Matches any element A that has the specified attribute with a value that is equal to or begins with the provided value. It is most often used to select languages, as shown here. `a[lang|="en"] {background-image: url(en_icon.png);}`
`A[att^="val"]`	Beginning substring attribute selector	Matches any element A that has the specified attribute and its value *begins* with the provided string. `img[src^="/images/icons"] {border: 3px solid;}`
`A[att$="val"]`	Ending substring attribute selector	Matches any element A that has the specified attribute and its value *ends* with the provided string. `img[src$="/images/icons"] {border: 3px solid;}`
`A[att*="val"]`	Arbitrary substring attribute selector	Matches any element A that has the specified attribute and its value contains the provided string. `img[title*="July"] {border: 3px solid;}`

Pseudo-class selectors

Selector	Type of selector	Description
`a:link`	Link pseudo-class selector	Specifies a style for links that have not yet been visited. `a:link {color: maroon;}`
`a:visited`	Link pseudo-class selector	Specifies a style for links that have already been visited. `a:visited {color: gray;}`
`:active`	User action pseudo-class selector	Selects any element that has been activated by the user, such as a link as it is being clicked. `a:active {color: red;}`
`:focus`	User action pseudo-class selector	Selects any element that currently has the input focus, such as a selected form input. `input[type="text"]:focus {background: yellow;}`
`:hover`	User-action pseudo-class selector	Specifies a style for elements (typically links) that appear when the mouse is placed over them. `a:hover {text-decoration: underline;}`
`:target`	Target pseudo-class selector	Selects an element that is used as a fragment identifier. `h1:target {color: red;}`
`:lang(xx)`	Pseudo-class selector	Selects an element that matches the two-character language code. `a:lang(de) {color: green;}`
`:root`	Structural pseudo-class selector	Selects an element that is the root of the document. In HTML, it is the `html` element. `:root { background: papayawhip;}`
`:nth-child()`	Structural pseudo-class selector	Selects an element that is the nth child of its parent. The notation can include a number, a notation, or the keywords odd or even. `tr:nth-child(odd) { background: #DDD;}`
`:nth-last-child()`	Structural pseudo-class selector	Selects an element that is the nth child of its parent, counting from the last one. `li:nth-last-child(2) { color: green;}`

Selector	Type of selector	Description
`:nth-of-type()`	Structural pseudo-class selector	Selects the nth element of its type. `img:nth-of-type(even) {float: right;}`
`:nth-last-of-type()`	Structural pseudo-class selector	Selects the nth element of its type, counting from the last one. `img:nth-last-of-type(odd) {float: right;}`
`:first-child`	Structural pseudo-class selector	Selects an element that is the first child of its parent element. `p:first-child {border-top: 1px solid;}`
`:last-child`	Structural pseudo-class selector	Selects an element that is the last child of its parent element. `p:last-child {border-bottom: 1px solid;}`
`:first-of-type`	Structural pseudo-class selector	Selects an element that is the first sibling of its type. `dt:first-of-type {font-weight: bold;}`
`:last-of-type`	Structural pseudo-class selector	Selects an element that is the last sibling of its type. `li:last-of-type {margin-bottom: 1em;}`
`:only-child`	Structural pseudo-class selector	Selects an element that is the only child of its parent. `aside:only-child {line-height: 1.5;}`
`:only-of-type`	Structural pseudo-class selector	Selects an element that is the only sibling of its type. `dt:only-of-type {font-weight: bold;}`
`:empty`	Structural pseudo-class selector	Selects an element that has no text and no child elements. `tbody td:empty {background: #000; }`
`:enabled`	UI pseudo-class selector	Selects a UI element if it is enabled. `input[type="tel"]:enabled {border: 1px solid red;}`
`:disabled`	UI pseudo-class selector	Selects a UI element if it is disabled. `input[type="tel"]:disabled {color: #ccc;}`
`:checked`	UI pseudo-class selector	Selects a UI element (radio button or checkbox) that is checked. `:checked {background-color: yellow;}`
`:not(X)`	Negation pseudo-class selector	Selects an element that does not match the simple selector X. `:not(pre) { line-height: 1.2 }`

Pseudo-element selectors

Selector	Type of selector	Description
`:first-letter` (`::first-letter` in CSS3)	Pseudo-element selector	Selects the first letter of the specified element. `p:first-letter {font-size: 4em;}`
`:first-line` (`::first-line` in CSS3)	Pseudo-element selector	Selects the first letter of the specified element. `.note:first-line {letter-spacing: 4px;}`
`:before` (`::before` in CSS3)	Pseudo-element selector	Inserts generated text at the beginning of the specified element and applies a style to it. `p.intro:before {content: "start here"; color: gray;}`
`:after` (`::after` in CSS3)	Pseudo-element selector	Inserts generated content at the end of the specified element and applies a style to it. `p.intro:after {content: "fini"; color: gray;}`

INDEX

Get even more for your money.

Join the O'Reilly Community, and register the O'Reilly books you own. It's free, and you'll get:

- $4.99 ebook upgrade offer
- 40% upgrade offer on O'Reilly print books
- Membership discounts on books and events
- Free lifetime updates to ebooks and videos
- Multiple ebook formats, DRM FREE
- Participation in the O'Reilly community
- Newsletters
- Account management
- 100% Satisfaction Guarantee

Signing up is easy:

1. **Go to: oreilly.com/go/register**
2. **Create an O'Reilly login.**
3. **Provide your address.**
4. **Register your books.**

Note: English-language books only

To order books online:

oreilly.com/store

For questions about products or an order:

orders@oreilly.com

To sign up to get topic-specific email announcements and/or news about upcoming books, conferences, special offers, and new technologies:

elists@oreilly.com

For technical questions about book content:

booktech@oreilly.com

To submit new book proposals to our editors:

proposals@oreilly.com

O'Reilly books are available in multiple DRM-free ebook formats. For more information:

oreilly.com/ebooks

O'REILLY®

Spreading the knowledge of innovators   oreilly.com

Have it your way.

O'Reilly eBooks

- Lifetime access to the book when you buy through oreilly.com
- Provided in up to four, DRM-free file formats, for use on the devices of your choice: PDF, .epub, Kindle-compatible .mobi, and Android .apk
- Fully searchable, with copy-and-paste, and print functionality
- We also alert you when we've updated the files with corrections and additions.

oreilly.com/ebooks/

Safari Books Online

- Access the contents and quickly search over 7000 books on technology, business, and certification guides
- Learn from expert video tutorials, and explore thousands of hours of video on technology and design topics
- Download whole books or chapters in PDF format, at no extra cost, to print or read on the go
- Early access to books as they're being written
- Interact directly with authors of upcoming books
- Save up to 35% on O'Reilly print books

See the complete Safari Library at safari.oreilly.com

Spreading the knowledge of innovators.   oreilly.com